INN
SPOTS

By
Nancy and
Richard Woodworth

&
MID-ATLANTIC
NEW YORK/VIRGINIA

SPECIAL
PLACES

*A guide to
where to go,
stay, eat and
enjoy in 35
of the region's
choicest areas.*

Wood Pond Press
West Hartford, Conn.

The authors value their reputation for credibility and have personally visited the places included in this book. They have seen them all, which gives them a rare perspective in the field. Unlike others, they do not ask the owners to fill out information forms or to approve the final copy. Nor do they rely on researchers or field inspectors with varying perspectives and loyalties to do their leg work. They make their recommendations based on their experiences and findings. No fees are accepted or charged for inclusion.

Prices, hours and menu offerings at inns and restaurants change seasonally and with business conditions. Readers should call ahead to avoid disappointment. The prices and hours reported in this book were correct at presstime and are subject, of course, to change. They are offered as a relative guide to what to expect. Rates quoted are for bed and breakfast, unless otherwise specified (MAP, Modified American Plan, breakfast and dinner; EP, European Plan, no meals).

For updates between editions, check out the Wood Pond Press web site at www.getawayguides.com. Favorite inns, B&Bs, restaurants and attractions from this book and from others by the authors are detailed under Getaway Guides On Line.

The authors welcome readers' reactions and suggestions.

Cover Photo: Breakfast table at The Inn at Perry Cabin, St. Michaels, MD.

Graphics by Jay Woodworth

Contents

Introduction

This is yet another inn book. But it's far more, too.

We enjoy reading others, but they rarely tell us what we *really* want to know – which inns and B&Bs are especially good and what they are like, where to get a good meal and what there is to do in the area. No inn is an island – they are part of their locale. With their neighbors, they share a sense of place.

These insights are what we now share with you. We start not with the inn but with the area (of course, the existence of inns or lack thereof determine the 35 special destination areas to be included). Then we tour each area, with the eyes and ears of the first-time visitor and the perspective of seasoned travelers and journalists. We visit the inns, the restaurants and the attractions. We *work* these areas as roving journalists, always seeking out the best and most interesting. We also *live* them – staying in, eating in, and experiencing as many places as time and budget allow.

The result is this book. It's a selective compendium of what we think are the best and most interesting places to stay, eat and enjoy in these 35 special destinations, some of them the Mid-Atlantic's best-known and some not widely known at all.

The book reflects our tastes. We want creature comforts like private bathrooms and comfortable reading areas in our rooms. We like to meet other inn guests, but we also cherish privacy. We seek interesing and creative food and pleasant settings for meals. We enjoy unusual, enlightening things to do and places to see. We expect to receive value for our time and money.

While touring the past year to research this book as well as the fifth edition of its companion, *Inn Spots & Special Places in New England,* we continue to be surprised by how many innkeepers say we are among the few guidebook writers who actually visit their facility and do not expect them merely to fill out a questionnaire and forward it with a considerable fee.

We also were struck by how many inns report, quite suddenly, an impact from the Internet. They say increasing numbers of travelers find places to stay and book reservations via the Net. The prospective guest likes the immediacy, the ability to see pictures and get detailed descriptions, the instant gratification of a quick, visual reservation. And yet, the realists among both innkeepers and browsers worry that the Web traveler finds only what the Web site wants them to know. They miss the insights offered by well traveled observers who have been there.

The inn experience is highly personal, both for the innkeeper and the inn-goer. The listing services, the advertising and the Web site hype do not have an objective perspective. Nor can they convey the personality of the place.

That's the role of experienced guidebook writers who make the rounds year after year and report things as they see them. Yes, the schedule is hectic and we do keep busy on these, our working trips that everyone thinks must be nothing but fun. One of us says she never again wants to get up in the middle of the night and cope with a strange bathroom. The other doesn't care if he never eats another bedside chocolate.

Nonetheless, it's rewarding both to experience a great inn and to discover a promising B&B. We also enjoy savoring a good meal, touring a choice musuem, poking through an unusual store and meeting so many interesting people along the way.

And that's what this book is about. We hope that you enjoy its findings as much as we did the finding.

Nancy and Richard Woodworth

About the Authors

Nancy Webster Woodworth began her travel and dining experiences in her native Montreal and as a waitress in summer resorts across Canada during her McGill University years. She worked in London and hitchhiked through Europe on $3 a day before her marriage to Richard Woodworth, whom she met while skiing at Mont Tremblant. They lived for the first ten years of their marriage in upstate New York and became familiar with the Mid-Atlantic during trips to visit his brother in Baltimore and his parents in Lynchburg and Smith Mountain Lake, Va. She started writing her "Roaming the Restaurants" column for the West Hartford (Conn.) News in 1972. That led to half of the book, *Daytripping & Dining in Southern New England*, written in collaboration with Betsy Wittemann in 1978. She since has co-authored *Inn Spots & Special Places in New England, Weekending in New England, Getaways for Gourmets in the Northeast, Waterside Escapes in the Northeast*, and *The Restaurants of New England*. She and her husband have two grown sons and live in West Hartford.

Richard Woodworth has been an inveterate traveler since his youth in suburban Syracuse, N.Y., where his birthday outings often involved train trips with friends for the day to nearby Utica or Rochester. After graduation from Middlebury College, he was a reporter for newspapers in Syracuse, Jamestown, Geneva and Rochester before moving to Connecticut to become editor of the West Hartford News and eventually executive editor of Imprint Newspapers. With his wife and their sons, he has traveled to the four corners of this country, Canada and portions of Europe, writing their findings for newspapers and magazines. With his wife, he has co-authored five editions *of Inn Spots & Special Places in New England* and *Getaways for Gourmets in the Northeast*, as well as *The Restaurants of New England*. Between travels and duties as publisher of Wood Pond Press, he tries to find time to ski in the winter and weed the garden in summer.

Excerpts from the authors' books are on line at **www.getawayguides.com**

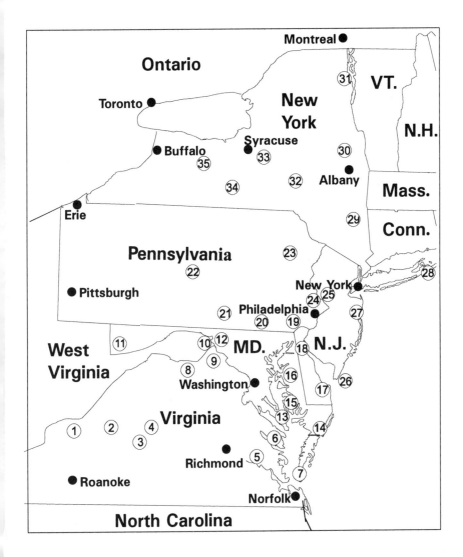

1. Hot Springs
2. Staunton
3. Charlottesville
4. Orange
5. James River
6. Northern Neck
7. Cape Charles
8. Washington
9. Loudoun County
10. Harpers Ferry
11. Deep Creek Lake
12. Frederick
13. Solomons
14. Snow Hill/Berlin
15. St. Michaels
16. Chestertown
17. Lewes
18. New Castle
19. Chadds Ford
20. Lancaster County
21. Gettysburg
22. State College
23. Canadensis
24. Bucks County
25. Lambertville
26. Cape May
27. Spring Lake
28. East Hampton
29. Rhinebeck
30. Saratoga Springs
31. Westport/Essex
32. Cooperstown
33. Cazenovia
34. Ithaca
35. Canandaigua

Championship golf courses are among attractions at Hot Springs and The Homestead.

Hot Springs, Va.
The Lure of the Baths

Since the days of Washington and Jefferson, the warm medicinal springs that emanate from the valleys of the Allegheny Highlands have lured the nation's elite. Their curative powers and social importance are legendary, having spawned two of America's world-class resorts, The Homestead at Hot Springs and The Greenbrier in White Sulphur Springs, W.Va.

This remarkably scenic area tucked between mountain ridges along the Virginia-West Virginia border offers much for today's visitor. You can soak in the "baths" in the same structures that Thomas Jefferson and Mrs. Robert E. Lee did. You can revel in contemporary spa treatments that would do California proud. You can play golf on some of the world's most challenging and scenic courses. You can partake of the good life at the Homestead and the Greenbrier.

You also can bask in one of the most picturesque, unspoiled regions we know. Verdant mountains, idyllic valleys, backroads hamlets, untrafficked byways and an exhilarating climate are the draws. Ninety percent of Bath County – so named because its warm waters reminded the earliest settlers of those in Bath, England – is forested. And half of that is part of the George Washington National Forest. The entire county has neither an incorporated town nor a traffic light. About the only signs of commercialism – and they're a lovely, colorful touch – are the trademark wildlife mailboxes donated to every Bath County homeowner by the local Bacova Guild Factory. The guild exports the fashionable mailboxes to paying customers across the country.

What this area offers are endless tranquility and rural pleasures, from walks to waterfalls. Its mountain air yields cool, restorative summer days and nights, as well as long springtimes and spectacular autumns (the fall foliage outshines even the showy redbud and dogwood that light up the hillsides in spring). Small inns and B&Bs contrast nicely in scale and price with the grand resorts, and their guests can take advantage of Homestead and Greenbrier facilities.

Even those ensconced at one of the resorts (and paying dearly for the privilege) should get out and about to enjoy fully a region of uncommon beauty. If you're staying at the Homestead, visit the Greenbrier for lunch, or vice-versa. Stay at one of the smaller inns or B&Bs and the money you save will allow you to do both.

Some people do energetic things, like hiking, fishing and golfing. Others never get beyond the front veranda or backyard hammock.

Inn Spots

The Homestead, Hot Springs 24445.

The Homestead and Hot Springs have been synonymous, ever since the first hotel was built around the hot springs in 1766. In fact, The Homestead *is* Hot Springs, its presence dominating the small community in every respect. The hotel exudes tradition and grandeur, Southern style.

Becoming frayed at the edges and near bankruptcy in 1993, the oldest family-run resort in the world entered into a joint venture with the Dallas-based Club Resorts Inc., one of the nation's leading owner/operators of golf and conference resorts. More than $25 million was invested to "restore this grand dame of American resorts to the splendid glory it has boasted for more than 200 years," in the words of new president Gary K. Rosenberg.

The Homestead's setting is stupendous. The landmark hotel tower is the only real break in 15,000 privately owned acres of Allegheny Mountains and valleys. The 521 rooms and suites, most in low-rise wings, look out onto hillsides and golf fairways. Most are spacious and have all the amenities.

Our parlor suite at the far end of what the staff calls "the older and more elegant" West Wing had a kingsize bed, a loveseat and two side chairs, a writing desk, a console TV, no fewer than four telephones and a full-length, screened veranda big enough to seat a party of twenty. Extra touches included European percale sheets, good reading lights, maid service twice daily and a walk-in closet that lighted automatically.

Gone are traditions such as nightly turn-down service (now available only on request), a holdover from the days when old-name families like

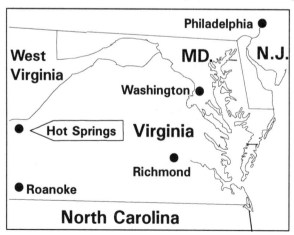

the Vanderbilts arrived with their trunks for the summer. The new management concentrates on things it deems more important to today's visitor.

Guests are still greeted in the majestic Great Hall, where afternoon tea is accompanied by live music and guests mingle at all hours in a living-room setting. They eat and drink in ten dining and entertainment venues (see Dining Spots). They play golf on three championship eighteen-hole courses. They play tennis on fifteen courts, swim in three pools, bowl on eight lanes, dance during dinner and take in a movie in the theater afterward. In winter, they ski at the South's first ski area.

The original hot springs are incorporated into The Homestead's European-style spa, built in 1892 and recipient of a state-of-the-art renovation in 1996. Their 104-degree waters provide a variety of treatments from $15 for a mineral tub bath to $25 for a combination bath. The Homestead also operates the original baths at Warm Springs.

The new look at The Homestead blends seamlessly with the old. Landscapers have added thousands of flowers to the grounds. Brick pavers replaced asphalt in the porte cochere entry. The entire East Wing with 86 guest rooms was refurbished. The hotel's main floor received new carpeting, long a sticky point with the AAA rating inspectors. The vast dining room was reconfigured and acquired a spiffy new wine room. The Grille was being renovated at our 1997 visit. The Tower Corridor of shops was transformed into a boutique setting opening one into the next like the rooms of a house. Archival photos line the refurbished corridors of the West Wing, and portraits of thirteen presidents who have visited the Homestead hang in the Presidents' Lounge. Murals tracing the history of Hot Springs enhance the Jefferson Parlor. The Casino, located between the spa building and hotel, was converted into a sports shop and a casual, indoor/outdoor grill. A new Homestead Kids' Club program operates behind the casino. The old Tower Lounge was transformed into a richly paneled library, game room and historical museum.

(540) 839-1766 or (800) 838-1766. Fax (540) 839-7670. Four hundred forty rooms and 81 suites with private baths. Rates, MAP. May-October: doubles, $374 to $470 weekends, $334 to $440 midweek; suites $554 to $1,194 weekends, $506 to $1070 midweek. Rest of year: doubles, $264 to $382; suites, $410 to $1,032.

The Greenbrier, White Sulphur Springs, W.Va. 24986.

If the Homestead is the grand dame of genteel Southern tradition, The Greenbrier just across the West Virginia border is the vivacious debutante – or maybe post-debutante, for surely this five-star, five-diamond resort has come of age.

The Greenbrier is new money rather than old, corporate-owned rather than family-run (as The Homestead had been until lately), glittering and eye-popping. Where it lacks the scenic setting of The Homestead, it compensates with spectacular landscaping and flowers. Splashes of vivid colors and chintzes in the Dorothy Draper style make the

Horses await at The Greenbrier entrance.

interiors of its Virginia counterpart look a bit pale. Its three eighteen-hole golf courses are not quite so highly rated as The Homestead's, but the new Spa, Mineral Baths and Salon building is state-of-the-art. In fact, everything at The Greenbrier is up to date and spiffy, and not in any understated way.

Here you'll ogle an indoor pool to end all pools with a billowing white sailcloth above, peach-hued walls and wicker furniture all around. Pause at the bar for "healthy-living drinks" made of whole fruit. The black and white marble floors of the Georgian lobby reflect the sunlight from sixteen-foot windows and french doors dressed in the brilliant florals that made Draper and protégé Carleton Varney, who redecorated The Greenbrier, famous. The entry lobby gives way to a succession of smaller lobbies and living rooms, each a study in interior design. From wallpaper to china, Draper's signature rhododendrons accent the columned dining room (see Dining Spots). Crystal chandeliers contrast with pecky wood walls and are a sight to behold in the Old White Club, the deluxe lounge named for the former hotel on the site, called the Old White. Draper's Cafe serves informal meals of cutting-edge cuisine. Such grandeur prompted columnist Elsa Maxwell to write, upon the hotel's reopening after service as a military hospital in World War II: "The Greenbrier is perhaps the most beautiful hotel in the world."

The public spaces tend to overshadow the 650 guest rooms, including 49 suites and 69 cottages, all decorated in the Dorothy Draper style and no two exactly alike. Draperies and wallpapers are color-coordinated and the refreshment center in each room matches the furniture. Our room, more spacious than many we saw, was most comfortable and provided every amenity but was not as superlative as the public facilities. We admit we did not visit the fourteen-room Presidential Suite that covers two floors.

Always upgrading, The Greenbrier now offers LaVarenne at The Greenbrier, bringing in its French founder to supplement the original resort cooking school founded in 1977. The adjacent Greenbrier Clinic performs complete health diagnostic evaluations. The Gallery of Shops on the lower level includes some of the fanciest we've seen, and makes you wonder how they manage to stay open with only a limited, though captive, audience.

A veteran staff of 1,600 (average tenure: thirteen years) caters to the needs of guests, who number no more than 1,400 at a time. The clientele here appears to be as rich as the facility, but as hotel historian Robert Conte pointed out during a tour, guests "stay as long as the money holds out – it used to be weeks, and now it's usually days."

(304) 536-1110 or (800) 624-6070. Fax (304) 536-7834. Five hundred thirty-six rooms, 33 suites, 30 cottages and 73 guest houses with private baths. Rates, MAP. April-October: doubles, $404 to $652. Rest of year: $320 to $510.

The Inn at Gristmill Square, Box 359, Warm Springs 24484.

This good-looking complex of guest rooms, recreation facilities, a shop and a restaurant resembles a small village and, indeed, is the biggest enterprise in the dear little hamlet of Warm Springs (population, 250, and every building redone in the last few years, according to innkeeper Janice McWilliams). Former owners of a ski lodge in Vermont, the McWilliams family took over this going concern in 1981 and have continued to expand.

Seventeen guest accommodations are scattered in four 19th-century buildings around an old gristmill that now houses a good restaurant (see Dining Spots).

Meadow Lane Lodge is centerpiece of a rural, sixteen-acre farm estate.

Rooms vary widely in size and decor. Each has antique furnishings, TVs, refrigerators, hair dryers and phones, and half have fireplaces. One is called the Silo for obvious reasons, and the two-bedroom Tower Apartment has a round living room and a fantastic tin chandelier. The Blacksmith Shop containing the inn's office has a Loft Room with kingsize bed and deck and the Spring Suite with a living room, a jacuzzi tub and a queensize bed in the bedroom, which opens to a private patio beside babbling Warm Spring Run. We enjoyed the Board Room, cozy and dark in barnwood with two double beds and a clawfoot tub. Others are partial to the extravagant Singapore Room and its two-part bathroom, one part being a tub in a niche behind a screen.

A country flavor prevails in the adjacent Miller's House, which offers two rooms and two suites. Four smaller rooms are across the street in the Steel House, close to the pool, a small sauna and three tennis courts. One hundred miles of walking and riding trails surround the property.

In the morning, Mrs. McWilliams delivers a picnic basket to each room. It contains juice, coffee and breads, plus the day's Richmond Times-Dispatch.

(540) 839-2231. Fax (540) 839-5770. Twelve rooms and five suites with private baths. Doubles, $80 to $100 B&B, $155 to $170 MAP. Suites, $85 to $140 B&B, $160 to $210 MAP.

Meadow Lane Lodge, Star Route A, Box 110, Warm Springs 24484.

The rural tranquility that is this area's main allure is perhaps nowhere more alluring than at Meadow Lane Lodge. The tradition launched by the late gentleman-farmer, Philip Hirsh, is being continued by his wife Catherine and grandson, Carter Ancona, who offer a variety of rooms with private baths in their lodge and two cottages on a 1,600-acre estate complete with fishing streams, fields and woods. A big white barn is full of exotic animals, from peacocks to nubian goats.

Set well back from Route 39 at the end of a long driveway, the accommodations are spacious and luxurious in a country-manor kind of way. Fireplaces at either end, antiques, sofas and a big table full of magazines attract guests to the lodge's long common room. The lodge includes a kingsize suite, an upstairs suite with sitting area and a screened porch and, most in demand, a small room with a corner porch affording the best view. The Snuggery, with a loveseat and TV tucked beneath the eaves, attests to the late owner's knack for architectural design. Furnishings are a mix of items from the Hirshes' travels. Phil was the third generation of a thoroughbred horse-breeding family (his father was the author of Yale's "Boola Boola"), and his wife still occupies the main house next to a swimming pool (available to guests by invitation).

Near the lodge, Craig's Cottage contains a suite with a small kitchen and living room, plus a fireplaced room with a kingsize bed and a bay window. The Car Barn has two more contemporary bedrooms sharing a living room.

The newest accommodations are in the Granary – three bedrooms, living room and kitchen in a converted 19th-century grain barn at the rear of the property.

Grandson Carter, now resident innkeeper, and a couple of longtime Hirsh assistants serve a full Southern breakfast. Expect things like curried scrambled eggs, sweet pea omelets, creamed turkey and chicken, batter bread and fried grits, many of the ingredients coming from the farm. The meal is taken in a sunny breakfast room at tables set with floral mats.

Outside are a tennis court, a croquet court, the owners' pool, fifteen miles of walking trails and the Jackson River, two private miles of which pass through the property. You can swim there, fish or go canoeing. A favorite spot is a wooden deck, built atop a cliff overlooking a slough and the river bottom below. Guests take cocktails and even picnic suppers here to watch the beaver, deer, herons, ospreys and such.

Few can resist stopping in the barn to check out Harvey the donkey, Mrs. Hirsh's favorite, who bunks with Nelson the horse. You'll hear guinea hens squawking and geese honking. Peacocks and Japanese silkies, a type of chicken with black skin and white feathers, parade about.

The Hirshes conceived, built and operated the Inn at Gristmill Square in Warm Springs before selling it in 1981 to concentrate on their home property. They retain a two-bedroom cottage for guests in Warm Springs.

Carter hoped to find a way to restore dinner service for guests on weekends in season.

(540) 839-5959. Fax (540) 839-2135. Four rooms, three suites and three cottages with private baths. Doubles, $105 to $125. Suites, $115 to $125. Cottages, $125 to $450. Two-night minimum on peak spring and fall weekends. Children over 5 in cottages.

King's Victorian Inn, Route 220, (Route 1, Box 622), Hot Springs 24445.
Atop a sloping lawn, this turreted Victorian house with a wraparound veranda overlooks the Homestead golf course. Inside, all is crisp and country elegant, with none of the clutter and darkness often associated with the period. "I like it light and airy," explains ex-Richmonder Liz King, innkeeper with her husband Richard, who is with the U.S. Postal Service in Staunton.

They have decorated six guest rooms, four with private baths, in traditional Williamsburg colors against a backdrop of reproduction antiques. A solid mahogany Charleston rice bed graces one room with two sitting areas, one in a sunny alcove over the living room, and a bath with a double vanity and colored soaps arrayed in a wicker basket. Another room, pretty in teal and rose, has a step-up bed

Guests at King's Victorian Inn enjoy turrets and wraparound porches.

and a wicker sitting area. The Victorian Room contains a porch-like nook, a fireplace and a sitting area with a double bed. Two bedrooms on the third floor share a bath and sitting area beneath a colorful glass ceiling.

The Kings offer cottage accommodations in an adjacent former ice house. It comes with a deck, an efficiency kitchen, a sofa and TV, plus an upstairs bedroom with a queen bed and a shower bath. Lately, they acquired and refurbished a duplex cottage next to the Homestead's Cascades Inn. Each side of the duplex contains two bedrooms, a kitchen and living area and a porch.

Public areas in the main inn include a second-floor garden room with wicker and TV, a smashing living room with a mauve carpet, two enormous sectional sofas dressed in a yellow floral print and a card table in a sun room alcove, and an elegant parlor with a white sofa, two rose wing chairs and an oriental rug. A raised fireplace with three stained-glass windows above, silver service on the sideboard and an 18th-century reproduction Chippendale table and chairs enhance the dining room. A piano is tucked in a hallway alcove beneath the stairway.

A full breakfast might include sausage and eggs with homefries, fried apples and coffee cake. Tea, crackers and cheese are offered in the afternoon.

(540) 839-3134. Four rooms and three cottages with private baths; two rooms with shared bath. Doubles, $85 to $105. Cottage, $115. Two-bedroom cottages, $120 to $150. No young children. No smoking. No credit cards.

Vine Cottage Inn, Route 220, Box 918, Hot Springs 24445.

"We're the next best thing to the Homestead," say the owners of this B&B just a stone's throw away. Most of the resort facilities are available to guests on a fee basis, as they are to Homestead guests who are not on package plans. Here you can pay for golf, horseback riding, bowling, the spa and meals and enjoy the Homestead experience at a fraction of the price.

Upstate New Yorkers Sandy and Joel Reber and her sister, Jean Rapp, took over in 1997 what had been a lodging facility since 1905. Their predecessors had adapted the late Victorian theme to what they called "country comfortable." There's a big TV in the comfy living room full of books. At the other side of the entry is a large, fireplaced dining room in red and blue.

Upstairs are eight guest rooms with private baths, four with shared baths and three former bunk rooms now billed as "family rooms" that accommodate three to five persons and share baths. Rooms come in quite a variety of configurations, but most of those with private baths have queen or kingsize beds. Biggest rooms are on the third floor, where the Presidents' Room with kingsize bed is decked out in red, white and blue and the Honeymoon/Anniversary Room on the end has a kingsize bed covered in lace, framed anniversary cards, wedding photos and a statue of a kissing couple.

The Rebers have enhanced the breakfast fare. They serve a fruit cobbler or apple crisp with homemade breads or sticky buns. These are preliminaries to a hot dish, perhaps stuffed french toast, blueberry pancakes or an egg casserole.

The new owners also were adding showers to some of their old-fashioned bathtubs and were accepting young children and pets in certain rooms.

(540) 839-2422 or (800) 410-9755. Eight rooms with private baths; four double rooms and three family rooms with shared baths. Doubles, $70 to $75 with shared bath, $80 to $90 with private bath. Family rooms, $80 for three occupants to $120 for five. Children and pets welcome.

Hidden Valley Bed & Breakfast, Hidden Valley Road, Box 53, Warm Springs 24484.

Hidden in the back of beyond beside the Jackson River, three roundabout miles west of Warm Springs, is this many-dimensioned treasure that was the setting in 1992 for the movie "Sommersby." Hidden Valley is at once a small and historically true antebellum B&B, an ongoing archaeological dig, a teaching site, and a wilderness mecca for hikers and trout fishermen. It's also quite a story.

The story begins more than 9,000 years ago with the Indians; the resident archaeologist and college students have catalogued thousands of artifacts from the area. Fast forward to 1848 when Bath County Judge James Warwick began construction of Warwickton, one of the finest Greek Revival mansions in western Virginia. It eventually fell into disrepair as a hunt club, a school and a hay barn. Fast forward to 1965, when the George Washington National Forest acquired the 6,400-acre tract for recreational purposes but had no use for the mansion, which is listed on the National Register of Historical Places. Enter Pam and Ron Stidham from Ohio, who had fallen in love with the place in 1978. "I wanted a brick house with a babbling brook and Ron wanted a house in the mountains with solitude," recalls Pam. "We got the best of both worlds here."

They also got more than they bargained for. It took years of pleading and bureaucratic maneuvering for the Stidhams to persuade the U.S. Forest Service to lease them the house and issue a special-use permit to run a B&B. The unprecedented agreement allowed the Stidhams to operate a commercial venture for 30 years in return for restoring the structure and opening it to the public for tours. They moved in 1990 into a house "in dire need of massive restoration."

Hidden Valley Bed & Breakfast provides historic plantation experience.

Some of the restoration coincided with the filming of "Sommersby," which required an antebellum mansion and a 360-degree panorama without a sign of modern civilization. The moviemakers built a set of eighteen structures (only two of which are left), but also delayed the Stidhams' plans for opening. They could do no restoration work during the six months of production, and then spent months returning the mansion to the condition it was in before the film crews arrived. Meticulous to a fault, Pam stripped off nine coats of paint that a set artist had applied to one fireplace mantel for a faded marble look because it was not the color used when the house was built. Her work was continually interrupted by curious sightseers who stopped to visit the interpretive center in the new, film-built summer kitchen and to visit the mansion (tours by appointment, $4).

"People said we were crazy," Pam recalled, "but all this work was worth it. You just sit out on one of the porches and you'll realize it." Pam and Ron, who works full-time for the Virginia Department of Corrections, opened their B&B in 1993. They offer three spacious, antiques-filled bedrooms, served by three private baths in a special bath and laundry wing. They also offer fine formal furnishings and antiques collected over 25 years and displayed in "a house that tells a story as it unfolds," according to Pam. Guests enjoy a Music Room and a high Victorian parlor, which holds an 1844 square grand piano. A formal dining room is the setting for a full plantation breakfast, including fresh fruit, banana or zucchini bread and perhaps a five-cheese egg strata. There are a couple of porches and a gazebo for taking in the utter stillness and marvel of it all. "When you enter the valley," as Pam says, "you leave the world behind."

There's really no choice. Hidden Valley is not just a B&B. It's a way of life.

(540) 839-3178. Three rooms with private baths. Doubles, $89. Children over 6. Pets welcome. No smoking. No credit cards.

The Anderson Cottage, Old Germantown Road, Box 176, Warm Springs 24484.
A two-story-high, wraparound veranda distinguishes this rambling house whose original four rooms were an 18th-century tavern. It then was a girls' school and an inn, and now is a private home-turned-B&B with two houses joined together. Jean Randolph Bruns, whose family has owned it since the 1870s, has been known to open it for tours for Homestead guests.

She offers a first-floor suite with a queensize bed, well-worn oriental rugs, a huge fireplaced parlor and the only modern bath in the house. Upstairs is a second suite with a queen bed, a clawfoot tub, and a parlor with a twin bed and a wicker sitting area. After staying here, guests from Chicago told Jean they were through looking for real estate – "they wanted to buy their room!"

A bedroom with a queensize bed comes with private bath. A large end room with beamed ceilings, working fireplace and a double and a single bed has a shared bath. A fifth large bedroom is seldom rented – "it's my museum room and pulls everything together on my historical tours," says Jean. With exposed chestnut log walls, it contains a little desk from the time it was a school, old textbooks and a museum-quality quilt of homespun, hand-stitched French fabric on the double bed.

Out back is an 1820s brick kitchen cottage with two bedrooms and a fireplaced kitchen-dining room, available for families and long-term rentals.

Guests pick out a mug from a huge collection and help themselves to coffee in the country kitchen, the only room in the house without a fireplace because it started as a porch. Breakfast, taken at a long table in the dining room, might include sausage, cheese strata and apples baked with brown sugar. The guest parlor opens onto the veranda, where church pews and rockers overlook two pleasant acres. The stream out back flows from the warm springs pools and is so tepid that "my grandchildren think all mountain streams must be warm," Jean reports.

(540) 839-2975. One room, two suites and two-bedroom cottage with private baths; one room with shared bath. Doubles, $60 to $70. Suites, $80 to $90. Cottage, $120. Closed December to early March. Smoking restricted. No credit cards.

Hummingbird Inn, Wood Lane, Box 147, Goshen 24439.

Their children grown, Diana and Jeremy Robinson decided to chuck their high-pressure careers for a lifestyle change in the Shenandoah Valley. Jerry had been an editor-in-chief and book publisher in New York and British-born Diana had been a registered nurse when they met up with the aborted Rose Hummingbird Inn, which had variously been an inn, boarding house or a residence since 1853. They upgraded guest rooms, added more rooms and serve meals of distinction in a destination inn just west of Goshen Pass, a spectacular gorge favored by fishermen, hikers and picnickers. "People seek us out to be in the middle of nowhere," says Jeremy.

Nearly a dozen hummingbird feeders surround the unusual fourteen-room Victorian Carpenter Gothic villa located along a residential street across from a seldom used railroad track. Hummingbirds are on view from the front-corner solarium as well as the two-story verandas that wrap around part of the main structure built in 1853. Guests also enjoy an elegant, chandeliered parlor with a fireplace and a rustic, paneled and beamed den with TV and a fireplace, located in a section of the house dating to 1780 and still with its original floor.

The Robinsons started with four queen-size bedrooms with private baths, each equipped with ceiling fans, natural-fiber linens, down comforters, fine antiques and handsome scatter rugs on the polished wood floors. The fireplaced Eleanor Room appears much as it did when Eleanor Roosevelt slept here in 1935; its antique bird's-eye maple bedroom set includes a unique serpentine-front dresser, vanity and chaise lounge. Deciding to stick with the names of presidents or their wives, the Robinsons created the rear Franklin Room with a rice-carved four-poster canopy bed, a mahogany Empire chest and a jacuzzi tub. Another serpentine-front oak dresser graces the Abigail Room with its queensize brass bed and a good view of the side perennial gardens. A gas fireplace and a double jacuzzi were added to the largest Martha Room with a corner sitting area. A new ground-floor room has a canopied Sheraton field bed and a private veranda.

Guests are welcomed with tea and English shortbread, served on antique Meissen china in the parlor. By reservation on weekends, Diana cooks a four-course dinner ($22.50 prix-fixe, with complimentary wine). A typical meal by candlelight includes potato and roasted garlic soup with orange-pepper puree, a mixed salad dressed with raspberry vinaigrette and a choice of two main courses, always filet mignon and perhaps salmon with dill sauce, chicken with porcini mushrooms or pork tenderloin with pink peppercorn sauce. Dessert could be a lemon tart or chocolate mousse terrine.

Breakfasts are bountiful. Start with fresh fruit or fruit compote, homemade muffins, raisin scones and rose-geranium bread. The main course could be omelets, cornmeal pancakes or french toast baked in honey and cinnamon, with bacon, ham or sausage. Jerry, a connoisseur of such things, grinds and blends his own coffee.

(540) 997-9065 or (800) 397-3214. Fax (540) 997-0289. Five rooms with private baths. Doubles, $95 to $125 weekends, $75 to $105 midweek. Children over 12. No smoking.

Three Hills Inn, Route 220, Box 9, Warm Springs 24484.

Built in 1913 as a residence by early feminist novelist Mary Johnston, this is a stunner – a large mansion occupying a hilltop site with a wondrous view of the Warm Springs Gap and the Alleghenies beyond. A novelist and her sisters operated the mansion as an inn, and a subsequent owner turned it into apartments. In 1984, a German woman purchased it and spent millions restoring it to its former status as an inn, which never measured up to its potential. She finally sold it in 1994 to Charlene and Doug Fike from Indiana.

The Fikes moved to Three Hills and planned to build a home on the 38-acre property. They also built a fitness center with an outdoor hot tub and a small conference center. Charlene wanted to continue her career of leading training sessions for small businesses and Doug, as executive director of a Mennonite organization, planned retreats for clergymen of various faiths. "We were both on the road traveling in separate directions and decided it was time for a change," Charlene said. "We wanted to pick a beautiful spot where instead of us going out all the time, people would come to us."

A more beautiful spot is hard to imagine. The Fikes set to work renovating and redecorating the entire inn and plan to offer dinner to inn guests and the public. (A highly acclaimed restaurant operation, The Muse, did not renew its lease after the 1997 season).

The Fikes inherited most of the heavy, European-style furnishings in the rambling main house and four older cottages. They lightened up the decor and modernized some of the bathrooms. The twelve guest accommodations in the main house still show their apartment heritage. Five are "hotel rooms" with double, queen or king beds. Three are one-bedroom junior suites with separate living room or kitchen. Four are master suites with one or two bedrooms, living room with fireplace and a kitchen. All have private baths and TV. The second-floor Birch Suite in front includes a formal living room with fireplace, kingsize bed, a huge mirrored armoire and a private deck on the porch roof. The rear Dogwood junior suite, with a kingsize bed and twin sleeper sofas in the wicker-furnished living room, overlooks the English boxwood garden.

Two cottages ranging from two to four bedrooms are available near the main house.

Resident innkeepers serve a full breakfast in one of the chandeliered dining rooms. Fresh fruit and muffins precede a main courses of fruit crêpes, puffed apple pancakes, stuffed french toast or individual omelets. Tea is offered on weekend afternoons.

Families are welcome, and the inn's new brochure promotes Three Hills as an environmentally conscious "green inn."

(540) 839-5381 or (888) 234-4557. Fax (540) 839-5199. Five rooms, seven suites and two cottages with private baths. Doubles, $59 to $99. Suites, $119 to $179. Cottages, $139 and $189, two-night minimum. Children and pets welcome. No smoking.

Dining Spots

The Greenbrier, White Sulphur Springs, W.Va.

The dining experience at The Greenbrier is as extravagant as everything else about this world-class resort. Most guests take dinner in the handsome **Main Dining Room,** a long space notable for enormous artworks on its pink walls, crystal chandeliers and arched windows onto the gardens. It's nicely broken up by columns, dividers and a center platform where a pianist and violinist entertain nightly. Vichyssoise and a famous dessert of peaches and cream are traditional favorites. Everything is prepared from scratch by the culinary staff of 135, many of whom received their training through The Greenbrier's Culinary Apprentice Program instituted in the 1957 to ensure the resort an ample supply of quality chefs.

The short MAP menu changes daily and is contemporary as can be. Start perhaps with corn and oyster chowder or an appetizer of blackened quail with grilled marinated vegetables and orzo pesto, and a spinach and arugula salad with marinated tomatoes and black olives. Main courses range from smoked arctic char with saffron seafood risotto to grilled veal filet with crayfish and lentil chili to roast leg of lamb with roasted garlic spoonbread. We've enjoyed several dinners here and were impressed both by the food and the flawless service.

Five-course dinners arrive beneath silver domes in the dark and masculine **Tavern Room.** Cooking is at open rotisseries and the cuisine is contemporary, as in an appetizer of honey-smoked breast of pheasant with marinated peppers and warm cilantro potato salad or an entrée of charbroiled veal T-bone steak with morel cream sauce and a roasted barley pilaf.

Colorful in rose, white wicker and chintz, **Draper's Cafe** serves à la carte breakfast and lunch. For a mid-day treat, one of us enjoyed black bean soup topped artistically with jalapeño pepper and sour cream and a cobb salad that was tossed instead of composed in the traditional style. The other had an excellent seared salmon steak with green and red tomato salsa, sweet California mustard and salad greens and the specialty dessert, a Greenbrier peach on rum-raisin ice cream topped with blackberry sauce.

Want a different experience? Head for the Greenbrier Golf Club, where the old dining room and veranda were transformed in 1997 into **Sam Snead's at the Golf Club** and **Slammin' Sammy's** sports bar. Here chefs employ a wood-burning oven in an open kitchen to prepare lunch and dinner in more casual surroundings. Seafood cappellini, roasted stuffed Maine lobster and hickory-flavored rotisserie chicken may be on the menu.

Dramatic open grill and table presentations are featured in Homestead's refurbished Grille.

Food and drinks also are available in the **Old White Club** and the **Rhododendron Pool Lounge.**

(304) 536-1110 or (800) 624-6070. Lunch, 11:30 to 2:30, to 6 in café. Dinner nightly by reservation, 7 to 9 or 10.

The Homestead, Hot Springs.

"You eat at The Greenbrier and you dine at The Homestead," we were advised by several of the latter's admirers – and they are legion.

The Main Dining Room is an L-shaped, football field-size expanse of the old school (lately enhanced with french doors, columns and greenery to serve as room partitions). At dinner, a band was playing for dancing as we gazed out at a sea of white tables and hovering staff. The dinner menu, somewhat pedestrian and passé at our first visit, has been elevated with the elimination of such traditional fixtures as tomato juice, vichyssoise and omelets. Now, along with the tried and true, the night's menu (available prix-fixe to the public for $60) might yield innovations like an appetizer of carpaccio of pork with dill-mustard sauce, a salad of belgian endive on mesclun with herbed cheese and taro root chips, and a main course of grilled ginger-marinated sea scallops, shrimp and swordfish with Turkish saffron rice and wilted spinach.

At our latest visit, we were well satisfied with appetizers of country pâté with foie gras in the middle and a lump crab and shrimp cocktail with rémoulade sauce, plus a couple of exotic salads. One of us had roast prime tenderloin with armagnac sauce, green peppercorns and grapes, served with ratatouille and macaire potato. The other chose rack of lamb with carrots, snow peas and a timbale of polenta with spinach. Desserts were blackberry pie and hazelnut-coffee ice cream pie, followed by cappuccino and espresso.

A delicious breakfast buffet was served in the dining room the next day. From the table with a fantastic array of fresh fruits (including gigantic strawberries, mangoes and kumquats) to the hot dishes of creamed beef, broiled fish, eggs and grits, it was a Southern treat to be remembered.

The pride of The Homestead is **The Grille,** a handsome room with huge windows onto the golf course. We found its French/American dinner menu (prix-fixe, $60) more innovative than that of the dining room.

Light fare is available seasonally in the casual new indoor-outdoor 19th-hole grill at the Club Casino adjacent to the first tee of the Homestead Course. Golfers are partial to eating in the **Cascades Club Restaurant** or the **Lower Cascades Clubhouse Restaurant.** The Homestead also operates **Cafe Albert** and **Sam Snead's Tavern,** which are popular with the public as well.

(540) 839-1766. Dinner nightly in dining room, from 6:30, jacket and tie required. Grille, nightly from 6:30, jacket required; closed some nights in off-season.

The Waterwheel Restaurant, The Inn at Gristmill Square, Warm Springs.

Fed by Warm Spring Run, the old waterwheel rotates constantly outside this 1900 gristmill, now transformed into an appealing restaurant with barnwood walls, beamed ceilings and ladderback chairs at tables on different levels. Gears and cogs of the gristmill are still in evidence, but free-standing candles, fresh flowers, linens and service plates emblazoned with a waterwheel logo create an elegant ambiance. Off to one side is a small, ten-seat tavern called the Simon Kenton Pub.

One unusual touch: there's no wine list. Instead, diners descend to a wine cellar to pick their choice from bins of bottles. The hazard is that in winter, the cellar occasionally gets so chilly that the red wines have to be warmed before serving.

Innkeeper Janice McWilliams's son Bruce oversees the dining operation, which is highly regarded. His wife Gloria is the chef. Among appetizers, we liked the mountain trout smoked over hickory chips and the country pâté of sausage, chicken livers and pork tenderloin blended with brandy and spices and served with the house chutney. Entrées range from baked stuffed trout and broiled swordfish to veal cordon bleu. Our choices were tenderloin en croûte and New York sirloin with horseradish butter, each accompanied by a sprig of plain steamed broccoli and nothing else. Profiteroles, cheesecake, zabaglione, bourbon pie and walnut torte were dessert choices.

(540) 839-2231. Entrées, $18.75 to $22.50. Dinner nightly, 6 to 9 or 10. Sunday brunch, 11 to 2. Closed Mondays, November-April.

Sam Snead's Tavern, Main Street, Hot Springs.

Located in an historic bank building in the center of town, this was renovated by golfer Sam Snead in 1980. Its symmetry and weathered gray barnwood exterior give it a distinct Wild West look. Golf memorabilia is at the entry, naturally, and wines are stored in the original bank vault. Staff clad in Sam Snead golf shirts serve patrons in a small, paneled dining room with green leather booths and chairs, or the larger dining area in the tavern with a fireplace and a dance floor. A porch on the second story is favored for outdoor dining in season.

The menu takes a golf theme, from chip shots for starters to the 19th hole for beverages. Dinner items range from pecan-crusted mountain trout with pecan crust to T-bone steak. Start with Buffalo wings, crabmeat chimichanga or a Gulf Coast shrimp cocktail. Finish with berry shortcake, ice-cream pie or rainbow sherbet.

(540) 839-7666. Entrées, $12.50 to $21.95. Lunch, Thursday-Sunday 11 to 4. Dinner, Thursday-Sunday 5 to 10. Hours vary.

Cafe Albert, Cottage Row, The Homestead, Hot Springs.

Light, casual fare is offered inside and out at this appealing cafe in the Homestead's quaint Cottage Row of shops and services. Jaunty umbrellaed tables on an outdoor deck provided the setting for our lunch of cold Virginia apple soup, a delectable croissant of turkey and spinach leaves and a good potato salad, and a tropical chicken salad sandwich on rye. Excellent chocolates, honey cookies and bread fresh from the Homestead's 19th-century ovens can be purchased along with meats, cheeses and other specialty items. Desserts range from pastries to sundaes.

(540) 839-7777. Open daily in summer, 9 a.m. to 8 p.m. Hours vary.

Diversions

The Springs. As did their forefathers, today's visitors can take part in the ritual of the baths. The Homestead's **Warm Springs Pools** remain as they were upon opening, the men's pool in 1761 and the ladies' pool in 1836. Thomas Jefferson took the waters here for his health. He is credited with designing the octagonal bathhouse that surrounds the men's pool, which has been in continuous use longer than any of its kind in the country. The crude device that lowered the ailing widow of Robert E. Lee into the restorative waters is still on view in the circular women's bathhouse. The waters, a constant 98 degrees, contain a greater variety of minerals than others in the valley. Visitors pay $6 for a towel, a very basic changing room and an hour's communal soak (in the nude for men) in a six-foot-deep pool that's 40 feet across and so clear that you can distinguish the stones on the bottom. The water has a gentle fizz of tickling bubbles. Bathers lie back against steps or float along ropes, but "this is not for swimming, it's for bathing," Steve the attendant advised at the men's bath. Shirdell Pryor, the women's attendant, makes the brightly colored calico bathing shifts trimmed with rickrack rack during the winter when the pools are closed. Women can bring a bathing suit, wear one of the shifts or bathe as the men do. Springs open Tuesday-Saturday 10:30 to 5, Sunday 1 to 5, mid-April through October; $12 per session. The **Hot Springs** at The Homestead are warmer, averaging 104 degrees. Attendants in the bathhouse built in 1892 use a variety of springs and follow practices of old European spas in offering mineral baths, sauna, steam room and massage at various prices year-round.

The Spa. The Greenbrier's $7 million Spa, Mineral Baths and Salon occupies a full wing of the legendary resort begun 217 years ago because of its healing waters. This is another of the few American spas to follow the European treatment of using fresh, natural mineral waters. The spa's bath facilities include walk-in whirlpool baths, Swiss showers, Scotch spray, steam, sauna and therapy rooms for massage and body wraps. Nineteen treatments are available, varying from 25 to 80 minutes in length. We tried the basic Greenbrier treatment ($60). The hour-long assault and battery of aching showers and massages combined with relaxing baths and body wraps left one of us so relaxed he literally could not walk his normal double-time pace back to the room. It took an hour's nap to revive him for dinner.

Garth Newel Music Center, Route 220, Hot Springs, (540) 839-5018. The hillside estate of a former dean of the Yale School of Fine Arts is a destination for chamber music lovers. It's been called the Marlboro of the South. Summer weekend concerts feature the Garth Newel Chamber Players and guest artists Saturdays at 4 and Sundays at 3, early July through Labor Day. The architecture and acoustics of air-conditioned Herter Hall are perfect for chamber music, and the mountain setting is unsurpassed. In the spring and fall, center directors Arlene and Luca DiCecco, who double as violinist and cellist with the Chamber Players, offer special Garth Newel holiday weekends. Up to twenty guests enjoy overnight accommodations and gourmet meals, wine and nightly concerts.

George Washington National Forest. About half of Bath County lies in the George Washington National Forest, which encompasses numerous recreation areas, trails and campgrounds. Surrounded by the national forest, **Lake Moomaw** extends twelve miles along the Jackson River and offers boating, swimming and fishing.

Shopping. The **Tower Corridor** shops on the main floor of The Homestead are elegant and pricey, as you'd expect. Particularly impressive is the new **Southern Taste,** a gourmet food and kitchen shop with an espresso bar. Outside in the **Cottage Row,** shopping is slightly more down to earth. We particularly liked the interesting jackets made of old quilts and the fabric plant sculptures at **Quilts Unlimited,** the toys at **Just for Fun** and the women's apparel at **Lemon Twist.** Hunting and fishing equipment is featured at **The Outpost,** whose young owners also run the **Bear Paw Bookstore** at The Homestead. The artworks, ceramics and kitchenware at the **Gallery of Hot Springs** and the variety of items at **The Gift Caboose** along the old railroad platform are highlights in the center of Hot Springs.

Warm Springs Gallery, at the foot of Courthouse Hill in Warm Springs, features original art and fine crafts by regional artists.

The **Greenbrier Creative Arts Colony** is in a group of cottages known as Alabama Row at the Greenbrier. Craftsmen are among those who work and sell their wares here. The extravagant Gallery of Shops at The Greenbrier includes **The Candy Maker,** where the resort's famous chocolates are made by hand; the **Greenbrier Shop,** purveying Greenbrier signature merchandise, including the rhododendron-patterned china; the **Best of West Virginia Shop,** showcasing handiwork of local artisans; the **Carleton Varney Gift Gallery** and the **Greenbrier Gourmet,** one of the best kitchen shops we've seen. Orvis, Steuben and **Polo Ralph Lauren** also are represented here.

Extra-Special ⸻

Bacova Guild, Main Street, Hot Springs.

The mailboxes with wildlife scenes that the Bacova Guild gives to every household in the county are made at the factory in the charming company town of Bacova, a few miles west of Warm Springs. The BA stands for Bath, CO for county and VA for Virginia. The owner of the entire town of 45 cottages, grocery and company commissary teamed up with local wildlife artist Grace Gilmore to laminate her works around objects such as mailboxes, service trays, ice buckets and such. The distinctive birds, deer and the like on pale yellow backgrounds are prized everywhere and available at the Guild's factory-outlet showroom in downtown Hot Springs, which also sells clothing and gifts for the sporting life. The mailboxes, which retail for $65 to $95, are the biggest seller. The guild does a large mail-order business.

(540) 839-2105 or (800) 298-2777. Open daily, Monday-Thursday 9 to 4, Friday and Saturday 9 to 5, Sunday 10 to 2.

Dogwoods are in bloom along brick sidewalks in front of Woodrow Wilson Birthplace.

Staunton, Va.

A Frontier Town Grown Up

The first thing you should know about Staunton is that its name is pronounced STAN-ton. The second is that this is Virginia's oldest town west of the Blue Ridge Mountains and was part of America's first western frontier. The third is that it is the Queen City of the Shenandoah Valley, a showcase for architecture and the arts.

Founded in 1732, just a decade later than Richmond, Staunton was settled by the first wave of immigrants heading west from the thirteen original colonies into Appalachia and beyond. Its boom days lasted from the Civil War past the turn of the century. Lately, its downtown has been held up as an example of historic rejuvenation.

Staunton is what you might call a frontier town grown up.

Thanks to local architect T.J. Collins, who designed or remodeled more than 200 local buildings between 1891 and 1911, Staunton has an architectural importance far greater than its population of 25,000 would indicate. It contains no fewer than five historic districts. One is the wharf area – a wharf without water, incidentally – where the coming of the railroad produced the largest collection of Victorian warehouses still standing in Virginia. The wharf area is now the center-piece of a downtown revitalization known for dining spots, shopping and lodging.

A city of hills that some think give it a European look, Staunton is wonderfully focused for the visitor. Most attractions are within walking distance of the tight little downtown, which, as local innkeeper Michael Organ likes to say, embraces "ten delicious dining experiences within ten blocks, all in historic buildings."

Old buildings thrive in new incarnations. The Belle Grae Inn, offering both guest rooms and dining, grew up around a Victorian mansion. The Frederick House harbors lodging in five restored townhouses and two older houses. An old grain mill is now the Mill Street Grill. McCormick's restaurant grew out of the old YMCA. Part of the train station houses The Pullman Cafe and a Victorian ice-cream parlor and another part the Depot Grille.

Staunton's best-known attraction is the Woodrow Wilson Birthplace, lately expanded with the addition of a full-fledged museum. Up and coming is the new Museum of American Frontier Culture, a state-backed museum of living history showing early farm life. The Statler Brothers Complex is of interest to fans of the red-white-and-blue country singers who for 25 years favored their hometown with a Happy Birthday USA celebration every July 4. Some fine little shops and unusual garden enterprises are scattered around the countryside.

Staunton is surrounded by schools: Mary Baldwin College, Stuart Hall prep, the College of the Holy Child Jesus for students from Spain. And it is surrounded by scenery: the Blue Ridge Mountains, the Appalachian foothills and Shenandoah National Park. It makes a good base for exploring a compact area bounded by historic Lexington, Charlottesville, Hot Springs and the Skyline Drive.

This old frontier town has matured well, indeed.

Inn Spots

Sampson-Eagon Inn, 238 East Beverley St., Staunton 24401.

Some B&Bs seem to have everything going for them, and this is one. Restorationists Frank Mattingly and his wife Laura, business dropouts from the Washington area, renovated the 1840 house into a deluxe B&B that won the Historic Staunton Foundation's annual Preservation Award in 1992. A marker relates that the house is on the site of a blacksmith shop in which the first United Methodist Church was organized in 1797 and from which the fashionable Gospel Hill area derived its name. The house is "an absolute textbook of architectural styles," says Laura, including Empire, Greek Revival, Egyptian Revival, Colonial Revival and Victorian.

The main floor contains one guest room, a guest living room and a center dining room, plus a side porch with a two-seater swing overlooking the garden. They and

the upstairs rooms showcase the couple's various collections. "We had a small antiques business and our dream was to have a place to show our collections," explains Laura. They range from antique delft to horse brasses.

Each of the five guest accommodations is large enough for a queensize canopied bed with down pillows, reading chairs, a desk, TV/VCR, telephone and private bath. We liked the

Sampson-Eagon House won Historic Staunton's annual preservation award.

Eagon master suite with a sleeping porch outfitted in wicker and balloon curtains, and an immense T.J. Collins-designed bathroom. The designer sheets were neatly folded back on a diagonal atop the bed covers. Rooms are decorated to perfection and with great attention to detail – from flashlights to hand-held mirrors, from albums of local restaurant menus to bottles of mineral water in each room. A guest refrigerator hidden off the second-floor hallway holds juices, mixers, ice and wine glasses. A pail at the foot of the stairway is full of candies, and gourmet chocolates are put out at nightly turndown.

A full breakfast is served on Royal Doulton china in the formal dining room. Ours started with fresh raspberries and blueberries with lemon yogurt made by Frank, along with homemade breads, including cranberry, apple and Laura's favorite bourbon-pecan. The pièce de résistance was Laura's specialty grand marnier soufflé pancakes with ham and grand marnier-strawberry and orange syrups. Eggs benedict, pecan belgian waffles and Frank's special sugar and spice baked apples are other favorites.

After breakfast, Frank, an avid Staunton booster and Virginia B&B leader, will supply enough ideas to keep you busy around here for a week.

(540) 886-8200 or (800) 597-9722. Three rooms and two suites with private baths. Doubles, $94. Suites, $115. Two-night minimum weekends, May-October. Children over 12. No smoking.

Frederick House, 28 North New St., Staunton 24401.

A total of twenty rooms and suites varying in size from small to vast are offered in five side-by-side townhouses and two houses across the street. All have been grandly restored by Joe Harman, one of the few Staunton natives we encountered on our rounds here. The ex-Washington banker came home to purchase a jewelry store and to save from demolition a cluster of empty buildings. He and wife Evy turned them into a small hotel at the edge of downtown, a task that took ten years to complete and was continuing at our latest visit.

"We've taken this little corner and made it nice," says Joe in an understatement masking the massive effort and expense that have gone into the undertaking. Theirs is a comfortable refuge of uncommon appeal and value.

Because of the buildings' heritage and layout, rooms vary widely. Those in the original townhouses range from a second-floor suite reached by a graceful, curved stairway and containing a large living room and two bedrooms to a walkout English basement bedroom with a queensize bed and a sitting area with floral sprigged wallpaper. Works of Virginia artists, American antiques, ceiling fans, good reading lamps, phones, TVs and terrycloth robes are in each room. All have modern baths.

Most rooms have private entrances, and guests are not likely to run into each other except on the nicely landscaped cobblestone terrace, an outdoor gathering spot, or in the spacious tea room below, where breakfast is served by the hands-on innkeepers, who live upstairs.

In 1997, the Harmans added more rooms, suites and common facilities in two substantial residences across the street, one dating to 1820 and the other to 1898. Decorated to the period, some have fireplaces and jacuzzis. We admired a new suite with twelve-foot-high ceilings, a solid walnut canopy bed and an armoire with TV/VCR – a considerable value for $125. The new properties include meeting and dining rooms for groups, and add to the Frederick House's billing as "a small hotel in the European tradition."

As classical music played, we enjoyed a breakfast of orange juice, grapefruit and a choice of ham and cheese quiche or egg casserole with whole wheat toast. Upon request, Joe Harman played tapes of the Statler Brothers country singers, hometown boys who made good.

(540) 885-4220 or (800) 334-5575. Fax (540) 885-5180. Ten rooms and ten suites with private baths. Doubles, $75 to $105. Suites, $95 to $170. Children accepted. No smoking.

The Belle Grae Inn, 515 West Frederick St., Staunton 24401.

The first of Staunton's innkeepers, Michael Organ started in 1983 with a rambling 1873 Victorian mansion. He now has nineteen rooms and suites in six restored houses encompassing nearly an entire block in a residential section just west of downtown. "You can tell our matriculations by our restorations – 1983, '85, '87, '89, '91 and '93," says he. "That also tells where our heads were." In more recent years, he has changed some of the smaller rooms into suites with bedrooms, sitting areas and fireplaces.

The main red brick house harbors a restaurant (see Dining Spots), a parlor and a garden room with chess and backgammon games on the first floor, plus seven guest rooms of varying size with antique beds and private baths. A rocking horse is in one, a wicker seating area in another and armoires are in most. Choicer accommodations appealing to business types are found in four restored Victorian houses called the Townhouse, the Bungalow, the Bishop's House and the Jefferson House. The last is a two-story duplex, where four suites are outfitted with sitting areas, wet bars, TVs, phones, queensize four-poster beds and courtyard verandas. Gilchrist & Soames toiletries and decanters of sherry abound. The various buildings and a conference center in a cottage are joined by pathways and boardwalks across a pleasant garden terrace.

Rooms keep getting a new look because the contents are for sale. "If you like your bed," says Michael, "you can take it home with you."

Thornrose House at Gypsy Hill faces a 300-acre municipal park.

Breakfast involves what Michael calls "innkeeper's fare," anything from french toast to steak and eggs and perhaps including roast pork with cheese soufflé.

The inn derives its name from two nearby mountains, Betsy Belle and Mary Grae, named by Scotch-Irish settlers for landmarks in Scotland.

(540) 886-5151 or (888) 541-5151. Fax (540) 886-6641. Seven rooms and seven suites with private baths. Doubles, $125 to $150 weekends, $95 to $115 midweek. Suites, $170 weekends, $140 midweek. Two-night minimum weekends (and $10 surcharge) in May and October. Children 12 and over. Smoking restricted.

Thornrose House at Gypsy Hill, 531 Thornrose Ave., Staunton 24401.

The previous owners got this "B&B in the English manner" off to a good start. But it has come of age with considerable sophistication under new owners Suzanne and Otis Huston, who were widely traveled during his career as an executive with du Pont.

They lightened up the decor with lace curtains and good-looking fabrics, added two bedrooms (with private baths), restored the masterful gardens surrounding a brick terrace and a couple of pergolas, and imbued the place with their enthusiasm and hospitality. Although some rooms are on the small side, not so is the master bedroom, with two twins joined together as a kingsize bed and windows on three sides. Suzanne's favorite is the smallest – the rear Yorkshire Room with a clawfoot tub, overlooking the gardens. A daughter's bedroom was converted into a cozy guest sitting room when she left the nest.

The Hustons continued the tradition of British tea, served in season on the inviting veranda or beneath the pergolas by the gardens. On cooler days it's taken in the living room, where a gas fireplace, grand piano and a TV are among the amenities. Breakfast, served in a cozy dining room, might feature crêpes stuffed with strawberries or vanilla yogurt, mushroom and cheese omelets, banana-pecan pancakes or oat whole-grain waffles with apples along with choice of juices and, at our visit, cantaloupe with blueberries. Otis makes his own muesli, for which guests frequently request the recipe.

Besides enjoying the Hustons' gorgeous property, guests only have to cross the street for golf, tennis, swimming and walking in the 300-acre Gypsy Hill Park.

(540) 885-7026 or (800) 861-4338. Fax (540) 885-6458. Five rooms with private baths. Doubles, $60 to $80. Children over 4. Smoking restricted.

The Inn at Keezletown Road, 1224 Keezletown Road, (Route 1, Box 14), Weyers Cave 24486.

Pastel pink with white gingerbread trim, this handsome B&B is located in a rural village with an odd name about ten miles north of Staunton. It's favored by those who want to be out in the countryside and near the new Shenandoah Valley regional airport (for quick hops to the big cities).

Sandy and Alan Inabinet from Northern Virginia chose this area for a B&B in 1994 because they were familiar with it from having a weekend ski home in Massanutten. They redid the 1896 valley Victorian farmhouse into a refuge of style and comfort.

The four guest rooms, all with private baths bearing the inn's own amenities, come with sitting areas and small TVs. They're furnished with Shenandoah Valley antiques, oriental rugs, ceiling fans and down comforters. The Rose Room with a gas fireplace and a high, step-up antique queen poster bed is on the ground floor. The others are upstairs. Beds vary from canopied queens to two twins joined as kingsize.

Besides enjoying a parlor with a fireplace, guests like to rock on the unusual, inverted-curved front porch or hang out at umbrella-shaded tables on the brick terrace situated between several rear outbuildings. One is the attached wash house in which the Inabinets reside; another is a small building in which Sandy was about to open a small antiques shop at our visit. The rear yard harbors a lily pond, an herb garden, a flower garden that provides bouquets for the rooms and edible garnishes, and the chicken house. The hosts' chickens lay unusual green, blue, brown and pink tinted eggs that turn up for breakfast in the morning.

The first wakeup call may be issued by Benny, the Aracuana rooster. Guests gather later for a hearty southern meal served in the dining room or in a delightful skylit garden porch overlooking the rear patio. Sandy's North Carolina upbringing stands her in good stead for the likes of country ham biscuits, pumpkin pancakes, grand marnier french toast, cheese grits, sausage and fruit compote. Four-course BYOB dinners are available Saturday evening by advance reservation, $30 all-inclusive.

(540) 234-0644 or (800) 465-0100. Four rooms with private baths. Doubles, $85 to $95. Children over 14. No smoking.

The Iris Inn, 191 Chinquapin Drive, Waynesboro 22980.

Stands of iris line the wide, curving driveway leading up to this stunning structure on a forested, 21-acre hillside overlooking the western mountains. The irises reflect one of the themes that Iris Karl, innkeeper with her husband Wayne, have executed throughout their very personalized inn.

Be advised that this is very different from the "old" inns with which Virginia is well endowed. The Karls looked at scores of potential properties to restore as a B&B when Wayne retired from the Federal Aviation Agency. "He was an engineer and always saw the things that were falling down," says Iris. "One day he said, 'why don't we build?' We started looking for land and never looked back."

White gingerbread trim graces pink facade of The Inn at Keezletown Road.

They found a secluded hilltop high above an I-64 interchange just southeast of Waynesboro, the sister city of Staunton in Augusta County. An architect designed a sprawling, two-story inn with seven guest rooms and suites off two 92-foot-long porches running the width of the structure, a lookout tower above a whirlpool spa and a soaring, 28-foot-high great room enhanced with a large and realistic wall mural of a woodland scene. They since have added two more deluxe suites with fireplaces, wet bars and what a fellow innkeeper calls "the world's only rolling bed," which slides in and out of a wall to be hidden away for meetings. "You don't have to be in an old, historic building to succeed in this business," Iris contends. Thanks to a receptive business clientele (one du Pont Co. physician books here every month, and two Texas businessmen stayed for six months), the inn enjoys unusually high occupancy year-round. "People like a place that's new, spacious and comfortable," says Iris.

Our quarters were in the Bird Room, the last available that evening. A kingsize bed, modern bathroom, refrigerator-wet bar and TV blended nicely with the bird theme, which included pictures of birds, birds on the wallpaper border, birds pictured along the tiled bath, a bird in a nest resting on the sink and a melange of bird feeders outside. Other rooms are larger; some have day beds and jacuzzi tubs. Iris has decorated all to the nth degree in accordance with their names, from Deer to Hawk's Nest. The Woodland Forest even adds a Secret World for little children, an attic alcove with a single bed and a teddy bear's picnic.

The new Garden Path suite with kingsize canopy bed has a vaulted ceiling, a corner fireplace and a wraparound deck overlooking the valley. Potman, a lifesize figure made of different-size clay pots, occupies a niche overlooking the sitting area, and a squirrel is painted on a kitchen drawer with a hole for acorns. A spiral staircase leads to a loft with treadmill, recumbent bicycle and day bed.

The rear Deep Woods suite, where pocket doors hide the movable bed, comes with a jacuzzi and fireplace. Paw prints painted on a wall were left by a koala bear

Breakfast is taken beside remarkable wall mural in Great Hall at The Iris Inn.

in a tree on the loft, and creatures of the woods are found inside a hanging lamp above the dining table.

Breakfast is an event in the Great Room, alongside the remarkable wall mural. At our visit, a plate of fresh fruit preceded a choice of light, heart-shaped belgian waffles or baked eggs with crabmeat. Banana bread, good bran muffins and bird-shaped rolls accompanied. The treats began with a glass of milk and homemade chocolate-chip cookies from a bottomless jar the evening before. They culminated with a loaf of "road bread," wrapped in saran with a plastic knife, and a hug from Iris upon departure.

What will energetic Iris think of next? She was planning a celebratory Iris Weekend for May 1998, free for anyone named Iris. And if not enough authentic Irises signed up, the first named for other flowers were to be guests at half price.

(540) 943-1991. Seven rooms and two suites with private baths. Doubles, $80 to $95 weekends, $75 to $90 midweek. Suites, $140 weekends, $130 midweek. Children over 10. No smoking.

Dining Spots

Belle Grae Inn, 515 West Frederick St., Staunton.

Occupying the front portion of the main floor of this inn are three elegant Victorian dining rooms plus a veranda and a garden terrace, as well as an art deco bistro for lighter dining and entertainment.

We dined in front of a fireplace amidst tables dressed in white and pink with blue china and glassware and an assortment of family keepsakes and heirlooms. Tables are well spaced and some seating is on couches. The short, contemporary menu might list such entrées as fillet of sole with cardamom and sherry cream, roast duckling with black currant-caramel sauce, fennel seed-crusted braised lamb shank with lemon-dill risotto, and Chincoteague crab cakes with puree of sweet red pepper and herb mayonnaise, a seasonal treat that we had enjoyed earlier here at lunch (since discontinued). Tasty appetizers included a smoked chicken, fig and roast shallot tart, terrine of lobster and boursin with herb puree, and roast quail with leek stuffing and corn vinaigrette. The basket of "bubble bread," spicy with caraway, was so good we readily accepted a refill. That meant we had to forego such desserts as almond-amaretto torte, chocolate-mocha crêpe and chocolate mousse pie.

"Fun dining" is offered in the airy Garden Room bistro, billed as Staunton's only indoor-outdoor cafe, with lots of glass. The short menu ranges widely from herb-roasted chicken with roast garlic and lemon cream over angel-hair pasta to beef carmello with mushrooms, peas and rice pilaf.

(540) 886-5151 or (888) 541-5151. Entrées, $17.95 to $21.95; bistro, $8.95 to $14.95. Breakfast daily, 7 to 9. Dinner nightly, 6 to 9.

L'Italia Restaurant, 23 East Beverley St., Staunton.

Highly regarded is this new branch of the well established L'Italia Restaurant of Harrisonburg, which took over the site of the late lamented 23 Beverley restaurant. Owner Emilio Amato retained the elegant decor and even the china, and filled the recessed niches in the walls with paintings by art students from James Madison University.

The extensive dinner menu, more Sicilian than northern Italian, may suffer from the breadth of more than four dozen choices. They include fifteen pastas (from manicotti to fettuccine alfredo with shrimp). As Neapolitan love songs played during the dinner hour, we enjoyed the shrimp scampi with honey-mustard glaze over angel hair pasta and a house salad with red wine vinaigrette. Less satisfactory was the veal saltimbocca, billed as a house specialty.

The appetizers are predictable, although the low prices may not be. How about antipasto salad for two for $6.90? Ditto for desserts, from spumoni and cannoli to grasshopper pie and tirami su. A few Virginia wines are on the primarily Italian wine list, priced primarily in the teens.

Many of the same dishes turn up at lunch time, when you can order anything from an Italian hoagie to veal parmigiana.

(540) 885-0102. Entrées, $7.50 to $13.50. Lunch, Tuesday-Saturday 11 to 3:30. Dinner, Tuesday-Saturday from 3:30, Sunday noon to 10.

The Depot Grille, 42 Middlebrook Ave., Staunton.

Immensely popular is this steak and seafood house opened in part of the old C&0 facility, called Staunton Station. It's one of the few complete train complexes in the country and lately rejuvenated by developer Victor Meinert. By complete we mean an operating passenger terminal with a couple of new eateries. Also a stunning curved outdoor concourse that's the scene of a series of free outdoor Shakin' at the Station concerts in summer. Plus a free-standing signal tower, a freight depot, and three cabooses and three baggage cars that have been turned into antiques shops and boutiques.

The old terminal houses the **Whistlestop Soda Shop,** with an extraordinary 1880s ice-cream parlor and pharmacy interior for which Vic Meinert outbid the Smithsonian. Ice-cream treats are featured beneath four massive bronze and stained-glass chandeliers salvaged from the old Milwaukee train station. Occupying part of the station concourse is the **Pullman Restaurant,** where we admired the ornate bar with swinging doors as we lunched on a crab cake sandwich and the offerings from a help-yourself salad bar that was more interesting than most. A new chef from Duner's in Charlottesville has a great New Orleans flair.

The depot restaurant contains a 50-foot-long, 19th-century oak bar obtained from an old New York hotel and believed to be the longest in the country. It also has a solarium with windows opening onto the outdoors and a vast dining room displaying railroad memorabilia and lit by oil lanterns even at noon. There's an old shoeshine chair at the door.

The all-day menu appeals to all tastes, and the seafood and nightly specials come highly recommended. We hear good things about the backfin crab cakes, the mesquite-grilled chicken, the black angus sirloin steak and the grilled shrimp and feta pizza. The prices certainly are right, and salad and two choices of fries, applesauce, coleslaw, steamed vegetables, rice or new potatoes come with. Heath Bar crunch is a favorite dessert.

(540) 885-7332. Entrées, $9.95 to $14.95. Open daily, 11 to 10:30.

Mill Street Grill, 1 Mill St., Staunton.

If this restaurant in the first Wharf Historic District building to be restored looks a bit like a gallery, thank the former owner whose wife also used to own the interesting art gallery upstairs (now a noisy sports bar).

Six panels of stained glass are a focal point of the decor of the old White Star Mills flour mill. Done by a local couple, they depict the journey of wheat from the harvesting to the baking of bread. There's much to look at on several levels with exposed beams and thick fieldstone walls: paintings and collages, old light fixtures, etched glass and copper rails.

Tablecloths and candlelight are the setting for dinner. The specialty here is ribs, slow-cooked baby back ribs and beef ribs in the Midwest style. A barbecue platter yielding samples of both costs $11.95. One well-traveled innkeeper calls them the best ribs she's ever had. She says the rest of the food has zip as well. The menu ranges widely from raspberry chicken or curried pork tenderloin to filet mignon sautéed in peppercorn cream sauce. Grilled mahi-mahi, charbroiled yellowfin tuna, crab cakes and pastas are among the offerings.

Appetizers run to steam spiced shrimp, Buffalo wings, potato skins and chicken nachos. Key lime, hazelnut-cappuccino and Reese's peanut butter pies are featured desserts.

(540) 886-0656. Entrées, $9.95 to $15.25. Dinner nightly, 4 to 10. Sunday brunch, 11:30 to 3. Closed in January.

J. Rugle's Warehouse, 18 Byers St., Staunton.

Gourmet pizzas and pastas are the specialties at this informal downtown restaurant in a restored warehouse with a large bar area, an upstairs dining room and, in season, a popular sidewalk cafe. The restaurant is part of developer Vic Meinert's group of restorations, which also includes the Depot Grille and the Pullman Cafe.

The specialty pizzas come in various sizes and with a variety of toppings, so in effect you create your own. Or you can choose one of the "history-making combinations:" spinach and artichoke hearts, cajun chicken or white cheese and pesto.

There's more. Entrées, served with house or caesar salad, include things like steamed crab legs, blackjack chicken (flamed with Jack Daniels), chicken pesto, steak kabobs and New York strip steak. There also are sandwiches and appetizers, from potato skins to nachos to mozzarella sticks.

Homemade desserts range from snicker bar pie and fried ice cream to tirami su. Cappuccino, lattes and Italian wines also are featured.

(540) 886-4399. Entrées, $9.95 to $13.95. Dinner nightly, 5 to midnight.

The Heavenly Bake Shop, 101 West Beverley St., Staunton.

A wall mural of clouds painted by one of the owners enhances this new downtown favorite for lunch and dinner. The baked goods and pastries are imported from Charlottesville, but the son of one of the owners prepares the sandwiches, salads and lunches, including a handful of vegetarian items.

Stop in for a breakfast snack of scones, muffins or sour cream coffee cake to go with a cappuccino or latte. For lunch, try a smoked turkey cobb sandwich or roast beef with watercress and alouette cheese on French bread. Or how about the California Dream salad – greens tossed with marinated chick peas, avocado, steamed broccoli, mushrooms, tomato, red onion and sprouts, garnished with cilantro? Or a caesar chicken salad? Prices are in the $4 to $5.50 range.

(540) 886-4455. Open Monday-Saturday, 9 to 5.

The Pampered Palate, 26-28 East Beverley St., Staunton.

The old Atlantic Lunch hot-dog stand has been transformed into this sprightly deli and gourmet food and wine shop. There is dining upstairs in a tearoom atmosphere (seven tables and a high chair) and downstairs in an ice-cream parlor setting.

Sandwiches with local names are "the Palate's pride." We liked the New Theater (vegetables, mushrooms and havarti) and the Statler (a quartet of meats and cheeses). Both were stuffed in pita bread. A few salads, quiche, pampered potatoes, cheese boards, bagels and sweets round out the fare. The menu is priced in the $3.50 to $5 range and everything's available to take out.

(540) 886-9463. Open Monday-Saturday 9 to 5:30, Sunday 11 to 2:30. No smoking.

Diversions

Historic Walking Tours. The Historic Staunton Foundation, founded in 1971 to promote preservation over demolition, has concentrated its efforts in the downtown and adjacent residential areas. That makes it easy to view the results on foot. Indeed, as county tourism coordinator Sergei Troubetzkoy noted, visitors can arrive at the restored railroad station by Amtrak, walk to lodging and restaurants, and never need a car – a rarity for a small town these days. The foundation's walking tour map and brochure focuses on 59 sites of outstanding architectural or historic merit in the Downtown, Wharf Area, Newtown, Gospel Hill and North End. Many sites were designed or remodeled around the turn of the century by local architect T.J. Collins, whose son continued the tradition. Visitors accustomed to Virginia's formal Jeffersonian brick styles will be struck by Staunton's exuberance, the result of one family having a major impact on the design of a community.

Woodrow Wilson Birthplace & Museum, 18-24 North Coalter St., Staunton.

The Presbyterian manse in which America's 28th president was born in 1856 is a registered National Historic Landmark. On guided tours every half hour, visitors see the room where he was born, the crib in which he slept and the chair in which his mother rocked him. The tour and furnishings emphasize the way of life of

Stauntonians in the 1850s – "the way they would have lived as a Southern family," according to our guide. You see twelve rooms containing many items that belonged to the Wilson family. The rear balcony affords a view of the historic gardens restored by the Garden Club of Virginia, the cream-colored buildings of Mary Baldwin College and the downtown. "Now you're part of the family," says the guide at tour's end. "You get to leave by the back door."

Before the tour, browse through the only museum in the country spanning Wilson's entire life. Seven galleries cover everything from his parentage to his funeral. The re-creation of his Princeton University study contains his old Hammond typewriter. Other galleries trace his economic and social reforms, the tumultuous war years, and his search for peace and a new world order. The well-spaced displays are tasteful, significant and not at all overwhelming. A highlight is his beloved 1919 Pierce-Arrow White House limousine, donated by his widow to be shown in his hometown in a large garage beside the museum. An attractive gift shop adjoins the garden.

(540) 885-0897. Open daily 9 to 5, March-November, 10 to 4 rest of year. Adults, $6.

Statler Brothers Complex, 501 Thornrose Ave., Staunton, (540) 885-7297. Opposite Gypsy Hill Park is this renovated school building, now the corporate headquarters of the Statler Brothers country singers, all of whom reside in the area. Still on view is the gymnasium stage where the brothers won their first talent show in 1955. Hallway cases sparkle with Grammys and records. One tour a day is given Monday-Friday at 2. Gift shop hours are weekdays, 10:30 to 3:30.

P. Buckley Moss Museum, 2150 Rosser Ave., Waynesboro.

On a hilltop overlooking Waynesboro, the stately brick Moravian mansion that celebrated artist Pat Moss designed herself in 1989 showcases many of her works. She still paints at her home and barn two miles to the south, her studio since the early 1960s, although her official residence now is in St. Petersburg, Fla. Three floors of the mansion trace her evolution from her Pennsylvania childhood through her time as a designer in the New York garment district to the height of her "Valley style." Her fame has spread mainly since the mid-1980s through the marketing efforts of her husband-manager, Malcolm Henderson. Most of the art here reflects the Amish and Mennonite "Plain People" in local and Pennsylvania scenes. Exceptions such as one of sailing on Tampa Bay and a Washington mountain landscape come as surprises. Her watercolors and original prints in the large shop start at $30 and go way up. An oil of Sedona in the Gallery/Studio was listed at $48,000.

(540) 949-6473. Open Monday-Saturday 10 to 6, Sunday 12:30 to 5:30. Free.

André Viette Farm and Nursery, Route 608, Fishersville, (540) 943-2315. In early spring, the rolling countryside here is ablaze with tulips. These spectacular perennial gardens continue with poppies, peonies, iris and, their real claim to fame, lilies. André Viette's fame, spread through his national gardening radio program, draws people from afar to his garden center and flower clinics.

Shopping. As you walk around downtown, you'll surely be struck by the interesting plants and gardens that are the work of a fulltime city horticulturist. **The Emporium** at 101 East Beverley St. stocks nice pottery, baskets, windsocks, unusual birdhouses, silk flowers, stuffed animals and the like. Tommie Duke and Stephen Fitzpen offer exceptional garden furniture, accessories and antiques with a New Orleans accent at **The Garden Room.** The new **Avery Studio Gallery** is an

Rear of Woodrow Wilson Birthplace overlooks restored gardens.

outstanding gallery of contemporary art. **Turtle Lane** is filled to the brim with appealing gifts. We liked the jewelry from exotic places at **Silver Linings**. **Honeysuckle Hill** offers antiques and collectibles. **Depot Antiques** carries interesting folk art, primitives and Shenandoah Valley furniture; we were struck by the rustic twig chair with a birdhouse on top for $150. If you're into oriental rugs, one of the best selections on the East Coast is opposite the train station at **Victorian Rug Co.**, 9 Middlebrook Ave. Quite a sight is the old automobile showroom now housing **Bruce Elder Antique and Classic Automobiles;** it has an elevator to transport cars to all three floors.

The **Virginia Made Shop** at Exit 222 from I-81 is full of local items. If you'd like a peanut basket – with peanut soup, peanut butter and an assortment of peanuts – this is the place. It's connected with the new **Bacova Guild Company Store.** The Staunton-Augusta **Farmers' Market** is a Saturday fixture; all participants produce what they sell.

Side Trips. Don't miss the jaunt about eighteen miles south of Staunton to the hilly, rural Raphine area. Here, almost side by side along Route 606 west from I-81 Exit 205, are two must stops:

Buffalo Springs Herb Farm, Raphine Road, Raphine.

Former florists from northern Virginia restored a 1793 brick and stone homestead and a big red barn beside a rushing creek, a grand space that lent itself to workshops, drying and demonstration areas and an exceptional shop. Don Haynie and Tom Hamlin offer herbal products, dried flowers and designs, garden books, herb plants in season, nature trails, an arbor garden and herbal happenings, from workshops to picnics to herbal lunches by reservation. Their 170-acre educational farm is so scenic that it's been a setting for weddings.

(540) 348-1083. Open April through mid-December, Wednesday-Saturday 10 to 5, also Sunday 1 to 5 except June-August.

Wade's Mill, 55 Kennedy-Wade's Mill, Raphine.

This neat place is one of the few operating gristmills actually producing flour as  a business in this country. The miller and his wife are Jim and Georgie Young, ex-Washington bureaucrats who bought the circa 1750 mill in 1991. Now Jim grinds a couple of thousand pounds of flour exclusively on mill stones each week. They also sell fresh breads and muffins in the fall, run cooking classes and occasional brunches in their renovated farmhouse, published a cookbook now in its second edition, and give tours and demonstrations in their mill, which is powered by a 21-foot water wheel fed by the nearby stream. Georgie's shop features local pottery and baskets, buckwheat pancake mixes and apple syrup, and a cook's corner with everything you need to cook and bake with flour.

(540) 348-1400. Open same hours as Buffalo Springs Herb Farm.

The Cyrus McCormick Farm, Route 606, Steele's Tavern.

Cross a little creek from the wayside parking lot at Walnut Grove Farm to the old gristmill, powered by water from a mill pond, and the blacksmith shop. This simple little farm smithy was the birthplace in 1831 of the first mechanical reaper, a horse-drawn harvesting machine. Young Cyrus McCormick's invention ushered in the age of farm mechanization and hastened the westward expansion of the United States. The story unfolds in a simple museum above the blacksmith shop, where reproductions of early reapers are on display.

(540) 377-2255. Open daily, 8 to 5, April-December. Closed weekends in winter.

Extra-Special

Museum of American Frontier Culture, Route 250 at I-81 Exit 222, Staunton.

Curiously juxtaposed next to the interchange of two interstate highways, this outdoor, living-history museum opened in 1990 to interpret the American frontier. This is not the frontier of the Wild West, but rather of America's first frontier – the Shenandoah Valley. The state-owned tract has four reconstructed farmsteads, three of which are from European nations (England, Northern Ireland and Germany) that the pioneers left behind. They are authentic reconstructions of historical working farms from each country, and costumed interpreters demonstrate daily life to visitors. The fourth and largest farm is the American synthesis, reflecting the melding of European influences. You might see a carpenter making pegs for the German barn, a pig-calling contest at the English farm, rare Kerry cattle, wonderful fencing in different styles and even stray farm cats. This is a special place for the young and the young at heart. The contemporary visitor center and the sounds of interstate traffic are in marked contrast to the farmsteads from the 18th and 19th centuries.

(540) 332-7850. Open daily, 9 to 5, winter to 4. Adults, $8.

Thomas Jefferson's Monticello lures visitors to Charlottesville.

Charlottesville, Va.

Jefferson's Lively Mountain Eden

History. Mountain vistas. A lively university town. Vineyards and wineries.

These are among the assets that draw visitors to Charlottesville, the Piedmont area favored by Thomas Jefferson. He built Monticello, his "little mountain" home, in the rolling countryside he later described as "the Eden of America." It overlooks the Blue Ridge Mountains, the town and the University of Virginia, which he founded.

Jefferson also persuaded his friend and fellow president, James Monroe, to build a home nearby. Another colleague, James Madison, lived two dozen miles to the north in Orange.

Jefferson's influence is everywhere obvious in the Charlottesville area. The University of Virginia that he designed is the region's major presence. Thousands of tourists are directed to Monticello from a large visitor information center at the foot of its access road. A dozen or more small wineries fulfill the hopes of Jefferson, a wine connoisseur and would-be grape grower.

The Blue Ridge Mountains to the west are a spectacular backdrop for a prosperous university town tugged between tradition and change. The visitor to Charlottesville detects few Southern accents, testimony to the influx of outsiders and their amalgamation into a sophisticated, academic culture. The city is rife with dining, lodging, shopping and cultural opportunities. A new indoor skating rink called the Charlottesville Ice Park and a six-screen movie theater thrive at the edge of downtown.

Traditionalists lament some of the changes. They contend that Charlottesville (now with a metropolitan population of 125,000) isn't the nice little place it used to be. Rush-hour gridlock stalls traffic on the expressways, and shopping malls have sprung up on farmlands. But this is urban sprawl with a difference: highways and commerce co-exist with antebellum plantations and an amazing number of palatial new homes, each with sizable property and a view of the surrounding Blue Ridge.

Sir Bernard Ashley chose the Charlottesville area as the site for his third and largest country-house hotel. He was struck by the beauty and heritage of the town and countryside. "It's not just a modern, thrown-up town," he said. "It has heart."

Inn Spots

Clifton – The Country Inn, 1296 Clifton Inn Drive, Charlottesville 22901.

Superlatives and Clifton go hand-in-hand. But for a gracious plantation built by Thomas Mann Randolph, who married Thomas Jefferson's daughter Martha and was an early governor of Virginia, this luxurious inn is surprisingly unpretentious. A hilltop away from Monticello on a cliff astride the Rivanna River, it has fourteen spacious rooms and suites, each with wood-burning fireplace and private bath. The 45 acres of verdant grounds off Route 729 in rural Shadwell harbor a sunken croquet pitch, a hard-surface tennis court, a neat swimming pool with terraced waterfall and lots of loungers amid the landscaping, an outdoor spa heated year-round, a 26-acre private lake, walking trails and wildlife, plus a couple of resident sheep.

"We want the atmosphere to be relaxed and casual, yet elegant," says Craig Hartman, hands-on innkeeper for owner T. Mitchell Willey, the Alexandria attorney who bought Clifton in 1984 and turned it into one of our favorite inns anywhere. "We don't want to lose the quaint, Jeffersonian feeling."

That is not to say rustic. Clifton is anything but. The six guest rooms in the main house offer lots of space and border on the majestic. Among their various accoutrements are antique beds with canopies built into the high ceilings and draped at the corners, cedar closets and comfortable sitting areas or rooms. Our most recent stay was in the refurbished Rivanna Suite, which has a huge bathroom with one of inn's five new walk-in spray showers, a clawfoot tub and a plump settee, not to mention a fireplace beside the queen bed in the bedroom and a sitting room with a sofabed and window seat. Evening turndown service provided ice, Perrier and fresh towels. Fruit, coffee and the morning paper were delivered the next morning.

At another visit, our quarters in the cathedral-ceilinged carriage house involved an expansive living room with a fireplace and french windows on both sides opening to let the breeze flow through, plus a queensize bed in a loft. Two guest rooms on the lower floor of the carriage house also have full-length windows across the back.

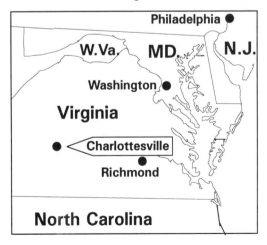

They and two large rooms fashioned from Randolph's old law office share a garden courtyard and a number of historic fixtures from the recently dismantled Meriwether Lewis home in Charlottesville. We've also stayed in one of the three suites in the secluded Livery. It came with a queensize bedroom, full bath with separate shower and a sunken sun room with sofabed and fireplace, and opened onto a patio and garden sloping toward the lake.

Clifton occupies mansion built by Thomas Jefferson's son-in-law.

Guests enjoy the run of the inn's sumptuous main floor. Here are a formal living room, a country library, a paneled dining room, a garden room and a rear dining porch, created by enclosing the old veranda, overlooking a new rear patio. Afternoon tea is put out in the garden room. At our latest visit, the copious spread teamed hot tea, herbed cranberry punch and lemonade with scones, rich chocolate cake and luscious canapés of goat cheese.

Breakfast is served on white linens and Villeroy & Boch china at five tables in the dining room or, our choice on a lovely summer morning, at individual tables on the rear dining porch. A fruit smoothie (orange, pineapple and banana juice) and apple-bran muffins began one repast; a platter of fresh fruit and apple coffee cake the next. The main dish at our latest visit was spectacular: poached eggs on a toasted croissant topped with a sauce of potage lyonnaise, tomatoes and chèvre. "I made it up in my head last night," the sous chef said when we asked the ingredients.

That didn't particularly surprise us, given the quality of dinner the preceding evening. Innkeeper Craig, the acclaimed chef who had greeted us upon arrival and helped get our luggage to the room, takes the stand during the evening cocktail hour to recite the dinner treats ahead. Ordinarily, this can be tedious, but Craig is a pro and we found his commentary as exceptional as the meal. A Culinary Institute of America grad, he and his wife Donna moved here in 1992 after cooking at Pinehurst and running a pastry shop and deli in Nag's Head, N.C.

Our latest dinner began with potage paysanne with chive oil and crème fraîche and a salad of greens, stilton and fresh apples with walnut focaccia. A tart passionfruit ice, served in a brandy snifter, cleared the palate an exceptional breast of duck with mulberry demi-glace, basmati rice and a julienne of carrots and haricots verts. Dessert following such a superb feast was hardly an anti-climax: dark chocolate cognac pots de crème with shaved chocolate, fresh berries and whipped cream.

The prix-fixe dinner, with a choice of two entrées, is five courses on weekdays and six courses on weekends, when there is live music by a pianist. Dinner is open to the public by reservation.

At our latest visit, Craig proudly showed the new 10,000-bottle wine cellar with an African mahogany ceiling. Like a fine wine, Clifton continues to improve with age.

(804) 971-1800 or (888) 971-1800. Fax (804) 971-7098. Seven rooms and seven suites with private baths. May to mid-November and weekends rest of year: doubles, $150 to $265; suites, $285 to $315. Mid-November to April: midweek, doubles $150 to $175, suites $200. Two-night minimum weekends. Children accepted. No smoking.

Prix-fixe, $48 on weekdays, $58 on weekends. Dinner nightly by reservation, 7:30.

Keswick Hall, 701 Country Club Dr., Keswick 22947.

"Absolutely spectacular" was the advance billing for this 48-room country-house hotel developed by Sir Bernard Ashley of Laura Ashley fame. It's the jewel in the crown of his Ashley House triumvirate, which began in 1987 with the acquisition of Llangoed Hall in Wales and continued in 1990 with the purchase of the Inn at Perry Cabin (which see) in St. Michaels, Md.

Also in 1990, Ashley House acquired the bankrupt Keswick property, 600 acres of rolling countryside east of Charlottesville next to Shadwell, first owned by Thomas Jefferson's father. It set out to make this the largest Ashley hotel and the first to include a private golf club and a development of 100 homes in the $1 million price range.

The $40 million rejuvenation of the Keswick estate was executed in the traditional Ashley idiom, a personalized mix of old and new.

First, the existing eighteen-hole golf course, designed by Arnold Palmer, was reopened and a posh pavilion built with fitness facilities to serve as a clubhouse. Next, a residence, the $1.5 million Keswick House, was built to showcase the private residential development. Finally, a 40-room wing was added to the original Italianate-style Villa Crawford, built in 1912 and serving as the original clubhouse. It became the hotel and restaurant.

"In the hotel," envisioned Sir Bernard – or "B.A." as his staff fondly calls him – "I want to wear what I like and sleep when I like. And if there are to be excitements, let them arrive at the dining table or on the golf course." The hotel could be intimidating, but this is not his intent, according to Anne E. Hooff, marketing director. "The idea is to escape. Comfort is the key, not elegance. He wants you to feel that this is his home and that you are his guest."

Our quarters in the third-floor Regency Room with its kingsize pewter bed was large and assuredly comfortable. One of eleven "studios," it ranked in price behind four suites and ahead of twenty-one state rooms and twelve house rooms. All are furnished in a mix of European antiques and appointments from the Laura Ashley collection, and no two are alike.

Every decision down to the selection of dessert spoons awaited Sir Bernard's final approval, although the execution was left to son Nick and a decorator from Bethesda, Md. Most accommodations have king or queen beds, but a few have twins or doubles. Each has a different armoire, a writing desk and an old reproduction radio. A handful of bathrooms possess oversize jetted tubs with separate showers.

More showy are the public rooms: the Great Hall in which arriving guests are greeted by a butler, the comfortable Morning Room (a study in off-white), the main Drawing Room outfitted with furniture from Sir Bernard's former house in

Keswick Hall (left) overlooks Keswick Club and golf course.

Brussels (and a number of his personal family photos here and there), a snooker room with a billiards table and a beautiful fireplace, and the large Crawford Lounge at the foot of a majestic staircase. Downstairs is a board room with state-of-the-art audio-visual equipment and antique trains perched on a high shelf. After a tour, we toddled down the path to the Keswick Club Pavilion for a swim in the pool, surrounded by beautiful terraces. Overnight guests are granted access to the pool, tennis courts, spa, sauna and steam rooms. Golf costs extra.

Meals are served in three serene dining rooms, dressed in light pastels with white tablecloths and striped and patterned upholstered chairs. Native Virginia chef Rick Small was invited to cook a James Beard Foundation dinner in New York, and in 1997 the chefs from all three Ashley properties combined talents for an encore at the James Beard.

Dinner is prix-fixe in four courses. One of us sampled the salmon argenteuil with asparagus and a sauce of roma tomatoes and basil, followed by grilled turbot on an exquisite sauce with broccoli. Dessert was pear sorbet served with wafer-thin crystallized slices of pear. The other enjoyed the bouillabaisse terrine in aspic, braised monkfish and shrimp with salsa and baby bok choy, and a stellar iced lemon soufflé with berries. A pink champagne sorbet was served between courses; coffee and mignardises followed. A bottle of Groth sauvignon blanc accompanied an impeccably presented, memorable meal.

Breakfast the next morning was another culinary treat. It began with unlimited fresh orange juice and an iced pineapple surprise that was like a sorbet. A basket of croissants, blueberry muffins and Virginia ham biscuits preceded the main dishes, a tomato and sausage frittata with hash browns and a platter of fresh fruits with fruit compotes. We'd return anytime to partake of the English mixed grill with eggs, tomatoes, blood sausage, mushrooms and the like.

A fairly exotic lunch menu in the Garden Room is available à la carte. The

Pavilion clubhouse serves three meals a day. Breakfast and afternoon tea are included in the rates.

(804) 979-3440 or (800) 274-5391. Fax (804) 977-4171. Forty-four rooms and four suites. Doubles, $195 to $545. Suites, $595 to $645. Prix-fixe, $58. Lunch, Monday-Saturday noon to 2:30. Dinner nightly, 6 to 10. Sunday brunch, noon to 3. No smoking.

The Inn at Monticello, 1188 Scottsville Road (Highway 20), Charlottesville 22902.

Nestled at the foot of Monticello Mountain on spacious dogwood-dotted lawns set back from quiet Route 20 is this small country manor house, ideally located near Charlottesville's main attractions. The house dates to 1850 but does not seem that old in its new incarnation. It was converted in 1989 into a comfortable, welcoming B&B and expanded in 1997 by new owners Norm and Becky Lindway, retired educators from Cleveland who were "not ready to retire."

The Lindways offer five air-conditioned guest rooms with private baths, each decorated in a different period with antiques and reproductions. Cotton sheets and down comforters are on every bed, now all king or queensize. Our quarters on the first floor, fashioned from the former dining room, had a high, step-up queensize bed and a private screened porch. Another favorite is the second-floor Victorian room with a carved walnut Eastlake bedstead and an antique mantel over the working fireplace. A loveseat slants across a corner. Guests in the other upstairs front bedroom can look out to adjacent Willow Lake, a pond with catfish and snapping turtles, at the edge of the property. Another main-floor bedroom has an arched canopy queen bed.

Homemade chocolate-chip and oatmeal cookies, tea and other beverages are offered in the long, comfortable common room outfitted with Virginiana. Breakfast is served at a dining table beside the fireplace in the common room. The fare the day of our visit included orange juice, melon and strawberries, a frittata with peppers and mushroom, and diced potatoes flavored with rosemary.

(804) 979-3593. Fax (804) 296-1344. Five rooms with private baths. Doubles, $110 to $145; 10 percent less in off-season. Two-night minimum weekends. Children over 12. No smoking. No credit cards.

200 South Street, 200 South St., Charlottesville 22901.

Two side-by-side houses at the edge of downtown were a shambles when a team of investors acquired them in 1986. After $1.5 million worth of renovations and at least that much in antique furnishings, they were opened as a suave in-town B&B in the Charleston and Savannah idiom. Most downtown restaurants are within walking distance.

Seventeen rooms and three suites are handsomely outfitted with 18th- and 19th-century antiques from England and Belgium. Most have queensize canopy or four-poster beds and sitting areas, and a few add fireplaces and whirlpool baths.

At our visit, a scrapbook in each room detailed the furnishings, most of which were for sale. In our first-floor front room, we were informed about the Georgian mahogany armoire circa 1800, the mahogany bow front chest of drawers (1815 and apparently having been sold, the more ornate replacement not being described), and eight other prized pieces, down to the Seljuk rug and brass candlesticks on the mantel. A clock-radio and a telephone equipped with modem were concessions to the times, and a TV set was available beneath the eaves in a small third-floor lounge (more than half the rooms now have TVs). The room was extra-comfortable and, given its proximity to the street, surprisingly quiet.

Afternoon tea as well as wine and cheese are set out in the main inn's library, chock full of local reading material. The library also has three scrapbooks portraying the inn's restoration plus more descriptions of all the antiques in living color. A buffet breakfast is served here and on the side veranda and a tranquil terrace courtyard. On a warm morning on the veranda, we were blessed with a breeze along with fresh orange juice, cantaloupe and cut-up fruit, cereal, molasses muffins, scones and blueberry cake.

Brendan Clancy, one of the early investors, and his wife Jenny bought out their early partners to "run the inn the way we wanted it." They have upgraded the furnishings and switched four rooms with twin beds to kingsize.

(804) 979-0200 or (800) 964-7008. Fax (804) 979-4403. Seventeen rooms and three suites with private baths. Doubles, $100 to $170. Suites, $190 to $200. Children accepted. No smoking.

The 1817 Historic Bed & Breakfast, 1211 West Main St., Charlottesville 22903.

Owner Candace DeLoach is an antiques dealer, and all the furnishings in the B&B beside her DeLoach Antiques Shop are for sale. The two adjoining townhouses were built by one of Thomas Jefferson's master craftsmen, an Irishman who was the principal carpenter for Monticello and for the Rotunda at the University of Virginia, a few blocks away.

A Georgian who formerly was an interior designer in New York, Candace has imbued her B&B with a spirit as eclectic as the decor. The living room is appointed with American Empire chests, Venetian tables, Biedermeier chairs, a large zebra-skin rug and a bowl of M&Ms.

Upstairs are four bedrooms with private baths. Rooms vary widely and décor changes as furnishings are sold. One room in the interior has no windows whatsoever (it's air-conditioned, our guide pointed out). Miss Olive's Room in the rear has a kingsize poster bed, a sitting area and a marble bathroom with shower. The Mattie Carrington Suite in front has a kingsize four-poster in the bedroom and a queensize mahogany bed in the purple parlor with French antiques and a glass chandelier. That room can be rented instead as part of the more formal James Dinsmore Suite in the adjacent townhouse, which comes with a study with a sofabed and a queensize pencil-post bed in the bedroom.

All quarters have TVs, and the three largest also have telephones. The other two have double beds, one an antique rope four-poster.

Candace serves a continental breakfast of fresh fruit, granola, and homemade muffins and breads.

A friend, Vickie Gresge, runs the **Tea Room Cafe** on the site with her husband Mark. The cafe occupies a sun porch and dining room and serves exotic sandwiches, salads, desserts and teas (a different flavor daily) Monday-Friday from 11 to 3.

(804) 979-7353 or (800) 730-7443. Fax (804) 979-7209. Three rooms and two suites with private baths. Doubles, $89 to $149. Suite, $179 to $219. Children accepted. Smoking restricted.

Silver Thatch Inn, 3001 Hollymead Drive, Charlottesville 22911.

A New England look and air pervade this rambling white clapboard house, built by Hessian soldiers who were imprisoned on the site during the Revolutionary

Silver Thatch Inn is known for fine dining and lodging.

War. The original 1780 log house now is a small common room. Later owners expanded so that the inn backing up to a residential subdivision has seven guest rooms with private baths, a cozy bar and three dining rooms (see Dining Spots).

New innkeepers Rita and Vince Scoffone from Arlington "took over a going concern" and only had to remodel three bathrooms. The guest rooms, all named after presidents, remain the same. Watermelon stenciling, wooden slices of watermelon and a watermelon wreath grace the bright and airy James Madison Room, a Federal period room upstairs in the main house with pencil-post queensize canopy bed, working fireplace and square bathtub. A brick patio and a sitting area are available for guests who stay in the four rooms in the adjacent cottage. The burled wood armoire in the George Washington Room is so tall that the ceiling had to be cut back for it to fit. Less formal is the Tyler Room with country pine furniture, deep mulberry walls, an old quilt and a fireplace. Country pine also is used in the upstairs Harrison Room, which has an antique iron double bed and a strawberry motif.

Coconut-granola-honey or chocolate-chip cookies are placed at bedside at night. Breakfast in a cheery sun room is continental-plus, from melons, berries and muffins to cereals and what our informant described as the best granola ever.

Guests have access to a large pool at the adjacent Hollymead neighborhood association.

(804) 978-4686. Fax (804) 973-6156. Seven rooms with private baths. Doubles, $115 to $150. Two-night minimum weekends in spring and fall. No smoking.

The Inn at Sugar Hollow Farm, Sugar Hollow Road, Box 5705, Charlottesville 22905.

Thirteen miles west of Charlottesville at the back of beyond is this sophisticated rural retreat. It's part of a 70-acre farm well past the hamlet of White Hall, at the edge of the Shenandoah National Park. Dick and Hayden Cabell built their handsome, contemporary clapboard house with the idea of sharing it with B&B guests.

The Cabells provide a number of comfortable common areas. On the main floor are a family room with a stone fireplace, a library with TV set, a cheerful sun room and a living room with a large palladian window. There's a reading nook off the upper foyer leading to the second-floor deck. Tea and other beverages from the butler's pantry may be taken to the nook or outside, where a passing stream is within earshot. Birds and butterflies thrive in the organic fruit, vegetable and flower gardens around the property.

A stairway with a teddybear on every step leads to five bedrooms with private baths, light-colored walls, plump beds, quilts and cheery fabrics. Handpainted wall designs add interest. The Wildflower master suite comes with a fireplace, a double jacuzzi and a kingsize four-poster bed with a canopy of white organdy. A window seat is in front of a bay window with panoramic views of the Blue Ridge Mountain. A kingsize rice poster bed, fireplace, double jacuzzi, a sofa and accents of Battenburg lace are attributes of the Country Manor Room. Barnwood paneled walls warm the Woodland Room, with queen bed, fireplace and handpainted flowers. The Hunt Country Room has a queen bed and fireplace, while the traditional Colonial Room furnished in cherry has extra-long twin beds.

Wild turkeys and deer may wander across the pasture during breakfast, served at a long table for eight beside a large bay window in the dining room. Egg dishes, cinnamon french toast or buttermilk pancakes may be the main dish. Fresh fruits, juices, homemade muffins and biscuits accompany.

"After searching for just the right setting for our inn," said Dick, "we finally found our corner of paradise in Sugar Hollow." Some might find it a mixed blessing, in that the nearest place for dinner is a dozen roundabout miles away. The Cabells oblige by offering family-style diners to guests by reservation ($23 per person) on Saturday nights.

(804) 823-7086. Fax (804) 823-2002. Five rooms with private baths. Doubles, $95 to $145. Two-night weekend minimum. Children over 12. No smoking.

High Meadows, High Meadows Lane, Scottsville 24590.

The sign out front dates High Meadows twice, 1832 and 1882, to reflect an oddball, two-in-one house. But that's only the half of it. It seems that in 1882, this was a house divided. A new owner wanted to raze the brick Federal structure in back so as not to block the view of his Italianate-Victorian white stucco villa going up in front. His wife and children said no way. What to do with the back porch already built, facing the old house rather than the countryside? He turned it into a longitudinal breezeway and two-story hall connecting the two structures. Thus were preserved two very different modes of architecture and lifestyles in one unusual dwelling.

The two modes are everywhere in whimsical contrast, from the clutter of the Patrick Henry Parlor and the historic aura of the brick-floored downstairs breakfast room to the main-floor Fairview guest room in the Victorian section with a clawfoot tub at the edge of the room facing the fireplace or, a floor below, the paneled Meadow View bedroom with a whirlpool tub, queen bed and a foldout murphy bed. The Fairview is a trove of Victoriana with swaths of netting crisscrossing the queensize blanket-roll rope bed and a bay window overlooking the azalea garden; the Meadow View is barely a cut above a basement den. Possibly more conventional is the Surveyor's Suite on the main floor of the Federal structure. It has an ornate fireplaced sitting room with heartpine floors and the original nine-over-nine window, plus a bath with clawfoot tub and a queensize brass bed in a room with windows on three sides off a porch. All told, there are five bedrooms and two suites, plus a carriage house with a fireplaced bedroom and a new suite with a fireplace and hot tub. The last overlooks the inn's antique rose garden, which contains 40 kinds of roses, some from pre-Roman days.

Each room contains a bound memorabilia book detailing guest information, photos on the restoration and verses about the room. Each also has a crystal decanter of port, and homemade cookies and fruit are set out in a parlor. Besides three common rooms, the inn has four porches to view 23 acres of gardens, woods and vineyards (the pinot noir grapes are sold to Jefferson Vineyards). Billed as a vineyard inn, it's the only one in Virginia that combines a place on the National Register of Historic Homes with a new viticulture happening.

High Meadows offers four more guest rooms in a 1907 residence a four-minute walk down the north meadow. All but one have decks or porches and fireplaces. This section is called the Mountain Sunset Inn to differentiate it from the main Vineyard Inn, both of which go under the original High Meadows umbrella.

Owners Peter Sushka and Mary Jae Abbitt live on the property, although she works at a brokerage in Richmond during the week. Peter is assisted by a fulltime chef and two resident innkeepers. The chef prepares a six-course dinner on Saturday, available by reservation for $40 per person in two lower-level dining rooms. A bistro dinner is offered Thursday, Friday and Sunday for $40 to $60 a couple, including wine. Other nights you can get a European evening basket of hot and cold foods ($50 for two with wine). The basket fare might be chicken chablis on puff pastry, beef bourguignonne or lasagna with a couple of salads, fresh fruit and dessert. Peter says they put it in a big picnic hamper with flowers and silver, a bottle of Virginia wine and a book of poetry and send guests "out to the fields or the gazebo for a romantic dinner."

The dinner option follows a wine-tasting of Virginia vintages in the Grand Hall or the West Terrace. A full breakfast the next morning might involve fresh orange juice and muffins, a main dish ranging from shirred eggs with turkey to various stratas, followed by a fruit dish, perhaps pear and currant crisps or a compote with yogurt.

(804) 286-2218 or (800) 232-1832. Fax (804) 286-2124. Nine rooms and five suites with private baths. Doubles, $99 to $149. Suites, $119 to $185. Add $80 MAP for Saturday stays. Two-night minimum most weekends. No smoking.

Dinner by reservation, Monday-Wednesday at 6:30, Thursday at 7, Friday-Sunday at 7:30.

Dining Spots

Metropolitain, 214 West Water St., Charlottesville.

Tops on most lists of local dining favorites is this establishment that moved in 1997 from its former downtown diner quarters into fancy mod digs in a onetime hardware store a couple of blocks away. The décor is minimalist in pale yellow and black, with high ceiling, well spaced tables and black banquettes.

Great food emanates from the open grill and deep fryer installed owners Vincent Derquenne, a young Frenchman, and partner Tim Burgess. They also have expanded their choice wine cellar, adding a reserve list.

Good sliced bread, a plain salad of Boston lettuce with a mustardy vinaigrette and a simple muscadet from a wide-ranging wine list were mere preambles to the triumphs that were ahead the night we dined. Among entrées, a paillard of plate-cooked (and barely cooked) salmon with basil puree, diced tomatoes and shoestring vegetables was a masterpiece, magnificently presented on an oversize plate speckled with parsley flakes. Equally presented was the grilled pork loin with spring onion puree, absolutely delicious fried cilantro wontons and cabbage slaw, the dish so ample that even two of us could not finish.

We had to save room for dessert. Good thing, because the champagne granité with fresh citrus and mint goes down as one of the most refreshing finales we've had. A close runnerup was the grilled banana bread with homemade honey vanilla ice cream and warm praline sauce. The descriptions hardly do justice to the presentations, again on oversize plates – one with a rainbow of strawberries, peaches and grapefruit; the other surrounded by squiggles of caramel and powdered sugar.

The two young innovators are equally at home with starters. How could one choose among wild mushroom bisque with fried leeks, seared venison carpaccio with red shiso and blackberry vinaigrette, duck quesadilla with adzuki bean salsa and chipotle cream, and gâteau of portobellos with grits and fried leeks?

Every menu gets more interesting, and dinner has become such a successful production that weekday lunches have been terminated.

Lunch and more casual dinners continue at **Bizou,** the owners' high-style diner restaurant in the deco space at 119 West Main St. where we first knew the Metropolitan.

(804) 977-1043. Entrées, $18.95 to $21.95. Dinner nightly, 5:30 to 9:30 or 10.

Ivy Inn, 2244 Old Ivy Road, Charlottesville.

A new chef-owner and his wife have updated this landmark traditionally favored by sedate types on the outskirts of town. Angelo Vangelopoulos, an American whose father was born in Greece, and his wife Farrell brightened up the interior of the lovely old red brick dwelling built around 1800. In partnership with his parents, who were in the restaurant business in Washington, D.C., they added oriental carpets and more gold and ivory tones to the small and intimate dining rooms upstairs and down. They seat 90 diners on two floors, plus 30 more in season on a canopied patio.

Angelo's modern American fare appeals to the sophisticated tastes of a younger clientele. Trained in classical French style with northern Italian overtones, he features local product on a dinner menu that changes nightly.

Meals may be ordered à la carte. Or the chef suggests a five-course tasting menu for $39.

A typical autumn night offered a dozen entrées, among them grilled local mountain trout with smoked bacon and pecans, grilled swordfish with rock shrimp and toasted pumpkin seed sauce, Virginia crab cake with red bell pepper sauce, local venison with dried cherry sauce, fricassee of rabbit with chanterelles in pommery cream, and a trio of local lamb.

Starters included a smoky three-bean soup with grilled rabbit sausage, marinated shrimp with cheese grits and creole tomato sauce, and a smoked salmon and potato napoleon with horseradish cream.

Among desserts were chocolate-macadamia decadence cake, warm apple crisp with homemade cinnamon ice cream, chocolate bourbon fudge cake with wild turkey crème anglaise, and profiteroles with cappuccino-kahlua ice cream.

The wine list is as select as the rest of the menu, with the preponderance of offerings priced in the high teens and twenties. Six local vineyards are included.

(804) 977-1222. Entrées, $16 to $24. Dinner nightly, 5 to 10. Sunday brunch, 11 to 2.

Memory and Company, 213 Second St. S.W., Charlottesville.

We tried four times to eat at this restaurant in a lovely old townhouse across from the 200 South Street inn. The first time its 45 seats were fully booked. The second time owners Ann Memory and her husband Hans had closed for a few days to recover from the University of Virginia graduation weekend. They did show us around, however, and gave us a sample of one of their splendiferous desserts – homemade coffee ice cream laced with rum on chocolate meringues. Yum! The third time we succeeded, only this time the couple were away on vacation and our experience suffered as a result. And the last time, surprise! The Memorys were only a memory, having sold the restaurant that evolved from the cooking school Ann started here in 1981.

The memory continues, however. Chef-owner John Corbett worked with Ann Memory before he took over in 1994. He retained the same style and concept. But with fourteen years' experience in California, the native Philadelphian added California and Southwest influences to the country French and Italian fare.

Dinner is prix-fixe for several courses, the price fluctuating with the seasons. Starting with an amuse-gueule of basil pesto savory cheesecake, you might choose among cream of shiitake mushroom soup, house-smoked salmon with sweet mustard sauce or a terrine of eggplant, sweet red peppers and chèvre with a parsley sauce. There are usually three entrées: maybe red snapper in parchment with tomatoes and crème fraîche, local braised rabbit with homemade fettuccine or angus beef tenderloin with red onions caramelized in madeira. A salad of baby greens follows the main course. The dessert choice could be lemon meringue pie, cheesecake with a raspberry and strawberry puree or homemade chocolate ice cream.

John bought Hans's extraordinary wine inventory, which has awards from Wine Spectator. With more than 1,250 bottles, about 100 in the $25 range, Memory and Company attracts serious oenophiles.

Dining takes place in a front room with starched cloths, heavy silver and jam jars filled with fresh flowers, a larger rear dining room where you may view the open kitchen or on a back patio beside the herb garden.

(804) 296-3539. Prix-fixe, $35 to $40. Dinner, Wednesday-Saturday 6 to 9.

Duner's, Route 250, Ivy.

From the outside it looks like a roadhouse, but locals as well as itinerant chefs on their nights off pack the place for some of the area's most inventive fare. Beyond a main room with booths and tables overshadowed by a brass canopy-topped bar lies a porch, dressed up with brick walls, patterned wallpaper above wainscoting and seven white-clothed tables with oil lamps and flowers in bud vases.

The water comes in beer mugs. The noise level is high, and so is the lighting. No matter. The food is good to excellent, especially the dozen or more nightly specials that supplement a fairly pedestrian menu. For starters, how about grilled duck and spinach salad tossed with pinenuts and a peach-cherry dressing or poached calamari in coconut milk and Moroccan spices? The latter dish came spiced with lots of coriander and a soupy broth that was great for dipping the accompanying monkey bread.

Among entrées, we felt the somewhat dry crab cakes cried out for a sauce. "No sauce," the waitress advised. "Needs sauce," we insisted. The kitchen obliged with an interesting chile tartar sauce that filled the bill. The veal sweetbreads with shiitake mushrooms and cream sauce were heavenly, though a minimal portion. A zesty salad with Greek olives and red onions accompanied. One of us wanted to splurge for the night's "entrée salad" of Louisiana oysters with greens tossed in caesar dressing for an extra $12.95. Ginger pound cake with local mulberries, strawberries and raspberries and a peach and pistachio crumb tart were satisfying endings.

A local Montdomaine chardonnay was a good choice from an extensive wine list, which contained a front page of specials under $20. A restaurant since the 1950s, Duner's was named for a former owner, a Turk whose wife bought it for him as a toy. It was about to close in the late 1980s, when former manager Robert Caldwell took over and saved the day. "It's a crazy place," our waitress acknowledged, "but a lot of good chefs have come through here."

(804) 293-8352. Entrées, $13.95 to $19.95. Dinner nightly, 5 to 10. Sunday brunch, 10 to 3.

C&O Restaurant, 515 East Water St., Charlottesville.

"The least prepossessing fine restaurant in America," the Washington Post calls it. A Travel-Holiday writer considers it the homeliest and "best restaurant in America." National food writers wax rhapsodic about the food, if not the atmosphere.

The local consensus seems to be that the C&O is resting on its laurels, however. Certainly our experience in the smoke-filled downstairs Bistro did not measure up, nor did that of fellow inn guests who termed their meal inedible. Another countered that her dinner was one of the best she'd had, a claim echoed by others at our most recent visit.

The contradictions emanate from a small brick building – identified by an old-fashioned Pepsi sign – across from the old Chesapeake & Ohio Railroad station. Upstairs is high-style, no-smoking dining area for 30 patrons in a simple room with high windows, pale yellow walls, high-back chairs and little to distract from the food. The traditional formal menu upstairs was discarded in 1997, and the bistro fare was upgraded and available upstairs and down.

Downstairs is a dark, noisy and claustrophobic little bistro with a long bar where smokers seem to gather. The bar is cheek to jowl with nine white-linened tables for two amid brick and barnwood walls, considerable bric-a-brac and illumination from three wagon-wheel chandeliers with every other light bulb off.

Our bistro dinner began with generous drinks and a decent artichoke pâté with good French bread. Disappointment set in with the wine list, an exorbitantly expensive affair starting in the mid-$20s and with many in the hundreds. We liked the steak chinois (flank steak) sliced with tamari and ginger cream sauce, but found the chicken breast with eggplant-avocado salsa bland beyond redemption. The small plates were overcrowded with new potatoes, tomatoes, carrots and onions. We passed up dessert, but heard that the crème caramel was perfect.

The offerings change nightly. Expect appetizers like Thai crab cake with peanut sauce and veal sweetbreads in marsala cream over sliced prosciutto. Main courses range widely from broiled salmon with spinach-gruyère-grand marnier mornay to beef tenderloin with a port-stilton glaze. Desserts run to coupe maison, seasonal sorbets and baba au rhum.

(804) 971-7044. Entrées, $12.50 to $22. Lunch, Monday-Friday 11:30 to 3. Dinner nightly, 5:30 to 10 or 11.

Silver Thatch Inn, 3001 Hollymead Drive, Charlottesville.

The restaurant here, always highly regarded locally, is said to be better than ever under owners Rita and Vince Scoffone and chef Bryan Holleman. The two-level main dining room is pretty and pristine with huge spindle-back windsor chairs at well-spaced tables draped in white linens. A quilt spreads across one wall, baskets hang from an old ladder, and Villeroy & Boch china graces the tables. Windows look onto lawns and gardens. A smaller English dining room is pretty in green and rust, and diners in the lower sun room almost feel they're outside.

The complex dinner fare, described by Rita as "beautiful modern American," changes every six to eight weeks. Typical among the eight main courses are a sesame sauté of soft-shell crabs served over coriander perfumed rice, grilled breast of duck with star anise ginger sauce, pan-roasted pork loin with an apple-chipotle-pepper chutney and grilled tenderloin of beef with mustard-shallot sauce. The day's catch might be grilled salmon crusted with roasted pecans and spices, splashed with a mango-papaya vinaigrette flavored with cardamom and cayenne pepper, and served over baby greens with fresh mulberries and flower petals.

Appetizers intrigue, perhaps a roasted pumpkin salad with country ham and saga blue cheese, grape leaves stuffed with lamb and pinenuts, and Southwestern steamed mussels in a beer-ancho pepper-lime broth. Desserts follow suit: maple-pecan cheesecake with maple cream and white chocolate maple sauce, chocolate-caramel-almond mousse cake and honey-almond tarts with honey crème anglaise and fresh mulberries.

The wine list, honored by Wine Spectator magazine, features Virginia wines at the low end of the price spectrum. Guests like to pause before or after dinner in the dark and comfy bar.

(804) 978-4686. Entrées, $19 to $24. Dinner, Tuesday-Saturday 5:30 to 9. No smoking.

Tastings, Market and Fifth Streets, Charlottesville.

This American grill and wine bar is an adjunct to a wine shop in the Downtown Parking Garage. It claims to be the first such combination of its kind on the East Coast, and boasts a wine list as big as its shop. Unlike many Virginia restaurants, which do not segregate smokers, this is a totally non-smoking restaurant. The changing menu features items from a wood grill.

Dinner might include such treats as chef William Curtis's secret crabmeat casserole, available as an appetizer or as an entrée. Grilled salmon with béarnaise sauce, roasted tawny duck with spicy orange glaze and herb-crusted rack of lamb were among recent possibilities. Desserts could be caramel apple tart, Vermont maple cream flan and chocolate mousse with sundried cherries. Or you could order a late-harvest riesling or port for what Tastings calls "dessert in a glass."

Meals are taken in an informal room at tables made from the tops of wine crates, or at stools at a bar for six in the wine shop. A real plus is that the entire 1,000-bottle inventory is available for a $5 corkage fee, meaning splurgers can sample a $40 burgundy for a bargain $45. More than 100 wines are available by the glass or half-glass, some as part of a sampling of three.

(804) 293-3663. Entrées, $15.95 to $19.95. Lunch, Monday-Friday 11:30 to 2:30. Dinner, Tuesday-Saturday 6 to 10. No smoking.

Extra-Special

Historic Michie Tavern, Route 53, Charlottesville.

Southern cooking is featured in the 200-year-old converted log slave house called The Ordinary beneath one of Virginia's oldest homesteads.

And it's like no ordinary "Southern" cooking. That is, it's – dare we say? – tasty and not cooked to smithereens. Food with a bit of a kick is how we'd describe it. You stand in a cafeteria line, help yourself to the buffet, and sit at communal tables

Historic Michie Tavern houses a museum and a restaurant featuring Southern cooking.

in the old log-walled tavern or at picnic tables in an enclosed garden courtyard. You may have a bigger meal than you want at midday, for a hefty pricetag, plus $1 each for beverage and dessert.

Our fried chicken was moist and tender, the black-eyed peas and coleslaw fine, the stewed tomatoes interesting and the green beans had a nice herbed flavor. Good biscuits and cornbread came with, and the apple cobbler was far better than institutional fare. Ice water and a half bottle of Autumn Hill chardonnay were served in tin cups. Waitresses in Colonial costume refilled plates with items of the diner's choice.

Before or after, you can tour the tavern-museum, which has a large collection of pre-Revolutionary furniture and artifacts. The Meadow Run Grist Mill, a separate building down a steep hill, contains the good **General Store** and the small **Virginia Wine Museum.**

(804) 977-1234. Buffet, $9.95. Lunch daily, 11:30 to 3. Museum and store, daily 9 to 5.

Diversions

The Monticello Visitors Center is located off I-64 at Exit 121 along Route 20 south, near the entry road to Monticello. It houses one of the larger local information centers we've seen, plus the Thomas Jefferson at Monticello Exhibition and a museum shop. The center offers a combination ticket for tours of Monticello, Ash Lawn-Highland and Historic Michie Tavern Museum for $20.

Monticello, Route 53, Charlottesville.
Starting in 1768, Thomas Jefferson designed and built his showplace hilltop home over 40 years, transforming his "essay on architecture" into an amalgam of Italian villas, Rome's Pantheon and a townhouse he observed in Paris while he

Docent demonstrates spinning wheel at Ash Lawn-Highland.

was there as U.S. ambassador. Now as then, it is the area's chief attraction, having been saved by a private foundation in 1924. It draws more than 550,000 visitors a year who wait in line up to three hours for the privilege. Go early or late, and you may face only a twenty-minute wait, as we did, from the time you board a bus at the shuttle station until the lineup outside the rear of the house is shepherded inside, 25 at a time.

The 35-minute guided tour of the main floor is an unfolding revelation of Jefferson's inventive mind: a calendar clock in the entry "museum," automatic sliding doors, an upside-down mirror, a revolving bookstand, a contraption that made copies of everything he wrote, a rotating pole to hold clothes, and dumb-waiters for wine at either end of the fireplace in the dining room. Although ahead of his time with skylights and such, his was a house better suited to a bachelor than a family, one of us thought. The tour ends somewhat abruptly outside. Visitors are left to troop on their own around lavish gardens and through the basement passageway past the kitchen to the household service dependencies built into the hillside.

We particularly liked the optional half-mile walk back down to the shuttle station, past flourishing vegetable gardens (said to include nineteen varieties of peas, Jefferson's favorite, all staked on branches and ready to pick at our mid-May visit). Pause at the family graveyard, where Jefferson's obelisk notes his fathering of the University of Virginia and his authorship of the Declaration of Independence and the Statute of Virginia for Religious Freedom, but makes no mention of his presidency. One family gravestone was as recent as 1988.

Back at the shuttle station, visit the **Thomas Jefferson Center for Historic Plants;** plants and seeds are available for purchase at a shop beneath a tent. The primitive **Little Mountain Luncheonette** serves a nice variety of sandwiches and salads in the $3 to $5 range. Top them off with Virginia apple cider.

(804) 984-9822. Open daily, March-October 8 to 5, rest of year 9 to 4:30. Adults, $9.

Ash Lawn-Highland, Route 795, Charlottesville.

The charming home of President James Monroe is dwarfed by its better-known neighbor, Monticello, whose gift shop is visible two miles away up a path from the front door. Thomas Jefferson persuaded Monroe to move to Highland to "create a society to our taste." Monroe's "cabin castle" is very different from Monticello, however. The squawks of resident peacocks could be heard (and their plumes seen) as our small group was led on a guided tour that was both more informative and more personal than the one at Monticello. This was a more lived-in and livable house than Jefferson's, and locals advise seeing it before Monticello, which they consider so novel and different. Monroe was forced to sell the house because of financial difficulties in 1826. It was bequeathed by one of its subsequent owners in 1974 to the College of William and Mary, which has just completed a major restoration. The tour ends when the guide turns you over to an "herb lady" for a five-minute talk on plants and herbs (we enjoyed her chat about nosegays). You can stay on to enjoy "lunch on the first lady's lawn." The **Kortright Cafe,** honoring Monroe's wife of 44 years, features foods from the Monroe table (from baked ham sandwich to a pâté plate), served with a cloth in a picnic basket to enjoy on the grounds. *(804) 293-9539. Open daily, March-October 9 to 6, rest of year 10 to 5. Adults, $7.*

University of Virginia. This prestigious university of 17,000 students was founded in 1819 by Thomas Jefferson, who designed its buildings, planned the curriculum and was its guiding spirit as "a hobby of his old age," according to our guide. Its heart remains the "academical village" along the Lawn, focusing on the Rotunda – a design rated by the American Institute of Architects as the outstanding achievement in American architecture. Free hourly guided tours show visitors the finer points of the Rotunda, a masterpiece patterned after the Roman Pantheon. Our tour was led by a most informative graduate student in English. We peeked into some of the 52 rooms occupied by students as well as two-story faculty pavilions along the Lawn and overheard one guide telling prospective students that these fireplaced rooms are the most coveted housing for seniors who have distinguished themselves on campus, offering heat but no lavatories. Piped up one prospect's mother: It's an 'honor' to live in rooms without bathrooms?" Deadpanned the guide: "Yes, they have heat." Walk the magnificent campus, see Room 13 where Edgar Allan Poe resided (a raven is on his desk and there's a recorded commentary) and admire the gardens framed by serpentine walls throughout the academical village.

The Downtown Mall. Charlottesville's historic district, especially the Courthouse area and Market Street, surrounds its downtown pedestrian shopping mall. Main Street and its cross streets have been closed to vehicular traffic. The result is a pleasant, tree-shaded brick walkway interspersed with planters, benches, whimsical cut-out figures, sidewalk cafes and frequent directory signs as in enclosed shopping malls. The downtown is struggling, having lost major stores to outlying malls. But specialty shops and restaurants have remained (or emerged), and this is one downtown that appears the place to be on a nice day. Good for browsing are such shops as **Palais Royal** (French linens for bed, bath and table), the outstanding **Signet Gallery,** handcrafted cherry furniture at **Thorn & Co.,** **O'Suzannah** advertising "contemporary art and soul," the **Copernicus** toy store, and **The Cat House** boutique for cat lovers.

More Shopping. College types gravitate to **The Corner,** an area of shops and restaurants centered along West Main Street between 14th Street and Elliewood

Avenue. Upscale shops are concentrated at **Barracks Road Shopping Center,** where you'll find **Laura Ashley** and **Talbots** as well as such local prizes as the **Happy Cook** kitchen shop, the extraordinary **Plow and Hearth** and **Nature by Design** stores, **Beecroft & Bull** for men's clothing and the **Virginia Shop** with everything from Smithfield hams to Williamsburg candles. **HotCakes** is a nifty bakery, cafe and gourmet-to-go shop here.

If you love browsing through unusual grocery stores as much as one of us does, don't miss **Foods of all Nations** at 2121 Ivy Road. Everything Indian, Mexican and Indonesian, for example, is here. So is a huge selection of wines, takeout salads and sandwiches for picnics. If we lived in Charlottesville, we'd be here every week.

Wineries. Thomas Jefferson failed in his effort to cultivate grapes for wines at Monticello, but he would be proud of what has been accomplished in Virginia in

recent years. Charlottesville bills itself as the winemaking capital of Virginia, claiming five wineries in Albemarle County and a dozen more in the surrounding area. The most impressive here is **Oakencroft Vineyard & Winery,** whose colorful red-barn winery occupies a stunning site between a farm pond and mountains in estate country just northwest of town. Owner Felicia Warburg Rogan started with a self-taught female winemaker, giving hers the distinction for nearly a decade as the only winery in America to be run by two women. Gabriele Rausse, described as "the sage of Virginia wines," is the legend behind **Jefferson Vineyards** (formerly Simeon Vineyards**),** just up the road from Monticello. You can sample quite a variety (from sauvignon blanc to chardonnay to merlot to a rare pinot

Wines and view at Oakencroft Vineyard.

grigio, $8 to $18) in the new tasting room with outdoor deck. Jefferson wines also are available at the affiliated **Simeon Farm Store,** where you can pick up a cream cheese and olive or chicken sandwich or a baguette and cheese for a picnic between Monticello and Ash Lawn.

An unbelievably scenic, mountainous route leads to **Afton Mountain Vineyards** in nearby Afton. Former NBC News producer Tom Corpora and his Japanese wife, Shinko, produce stellar chardonnays, rieslings, cabernets and pinot noirs in the $9 to $15 range. Theirs is an unusual venture, combining state-of-the-art equipment with ancient technology – a gravity processing system and a unique, 100-foot-long wine storage cave. Their showroom offers wine tastings plus gourmet picnic foods that can be eaten in the second-floor luncheon room or on tables outside. We took home a $10 chardonnay to recapture the memories of a picturesque and true place.

Crowd gathers at Montpelier in Orange for annual Steeplechase races in November.

Orange County, Va.
On the Trail to Discovery

Few people outside central Virginia have heard of Orange County, much less been there.

Its county seat, Orange (population 2,700), is "still a sleepy little Southern town," in the words of a local restaurateur. Its landed gentry maintains a lower profile than that of its neighbors to the south in Albemarle County surrounding Charlottesville. "People come here from urban centers to escape to the country," says local booster Donna Bedwell. One writer even wrote a piece in a Charlottesville magazine about taking a country weekend respite from the stresses of Charlottesville in Orange, a mere twenty miles away.

But this dormant, unspoiled, scenic countryside that spawned presidents James Madison and Zachary Taylor is taking on a new role. A marketing director has been hired to double the attendance at Montpelier, the lifelong home of James Madison, now undergoing a major restoration. With that increase will come an inevitable influx of tourism accompaniments along Route 20, the Constitution Trail (so named for the number of homes of presidents and governors along its path) that meanders through the heart of the county.

The horsey set of northern Virginia hunt country is moving toward Orange. The area is the center of the state's winemaking industry, Orange having more acres in grape production than any other Virginia county. B&Bs are emerging to supplement the more established inns. The area "is beginning to be discovered," says Suzie Blanchard, a former Chicagoan whose market research led her to this part of Virginia to establish the Inn at Meander Plantation.

Meanwhile, it retains the sense of history and unspoiled countryside of old Virginia, suspended in a time warp against the encroaching pincers of Charlottesville to the south, Fredericksburg to the east and Washington to the north. The picturesque charms of the rolling Piedmont, the wineries, the emerging Montpelier, a couple of museums, the Civil War battlefields – all make an interesting destination for those who cherish peace and quiet.

Inn Spots

The Hidden Inn, 249 Caroline St., Orange 22960.

Hidden down a hillside beneath Route 15, this century-old Victorian inn offers tranquility on five wooded acres deeded from the forebears of Zachary Taylor. It also has some of the fanciest guest rooms around.

Ray Lonick, innkeeper with his wife Barbara and serving as mayor of Orange, greets guests with his own map and suggestions for touring and shows off his back yard containing "just about every tree that grows in Virginia." The Lonicks – he an early-retired Xerox sales executive from New Jersey – acquired the inn in 1987 and totally redecorated, adding Barbara's samplers, her mother's quilts, family photos and their homemade bath salts and cinnamon soaps. They offer five-course dinners Saturday by reservation, compiled a cookbook, and have added two deluxe suites in outbuildings and three guest rooms in an adjacent house.

Rooms now total ten, all with private baths and period furnishings and some with jacuzzi tubs and fireplaces. Our expansive quarters in the Verandah Room, upstairs and to the rear, included a queensize pencil-post bed with a fishnet canopy and ruffly pillows, a chaise lounge, an enormous bathroom with windows on two sides and, crowning touch, a private balcony with wicker furniture for viewing the back yard. Also special is the large upstairs room in the rear carriage house, dark and masculine with a rooftop balcony, jacuzzi, and paisley sheets and pillowcases matching the bathroom wallpaper. A newer treat is the garden cottage, pink and flowery with a skylight, a queensize four-poster, TV, jacuzzi and rear deck.

The Lonicks offer candlelight picnics and bubble bath in the rooms of late-arriving guests on Fridays and for those on romantic getaway packages. Saturday's optional five-course dinner, priced at $37, begins with a wine reception featuring area vintages in the living room. Typical fare includes artichokes romano, asparagus soup, hearts of palm salad, filet of beef with chasseur sauce or chicken with mushrooms in puff pastry, and cheesecake or white chocolate mousse pie.

For our breakfast, Ray cooked french toast made with thick homemade bread and sausage following openers of peach-orange juice, cut-up grapefruit and carrot muffins. Orange-granola pancakes and cheese eggs with ham and biscuits are other favorites.

(540) 672-3625 or (800) 841-1253. Fax (540) 672-5029. Eight rooms and two cottages with private baths. Doubles, $79 to $159. Cottages, $169. Two-night minimum weekends. Children accepted. No smoking.

Dogwoods and azaleas provide springtime welcome to The Hidden Inn.

Mayhurst Inn, off Route 15, Orange 22960.

This stunning white Italianate Victorian mansion built atop a hill in 1859 by Col. John Willis, great-nephew of President James Madison, looks like a wedding cake. The inside is tasty as well.

Undertaking two years of top-to-bottom renovations in 1996, new owners Peg and Bob Harmon from Colorado have endowed it with a true sense of style and nine comfortable guest accommodations with private baths. They also serve hearty breakfasts and Virginia wines and appetizers in the afternoon.

Hundreds of visitors oohed and aahed over the Mayhurst restoration during the annual Orange County Holiday Tour in December 1997.

Former owners had abandoned the inn in the early 1990s. Part of a 1,700-acre plantation, it was the Northern Virginia army headquarters during the Civil War under Gen. A.P. Hill and was host to Stonewall Jackson and Robert E. Lee. "It's really something to think that three generals slept here," says vivacious Peg. The fanciful architecture includes a rare spiral staircase in an oval shape, ascending four stories to a rooftop gazebo.

The Harmons invested big bucks and employed Peg's eye for style in redoing six guest rooms and three suites, six with fireplaces and most with queensize beds. She calls the prized Italian Suite "neo-Caesar in mode," decorated in black and cream with gold accents. It has a double jacuzzi of black granite in its sitting room, which also offers a fireplace and a rear balcony. The bright scarlet wallpaper in the king-bedded Madison Room wallpaper happens to be a reproduction of Dolley Madison's bed hangings. The rear General's Room, furnished with antiques from the 1860s, is done in Confederate gray with gold touches.

The ground level contains a Garden Room, done in a floral motif and with a bathroom that looks like a garden terrace with its slate floor, shower wall and vanity.

The Harmons may eventually serve dinner by reservation to house guests on Friday and Saturday nights in the 22-seat dining room on the ground level, handsome in blue and white with buff walls and antique German china. They offer

White Italianate Victorian mansion housing Mayhurst Inn looks like a wedding cake.

breakfast in guests' rooms or on the screened porch. Bob's specialty is made-to-order omelets.

(540) 672-2243 or (888) 672-5597. Six rooms and three suites with private baths. Doubles, $110 to $150. Suites, $160 to $195.

The Inn at Meander Plantation, James Madison Highway (Route 15), Route 5, Box 460, Locust Dale 22948.

"It's a real treat to be in a house where so many historical figures have tread the floors." So says Suzie Blanchard, co-innkeeper with her husband Bob of the Inn at Meander Plantation. They know. Their stately Colonial manor house with six pillars in front was built in 1766 by Henry Fry Sr., whose close friend, Thomas Jefferson, often stopped here on his way to and from Monticello. A print of the first official map of Virginia, as surveyed and drawn by the fathers of both Fry and Jefferson, hangs on their living room wall. And Robert E. Lee rested in the shade of a sycamore on Meander land while a blacksmith shod his horse and Confederate troops crossed the Robinson River en route to the Civil War Battle of Cedar Run.

Today, guests who stay at this new inn can tread in the same footsteps. They are greeted in a reception room behind the pillared portico that's large enough to hold a grand piano. They gather in the sunken living room, long and comfortable, and on the rear porches of the L-shaped house. They stay in one of the four bedrooms, one of them a two-room suite. All have private baths and queensize four-poster beds and are elegantly furnished to the period with lacy pillows, down comforters, wing chairs, armoires and oriental rugs on the polished heartpine floors. The suite and a downstairs room both open onto the rear porches. The adjacent groom's cottage holds a sitting room with a sofabed, a queensize bed and a kitchenette. A former summer kitchen now holds a deluxe two-room suite with living room down and king bedroom above. Guests also enjoy some fairly exotic meals whipped up by Suzie, a food writer for Pioneer Press newspapers in suburban Chicago. The former publisher there, Suzanne Thomas, shares innkeeping duties here with the Blanchards.

Breakfast, as delivered by these two articulate women, is a convivial affair in the formal dining room. You might start with fresh fruit (a seasonal favorite is sautéed orange slices and cranberries), a choice of juices and a spicy upside-down sausage cornbread. Next come scrambled eggs flavored with herbs from the garden and baked hash browns, Sour cream coffee cake, poppyseed bread or croissants might accompany. Others of Suzie's specialties include wild rice and walnut pancakes, spinach strata, crab or asparagus quiche and grits.

Dinner is offered by reservation for $37.50 a person. A typical meal might be spicy shrimp with homemade rémoulade sauce, crab bisque or cream of broccoli soup, a salad of baby greens with grilled portobello mushrooms, and a main course of grilled game hen with soy-pineapple marinade, accompanied by green beans with red pepper slices and garlic. Dessert could be a fresh strawberry tart. Virginia wines are available for purchase.

Adjourn to one of the white rockers on the expansive back porches to survey the scene. The 80-acre property contains formal boxwood gardens, a portion of the Robinson River and pastures for seventeen resident horses.

(540) 672-4912 or (800) 385-4936. Three rooms and three suites with private baths. Doubles, $95 to $140. Suites, $175 to $195. Children and pets accepted. No smoking.

Willow Grove Inn, 14079 Plantation Way, Orange 22960.

Perched on a hillside with 37 acres, this Federal and Classic Revival plantation home commands attention. You can see it as you approach from the south, and the number of cars in the parking lot attests to the popularity of its restaurant (see Dining Spots).

Like many houses of its size, Willow Grove had fallen on hard times when it was purchased in 1987 by Angela and Richard Mulloy to operate as a restaurant and inn. They're proud that the woodworking in the original 1778 portion was done by the artisans who crafted Montpelier, and that the brick portion was built in 1820 to Thomas Jefferson's design by workmen who had just finished his University of Virginia campus. The Mulloys are restoring the Victorian gardens and primping up the sloping lawns with their stately magnolias, English boxwood and the willows for which the place was named.

Three guest rooms and two suites on the second and third floors are named for Virginia presidents born along the Constitution Trail and decorated to the appropriate period. The corner Washington Room is an elegant space with six windows, double cherry poster bed with tester, sitting area and fireplace. It contrasts in style and price with the mid-18th-century Harrison Room tucked under the eaves. Here you'll find a double Jenny Lind bed, an antique washstand in the room and what Angela calls a sailboat's bathroom with a toilet beyond the step-through shower. The Taylor-Monroe Suite offers adjoining corner rooms, one with a 19th-century tiger maple poster bed and fireplace and a sitting room with a sofabed. The Wilson Suite has two bedrooms (one with a double brass and iron bed and the other with twin beds), a sitting room and a turn-of-the-century motif.

Five newer accommodations, all with whirlpool tubs and separate showers, are housed in antebellum outbuildings around the lovely property. The prized Weaver's Cottage offers a kingsize mahogany poster bed, a sitting room, fireplace and a private veranda. The Summer Kitchen, relocated from the Shenandoah Valley, has a kingsize brass and iron bed and a sitting area with antique wicker furniture. The Butler's Quarters is an English country-style suite with kingsize mahogany sleigh bed and separate sitting room.

All rooms are handsomely furnished, contain beds with triple sheeting and down pillows, and possess such amenities as Saratoga water and a large basket of assorted toiletries, many of them Neutrogena.

A hearty breakfast of fresh fruit with scrambled eggs, frittatas or french toast is served in the front tavern room, full of hunting prints and atmosphere.

(540) 672-5982 or (800) 949-1778. Fax (540) 672-3674. Three rooms, two suites and five cottages with private baths. Doubles, $220 to $330 MAP. Cottages and suites, $275 to $330 MAP. Children welcome. Smoking restricted.

The Shadows, 14291 Constitution Hwy., Orange 22960.

"I target the child in every adult," says Barbara Loffredo, who goes so far as to put rubber duckies in the bathrooms so you can play in the tub. Ex-New Yorkers Barbara, a legal secretary, and husband Pat, one of New York's Finest, fell in love with the area, bought the 1913 stone craftsman's cottage and opened in 1987 as a B&B. "Our debut was the Christmas tour," recalled Barbara, "and 320 people came through."

The house is up a long and winding drive through many trees (hence the name Shadows). The Loffredos have added lush cutting gardens of flowers and herbs to the side around a gazebo. As you tour the grounds you might be accompanied by the couple's dog, James Madison, found at – you guessed it – Montpelier.

With Stickley furniture and a staircase that architects make a special trip to see, the downstairs common areas are charming. Lots of antiques and pieces the couple have collected decorate the four upstairs bedrooms, all with private baths. We like best the Rose Room, which has a huge private veranda overlooking the lawns and the Loffredos' goat, Nanny, grazing near the barn (guests feed her flowers and dog food to gain her affection). The Blue Room has a cedar-lined bathroom and a queensize walnut bed pre-dating the Civil War. The smaller Peach Room with a king bed of burled walnut is particularly pretty, and the Victoria Room is full of ruffles.

Also on the property are two outbuildings converted into sleeping quarters. The two-room Cottage has a separate sitting room with wicker furniture and its own deck. The Rocking Horse Cabin, also with two rooms and a porch, is all natural wood on the inside and decorated with country crafts. There's an array of rocking horses, and the horse motif extends from the cover on the kleenex box to the toilet lid. It has a queen bed and a new gas fireplace.

Pat is in charge of the wonderful breakfasts served on fine crystal and china: maybe a fruit course like poached pears in grand marnier cream or a big bowl of local strawberries. Stuffed french toast with cream cheese sauce and a dish of sautéed apples that comes out like a soufflé is a favorite. The ham, cheese and egg bake uses local eggs, their yolks so yellow they make the orange juice look pale, Pat says. Barbara calls his buttermilk biscuits the best around.

From refreshments like hot spiced cider or iced tea upon arrival to a homemade sachet when you leave, you'll be treated with TLC and a lot of mothering at the Shadows.

(540) 672-5057. Four rooms and two cottages with private baths. Doubles, $80 to $95. Cottages, $100 and $110. Children over 10. No smoking.

Sleepy Hollow Farm, 16280 Blue Ridge Tpke. (Route 231), Gordonsville 22942. Nestled in a hollow off Route 231, Orange County's prettiest byway, Sleepy

Main house at Sleepy Hollow Farm is surrounded by lawns, woods and pastures.

Hollow is a paradise of sorts. Beverley Allison, innkeeper with her daughter Dorsey, moved to the house as a bride in 1950 and calls it "a poor man's Montpelier, a humble little frontier house in the midst of all the estates." Expanded over the years, the house is beautifully but comfortably furnished and has a lived-in feeling. It is surrounded by lawns, woods and pastures. In front is a farm pond beside a gazebo, a dock that says "swim at your own risk" and, at our visit, a bunch of ducklings scurrying after their mother.

Beverley, an ABC News journalist turned Episcopal missionary, calls hers an organic house that's still growing and evolving. The process continued with the conversion of a TV room into a sixth guest room with a queen bed, fireplace and jacuzzi and the enclosing of the adjoining terrace for a new TV room. The jacuzzi is "bowing to the trend," Beverley acknowledges, "even though this is a place for people not to lie in a bathtub but to go birding, to discover the wildlife, to smell the flowers."

Guests have plenty of space to spread out in a cozy living room, a beamed dining room and what used to be a country porch, now expanded into an enormous sun room with a showpiece dollhouse (Beverley provides a less precious one for the kiddies to play with). This is the setting for a breakfast of fruit compote, farm-fresh eggs (from Dorsey's chickens) or pancakes, and extra-good coffee because the water comes from a deep spring on the property.

Accommodations include a main-floor master bedroom with a queensize canopy four-poster, dressing room, full bath and a stunning handpainted chest from the Orient. Others are the downstairs Squire Room with a queen bed and a large bathroom with whirlpool tub overlooking the pond. Upstairs is a small bedroom known as the Ghost Room, though the ghost has not been seen since the house was blessed. What's called the children's suite has two bedrooms connected by a bath. Just outside is the Chestnut Wood Cottage made up of two suites: the kitchen house, which obviously has a kitchen, and the older and smaller slave house. Each has a deck, a fireplaced sitting room with a pullout sofa and a bedroom and bath upstairs. A recent two-story addition to the kitchen house made room for a larger bedroom upstairs and a whirlpool tub room below.

Baskets of fruit and Virginia peanuts are in the rooms. Beverley serves refreshments, from tea to local wine, upon guests' arrival.

(540) 832-5555 or (800) 215-4804. Fax (540) 832-2515. Three rooms and three suites with private baths. Doubles, $65 to $95. Suites, $85 to $135. Children and pets accepted.

The Holladay House, 155 West Main St., Orange 22960.

This in-town, Federal-style brick house dating to 1830 offers six guest accommodations with private baths and, a treat for some, breakfast in your room. "My grandfather bought this place in 1899," says genial host Pete Holladay, "and some of the family have been here ever since." His father was raised in the house and, though Pete and wife Phebe had long talked of doing a B&B, it wasn't until 1989 when their kids were through college that they opened. He'd been in charge of food and housing services at private schools for 30 years, so considered this a logical move.

Pete prepares a full breakfast, heavy on fruits, fresh breads, perhaps scones with eggs or baked eggs with tomatoes and popovers, biscuits, peach puffs or apple muffins that were voted the best in Virginia by the state B&B association. He serves the meal in guests' rooms, anytime between 6 and noon, saying that's the way people want it. A lovely formal dining room is put into use if groups want to eat together.

Each bedroom is furnished with family pieces, including armoires, sleigh beds and four-posters, as well as a table and chairs for breakfast service. A ground-level suite contains a small sitting room, a large bedroom and a bath with a whirlpool tub and walk-in shower. It can be rented in conjunction with an existing ground-floor bedroom with kitchenette and bath.

The Holladays recently opened a recreation/game room on the ground floor. Guests also enjoy a side porch and two outdoor decks.

(540) 672-4893 or (800) 358-4422. Fax (540) 672-3028. Four rooms and two suites with private baths. Doubles, $95 to $135. Suites, $175 and $195. Children accepted. No smoking.

Rabbit Run B&B, 305 North High St., Box 535, Gordonsville 22942.

"We saw rabbits running around outside the house when we were looking to buy," said Virginia Hulvey. So Rabbit Run became the name of the B&B she operates with her daughter, Elizabeth Hupp. "We love rabbits. They're a sign of goodness and innocence."

Those traits also characterize this homey B&B in a 1880s farmhouse in a shady residential section at the edge of Gordonsville. "We don't have fancy antiques," advises Virginia. "Just family pieces." They added private baths and closets for the three guest rooms, but otherwise a visit here is like coming home to a favorite aunt. The bedrooms are snug and warm, with quilts and country accessories. The nicest is a queen-bedded room in the rear. There's also a small single that shares a bath.

Guests enjoy a cozy TV/library and a larger living room on the main floor, as well as more than two acres of grounds. A typical breakfast includes juices and fresh fruit, homemade bread and muffins, and eggs any way. "I make a mean omelet," says Virginia. Tea is offered in the afternoon.

(540) 832-2892 or (800) 791-9204. Fax (540) 832-0801. Three rooms with private baths. Doubles, $75. Children over 5. No smoking.

Prospect Hill Plantation Inn offers rooms in dependencies as well as in main house.

Prospect Hill Plantation Inn, 2887 Poindexter Road, Trevilians 23093.

Although often thought of in connection with Charlottesville, which is fifteen miles to the west, this renowned inn is closer to Orange, and is recommended by Orange innkeepers for its dining.

Out in the middle of nowhere, the place is idyllic: a thirteen-room country inn and restaurant (see Dining Spots) on a 40-acre wheat plantation dating to 1732. A stunning boxwood hedge lines the driveway leading to the handsome, pale yellow main house, the oldest continually occupied frame plantation manor in Virginia. Boxwoods also frame paths to the original dependencies, all transformed into deluxe lodgings tucked away in the trees. All but one room have fireplaces and more than half have double jacuzzis. Afternoon tea, a fixed-price candlelight dinner and breakfast in bed are included in the tariff. A basket of fresh fruit, a box of raisins, homemade cookies and a half bottle of red wine are in each room.

The five guest rooms in the manor house vary in size from servant quarters to the Overton. The latter is dark, quiet and rich in blue with a high queensize four-poster bed, sitting area and a balcony overlooking the back lawn.

Most coveted are the eight suites in dependencies on either side of the manor house. They are cherished for their privacy as well as their comforts. The original summer kitchen is dark and historic and offers a double jacuzzi. The carriage house contains two expansive suites with sitting areas. The walls of the boys' cabin, oldest on the property (1699), are exposed logs, reminding one of us of summer camp long ago. Overlooking the inn's swimming pool, it has a large cedar bathroom (nothing like the shower houses of summer camp) and a double jacuzzi.

Twittering birds, bees and butterflies kept us amused on the afternoon deck of the Overseer's Cottage, which came with a sun porch/sitting room outfitted with wicker and an oriental carpet, a queen poster bed near the fireplace in the bedroom and a covered morning porch. It was here we learned that Prospect Hill is part of the Green Springs National Historic District, a pristine area of thirteen plantations, stores, chapel and other historic houses preserved as "a gently civilized countryside" – of which we felt a part, if only for an evening.

The next morning, our sun porch proved a delightful setting for a breakfast of exotic fruit, orange juice and french toast, strewn with raspberries and blueberries and garnished with pansies.

Founding innkeepers Bill and Mireille Sheehan, who converted the plantation into an inn in 1977, have turned day-to-day operations over to their son Michael, his wife Laura and caring managers.

(540) 967-0844 or (800) 277-0844. Fax (540) 967-0102. Five rooms and eight cottage suites with private baths. Doubles, $245 to $285, MAP. Suites, $290 to $325, MAP.

Dining Spots

Willow Grove Inn, 14079 Plantation Hwy., Orange.

The rural setting is tough to beat and the dining rooms are as luxurious as can be. The dining experience has its ups and downs, according to local reports, but all concede it is Orange County's most ambitious food and lodging undertaking.

Dining is in three interior venues, plus a garden veranda in season. The Jefferson Library is a comfortable room dressed in white with different floral china at each table (as is the case throughout the inn). The larger and more formal Dolley Madison Room has a crystal chandelier, Queen Anne chairs and deep rose swags over the windows. The casual, ground-floor Clark's Tavern sports a bar of heartpine, hand-hewn beams and assorted antique china on the tables. Service was leisurely at lunch (no longer served), when we sampled a mesquite chicken salad and poached salmon with a cucumber salad. We also enjoyed the inn's specialty, Willow pie, a decadent concoction with chocolate chips, walnuts and bourbon in a puff pastry shell topped with real whipped cream.

The cuisine is regional American, and meals upstairs are prix-fixe. Typical main courses are cornmeal-crusted local trout with Virginia ham and black walnuts, pan-seared fillet of salmon with saffron-crayfish sauce, napoleon of grapevine-smoked chicken breast with forest mushrooms and grilled black angus beef tenderloin with bourbon sauce.

Starters could be wild watercress vichyssoise, homemade duck pâté with fruit compote, mushroom strudel with roasted shallot sauce, and baked walnut-crusted goat cheese with field greens and raspberry-walnut vinaigrette. For dessert, how about bourbon-walnut-chocolate pie, fruit cobbler or frozen white chocolate mousse with praline sauce?

Virtually the same menu is offered à la carte downstairs in the tavern. Dinner is available to house guests on weeknights.

A vocalist and pianist entertain on weekend evenings, and live jazz is played at brunch.

(540) 832-2892 or (800) 791-9204. Prix-fixe, $38; tavern entrées, $17 to $23. Dinner, Thursday-Saturday from 6, Sunday from 4. Sunday brunch, 11 to 3.

Prospect Hill, 2887 Poindexter Road, Trevilians.

Dining is an event at this plantation inn, so secluded that it feels it must offer dinner to house guests who have nowhere else to eat, but so special that it draws outsiders from Orange, Charlottesville and beyond.

Executive chef Michael Sheehan changes the menu for the set (no choice), five-course meal nightly. Guests are invited into the manor house half an hour before the appointed dinner hour to help themselves to complimentary wine and cider in the entry hall, relax by a fireplace in the parlor or stroll the grounds. When the innkeeper rings the dinner bell, everyone is seated at a private table – in the front dining room, the Rose Room or the Conservatory. The innkeepers introduce themselves to the diners in each room, describe what they are about to be served, offer a grace and the meal begins.

Although we're partial to the Conservatory with its summery wrought-iron chairs and view onto the back lawns, we think each room is pretty as a picture. Tables are set with cut glass, fine china, heavy silver (including four forks) and a vase of alstroemeria. Michael has added contemporary and international accents to the inn's traditional French cooking that reflected his mother's background in Provence.

Our dinner began with an ethereal strudel of rabbit mousse with Asian pear slices over alfalfa sprouts, a warm hazelnut vinaigrette and beet relish. Watercress soup and a salad of baby greens with shaved red onions came next. The main course was seared veal tenderloin medallions with shiitake mushrooms, accompanied by a yucca root puree with smoked tomatillo and haricots verts. A lemon cloud mousse, presented in pastry cups with chilled blueberry coulis and fresh berries, was a refreshing ending to a memorable meal.

There's an excellent wine list. A nightly special offered at $20 a bottle, in our case a Côtes du Rhone, is perfectly adequate..

(540) 967-0844 or (800) 277-0844. Prix-fixe, $45. Dinner by reservation, Sunday-Thursday at 7, Friday and Saturday at 8.

Toliver House Restaurant, 209 North Main St., Gordonsville.

This Victorian house converted into a restaurant has undergone major changes and expansion lately. Owner Mike DeCanio brought in two friends from the Midwest as partners, chef Gary Johnson and manager Jim Reber. They added a screened dining porch, a new kitchen and a new lounge, and redecorated existing dining areas in the front parlor, dining room and paneled library. The result is a spiffy, white and green decor that varies from room to room with more seating for dining on the porch and in the lounge. The new chef added excitement to a menu that had barely changed in years.

White tablecloths, colored overcloths and candlelight are the backdrop for an extensive menu with an emphasis on fresh seafood and down-home Southern cooking. Dinner entrées ranges from chicken breast in a lemon and parsley cream sauce to filet mignon and porterhouse steak. The specialty is crab cakes, available as an appetizer or a main course. Other favorites are broiled jumbo shrimp stuffed with sherried lobster filling, grilled swordfish or salmon, and charbroiled pork chops topped with fried apples. A fried oyster sandwich is a luncheon standout. Popular starters include Brunswick stew, french onion soup with madeira and gruyère, smoked salmon and shrimp cocktail. The dessert tray might hold pumpkin or brandy-alexander cheesecake, coconut-carrot cake and sweet potato-pecan pie.

Chef Johnson added ethnic fare on Thursday nights, the themes changing monthly and planned a year in advance. An all-you-can-eat fried chicken dinner is offered every Sunday night in honor of Gordonville's onetime claim to being the "fried chicken capital of the world – if not the universe," according to Mike.

Tinted photos of Gordonsville and area are displayed in the new Nathaniel Gordon lounge, named for the town's founder and featuring an oak bar custom-made by a cabinetmaker from Charlottesville. The lounge, where the dining tables are topped with cloths and kerosene lamps, is the only room in which smoking is allowed. The restaurant serves wines from Virginia exclusively.

(540) 832-3485. Entrées, $12.95 to $17.95. Lunch, Tuesday-Saturday 11:30 to 2:30. Dinner, Thursday-Sunday 5:30 to 9. Sunday brunch, 11:30 to 2:30.

Morgan's, 182 Byrd St., Orange.
New owners took over the highly rated Orange Gourmet in 1997 and renamed it Morgan's. Rich and Laura Baker went after the local trade with a downscaled menu and lower prices and, after a somewhat rocky start, quickly hit their stride.

Arrive and you might think you've got the wrong place, for the cinderblock building isn't terribly attractive and doesn't even look like a restaurant. The bar in which we once had lunch now is a function room. The bar has been moved to the center of the building and most dining takes place in a large rear dining room with windows onto a little garden.

The menu is more pedestrian than when we ate here. Now the lunchtime fare consists of sandwiches, spuds and salads. The signature baked potato soup with bacon, cheddar cheese and scallions is said to be first-rate. So is the caesar salad.

Dinner is more basic as well. The six entrées include grilled swordfish, seafood pasta, broiled pork chop and New York strip steak, served with salad, starch and vegetable. Appetizers are of the nachos, baked potato skins and chicken fingers school. Cheesecake and Kentucky derby pie are favored desserts. Most of the wines are priced in the teens.

(540) 672-0800. Entrées, $9.95 to $12.95. Lunch, Friday and Saturday from 11:30. Dinner, Tuesday-Sunday 4:30 to 9 or 10.

Firehouse Cafe & Market, 137 West Main St., Orange.
The old firehouse with its high ceilings, tall front windows and abundant greenery provides lots of atmosphere for this cafe and market, which features gourmet foods and Virginia wines. Partners Dornin Formwalt and Marty Van Santvoord offer breakfast, lunch, deli takeout fare and weekend dinners, plus a house band on Friday nights, when we're told that local yuppies have made it the place to be and people often end up dancing in the streets.

Things were quieter at our lunchtime visits. We enjoyed a cup of gazpacho, a pasta salad, and a vidalia onion quiche with house salad on one occasion, and a turkey quesadilla, a cup of sweet onion soup and half a pastrami sandwich the next. Specials included cold curried broccoli and cold zucchini soups, minted fruit salad and chocolate-almond torte. The menu is limited, but you'll find nachos, a burrito plate, deli sandwiches and desserts, and everything is in the $2.75 to $5.95 range.

The dinner menu reflects higher aspirations. Typical main courses range from pan-fried catfish with fresh tomato salsa and broiled salmon with Mediterranean orange and olive compote to roasted pork tenderloin with blackberry sauce and grilled New York strip steak topped with button mushrooms. The signature dish is filet mignon, topped with béarnaise sauce.

(540) 672-9001. Breakfast, Monday-Friday 7 to 10, Saturday 9 to 11. Lunch, Monday-Saturday 11:30 to 3. Dinner, Thursday-Saturday 5:30 to 10. Sunday brunch, 11 to 3.

Mario's, 269 Madison Road, Orange.
A chef from Sicily is plying his trade at this modest new eatery, "home of the authentic pizza and real Italian cuisine." He's so proud of his pizzas that he

challenged Pizza Hut to a head-to-head competition one year at the Orange County Fair (we didn't hear the results, but we certainly can guess). "There's a big difference between the big chains and the independent pizzeria and you can taste that difference right here," he advertises.

Neapolitan, Sicilian and white pizzas, strombolis and calzones are among the offerings on the enormous menu. Also available are pastas, chicken and veal dishes (we hear great things about the veal marsala), hot subs, hoagies and spinach calzones that are said to be out of this world. There are a few beers and wines to go with.

(540) 672-3344. Entrées, $6.95 to $9.95. Open Monday-Saturday, 11 to 11 or midnight.

Diversions

Montpelier, Route 20, Montpelier Station.

A Johnny-come-lately as tourist attractions go, the home of President James Madison was opened for public tours in 1987 by the National Trust for Historic Preservation. It's very much a restoration in progress, so don't expect to find a furnished home as at nearby Monticello or Ash Lawn. Do expect to see what was – and will be again when finished – a showplace renowned for entertaining. Started as an eight-room house, it was expanded over the years to the point that when the National Trust inherited it from Marion du Pont Scott, it was a 55-room mansion that the du Pont heiress had made into a hunt-country mecca. Since 1984, it's been the site of the Montpelier Steeplechase races, staged annually the first Saturday in November. The trust is restoring the house to show both the Madison and du Pont influences. A bus shuttles visitors from the excellent gift shop called the **Montpelier Supply Co.** up a pretty hillside drive to the imposing home, somewhat the worse for years of neglect. Interior highlights include the Corning Glass fireplace with enormous mirror above in "La Modern" Red Room, all art-decoed up by Marion du Pont, the horsewoman. She was also responsible for the Adams Room, the most "furnished" room with a rare Persian carpet, reproduction Steinway piano and gilt ceiling. Another part of the house will show how the Madisons lived. Visitors can amble through the restored double-tiered gardens, quite a sight against a forested hillside backdrop, and follow a tree walk brochure that points out 40 trees from across the world. The shuttle bus traverses a portion of the 2,700-acre estate, which has 100 other structures including houses, a bowling alley and stables, plus race courses, thoroughbred horses and working farmlands leased to tenants. On the way out, notice the Montpelier station the owner built in 1910 at the entrance to the estate. Although the train no longer stops, the station lives on as a post office. And Montpelier lives on as a social center for the county, hosting wine festivals, the county fair and such – preserving not only the architecture but the cultural heritage of the area.

(540) 672-2728. Open daily 10 to 4, March-December; weekends only, January-February. Adults, $6.

James Madison Museum, 129 Caroline St., Orange.

This small downtown museum is an excellent complement to Montpelier, showing possessions of the president and his wife Dolley, furnishings from Montpelier, presidential correspondence and books from his library. Downstairs is a fine Hall of Agriculture exhibit in tribute to Madison's farming techniques.

(540) 672-1776. Open Monday-Friday 9 to 4, weekends 1 to 4. Closed weekends in winter. Adults, $4.

Barboursville Ruins area is backdrop for winery and, in summer, Shakespeare plays.

Barboursville Vineyards and Ruins, 17655 Winery Road (Route 777), Barboursville, (540) 832-3824. Virginia winemaking started here in 1976, nearly two centuries after pioneering vintner Thomas Jefferson's vineyards of European stock were blighted. The Zonin family from Italy were the first in the state to plant viniferas successfully and have many awards to show for them. Specializing in premium wines, winemaker-manager Luca Paschina offers an excellent chardonnay for $9.99 and limited releases of pinot noir ($10.99) and merlot ($11.99) in an impressive tasting room with a Mediterranean facade. Visitors get to sample at least four of the twenty wines. Seventy-five scenic acres are under grape cultivation and more than 10,000 cases are produced annually. Nearby on the property are the **Barboursville Ruins,** the Jefferson-designed home of Gov. James Barbour, which was destroyed by fire in 1884. Open to public view behind dense shrubbery, the shell of the mansion is remarkably close to two handsome outbuildings, joined into one and lived in today as the primary residence of the estate.

Ruins on view, Monday-Saturday 10 to 4:30, check in at winery office. Winery: tastings, Monday-Saturday 10 to 5, Sunday 11 to 5.

Shakespeare at the Ruins, Barboursville, (540) 832-5355 or (800) 768-4172. The Barboursville Ruins are a spectacular backdrop for the annual Shakespeare at the Ruins each August. The Four County Players, Central Virginia's longest-running community theater, stages one of its year's five productions on the grounds of the mansion, combining Renaissance costumes and music with a Shakespearean play on three weekends. A catered buffet dinner and wines are available from the winery for a picnic before the show.

Horton Cellars, 6399 Spottswood Trail (Route 29), Gordonsville.
Although it had been growing grapes behind the Hidden Inn in Orange and producing wines in connection with Montdomaine Cellars south of Charlottesville, Horton Vineyards now has a large new underground winery topped by an impressive sales room looking rather like an English Tudor château. Dennis and Sharon

Horton, who have produced a number of award-winners, were earning acclaim for their new Horton norton ($11). An oak-aged wine patterned after the 19th-century Monticello Wine Co.'s original claret, it incorporates red hybrid norton grapes propagated in Thomas Jefferson days. Horton has committed to other French Rhone-type grapes, including one of the largest plantings of viognier, a rare substitute for chardonnay. Horton's 1994 viognier ($20) was rated best in the nation. Wine writers consider the Horton cabernet franc one of the better reds produced in Virginia.

(540) 832-7440. Tours and tastings daily, 11 to 5.

Shopping. Downtown Orange got a shot in the arm with the conversion of its old railroad depot into a transportation center and visitor center with a park beside. New businesses were already opening, among them **Not the Same Old Grind at 113 East Church St.** Jim and Nancy Bosket offer specialty coffees and teas, New York-style bagels, sandwiches, baked goods and chocolates, plus a sofa and a few tables for partaking. Pick up some reading material from **Bookends,** a new and used bookstore also in the building.

We liked the wares at **The Country Mouse,** 143 East Church St., an herb cottage where several rooms are filled with baskets, baby and bath things, hats, herbs, spices, organic foods, garden items and great jewelry, especially that depicting animals. The relocated **Somerset Shop,** part of a larger store at 110 East Main St., has every kind of country gift, handcrafted item and accessory you could imagine. Back near its old home in Somerset is the **Old Somerset Print Shop & Fine Art Gallery,** an excellent gallery specializing in upscale watercolors, mostly pastoral scenes from the English countryside. We love the paintings of the Blue Ridge Mountains by Frederick D. Nichols, but they are out of our price range. See them at **Beth Gallery,** Route 678 in Barboursville. Appointments are advised. Antiques, scented items, herbs, birdhouses, books and much more are on display at **Barboursville Gift Gallery,** Route 20 north.

Extra-Special

Ed Jaffe Gallery, 108 West Main St., Orange.

This 5,000-square-foot studio and gallery – "unlike any other north or south of Manhattan," according to its creator – opened in a former five-and-dime store in downtown Orange in 1994. Sculptor Jaffe had tired of the way traditional galleries showed his sculptures for twenty years on the East and West coasts. As the middle-man, "the gallery tends to put up a wall between the artist and the collector," Ed said. He liked having collectors visit his farmhouse-studio in southern Vermont, discovering "a bond that comes from direct contact." He also didn't care for the way the galleries handled pieces that were as dear to him as family members, so he "pulled all my babies home" and decided to open his own gallery. The question was where. He didn't want to return to New York City, where he'd worked as a professional photographer, and a Vermont mountain top was not the place to reach a broad market. His search took five years; the change took five months. The center of his universe is now downtown Orange, which he calls the heart of the nation's North-South corridor. He converted part of the store into a studio and his living quarters, and the rest is like a museum in need of a few more exhibits. The entire space is devoted to the works of one man, mostly sculptures but some paintings. They carry pricetags from $300 to $15,000.

(540) 672-2400 or (800) 672-8588. Open most Saturdays 11 to 5, and by appointment.

James River Plantation Country

Where Time Is On Hold

Plantation Country. The name evokes images of early aristocracy, vast tracts of farmlands, lazing riverboats, manor homes, belles in hoop skirts and gentlemen attired for the hunt.

What could be more Southern? And where – with the possible exception of Natchez – is that Southern lifestyle more in evidence today than along the James River in Virginia's Tidewater? Its way of life has been established since the area was settled during the first westward expansion of English-speaking America in the early 1600s and the James became the highway to inland commerce.

Close to Virginia's busy Historic Triangle (Williamsburg, Jamestown and Yorktown), plantation country goes its own way just inland along the James. Time has been put on hold in this rare Southern oasis where American history officially began.

About a dozen plantations of note still thrive, and half are open to the public. Miles of fields, farmlands and forests give way to the occasional river vista in this far-flung, sparsely populated stretch along both sides of the river.

There are no cities. Indeed, Charles City County, home of most of the great plantations on the river's sylvan north side, is really a county without a city. Charles City, a one-horse hamlet with little more than a courthouse and a school, stands in stark contrast to its neighbor to the east, touristy Williamsburg. The main route along the north bank, Route 5 (also called the John Tyler Highway), is America's oldest highway and appears nearly deserted.

Upriver and across the James is Hopewell, America's busiest port during the War Between the States. A visit to Grant's Headquarters at City Point is a welcome contrast to plantation tours. As the region's nearest urban link, Hopewell offers accommodations, riverfront restaurants, and antiques and collectible shops.

Down river on the south side are two relatively undiscovered prizes. Surry, population 300, is the center of peanut country and a lazy Southern hamlet, if ever there was one. Smithfield, population 4,700, is a 1750s river town that produces the world's most famous ham. It's the epitome of Tidewater and the center of the aptly named Isle of Wight County.

Only at the far ends of Plantation Country does one sense a few urban encroachments from Williamsburg, Norfolk and Richmond. Otherwise, all is peaceful and quiet at the plantations as the Harrisons, the Tylers, the Carters and the rest go about their business. They reflect to this day the web of kinship that has linked Virginia aristocracy from the beginning.

Original family is still in residence on Shirley Plantation complex beside James River.

Inn Spots

Several plantations take in overnight guests, and a few B&Bs have sprung up on both sides of the river. More traditional and more numerous accommodations are available in Williamsburg and Hopewell.

Edgewood Plantation, 4800 John Tyler Memorial Hwy., Charles City 23030.
When in Plantation Country, why not stay in a plantation, even if it is not a typical manor house and is relatively small in comparison? Don't stay here, mind you, if you want to be in the thick of Williamsburg activities, don't care for antiques, dislike clutter and want a large bathroom.

Prepare to be overwhelmed. Dot and Julian Boulware have assembled a collection to end all collections at their home and B&B. They created it in 1984 from an ugly duckling of an 1849 Gothic Revival that no one else wanted across from, and once

Bedroom at Edgewood Plantation holds canopied bed, loveseat and perambulator.

part of, the Berkeley Plantation. Dot, a Richmonder who has an eye for displaying things stylishly, has furnished the place with "a little bit of everything" – and lots of it. She must have thousands of dolls, books, buggies, dollhouses, hat boxes, hats and antiques and they are everywhere. At our first July visit, she still had some of her eighteen Christmas trees up and lit.

A gorgeous spiral staircase, its banister draped in lace, pink satin, baby's breath and evergreen branches, winds to the second floor. Here off a central hall are four bedrooms, all with private baths, fireplaces and at least fourteen pillows on each bed.

"Each room is a fascination," says Dot. She's tried to hide the TV/VCRs that she recently installed in each room, "because I hate them, and you have plenty of entertainment anyway." Roses abound, for Edgewood caters to romance. "This is a lady's house," explains Dot. "The men ask, 'where do we sleep?'" That's no idle question. Although the beds are high and comfy, Dot must remove all those pillows and layers of antique coverings at night. Empty your pockets before retiring and you could lose their contents in all the collections, for there's not an uncovered space to be found. If you head for the bathroom in the dark of night, you might mistake a headless mannequin costumed in white for the resident ghost and land, as one of us nearly did, in a waiting perambulator. Showering the next morning in what must be the world's smallest bathroom was a feat. The bathrooms aren't big, Dot concedes, but contain "everything you need to have."

On the third floor is a sitting area, set with a teddy bears' tea party and a TV ensconced in a dollhouse, between two bedrooms that share a bath.

Upstairs in the old slave quarters behind the house are two more rooms, one a honeymoon suite called Prissy's Quarters. Grapevines strung with dried flowers festoon the pencil-post queen bed and the quilt is patched with hearts. The country decor is simpler than in the main house, and amenities include a small kitchen and a sitting area with TV.

What next? "I'm not finished yet," said Dot as she talked of more rooms in a 1725 grist mill built by Benjamin Harrison at the side of the property. Julian has planted a large, symmetrical boxwood garden with gravel walks lined in brick, a trickling fountain and a tiered terrace descending to a pond.

Already, Edgewood offers a swimming pool and hot tub, a side patio, two gazebos, a front veranda overlooking colorful landscaping, a 38-foot-long living room full of Victoriana, a formal dining room and a country kitchen so cluttered it's a wonder that breakfast can be prepared. But prepared it is, and served by candlelight at a long, lace-covered table in the dining room. At our visit, orange juice in a pewter cup and fresh berries and other fruit in a pewter dish preceded delicious thick french toast with cinnamon and powdered sugar. The hostess sits with her guests and keeps up a running commentary on all the fascinations of her place.

The house is open daily except Monday for tours ($7, including second-floor bedrooms), led by Dot in Victorian costume. She also serves lunch and tea by appointment ($20 to $30) in the downstairs tavern and tea room, as chock full as the rest of the house.

(804) 829-2962 or (800) 269-3343. Five rooms and one suite with private baths; two rooms with shared bath. Doubles, $158 to $188 with private bath, $125 with shared bath. Suite, $188.

North Bend Plantation B&B, 12200 Weyanoke Road, Charles City 23030.
This unpretentious, 1819 Greek Revival house at the end of a long road harbors a lot of history. Owner George Copland is a great-great grandson of Edmund Ruffin, the Southerner who fired the first shot of the Civil War. Union General Sheridan used the house as his headquarters. And the owner still farms the plantation, when he's not busy with his four-room B&B.

George and his wife, Ridgley, a family nurse practitioner, offer four large guest rooms, all with private baths. Each is furnished with family antiques and collectibles in the spare Federal style. The rear Magnolia Room overlooking the swimming pool has a canopied queensize rice bed and a connecting bedroom in the maid's quarters. The Sheridan Room features a canopied step-up queen tester bed bearing a gunshot wound from the Civil War and covered by a floral comforter. Also here are a velvet settee, a rocker and the general's Civil War desk containing special orders from New York. The Rose Room, also with a queen canopy bed and a chaise lounge, has a more feminine look with dolls and pillows. The Federal Room contains an 1850 sleigh bed, a rich patterned gold loveseat and a cast-iron bath.

Guests watch passing deer in the fields and listen to chattering birds from an enclosed upstairs sun porch outfitted in wicker. Downstairs are a double parlor, a dining room with an old billiards table with a marble base at one end and a homey kitchen where most guests prefer to eat as George whips up his specialty waffles. Eggs with sausages and biscuits are another breakfast favorite.

(804) 829-5176 or (800) 841-1479. Four rooms with private baths. Doubles, $115 to 135. Children over 6. Smoking restricted.

Jasmine Plantation B&B, 4500 North Courthouse Road, Providence Forge 23140
Candles are lit in every window of this handsome, gabled white and green 1750s

farmhouse on 47 rural acres. Chickens and roosters are on display in back, and walking trails wind through the woods past tranquil sitting areas.

A country store off the front foyer, where guests check in, is stocked with antiques for sale. Owners Joyce and Howard Vogt, who live next door on the property, offer six guest rooms, four with private baths and working fireplaces. The two oldest rooms in the 1700s section share a bath and are furnished with antiques dating to the 1600s. The George Morris Room, the most spacious, is furnished in Empire style and has a fireplace, sitting area, TV/VCR and private bath with clawfoot tub and separate shower. Period antiques also prevail in the other rooms. Two are Victorian and the Rose Room has a 1930s theme.

Three working fireplaces are evident on the main floor, all of which is devoted to common areas. Among them are a formal parlor, a rear den with TV and a couple of dining areas. The Vogts serve a country breakfast of fresh fruit, bacon and Surry ham, and an entrée of perhaps omelets, waffles or french toast.

(804) 966-9836 or (800) 639-5368. Fax (804) 966-5679. Four rooms with private baths and two rooms with shared bath. Doubles, $75 to $105. Children over 12. No smoking.

Piney Grove at Southall's Plantation, 16920 Southall Plantation Lane, Box 1359, Charles City 23030.

Out in the middle of nowhere is this delightful restoration, not really a plantation home of the dimensions considered hereabouts but a remarkably historic and appealing place nonetheless. Restorationists Joan and Joseph Gordineer of Williamsburg first purchased a general store and residence that had begun life in 1800 as a log corn-crib.

With son Brian, whose graduate thesis focused on tourism in the James River Plantation Country, they opened a B&B with one room in the National Register-listed main house that's as atmospheric as can be. In 1989, they moved a modest Greek Revival plantation house from Ladysmith to a site behind the main house. It backs up to woods and a farm corral, and faces gardens and loblolly pines and an open shed housing Joseph's collection of old cars. At its side is a gazebo next to an idyllic, hidden swimming pool surrounded by lounge chairs. The Gordiners now offer three guest rooms and a suite with private baths and considerable comfort.

Brian and his father did the restoration of the Ladysmith house themselves. The son's artistry is evident in the stenciling and in the ongoing mural of Greek buildings working its way around the walls of both floors of the center hall. The four rooms on either side of the hall, upstairs and down, have been granted extra space, thanks to a rear addition that holds the bathrooms. Each high-ceilinged room has a fireplace and comes with a double bed (two also have a twin), loveseats, wing chairs and/or rockers, mini-refrigerator and coffeemaker. One is a two-bedroom suite suitable for three people.

A decanter of apple brandy is in the hall, and mint juleps or hot toddies are served upon arrival. A farm bell is rung ten minutes before breakfast is ready in the main house. It's served at three tables in the parlor/library of the oldest, log-walled section. The fare includes juice, fresh fruit, Virginia ham or sausage, home-made breads and one of six casseroles made from fresh eggs. Afterward, adjourn to the neatest little screened porch, snug with two wicker chairs facing a wicker loveseat and screened from the odd passing vehicle by a boxwood hedge, or linger by the fire in the formal parlor with its rich blue walls, wood moldings and stenciling.

Rows of rose of sharon trees, hibiscus gardens, pear and plum trees, trellised

Horses graze outside Piney Grove at Southall's Plantation.

grapes and raspberries, a corral holding ducks, geese, sheep and a goat, and the swimming pool offer plenty of diversion. A nature trail leads through the woods to a ravine with springs and a swimming hole.

(804) 829-2480. Three rooms and one suite with private baths. Doubles, $125 to $140. Suite, $160. Children accepted. No smoking.

Seward House Inn, 193 Colonial Trail East (Route 10), Box 352, Surry 23883.
British-born Cynthia Erskine was picking pole beans and cucumbers in her back-yard garden at our first visit. She led us in the back way past the kitchen, the dining room and the living room, where a TV shared space at the time with a sewing machine "because we're still making curtains."

The B&B was opened in 1990 by Cynthia and a Norfolk friend, Jacqueline Bayer. It is homey and welcoming, from the pictures of Jackie's children in the front hall to the jars of basil jelly that Cynthia makes and gives to guests. The sewing machine is long gone, but there's now a piano in the hall.

The four guest quarters are furnished with mementos of three generations of their families, including handcarved beds, old toys, bits of needlework, a handcarved trunk, and prints of Andrew Wyeth and Maxfield Parrish. The front corner downstairs room has a private bath. A bathroom with a clawfoot tub serves two upstairs bedrooms, one with a queensize bed. The other has twin beds, a teddybear on a trunk and a fireplace mantel bearing a miniature sewing machine and toy soldiers. We stayed in a small guest cottage at the side is called the Surgery; this is the office in which Jackie's great uncle used to practice medicine. It now offers a full bath, a queensize bedroom and a living room with a rattan loveseat and chair.

Although almost in the center of town (what there is of it), the inn is surrounded by fields of soybeans and corn. Guests enjoy a front veranda and a trellised side deck overlooking the tranquil scene, including a small fish pond. A jigsaw puzzle is at the ready in the living room of what Cynthia calls "a family-friendly house."

For breakfast, "we do things family style, and lots of it." Ours was an omelet with shiitake mushrooms, parsley and parmigiano-reggiano cheese, with a side of country ham from the nearby Edwards Virginia Ham Shoppe. Or the main course could be waffles containing pecans picked from trees outside. Spicy sausage gravy over biscuits has been a hit lately. Overnight guests may use the hosts' barbecue grills for dining al fresco on the trellised deck or have dinner prepared by reservation. The tab averages $25 for something like organically grown salad with homemade dressing, biscuits, French bread, pasta with garden vegetables, fruit and cheeses. In winter, Cynthia might do a roast or chicken. Upon request, they also pack picnic lunches.

Besides the basil jelly, Cynthia puts up wild blackberry jam and sent us on our way with a small jar. It sure did liven up our toast while it lasted.

(804) 294-3810. One room and one suite with private baths; two rooms with shared bath. Doubles, $65 to $70. Cottage, $80. Children accepted. Smoking restricted.

Mansion on Main, 36 Main St., Smithfield 23430.

This yellow and red Victorian residence, nicknamed "the mansion" when it was built in 1889 as one of the largest in town, was converted into a B&B in late 1997. Sala Clark, a young Smithfield resident, was doing it by herself, so the structure was a work in progress at our visit.

Sala opened with three second-floor guest rooms, all furnished in Victoriana and mostly with period antiques. One with two double beds has a private bath. Two others, one with queen bed and one with a double, share a bath and can be rented as a suite. In early 1998, Sala started work in the attic on another bedroom with private bath and a sitting area. Eventually, she planned to convert a rear carriage house into a fifth guest room.

Guests are served a traditional Southern breakfast of fresh fruit, eggs, Smithfield ham, hash browns and muffins at a huge table in the dining room. Tea and sweets are offered in the afternoon. Guests also enjoy a parlor and a library.

Sala opened an antiques shop on the main floor, the Collector's Corner, borrowing on the experience of her mother, an antiques dealer.

(757) 357-0006. One room with private bath and two rooms with shared bath. Doubles, $55 to $75. Suite, $125.

Smithfield Station, 415 South Church St., Smithfield 23430.

Built in 1986 and with water on three sides, this was designed by a local businessman/sailor to look like a Victorian Coast Guard station. Its busy marina and restaurant (see Dining Spots) draw crowds, but overnight guests can be above the hubbub in fifteen guest rooms on the second and third floors, or away from the fray in two suites in a lighthouse.

In contemporary motel style, the upstairs rooms are attractive with pine furnishings, kingsize or two double beds, TV, phone, a table with two chairs and waterfowl pictures on the walls. By far the most appealing are those overlooking the Pagan River and Cypress Creek across deep rear balconies running the length of the building. Our balcony would have gotten a workout except that we were there during weather so torrid that we couldn't venture outside our air-conditioned room even after the sun had gone down.

A continental breakfast is served buffet-style on weekdays in one of the dining rooms. Juices, fruit, danish and homemade rolls filled with Smithfield ham are the fare.

Seward House Inn and small adjacent cottage offer four guest accommodations.

Lately, owners Ronald and Christina Pack added a boardwalk with gazebos, a swimming pool and an outdoor bar and grill. They built a lighthouse for use as two deluxe suites and a conference center, surrounded by water. The Captain Sinclair features a king bed, gas fireplace, microwave and wet bar, double whirlpool tub, steam shower and a spiral staircase to the cupola of the lighthouse for the best view in Smithfield. The Captain Todd offers a kingsize murphy bed, fireplace, kitchenette and dining area as well as a site for small business meetings.

(757) 357-7700. Fifteen room and two suites. Doubles, $59 to $99. Suites, $175 and $225.

Isle of Wight Inn, 1607 South Church St., Smithfield 23430.
Its location among relatively new buildings along a commercial strip at the southern entrance to town surprises. Which came first – the inn or the strip? The latter, apparently, for this was built as an office building and renovated later into a twelve-room inn and antiques shop.

The residential exterior masks its origin, and inside all is dark and antiquey. The parlor is part of the antiques shop, which specializes in period furniture and old clocks. Off the parlor is a dining room, where clocks tick away as guests help themselves to a continental breakfast of fruit, danish and Smithfield ham biscuits.

The first and second floors contain a variety of guest rooms, each with private bath, TV and telephone. Four are large suites with private entrances, two with jacuzzis. One we saw had a huge corner fireplace, a canopied step-up queensize four-poster and a double jacuzzi with tall candles beside a mirrored wall in the bathroom. A large efficiency on the lower level is decorated in country style.

(757) 357-3176 or (800) 357-3245. Eight rooms and four suites with private baths. Doubles, $59. Suites, $119.

Four Square Plantation, 13357 Four Square Road, Smithfield 23430.

Amelia and Roger Healey moved in 1994 from a small B&B in Wrightsville, Pa., to a larger and older home built in 1807 as the centerpiece of a 23-acre plantation. Here, in a house listed on the National Register and declared a Virginia Landmark Property, they offer three large bedrooms with fireplaces and private baths.

A Pennsylvania quilt graces the kingsize poster bed in the Thomas Room, comfortable with thick carpeting and two armchairs. A secluded bedroom in the rear of the house is nineteen feet square and furnished in the Empire style with a queen bed and large walnut armoire.

European and American antiques enhance the public rooms. A Spanish portable writing desk dating to the 1600s takes center stage in the parlor. The dining room holds a French trestle table from a monastery, dating to the 1500s and the oldest piece in the house. Quite a collection of French tinkers' miniatures (copper pots and pans) adorn one wall.

Amelia serves a full breakfast – a Southwest omelet with Virginia ham and banana bread the day of our visit. Fruit compote, lemon-poppyseed muffins and blueberry pancakes were on the docket the next day.

(757) 365-0749. Three rooms with private baths. Doubles, $65 to $75. Smoking restricted.

Dining Spots

Indian Fields Tavern, 9220 John Tyler Hwy., Charles City.

In an area of few people (other than plantation-goers, many of whom don't spend the night), a young man who grew up on one of the biggest plantations is making a go of it with a most appealing restaurant. In 1988, Archer H. Ruffin Jr., a relative of the family that owns nearby Evelynton Plantation, turned a ramshackle, century-old farmhouse into a bustling eatery accommodating 90 patrons in four dining rooms upstairs and down, plus 30 more on screened porches. The name derives from the surrounding fields, which natives were farming when the first English settlers arrived in Virginia.

Archer's mother and his sister-in-law helped with the decor. They went with an early tavern look and a burgundy, green and beige color scheme. Bare hardwood floors, windsor chairs and well-spaced tables topped with burgundy cloths, votive candles and bud vases bearing large lilies set the stage for an ambitious dinner menu, which changes frequently.

For starters, we sampled the night's gazpacho and the huge Indian Fields garden salad with dijon vinaigrette as we munched on homemade sweet Sally Lunn bread. Other possibilities were grilled wild mushrooms with red wine and stilton cheese and pan-seared oysters over grilled sweet corn bruschetta and red pepper rouille. Among entrées, we liked the soft-shell crabs served with a spicy pecan butter, carrots and yellow squash. Also excellent was the mixed grill of lamb, quail and Surry sausage with a brandied pear demi-glace, accompanied by broiled potatoes and haricots verts. We hear great things about the oysters or crab cakes harrison, new signature dishes served with hollandaise sauce over Smithfield ham and toasted Sally Lunn bread

The wine list is quite select and reasonably priced. Desserts are to groan over, particularly if you're into cakes or bourbon-chocolate-pecan pie. The raspberry cheesecake was extra-good.

Indian Fields also serves interesting fare in the $5.50 to $11.95 range for lunch

Archer H. Ruffin Jr. turned ramshackle farmhouse into Indian Fields Tavern.

and Sunday brunch. The throngs pouring in for weekday lunch at our latest visit attested to the success and drawing power of a restaurant way off the beaten path.

(804) 829-5004. Entrées, $15.95 to $21.95. Lunch daily, 11 to 4. Dinner nightly, 5 to 9 or 10. Sunday brunch, 11 to 4.

Coach House Tavern, 12602 Harrison Landing Road, Charles City.

Once the place where Benjamin Harrison garaged his coaches, this small outbuilding at Berkeley Plantation has been transformed into a thing of beauty for special-occasion dining. With blue over white cloths and fanned napkins, large tables on two levels look through french doors onto an expanse of lovely gardens.

Votive candles flicker on wall sconces among dark beams and posts at night, when the room is positively magical. Dinner is leisurely and the table is yours for the evening. The concise menu offered by Sandra Capps and Steve Danz changes often. Entrées might include pan-seared salmon with herbed butter sauce, quail with apple-walnut stuffing, veal marsala and loin lamb chops with rosemary wine glaze. Start with a signature french onion soup "served en boule," oyster stew or baked mushrooms stuffed with crab imperial.

At lunch, waitresses in Colonial dresses pour non-stop iced tea. Between plantation tours we enjoyed a crab cake sandwich and a seafood salad in a halved avocado. Pretty as a picture, the latter was garnished with an abundance of fresh fruit, from strawberries to kiwi to honeydew. It came with potato salad and cold roasted peppers. The crab sandwich arrived on thick toasted bread described as "baked bass." Was it Sally Lunn bread? "No, suh, it's fresh baked bah-us." For dessert, the famous Berkeley rum cake lived up to its billing. Surrounded by blue-berries, raspberries and strawberries and resting on crème anglaise, it was one of the best cakes we've tasted.

(804) 829-6003. Entrées, $21.95 to $26.95. Lunch daily, 11 to 4. Dinner, 6 to 9, Sunday 11 to 5.

David's White House Restaurant, 3560 Courthouse Road, Providence Forge.
The original chef and partner from Indian Fields, David Napier, opened his own restaurant to equally good reviews. The setting is a turn-of-the-century house built by the town miller in the center of historic Providence Forge. Well-spaced tables in four dining rooms are dressed with white cloths and fresh flowers. David set out to offer "fine dining in plantation style" with an added embellishment: the food at this White House "could easily by served at any state dinner held at the one in Washington."
The regional food press agreed. David earned considerable acclaim for dinner appetizers like sherried crab, grilled oysters on corncakes topped with chipped Smithfield ham, and homemade hunter's sausage, patties of venison, lamb and tenderloin seasoned with sage and fennel seed and topped with berry glaze. His Big Daddy seafood gumbo blends shrimp, okra and garlic with French bread croutons.
Main courses range from baked Virginia ham with bourbon-glazed apples to grilled quail stuffed with hunter's sausage. A sampler plate teams three house favorites: sautéed oysters topped with Smithfield ham, filet mignon with a red wine and roquefort glaze, and slow-roasted baby pork ribs. Crab cakes with caper mayonnaise and grilled duck breast with fried grits are other favorites.
(804) 966-9700. Entrées, $13.50 to $18.50. Lunch, Tuesday-Saturday 11 to 4. Dinner, Tuesday-Saturday 5 to 10. Sunday, brunch 11 to 4, dinner, 4 to 10.

The Smithfield Inn, 112 Main St., Smithfield.
The stylish restaurant at this newly restored and reopened inn – built in 1752 and one of the oldest buildings in town – receives high marks from locals.
Beyond a front veranda with a lineup of rocking chairs are two dining rooms, elegant and formal in Victoriana. Fringed lamps and fancy glassware are on each large, well spaced table. More dining is available in the English-style William Rand Tavern and on a side brick patio outfitted with white wrought-iron furniture.
The fare is contemporary American with a Southern accent. Expect dinner entrées like pecan-crusted rainbow trout on a sauté of Smithfield ham and granny smith apples, lump crab cakes over Smithfield ham, game stew, brochette of pork, venison chops with a currant compote and medallions of lamb with a rosemary concasse. Appetizers could be oysters fontina, tempura shrimp and grilled quail. Other favorites are crab and spinach soup, brunswick stew and oyster stew.
Appetizers, soups, stews and sandwiches are available for supper in the tavern. Similar fare is offered on the lunch menu. We'd like to try the oyster fritter and the open-face lump crab cake sandwich.
After a million-dollar plus restoration, the inn – now owned by meat packer Joe Luter III of Smithfield Foods – offers five upstairs suites for overnight guests. They're said to be elegant and pricey. We were unable to verify because when we tried, the manager relayed a curt message that the inn was not interested.
(757) 357-1752. Suites, $145. Entrées, $14.95 to $22.95. Lunch, Tuesday-Sunday 11:30 to 3. Dinner, Wednesday-Saturday 6 to 9. Tavern, Tuesday-Saturday 4 to 10. No smoking.

Smithfield Station, 415 South Church St., Smithfield.
Nicely nautical to go with its setting, the main floor of this contemporary hotel-marina-restaurant has four dining areas including a lounge, plus a solarium and a waterside deck, and seats up to 150.
The extensive menu has something for everyone, from baked chicken stuffed with Smithfield ham, swiss cheese and roasted peanuts to pork oscar and T-bone

steak. Seafood is king here, along with ham. It comes as nautical pasta, blackened catfish, crab norfolk, seafood rockefeller, surf and turf (crabcakes and Smithfield ham), and what have you. We can vouch for the sampler of Smithfield ham, the Station pasta combining shrimp, smoked salmon and Smithfield ham chunks over spinach fettuccine, and seafood norfolk, accompanied by yellow squash parmesan. A peach-berry sundae, marinated in triple sec and served over vanilla ice cream, made a refreshing ending.

A Smithfield ham platter, served with fried apples and vegetable of the day, is a favorite at lunch.

Outside on the new boardwalk along the Pagan River bridge, the **Boardwalk Raw Bar & Grill** serves Wednesday-Saturday from 4 to 10 or 11, Sunday 1 to 10.

(757) 357-7700. Entrées, $14.95 to $21.95. Lunch daily, 11 to 4. Dinner nightly, 4 to 9:30.

Surrey House Restaurant, Routes 10 and 31, Surry.

Predictable Southern cooking is served up with lots of local color at this oldtimer in the heart of peanut country. New owner Michael Stevens expanded the menu, but retained the old favorites rendered by longtime owner Helen Gwaltney Lenox. Even though it now serves Williamsburg wines, iced tea with frequent refills remains the beverage of choice at noon or night.

At lunchtime, one of us sampled a cup of peanut soup, a creamy chicken broth with spices and crunchy peanuts, and a club sandwich like those we remember from thirty years ago, overflowing with Edwards ham, bacon, turkey, cheese, lettuce and tomato. The other went for the surf and turf ($12.99), a midday whopper of Edwards ham with a crab cake, plus a trip to the salad bar, an apple fritter, hushpuppies and rolls. Four kinds of sauces in a pewter relish tray accompanied.

Those in the mood can sample the famous Surrey House peanut butter board ($4.99). This do-it-yourself affair involves slices of white and brown bread, a jar of peanut butter, down-home honey, a rasher of bacon, raisins, jelly, a whole ripe banana, apple wedges and cheese, served up on a Surry County pine cutting board.

Ham comes any number of ways, from eggs benedict at breakfast to a dinner special with fried oysters. The all-day menu also offers local seafood, fried chicken, delmonico steak and roast turkey.

The paneled dining room is down-home homey, with booths, banquettes and a hodgepodge of art on the walls. Waitresses in vaguely Colonial ankle-length dresses with puffed sleeves provide quick service. The Carriage Room is more formal with white and blue tablecloths.

(757) 294-3389 or (800) 200-4977. Entrées, $5.25 to $15.99. Breakfast daily, 6:30 to noon. Lunch and dinner, 11 to 9.

The Backfin Seafood Restaurant, 1193 Jamestown Road, Williamsburg.

Folks in Surry swear by this modest eatery, a twenty-minute ferry ride across the James River and five miles from the Jamestown ferry landing. Hard to find, this is not a tourist restaurant, our informants insisted – just a casual place for seafood, nicely served by a young staff.

We stopped for lunch, sampling the specialty crab cake sandwich and a soft crab "sea basket," at $5.95 the priciest of eight seafood baskets served with fries, coleslaw and hushpuppies. A basket of cornbread staved off hunger as we awaited our choices on the covered, trellised outdoor picnic deck overlooking the rear of a shopping plaza parking lot.

The dinner menu is basic, from fried catfish and fried oysters to the specialty crab cakes, soft-shell crab and a broiled or fried seafood platter.

(804) 220-2249. Entrées, $7.95 to $11.95. Lunch, Monday-Saturday 11 to 3. Dinner, Monday-Saturday 4:30 to 9.

Smithfield Gourmet Bakery and Café, 218 Main St., Smithfield.

Bon Appétit magazine requested the recipe for the orange muffins at this prized little bakery and homey café seating 40 diners.

Owner Carolyn Burke is better known for her cheesecakes. Patrons wax enthusiastic over her sandwiches, including one called the Windsor Castle stuffed with roast turkey, cheddar, grilled onions, honey mustard, lettuce and tomato on grilled tomato-basil bread, a steal for $4.19 – the top price, except for a hamburger or a grilled chicken sandwich. The breads are fresh baked, the ham is Smithfield, and the sides of potato, garden or pasta salads first-rate. For dessert, the coconut cake comes highly recommended.

(757) 357-0045. Open Monday-Saturday 9 to 6, Sunday 11 to 5.

Diversions

Most visitors come here to see the plantations (only a few of which are open to the public). Be advised that there also are a couple of historic towns, a marvelous state park with a model farm, peanut farms, purveyors of Smithfield hams, and more peanut, tobacco, soybean and cotton fields than we ever thought we'd see.

Plantations. Of the dozen or so landmark plantations, some like **Brandon** and **Westover** are open to the public only by appointment and during Historic Garden Week. Others like **Weston** and **Appomattox Plantation** are off the beaten path in Hopewell. Still others like **Bacon's Castle** and **Smith's Fort** are undergoing restoration, and **Chippokes** was inexplicably closed when we were there. Those plantations that are open help support their upkeep by charging for tours. Our favorites:

Shirley Plantation, 501 Shirley Plantation Road, Charles City.

Started in 1613, the home of ten generations of Hills and Carters (and the mother of Robert E. Lee) is perfectly poised with a long view up the James River. Its dependencies form the only Queen Anne forecourt in America, and here you may encounter the Carter pets at play. We found this to be the most personal of plantations, the only one in its original condition and the only one with direct descendants of the original family still in residence. Charles Hill Carter Jr., the county supervisor and handyman about Shirley, lives upstairs with his wife, who runs the gift shop, and two sons who eventually will take over Shirley but who had just opened a clay shooting course at our visit. Guided tours run continuously and there are no roped-off areas. You'll learn the intriguing story behind the family portraits done by an itinerant painter, see dates etched in the dining-room window by ladies testing the quality of their diamond rings, spot two spigots beside the dining-room fireplace for cleaning dishes, and marvel at a unique free-standing square staircase with no visible support in the foyer. The family's silver, coats of arms and other heirlooms are out for all to see.

(804) 829-5121 or (800) 232-1613. Open daily, 9 to 5. Adults, $7.50.

Evelynton Plantation, 6701 John Tyler Hwy., Charles City.

An air of modern luxury pervades Evelynton, to our minds the most appealing

and livable of plantations. It's on a shady, tiered lawn overlooking Herring Creek. The impressive Georgian Revival manor house was built in 1936 on property purchased in 1847 by Edmund Ruffin Jr., the states' rights activist and agricultural reformer who fired the first shot in the Civil War at Fort Sumter. The war came to Evelynton when Union General George McClellan occupied the area, burning the original house belonging to the Southern martyr. Today, rope hammocks and two Adirondack chairs flank a cannon and a plaque commemorating the Battle of Evelynton Heights. Ruffin's great-grandson built the showplace home that stands today as testimony to the good life. A guide points out the Chippendale necessary chair in the front bedroom, a sunken family garden room glamorous in brick and chintz, the carved moldings along the ceilings, the formal dining room with an 18th-century Heppelwhite curved buffet, and recent portraits of the four offspring of Saunders Ruffin, current occupant. Portions of three movies were filmed here. The canopied rear terrace was added lately as a setting for weddings and functions.
(804) 829-5075 or (800) 473-5075. Open daily, 9 to 5. Adults, $7.

Berkeley Plantation, 12602 Harrison Landing Road, Charles City.
The most obviously commercial of the plantations, this is known for its firsts. It was the site of the first official Thanksgiving in 1619. It was the birthplace of Benjamin Harrison (signer of the Declaration of Independence) and of William Henry Harrison, ninth U.S. president, and the ancestral home of 23rd president Benjamin Harrison. And "Taps" was composed here in 1862. Following a slide show, costumed guides shepherd visitors through the main floor of the 1726 house, admonishing them not to touch or lean on the furniture. Exceptional Heppelwhite, Chippendale and Louis pieces abound. Octogenarian owner Mac Jamieson rides around on a golf cart to oversee the magnificent gardens; often mistaken as a groundskeeper, he loves to talk with those who approach.
(804) 829-6018. Open daily, 8 to 5. Adults, $8.50.

Bacon's Castle, Route 617, Surry.
The oldest documented brick house in English North America (1665) holds particular fascination. The high Jacobean-style structure is in the process of restoration, which gives insights into construction techniques as well as history spanning three centuries. A ten-minute audio-visual presentation precedes an informative 45-minute guided tour. Visitors see graffiti on a wall (one child's scrawl dated 1886 says "this day I am sick"), a love letter written in glass, a 1710 one-hand clock and a room full of artifacts acquired in archaeological digs on the property, from clay marbles to egg shells. Outside, what was thought to be a 19th-century garden turned out to be a Renaissance-style English garden from the 17th century. Uncovered in 1985, it prompted the New York Times to declare it the "earliest, largest, best-preserved and most sophisticated garden that has come to light in North America." The resident gardener likes to show off its prizes.
(757) 357-5976. Open Tuesday-Saturday 10 to 4, Sunday noon to 4. Adults, $5.

Smithfield. Known for its hams, the hog capital of the world also is a case study of an early river port. Some say Smithfield's collection of 60-plus historic houses represents the best selection in Tidewater because it spans both 18th and 19th centuries. The Chamber of Commerce's walking-tour map notes a blend of more than 60 Colonial, Federal, Georgian and Victorian structures side by side – including Victorian Row, which would do Cape May proud. We chanced upon Hayden's Lane, a brick walkway beneath a canopy of flowering crape myrtle trees leading to Hayden Hall. Check out the old-time country store complete with early postal boxes, pot-bellied stove and revolving stools in the Barlow Gallery at the **Isle of Wight County Museum,** housed in two bank buildings.

Smithfield's is the kind of downtown where the Lord's Vineyard (cards, gifts and Bibles) occupies space next to Hamtown Barber & Styling. **Ashton Galleries** stocks fine gifts and accessories. At **Joyner of Smithfield's** downtown retail shop, you can sample and purchase a variety of Smithfield hams, their pungently salty and smoky taste distinctive partly because the hogs are raised on local peanuts. The shop also features peanuts. **Basse's Choice Ham Shop** features Gwaltney's hams. Also a specialty foods store, it stocks a variety of mostly Virginia-made products, from dips and hot pepper jelly to chocolates and wines. For deli sandwiches or desserts, check out the **Smithfield Confectionery and Ice Cream Parlour.** Art and handcrafts are offered at the interesting **Collage Art Gallery,** ensconced in one of the five Victorian Row houses. Twenty-three dealers show their wares in the **Smithfield Antiques Center** co-op.

Surry. Named for the English county of Surrey, this was the home of some of the first black settlers in America. Today, peanuts rule (the little Smithfield-Surry phone book carries two pages of listings for peanut products in its yellow pages). The annual Pork, Peanut & Pine Festival draws thousands on a mid-July weekend to **Chippokes Plantation State Park,** the oldest continuously farmed property in the country. Besides swimming, picnicking and hiking, the park offers an 1854 mansion with formal gardens, a visitor center with windows onto the James River, and a model farm and forestry museum illustrating agricultural life as it was in Colonial times. The farm tour alone is worth the trip. The **Surry-Jamestown Ferry,** one of Virginia's last, links the two sides of Plantation Country. In town, tours of the smokehouse are offered hourly on the half hour at **Edwards Virginia Ham Shoppe,** where you can snack on such local specialties as ham rolls, sausage sandwiches, peanut soup and Brunswick stew. **Farmer Joe's** gift shop sells flowery items and plants.

Extra-Special

St. Luke's Church, 14477 Benns Church Blvd., off Route 10, Smithfield.

Hidden English-style in the middle of a forested cemetery beside a creek, this is America's only original Gothic church and its oldest English-speaking church (1632). Its original traceried windows, stepped gables and buttresses are unique in American architecture. A guide points out the stained-glass window commemorating Pocohontas, the first convert in Virginia to the gospel. The pews were put together with wooden pegs on a raised platform to keep the feet warm. The triple-decker pulpit bearing the rector's hour glass is topped by a sounding board that served as an amplifier. A spectacular 1665 English organ has wood pipes in the shape of a three-dimensional hallway. The church's construction at a time when the Indians were still hostile explains the recessed doorway; "they would trip or hit their heads if they ran too fast, giving time for the men in the back of the church to get their guns," the guide said. Today the Anglican church is used once a year for a non-denominational service. Outside the Old Brick, as this precious church is called, the setting is shady and tranquil, like that of an English churchyard. There are benches, a sundial, and graves of the locally ubiquitous Jordan family.

(757) 357-3367. Open daily except Monday, 9:30 to 5. Donation.

All is tranquil in inlet scene typical of Virginia's Northern Neck.

The Northern Neck, Va.

Tidewater's Bypassed Treasure

A National Park Service film calls this "The Athens of the New World." Historians consider it "the Cradle of the Nation." George Washington described it as "the Garden of Virginia."

High praise for an area that many people outside Virginia have never heard of. Known as the Northern Neck, Tidewater's treasure is a peninsula wedged between the Potomac and Rappahannock rivers on the western shore of the Chesapeake Bay.

Locals would scoff at the "Athens" title, knowing how relatively impoverished and how off the beaten path the area is today. They know that the 20th century favored Williamsburg and Norfolk to the south and Richmond and Fredericksburg to the west. The Neck was left to languish in nostalgia, its watermen fishing for a livelihood and its planters harvesting their crops. No town of size or reputation developed, with the possible exceptions of Reedville – which the unique menhaden fishing industry once made the richest per capita in the country – or Irvington, to which the posh Tides Inn lures golfers, yachtsmen and retirees.

"We're really undiscovered, and the people who have discovered us don't tell anybody," says Francene Barber, former head of the Northern Neck Travel Council. The folks are so friendly that motorists quickly pick up what part-time resident Roger Mudd described in an article as the Northern Neck wave – two fingers lifted off the steering wheel. No one locks houses or cars except in July, according to local lore, and then simply to avoid receiving unwanted zucchinis.

Only lately have newcomers – mostly retirees from Richmond, Norfolk and northern Virginia – created something of a tension between new and old. The "come heres" savor the slower lifestyle but lament the lack of amenities. The "from heres" welcome the economic shot in the arm but worry, probably unnecessarily, that the Neck will become one elongated suburb of Washington and Virginia Beach.

The area's first tourist actually was Capt. John Smith, whom Pocohontas saved from the Indians in 1607. "Heaven and earth never agreed better to frame a place for man's habitation," said he. Three of the nation's first five presidents agreed, and one of the four counties that make up the Neck produced more American statesmen than any other.

Now, some people come here to see ancient churches, George Washington's birthplace and the Stratford Hall childhood home of Robert E. Lee. Others are drawn by the mysterious, often hidden presence of water. The bay, rivers and wide creeks offer miles of uncharted shoreline, and almost every road ends at the water.

Here, more than in most places, travelers must detour from the main highway to discover the joys of picturesque inlets and historic sites at the end of nowhere. "History abounds and water surrounds," the local Travel Council proclaims. But the visitor must seek them out.

Most sightseeing attractions are at the more primitive top end of the neck, while most inns and restaurants are at the more affluent southern end. State Route 3 is the main highway running up the center of the neck. Creeks and rivers rambling hither and yon often make road access roundabout and time-consuming.

Inn Spots

The Tides Inn, King Carter Drive, Box 480, Irvington 22480.

For more than 50 years this family-run waterside resort has been attracting the Cadillac set, who return year after year to enjoy what the Stephens family owners call "the company of the finest people in the world, your genteel fellow guests." Now run by general manager Michael Thomas with grandsons Lee and Randy Stephens (their uncle oversees the equally resorty but less plush Tides Lodge across Carters Creek), this is a bastion of elegance and service. The entire staff exudes uncommon friendliness and, distancing itself from its rather reclusive past, the inn increasingly is taking an active role in the surrounding community.

The wonderfully land-scaped setting on a narrow peninsula jutting into Carters Creek as it empties into the two-mile-wide Rappahannock is unsurpassed. Many of the 134 elegant, hotel-style rooms in connecting tiered, three-story lodges take full advantage, especially those with balconies in the Garden House extension and its latest addition, 24 larger rooms with balconies that opened in 1997. Positively idyllic are the twenty rooms and semi-suites in the Lancaster and Windsor houses. Here the floral comforters match the draperies and valances, the TVs are hidden in armoires or behind shutters in the walls, the bath/dressing rooms are extra-large and outfitted with Smith & Vandiver toiletries, and the beds are kingsize or two doubles and "triple-sheeted for comfort." The private balconies are of the "wow" variety. Any business transacted in the Lancaster's picture-windowed meeting room surely plays second fiddle to the view. Standard and even superior rooms in the main lodge are smaller and somewhat dated; we'd save our shekels for a splurge in the Lancaster or Windsor houses.

Oriental rugs grace the floors and crystal chandeliers the ceilings of the public rooms. Along a hallway is a tony shop, its display windows beckoning to passersby. But nothing competes with the view of the water through floor-to-ceiling windows as the bellman opens the doors at the porte cochère.

Luxuries include a heated saltwater pool beside a sandy river beach at the tip of the peninsula, a beachside boardwalk, the inn's cruising yachts, four tennis courts, a fitness and health facility, a regulation croquet course and the beautiful grounds, dotted with seats here and there. The crowning touch is 45 holes of golf, including the inn's nearby Golden Eagle Golf Course, ranked among the top three in Virginia.

Rates include two meals daily. Lunch is served aboard the resort's signature 127-foot yacht Miss Ann, at Commodore's, a colorful, beachy waterside restaurant where you feel as if you're on a boat, or at Cap'n B's restaurant at the Golden Eagle golf course. Jackets are required for dinner in the resort's two adjoining dining rooms, all windows onto the water (prix-fixe dinners are available here to the public). Our meal began with the acclaimed hot oyster cocktail and a shrimp and scallop tostada. Next came a succession of relishes and breads, plus caesar or grapefruit and avocado salads. Main courses of crab imperial and soft-shell crabs were accompanied by vegetables served family style. Peaches poached in champagne and a creme de cacao parfait ended a fine meal.

The next morning produced the kind of breakfast that makes lunch redundant. The golfers' buffet looked like the usual, so we ordered a couple of treats: a ham and cheese omelet with Northern Neck fish roe cakes and an abundant mixed grill. Biscuits came first and spoonbread came with.

The resort has more than two staff members for each room and claims an employee turnover rate of less than ten percent annually. Patriarch Bob Lee Stephens writes a newsletter to "old friends" three times a year. He and his sons and their wives host a weekly cocktail party for guests. Contrary to some of its peers, only twenty percent of its trade is conferences, and the Tides has increased children's activities to boost its family trade. "Only 25 percent of our guests play golf," says Michael Thomas. "But 90 percent go out on Miss Ann. That yacht is our real treasure."

(804) 438-5000 or (800) 843-3746. Fax (804) 438-5222. One hundred eleven rooms and suites with private baths. Rates MAP: doubles, $260 to $350. Semi-suites, $306 to $326. Suites, $476 to $688. Closed January to mid-March.

Prix-fixe, $40. Lunch daily, 11 to 3:30. Dinner nightly, 6:30 to 9.

Cedar Grove, Fleeton Road, Route 1, Box 2535, Reedville 22539.

One of the more appealing rooms we have stayed in was at this light and airy, Colonial Revival B&B overlooking the Chesapeake Bay from the affluent peninsular hamlet of Fleeton. It's the Lighthouse Suite, with a nifty bay-window seat outfitted in chintz, from which you can view the Great Wicomico River as it enters the bay. That is if you're not already ensconced on the spacious rear porch, up a

Grounds of Cedar Grove B&B back up to Chesapeake Bay.

couple of stairs from the room and screened to the floor on three sides. With its white wicker furniture it's a perfect spot in which to enjoy the breeze as you look through the thoughtfully provided binoculars at the nearby lighthouse, the wildlife and the broad sweep of the bay south toward Norfolk. Ceiling fans whirring on the porch and over the queensize bed kept the room cool enough that we could sleep without using the air-conditioning on a hot summer night.

Two smaller front rooms that sometimes had gone begging were converted in 1998 into a handsome new suite with a queen bed and a sitting room furnished in antiques. They open onto a new rooftop deck that offers another good view of the water. Cable TV and telephone modems were installed in each suite as part of the upgrade.

Sue and Bob Tipton, early retirees from IBM in Poughkeepsie, N.Y., have furnished their 1913 house in a light, uncluttered style. Victorian Eastlake pieces dignify the comfortable living room. Guests also enjoy a sun room with a TV.

Breakfast to the strains of classical music (we enjoyed "Spring" from Vivaldi's Four Seasons) is served beneath a crystal chandelier in the formal dining room, handsome in pale green and rose. Sue, who took courses at the Culinary Institute of America in Hyde Park, offers a choice of juices served in her grandmother's dainty glass mugs, fresh fruit like the bursting-with-flavor local cantaloupe topped with yogurt sauce and blackberries, and an entrée like an Italian vegetable omelet with rashers of bacon. Remarkably good blueberry muffins made with oatmeal and lemon zest might accompany. Poached pears with melba sauce, peach french toast, vegetable frittata, banana buttermilk griddle cakes and crab omelets are other possibilities.

The Tiptons offer beverages in the evening and cream sherry at bedside.

Besides the water views from their suites, guests also enjoy a deep back yard with a garden and, through a field, a little beach on the bay.

(804) 453-3915 or (800) 497-8215. Fax (804) 453-3915. Two suites with private baths. May-October: $125. Rest of year: $100. Two-night minimum special weekends. No children. No smoking.

The Bailey-Cockrell House, Main Street, Reedville 22539.

Up-and-coming Reedville gained yet another stylish B&B in 1995, this one housed in a former physician's home dating to 1884. Charlotte and Alf Braxton, who own the Country House antiques and gift shop in nearby Burgess, have, after an extensive restoration, outfitted their home with handsome antique furnishings and accessories. Yellow with white trim, the house backs up to Cockrell's Creek, with a sloping lawn leading to a dock, where a paddle boat awaits guests. A wicker-filled front veranda faces Main Street. Guests also have use of an elegant parlor and a study equipped with TV.

All four accommodations come with antique double beds, private baths and cable TV/VCRs. The rear Federal and Americana suites, furnished according to their names, have sitting areas with views of the water. The Americana, with a rope bed, also has a day bed in its wicker and oak sitting room. The Victorian Room on the street side is furnished in the early 1900s style.

The Braxtons serve a full breakfast by the fireplace in an elegant dining room crowned with an oversize crystal chandelier. Fresh fruit, juice and muffins precede the main course, which might be Alf's egg and ham casserole or his stuffed french toast.

(804) 453-5900. Two rooms and two suites with private baths. Doubles, $85. Suites, $95.

The Morris House, Main Street, Box 163, Reedville 22539.

Young North Carolinians Erin and Heath Dill took over the Elizabeth House B&B in 1996. They redid the place from top to bottom and renamed it for Albert Morris, a Reedville founder and menhaden fishing magnate, who had built the house in the Queen Anne style in 1895.

The fine architectural detail appealed to the Dills, who saw it as a place to house antique furniture and collections passed down from their families. Writeups in each bedroom detail the contents. Note all the original carved oak in the entry hall, ornamented with carved ribbons, bells, bows on the banister posts and shells on the doors.

Common space includes a fireplaced living room and a second-floor study/TV room opening onto a rear porch overlooking wide Cockrell's Creek, to which the large rear lawn backs up (it's deep enough for swimming and boating). Equestrian antiques are displayed around the antique walnut double bed in the main-floor Hunt Room, which has a large sit-down shower. The second floor holds a queen room with clawfoot tub and separate shower, outfitted with native American memorabilia, and a Balcony Suite with queen canopy bed, a double jacuzzi in the sitting room, collections of miniature furniture and a private balcony the front overlooking the mouth of the Great Wicomico River and the Chesapeake Bay. The pièce de résistance is the Turret Suite, encompassing the entire third floor. It has a kingsize poster bed, day bed, gas fireplace, and large bath with jacuzzi. The sink is in a reproduction writing desk, and the sitting room contains a TV/VCR, a wet bar and a doll collection from around the world. A raised window seat in the turret overlooks the scene, inside and out.

Lest the antiques and collections mislead, the Dills are quick to point out theirs is not a museum. Decor has been done simply yet with flair, and the furnishings are user-friendly, down to the urethaned bedside tables "so you needn't worry about setting down your drinking glasses."

A great blue heron parades every morning past the rear waterside cottage, a huge space with an enclosed porch and enough beds and sofabeds to sleep eight. Designed for families and fishing groups, it displays some rare sports equipment from Heath's playing days.

Talented Heath, who was looking next to restore the carriage house, is the breakfast cook. He does cheese blintzes with strawberry puree and crab quiches, but is best known for blueberry pancakes from his grandmother's recipe.

(804) 453-7016. Two rooms, two suites and one cottage with private baths. Doubles, $85 to $98 weekends, $75 to $88 midweek. Suites, $130 to $150 weekends, $115 to $135 midweek. Cottage, $150 weekends, $135 midweek. Children and pets accepted in cottage. Smoking restricted.

The Gables Bed & Breakfast Inn, Main Street, Box 148, Reedville 22539.
"There's something about this house that begs to be shared with the public," says Barbara Clark. So share she does, with an avowed "sense of noblesse oblige." Overnight guests in two bedrooms face enough ultra-Victorian common areas and exotica to qualify the place as a museum. "If we had a sign out front," says Barbara, who does not advertise and has no inn brochure, "I'd be answering the doorbell all day to give tours."

Built in 1909 by a sea captain who was one of Reedville's menhaden industry titans, the Queen Anne Victorian has eight sides and eight gables, configured on the points of a compass rose. The mast of the captain's schooner, built into the center of the top floors, supports the roof and the ship-like appointments within. The house is an architectural treasure, from its exterior walls of custom-made pressed bricks speckled with steel to the slabs of marble on the floors and the glazed brick in the kitchen, baths and entry way. Barbara and her husband Norman, a dentist with the Public Health Service, bought the Gables as a potential retirement home in 1982. While he practices in Maryland during the week, she holds down the fort here, "singlehandedly stripping all the paint from the woodwork" and collecting curiosities ever since.

For Barbara, who's addicted to her house and its history, the B&B is almost an after-thought. She's like a museum docent as she guides visitors through the guest rooms, one with a bedroom set from Wales and the other with a kingsize four-poster bed and well-worn oriental rugs. She's more interested in showing the master bath across the hall from the first bedroom. It's huge, with chandeliers, glazed brick walls, marble floors, a clawfoot tub and a corner shower. Guests in the other bedroom use a private bath tucked into a gable on the third floor. And that third floor is like none we ever saw – a huge open sitting room punctuated with gables in the corners. The ship's mast extends through its center (and up to the fourth-floor crow's nest). A munitions cabinet at the head of the stairs displays assorted memorabilia. Two leather sofas form a seating area beneath a window, and a third leather sofa faces a TV set in one gable.

Although the third floor is most unusual, rooms on the main floor are no slouches. A dark double parlor is outfitted with Victorian museum-piece furnishings and gilt-edged mirrors. A lace-clothed table in the dining room rests beneath an ornate, pink-glassed chandelier from Vienna, and Barbara may rummage through sideboard drawers filled not with dinnerware but papers to shed more light on the subject at hand. At either end of the second floor are sun rooms, one in the rear for the morning with a spectacular view onto Cockrell's Creek and the Chesapeake Bay

The Morris House occupies home built in 1895 for a founder of Reedville.

and the other in front for the afternoon sun and the sunset. A screened veranda wraps around three sides of the main floor.

Barbara's breakfast specialty is apple fritters, light and fluffy and served with sausage or bacon. Fresh fruit or grapefruit meringue precede. Soufflés and rum french toast are other possibilities.

(804) 453-5209. Two rooms with private baths. Doubles, $85 to $95.

The Inn at Levelfields, Route 3, Box 216, Lancaster 22503.

Warren and Doris Sadler – he from Chicago and she from Memphis – were the first of the Northern Neck's latter-day innkeepers. They acquired their antebellum manor house set well back from Route 3 in 1984 and turned it into an inn with a small, part-time restaurant.

The main floor has two formal dining rooms (where the inn the inn no longer serves dinner but caters private parties), a kitchen through which overnight guests often enter the inn, and a homey common room doubling as an office that guests share with the innkeepers and their two large and loving brown labrador retrievers. Out back is a fenced-in swimming pool. The rest of the 54 acres left from the original 1,200-acre Dunaway plantation involves crops and forests.

Upstairs off a wide central hallway are four lofty corner bedrooms, each with fireplace and private bath and done in bright Colonial colors. One is in olive green with a bathroom all in pink. Another is yellow and a third is painted barn red. Our room, in blue and white with a high-rise four-poster king bed, was charmingly quirky. It was big enough to rattle around in, but had only one easy chair (one of us had to bring over a desk-type chair from a far corner as we read before dinner). After dinner, we crouched through the bottom of a half door in the bathroom to get to our private balcony, with a view out the long driveway. It's the spot to listen to the loudest tree frogs around as you watch the stars sparkling in a pitch-black sky. The next morning one of us showered beneath an eight-foot-high spigot, which was like standing outside in a drizzle. The other enjoyed the extra-long bathtub.

Doris cooks and Warren serves breakfast in the front dining room. Fresh orange juice, succulent local cantaloupes, coffee cake and eggs any style with crisp bacon, sliced local tomatoes and English muffins were the fare at our visit.

(804) 435-6887 or (800) 238-5578. Four rooms with private baths. Doubles, $95.

The Hope and Glory Inn, Box 425, Irvington 22480.

An advertising agency principal from Minnesota, Bill Westbrook, has poured big bucks into the restoration of an 1890s schoolhouse that had been the rather ramshackle King Carter Inn. It's handsomely dressed in pale yellow with white and black trim and embellished by landscaping and gardens. His creative flair shows, in the offbeat decor that rated a writeup in Southern Living magazine, collections of folk art and a suave brochure that cites the upstairs bedrooms as "rather hopelessly romantic."

They certainly are unexpected. On the second and third floors, they consist of queen or double beds, minimalist decor and not much else. They do not have rugs on the floors, curtains on the windows or comfortable chairs to sit on. The floors are painted, cloths are swept back to screen the windows, hats serve as lamp shades and old sinks are skirted in fabric. The walls might be painted gray and the floor black, and one room is all white. The suite has a queen bed and a queen sofabed in the sitting area. Room 7 places a double bed sideways against a window alcove, with only one way in and out. The only other furniture is a round table with two wood chairs. Room 6 has a clawfoot tub (no shower) in the bedroom. The upstairs sitting room consists of three overstuffed chairs, woven rugs on the floor, and a chess set of oversize salt and pepper shakers.

More comfortable, perhaps, are four rear cottages grouped plantation-style around a landscaped brick courtyard with fountains, birdhouses, an herb garden and an outdoor shower with clawfoot tub. The cottages continue the simple, summery look. Most have private outdoor sitting areas as well as small indoor sitting rooms furnished with a couple of chairs. One cottage has a queen bed and the others have doubles or twins.

The main floor of what advertising jargon calls "a fine small hotel" is a sight to behold. The open, columned lobby sweeps past a central staircase through a library and game room into a country dining room with a table for fourteen. At our visit, we thought the lobby furniture had been shoved aside for a large catered luncheon, but no. That's the way it always is, we were advised. "Intimate conversational settings," they call it.

Fabulous folk art from a local artist adds eye appeal. Managers who live off-site prepare a full breakfast, perhaps stuffed french toast with cream cheese, orange marmalade and caramelized pecans, or pavlova egg meringue filled with pineapple sorbet or fresh fruit.

(804) 438-6053 or (800) 497-8228. Fax (804) 438-5362. Six rooms, one suite and four cottages with private baths. Doubles, $95 to $120. Suite, $135. Cottages, $135 to $175. Children accepted in cottages. No smoking.

Linden House, Route 17, Box 23, Champlain 22438. Champlain.

Horses and cows graze in the pastures beside this restored planters' home, set well back from the highway on 200-plus acres northwest of Tappahannock. "You want to see a bull so spoiled he eats apples right out of my hand?" asks innkeeper Sandra Pounsberry. She proceeds to feed the critter apples that she picks from a

Restored 1890s schoolhouse is now home of The Hope and Glory Inn.

tree just beyond his reach, while his companions settle for fallen apples on the ground.

Sandra and Ken Pounsberry from Maryland's Prince Georges County bought the 1750 house, which had not been lived in for 25 years, and set about restoring it into a comfortable B&B.

They offer two bedrooms and a suite in the main house, plus two larger rooms and a suite in the coach house they built next door. All have queensize beds, TVs, refrigerators and robes. They are nicely appointed with country furnishings and antiques, and Bibles are on display in each. Fireplaces and sitting areas, one with an oversize chair and a half with matching ottoman, are features of the spacious second-floor Robert E. Lee and Jefferson Davis rooms, one with a double jacuzzi and steam shower. A very narrow staircase tiptoes to the third floor, site of the Linden Suite with a cannonball queen bed and a daybed in the alcove.

Rooms in the adjacent coach house come with queensize beds and private baths. The ground floor is devoted to the Carriage Suite, with wicker seating in front of a working fireplace and an enormous bathroom with corner shower and space earmarked for a jacuzzi. It opens onto a covered front porch with brick floor and an antique sleigh for a seat. Two rooms upstairs share a little rear balcony.

Back in the main house are a variety of handsome common areas. The "receiving room" almost looks like a museum piece with antique furnishings and a spinning wheel in the corner. More livable is the rear family room, where guests can watch TV in front of shelves holding the hosts' collections of depression glass and beer steins. A side smoking porch overlooks the herb garden, while the wicker-filled back porch enjoys a view of the yard, woods and gazebo. Still another arched nook under the front porch entry holds blue wrought-iron chairs for an intimate tête-à-tête. Inside, the white textured walls are striking with restful pale blue doors and trim on the main floor, celery green trim on the second floor, pink trim on the third and yellow trim on the ground floor. The latter floor holds a large dining room with tables for sixteen and a country kitchen.

Here is where Sandra, a caterer, serves a hearty breakfast. The plantation special consists of half a belgian waffle and an omelet incorporating green peppers, onions, cheese, tomatoes and ham, plus bacon and sausage. A plate of fried green tomatoes or fried corn might accompany. A fresh fruit plate and juice precede.

Sandra's cooking talents also are displayed at dinner, served by reservation to ten or more for $16.95 to $22.95. The night before our visit she served caesar salad, New York strip steak, baked potatoes, green beans amandine and peach cobbler with ice cream. Maryland crab cakes and breast of chicken are other main-course possibilities.

(804) 443-1170 or (800) 622-1202. Fax (804) 443-0107. Four rooms and two suites with private baths. Doubles, $85. Suites, $135.

Dining Spots

Elijah's Restaurant, Main Street, Reedville.

This welcome addition to the Northern Neck dining scene was opened in 1996 by Taylor Slaughter, great-grandson of Elijah Reed, founder of Reedville, whose portrait hangs over the bar. He restored the town's original mercantile store into a three-room restaurant seating more than 100, with a back room overlooking the water, a small front cafe and a front deck for steamed hard crabs. The original wainscoted walls convey a rustic lodge look; beige tablecloths with colorful napkins add charm. The lineup of rocking chairs on the restaurant's long side porch remind Taylor of Virginia Beach, where he started in the restaurant business at age 14.

Taylor is the working chef, and his fare is fresh, abundant and first-rate. Seafood is the specialty. Expect appetizers like bacon-wrapped scallops and chicken tenders with honey mustard. Main courses could be fisherman's penne, shrimp with artichokes over pasta, baked salmon fillet with roasted hazelnut-butter sauce, fried oysters with hush puppies and grilled ribeye steak with onion rings. A lengthy casual menu offers everything from spicy chicken fajitas to breaded catfish.

(804) 453-3621. Entrées, $11.25 to $14.95. Lunch, Wednesday-Sunday noon to 3, weekends only in off-season. Dinner, 5 to 9. Closed January and February.

dé Medici, 51 School St., Kilmarnock.

Chef David Coontz, a Culinary Institute of America-owned chef, tired of the pace of cooking in hotels after ten years and opened this stylish restaurant in a storefront in 1997. His specialty is Italian cuisine, which was underrepresented in the area, and "I love the Northern Neck," so the match was a good fit.

He and his fiancée, Jennifer Pittman, fashioned an urbane little establishment with a big-city look. A banquette lines one wall, tiny white lights provide dim illumination, and showplates provide accents on the white-clothed tables. A bar along one side is slick in pink and black granite.

Bread sticks arrive with a bowl of garlicky olive oil for dipping as you study the extensive menu. The extensive menu ranges widely from chicken piccata to vitello della casa, sautéed with shrimp, scallops, lump crab and mushrooms in parmesan cream sauce. Tuna puttanesca, salmon dijonnaise, flounder italiano, seafood posillipo, tournedos gorgonzola and osso buco are among the possibilities. Start with bruschetta, carpaccio or the house antipasto. Finish with ricotta cheesecake, spumoni meringue or tirami su.

David makes his own breads and pastas. Early diners gave the food high marks.

(804) 435-4006. Entrées, $7.99 to $17.99. Dinner nightly, from 5. Sunday brunch, 11 to 2. Closed Tuesday in off-season.

The Crab Shack at Rappahannock Seafood, Route 672, Kilmarnock.
Here's the kind of place we'd hoped to find all across the Neck: A sprightly solarium with an array of tables covered with red and white checked cloths, fresh seafood from the adjacent market, picnic tables outside by the water, and a grand view of Indian Creek and the Chesapeake Bay. Although when we first met this place it was called the Rappahannock Cafe and was open only for lunch, at our latest visit it also was serving dinner nightly as The Crab Shack.

At our first lunch, the ice water came in paper cups with a slice of lemon – now that's class – as we sampled very spicy peel-and-eat shrimp said to be mildly seasoned and coconut shrimp with apricot-onion marmalade sauce, with a side salad.

We liked our lunch so much that we returned to the seafood market the next day to acquire crab cakes and fresh crabmeat to take home, and to add our suggestion that they ought to serve dinner.

The suggestion quickly became reality. The cafe in a section of the seafood market and its former gift shop was transformed into the high-style Crab Shack. Some shack, this, with dark green walls trimmed in white, a thatched "hood" over the bar, brightly patterned fish cloths and fresh flowers in Perrier bottles on the tables, and potted palms and hanging plants all around. Before sunset, ducks waddled up to the windows, as if looking for handouts, as we shared a dinner appetizer of fabulous crabmeat nachos. The house raspberry vinaigrette dressed good salads that come with each entrée. Choices ranged from baked clams marinara over pasta to veal chop with wild mushroom ragout. We were pleased with the plate of crab cakes and the seafood sampler that teamed a crab cake and soft-shell crab with flounder, trout, shrimp and a side of rice. The key lime pie and tropical fruit tart were excellent, and two peppermints came with the bill.

(804) 435-2700. Entrées, $9.75 to $18.95. Lunch daily, 11 to 3. Dinner, Friday-Sunday, 5 to 9. Closed in January and February.

Chesapeake Cafe, Route 3 north, Kilmarnock.
This new restaurant could be anywhere, but hits the spot along the commercial strip north of Kilmarnock for fresh seafood prepared with flair. It's a large space with well-spaced booths and tables covered with beige vinyl cloths, dim lighting from wall sconces and cut-glass oil lamps, and a prominent lounge.

Our lunch was a mixed success: a fine grilled chicken caesar salad and a so-so seafood gumbo with a cobb salad lacking most of the traditional cobb salad ingredients. Dinner may be a better bet. The ultimate for crab lovers is a dish called "crab on crab:" two soft-shell crabs topped with sautéed crabmeat. Otherwise, expect things like grilled yellowfin tuna, prime rib and ribeye steak, touted as owner Carroll Webb's favorite.

(804) 435-3250. Entrées, $9.95 to $18.95. Lunch and dinner, Monday-Saturday.

Lancaster Tavern, Route 3, Lancaster.
The aromas of good home cooking nearly overpowered as we entered the kitchen of this restaurant of the old school. Lindy Grigsby has taken over for her mother, Ann Parsons, who retired after many years or running this Southern-style dining room in her house which dates to 1790. There's no menu and no liquor. Folks dine communally at one of four oilcloth-covered tables and take pot luck.

When we stopped by, Lindy was preparing chicken and dumplings and pot roast for the evening's dinner. Among her other offerings that night was Colonial gazpacho, so called "because we're serving it in Lancaster County." The night's salads were lemon cream congealed salad and apple sauce. Veggies were green beans, whipped squash and broccoli casserole. A yellow cake with coconut cream frosting concluded.

Lindy says she can seat 30 people at once "if they're on good speaking terms." Meals are served family-style, all you can eat for $6 at lunch, $9 at dinner.

Lunch that day was stuffed shells with three kinds of cheese, accompanied by beans, squash, coleslaw, cucumbers and gazpacho. The place is highly rated for home cooking and local color.

(804) 462-5941. Prix-fixe, $9. Lunch, Thursday-Sunday 11 to 2. Dinner, Thursday-Saturday 5 to 8, also Sunday in season.

White Stone Wine & Cheese Co., Route 3, White Stone.

This is a good place to pick up a sandwich for a picnic or to eat at one of the tables here. Specialties include a chicken fajita pizza served on pita bread with green salad and salsa, a veggie burger, a pâté platter and chicken française at prices from yesteryear. Salad favorites are chicken tarragon and apple-walnut tuna. One of the sandwiches might be brie and prosciutto. You also can get applewood-smoked Virginia trout, chili, Maryland crab soup, and key lime or snickers pie. Sticky buns on Saturday are special.

Of course, there's a good selection of cheese, and the wine selection is the best on the Neck.

(804) 435-2000. Entrées, $3.75 to $5. Open Monday-Saturday, 10 to 5.

Cafe Lotte, Route 360, Lottsburg.

Don't you love the name? The Northern Neck's only real coffee emporium plays on the town's name and dispenses a dynamite latte, along with other coffees and teas and a handful of brunch items (sausage and egg biscuit, soups, homemade barbecue or chicken salad on bialy) and homemade desserts like peanut-butter bonbons and bread pudding with orange sauce.

There's more. This occupies only a portion of the **Little People's Guild** store, a ramble of shops offering all kinds of wares, from Christmas dolls and carved driftwood birds fashioned by owners Joyce and Marty Stewart. They started in two rooms and the enterprise mushroomed. They show works of local craftsmen, have a neat bird room with all things bird-oriented, and oversee the new Northern Neck Farmer's and Watermen's Market in a shed out back. They were even thinking of adding a three-room B&B upstairs.

(804) 529-5938. Open Monday-Friday 10 to 6, Saturday 9 to 5.

Peppermint's, Main Street, Reedville.

This cute, bright pink sandwich and ice cream shop is the place where everyone goes in Reedville to share the day's news. Owner Patsy Self obliges with a short list of simple sandwiches ($1.50 to $2.25), ice cream dishes and the like. Crab soup and crab melt were specials the day we were there. The place was so jammed we couldn't find a table, however. On nice days, the crowd spills onto an outdoor deck at the side.

(804) 453-6468. Open Monday-Saturday 10:30 to 8, Sunday 2 to 8. Extended hours in summer.

Diversions

History and water are the main attractions here and they pop up in unexpected places. Head down almost any side road and you'll likely see an historic marker, an old church, cornfields, a hodgepodge of houses with perhaps a manor in between and, eventually, water – in the form of creek, river, bay, inlet or what have you. The water here often seems elusive, but it's all around.

Stratford Hall Plantation, Route 214, Stratford.

The birthplace of Robert E. Lee in 1807 was built about 1738 by Thomas Lee, a distant relative. Thomas, president of the Council of Virginia, was father of the only two brothers to sign the Declaration of Independence, Richard Henry and Francis Lightfoot. The H-shaped brick manor house, situated high above the Potomac, is one of the largest private dwellings of the Colonial period open to visitors. Costumed guides show the house, usually starting in various bedrooms, a school room and a winter kitchen on the ground floor. The grander rooms are upstairs, including the 29-foot-square Great Hall, supposedly one of the most beautiful rooms in America. Everyone enjoys seeing Robert E. Lee's cradle in his mother's room. After touring the house, visitors wander around the various gardens and dependencies, including the kitchen, where ginger cookies and cider are served. Usually one can drive to the bluffs for a good view of the Potomac, seven miles wide here, but at our visit the road was closed after a storm had turned it to mud. Also on the property is a restaurant in a log cabin, with a large screened porch overlooking a forested ravine where we felt as if we were eating in the treetops. Our Plantation luncheon ($7.95) included Virginia ham or southern fried chicken, candied sweet potatoes, coleslaw, hot biscuits and preserves and beverage (and everyone seems to drink iced tea). Of course, you can get the ubiquitous ham biscuits and crab cakes. Lunch is served from early March through October, daily 11:30 to 3.

(804) 493-8038. Plantation open daily, 9 to 4:30. Adults, $7.

George Washington Birthplace National Monument, Route 204, Oak Grove.

A 51-foot-tall granite obelisk rises unexpectedly at the end of a country byway. The miniature Washington monument is appropriate but somehow startlingly out of character at the restoration of George Washington's birthplace and memorial house, the re-creation of the site as it was in the early 1700s. It was on this point overlooking Popes Creek and the Potomac River that the president spent the first three years of his life, and he returned here frequently as a teenager. Destroyed by fire in 1779 while Washington was leading the Continental Army, the house was rebuilt in 1930 as a memorial. It's a lovely, livable house, made even more appealing by its tranquil surroundings. Costumed docents spin wool in the hallway, make candles outside and cook waffles in the kitchen house. The 200 or 300 visitors a day to what one docent called "the government's best-kept secret" enter through a modern visitor center, see a fourteen-minute film and walk to the restoration site for a tour. Then they're on their own for a look at the farmlands, the family burial ground and a picnic area. There's even a beach, where one can frequently find shark's teeth washed up from the river bottom.

(804) 224-1732. Open daily, 9 to 5. Adults, $1.

Mary Ball Washington Museum and Library, Route 3, Lancaster.

This historic complex including an old jail and an old clerk's office in the center of tiny Lancaster honors "the mother of the father of our country." The museum is of less general interest than, say, the George Washington Birthplace or Stratford Hall. But genealogists come from across the world to trace the lineage of early Virginians from documents dating to 1651.

(804) 462-7280. Open Wednesday-Friday 10 to 5, Saturday 10 to 3. Donation.

Reedville Fishermen's Museum, Main Street, Reedville.

The trash fish, menhaden, was money in the bank to Reedville, which at the turn of the century was purported to be the richest town per capita in the country. Oils of the menhaden are used today for paints, cosmetics and soaps, and Reedville is the home of Ampro Fisheries and of Zapata Haynie Corp., the largest fish oil producer in the United States. The quaint Victorian hamlet – a long one-street National Historic District without so much as a general store – is considered the charter fishing capital of the country. The little William Walker House was opened in 1990 as a museum to detail the menhaden industry. Out back along the banks of Cockrells Creek, a new museum structure has enlarged the exhibition space. The original museum was converted into a typical waterman's home of the late 19th century.

(804) 453-6529. Open daily 10:30 to 4:30, May-October, weekends 11 to 4 rest of year. Closed January to mid-February. Donation.

Westmoreland State Park, Route 347, Montross. Situated on cliffs overlooking the Potomac between the birthplaces of Washington and Lee is one of the more attractive state parks we've seen and one of the few with a visitor center. Miles of wooded trails draw hikers. A sand beach is popular with sunbathers (the swimming is better in the adjacent pool, we're advised). Paddleboats are available for exploring the Potomac. There are campgrounds and cabins for overnighters.

Ingleside Plantation Vineyards, Oak Grove.

The plantation house here designates one of Virginia's larger and more enterprising wineries as a registered National Historic Place. It's owned by the Carl Flemer family, whose 2,500-acre plantation embraces three manor homes, the East Coast's biggest wholesale nursery and 45 acres of vineyards planted with fifteen varietals. The modern winery produces 15,000 cases annually under the direction of Belgian winemaker Jacques Recht, who paused here with his wife on a round-the-world sailing expedition and stayed. Jacques is in considerable demand as a consultant, but oversees production of some fine chardonnays, cabernet sauvignons and a limited-edition pinot noir. His sparkling wine was voted one of the top ten in the country. A large tasting room offers samples of up to a dozen offerings, priced from about $6 to $17. There are tours, a gift shop, historic artifacts and a video presentation.

(804) 224-8687. Open daily 10 to 5, Sunday noon to 5.

Driving Tours. Pick up a detailed Northern Neck map to find your way along back roads to favorite spots. They include **Fleeton,** a summer colony built by prosperous Reedville fishermen to escape the smell of menhaden; **Kinsale,** described to us as a New England-type harbor town, but that's stretching it; **Sharps,** a one-street Victorian village centered by a big Presbyterian church; **Weems,** a beachy-looking summer colony on the way up, and **Irvington,** where some of the yachts are as expensive as the homes along Carter's Creek. Two free state-run **ferries** make a couple of the trips shorter on either side of the Neck. The Sunnybank ferry has a more picturesque crossing than the Merry Point. Each takes two vehicles at a time and, supposedly, you honk your horn if the ferry is waiting on the opposite shore.

Near Irvington, historic **Christ Church,** the only virtually unchanged Colonial church in America, was built in 1734 by Robert "King" Carter, the agent for the English proprietor of the Northern Neck, whose descendants included eight governors of Virginia, two presidents and something like 250 Carter listings in the local telephone directory. Cruciform in design, it has a rare three-decker pulpit that is still used for services in summer. While Christ Church is exquisite in its perfection, **St. Mary's White Chapel** near Lively is charming in its simplicity. Dating to 1669, it contains the oldest altar boards in Virginia – three tablets reciting the Lord's Prayer, the Ten Commandments and the Apostles Creed. Churchwomen did the spectacular needlework for the curved kneeling pads at the altar.

Nature Preserves. Birding is big in a couple of new wildlife preserves. Hughlette's Point Nature Preserve, Route 605 north of Kilmarnock, a Virginia Wildlife Preserve, has a mile-long trail winding through the pristine wood to a sandy beach along the Chesapeake Bay. A Nature Conservancy tract called **Voorhees Nature Preserve,** Route 637 at Westmoreland Berry Farm, Oak Grove, offers several miles of woodland trails with observation points overlooking the Rappahannock River and marshes.

Shopping. You're not going to go crazy shopping in this area, but there are little antiques stores dotted here and there, and a few local artisans. Irvington is home to a few nifty stores like **The Dandelion** for the local gentry, the **Grapevine** with pained and mosaic designs, and **The Bay Window,** an amazing studio-shop with colorful squiggles on the walls, where owners Mary Ragland and Candy Terry silk-screen their own T-shirts. A lobster trap hangs from the ceiling at **Wood-A-Drift Artifacts Shop,** chock full of decoys, shells, lamps, nautical gifts, books, paintings and more. Artist-owner Graham Bruce stocks unusual items like a crab shell transformed into a Santa for the Christmas tree and walking sticks with white pine duck heads on top.

Bay Gallery and Gifts, Route 360, Heathsville, carries works of local artists. The **Barn Shop at Mary Young's Herbs,** Route 202, Hague, offers perfectly beautiful wreaths, dried flowers, potpourri, herbal gifts and more. The biggest mercantile enterprise around is Joyce and Marty Stewart's **Little People's Guild** in Lottsburg (see Cafe Lotte above), the old general store filled with all local arts and crafts.

Extra-Special

Nadji Nook, 303 Queen St., Tappahannock.

Just across a bridge from the Northern Neck is the antiquey town of Tappahannock, which boasts an appealing riverfront historic district and St. Margaret's School, an Episcopal boarding school for girls. The star among antiques shops is this glittering emporium, where old saws and a railroad lantern hanging from the ceiling are overshadowed by a fourteen-tiered chandelier. A born collector, late owner Jackie Allen Fisher was known to dicker, but not much, as antiquers sought her one-of-a-kind prizes. Her husband Randolph continues the tradition. You might find a rare music box for $8,750 or a restored carousel horse for $9,500. We picked up a couple of odd salt and pepper shakers for a gift for considerably less.

(804) 443-3298. Open Monday-Thursday 10 to 5, Friday and Saturday to 6, Sunday 1 to 6.

County seat at Eastville stores oldest court records in America.

Cape Charles, Va.
The Town that Time Forgot

Founded in 1884 as a planned community by railroad/ferry interests, this johnny-come-lately settlement at the southwestern tip of Virginia's historic Eastern Shore grew rapidly to become its largest and busiest town.

Railroad magnates William H. Scott and Alexander Cassatt laid out Cape Charles in perfect square blocks stretching back from the Chesapeake Bay. The seven

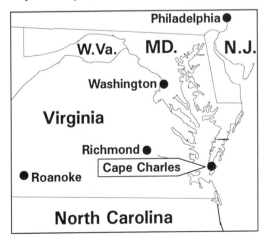

avenues were named for famed Virginians and the six cross streets for fruits and trees. Substantial homes were built to house railroad executives and entrepreneurs attracted by climate, harbor and prosperity. The town thrived for more than half a century because anyone who traveled up and down the Eastern Shore had to pass through it. Up to two million people arrived annually by train or car to catch the steamer or ferry to or from Norfolk.

After World War II, however, the ferry terminal relocated south of town and the trains stopped carrying passengers. The Chesapeake Bay Bridge-Tunnel, which opened in 1964, provided access to the mainland and a new highway bypassed the town.

Time virtually stopped in Cape Charles after the last steamer left in 1953. Fewer than 40 buildings have been erected in the post-war era. Most of its 568 original structures were built between 1885 and 1920, producing one of the largest concentrations of turn-of-the-century buildings on the East Coast. In 1991, the historic district was placed on the National Register.

Today, the bayside town is undergoing a renaissance. New enterprises are reviving a downtown that had been eerily abandoned. Newcomers are restoring aging houses as vacation or permanent homes. B&Bs and restaurants have emerged to promote Cape Charles as a destination area for tourists. "This is a town on the way up" and "you won't recognize the place in five years" are themes heard time and again from the most diverse of sources.

In 1996, ground was broken for the nation's first eco-industrial initiative, the Port of Cape Charles Sustainable Technology Industrial Park along the sleepy harbor. The first two enterprises got started quickly, a museum of local African American history was emerging in the old black high school, and a technical center was planned to attract visitors.

In 1997, a Virginia Beach developer won approval for a luxury retirement community called Bay Creek. It will encircle the town with up to 3,000 residential units and two eighteen-hole golf courses designed by Arnold Palmer and Jack Nicklaus.

Intriguing contrasts abound. Neighboring Eastville has a courthouse where visitors can inspect the oldest court records in America, dating to 1632. The national wildlife refuge has a state-of-the-art visitor center that the ranger on duty believed to be the most advanced in the country. A longtime merchant has furnished a turn-of-the-century general store as a museum. A block away a Library of Congress staffer has created a gift shop that would be at home in Georgetown or Manhattan. A food retailer has turned a truck stop into something of a gourmet restaurant. A Washington chef has opened a true gourmet restaurant in a Victorian mansion.

Excitement is in the air, but don't be surprised to find half-blocks of abandoned stores between the rising stars or ramshackle eyesores amid the residential restorations.

"I tell prospective visitors that if they're looking for fun and cha-cha, don't come here," says Chris Bannon, dean of local innkeepers. "But if they want the beach, birding, friendly people, rural Americana and history, we've got them all."

Inn Spots

Cape Charles House, 645 Tazewell Ave., Cape Charles 23310.

Looking for a lifestyle change, Bruce and Carol Evans stayed at the Sea Gate B&B (see below) with innkeeper Chris Bannon and put in a bid for this Colonial Revival frame house built in 1912 the same week. They started renovating and upgrading the house, turning it into one of the grandest on the Eastern Shore. Bruce became chairman of the town planning commission and the county's industrial development authority. Carol serves on the zoning board and is president-elect of the chamber of commerce. They opened their B&B in 1994, and have been entertaining guests in a house party atmosphere and touting the charms of Cape Charles to one and all ever since.

The pair come with credentials as well as enthusiasm. Bruce retired as a store

Carol and Bruce Evans, in front of Cape Charles House, are among the town's guiding spirits.

manager for Sears. His wife, who trained in fashion design, was teaching microwave cooking for Sears and writing for a national cooking magazine. All these talents are manifest in their B&B.

Their two parlors offer plush seating, oriental rugs and some of Carol's collections: an old silk spool cabinet, paperweights and her grandmother's samplers. The chandeliered dining room, transformed from a library, is snazzy in hunter green and burgundy with a Schumacher print wallpaper border, roman blinds and matching antique glass on the fireplace mantel.

Corinthian columns frame the staircase to the second floor, which harbors five spacious guest rooms with king or queen beds and private baths. Each is identified with someone important in Cape Charles history. We were comfortable in a side room named for William Scott, the multi-millionaire who tried to get the Pennsylvania Railroad to come to town and finally put up the money himself. Five antique rug beaters were fanned on the wall above the queensize bed. A sofa and writing desk were situated against the bay windows, and a couple of old trunks held a decoy collection as well as our luggage. The large bathroom contained a clawfoot tub and shower.

The most coveted room is named for the original occupant, Julia Wilkins. It's a beauty in blue and white, with a kingsize bed, a border of Royal Copenhagen plates beneath the ceiling, a settee, a wicker loveseat, a private balcony and a bathroom with a jacuzzi. The rear B.F. Kellogg Room is cheery in yellow, while the front Alexander Cassatt Room in apricot colors is hung with Carol's prints.

Breakfast was a gourmet treat, quite amazing given that the Evanses were hosting a reunion of old friends and his fellow barbershop quartet singers and their wives for the weekend, making a total of sixteen hungry people at two seatings. Orange juice and cut-up mixed fruit preceded a work-of-art baked stuffed croissant bearing cream cheese, peaches and cinnamon, garnished with bacon and grapes and served with plain and hazelnut-flavored maple syrups. Other specialties include creamed eggs and mushrooms in dill sauce over homemade dill bread, an egg and cheese quesadilla with herbs and bell peppers, grits and cheese soufflé and banana-stuffed french toast. Carol was preparing a cookbook of favorite recipes, and offers five-course dinners for groups of guests by reservation.

Wine, cheese and hors d'oeuvre are offered in the early evening. Chocolate mints are bedside treats.

(757) 331-4920. www.capecharleshouse.com. Five rooms with private baths. Doubles, $80 to $105. No smoking.

Wilson-Lee House, 403 Tazewell Ave., Cape Charles 23310.

David Phillips is a stage designer and Leon Parham an architect, so they knew what they were doing when they started restoring this 1906 Colonial Revival four-square house, built for the owner of the old Wilson's Department Store and one of the finest residences in town. "This house spoke to us," David said as he recalled the purchase and subsequent weekends of commuting from New Jersey during nine months of renovations. The partners ran a two-bedroom townhouse B&B in Jersey City to try their hand at innkeeping before deciding to transplant their success to their native South.

They opened in late 1996 with six up-to-date rooms with tiled baths and pedestal sinks, queensize beds, dramatic decor, clock radio/CD players, hair dryers and terrycloth robes. Rooms come with the inn's own toiletries and chocolate mints on the pillows.

Named for members of the original family, the bedrooms are striking for their theatrics, especially the artworks and the bed covers and window treatments fashioned by a friend. They are furnished with a mix of contemporary accessories and period heirlooms from David's family. The Alyce Wilson Room has an imported French iron canopy bed whose lines convey a stark simplicity. The James Wilson Room is Victorian in hunter green and red, with a stately carved walnut bed and bureau and thick carpeting. The bed and the bureau are art deco pieces in the Georgia Wilson Room. The third-floor Anna's Room has a walnut spool bed and an antique platform rocker. The premier James W. Lee Room, named for the Norfolk architect who designed the house, is designed in architectural and post modern style with contemporary waffle steel chairs. A glass block wall conceals a jacuzzi tub in the bath area and a double vanity.

David, an accomplished cook, prepares a Southern breakfast featuring biscuits and country ham, as well as a main dish like cheese grits soufflé, eggs florentine, oven-baked pancake with apples or a hash brown and sausage frittata. Coffee-walnut-chocolate chip muffins might accompany. The meal is served in a dining room appointed in black and burgundy or on a screened-in section of the wrap-around veranda.

Consummate hosts, the partners have succeeded in restoring the house to what they said was its original purpose: "fun and entertainment." They stock a butler's pantry for "guests to make themselves at home." By reservation, they will arrange for sunset sails with cocktails and a cookout on their deck.

(757) 331-1954. Six rooms with private baths. Doubles, $85 to $120. Children over 12. No smoking.

Sea Gate B&B, 9 Tazewell Ave., Cape Charles 23310.

A tropical look prevails at this delightful B&B. Chris Bannon, a hospitality professional who had run the Holy Family Monastery's retreat weekends in Connecticut, tired of wintry weather and decided to return to his native Norfolk area. He settled on Cape Charles and opened the first B&B in town in 1988.

Sea Gate started bed-and-breakfast movement in center of Cape Charles.

"I always wanted a palm tree and now I have three," he says by way of explanation for the swamp palms beside the front door of a house painted a summery peach color. The screened porches full of plants add to a tropical look that Chris likes to call eclectic.

The main floor is a happy melange of side dining porch at one end, a large foyer, a country kitchen and a formal living room, both opening onto a solarium porch furnished in rattan. A spiral staircase wends its way through the solarium greenery to a second porch overhead.

Upstairs are four spacious corner bedrooms. Two in back have queen beds, one with a stunning blue and yellow quilt, and private baths. A front room has a king bed with half-bath in the closet, while the other also has a lavatory and opens onto the upstairs porch above the solarium. These two share a full bath.

Chris puts his hotel-restaurant background to the test, preparing and serving a hearty breakfast of juice, fresh fruit, two or three breakfast meats and a main dish, perhaps french toast, omelets or a Mediterranean egg dish with cheese and tomatoes. It's taken at individual tables on the dining porch between 8 and 10.

The personable host occupies "the Cloister" on the third floor when he's not entertaining guests, serving on the Town Council, ecumenicizing the local Catholic church into a community center or drumming up enthusiasm for Cape Charles. This one-man band lends to civic duties the same passion he extends to innkeeping.

(757) 331-2206. Two rooms with private baths and two rooms with private lavatories and shared bath. Doubles, $75 to $85.

Bay Avenue Sunset Bed & Breakfast, 108 Bay Ave., Cape Charles 23310. This gray clapboard house with rust-red shutters faces the Chesapeake Bay across Bay Avenue and was thoroughly updated upon opening in 1993 to meet or exceed

AAA three-diamond ratings requirements, of which the owners are exceedingly proud. Al Longo and Joyce Tribble call theirs "a 1915 cozy Victorian," but actually offer a variety of styles.

The four guest rooms have private baths, ceiling fans, central air, queen beds, cable TV, clock radios and toiletries that surpass AAA standards, Al points out. Each room is different. Courtney, the smallest but in front with a super view, has wicker furniture, a sit-down shower, a glass dolphin hanging from the fan drawcord and a beachy theme in terms of accessories on display. Abigail in back is bigger and done in Colonial decor.

The two most prized rooms are on the third floor. Intricate wallpaper treatments and borders convey a Victorian theme in the rear Victoria room, notable for an old cherry bedroom set that was in Al's family. An ancient but still working radio rests on an old Singer sewing machine in its entry and a clawfoot tub is in the bathroom. The Victoria has a new Vermont Castings gas stove. So does the front Sheena Room, contemporary in decor with rattan and "touches of rain forest," Joyce says, plus two chairs and a futon couch that opens into an extra full-size bed.

A small common area on the second-floor landing is furnished in wicker and proves a popular place for viewing the bay. The main floor holds a small parlor and a fancy dining room with glass in a display case and a silver spoon collection on a wall. An enclosed side porch contains a refrigerator, bikes and beach chairs for guests' use.

A full breakfast of fresh fruit, homemade breads or muffins and perhaps stuffed french toast, strata or sausage casserole is served at a table for eight in the dining room.

(757) 331-2424 or (888) 422-9283. Fax (757) 331-4877. Four rooms with private baths. Doubles, $85 to $105, mid-March to mid-November, $75 to $85 rest of year. Two-night minimum weekends in summer. Children over 10. No smoking.

Nottingham Ridge, 28184 Nottingham Ridge Lane, Cape Charles 23310.

A beautiful brick manor house built in 1975. A sandy beach alongside the Chesapeake Bay. A secluded, hundred-acre property two miles off the main road.

These are among the attributes of Bonnie Nottingham's home, which she shares with guests in four B&B rooms. "The sun sets in our back yard," says Bonnie. "We take it for granted, but guests are so awed by it."

She and her sister-in-law, Sara Nottingham Goffigon, who runs the Pickett's Harbor B&B, are the original B&B hostesses in this section of Virginia's Eastern Shore. Their substantial houses also are the only ones along a half-mile stretch of dirt road called Nottingham Ridge Lane, nestled between woods and farmland on one side and the bay on the other.

Guests enjoy nettle-free swimming from a sandy beach that stretches as far as the eye can see in either direction. They also enjoy the showy azaleas and rhododendrons in the backyard and the view over the dunes from the screened porch across the rear of the house.

Inside are a fireplaced family room in which a wide cabinet displays Bonnie's collection of blue and white china, an elegant front living room with a fireplace, and a formal dining room where breakfast is served when it's too cool to be outside on the porch. A main-floor guest room, pretty in pale yellow with green trim, comes with a queensize iron bed and a full bathroom with a view of the bay.

Upstairs are three more bedrooms, all quite spacious and with private baths. One in the rear with bay views has a double mahogany sleigh bed, a writing desk and two chairs. A front bedroom offers a queen poster bed, floral fabrics, two rattan chairs and a bathroom with a sit-down shower. At the far end of the house is a suite with a queensize spool bed, Duncan Phyfe sofa, antique cedar chest, oriental rugs and a TV/VCR. An ante room with a twin bed turns it into a family suite.

Bonnie serves a full breakfast. The day of our visit she chose grapefruit, muffins, scrambled eggs with bacon and fried apples. Other main courses include sweet-potato biscuits with Smithfield ham, egg casserole, quiche and french toast. Wine and cheese are offered in the afternoon.

(757) 331-1010. Three rooms and one suite with private baths. Doubles, $90 to $100; suite, $100 to $130. Two-night minimum weekends, April-October. Children over 8. No smoking. No credit cards.

Pickett's Harbor B&B, 28288 Nottingham Ridge Lane, Cape Charles 23310.

Sara Goffigon gets up at 4 a.m. some days to prepare breakfast for guests before leaving for her job as a teacher of advanced placement courses at a private school up the shore. How can she maintain the pace? She and her husband Cooke raised five children, "so everything has been easy ever since."

Part of the Nottingham family that has farmed 100 secluded areas along the Chesapeake Bay since the 1600s, Sara started taking in B&B guests in 1982 in a handsome brick and gray clapboard house the couple built to look old in 1976. The rambling house is nestled in a forest of oaks and loblolly pines, with land-scaped grounds leading toward the sand dunes along the bay.

The Goffigons offer six guest rooms in a variety of configurations. Three have private baths and the others share two baths. Three have queen beds, two are doubles and one is a three-quarter bed. We looked into a couple of rooms with country antique furnishings and handsome wood floorboards obtained from a tobacco warehouse in Richmond.

Guests take breakfast in a stunningly handsome formal 18th-century dining room with oriental rug and fireplace or on the back porch looking toward the bay. The fare includes fresh fruit, sourdough bread or muffins, Virginia ham and a main dish such as asparagus quiche or cheese, sausage and egg casserole.

(757) 331-2212. Three rooms with private baths and three rooms sharing two baths. Doubles, $75 to $125. No smoking.

Chesapeake Charm B&B, 202 Madison Ave., Cape Charles 23310.

Pale yellow with green trim, this square house built in 1921 is furnished with 1930s family heirlooms. Barry and Phyllis Tyndall from North Carolina moved here in 1995 to open this as a B&B. He commutes daily to work in Virginia Beach, while she runs the house and takes care of their toddler.

The Tyndalls did all the renovation work themselves. The second floor holds three guest rooms with private baths. Granny's Treasures is furnished with items made by or given to them by their four grandmothers, including a double bed with a hand-carved headboard. The Eastern Shore Room has a rolled oak queensize bed, pictures by Eastern Shore artists and a jacuzzi tub in the bathroom, the ceiling and walls of which talented Phyllis wallpapered and painted to resemble pressed tin. The Queen Anne's Lace Room has an Eastlake queen bed with a lace crocheted cover and pillows, two wood upholstered chairs and a vintage pedestal tub in the bathroom.

Downstairs is a pump organ in the vestibule. Beyond the living room is a dining

Dogwoods and azaleas brighten grounds of Nottingham Ridge manor house in spring.

room where breakfast is served. Barry cooks on weekends and Phyllis on weekdays. Expect fresh fruit, homemade muffins and perhaps Barry's apple pancakes or Phyllis's unique strawberry omelets. Afternoon refreshments include many of their grandmothers' Southern treats, including cookies, pound cake and lemonade.

(757) 331-2676 or (800) 546-9215. Three rooms with private baths. Doubles, $65 to $85. Children over 2. Smoking restricted.

Dining Spots

Eastville Manor, 6058 Willow Oak Road (Route 631), Eastville.

Since this restaurant's opening in 1996, there's no doubt among Eastern Shore gourmands that they have a treasure in their midst. William Scalley, a chef who had cooked at the Mayflower and Four Seasons hotels in Washington, D.C., and his New Orleans-born wife Melody bought an 1886 Victorian mansion on the outskirts of Eastville and opened a restaurant of distinction. They did so with trepidation because, Melody said, "we're offering the only fine dining in the county and the locals find us expensive."

Doing much of the renovation work himself, Bill – whom his wife describes as a Renaissance man – created three small dining rooms with well spaced tables dressed with votive candles and fresh flowers. He made the stained glass for the front door and crafted the corner shelf for a collection of show plates. Wrought-iron overhead trim in the doorways separate two rooms done in pale yellow atop blue patterned wainscoting. Masses of colorful zinnias – grown by a waitress and still blooming at our mid-November visit – decorated the foyer. Melody planted 5,000 bulbs amid the majestic boxwoods and gardenia plants "taller than I am" on the showy grounds outside.

Flowers turned up as garnishes on our dinners, starting with an appetizer of a delicious crab cake decorated with a baby mum, carrot curls, an onion blossom and coriander. Basil butter accompanied a basket of sensational breads, among them corn and sourdough. The short menu bore prices that would have been expected at lunch in many a city restaurant. Main-course choices ranged from grilled tuna with roasted red peppers, jicama, peanuts and sesame seeds in curry butter to roasted chicken breast stuffed with spinach, Smithfield ham and sundried tomatoes with cheddar grits in a grainy mustard sauce. We were impressed with our selections: medallions of duck with fried plantains in a ginger-orange sauce and sliced beef tenderloin in a cabernet-tarragon sauce. Each was abundantly presented in something of a hodgepodge atop a couple of dozen fresh vegetables and sides. Eight fantastic-sounding desserts included a quartet of exotic, homemade sorbets that were a refreshing ending to a memorable meal.

Chef Bill, who mans the kitchen from 9 a.m. to midnight, offers five-course wine-tasting dinners monthly. He serves lunch in season, and cooks a full breakfast for overnight guests who book the manor's upstairs suite with queen bed and double whirlpool tub for $160 a night.

(757) 678-7378. Entrées, $10.95 to $14.95. Lunch, Wednesday-Friday 11:30 to 2, spring and summer. Dinner, Wednesday-Saturday 5:30 to 9. Closed in January.

Sting-Ray's Restaurant, 26507 Lankford Hwy. (Route 13), Cape Charles.

They dub it "Chez Exxon," this semi-gourmet restaurant that Ray Haynie built from a twenty-seat truck stop he bought in 1985. With a background in food retailing, he expanded the rear restaurant with an open kitchen into more than 100 seats in three usually packed dining areas.

"I'm Sting-Ray," he said when introduced, having taken the name when he entered chili cook-offs in which his version was honored for its deep, smoky flavor that stings on the palate. "We make everything from scratch," said Ray, who now has an enormous kitchen staff and spends most of his time greeting customers out front. He features fresh seafood and angus beef, plus Southern side vegetables and inspired homemade desserts that keep regulars coming back.

The fare is truck stop by day, upscale at night. Decor is basic: bright lighting and bare booths and tables, each dressed with a ketchup bottle, salt and pepper shakers, an ashtray and packages of artificial sweeteners. You order from a blackboard menu at the counter, and waitresses bring the meal.

At our visit, the menu offered a staggering 22 entrées (after a couple had been erased because they'd sold out by 5:30). They ranged in price from fried oysters or pan-fried pork chops to shrimp or flounder stuffed with crab imperial. The salmon is to die for, according to one fan. So is the Smithfield crab imperial, layered with Smithfield ham and topped with cheese. It's almost everybody's favorite, except for oldtimers who disdain the fancy choices and opt for pork ribs, delmonico steak or the dinner platter of roast beef with gravy. Creamy crab soup is the starter of choice. Sweet potato pie and Tennessee bread pudding are among the desserts.

An extensive selection of wine is displayed on racks as you enter the restaurant area from the service station/convenience store. Customers so inclined pick out their choices, pay the retail price and there's no corkage fee. But wine imbibers might feel conspicuous among all the beer-guzzling and iced-tea sipping locals.

(757) 331-2505. Entrées, $8.95 to $17.95. Open daily from 5:30 a.m. Dinner, 4:30 to 9 or 9:30.

Tastefully Yours, Too, 307 Mason Ave., Cape Charles.

Two nuns from the order of Sisters for Christian Community run this new restaurant, a branch of their original up the Eastern Shore in Jamesville and featuring

Italian cuisine – heat-your-own with a microwave at lunch and, in the plans, classic and leisurely in eight courses at dinner.

Sisters Connie Karli and Maureen Miele, retired teachers who also did prison and social work, opened in 1997 in downtown Cape Charles with a mission: to help boost Eastern Shore employment, particularly among the handicapped and those on welfare. They also focus on delivering to local businesses.

Locals lunch on garden furniture, amid large photos of Italy, hanging arrangements, wreaths and such on the walls. Choosing from the week's short menu, we nuked our tortellini soup, linguini with white clam sauce, mushrooms and black olives, and acorn squash stuffed with sausage, apples and nuts. Everything was homemade and delicious, and we surely appreciated the fact that we spent all of $8.50, even if we had to serve and bus the table ourselves. Nothing costs more than $4.50, with most dishes in the $3 range. Interspersed with the listing of lunch dishes are the delightful comments of the sisters, as in "Connie's angel hair salad – it tastes as if an angel made it." We passed on dessert, even though a fellow patron wanted us to take a bite of her cheesecake, which she said was the best ever.

Another part of the sisters' mission is for people to get to know each other. They planned to initiate classical Italian eight-course dinners Thursday-Saturday. These start at 7:30 with wine and hors d'oeuvre and mingling, go on to wedding soup or clam bisque, antipasto, pasta, intermezzo of orange sorbetto, entrée, fresh fruit and nuts, and dessert. Dinner takes three hours, and people dine communally. Special nights for ex-New Jerseyites, or ex-Richmonders, for example, will be a chance for them to get acquainted. The ambitious sisters also planned to serve Sunday brunch, and to have outdoor seating for lunch in season.

(757) 331-1950. Open Thursday-Saturday 9 to 6. Dinner by reservation, Thursday-Saturday at 7:30.

Rebecca's, 7 Strawberry St., Cape Charles.

Home cooking of the greasy spoon school is the strength of this establishment likened to a Southern hometown cafe of 50 years ago.

At our initial Cape Charles visit it was the only place in town open for lunch, other than the soda fountain at Rayfield's Pharmacy. So we settled in for a crab cake sandwich and a fried oyster dinner with coleslaw and french fries, tasty and filling. The menu reads like the 1950s, with things like a BLT and fried chicken featured at lunch. The dinner menu yields liver and onions, steamed shrimp, softshell crab, crab imperial and fried or broiled seafood platter, with a choice of ten side vegetables.

Homemade cobblers, pies (pecan and white chocolate/banana cream) and bread pudding are among the desserts. Beer and wine are available.

Decor is plain: a pine-paneled room with basic booths, tables and chairs. As elsewhere in town, everyone seems to know each other.

(757) 331-3879. Entrées, $4.75 to $13.95. Open daily except Tuesday, 11 to 9.

Diversions

Nature, history and old-time Americana are the draws here.

The area has one of the highest Christmas bird counts (more than 150 species) north of Florida. The October birding festival attracts thousands, and more species are sighted here than in better-known Cape May, N.J. Monarch butterflies migrate through. Birders band everything from hummingbirds to bald eagles.

Eastern Shore of Virginia National Wildlife Refuge, 5003 Hallett Circle. This 750-acre wildlife refuge at the northern end of the Chesapeake Bay Bridge-Tunnel was established in 1984 to manage and protect habitats for migrating birds along the Atlantic Coast flyway. Audio-visual displays in the state-of-the-art visitor center detail everything one could want to know about shore wildlife. Two stationary telescopes and two sets of binoculars in an observation room with large glass windows yield close-up views across the salt marshes toward the barrier islands. Pictures identify birds frequently sighted. Young and old enjoy what a ranger called the "think tank," a touch-and-feel display of exotic shells and skeletons. Twenty-seven videos lasting from four minutes to an hour are available for showing in the auditorium. In front of the replica of a waterman's shack, we listened to a recording of Cigar Daisey of Chincoteague talking about decoy carving. Outside, a half-mile interpretive trail loops past an old graveyard to a World War II bunker, where a 60-foot-high observation platform overlooks marshes, islands, inlets and ocean. Offshore beneath the bridge is the Fisherman Island wildlife refuge, a special haunt for birders.
(757) 331-2760. Open daily, 9 to 4. Free.

Kiptopeke State Park, 3450 Kiptopeke Drive, (757) 331-2267. Situated along the Chesapeake Bay three miles north of the bridge-tunnel is Virginia's newest state park, established in 1992 and under development as a mecca for nature lovers. Near the boat ramp is the old terminal building for the ferry service that moved here from Cape Charles in 1950. The 375-acre park has a swimming beach, picnic areas, camping facilities, a hiking trail, a fishing pier, a hawk observatory and a bird banding station. Visitors join volunteers in bird banding on fall weekends.

Touring Cape Charles. Points of interest are detailed in a brochure and map published by the town's B&B association. Sights vary from several Sears, Roebuck mail-order houses to two houses that have settled toward each other to the point where their roofs overlap. The landmark water tower visible as you approach town turns out to have been designed in 1992 and patterned after the old Cape Charles Lighthouse. Nearby, the old Delmarva Power Plant was being converted into the **Cape Charles Museum and Welcome Center,** open weekend afternoons. Two railroad cars were being restored behind the museum for excursions to neighboring towns. Virginia's first memorial library is housed in an old Presbyterian church at Tazewell and Plum. Visit the gazebo at the foot of Randolph Street, where a dolphin sculpture is beside the path to the public beach. A narrow boardwalk parallels the beach along Bay Avenue. There's a new jetty pier at the harbor, where Applaud the Sunset parties are staged in the Key West idiom. A parade is the highlight of the annual Cape Charles Day celebration in September. The Pride of Baltimore showed up in 1997 at the annual Schooner Feast, part of the Great Chesapeake Bay Schooner Race from Norfolk to Baltimore. The Fourth of July fireworks here are considered the best on the Eastern Shore.

Look across the harbor for the pioneering **Port of Cape Charles Sustainable Technologies Industrial Park,** the first of four in the nation. It is designed for companies that do not generate waste or that use as a resource the discharge of those that do. A technical center is expected to be of interest to visitors.

Eastville. Compared with nouveau Cape Charles (founded 1884), the somnolent Northampton County seat about six miles north appears positively historic. It was settled shortly after Captain John Smith explored the peninsula in 1608 on his way to establishing the first permanent English colony in Jamestown. The Colonial Courthouse, built about 1731, contains the oldest continuous court records in the nation, dating from 1632. They can be examined at the court clerk's office on the first floor. Outside on the tiny Courthouse Green are a confederate monument, a debtor's prison, an ancient whipping post, and a couple of ancillary buildings that now are attorney's offices.

Shopping. Abandoned storefronts, indeed blocks, strike visitors along Mason Avenue, the once thriving main street. Between them, however, are some promising newcomers, as many as ten in 1997 alone. The standout is **Cape Charles Trading Co.**, which started as an antiques shop but evolved into an eclectic gift shop. Owner Paul Dwyer commutes weekends from his work at the Library of Congress to oversee a veritable bazaar of one-of-a-kind gifts and collectibles that you don't expect to find in Cape Charles. Nearby is the small retail showroom of **Delisheries, Ltd.**, wholesaler of gourmet baking mixes. Patterned after his mother's Sugar Plum Bakery in Virginia Beach, the enterprise is overseen by Chris Marshall and his fiancée, Meg Nash, who were preparing "easy, one-bowl mixes" for cookies and muffins in the back production area. One of the first participants in the new Sustainable Technologies Industrial Park, the pair plan to train handicapped workers to help with production. Artworks by Eastern Shore artists, some of them quite spectacular, are carried by Felix Torrice at his new **12 Peach Gallery** at 12 Peach St.

A special place up the shore at Onley is **Turner Sculpture,** the foundry and gallery where world-renowned artists David and William Turner produce remarkable bronze sculptures of wildlife in action. One of their pieces, two Canada geese about to land, is on display outside the entrance to the visitor center at the Eastern Shore of Virginia National Wildlife Refuge.

Extra-Special

Charmar's Old Country Store Museum, 213 Mason Ave., Cape Charles.

This is a turn-of-the-century country store like no other – partly because it's a museum and nothing's for sale, partly because it's one man's labor of love, and partly because everything is authentic (the soap boxes and containers are full, not cardboard or metal showpieces). Antiques dealers Charles and Margaret Carlson opened the museum by happenstance in 1979 in a storefront next to their **Charmar's Antiques** shop. Why? "It's a long story," says Charlie, holding forth in his museum. "My wife says I'm a sucker for buying anything." It seems a friend called one day to offer a 21-foot store counter and cajoled the dealer into accepting it if it was delivered. "We stuck it in here and I started filling it up with all the boxes of stuff I had collected." Soon he had a full-fledged country store, with a post office in the back, a potbelly stove, shelves of merchandise (from cow tonic to lice killer to Blossom Bloomers to a can of Caster Oil axle grease). We could relate to all the old soap detergents of our youth, if not to the strange wire contraption he called a chicken catcher. "See my customer," he pointed to a mannequin. "And my butcher." Quite the character, Charlie has great fun showing one and all the intricacies of his special collection. School groups visit to observe and hear his tales of life in the past.

(757) 331-1488. Open by appointment or by chance via the antiques shop, Monday-Saturday 10 to 5. Donation.

Washington, Va.

The Place That an Inn Built

After seventeen-year-old surveyor George Washington laid out its streets in 1749, this was to become the first of 28 towns named for the father of our country and the only one so designated before he became president. Not until rather lately had it been lifted from obscurity by an unlikely catalyst, a restaurant and inn playfully called The Inn at Little Washington.

This was "almost a ghost town," in the words of Patrick O'Connell. He teamed with Reinhardt Lynch to convert what once was a garage at the main crossroads into a restaurant in 1978. Rave reviews quickly attracted the movers and shakers from big Washington, along with food and lodging cognoscenti from around the world. Because their clientele complained of the late-night drive back to the other Washington, the partners eventually added bedrooms and suites to become a full-service inn. Not an ordinary inn, mind you, but a pricey paragon that has been exalted to incredible heights. It is the only establishment ever to capture five-star awards for both dining and lodging from the Mobil Travel Guide and the first inn to receive five-diamond awards for both food and loding from the AAA.

Its accolades – and the adulation of the nation's elite – have put on the map, for better or worse, the two-bit hamlet in which it resides. But, its press to the contrary, this is no one-inn nor one-restaurant town. Others have popped up in the inn's footsteps.

Happily, success has not spoiled little Washington. The entire village is designated an historic district and remains unscathed by development.

Washington is the county seat of Rappahannock County, though you'd scarcely know it from the unassuming government buildings a block off Main Street. With 6,000 people, Rappahannock is the second smallest of Virginia's counties. It's a relic of the past, situated between prosperous hunt country to the east and the bucolic Blue Ridge Mountains to the west. It's a detour off the main road and not really on the way to anywhere else.

The village's estimated population of 232 ranks it as the county's largest, ahead of Sperryville and Flint Hill. The mountainous county has more cows than people and more apple trees than cows. There are no traffic lights (only a couple of flashers), no supermarkets or chain stores. It is a spectacularly scenic mountain area, yet tranquil and gentle. A few good shops, wineries and outdoor activities, plus the area's cachet, make it a destination for weekenders (almost everything is closed early in the week).

Exotic plants are featured in inner courtyard at The Inn at Little Washington.

It's a diverse area because it is home to the poorest of the poor as well as the richest of the rich. Sometimes it's hard to tell which is which because almost everybody drives a pickup truck – except for visitors, most in luxury cars, whose destination is the Inn at Little Washington.

Inn Spots

The Inn at Little Washington paved the way, but others have followed – and are much in demand as lodging alternatives for visitors who don't wish to pay top dollar. Like the inn, some of the B&Bs carry surcharges for weekends and the month of October. Although 75 percent of their business at certain times comes as a result of overflow from the inn, each is increasingly able to stand on its own.

The Inn at Little Washington, Middle and Main Streets, Washington 22747.
There's no sign to detract from its aura of exclusivity. Only by the process of elimination does the visitor determine that the unremarkable, three-story white building festooned with flags at what passes for the village crossroads is, indeed, the celebrated Inn at Little Washington. Depending on the time of day, the handful of fancy cars parked in pickup territory might give it away. But lace curtains on the windows and a closed entry thwart the gaze of curious passersby.

This is an inn turned inward unto itself, as one might find in a large city. From the inn's perspective, the village is not particularly compelling, and those with the wherewithal to spend a night or two here seem to want to screen themselves from the outside. Owners Patrick O'Connell and Reinhardt Lynch provide a cocoon of luxury patterned after an English manor home. Everything has been draped, flounced and swagged by a London stage-set designer who, curiously, never saw the place until she attended the grand-opening party. Her elaborate conceptual drawings of each room hang in the hallways.

The restoration of the two-story lobby alone cost more than the original building. Its gilt ceiling is decorated with a collage of 500 hand-drawn blocks that resemble stained glass. Surely the inn's reported $2 million renovation tab does not include the furnishings. Otherwise, the reports of bedspreads costing $10,000 are apocryphal.

The banister leading upstairs to a second-floor lobby favored by overnight guests for tea or cocktails is wrapped in velvet. The twelve accommodations here range from standard (one) to intermediate (three) and superior (four) to suites (four). An additional intermediate room and suite in the inn's guest house above the Rare Finds gift shop down the street are described by its proprietor as "just as nice if not nicer" in comparison with the main accommodations. The latest in a 1997 addition behind the inn are the ultimate. Called junior suites and under construction at our visit, they are side by side on the second floor atop a new kitchen and share a wide rear balcony. Larger than the original rooms, one has a fireplace and a bathroom that's as big as the inn's smallest room.

The inn's 1997 expansion also produced a new library, a bar and lounge area, and a small private dining room in space freed up by vacating the old kitchen.

Each accommodation is "utterly decadent in detail," in the words of the inn's extravagant, sixteen-page brochure. All are decorated to the nth, up to the wallpapered ceilings and down to the oriental rugs on the floors. Each has a bathroom with countertops of Greek marble, heated towel racks, a shoe polisher and Gilbert & Soames toiletries. There are terrycloth robes, padded and removable coat hangers, a telephone but no TV or radio, lush beds draped within an inch of their lives, and double doors at the entry to eliminate hallway noise. All have a cozy chair with a hassock and a throw on top. Some have window seats and others have private balconies. Those looking onto the garden courtyard appeal more than those facing the street. Each is furnished with antiques and custom-made contemporary pieces, and "Mr. O'Connell is always on the lookout for new things," our guide offered. Clad in black and white, a staff of more than 60 attends to every detail and are quite a presence in the center of town as they move between buildings.

Two duplex suites, furnished and decorated similarly except for their color schemes, crown the inn's third floor. In the more striking of the two, an arched doorway leads to a sitting area with a velour sofa/banquette a dozen feet long, all draped in mulberry and awash with pillows. Walls are a soft sponged peach and

Colorful gardens welcome guests to Bleu Rock Inn.

oriental throw rugs cover the oatmeal-colored carpeting. A side balcony overlooks the garden. A wet bar and a stereo system separate the sitting room from the bathroom. The latter contains a jacuzzi in a window alcove, a double sink, a dressing area with a built-in seat, a w.c. and bidet behind one door and, behind another door, a shower stall for two with English hinged glass doors. One entire wall is mirrored. Upstairs in a loft is the bedroom with another balcony, from which you can see most of the village. Layered fabrics like those used in the sitting area decorate the kingsize bed. A stunning canopy is painted on the ceiling that slopes to the floor below.

Fresh flowers furnished by the inn's fulltime gardener (often supplemented by orchids grown for the inn by a nearby purveyor) greet guests. Bottles of mineral water await. Tea and a fruit and cookie tray are served in the room at check-in.

The patio beside an exotic garden incorporating oriental and native Virginia plants is a favorite spot for breakfast. Fresh fruits, juices and homemade breads and pastries like applesauce-walnut croissants are included in the rates. A hot breakfast that brings the acclaimed pan-fried rainbow trout or eggs scrambled with Scottish smoked salmon and cream cheese costs an extra $12 per person.

Is a stay here worth the expense? Yes, for those who aspire to the ultimate in decor and service, though some might find the cocoon claustrophobic. The cache of glowing press reprints in the lobby and the flyer headlined "Avalanche of Awards Hits Inn at Little Washington" dispel any doubts.

(540) 675-3800. Fax (540) 675-3100. Nine rooms and five suites with private baths. Doubles, $260 to $410. Suites, $420 and $545. Add $100 for all Fridays and month of October; add $175 for all Saturdays. No smoking.

Bleu Rock Inn, 12567 Lee Hwy. (Route 211), Washington 22747.

Morning may be the best part of the experience here, say staff and guests at this deluxe inn, a pretender to the Inn at Little Washington's throne. That's because of the lavish breakfasts served in a matchless setting: in a dining room beside the garden or on a rear terrace overlooking a Napa Valley-ish vista toward a pond, vineyards and the Blue Ridge Mountains.

The dominant inn cannot match the newcomer's complimentary breakfast, scenery or value. Consider the morning repast, which changes daily: perhaps grand marnier french toast, shrimp and tomato omelet, poached eggs with smoked salmon or omelets with shiitake mushrooms, chives and local goat cheese. Little drop biscuits, carrot and poppyseed muffins and blueberry and cinnamon rolls with three homemade preserves might accompany. "We try to do something extra," says co-chef Lynn Mahan in a reference to the lack of a full breakfast included in the rates at the other inn.

The Bleu Rock, which serves mighty good meals (see Dining Spots), also offers a spectacular, rural setting on 80 acres. It was opened in a converted farmhouse a few miles southwest of the village in 1990 by brothers Bernard and Jean Campagne, who operate La Bergerie Restaurant in Alexandria and are tinkering with this as a place to which they will retire.

The five unpretentious guest rooms with private baths are pristinely elegant (but why the small, stand-up balconies without chairs?) The four upstairs rooms have queensize beds. The largest is outfitted in peach and moss green colors with draped lace curtains. A nearby room, much smaller, is done in blues and yellows. Another room in deep blue has a dark blue comforter adorned with tulips. The shower curtains in most bathrooms match the bed covers. Fresh flowers, a hair dryer and fancy Kingsbridge toiletries, pretty dried wreaths and potpourri are hallmarks. Fruit baskets and candies are placed in each room. A downstairs room in blue-green and deep rose offers two double iron and brass beds and a large bath tiled in pink.

An attractive and spacious sitting room, quite elaborately furnished, harbors books and games and a fireplace. Out in front of the restored white stucco farmhouse with a tin roof and blue accents are colorful gardens and a trickling fountain. And in back, well away from Route 211, are the pond, vineyards and mountains, with plenty of seating to take them all in.

(540) 987-3190 or (800) 537-3652. Fax (540) 987-3193. Five rooms with private baths. Doubles, $195 weekends and October, $150 Sunday, $125 Wednesday and Thursday. Children over 10. Smoking restricted. Closed Monday and Tuesday.

The Middleton Inn, 176 Main St., Box 254, Washington 22747.
Uncommonly sumptuous for a B&B, this hilltop brick manor house was opened to guests in 1995 after eight months of top-to-bottom renovations. Mary Ann Kuhn, a former Washington Post reporter and CBS News producer, found a new calling as a restorer of old buildings and as a hostess par excellence.

Sparing no expense, vivacious Mary Ann produced plush common rooms and four deluxe guest rooms in the main Federal house built in 1850 by Middleton Miller, who manufactured the Confederate uniforms during the Civil War. She turned the former slave's quarters behind into a romantic little cottage and boarded her horses in a rear barn on the six-acre hunt-country estate.

The bedrooms are sights to behold. Each comes with a marble bath and a working fireplace. Fine linens dress the queen or king beds. Bottles of spring water are at the ready, and chocolates are placed at bedside during turndown service.

The queensize wicker Chartwell sleigh bed in the front-corner Ivy Room is a reproduction of one from Winston Churchill's family home in England. A leather loveseat and a wing chair take advantage of the mountain view from the other front-corner Hunt Country Room. An antique bookshelf becomes a closet in the rear Morning Room, pretty in yellow with floral fabrics. A large 1830s vanity topped by a mirror in the bedroom is the focal point in the Man's Vanity Room. Bath facilities are enclosed on either side.

Mary Ann Kuhn renovated her brick manor house into The Middleton Inn.

The most sought-after quarters are in the rear cottage. It has a small living room with TV, a little refrigerator and stove, and a bathroom with a jacuzzi tub from which you can look out the window at the mountains. Upstairs is a bedroom with beamed cathedral ceiling and a queensize sleigh bed.

Guests enjoy afternoon tea and wine in the formal drawing room. A focal point is an 1830s grand piano upon which rests a striking bronze sculpture of George Bush pitching a horseshoe, the work of syndicated cartoonist Patrick Oliphant, Mary Ann's ex-husband.

The most visually striking space is the dining room, where five round tables are dressed in long white linens, sterling flatware and Herrend china for breakfast amidst museum-quality hunting prints and an extravagant floral display. Every course arrives on a silver platter. Fresh orange juice, fruit and homemade muffins are preliminaries to such treats as raspberry pancakes with country sausage or eggs benedict with smoked trout and asparagus. Linger over coffee on the front porch and enjoy the view of the mountains.

(540) 675-2020 or (800) 816-8157. Fax (540) 675-1050. Four rooms and one cottage with private baths. Doubles, $260. Cottage, $375. Two-night minimum for October and holidays. Children over 12. No smoking.

Sycamore Hill House & Gardens, 110 Menefee Mountain Lane, Washington 22747.

Off by itself on 52 acres at the end of a mile-long driveway up Menefee Mountain, this is one of the few contemporary B&Bs in all Virginia. "No dolls, ducks or bunnies here," says Kerri Wagner, innkeeper with her husband Stephen. Just tasteful furnishings, exquisite flowers and plants, original artworks, three comfortable rooms with queen beds and private baths, gourmet food and a view that won't quit.

Kerri, a former lobbyist in the other Washington, and Steve, a well-known illustrator, spotted a for-sale sign on a Sunday drive in 1987. "We came back as a lark, saw the house and had to have it," says Kerri. "Steve's job was portable and mine was not, so that was the impetus for the B&B." They opened on New Year's Day in 1988, having decided the house was so big and the location so special that they ought to share it.

And share they do. Kerri greets summertime guests with iced tea and homemade cookies on the 65-foot, semi-circular veranda, where Amish bentwood rockers take in a 180-degree panorama of the Blue Ridge Mountains across Kerri's prized gardens. The originals of Steve's illustrations for Time-Life Books (and others) enhance each room. His illustration of the inn on a winter night with deer in the snow and a zillion stars is magical. It hangs in the master bedroom, where we awoke in a waist-high four-poster bed to a mist-shrouded vista that looked like an oriental landscape. No fewer than four arrangements of garden flowers decorated our bedroom, dressing room and the bathroom with its double sinks. A decanter of brandy had provided a nightcap beneath the stars on the veranda the night before.

Though the master bedroom is the biggest and has the best view, the other choices are no slouches. A closet that once blocked the view in the Peach Room has been opened up; wicker chairs and built-in shelves full of books and lush African violets have been added on either side of the new window. White wicker furniture gives the smaller Wicker Room its name; its bath across the hall was Kerri's rejuvenation project one winter.

All three rooms have sitting/reading areas. But most guests prefer to relax in the airy living room with its circular wall of glass and accents of plants or on the veranda beyond. That is, when they're not enjoying the grounds. The massed floral plantings are spectacular, and wildlife and birds are abundant. Kerri no longer grows the vegetables and herbs that were in such demand at local restaurants. Instead she has taken up running, finishing second among women over age 50 in the annual local Fodderstock marathon.

The glass table in the open dining room is covered with a pink cloth for breakfast at 9 o'clock. Classical music played as we enjoyed orange-pineapple juice, slices of melon and strawberries with ham, and Kerri's special apple puff, almost like a soufflé and served in a quiche dish. Other entrées could be steak and eggs, light-as-a-feather angel pancakes and sometimes a shrimp soufflé.

Good as they are, the breakfasts here necessarily play second fiddle to the setting. Not to mention the views.

(540) 675-3046. Three rooms with private baths. Doubles, $100 to $200. Two-night minimum spring weekends; three-night minimum holiday and fall weekends. Children over 12. No smoking. Closed Tuesday.

Blue Knoll Farm, 110 Gore Road, Castleton 22716.

If the Wagners provide a mountaintop setting and contemporary elegance at Sycamore Hill, Mary and Gil Carlson offer serenity and a spirit of whimsy in their restored Virginia farmhouse on five rural acres in the middle of nowhere.

This is now home for the Carlsons, who had moved twenty times in as many years during his service as a Navy submarine officer. Retired in Annapolis and "always wanting to do the B&B thing," they jumped at the chance to purchase a ready-made B&B in tiny Castleton, barely a dot on the map some ten roundabout miles east of little Washington. Gil built a double garage with a workshop and office that his wife calls "The Taj Garage" and set to work constructing a sundeck on the side of the house and a double-side Victorian glider for the lawn.

The Carlsons offer four guest rooms with private baths and king or queen beds.

Sycamore Hill House & Gardens, as portrayed by illustrator-innkeeper Stephen Wagner.

They range from Rebecca's Room, full of dolls and a dollhouse, with an old quilt behind the bed and the bath across the hall, to the master bedroom with an elaborate antique bed headboard and Ralph Lauren comforter, lacy curtains and a jacuzzi. The Meadowview Room with a kingsize bed at the back of the house is for those who cherish privacy. Our choice was the fireplaced main-floor Library, where a queensize brass bed shared quarters with shelves of books and an old desk bearing all the requisite accessories. "We've tried to make it fun," Mary advised as we remarked on the rooster-related pottery, "because this is not a really elegant house."

Guests spread out beside a wood stove in the front parlor, over afternoon refreshments at the breakfast table and on two great porches, one facing a farm pond. The latter porch was where we greeted the day over a masterful breakfast, punctuated by the mooing of nearby cows and the quacking of baby ducks. Mary's specialties include a prosciutto-provolone-basil breakfast strata and pineapple upside-down french toast. A lavish fresh fruit platter, lemon poppyseed breads and key lime or peach bran muffins might accompany. Fine china and linens, silver, fresh flowers and flickering candles transformed an ordinary picnic table into an entrancing setting.

(540) 937-5234. Four rooms with private baths. Doubles, $95 to $125. Two-night minimum on holiday weekends and during October. Children over 14. No smoking.

Sunset Hills Farm, 105 Christmas Tree Lane, Washington 22747.

The front doorbell chimes out a ragtime melody in this architect-designed, stone house in the Frank Lloyd Wright tradition high up Jenkins Mountain. Betty and Leon Hutcheson moved here in 1978 from Alexandria after their four offspring had left for college. They were responsible for bringing the principals of Bleu Rock Inn to a site below theirs along Route 211. In 1993, they started taking in overnight guests in their showplace of a house.

For starters, the Hutchesons offer three bedrooms, each with marble bath and

TV and furnished in traditional style. Two in the rear come with queensize beds and fieldstone walls made of stones from the property. The extra-large Gazebo Room has a kingsize poster bed, a sitting area with TV and a bath with jacuzzi tub, twin vanities and a wall mural of belgian horses painted by Betty and a friend. It has direct access to a large side deck, full of heavy Adirondack-style chairs and tables and prolific flowers, leading to a screened gazebo. Both are great spots for enjoying the farm gardens, the horses grazing near the sunken pond in front, and the Blue Ridge vistas.

Guests also enjoy a huge, circular, open living/dining room with a table for six looking somewhat lonely in the center. Here or in the gazebo is where Betty serves a full breakfast. Expect fresh fruit (the couple pick their own berries and peaches), juice, and perhaps pancakes or an egg casserole with blueberry muffins. Beverages come from an espresso-cappuccino machine. Afternoon treats include lemonade, iced tea and cakes. Bedrooms are stocked with soft drinks and fresh fruits.

The Hutchesons, who live in a separate section of the house, have plans for three more guest rooms and a library. Meanwhile, they oversee production of brandied peaches, fruit butters, other fruit products and gift baskets at their mountaintop Sunset Hills farm store and Christmas shop in a barn near their house.

(540) 987-8804 or (800) 980-2580. Fax (540) 987-9742. Three rooms with private baths. Doubles, $150 and $195. No children. No smoking.

Fairlea Farm Bed & Breakfast, 636 Mount Salem Ave., Box 124, Washington 22747.

For an edge-of-town residence, this fieldstone manor house has a remarkable setting. It's surrounded by a working 40-acre sheep and cattle farm and yields 180-degree vistas. "You really feel like you're in the country," says Susan Longyear, who with husband Walter moved here from Falls Church and opened their home as a B&B after raising a family. The property was the old county fairgrounds, and a shed near the backyard gazebo and shady flagstone terrace was once a concession stand.

Few would guess its background, for today all is quite elegant and comfortable, from the lovely living room with fireplace and oriental rugs to the four guest quarters with queensize beds and private baths. The Magnolia Room, so named because it looks onto a couple of magnolia trees, is the main-floor master bedroom with a sofa, bathroom with double vanity, and a collection of miniature mirrors (53 at last count) on one wall. Upstairs, the Meadow Room has a brass bed, while the Rose Room overlooking the rose garden contains a canopy bed. A suite in the walkout basement is fashioned from a paneled family room. It has a four-poster bed, a sofabed, a stone fireplace, TV and kitchenette.

Fresh fruit and flowers are in each room, and ice water accompanies nightly turndown. A sumptuous breakfast is served at guests' convenience. Expect things like strawberry-rhubarb compote, apple puff, egg casserole, crêpes with local fruit, homemade breads and muffins.

(540) 675-3679. Fax (540) 675-1064. Three rooms and one suite with private baths. Doubles, $75 to $105. Suite, $125. Children accepted in suite. No smoking.

Caledonia Farm - 1812, 47 Dearing Hill Road, Flint Hill 22627.

"I've been to 262 B&Bs in North America and we do it differently from any other," says broadcaster-turned-innkeeper Phil Irwin. And loquacious Phil, who was the Breakfast Show host on the Voice of America, is quick to tell you how he does it.

"We produce a custom breakfast on demand," says he. That means a choice of menu, from smoked salmon on a bagel with neufchatel cheese to eggs benedict, following Eastern Shore melon, juices and cereal. Aspenglow sparkling cider in a champagne glass opens the presentation; a hot apple strudel concludes. Breakfast is served at hourly intervals "because of our shared-bath situation." Which is fine if you get your hour of choice, but it's first come, first served, and no deviations are tolerated. You arrive late for breakfast and you may go hungry; you arrive late at night and your reservation may not be honored. Phil does things his way.

He really gets going as he leads guests on a tour of part of the 183-year-old stone house after sharing a glass of wine or beer in the late afternoon in a gorgeous front gathering room. Here you'll find exposed beams, a great stone fireplace, paneled window wells and cross-and-bible doors – some are "architectural impurities," Phil points out. Up a very steep staircase is a landing with seating to enjoy the mountain view and two guest rooms sharing a bath (lately, Phil has been trying to rent them as a suite). One has a double bed with old pine furniture and a fireplace; the other a single and a double. Both have oriental scatter rugs on wood floors, electric candles in the windows and "the thirstiest towels and the best foam mattresses money can buy." Phil assures, "you will have the best sleep you ever had." An oversize lantern, robes, a lighted makeup mirror and extra pillows and blankets in the closets are extra touches of hospitality that, Phil says, make his B&B unique.

Beyond a winter kitchen with a cooking fireplace is the Summer Cottage, billed as a honeymoon suite. It's connected to the main house by a breezeway with garden chairs. A huge spinning wheel rests in front of an enormous stone fireplace. A kitchenette offers a wet bar, mini-refrigerator and a microwave. Upstairs is a pretty bedroom with four-poster double bed, two armchairs and a full bath. "People often check in here and we never see them again," says Phil.

Those who are seen may enjoy three porches, stroll around the 52-acre working cattle farm crisscrossed by nearly a mile of stone fences, borrow bicycles, play badminton or climb the 3,000-foot mountain upon which the Skyline Drive passes behind the house.

(540) 675-3693 or (800) 262-1812. Two rooms with shared bath and cottage suite with private bath. Doubles, $80. Suite, $140. Fifty percent surcharge if only staying Saturday. Two-night minimum for holidays and October. Children over 12. No smoking.

Heritage House, 291 Main St., Washington 22747.

Gray with black shutters and two-story-high pillars, this attractive B&B is the village's closest in proximity to the Inn at Little Washington, a block's walk for dinner. The former owners' old Country Heritage shop next door accounts for the name given to an 1837 house that served as a Confederate general's headquarters during the Civil War.

Broadcaster Frank Scott, a former NBC vice president, and his wife Jean offer four guest rooms, all with private baths. Because of their years of world travel, the Scotts changed to "a more international decor." A Black Forest cuckoo clock, a Spanish ship model and drinking steins from Bavaria are on display in the public rooms.

A ground-floor corner space called the Lace Room fully lives up to its name;

frillier and lacier than ever, it has a kingsize bed outfitted in white and draped with lace. Upstairs are three guest quarters. The Victorian Suite with queen bed and authentic Polish village art has a slanted, creaky sun porch with wicker furniture and wild pink walls. The Amish Room is furnished in the simple Amish style with an antique double bed and rag dolls. David Winter cottages cover the mantel in the British Room, with antique double bed, loveseat and much Dickens memorabilia.

Afternoon refreshments, best enjoyed in the yard with a view of the mountains, might be sparkling cider, cookies and candy. The B&B has a license to sell Virginia wines and champagne. Resident innkeeper Cindy Brown, formerly with the acclaimed Kincaid's restaurant in big Washington, is known for her lavish breakfasts. Service is communal at 9 a.m. at a large table in a dining room outfitted with Bavarian steins and a collection of silver spoons. The menu, printed daily, might offer "Heritage Meritage of juice" (a blend of orange, carrot, beet and apple cider), golden pineapple with blueberries, pear-mint bread and blueberry-currant muffins, and smoked salmon hash with red potatoes, served with a poached egg in a pastry shell. Other main courses include curried cornbread pudding with baked eggs and monterey jack, poached eggs served in a pastry basket with zucchini, mushrooms and tomato, and eggs florentine.

Further exploiting her cooking talents, Cindy will serve dinner for four to eight guests by reservation. The meal, priced according to market availability, is served at the time of the guests' choice.

(540) 675-3207. Three rooms and one suite with private baths. Doubles, $105 to $120. Suite, $135. No children. No smoking. Closed Tuesday.

The Foster-Harris House, 189 Main St., Washington 22747.

The area's first B&B to emerge in 1984 in the shadow of the Inn at Little Washington, this 1900s-vintage frame farmhouse was acquired in 1997 by John and Libby Byam from Morgantown, W.Va.

They purchased it from a former caterer from big Washington who was known for her sumptuous breakfasts, and John said they hoped to "build on her reputation." The meal is served at 9 or 9:30 in a small dining room furnished with country antiques. Juice, fruit, muffins and tea breads precede such treats as egg, spinach and mushroom strata; a potato, cheese and egg casserole, or Southwest-style poached eggs with breakfast meats. In the afternoon, tea or lemonade and cookies may be taken in the parlor, on the front porch or beneath an old plum tree.

Between meals, the Byams tend the country-style perennial gardens that border the turn-of-the-century house. They also have improved the room configuration and formalized the Victorian farm-style decor with some of their own furnishings.

All five guest quarters offer private baths and all but one of the beds is queensize. John's favorite is the Mountain View suite with a wood stove, a bathroom with a whirlpool tub for two and a sun room with wicker chairs for taking in the scene. Another favorite is the side Garden Room, cool and serene and reminiscent of spring year-round. A mini sunroom with a table for two adjoins the rear Meadow View Room, where a duvet covers the step-up Eastlake bed. Folk art is the theme in the cozy Americana Room, which has a queen bed and excellent examples of faux painting in the full bathroom. The new Teal Room has a double bed.

(540) 675-3757 or (800) 666-0153. Four rooms and one suite with private baths. Doubles, $95 to $120. Suite, $145. Children over 12. No smoking.

Gay Street Inn, 160 Gay St., Box 237, Washington 22747.

This restored 1860 white pebbledash farmhouse at the end of Gay Street features three spacious guest rooms with private baths and antique double beds, plus a new suite with a full kitchen. Originally from Nantucket, Donna Kevis is innkeeper with her husband Robin, a carpenter, whose handiwork shows in the stacked bathrooms he added for two guest rooms as well as the soaring addition that serves as family quarters.

The darkish bedrooms are decorated with large patterned wallpapers and furnishings of the period. One downstairs has a canopy bed and a chair and a rocker beside the working fireplace. The chaise in Clyde's Room, which Donna named for her brother-in-law, was a wedding gift supposedly acquired at a Kennedy tag sale in Hyannis Port.

For some years, breakfast was served buffet style at tray tables in the Mount Vernon living room, so named because her mother-in-law's Mount Vernon prints are hung on the walls. In 1997, the Kevises added a glass breakfast conservatory off a brick terrace in the back. The meal involves juice, fresh fruit, homemade buttermilk muffins or coffee cake and perhaps french toast, a one-egg soufflé with vegetables or Donna's version of breakfast burritos – local eggs and shiitake mushrooms wrapped in a warm tortilla with homemade salsa.

Theirs is one of the few area B&Bs that accepts young children and pets.

(540) 675-3288. Three rooms and one suite with private baths. Doubles, $95 to $115. Suite, $135. Children and pets welcome.

Dining Spots

The Inn at Little Washington, Middle and Main Streets, Washington.

The restaurant here preceded the inn, Patrick O'Connell and Reinhardt Lynch having decided to settle down in one spot rather than expand the thriving catering business they had started in Virginia hunt country. With a teenaged kitchen helper as the only staff, they opened their dining room in a former garage on a January weekend in 1978. Seventy patrons showed up and the next weekend, a Washington Star reviewer visited and proclaimed it the best eatery within 150 miles of D.C. Since then, gourmands from across the world have joined the powers-that-be from that other Washington in seeking one of the 75 seats in culinary euphoria.

Today, they may snag one of the two chef's tables in the new, state-of-the-art European-style kitchen – said to be the first of its kind in the United States – and watch the behind-the-scenes proceedings. Here you can dine by the fire and watch "a great artist in a grand new studio," in the words of the inn's publicist.

Few are disappointed, but count us among them. We were unfortunate enough to encounter five-star lapses and gaffes in service along with five-star triumphs in food and surroundings.

First it should be noted what the inn is not. It is not particularly intimidating nor pretentious, unless you balk at a waiter refolding your napkin when you leave the table for the restroom. It is not unpopular; witness the need for reservations weeks in advance for weekends and the denial of up to 3,000 requests for dinner on a Saturday night. It is not inexpensive; meals are prix-fixe, $88 on weekdays, $98 on Fridays and $108 on Saturdays. A seven-course tasting menu is offered the entire table for $118 each ($158 with wines). A four-course vegetarian menu is available as well.

The main dining room and the smaller Terrace Room and Garden Room, both facing the inner courtyard, are as elegant as the rest of the inn. Peach-colored taffeta lampshades hanging over most tables in the main room are the decorative hallmark; the lamps cast a glamorous glow over patrons and more light over-all than one would expect. A ceramic swan holds a mass of flowers in the center of the rich but subdued room. More splashy is the Terrace Room, where a wall of banquettes faces the garden beneath fans whirring and fabric billowing from the ceiling.

Chef Patrick's menu blends classic French and new American creativity into what he calls "cuisine of the territory." The menu is relatively simple and straight-forward, eschewing European terminology to the point that grilled poussin is described parenthetically as "young succulent chicken."

The food is anything but simple, however. Dinner begins with a couple of items not on the menu – in our case, a delicate puff pastry of leeks and a canapé with foie gras, one for each person, plus a demitasse of chilled vichyssoise accented with sorrel. A basket of rolls and breads accompanied. We gladly would have tried any of the ten first-course selections. Eventually we settled on a stupendous (and famous) sauté of New York State foie gras with smoked goose breast and local ham on a vinaigrette of black-eyed peas and a dish called salmon four ways, which turned up in three rosettes and three puffs with an excellent dill-mustard sauce.

A half-hour delay between appetizers and our between-course selections of a mixed green salad and a grapefruit-tarragon sorbet signaled that something was amiss. Another half hour ensued before the arrival of our main courses, grilled rack of lamb and a sauté of veal sweetbreads. "Here's your lobster," the waitress said to the lamb-orderer, who was nursing a $36 bottle of Stag's Leap merlot, one of the least expensive wines from an extraordinary 14,000-bottle cellar. Informed that we had not ordered lobster, she whisked both dinners back to the kitchen. The original waiter in the team that served many tables returned five minutes later and asked how the lamb was to have been cooked. Five or so minutes later the waitress arrived with another salad and another sorbet without explanation; when asked what was going on, she replied "we thought you might be hungry." Fifteen minutes later the ordered main courses came with a perfunctory apology. Elapsed time between appetizer and entrée: more than an hour.

Only as he later cleared the main courses did the waiter offer to make amends: a complimentary after-dinner drink to follow dessert. Besides the chosen seven deadly sins (a sampler of the inn's remarkable offerings on a plate painted with strokes of chocolate and fruit sauces) and a trio of nut tarts with caramel ice cream, he also presented a complimentary "white chocolate mousse in bed between dark silky sheets." The house chardonnay that began our meal more than three hours earlier turned out to be on the house.

(540) 675-3800. Prix-fixe, $88 weekdays, $98 Friday, $108 Saturday. Dinner by reservation, 6 to 9:30, Saturday 5:30 to 10:30, Sunday 4 to 9:30. Closed Tuesday except in May and October.

Bleu Rock Inn, Route 211, Washington.
This newcomer with a misleadingly pretentious name (why not just "Blue?") aspires to the heights set by the Inn at Little Washington. We think it succeeds in food and service – at about a third of the cost – and its location is unsurpassed. Set against a backdrop of vineyards and mountains, it looks like an inn out of California wine country, with a French provincial accent.

Blue Ridge Mountains are backdrop for dining terrace at Bleu Rock Inn.

Dining is in three simple but elegant fireplaced rooms seating a total of 75, plus a spectacular rear terrace. One small room is striking for elaborately painted wall panels that remind one of Versailles. In the main dining room, tapestry chairs, white cloths over burgundy and pink, fanned napkins standing tall in wine glasses, white china, heavy cutlery, little lalique-style lamps and fresh flowers create an elegant backdrop for the food.

Owners Bernard and Jean Campagne, who also run La Bergerie Restaurant in Alexandria, assign cooking duties to chefs Richard and Lynn Mahan. The menu changes seasonally, but we wouldn't tamper with anything we tried. Among starters were an eggplant and goat cheese terrine with artichoke, tomato and zucchini, small but ever so good, and confit of duckling with orange onion marmalade and grilled radicchio. Fabulous rolls that turned out to be onion poppyseed with finely chopped sage accompanied.

Main courses range from Alsatian choucroute with champagne-apple sauerkraut to grilled local free-range lamb loin with shiitake and oyster mushrooms. The chicken fricassee with glazed apples, shiitake mushrooms and spaetzle we tried here was one of the best chicken dishes we've had; it was accompanied by an out-of-this-world Shenandoah cider sauce. Grilled shrimp paired zucchini and julienned vegetables in a tomato sauce over angel-hair pasta, all mounded in the shape of a lobster.

Dessert could have been an anti-climax, but not here. We sampled a peach shortbread tart with cassis sauce, and a terrine of three sorbets. The latter brought passionfruit, black currant and coconut on a plate painted with a mosaic of sauces, plus two ginger-molasses cookies.

An excellent Naked Mountain chardonnay accompanied from a choice, fairly priced wine list. (Nearby Oasis Vineyard makes wines from the inn's grapes under the Bleu Rock Vineyard label.) Service throughout was excellent, by waitresses so unobtrusive you hardly realized they were there. And the bill for near-perfection came to $86 for two, about one-third as much as we were to spend the next night at the other inn in little Washington.

(540) 987-3190 or (800) 537-3652. Entrées, $16.75 to $22.50. Dinner, Wednesday-Saturday 5:30 to 9:030. Sunday, brunch 11 to 3, dinner 5:30 to 9..

Four & Twenty Blackbirds, Routes 522 and 647, Flint Hill.

Two alumni of the Inn at Little Washington opened this urbane little place in an old general store in 1990. Chef Heidi Morf, who was dessert chef at the inn, and Vinnie DeLuise, a former waiter there, have generated an avid following who appreciate the creativity, the informality and the prices. It's the place to which local gourmands return time and again.

The main-floor dining room is colorful yet glamorous. The chintz draped around the windows matches the chair seats, walls are pale peach above the chair rail and deep green below, and the woodwork is deep purple. A downstairs room with a stone bar and red trim is more rustic.

We've enjoyed a sensational lunch here (since discontinued), but a subsequent dinner by candlelight with live guitar music proved even more delectable. Unusual hot bread sticks, curled up at the end like a fiddlehead fern, tasted of fennel and hot chilies. Among appetizers were a great California sushi roll with crabmeat and avocado and an assertive tart bearing smoked peppers, caramelized vidalia onions and maytag blue cheese. A small salad of assorted greens with a lovely dijon vinaigrette prepared the palate for the main courses. One of us had sautéed soft-shell crabs atop a shrimp jambalaya with hush puppies. The other tried the grilled rockfish with the best sundried tomato aioli ever and orange couscous, garnished with tiny johnny jump-ups. Sweet endings were strawberry shortcake on heart-shaped biscuits with homemade lemon ice cream and a fresh plum, nectarine and almond tart with Rappahannock raspberry sauce.

This is the stuff of which culinary dreams are made, at prices that won't break the bank. A good wine list is priced in the teens and twenties.

(540) 675-1111. Entrées, $17.50 to $20.95. Dinner, Wednesday-Saturday 5:30 to 9. Sunday brunch, 10 to 2.

The Flint Hill Public House, Route 522, Flint Hill.

High atop a broad lawn, this majestic old structure built in 1899 served as a grade school for most of its years. Lately it has been a restaurant with a variety of dining options, including a great outdoor deck lined with impatiens and overlooking prolific gardens.

New owners John and Denise Pearson, young and energetic, have given it its most successful incarnation yet. John, the chef, employs Virginia products whenever possible in a straightforward manner that contrasts nicely with the more eclectic fare of Four & Twenty Blackbirds down the street. "It makes for good neighbors," John says, and his admiring competitors agree.

Dining is in the paneled Public Room, with a bar in the corner, floral placemats on old English pub tables and oriental runners on the floor. Beyond is a wicker parlor with dining tables opening onto the rear deck, a great place for a summer meal.

All is quite stylish for contemporary fare that earns good reviews. Dinner might start with a choice of filé gumbo, polenta cakes with wild morels, fried Asian vegetable rolls and a salad of grilled cucumbers, vidalia onions and goat cheese. Expect main dishes like seared yellowfin tuna with pineapple-ginger glaze, monkfish with Israeli couscous, spicy soft-shell crabs with corn relish, roasted chicken with flageolets and seared beef tenderloin with roasted garlic mashed potatoes.

John has added thousands of bottles to his wine cellar, which he considers the area's best after the Inn at Little Washington. He also presents quarterly vintner's dinners and a variety of food events "designed to be a celebration of food in America today."

The Pearsons also have refurbished two spacious, high-ceilinged upstairs guest rooms with queensize beds and private baths, renting for $95.

(540) 675-1700. Entrées, $15.95 to $18.95. Lunch, 11:30 to 2:30. Dinner, 5:30 to 8:30 or 9:30. Sunday, brunch 11 to 2, dinner 5 to 8. Closed Wednesday.

The Appetite Repair Shop, Main Street, Sperryville.

The young waitresses wear T-shirts labeled "service technician" and there's much memorabilia from auto repair shops and gasoline stations all around. Owners Cindy and Gregg Gillies have spent a lot of time around auto shops, so the theme seemed a natural.

Their vast space is mainly kitchen fronted by a counter, where you place your order for burgers, sandwiches, "fluids" and accompaniments from the "parts department." But there are unexpected surprises like fresh flowers atop some of the bare wood tables and a pastry case that includes blackberry cobbler and red raspberry pie. There's even a summer music series with live entertainment here on Sunday evenings.

We did a test drive on a couple of sandwiches, the grilled chicken with lettuce and tomato and the pulled pork barbecue topped with cheese and bacon. Served with coleslaw and great fried potato wedges, both proved quite satisfactory for a bit more than $4 each. Other sandwiches were priced from $1.50 for grilled cheese or a hot dog to $4.90 for the "luxury model" Italian chicken fillet with provolone, sautéed onions and peppers. Dinner specials add things like pizzas, liver and onions, baked chicken, deep-fried catfish and steak.

Noticing the slogan "appetite repair at a price that's fair," we had to ask the owner if this was a takeoff on a famous nearby restaurant that was born in a garage. "No, I didn't know that," came the laconic answer. "We started in Madison County."

(540) 987-9533. Entrées, $4.50 to $8.50 Open Monday-Thursday 8 to 3; Friday-Sunday 8 to 8.

Diversions

The Blue Ridge Mountains, Skyline Drive and Shenandoah National Park bestow on this area a spectacular backdrop, plus scenic drives and hiking trails. Old Rag Mountain is a hiking favorite. Drive the Skyline Drive for awesome scenery – and perhaps lunch on top of the world at Skyland Lodge.

Walking Tour of Washington. The Rappahannock Historical Society sells a pamphlet-size treatise billed as a walking tour along the quiet, tree-shaded streets of "the first Washington of them all." There's no map, and the text is for the truly interested. The Washington Business Council provides a more readily available free map, geared to commercial interests. Others will be satisfied with a leisurely stroll along Main and Gay and their connecting side streets, stopping to see whatever charms them. This really is a small rural village; that's the beauty of it. There are a few county and municipal buildings, a couple of churches and three log houses. Note the neat old printing press outside the door of the Rappahannock News building. **First Washington's Museum,** run privately and commercially by its creator, Ruby Jenkins, is an 18th-century tavern and schoolhouse all aclutter with historic and local memorabilia. **The Theatre at Washington** stages movies, recitals and other events, usually one night a weekend.

Driving Tours. The most rewarding way to sense the area's tranquility and beauty is to drive along any of the back roads (obtain a county map to avoid getting lost). You can bicycle if you bring your own, but this is winding, hilly territory, not for the faint of heart. Some of our favorite rural byways are Route 628 between Washington and Flint Hill, Route 729 between Flint Hill and Ben Venue and beyond to Laurel Mills or Viewtown (really!), and Routes 635, 688 and 726 in the winery country around Hume, Linden and Markham. You'll stumble onto surprises like the 1842 Leeds Church and its big parish house, manse and graveyard out in the countryside south of Markham. In foliage season, these are the best ways to beat the bumper-to-bumper traffic along main Route 211.

Horseback Riding. This is the western edge of Virginia hunt country, so why not do as the Virginians do? Rent horses at Marriott Ranches, Route 726, in Hume. Guided 90-minute trail rides are offered by reservation daily except Monday.

Wineries. Three nearby wineries are blessed with gorgeous locations like those of the Napa Valley. They are destinations for those who enjoy scenery as well as wine.

Linden Vineyards & Orchards, Route 638, Linden.

On a hilltop facing east, this versatile winery yields quite a view and makes the most of it with an outdoor deck and picnic tables scattered about. All the better to enjoy a lunch pairing goat cheese, smoked trout mousse, pâtés and baguettes with a good bottle of chardonnay or a dry seyval, all available on premises. More Virginia wineries should do this, for owners Jim and Peggy Law have plenty of takers. The operation has grown rapidly since their 1988 opening. The Laws produce a good late-harvest vidal dessert wine that won the 1994 Virginia Governor's Cup as the best in Virginia. They offer pick-your-own fruits, including apples and blueberries. They also stage vintner dinners and seminars, barrel tastings and jazz days, and produce a snappy-looking newsletter-magazine.

(540) 364-1997. Open Wednesday-Sunday and Monday holidays, 11 to 5, March-December; weekends only, rest of year.

Naked Mountain Vineyard & Winery, 2747 Leeds Manor Road (Route 688), Markham.

Up a mountain and down a hairpin driveway lies this prize, nestled between hills and producing Virginia's most-honored chardonnay. Sold here for a bargain $11, it's so esteemed that it's one of only two East Coast wines served at Domaine Chandon's restaurant in California wine country. Not bad for what had been a hobby for amateur winemakers Bob and Phoebe Harper. Most of their 3,000 cases a year are chardonnay. A few rieslings, sauvignons and clarets also are produced. The cathedral-ceilinged tasting room overlooks a close-in vista that has been described as the most picturesque of any East Coast winery.

(540) 364-1609. Open Wednesday-Sunday 11 to 5, March-December; weekends only, rest of year.

Oasis Vineyard, 14141 Hume Road (Route 635), Hume.

This is one of Virginia's oldest and largest wineries. "We learned as we went and made every mistake," said Corinne Salahi, a Belgian married to an American, of the vineyard she and husband Dirgham established in 1975. They're best known for their sparkling wines, produced by the traditional méthode champenoise, and representing one-third of their 12,000-case production a year. Their chardonnays ($9) are also prize-winners. Visitors tour a large downstairs facility boasting oak barrels for chardonnay and concrete holding tanks from Italy. They sample wines upstairs on wine-barrel seats around tables facing the Blue Ridge. Lunch is available from the Oasis Cafe. Oasis also offers a cigar and wine menu on its new Cigar Patio. *(540) 635-7627. Open daily, 10 to 5.*

Shopping. Washington has a few excellent galleries, gift and antiques shops, many open only weekends or by appointment. Our favorite is Elaine Kramer's **Talk of the Town,** a wonderful shop with suave cards, jewelry, T-shirts, accessories, garden implements and such. She recently opened a downstairs gallery. She also connected her store to the showroom of her husband, master cabinetmaker Peter Kramer, "so now we're a mall!" His stunning furniture is much prized locally, and customers like to watch the cabinetmakers at work. **Rare Finds** is an antiques, gift and accessory shop, every bit as eclectic as the room and suite offered upstairs by the expanding Inn at Little Washington. The inn, incidentally, has an ultra-suave new gift shop of inn-related items across Main Street from the main building.

Sperryville harbors good shops, among them **The Church Mouse** gift shop and gallery in a converted country church, **Southern Drawl Artworks** and **Faith Mountain Company,** a two-story ramble of rooms full of dolls, prints, clothing, specialty foods and garden accessories, plus an outlet room in back. Out Route 211 west is the Mountainside Market Shopping Center, new home of **Cabin Fever Books,** relocated from little Washington, and the **Odyssey Collection,** with an exceptional array of jewelry, pottery, paintings and clothing, with a focus on native American and Indonesian art. **Mountainside Market** is a terrific gourmet, whole-foods emporium with a small deli section of prepared sandwiches and pastries. With tables out front, it's something of a community hangout. A sign on the door as you leave warns, "Beware of hitchhiking cats."

In fall, fruit stands pop up everywhere. One of the best is **Sperryville Farms,** where Hazel Hall's jams and jellies are much in demand at $4.95 for a large jar. How many preserves does she put up? "We had a thousand labels printed up last year and we're out of them," her husband responded.

Extra-Special

Laurel Mills Store, Route 618, Castleton.

The one-horse hamlet of Laurel Mills, population 15 (as tabulated on her fingers by Mary Frances Fannon, one of the fifteen), is the unlikely home of a general store, gallery and antiques shop. And Mrs. Fannon, whose husband is a prosperous oil dealer in big Washington, is the unlikely proprietress. When the store, dating to 1877, was about to be converted into apartments, she bought the place and "thought I'd have all this time to sit behind the counter and read books, as the former employees did." Not at all. She stocked the shelves, made sandwiches, lent books, manned the cash register and pumped gasoline, all the while chatting amiably with farmers, truckers and politicians who make the front porch their own and fill their coolers with water from the spring at the side. Mrs. Fannon has since branched out, restoring the stone cellar into an antiques shop and gallery called Down Under Laurel Mills Store. Here she showcases country antiques and one-of-a-kind pieces from area artisans and furniture-makers – an upscale adjunct to a down-home country store. She closed the Down Under store temporarily at the end of 1997, and was undecided what she would do there next.

(540) 937-3015. Open Monday-Saturday 7 a.m. to 7:30 or 8 p.m., Sunday, 8 to 6.

Loudoun County, Va.

Heart of Hunt Country

Less than 40 miles from the Washington Monument and the halls of Congress lies hunt country and some of America's most hallowed ground. The transition from the nation's capital to the horse and hunt capital to the west occurs rather suddenly around Leesburg in eastern Loudoun County. Left behind are Interstate 66, Washington Dulles International Airport and all the trappings of galloping suburbia. Ahead, the farms and pastures of horse country undulate toward the Blue Ridge Mountains.

It's a curious juxtaposition, this feeling of being so near, yet so far – so close to Washington, yet so far removed in body and spirit. The juxtaposition is most striking in Leesburg, the commercial seat of Loudoun County. Docents in Colonial costume spin tales and yarn beside the timbered cottage holding the Loudoun Museum's gift shop as shoppers converge on the municipal ramp parking garage in the center of town. On the outskirts, the congestion of residential subdivisions, highways and strip shopping centers yields abruptly to the tranquility of plantation estates, dirt roads and country stores.

If bustling Leesburg reflects Loudoun's commercial and historic interests, tony Middleburg represents the equine theme so imbued in the fabric of the region. In prime horse and foxhunt country, some of the horses live better than ordinary Americans, as the well-heeled farms around Upperville and Waterford attest. The retailing emphasis (Dominion Saddlery, the Sporting Gallery and The Tack Box Saddlery) and shop names (The Finicky Filly, the Upper Crust) tell the story. The Middleburg Police Department sports a red fox on its insignia. The paintings hung in homes, restaurants, inns and banks adhere to the theme.

Middleburg is the home of The Chronicle of the Horse, the weekly hunt newsmagazine. Leesburg is headquarters of the Masters of Foxhounds Association, the Morven Park Equine Medical Center and the U.S. Combined Training Association. The fact that one of the nation's richest counties declines to pave many of its roads is not a sign of impoverishment – it's simply better for the horses that way.

Horses and horse people are everywhere. That does not mean the casual visitor is likely to see a foxhunt, however. The hundred or so members of each of the dozen hunt clubs in the area usually ride with the hounds three times a week from fall through spring, but their territories are out of the public eye. More visible are the point-to-point races, steeplechase meets and polo games staged weekends in spring and fall.

Hounds lead foxhunters in front of Morven Park mansion in Leesburg.

Its proximity to Washington and its affluent lifestyle draw the rich and famous. The Roman Catholic church in Middleburg was built in 1963 for President John F. Kennedy; his family rented the Glen Ora estate locally and Jacqueline Onassis rode with the Piedmont Fox Hounds and Orange County hunts until just months before her death in 1994. Writer Russell Baker, actor Robert Duvall, philanthropist Paul Mellon, the Smothers Brothers and Washington business magnates like Donald Graham have homes here.

Spectacularly scenic is this rolling, manicured and serenely undeveloped landscape, crisscrossed with the pristine fences and corrals of horse country. It seems more English than England, in the words of one resident Brit, and not just in terms of topography. Loudoun retains its early hamlets, settled variously by Quakers, Scots and Germans. There's no more picturesque a Cotswolds hamlet than tiny Waterford, the entire village a designated National Historic Landmark and preserved as a community of a century ago.

Waterford, Lincoln, Aldie, Philomont, Lucketts, Upperville – these are the quiet places that add dimension to the Loudoun sheen forged by Leesburg and Middleburg. Some of the historic inns that housed the Lees and Washingtons have been upstaged by a flurry of small and promising newcomers. One plantation owned by descendants of America's first organized hunt takes in overnight guests.

The aura of history and the mystique of foxhunting are palpable here. Plantation

The Ashby Inn & Restaurant are headquartered in this white brick house built in 1829.

houses and museums, good restaurants, wineries, shops and recreation facilities help make Loudoun County uncommonly popular with visitors, especially on weekends. This is, after all, a place for escape. And Washington, eminently escapable, is so near yet so far.

Inn Spots

The Ashby Inn & Restaurant, 692 Federal St., Paris 20130.

When John and Roma Sherman purchased in 1984 the property that started this fine inn, it was an old farmhouse with one bathroom. Ten years later, they have an acclaimed restaurant, six guest rooms in the inn and four deluxe suites in building nearby. Theirs is a class act all the way.

The tiny town of Paris and its quiet main street, fortuitously bypassed by busy Route 50, are the setting for the whitewashed brick main inn, built in 1829. Its restaurant draws folks from Washington and beyond, and its four newer suites in the old schoolhouse – 60 paces, as the inn brochure says, down the street – draw from everywhere.

Two upstairs and two down, the suites are of the same configuration but each is painted in a different glowing color, one a dazzling pumpkin gold and ours a restful deep red. The upper rooms come with a cathedral ceiling and a high round window over the door to their own porch, through which we found it entrancing to watch the passing clouds. They could not be more comfortable with queensize canopy bed, fireplace, small TV, telephone, a cushioned window seat, a two-part bathroom with steeping tub and many amenities, including coffee service, and two wing chairs placed strategically in front of the fireplace. We even found a copy of "Middlemarch" in the bookshelf. Biggest treat of all is the covered porch, where we lounged in Adirondack chairs and watched black angus cows roam up and down the hill in back – a truly pastoral scene.

The six rooms the Shermans started with are upstairs in the main inn. Four have private baths. Two "dormer" rooms on the third floor share a full bath and separate water closet; each has its own sink. The grand Fan Room, with palladian window in back and a fan bed handmade by a friend of the Shermans, has its own entrance and balcony. All are handsomely furnished with antiques, oriental rugs and hunting prints.

A small front common room in the inn is available to overnight guests and to those coming in for dinner. Adirondack chairs dot the spacious lawns behind the inn, and the lavish gardens are a joy to behold.

Breakfast involves a choice of juices, muffins, eggs any style, pancakes, homefries, breakfast meats and grilled tomatoes. We particularly enjoyed the tomatoes alongside fat, juicy sausages.

British-born Roma, who hunts with the Blue Ridge Hunt and can tell the guest all about foxhunting, handles the breakfast detail. Husband John, an ex-journalist and Congressional speech writer, is ever present at dinnertime, keeping the four dining rooms running smoothly. He became enamored with food and restaurants during his Army days in France and, despite a high-profile Washington career that caused him to commute until lately, "always knew I eventually wanted to do this." He and Roma do it very well indeed.

(540) 592-3900. Fax (540) 592-3781. Four rooms and four suites with private baths; two rooms with shared bath. Doubles, $100 to $150. Suites, $190. Children over 10. No smoking.

Poor House Farm, 35304 Poor House Lane (Route 756), Round Hill 20141.

"If you have to end up in the Poor House, this is the one." So reads one of the adulatory notes in the guest book in the Cook House Cottage, a deluxe retreat fashioned from the cook house at what was first a plantation and later served as the Loudoun County home for the indigent.

Dottie and Fred Mace, transplants from Machias in the easternmost reaches of Down East Maine, bought the circa 1814 property in 1987, spent four years renovating the cottage and main house, and were on their way to producing some of the most appealing and comfortable B&B accommodations in Loudoun County.

This really is out in the country, an utterly quiet twelve acres reached by dirt roads. About the only "traffic" comes from the horses and hounds of the prestigious Piedmont Fox Hounds hunt club, which passes out front in its thrice-weekly rituals with occasional guests like the late Jacqueline Onassis.

The Maces started with a guest room and a small suite in the main house, both stylishly decorated and designed for comfort, and the romantic brick Cook House Cottage. The latter has an open living room with sofabed and armchair facing a small TV and a huge fireplace, a kitchen and dining area, and a second floor with a queensize pencil-post bed and a clawfoot tub in the bath.

In the works were two more fireplaced rooms in a former slave cottage, a two-level suite with a fireplace in the patent house, and a third bedroom in the main house, all with private baths, although plans were put on hold following Fred's untimely death in 1997. The Maces were expanding the main house to the rear, adding a new kitchen and freeing up space for a library and a cozy sitting room. That's in addition to the existing living room/dining area, a suave space where gorgeous china collections are displayed in cabinets on either side of the fireplace.

A full breakfast is served in the dining area or, our choice, on the wicker-filled side veranda overlooking the plantation outbuildings, rolling farmlands and a farm pond. Amid an abundance of flowering plants, Villeroy & Boch china and fine crystal, we feasted on bowls of perfect fresh fruit (raspberries, blueberries, grapes and sliced peaches), homemade scones and a feather-light quiche with ham, onions, vegetables and cheese. Another of Dottie's breakfast favorites is stuffed french toast with cream cheese.

Birds twittered and flitted in and out of a birdhouse dubbed "Nest and Breakfast" as we took in the tranquil scene from a chintz-covered wicker swing. Who wouldn't think, this is the life?

(540) 554-2511. One room with private bath and two rooms with shared bath in main house; one cottage with private bath. Doubles, $95 to $115 weekends, $85 to $95 midweek. Cottage, $145 weekends, $130 midweek. Two-night minimum weekends in May and October. Children over 12. No smoking.

The Norris House Inn, 108 Loudoun St. S.W., Leesburg 20175.

Elegant common rooms, a long side veranda, award-winning gardens and grounds, and an adjacent tea room are among the attributes of this handsome, three-story brick Federal residence built in 1806 at the edge of downtown Leesburg. Californians Pam and Don McMurray, former traveling business executives, searched the country before settling on Leesburg and the house owned by the Norris family, builders responsible for many of Loudoun County's better houses.

With painstaking renovation and attention to detail, they have imbued the property with taste and charm. Guests enjoy a main-floor library with built-in cherry woodwork, a formal living room with windows onto the side veranda (a particularly photogenic scene), and a formal dining room graced with sterling silver, crystal and antique Royal Doulton china. Especially enjoyable in the urban Leesburg setting is the spacious side yard with prolific gardens, an old magnolia tree and a 65-foot-tall black walnut tree, the biggest in Loudoun County. Take it all in from the wicker furniture on the side veranda, screened from the street by shrubbery and the living-room wing, where libations include wine from nearby Tarara Vineyard.

When it's time to retire, settle into one of six upstairs guest rooms, three with working fireplaces. We enjoyed the Norris Room, "which fulfills most guests' fantasies," in Pam's words. It is pretty in pink, blue and white, with a lacy canopy queensize bed, a plethora of pillows, beautiful sheets and towels, and a Victorian settee. It comes with a fireplace and a refrigerator stocked with Evian water and soft drinks outside the door. The second floor also contains three other bedrooms, one done with a hunt country look and another in English garden decor. The four share two commodious bathrooms. Two smaller rooms on the third floor also share a bath. Potpourri is in all the rooms, and you're apt to find handmade and handpainted chocolates on your pillow when the beds are turned down at night.

Pam serves a breakfast to remember. We liked the oven-baked pancakes, really more like crêpes, filled with fresh berries and served with Smithfield ham sausage patties. A frittata with red, yellow and green peppers, zucchini and roma tomatoes was on tap the next day. These are accompanied by fresh fruit and a special blend of coffee.

The McMurrays acquired the oldest stone building in Leesburg next door. They leased it to Sandy Ruefer, who operates it as **The Stone House Tea Room.** Here you can order cream tea, light tea or full tea ($5 to $12.50), complete with tasty treats like minced ham and pineapple sandwiches, mini-quiches, chocolate zucchini cake and lemon curd tartlets. The goodies are served at calico-clothed tables in two atmospheric rooms, one in which Henry Clay inscribed his name on the wall for posterity. Sandy makes and sells tea cozies, premium teas and gift baskets wrapped with ivy ribbons. She also serves light sandwich and salad lunches.

Veranda overlooks lawn at Norris House.   Breakfast on veranda at Poor House Farm.

You just know the energetic McMurrays aren't finished with the Norris House complex. They already manage and lease out six nearby rooms on weekends, and had their sights on adjacent properties for more accommodations and landscaping. The finicky guest hardly minds the absence of private baths or the lack of a parking area. You simply stash your vehicle a block away in the municipal parking garage and, trite as the saying is, step back in time, elegantly and with style.

(703) 777-1806 or (800) 644-1806. Fax (703) 771-8051. Six rooms with shared baths. Doubles, $105 to $145 weekends, $85 to $100 midweek. Two-night minimum weekends except in winter. No smoking. Tea room by reservation, Friday-Monday noon to 5.

The Longbarn, 37129 Adams Green Lane, Middleburg 20118.
A renovated century-old barn imparts Italian country-style elegance, thanks to Chiara Langley from Bologna, whose sister runs an inn in Italy. Chiara decided to do the same in Hunt Country in 1994 after moving from San Francisco with her American husband Roland, a high-powered Washington business executive. "I fell in love with this house," she explains. "You can see why."

Hidden back in woods and gardens behind a farm pond, The Longbarn is the epitome of a country-elegant retreat. It takes a good imagination to visualize this architect-designed restoration as a barn, despite the abundant barn wood and a loft above the glamorous, soaring living room, with two separate sitting areas below. "This house just keeps going on and on," says Chiara as she shows the "dinette" used for breakfast beside her large kitchen at one end of the structure and the Garden Room guest quarters at the other end. Here, with a view of the garden, you'll find a queensize bed dressed with a floral quilt and a down comforter, with matching pillows and fabric draped behind the bed.

Head upstairs to a loft dining area so big that the Langleys can entertain 40 for a Thanksgiving buffet dinner. It's warmed by a museum-quality art collection and terra cotta sculptures by Italian sculptor Don Gianni Gilli. Chiara enticed him to

Middleburg to create similar works for St. Stephen the Martyr Church, built three decades earlier for the Kennedys. Off the loft is an expansive deck facing gardens, gazebo and pond. Beyond is the Blue Room, named for its blue metal queen bed, again with private bath. Adjacent is a third, twin-bedded guest room that's often pressed into use, when it's not serving as the hostess's laboratory (she used to work as a scientist). You get the idea that Chiara will do more with the house, which has five bedrooms and five bathrooms. At our visit, she was hosting special events and talking of starting a small restaurant in the former milking barn out back, "but I'm going to move slowly."

That's the way to go, given the serene setting and the classical music that plays throughout the house. Chiara serves a lavish continental breakfast – from cereal to croissants, "everything but eggs." She has been known to give complimentary facials to guests, and sometimes a friend presents piano concerts in the great room. "We do enjoy this house," she says. "It's like living inside a violin, with all this wood paneling. It's such a joy to be here."

(540) 687-4137. Fax (540) 687-4044. Three rooms with private baths. Doubles, $100 to $130. No smoking.

Ivy Hall B&B, 12 Burke Circle, Hamilton 20158.
Built in 1881 by a Presbyterian minister who used it as a second home, this handsome Second Empire brick mansion is the largest residence in Hamilton. Young owners Georjan and Graham Overman from Fairfax County gutted the interior and set about its restoration from four apartments, a process that took far longer than planned. They finally opened in late 1997 with six guest rooms.

The structure was very much under renovation at our visit. A construction worker pointed out salient features of the large, high-ceilinged bedrooms with bay windows. Two on the second floor have private baths; four on the third floor share two baths. All have queensize beds and period furnishings. Some have fireplaces, and Georjan hoped eventually to have fireplaces working in all the rooms.

The main floor contains two parlors and a dining room, where Georjan serves a full breakfast. Fruit and homemade breads accompany an egg dish, quiche, french toast or pancakes. Tea is offered in the afternoon. Guests relax outside on a front porch beneath a huge poplar tree.

(540) 338-7426. Two rooms with private baths and four rooms with shared baths. Doubles, $125 to $135.

Welbourne, Welbourne Road, Middleburg 20117.
No inn property in the area better reflects the past than Welbourne, a time warp and truly a special place. It's not for everyone, but comes highly recommended by authorities ranging from Gourmet magazine to innkeeper John Sherman of the Ashby Inn, who advised that if he had to choose one place to spend an evening, it would be here.

Welbourne, a circa-1775 working plantation, is hardly your typical inn. It's a living museum, occupied by the seventh generation of the family of Col. Richard Dulany. He was the Civil War general who in 1840 founded the country's first horse show and hunt club, the Piedmont Fox Hounds. His great-great-grandson, Nathaniel Morison, a Piedmont board member, lives here today with his wife and children.

"I'm the host, not the innkeeper," advises Nat, who is proud that Welbourne has no brochure. To keep the place going, the family started taking in paying guests

Welbourne is a living museum of antebellum plantation life.

"by introduction" in the 1930s; the Morisons continue by word of mouth. "I call the experience faded elegance," says Nat, who fortuitously happened to arrive home in his pickup truck as we stopped by. "If you want interesting history and something real, it's here. If you want TVs and jacuzzis, it's not for you."

"Something real" pervades the entire 550-acre plantation in the heart of prime Middleburg hunt country, reached by the dirt road named Welbourne, County Route 743. The front foyer opens on one side into two living rooms, placed end to end and flanked by a great back porch. The other side opens into the library, where you can spot the date 1862 inscribed in a window and where some of the family's vast collection of miniature giraffes is housed along with such treasures as a sword from the Civil War and Stonewall Jackson's gloves. The library opens into a bedroom of majestic proportions, outfitted in vaguely oriental style with a canopy bed, clawfoot tub, a Tiffany set on the desk and a tray of bottled waters and mixers on a sideboard. F. Scott Fitzgerald and Thomas Wolfe stayed here, and you can, too, for $80 a night. A friend made a plaque to designate this as the Jeb Stuart Room, Nat says in his typical droll style, "but we never used it." So what do they call it? "The End Room."

Upstairs is the Over the Parlor Room, with two twin beds, and another room with two twins joined as a king. In back is the Over the Gun Room, Sherry Morison's favorite, because it gets lots of light. A settee and a window seat take advantage of the view through the vine-covered windows.

The five main guest rooms in the house plus two cottages have private baths; four smaller bedrooms share baths and are used for overflow. All come with family memorabilia reflecting a way of life. "I tell people it's like visiting Grandma's house as a child," says Nat. Most reply that theirs didn't have a house like this.

The household staff, who are like family, help oversee the place while Sherry is at work as a real-estate agent and while Nat is taking care of the 65 "retired" horses he boards here for owners who want them to live out their days with grace. The

Morisons and staff serve a grand southern breakfast amid much silver and china in the dining room, where the table is set for ten to fourteen. Bacon, eggs, sausage, grits and fried tomatoes are the usual fare, with pancakes reserved for Sundays.

When we'd arrived, Nat had said he has five friendly hound dogs that "you have to climb over to get inside," which we did. As we eventually drove away, we happened to look in the back seat of our car. There was Danny the hound, who had jumped in an open window, settled down for a nap and refused to budge. Nat's teenaged son Joshua had to be summoned to get Danny out.

(540) 687-3201. Five rooms and two cottages with private baths; four small rooms with shared baths. Doubles, $80. Cottages, $90. Small rooms, $60. Two-night minimum weekends in spring and fall. Children welcome.

Cornerstone Bed & Breakfast, 16882 Clarks Gap Road, Paeonian Springs 20129.

Molly and Dick Cunningham purchased this homey 1745 farmhouse from Arthur Godfrey's widow, raised their family and started taking in guests in 1989. They were following a precedent set by previous owners who ran first an 18th-century ordinary and later a 19th-century rail-stop guest house. The house occupies a hilltop spread between Leesburg and Waterford, near the Paeonian springs that attracted escapees from the cities in Victorian times.

This is a very much lived-in house, from the expansive front porch with its wicker glider and lineup of mountain bikes ready for the borrowing, to the rear sun room overlooking the pool. Guests also use a formal double parlor with sitting and dining areas, graced with handsome oriental rugs and bouquets of flowers that the Cunninghams, avid gardeners, grow on their property.

Upstairs are two guest rooms with private baths, furnished with antiques and family heirlooms. One in the rear has a queensize bed. The one in front contains a queensize poster bed.

Breakfast could be "about anything," Molly says. Favorites are eggs benedict with asparagus from the garden, corn fritters and blueberry pancakes. Occasionally, the couple serve a Southern breakfast with grits and country ham. The tomato juice is homemade.

(540) 882-3722. Two rooms with private baths. Doubles, $90. No smoking.

Stonegate Bed & Breakfast, 225 West Colonial Hwy., Box 100, Hamilton 20159.

Civil War memorabilia plays a role in this B&B run by retired Navy submariner Bill Gallant and his wife Vicki. They share their fieldstone Georgian home with guests in two bedrooms named for opposing Civil War generals.

The Grant Room has a double poster bed, private bath and quite a collection of hats. "Grant gets the smaller room in Virginia," quips Bill, who leads the way to the Lee Room, with a queensize bed, day bed, sitting area and a large bathroom with a whirlpool tub in what had been a pine-paneled play room. An antique crib holds two dolls in a corner.

A hat stand in the front foyer holds another array of hats. Guests enjoy a formal parlor and a side screened veranda where breakfast is often served, with music provided by chirping birds outside. Typical fare are belgian waffles or cheese strata with grits and ham cornbread.

Two acres of grounds offer lawn and trees, including a rare cucumber magnolia tree that Bill says is ranked No. 1 in Loudoun County and No. 2 in the state. Cajole him into telling tales of his role as a navigation expert on the first patrol of the nuclear submarine USS Lee.

(540) 338-9519. Two rooms with private baths. Doubles, $75 and $90.

Little River Inn, 39307 John S. Mosby Hwy. (Route 50), Box 116, Aldie 20105.
One of the area's earlier B&Bs, this was established by antiques dealer Tucker Withers, who had moved his shop here from Bethesda, Md. He bought his great-uncle's house for the first six rooms of his B&B in 1982. He later added the 1790 patent house and 1810 log cabin across the driveway and the newer Hill House across the road, and now offers an historic complex with ten guest quarters, six with private baths.

Aldie is built around a restored grist mill on the Little River. With his antiques shop and other interests in the hamlet, Tucker seems to be Aldie's chief landholder as well as its main persona. Breakfasts here are legendary as he spins tall tales and local recollections while a varied repast is served. The fare includes juices and fruit, homemade poppyseed muffins or banana bread, cereals, and main dishes like dutch apple baby, local sausages with eggs, baked french toast and pancakes. The meal is taken in a dining area beside the kitchen in the main house, at tables scattered through two atmospheric main-floor common rooms, out back at wrought-iron tables on the flagstone patio or in guest quarters in the outbuildings.

The bedrooms are furnished authentically and rather sparsely with double or twin beds, antique chests and bureaus, quilts, and hooked or braided rugs. One coveted room has a loveseat and a working fireplace. It shares a bath with another bedroom on the second floor, while a third room with double bed has a new private bath. Other chairs in the bedrooms we saw were wood and not the kind you'd feel comfortable sitting in for long. Traffic lumbers along busy U.S. Route 50 just outside. Quieter and more spacious are some rooms in the outbuildings. The Hill House has a fireplaced living room, dining room, kitchen and two bedrooms with private baths, plus a library with a sofabed and half bath. The terraced, two-acre yard contains towering boxwoods, an herb garden and a 50-foot pergola.

(703) 327-6742. Six rooms and cottages with private baths, four rooms with shared baths. Doubles, $80 to $95. Cottages, $145 and $160. House, $190 for two, $30 each additional.

The Red Fox Inn, 2 East Washington St., Box 385, Middleburg 20118.
A handsome four-story stone structure dating to 1728, this represents many people's vision of a large but quaint old inn from days of yore. Billed as America's oldest original inn, it's cloaked in all the appropriate honors, from sometime AAA four-diamond ratings to Travel/Holiday dining awards. Lately it seems to be resting on its laurels – or is it simply too big for its breeches? We found the welcome to be lacking, service indifferent, management not on hand and the guest rooms lack-luster and pricey.

The Red Fox advertises 23 "romantic accommodations" with private baths in the original inn and three nearby buildings. We were given keys to view two "typical" rooms up steep stairs on the third floor. The spacious Bridal Suite had the requisite kingsize canopy bed, a parlor with a sofa, two wing chairs and a huge built-in armoire, hooked rugs on wide-board floors, two TV sets and two telephones. Another kingsize bed graced the corner Martha Washington Room. Its two wing chairs were spaced twelve feet apart on either side of a bureau, facing the bed and not the TV set. The beds were covered with white chenille spreads that looked like Bates, the bathtubs were equipped with hand-held showers, the toiletries consisted of a Gilbert & Soames shoeshine cloth and sewing kit and a plain bar of Camay soap, and the welcoming touch was two bottles of local Meredyth wines in each room, "available for consumption or to take home, $16." An order form outlined fairly basic choices for a continental breakfast, to be delivered to the room at a specified time in the morning for $1 service charge per person. The front desk, which gave our queries short shrift, assured that what we saw was representative of the inn. We would hope that the newer rooms in the Stray Fox Inn annex on a side street behind the inn might be more inviting.

Tourists and big spenders gravitate to the downstairs dining rooms, full of atmosphere, in the main inn. Singles and families like Mosby's Tavern, the inn's barn of a pub nearby at 2 West Marshall St. Lunch and dinner are served in both venues daily.

(540) 687-6301 or (800) 223-1728. Fax (540) 687-6053. Fourteen rooms and nine suites with private baths. Doubles, $135 to $155. Suites, $150 to $245.

Dining Spots

The Ashby Inn & Restaurant, 692 Federal St., Paris.

If the name Paris brings culinary thoughts to mind, the Ashby Inn at the crossroads of this rural town obliges. Innkeepers John and Roma Sherman have created a restaurant of distinction with an unpretentious atmosphere and friendly, flawless service.

About 80 diners are accommodated in four small rooms, ranging from a cozy tavern to a room with high booths and small engraved plaques bearing names of friends and regulars, of which the Ashby seems to have many. A thunderstorm had rendered the handsome, wisteria-covered side courtyard out of commission the night we dined, but the sun porch dressed in white (the Ashby's favorite "color") proved as radiant as a bride. Rotating artworks by a Leesburg artist who paints in Provençe provide color throughout and sell briskly.

The waitress fulfilled a complicated dinner order without taking notes, as did innkeeper John Sherman at breakfast the next day. Great starters on the menu that changes nightly were a chilled carrot puree soup, artistically decorated with citrus crème fraîche, and a caesar salad with grated parmigiano-reggiano and unusual polenta croutons. The seven main dishes typically range from pan-seared bluefish with tomato-caper relish to grilled quail or fillet mignon with bourbon butter. We liked the Atlantic tuna sautéed with extra-virgin olive oil and white beans and the crab cakes (an Ashby Inn classic of 100 percent pure lump crabmeat with a bit of tarragon, moist and tasty as could be), accompanied by sides of potato ribbons and fresh spinach. Zesty grapefruit sorbet was a refreshing dessert from a choice that included crème brûlée, strawberry shortcake with biscuits and bittersweet chocolate torte with chocolate ganache and crème anglaise.

John has lovingly prepared a select wine list, whose spirit and underlying philosophy as described in the introduction are to be applauded. Though there are plenty of choices for a splurge, we felt quite comfortable ordering one of his recommended specials, a Honig sauvignon blanc for $16.50.

The Shermans are a major presence at Sunday brunch (a local institution), cooking omelets and carving ham at the buffet table set up in the sun porch.

(540) 592-3900. Entrées, $16.50 to $24.50. Dinner, Wednesday-Saturday 6 to 9. Sunday brunch, noon to 2:30.

The Lightfoot Cafe, 13 North King St., Leesburg.

This with-it establishment of recent vintage is billed as a progressive American bistro in the heart of old-town Leesburg. It takes its name from Francis Lightfoot Lee, a signer of the Declaration of Independence and a member of the Virginia family for which the town was named. Sisters Carrie and Ingrid Gustavson feature food that is "gently prepared, graciously served and sensibly priced."

In 1998, they were preparing to move around the corner from their original haunt at 2 West Market St. into an ornate 1888 bank building designed by the architect for Washington's Union Station. The two-story high interior with arched windows and marble pillars holds about 200 seats for dining. Carrie said the concept would remain the same – "this simply gives us room to expand."

Ingrid, the chef who trained at the Culinary Institute of America, categorizes her dinner fare under starters, light fare, main plates and pastas – a perfect setup for grazers.

One of us made a satisfying meal out of light offerings. The Lightfoot plate yielded a standout herbed feta cheese dip plus hummus and a tuna and calamata olive spread, served with herbed pita chips and toasted baguette slices. The salad of cafe greens was tossed with soybean sprouts and oven-roasted walnuts. A couple of mini shrimp and crab cakes were fired by a Thai red curry sauce. Large plates ranged from sautéed Swedish salmon with horseradish butter to grilled lamb on a bed of spring greens tossed with everything from asparagus and roasted cumin potatoes to anchovies, wild mushrooms and garlic aioli. The pasta de la casa, also an innovative melange, was hearty and tasty: chipotle fettuccine with shrimp, swiss chard, oyster mushrooms, tomatoes and prosciutto tossed with roasted garlic, extra-virgin olive oil and romano cheese. Desserts ranged from fresh berries to bread pudding, mocha ya-ya and shoofly pie.

(703) 771-2233. Entrées, $15.50 to $17.95. Lunch, Tuesday-Saturday 11:30 to 2:30. Dinner, Tuesday-Saturday 5:30 to 9:30, Sunday 11 to 9.

Tuscarora Mill, 203 Harrison St., Leesburg.

Popularly dubbed Tuskie's but far more sophisticated than that sounds, this was a working grain mill until 1985. Then it was moved a couple of blocks to form part of the restored Market Station shopping and business complex, which also includes a freight depot and station master's house, an 18th-century mill from Pennsylvania and a log cabin from West Virginia. The second-floor restaurant still holds many mill artifacts and equipment. Built into the floor is an old-fashioned scale that used to weigh bags of grain and now is occasionally tested by curious diners. Quilted wall hangings are spotlit on the soaring barnwood walls, and purple lacquered chairs and colorful patterned tablecloths provide plenty of color in the main bar and restaurant. Hanging plants and Victorian street lamp standards make the adjacent garden room, with walls of windows bridging the shopping complex below, a pleasant setting.

The menu covers are as artistic as the presentation of the fare described inside. At lunch, we were impressed by the gazpacho filled with crisp vegetables and topped with a bit of salmon and crabmeat, and a Thai chicken salad. Not so impressive was the wonderful sounding asparagus and crab salad marinated in tequila, lime and cilantro – great tasting but a niggardly portion for $7.95. Only a second helping of crispy rolls with herb butter and an order of frozen lemon mousse with strawberries and golden raspberries separated one of us from starvation.

The dinner menu incorporates many of the lunchtime appetizers and entrées, nearly half of which are available as small plates. Expect things like Japanese-style seared yellowfin tuna with wasabi cream, sesame-roasted salmon with ginger relish, beer-battered soft-shell crabs, grilled pork chops with bourbon-molasses glaze, and dijon-crusted rack of lamb.

Tuskie's wine selections earned the Wine Spectator award of excellence. Interesting imported beers are on tap, available by the pint or glass.

(703) 771-9300. Entrées, $12.75 to $25. Lunch and dinner daily, 11:30 to 9:30 or 10, Sunday from noon.

Back Street Cafe, 4 East Federal St., Middleburg. (540) 687-3122.

Some locals think this Italian-American restaurant and catering establishment of more than ten years' vintage is the best place to eat in town. Certainly its front patio is one of the more jaunty settings, and its salad bar is one of the better we've seen.

It's so good, in fact, that one of us decided to go with the consensus and made a fine lunch of the all-you-can-eat salad bar for $4.95. He got two hefty platefuls of mesclun, spinach and radicchio with a variety of accompaniments, plus such extras as tuna, curried chicken, three-bean and pasta salads. The other was satisfied with a cup of chilled cucumber soup and a toasted BLT with cheese.

Proprietress Tutti Perricone touts creative "pastas" on the dinner menu, ranging from chèvre cappellini and spinach pie to seafood cioppino over linguini and roasted pork chops topped with fontina cheese and served over polenta. The night's specials could be chicken al forno, grilled swordfish with a salsa of sweet bell pepper, avocado, tomato and mango, and strip steak with wild mushroom sauce. Steamed mussels, pizzas and crostini with crab and artichoke are among appetizers and light fare.

All this is served in a simple setting of close-together tables covered with green cloths or print mats, bentwood chairs and lots of ivy painted on the walls.

Entrées, $10.95 to $17.95. Lunch, Monday-Saturday noon to 3. Dinner, 5 to 9 or 10. Closed Sunday. No smoking.

Bistro Belle Fleur, 101 South Madison St., Middleburg.

Retired Washington engineering consultant Brad Johnston had never run a restaurant before, so when he took over the former high-style, northern Italian Tuscany Inn in 1996 he mailed out surveys to everyone in Middlebury to determine what locals wanted in a restaurant. The consensus was "casual, fresh and uncomplicated food, carefully prepared," said Brad, "This bistro is my response to that."

Friends also advised that if he was going to be in the restaurant business, he had to stay on top of it. "So I am," he noted, occupying one of three bedrooms above the restaurant in the 1790 Wright house, the second oldest home in Middleburg.

He lightened up two dining rooms with buttercup yellow walls, mint and yellow plates, and white tablecloths, each topped with a potted plant. He added a pleasant deck for dining outside, and redid the bar area so people who were alone could eat communally at the bar.

And he gave a French accent to the short dinner menu, which he calls modified table d'hôte, $26 for four courses. The meal starts with whims of the chef and soup or salad. There are choices for main courses, among them sautéed scallops, roast duckling and black angus filet mignon. Desserts also are at the whim of the chef.

Early reports were that the food was quite good, so we were surprised to find ourselves almost alone at lunchtime on a summer weekday. Lunch is à la carte and quite brunchy, especially such items as eggs benedict, omelets and shrimp and leek frittata. The menu was fleshed out with French fare like salade niçoise, beef tenderloin salad, "croque-and-a-Coke" and a reuben, the only sandwich.

Along with his quarters, Brad offers two guest rooms. One in which we stayed under the previous owner has a queensize bed with a private bath across the hall. A smaller room has a queen bed and shares a bath with the host-in-residence.

(540) 687-6456. Table d'hôte, $26. Lunch, Thursday-Sunday 11:30 to 2:30. Dinner, Thursday-Sunday 6 to 9. Doubles, $100 and $150.

Fiddler's Green, Loudoun and Stuart Streets, The Plains.

Hunt country foodies trek the back roads to this rambling establishment, perhaps the most visible landmark in The Plains. Beyond a large and attractive trellised

Rear dining room at Fiddler's Green.

patio – an idyllic spot for lunch or dinner – lies a rambling barn of a structure. It holds a lounge in front and an airy, two-story-high rear dining room, where tall windows display the outdoors and a stuffed giraffe in the corner surveys the scene. The decor here is country-stylish in peach and gray, with copper cooking pans hanging on walls and beams, an assortment of upholstered booths and round Shaker-style tables, and colorful, mismatched service plates at each setting.

The short, interesting menu is printed daily. For dinner, look for starters like chilled avocado soup with smoked tomato salsa, smoked trout crostinis with pommery mustard and horseradish, and carpaccio of beef with arugula and parmesan. Caesar salad with grilled shrimp and grilled salmon salad with french beans are listed under light fare. Entrées range from fettuccine with wild mushrooms, parmesan and cream to stuffed quail with country sausage and roasted shallots. Grilled rainbow trout with lemon and parsley, pork loin with honey-mustard sabayon and grilled T-bone with herbed butter are other possibilities. For dessert, how about apple-berry crisp, sour-cream cheesecake with strawberries, lemon chiffon pie with blueberries or tirami su with Bailey's Irish Cream and dark chocolate?

Many of the same items turn up on the appealing little lunch menu.

(540) 253-7022. Entrées, $11.50 to $18. Lunch, Tuesday-Saturday 11:30 to 2. Dinner, Tuesday-Sunday 6 to 9. Sunday brunch, 11:30 to 2.

Diversions

Horses and foxhunting are the chief draws in this area. Unless you have local connections or book with knowledgeable (and well located) innkeepers, you're not likely to see – let alone participate in – a foxhunt, which is a private affair for members and invited (paying) guests. But you may hear or catch a glimpse of one of the area's dozen hunts in pursuit of their quarry, generally three days a week from September to March. You're more apt to catch the equine flavor at one of the horse shows, polo matches or the point-to-point or steeplechase events, usually scheduled for weekends in spring and fall.

Quaint Hamlets and Scenic Drives. From uppercrust and horsey Upperville to antiquey Millbrook to the German enclave of Lovettsville, quaint hamlets abound. Perhaps the most quaint is Waterford (see Extra-Special). To best appreciate the area, shun the main highways and get off the beaten path, which is done easily only if you have a good county road map. Having toured most of the area, we're partial to Routes 662 and 665 out of Waterford, Route 734 (the Snickersville Turnpike) from Aldie to Bluemont, Route 709 (the Zulla Road past huge horse estates south of Middleburg), Route 626 (the Halfway Road) south of Middleburg, and particularly Route 626 (the Pot House Road) north of Middleburg past the Glenwood Racetrack, through forested hill and dale to the fabled and surprisingly remote Foxcroft School for young ladies.

Morven Park, 17263 Southern Planter Road, Leesburg.

Turkey buzzards haunt the fences and two black lion sculptures guard the pillared portico of Morven Park, the stately home of Virginia reform governor Westmoreland Davis, whose widow gave the entire 1,500-acre estate in trust to the public in his memory. The Greek Revival mansion, left as it was and decorated to the hilt in a Renaissance theme, is truly a museum. Four Brabant tapestries – said to be in better condition than those in the Vatican – hang in the front foyer, vying for attention with graceful cherubs over the doorway. Those into showy European decor will enjoy the guided, hour-long tour of the mansion's sixteen restored rooms, rich with Tiffany silver in the formal Jacobean dining room, Hudson River School paintings in the informal dining room, and a Hapsbourg crown mirror in the ladies' drawing room. Those into foxhunting will enjoy the twenty-minute film and the memorabilia in the **Museum of Hounds and Hunting,** which occupies the north wing of the mansion (the fabulously wealthy Governor Davis was master of the Loudoun Hunt). Others like the **Carriage Museum,** built around the 100-vehicle collection donated by a Warrenton horsewoman and on rotating display in the old coach house. It includes everything from a charcoal-burning fire pumper and a ladies' phaeton to surreys and a funeral hearse. The magnificent grounds are known for rare specimen trees, including the oldest small-leaf linden on the East Coast, and the **Marguerite Davis Boxwood Gardens.** The Morven Park Steeplechase Races are held here in mid-October. Nearby is the **Morven Park Equestrian Center.**

(703) 777-2414. Open Tuesday-Friday noon to 5, Saturday 10 to 5, Sunday 1 to 5, April-October, also weekends in November. Adults, $6.

Oatlands, Route 15, Leesburg.

The 1813 plantation house built by a descendant of Virginia's famed Robert "King" Carter is better known and has a higher profile than Morven Park, thanks to its operation by the National Trust for Historic Preservation. It was purchased in 1903 by William Corcoran Eustis (of the Washington banking and Corcoran Gallery family), and Mrs. Eustis used it as her English-style country house during the summer and foxhunting seasons until her death in 1964. Their daughters, who live nearby at Little Oatlands and Oatlands Hamlet, left the house and the 261-acre estate to the National Trust. Unlike Morven Park, this is a livable house rather than a museum, and visitors feel as if "the family has just stepped out for a spell," in the words of our tour guide. You'll see George Washington's dessert service displayed in the formal dining room and William Eustis's foxhunting garb in his dressing room. Four acres of formal, terraced gardens are open to visitors, as is the carriage house visitor center and gift shop.

(703) 777-3174. Open Monday-Saturday 10 to 4:30, Sunday 1 to 4:30, April-December. Adults, $6.

Tarara Vineyard & Winery, 13648 Tarara Lane, Leesburg.

This happening place is the "retirement project" of Margaret and Whitie Hubert, he a developer and contractor in Gaithersburg, Md. They bought a 475-acre corn and soybean farm along the banks of the Potomac River near Lucketts in 1985 and planted more than a hundred acres of grapes, fruit trees and nursery stock. They named it Tarara, Margaret explains, after the river flooded the year they bought the place. "We felt we'd landed and come to rest like Noah's Ark at Ararat up here on this cliff – but we didn't like the rat at the end of Ararat, so we spelled it backward." The centerpiece is the 6,000-square-foot winery and wine cave blasted out of a rocky cliff 30 feet deep, beneath their showplace of a house. The spacious tasting and sales rooms are full of interesting touches, among them the acrylic jewelry and baskets of artist-daughter Karen Hubert of Alexandria and the mixed-media artworks of daughter Martha Hubert. labels. Tarara sells its fruits to the public (we sampled a couple of delicious blackberries prior to the official pick-your-own weekend following our visit) and sponsors special events from wine dinners to grapevine decorating workshops to pig roasts to picnics to pony rides – all designed to bring people to the winery. Its barrel-fermented chardonnay ($12.99) and reserve cabernet ($15.99) are highly rated. We and others are partial to the unique non-vintage charval ($7.99), a sprightly blend of chardonnay and seyval blanc.

(703) 771-7100. Open Thursday-Monday, 11 to 5; weekends only January and February.

Piedmont Vineyards & Winery, Route 626, Middleburg.

Virginia's first commercial vinifera vineyard was established by Mrs. Thomas Furness in 1973 on 37 acres of a pre-Revolutionary farm called Waverly. Her daughter, Elizabeth Worrall, has made a name among connoisseurs for the boutique winery, producing 5,500 cases a year of some of the best white wines in Virginia. The small flagstone-floored tasting room, quite appealing with wicker furniture, is rather like a Southern veranda, and the picnic grounds among the trees beside a pond are enchanting.

(540) 687-5528. Open daily, 10 to 4.

Loudoun claims to be the birthplace of the Virginia wine industry, now the fourth largest in the United States. Other wineries in the area include the long-established but rather primitive **Meredyth Vineyard** south of Middleburg, **Swedenburg Estate Vineyard** east of Middleburg, the scenic **Willowcroft Farm Vineyards** perched alongside Mount Gilead (which offers panoramic Loudoun County views) and the new **Loudoun Valley Vineyards** in Waterford, a state-of-the-art winery with spectacular views and some great-sounding winemaker dinners.

Shopping. Leesburg is the commercial hub of Loudoun County, although most of its major and basic businesses have moved to strip plazas south and east of town. The Old Town downtown section has attracted antique dealers, some of whom show at **Leesburg Downtown Antiques** at 27 South King St. and the **Leesburg Antique Gallery of Shoppes** in an old church at 7 Wirt St. Also of interest are **Leesburg Vintner,** which serves up great deli sandwiches along with wines and beverages; the **Kitchen Shop,** and **Yesterday's Memories** (with a native American and New Age theme). The feline-lover among us had a field day at **Classy Cat Gifts,** while the other checked out the Civil War titles at **Clio's History Bookshop.** Stores seem to come and go in Leesburg's restored **Market Station** at the edge of downtown.

Tiny Middleburg is perhaps of more appeal to visiting shoppers. Its quaint, tree-lined downtown is chock-a-block full of stylish stores, many with an equine theme, and we were impressed with the showy potted hibiscus trees placed on the four corners at Washington and Madison streets. Established in 1956, **The Fun Shop** with the curious name is a mini-department store in a warren of rooms, stocking everything from table linens and clothing to toys, books, lamp shades and notions (it even offers a toll-free 800 phone number for customers from afar). Also quite big and au courant is **Gourmet Kitchen Plus,** a dream store for those interested in culinary matters. The **Irish Crystal Company** is the first store in Virginia to carry the fine Tyrone Crystal and, unlike most shops of its ilk, the owner urges visitors to touch the merchandise. **The Finicky Filly** offers wonderful women's wear; it's the female counterpart to venerable horseman Tully Rector's men's store. He also offers a "painting of your horse" as one of the services of **The Shaggy Ram,** specialist in country antiques, hunt items and English imports. **A Little Something from Middleburg** offers home furnishings and accessories. English and European garden antiques and furniture are offered at **Wickets Garden Style.** Equestrian books are a special feature of **The Book Chase.** Pick up a croissant or a sandwich at **The Upper Crust,** an excellent bakery.

Extra-Special

Waterford. Every state should have a Waterford, but precious few do. Reminiscent of the British Cotswolds, this treasured community of a few hundred souls is no longer an endangered species, having been saved by the Waterford Foundation. The must-see town, settled by Quakers in 1733, is one of the few communities totally encompassed on the National Register of Historic Places. Waterford's Quakers and thriving free black community supported the Union in the Civil War, when it was harassed both by Union forces because of its location and by Confederate forces because of its beliefs. Today, Waterford's buildings and rolling fields, wedged into a fold between hills, look much as they did a century ago. As you drive through on High Street (Route 662 northwest of Leesburg), don't make the mistake of thinking the town consists of a few nice houses, the Catoctin Presbyterian and Waterford Baptist churches and the red-brick Loudoun Mutual Insurance Co. Instead, head west down one of the side streets to Second and Main streets. Here you'll find a remarkable variety of log, stone and brick houses, the Peaceable Kingdom gift shop, the Waterford Forge, the mapmaker-historian and who knows what all. On a weekday you're likely to have the place to yourself. But come the first weekend of October, thousands are drawn here for the Waterford Foundation's annual house tour and crafts exhibit, one of the nation's best juried shows.

Potomac and Shenandoah rivers converge at Harpers Ferry.

Harpers Ferry, W.Va.
Worth the Voyage

The view of the convergence of the Potomac and Shenandoah rivers here is "one of the most stupendous scenes in nature – worth a voyage across the Atlantic."

So said Thomas Jefferson back in 1783. The view of Harpers Ferry continues to astound travelers, especially those emerging from the Baltimore-Washington megalopolis and suddenly confronting a different vista: one of rivers slicing between mountains, endless greenery and a rugged aspect all around.

Harpers Ferry, a boomtown that died after the Civil War, remains much the way it was during the days of John Brown's infamous raid. An old, hilly, European-looking town that never ceases to amaze, it's the start and the heart of this area known locally as West Virginia's Eastern Panhandle.

Beyond lies busy Charles Town, the Jefferson County seat where John Brown was tried and hanged. Young surveyor George Washington purchased his first land and settled members of his family here in 1748. More Washingtons lived here and more are buried in the Zion Episcopal Church graveyard here than anywhere in the country. Today, it's also distinguished by more traffic lights per capita than any small town we know of.

Make a triangle – that's the route the roads seem to take – from Harpers Ferry to Charles Town around to Shepherdstown, West Virginia's oldest town. It's across the Potomac from Sharpsburg, Md., and the bloody Antietam National Battlefield (see Frederick chapter). A quaint college town, Shepherdstown has retained the charm that bustling Charles Town seems to have lost.

This area is paradise for mountain climbers, hikers along the old Chesapeake & Ohio Canal towpath, Civil War buffs and the rest of us. Country inns and B&Bs arrived here late (about 1985), but seem to be making up for lost time. Zoning limits their presence in most of Harpers Ferry, the soul of the area.

The National Park Service has restored Harpers Ferry's lower town, which serves as a national model of historic preservation and draws more than a million visitors annually. Despite all the people, the view and the surroundings are just as Thomas Jefferson said they were.

Inn Spots

Except for the ancient Hilltop House, something of a time capsule that is appropriate for Harpers Ferry, accommodations here are generally limited to B&Bs of no more than two guest rooms. There is a new Comfort Inn, but that's uptown in Bolivar. Country inns and B&Bs prevail in Charles Town and Sheperdstown, each about six miles away as the crow flies.

Briscoe House, 828 Washington St., Box 1024, Harpers Ferry 25425.

The "Brit B&B" license plate on their van tells where Jean Hale's loyalties lie. She and her American husband Lin traveled around the world during his Army career, which is "why we needed a twenty-room house" for all their furnishings. In 1995, they bought the substantial 1880s residence known locally as the old Briscoe house, once the home of two black professors at the local college, and turned it into one of the area's more comfortable B&Bs.

The Hales put up guests in two front suites on the second floor, both with private baths and TV. The Ivy Room has a sitting room in front, an ivy-patterned comforter on the queen bed and sprightly décor. The Rose Room is named for the flowers on its comforter and pillows, has a sitting area and a mirrored jacuzzi tub in the bathroom.

The front parlor/dining room are outfitted in Victoriana. In her enormous kitchen, Jean prepares a four-course English breakfast: fresh fruit, coffee cake, cereal and, often, ham and eggs with fried potatoes. Guests "rave about her breakfasts," her husband advises.

(304) 535-2416. Two suites with private baths. Doubles, $85 weekends, $75 midweek.

Harpers Ferry Guest House, 800 Washington St., Box 1079, Harpers Ferry 25425.

This B&B looks and smells new. And it is. Al and Allison Alsdorf obtained

photos of the original Victorian house on the property, which had burned ten years earlier, and rebuilt it to look much the same.

They offer three sprightly bedrooms with queensize beds, private baths and TV sets. One on the main floor is designed for the handicapped. Quilts top the poster reproduction beds that were made in nearby Berkeley County. Alison is particularly

Wide front porch leads into Ransom-Armory House.

proud of her West Virginia kitchen, built by a retired industrial-arts teacher and his wife. The adjacent dining room is the setting for some grand breakfasts. Al cooks omelets and Allison prepares cornmeal or blueberry waffles to accompany juice, fruit and banana or lemon-poppyseed muffins.

Because of its newness, rooms in this house seem bigger than in the average Victorian. There's a large living room with TV. "Guests can be as private or as much a part of the house as they wish," says Alison.

The Alsdorfs moved in 1993 from New Paltz, N.Y., when Al was transferred to Gaithersburg, Md. He likes trains and, when he came across the railroad bridge, Harpers Ferry reminded him of home.

(304) 535-6955. Three rooms with private baths. Doubles, $85 weekends, $60 midweek. Children over 10. No smoking.

Ranson-Armory House, 690 Washington St., Harpers Ferry 25425.

A good-looking 1830 house, its original portion one room deep, was turned into a B&B in 1990 by John and Dorothy Hughes, he a retired teacher from Silver Spring, Md., and she lately the president of the state B&B association.

They offer two guest rooms with private hall baths. The room to the rear, with a view of Maryland Heights, has windows in four directions because of the one-room-deep layout. An antique quilt covers its double bed. A smaller front room, with windows on two sides, looks toward Loudoun Heights.

A stained-glass front door opens onto a big front porch full of rockers, well screened from the street by shade trees. Guests also relax in the parlor and on a flagstone terrace beside the lovely rear gardens.

Breakfast is served in an interesting-looking dining room with a fan-shaped window and balloon curtains. Dorothy's mainstay is stuffed french toast ricotta, accompanied by warmed maple syrup, grits or home fries and sausage. Other possibilities are an egg casserole or individual soufflés.

(304) 535-2142. Two rooms with private baths. Doubles, $75 to and $80 weekends, $65 midweek. No smoking.

Lee-Stonewall Inn, 1145 Washington St., Harpers Ferry 25425.

Opened in 1990, this is the most historic of Harpers Ferry's B&Bs. The Georgian-Federal brick structure dates to 1795 and is on the National Register. It takes its name from builder Richard B. Lee and Stonewall Jackson, who is believed to have occupied it briefly during the Civil War.

Gary and Regina Sharp, he a school guidance counselor in Virginia's Loudoun County and she an assistant principal in Washington County, Md., offer two guest accommodations with private baths. One on the second floor has a queen canopy bed, an antique rocking chair, an old fainting couch and stenciling around the chair rail. On the third floor is a two-bedroom suite, also decorated in Colonial style with antique brass and high-back oak beds.

Guests relax on the back porch or on lawn chairs in the back yard, where chickens were clucking around beneath a fragrant weeping myrtle imported from England and as old as the house. They also enjoy the fireplace in the French-style living room, which has interesting tapestry window treatments.

A hearty country breakfast, served fireside in the dining room, might start with chilled peach soup pureed with cream cheese or, in cool weather, baked apples. House specialties are eggs benedict and lemon-anise waffles.

Because they are located just across the town line in Bolivar and are not subject to Harpers Ferry's zoning regulations, the Sharps were thinking of adding two more rooms with private baths.

(304) 535-2532. One room and one suite with private baths. Doubles, $80.

Hillbrook Inn on Bullskin Run, Summit Point Road, Route 2, Box 152, Charles Town 25414.

This beauty of a Tudor mansion on fifteen levels and seventeen rural acres is an anomaly. It has earned national awards and magazine coverage, and yet is little known within the area and its brochures are not often available through visitor centers. Perhaps that's because innkeeper Gretchen Carroll is out to attract an upscale clientele that appreciates a richly furnished house in the English country style and prix-fixe gourmet dinners and is willing to pay for the privilege.

Only one room wide and in places only one room high, the stuccoed house of thirteen gables, timbered walls, windows with more than 2,000 panes of glass and an unmistakable English look tiptoes up a hillside. That makes things mighty interesting, inside and out.

Start in the living room, twenty feet high, with tall mullioned windows on two sides. It contains a battery of art objects, elegant furnishings and oriental rugs characteristic of the entire manor. Fireplaces on either end of the room add warmth in winter. Up one level from the living room is the large Bamford Suite with fireplace and porch, a queen bed in the corner and an old Vuitton steamer trunk for a luggage rack. The suite and the Cottage, reached by a private entrance and known as the room of the nine oriental rugs, command top dollar. The Cottage offers a queen bed, a glass-front wood stove, a red velvet chair and two side chairs, a balcony, and a deep red and blue paisley decor.

Tudor-style Hillbrook Inn on Bullskin Run offers lodging and fine dining.

Other rooms include Locke's Nest, entered high above the living room and harboring two beds with thick brass headboards that are polished every other week. The tub and the toilet retain the colors of what had been an all-purple bathroom. Two smaller rooms, the queen-bedded Lookout and the Point with antique double bed, are tucked into the eaves. Sloping walls create odd angles and spaces in the former, windows look out in three directions, and a Thai spirit house intricately carved in teak sits atop an ancient English oak table. A six-foot-long tunnel leads to the Point, which reflects the innkeeper's passion for oriental rugs, rich but dark fabrics and upholstery, and rare paintings from Europe and Asia.

The public spaces are sights to behold, especially the dining room that is higher than it is wide, where a seven-course dinner is served at 8 o'clock (see Dining Spots). There's a library full of interesting books. A smashing tavern with a box-beam ceiling, a grand piano and lots of wing chairs looks like an English gentleman's club. The dining porch used for breakfast overlooks gorgeous back lawns, an old boxwood grove, a tall willow tree and a duck pond. A full country breakfast features pecan pancakes with ginger butter, and french toast tatiana, served with warm cranberry-orange syrup and sour cream. The inn serves lunch by reservation, and English teas are offered Sunday afternoons from November to April at $20 a head.

Fresh flowers and a small box of Lake Champlain Chocolates from Vermont are in each room. The guest book is full of raves, the theme being "a special, magical place."

(304) 725-4223 or (800) 304-4223. Fax (304) 725-4455. Six rooms and one suite with private baths. MAP: Doubles, $370 to $430 weekends, $250 to $300 midweek.

The Carriage Inn, 417 East Washington St., Charles Town 25414.
New owners have added a personal welcome and creature comforts to this B&B in need of the caring touch of innkeeper/owners in residence. Al and Kay Standish from northern Virginia bought the establishment in 1996, did some refurbishing, added personal possessions and turned a rear carriage house into a suite.

Built in the early 1800s, the corner house hides behind huge shade trees on the town's main street. The former owner, a contractor, is credited with devising the sunken private baths found in former stairwells to the rear of the house. He also made the beds by hand. Named for the color of their wallpaper, the five guest rooms in the main house come with full baths and queen four-poster beds. Four have gas fireplaces. Some have day beds or a velvet loveseat with two side chairs, and one has its own enclosed porch with TV and refrigerator. The Blue Room has one of the highest step-up beds we've seen. You'd never know the Lavender Room on the third floor was once the attic; it has a four-poster bed, a sitting room with a daybed and a settee, and a franklin stove.

The Standishes converted the carriage-house apartment in which previous managers resided into a three-room suite. The main floor has a living room with a sofabed and a dining area, while the pine-paneled upstairs bedroom contains a queensize bed.

Guests enjoy a heavily shaded front veranda with a swing and a deep back yard. Breakfast with china and crystal is served at one large table and two small tables in the dining room. It includes tropical fruit juice, sliced fruit, and perhaps German baked eggs and sausage plus double chocolate-banana muffins.

Afternoon tea is available in the drawing room, which has twelve-foot-high ceilings, a piano and TV.

(304) 728-8003 or (800) 867-9830. Five rooms and one suite with private baths. Doubles, $115 weekends, $75 midweek. Suite, $135 weekends, $95 midweek. Children in carriage house suite only. No smoking.

Washington House Inn, 216 South George St., Charles Town 25414.

Built at the turn of the century by Samuel Washington, grand-nephew of the first president, this fine example of late Victorian architecture offers six rooms with private baths, a turret and a wraparound veranda dressed in wicker. Owners Mel and Nina Vogel, who moved with two teenagers from suburban Washington, have added fine antiques, family heirlooms and handmade quilts crafted by a distant relative from Charleston.

Unusual corner fireplaces – two of seven in the three-story house – back up to each other in the pink and maroon parlor and the pink lace-clothed dining room, which is set with Limoges china. Ensconced in the turret, the parlor is the place for games like backgammon and cribbage.

The dining room, with regal oxblood-colored walls, is the setting for Nina's breakfasts. Her cooking interests were inspired by her parents' restaurant in Ohio. Expect juice, fresh fruit, gourmet coffees and a main dish like caramelized french toast, sausage and eggs or cinnamon raisin french toast stuffed with cream cheese.

A prized original lithograph of Abraham Lincoln graces the downstairs foyer near the carved oak staircase. The Lavender Room in the turret and the Rose Room next door are decorated in pale colors, as is the third-floor Turret Room. More vivid is the Green Room, done in hunter green with a four-poster bed, desk and two side chairs. The walnut sleigh bed in the Dormer Room is topped by a faux canopy of hunter green moire and covered with an embroidered coverlet accented with a hand-crocheted throw made by Nina's mother. Some rooms have fireplaces and casablanca paddle fans. The modern baths have pedestal sinks and showers. Except for prized personal possessions, most of the furnishings are for sale.

(304) 725-7923 or (800) 297-6957. Fax (304) 728-5150. Six rooms with private baths. Doubles, $125 weekends, $75 midweek. Children over 10. No smoking.

New and old merge nicely at rural Cottonwood Inn.

The Cottonwood Inn, Route 2, Box 61-S, Charles Town 25414.

Black and white cows from the farm up the road were lying in the shade beside Bull Skin Run as we approached this nearly 200-year-old farmhouse out in the countryside about five miles east of town. Joe and Barbara Sobol left his oil and gas business in the Texas-Louisiana area in 1995 to launch a new business here – the production of European video travelogues in a studio at the rear of an existing B&B.

The six-acre property beside a stream, graced with prolific flowers, is quiet as can be. The seven guest rooms with private baths vary widely. Some, up an original staircase, are cozy and historic with clawfoot tubs, old beds and fireplaces. Others up narrow stairs in an older section are carpeted. One with a kingsize bed, a day bed and a full bath is cheery with white walls. A 1988 addition holds modern rooms that are quite inviting in their newness. All rooms have television, queen or king beds, sitting areas and air-conditioning.

Both the guest rooms and common rooms are designed for comfort. There's a large, beautiful living room with a grand piano in a corner and a well-stocked library at the far end. Its floral blue carpet picks up the pale yellow and apricot colors on the walls. Windsor chairs are at tables in the beamed dining room, site of a huge brick fireplace with a raised hearth and butter molds hanging along a beam.

Breakfast consists of juice, fresh fruit and an entrée such as puff pastry with smoked turkey and cheese or an egg, onion and cheese casserole, plus orange-blueberry muffins or apple-cherry coffee cake. Afternoon refreshments are taken on Adirondack chairs on the front lawn, looking toward those cows lazing beside the creek.

(304) 725-3371 or (800) 868-1188. Seven rooms with private baths. Doubles, $75 to $105. Two-night minimum in October and holiday weekends. No smoking.

Thomas Shepherd Inn, German and Duke Streets, Box 1162, Shepherdstown 25443.

An early American but comfortable feeling pervades this cream-colored brick Federal house at the main intersection in Shepherdstown, West Virginia's oldest town. The warmth comes from Margaret Perry, the hospitable hostess known for caring touches and gourmet meals.

The B&B, opened in 1985, has a rich, formal living room furnished with wing chairs, oriental scatter rugs and decanters of sherry at the ready. There are two dining rooms, the better to serve people at different times. Another favorite gathering space is the upstairs library, with a small TV and a stash of material on the area. Off it is a porch with rockers and lots of plants overlooking the rear garden.

Of the seven guest rooms, we liked Room 6 in back looking out over the garden; it comes with a canopied bed, a full bath and a loveseat. Other rooms vary: one is rather small with a double bed, another has a double and a twin, and still another a sleigh bed. A front corner room offers a partially canopied bed, two upholstered chairs and a large full bath with big, thirsty towels. A new bedroom on the main floor is bright and airy, furnished in wicker with a sitting area and TV. It overlooks the side garden.

Breakfasts here are special. "There's not a morning I don't get up and can't wait to get to the kitchen," says Margaret. The meal might begin with chilled orange-blueberry soup garnished with crème fraîche or a nectarine poached with ginger. Baked eggs florentine, omelets with asparagus and mushrooms, sour cream pancakes with homemade sage sausages or bread pudding with raspberry sauce follow. Herbed basmati rice with soy sauce and garnishes like nasturtiums, pansies and calendulas from her gardens could accompany.

Margaret, whose love for cooking is exceeded only by her hospitality, plies arriving guests with cookies and sherry and will fix dinner for guests by prior arrangement. She has been known to make little gifts of soaps and bags of potpourri for departing guests.

(304) 876-3715 or (888) 889-8952. Seven room with private baths. Doubles, $95 to $125 weekends, $85 to $95 midweek. Two-night minimum on weekends. Children over 8. No smoking.

Bavarian Inn and Lodge, Route 480 (Postal Route 1, Box 30), Shepherdstown 25443.

This was the area's first, starting as a restaurant in 1962 and adding lodging in chalet-style buildings overlooking the Potomac River in 1981 and a conference center in 1994.

Though the restaurant (see Dining Spots) remains the priority of Munich-born owner Erwin Asam and his English wife Carol, their overnight accommodations are attractive as well. Four Bavarian-style, beamed chalets bear exterior murals of mountains and castles. They contain 39 well-appointed rooms with queensize four-poster beds (mostly canopied), sitting areas with TV, many with sleep sofas, and private balconies high above the Potomac. Twenty-six have gas fireplaces and eighteen offer jacuzzi baths.

From our balcony we could watch canoeists below on the river and rabbits scurrying along the hillside and hear lovely bird calls at both dusk and sunrise. Only the noise of traffic from the nearby highway bridge pierced the tranquility. Inside our spacious, stucco-walled room in white and light brown were a couple of welcoming apples, two wing chairs and an archway to the entry and the bath, which included a dressing room with extra vanity and assorted Lord & Mayfair toiletries.

Thirty more rooms, nine with fireplaces and jacuzzis, plus a conference and exercise facility, are located in a newer building between the chalets and Route 480.

There also are three guest rooms in the main greystone inn and restaurant, uphill from the chalets. Twelve acres of nicely landscaped grounds include a secluded swimming pool. Breakfast is available at hotel prices in the restaurant.

(304) 876-2551. Fax (304) 876-9355. Seventy-two rooms with private baths. Doubles, EP, $115 to $175 weekends, $85 to $135 midweek.

Dining Spots

Hillbrook Inn on Bullskin Run, Summit Point Road (Route 13), Charles Town.

We don't know whether the setting or the food is more the attraction here. It could be both, but who knows? Only the flush tend to eat here because of the pricing structure, which commands a hefty $60 for a prix-fixe dinner on weekdays, $70 on weekends (the price includes table wines poured throughout the meal). Innkeeper Gretchen Carroll says the experience is designed to be relaxed and unpretentious, rather like a dinner party in a private home.

The dining room in this stunning Tudor mansion is taller than it is wide or long, which makes for an interesting sense of space. A brass chandelier comprised of old oil lamps casts soft shadows over a handful of tables showing the patina of old wood and set with brass service plates. Flickering candles in hurricane chimneys are reflected in the silver and crystal and in a brass teapot collection on the buffet, and the gold print on the wallpaper shimmers by candlelight. The adjacent breakfast porch, used for dinner overflow, overlooks the rear lawns and gardens that are spotlit at night.

Executive chef Christine Hale, a Pittsburgh Culinary Institute graduate who trained in France, oversees the prix-fixe, single-choice menu. The seven-course dinner is served at individual tables at 8 o'clock. It might start with white button mushrooms in a garden herb marinade, curried onion soup and penne with a tomato-caper sauce. The main event could be grilled marlin with tarragon butter, teamed with jasmine rice, sautéed squash with thyme, pernod cucumbers and oil-roasted green beans. A salad of red leaf lettuce with avocado and mango follows. The meal concludes with smoked havarti cheese with bremner wafers, honeydew melon and red grapes, and a dessert like poached pears with caramelized pecans, chocolate ganache and strawberry coulis.

A prix-fixe lunch ($20) offering a sampling of the inn's specialties is served by reservation on the enclosed dining porch or on the garden terrace.

(304) 725-4223 or (800) 304-4223. Prix-fixe, $60 to $70. By reservation only. Lunch daily, noon to 2. Dinner, nightly at 8. No smoking.

Yellow Brick Bank, 201 West German St., Shepherdstown.

Bright red apples hang from ficus trees in this colorful – make that flamboyant – restaurant inside an old yellow brick bank. In the main dining room, huge old posters decorate the pink walls, the chairs are pink and mauve, and the high coffered ceiling is edged in handpainted blue clouds. A casual dining room and bar, done up in white wicker, has tall windows onto a side patio.

At lunch, one of us enjoyed a bowl of sweet corn and jalapeño chowder, loaded with chopped ham and tomatoes and packing a spicy wallop, and an appetizer of shiitake mushrooms on lemon thyme toast. The other chose pesto pasta with chopped tomatoes, served in a big bowl with French bread alongside. We had no room left for desserts, among them lemon cheesecake with caramelized mascarpone, coffee ice cream with kahlua and coconut, and Mexican chocolate bread pudding with crème fraîche. On weekends, there are two sampler plates of four desserts each.

The dinner menu offers stellar pastas as well as entrées ranging from grilled salmon with dijon-balsamic glazed to grilled rack of lamb with curried mango chutney and creamed cucumbers. Bluefin tuna grilled with tamari and freshly grated horseradish, grilled rainbow trout with mango relish and grilled hanger steak are among the choices. The cooking here is assertive, to go along with the eclectic atmosphere.

A wood-burning oven and an applewood grill were being installed in a large kitchen addition at our latest visit to add even more contemporary flair to the menu.

(304) 876-2208. Entrées, $15 to $23. Lunch, Monday-Saturday 11:30 to 4:30. Dinner from 5. Sunday brunch, 11 to 4.

Bavarian Inn, Route 480, Shepherdstown.

This well-known dining room attracts diners from near and far. It's not the kind of place to which we were attracted for a Saturday lunch – we stopped, looked at the menu, saw all the staff and customers in dressy attire and decided to go on to a more casual place where we could eat outside. But it fit the bill perfectly for dinner at another visit.

The main dining room in the living room of the original greystone mansion resembles the interior of a Bavarian lodge with paneled walls, beamed ceiling, deer-antler chandeliers, a deer head over the huge stone fireplace and racks with displays of Bavarian china and beer steins. We preferred the pleasant, glassed-in terrace dining area with windows onto the gardens.

The extensive dinner menu covers all the bases, including Bavarian, continental, American, cold platters and "lean and healthy."

When in Bavaria, do as...and one of us did. Wiener schnitzel with red cabbage and pan-fried potatoes with caraway seeds was the real thing. The other sampled the grilled medallions of pork tenderloin with red cabbage and green beans, which was unmemorable. Good German bread arrived as we sat down. A small slab of the chef's mellow veal, liver and duck pâté with all the trimmings and house salads tided us over until the entrées came. A Bavarian nut ball – vanilla ice cream rolled in peanuts and topped with chocolate sauce and coconut flakes – was not cold enough but quite good.

There are interesting, reasonably priced international coffees and after-dinner drinks. You might want to adjourn downstairs to the **Rathskellar,** a very alpine place that wraps around the bar and offers weekend entertainment.

(304) 876-2551. Entrées, $12.75 to $21.95. Lunch, Monday-Saturday 11:30 to 2:30. Dinner, 5 to 10, Sunday noon to 9.

Charles Washington Inn, 210 West Liberty St., Charles Town.

The oldest home in Charles Town on property purchased from Charles Washington (for whom the town was named), this was known as the Tiffin House for most of its 203 years. New owners gave it a facelift and a new name, and expanded the dining capacity. Meals are served in three small fireplaced rooms, a casual one on the main floor and two fancier rooms upstairs, decorated in what the owners call "Colonial romantic" style. There are also a bar and a new garden dining room.

Crab cakes and veal dishes are the specialties, but the menu changes seasonally. For dinner, you might find cajun scallops, broiled salmon with lemon-dill beurre blanc, chicken sautéed with artichoke hearts and sundried tomatoes, veal saltimbocca, prime rib or filet mignon béarnaise sauce.

Start with stuffed mushroom caps or smoked trout. Finish with coconut cake, fresh strawberries or chocolate pâté with raspberry sauce.

(304) 725-4020. Entrées, $13.95 to $17.95. Lunch, 11:30 to 4. Dinner nightly, 5 to 9 or 10.

The Anvil Restaurant, 1270 Washington St., Harpers Ferry.

This oldtimer in the uptown Bolivar section packs in the tourists in a pub out front, a big early American dining room to the rear and an outdoor patio beyond. Although the dining room and patio were empty at our visit, there was a waiting line for lunch in the crowded pub and we couldn't wait.

Too bad, for this is considered the best place to eat in town. The menu is traditional continental-American. Seafood linguini en papillote is the house specialty. Blackboard specials at our visit were baked potato soup, chicken roulade and blackened grouper. Other entrées could be crab cakes, stuffed or broiled flounder, salmon en croûte, chicken parmigiana, veal cordon bleu and filet mignon.

Starters include clam chowder, crab soup, cheese sticks, shrimp cocktail and egg rolls. Among desserts are cheese cake, carrot cake and midnight chocolate cake.

(304) 535-2582. Entrées, $9.95 to $17.95. Lunch, 11 to 4:30. Dinner, 5 to 9 or 10. Closed Monday.

Diversions

Harpers Ferry National Historic Park, (304) 535-6223. The immensely picturesque area that Thomas Jefferson said was "worth a voyage across the Atlantic" to see is seen today by more than one million visitors annually, yet remains little changed from the 19th century. From an information center west of town (parking, $3 individual, $5 per carload), buses shuttle visitors every five minutes into the historic lower town, which is blissfully tranquil because vehicular traffic is light.

The town of Harpers Ferry boomed after it was designated a federal armory and arsenal, manufacturing many of the munitions used in the War of 1812 and the Civil War. The buildings were the targets of abolitionist John Brown's raid, aimed at arming the slaves for insurrection. The town of 3,000 declined rapidly because of destruction wrought by the Civil War and repeated flooding. It was a sleepy little hamlet when taken over by the National Park Service in 1944 and restored in what has since become a national model for historic park preservation. The park's four themes are industry, John Brown's raid on the arsenal, the Civil War and black history. The last is represented by Storer College, a normal school for the education of freed blacks that started in an abandoned armory dwelling in the upper town. Park employees in period clothing present living-history programs and guided tours in the streets and restored buildings during summer and on certain weekends.

Most of the sites are clustered along Shenandoah Street in **Lower Town.** The old Stage Coach Inn is now the Harpers Ferry Historical Association's excellent bookstore and an information center. The Master Armorer's House is a museum on gunmaking. Stop at the old dry goods store, where the 1850s price list puts neckties at 35 cents each. John Brown's Fort is the old armory firehouse where he

Shenandoah Street retains feeling of yesteryear in Harpers Ferry's Lower Town.

and his followers were captured. Other attractions include the Blacksmith Shop, Provost Office, John Brown Museum, Whitehall Tavern and a confectionery.

From the lower town, the town marches in European fashion up a steep hill without a 20th-century intrusion. The **Stone Steps** – we counted 56 of them – begin a trail to the upper town. A sign says the trail takes 45 minutes and is steep at the start, but the views of rivers, bridges, lower town and surrounding heights "are well worth it." First comes the 1775 **Harper House,** built by the town's founder, now restored as an 1850s tenant house to represent the crowded conditions and lack of housing in the town's industrial heyday. Opposite are spring houses and root cellars, small caves carved into the shale cliffside. Next is St. Peter's Roman Catholic Church, an 1833 stone church and a commanding presence, but difficult to reach by car for Sunday Masses. Beyond are the ruins of St. John's Episcopal Church and **Jefferson Rock,** vantage point for the "stupendous" view.

Other Towns. Charles Town, the busy county seat, does not have much to commend it to visitors unless they are Washington family buffs or racetrack fans. A Washington descendant still lives in Harewood, the 1770 home of Samuel Washington, but all six Washington family homes are privately owned and not opened to the public. A brochure illustrates a walking tour of historic points so spread out that most prefer to drive. Some are satisfied simply viewing the collections at the Jefferson County Museum. Thoroughbred racing is featured at the Charles Town Races and sports car racing at the Summit Point Raceway. More to our liking is quaint **Shepherdstown,** endowed with street after street of historic homes, good shopping and the campus of Shepherd College. Current and foreign films are shown in the Old Opera House, and the Contemporary American Theater Festival presents four new plays each July at Shepherd College.

Hiking. The **Appalachian Trail** crosses the Potomac on the same railroad-pedestrian bridge that tourists use to get near the railroad tunnel and onto the Chesapeake & Ohio Canal towpath. Favorite hikes are to Maryland Heights and

Overlook Cliffs, a four-mile round trip that rewards the hardy with the view of Harpers Ferry that is the trademark of the area. Other trails lead to Virginius Island, Jefferson Rock, Loudoun Heights and Bolivar Heights.

Shopping. We weren't particularly impressed with a lot of the shops in Harpers Ferry, most of them geared to tourists and the better ones tucked away out of sight. But there are exceptions: the handcrafted stoneware and porcelain at **Westwinds Potters,** the original folk art collectibles and handmade crafts in an 1829 dwelling called **Marmion House Gifts,** and the **Elegant Country Flowers & Antiques. Grape Expectations** offers "something grape for everyone," especially West Virginia wines, picnic baskets, glassware and ceramics. We like the jewelry at **The Spy Mountain Jewelry Company and Clothing Boutique,** the handicrafts at **Sleepy Hollow Creations** and the collectibles at **Stone House Antiques.** Almost every other building along High Street seems to be a snacky café, ice cream or coffee shop; their names (The Garden of Food, Hot Dog Haven, the Coffee Mill) indicate what they are about.

In Shepherdstown, **Dickinson & Wait** is an exceptional pottery studio and craft gallery. **Village Green** is a trove of gifts and decorative accessories, with **Village Finery** for women's apparel upstairs. **Cocoa** stocks accessories and gifts, and **O'Hurley's General Store** is a must stop. **Maggie's Marketplace** specializes in natural foods. For a snack there's **Ye Olde Sweet Shoppe,** a bakery that makes everything it sells, specializes in whole-grain European breads with no sugar or additives, and the coffee is 35 cents if you bring your own cup (otherwise, 45 and 80 cents). Wonderful artworks share the stage with coffee and espresso at **Lost Dog Coffee. The Old Pharmacy Café & Soda Fountain** is recommended for lunch and light supper. Besides coffee and candles, the **German Street Coffee & Candlery** offers oil lamps, glassware and garden accents.

Extra-Special

The Chesapeake & Ohio Canal National Historic Park.
With 74 lift locks and designation as a national historic park, the C&O Canal stretches 185 miles from the heights of Cumberland, Md., to Rock Creek in Georgetown. The towpath along the Maryland side is immensely popular with joggers, walkers and bicyclists because it's so level, and nowhere more so than in the Sharpsburg-Harpers Ferry area, where it incorporates six miles of the Appalachian Trail. Here a stone and dirt path follows the Potomac beneath a canopy of trees. Particularly interesting is the 3.5-mile stretch south of Shepherdstown to Antietam Creek, where you'll see the Antietam Viaduct, Lock No. 38 and the sites of two bloody Civil War battles along Antietam Creek. Park rangers lead periodic tours to various locks, aqueducts and even caves. Information is available at park headquarters in the impressive **Ferry Hill Place,** an 1813 plantation manor above the Potomac off Route 34 in Sharpsburg, Md., almost opposite the Bavarian Inn in Shepherdstown.
(301) 739-4200. Visitor center open daily, 8 to 4:30.

Deep Creek Lake, Md.
Mountain-Top Playground

A variety of both mountain and lake activities in one compact area draws those in the know to an area that many Americans have never heard of. Hiking, whitewater rafting, boating, swimming, skiing – all are available in westernmost Maryland's rural Garrett County, home of Deep Creek Lake.

Maryland's highest mountains first drew visitors as the frontier developed in the 19th century. The Baltimore & Ohio Railroad opened up the area, building summer resorts in Oakland and Deer Park. Presidents Grant, Harrison and Cleveland vacationed here and attended services in the old Garrett Memorial Church in Oakland, now called the Church of the Presidents. Henry Ford, Thomas Edison and Harvey Firestone camped at the foot of Maryland's highest waterfall in 1918, a visit commemorated in Swallow Falls State Park.

The area's popularity ebbed until manmade Deep Creek Lake was created in 1925 and Wisp Ski Resort rose above its shore. Originally a "cabin lake" favored by people from Pittsburgh less than two hours away, Maryland's largest freshwater lake has gone upscale in the last decade or so. A building boom has created substantial homes and condominiums along much of its meandering, 65-mile shoreline.

"We've changed from honky-tonk cabins to B&Bs and from spaghetti to French restaurants," notes Mary Bender, who opened the Carmel Cove Inn in 1994. A Pittsburgh resident, she credits the upscaling of Deep Creek Lake from its early Steel Town image over the last decade to an influx of people and money from Baltimore and Washington, D.C.

With an uncharacteristically wimpy name for a ski area, Wisp has the only downhill slopes in Maryland. Located astride Marsh Mountain, part of the Allegheny Range, it rises 610 feet from the lakeshore to an elevation of 3,080 feet. Wisp also has a golf course and a resort hotel that looks like a hospital.

The area's beguiling charms remain relatively undiscovered (the AAA Mid-Atlantic Tour Book barely mentions the area). Never mind. Those in the know

enjoy swimming and boating in a mountain lake that looks as if it's been relocated from the Adirondacks (a 30-foot power company easement along the shore ensures a natural, forested setting). Wilderness lovers enjoy the county's 70,000 acres of mountainous state park and forest lands, which offer everything from waterfalls to whitewater boating to cross-country skiing.

Carol McNiece Photo

Refreshments await visitors on stone porch overlooking Deep Creek Lake at Lake Pointe Inn.

The lake area is blessedly free of mosquitoes, and, in summer, is ten degrees cooler than nearby cities. Fall foliage colors rival those of New England and average yearly snowfalls of 100 inches create a winter wonderland.

Arts festivals and a few good restaurants and shops add to the mix. The only town is Oakland, the county seat with a population of 1,700.

Little changed is the unspoiled nature of an area populated partly by Amish and Mennonites and a Bible-belt mentality that bars the sale of alcoholic beverages on Sunday, a ban upheld in a recent county-wide referendum. "We're behind the times," says Ken Bock of the Savage River Inn. "We haven't had to lock our doors in the 25 years we've lived here."

Inn Spots

Lake Pointe Inn, 174 Lake Pointe Drive, Box 873, McHenry 21541.

Put aside your skepticism when you proceed through an emerging development of rather pretentious residences at the foot of Wisp Ski Area and face a trailer park across the lake. Ahead lies an 1890 farmhouse, partly hidden in pines at lake's edge, right beside the water and in a world unto itself.

The oldest house along Deep Creek Lake shore was built long before the lake was created, but was in such disrepair that the Lake Pointe developer planned to raze it. George and Linda Pettie, longtime lake vacationers from northern Virginia, saw its potential and stepped in to save it. A scrapbook details its extensive restoration in 1995 into a luxurious B&B in the style of an Adirondack lodge.

The stone house has an idyllic stone and pillared porch wrapping around the side and back. Here you can sit in wicker rockers and watch boats come and go on a cove with the main lake in the distance. Water's edge is a mere thirteen feet away. Power company easements require any structures dating after 1925 to be set back at least 30 feet from shore, but this property was grandfathered.

The lodge feeling continues inside, where the original wormy chestnut wood panels the walls and ceiling of the great room – dark and cool in summer, and warmed by a soaring stone hearth in the winter. The main floor also holds a couple of sunny breakfast rooms, a guest kitchen and pantry, a handicapped-accessible room and the living quarters for well-traveled innkeeper Carol McNiece, whose previous career was in corporate travel planning.

On the second floor are six small but comfortable guest rooms with private baths, queensize beds with down comforters and pillows, small TV/VCRs and telephones. Each is named for a local personage, whose life detailed in the room's scrapbook. Furnishings throughout are in the Arts and Crafts tradition.

We enjoyed the Browning Room with windows onto both lake and ski mountain. Its full bath with shiny brass fixtures was equipped with all kinds of luxuries, from huge Egyptian cotton bath towels to terrycloth robes to Neutrogena toiletries. The larger McHenry Room adds a double whirlpool tub. A shelf in the hallway was stocked with complimentary beverages and a video library, and coffee was ready here the next morning.

Originally planned as dormitory bunkrooms, two large rooms on the third-floor loft now have queen beds with daybeds as adjuncts. Each has a private hall bath.

Substantial hors d'oeuvre are offered upon arrival. Carol will prepare a light supper with advance notice any day but Saturday. The $15 tab includes hearty soup, salad and dessert or, in winter, cheese fondue.

The breakfast menu is posted daily. Ours included choice of juice, a delectable half grapefruit flavored with ginger sauce and vanilla beans, nutmeg-cinnamon muffins made with Vietnamese nutmeg, and creamy pesto eggs in puff pastry with ricotta cheese and asparagus, hash browns and maple-link sausage. Between courses, Carol took part in her morning ritual: feeding cashews to a cheeky chipmunk and getting a duck to eat out of her hand. She pointed out resident loons on the lake. Later she and assistant innkeeper Alison Dees, the inn's massage therapist, took us for a ride around the lake on the inn's speedy pontoon boat. We never did have time to try out the hot tub overlooking the cove.

(301) 387-0111 or (800) 523-5253. Nine rooms with private baths. Summer and winter: doubles $128 to $178 weekends, $113 to $163 midweek. Rest of year, $113 to $163 weekends, $98 to $148 midweek. Two-night minimum on weekends. Children over 16. No smoking.

Carmel Cove Inn, Box 644, Oakland 21550.

A former monastery has been transformed into the area's largest upscale B&B. Mary and Peter Bender from Pittsburgh acquired the Carmelite Fathers monastery in 1994 from a Carmel Cove developer who was superstitious about tearing it down. With their young children, they had been scouring the East to search for a B&B site and found it here.

The monks' "cells" were gutted to produce ten guest rooms, all with private baths and most with queensize beds. Two in the middle of the rambling, T-shaped house are decidedly small, five deluxe are slightly bigger and three premier rooms come with whirlpool baths and separate showers. One of the last opens onto an expansive new deck along the side of the building; the others on the lower floor have fireplaces or franklin stoves. All are bright and cheery, furnished simply but stylishly with matching bed covers and window treatments, herb wreaths on the doors and family antiques. Our deluxe room with queen bed opened onto the deck, and the only sounds to be heard were birds twittering at daybreak. The quarters

Former monastery is now home of Carmel Cove Inn.

were tight and the bathroom big enough only for a shower, but all the requisite amenities were at hand (or in a chest in the hall, for those who forgot), and breakfast was served on the deck outside our room the next morning.

And what a breakfast it was! Beforehand, we helped ourselves to juice, fresh fruit, coffee and date-raisin scones in the airy, cathedral-ceilinged dining room. At the appointed hour, the table on our deck was dressed with linens and set with a fruit platter. Each of us was given an oversize plate laden with a shiitake mushroom omelet (the mushrooms grown by the waitress), the best-ever blueberry-raspberry pancake of the melt-in-the-mouth variety with local syrup, a mound of hash-brown new potatoes accented with yellow and red peppers and lots of herbs, plus a plump local Mennonite sausage. We couldn't possibly finish, and couldn't face lunch until mid-afternoon.

The culinary treats began the day before when Mary and her resident innkeeper, Ed Spak, a well traveled California chef, put out wine and exotic goodies for guests in the afternoon, followed by sherry and chocolate-covered strawberries in the evening. These were served in the monks' former chapel, now an English-style great room. It has a billiards table at one end, a large TV/VCR at the other, and comfortable seating amidst an array of food and travel magazines plus four metropolitan Sunday newspapers in the middle.

The location off the beaten path in an area of substantial homes means the inn will always be secluded. The cove is a five-minute walk through woods for swimming or canoeing. Two tennis courts are available, and a hot tub is just off the deck.

The innkeepers go the extra mile for their guests. They even provided a bottle of wine and picked up a carryout dinner from Pizzeria Uno for us to enjoy on our deck because it was Sunday and restaurants either were closed or were not serving wine because of the county's blue laws. Such service prompted more than one couple to write in the guest book, "we felt like visiting royalty."

(301) 387-0067. Ten rooms with private baths. Doubles, $100 to $140 weekends, $80 to $120 midweek. Children over 12. No smoking.

Savage River Inn, Dry Run Road, Box 147, McHenry 21541.

A successful building contractor who later manufactured pushcarts for hot dog vendors, Ken Bock took on a new project in 1993. He added a floor to his hilltop

Contemporary residence on four levels has been converted into Savage River Inn.

farmhouse at the edge of the Savage River State Forest, installed new bedrooms and bathrooms, spiffed up the common areas and opened a B&B. "I used to be Mr. Hot Dog," says Ken, who's too active to think of retirement. "Now I'm Mr. Innkeeper."

His B&B hideaway – nicely secluded amidst 53 acres surrounded by state forest – is heaven on earth for hikers, cross-country skiers, nature lovers and others who prefer mountain solitude to the hustle and bustle of Deep Creek Lake eight miles to the west. Here, near the crest of the Eastern Continental Divide, is a panorama of mountains and valleys populated by deer, wild turkeys, grouse and the occasional bear.

The four-level structure, which bears few traces of its farmhouse past, is an architectural showplace. The ground floor holds a country kitchen and a two-story great room with vaulted ceiling and massive fieldstone hearth, large-screen TV, comfortable seating, a dining area and french doors onto expansive decks on two sides. The loft holds a library and leads to the kitchen and main entrance on the second level. Here also is an expansive suite with queensize bed, a bathroom hidden behind a mirror and a cozy sitting area with a franklin stove on a sun porch, where we would gladly have spent the evening had we not been lured outside by Ken onto the front deck for drinks and conversation. "Our guests need a little wine and cheese after driving three or four hours from Down East," he says, employing the local geographical reference to the Baltimore-Washington metro area.

On the third floor are two smaller guest rooms with queen beds and the country-pretty décor evident throughout the house. Sue Bock, who works fulltime as a nurse, designed the splashy window treatments, but her husband takes credit for the little flower-basket wreaths on the doors: "I made them myself."

The owners' quarters on the fourth floor were about to become a penthouse suite, accessed by an elevator. The Bocks were moving into a nearby barn, freeing space for guests in a side-by-side sitting room and bedroom with 24 feet of windows onto the mountains, not to mention a TV and fireplace and a full-width balcony.

They also were installing a kidney-shaped pool to supplement the outdoor hot tub.

Breakfast is taken at an Amish-crafted table for ten in the great room, or outside on a nicely landscaped, tiered patio-deck beside an ornamental lily pond. After serving orange juice and a fruit plate, Ken, who loves to chat, whipped up an admirable vegetable omelet with hash browns and toast with homemade raspberry jelly between conversational asides.

"I've never stayed overnight in an inn," says Ken. He's having too much fun with his own.

(301) 245-4440. Two rooms and two suites with private baths. Doubles, $80 to $100. Suites, $120 and $150. No smoking.

Harley Farm B&B, 16766 Garrett Hwy., Oakland 21550.

Hidden down a steep hill off the main highway between Deep Creek Lake and Oakland is this farmhouse B&B at the heart of a 65-acre working farm.

The exterior of the house and grounds can best be described as family farm, the front porch and yard cluttered with lawn chairs, swings and a trampoline. The inside is a beauty. The main portion, attached to the front of a 70-year-old brick house, was built in 1991 as a B&B by a previous owner. Wayne Gillespie, an Army retiree, and his wife Kam, who was with the World Bank, took over in 1993. They offer six spacious guest rooms in the main house, all with full baths and queensize four-poster beds, plus a two-room family suite. Each has different stenciling, eclectic art, Amish quilts and thick carpeting. Amenities include hair dryers, robes and – a different twist – slippers, for trips to the outdoor hot tub.

The newest accommodations are in a rear carriage house. A honeymoon suite on the second floor offers a kingsize brass bed, a bathroom with shower and heart-shaped jacuzzi, a kitchenette to make one's own breakfast and a living room with gas fireplace and TV. The concept proved so successful that the Gillespies replicated the suite on the floor below for 1998.

A hearty farm breakfast is served at a table for ten beside the fireplace in the dining room. Eggs benedict and homemade nut breads were the fare at our visit, but the possibilities range from blueberry soufflés to belgian waffles. Kam's signature frittatas are a Sunday morning treat.

Guests spread out in an expansive great room, full of objects from the owners' world travels, and a side TV room. Youngsters head outside to play on the lawn, fish in a stocked farm pond or watch horses grazing in three fields. As they depart, Ken is apt to load guests down with vegetables from his garden.

Harley Farm also operates as a retreat center for fitness and spirituality programs, yoga and art workshops.

(301) 387-9050 or (888) 231-3276. Six rooms and three suites with private baths. Doubles, $100 to $110 weekends; $90 midweek, July-October, $80 to $90 rest of year. Family suite, $120 to $150. Honeymoon suites, $150 to $185. Two-night minimum stay most weekends. Children over 10. No smoking.

Elliott House Victorian Inn, 146 Casselman Road, Grantsville 21536.

Located just off the first national road built in America and backing up to the Casselman River, this new inn on seven acres is part of a complex containing the Penn Alps crafts store and restaurant and the Spruce Forest Artisan Village.

While a dozen nearby log structures date to the Revolution, the Elliott House is a prim and proper Victorian. The house was owned by the last millers on the adjacent 1797 Stanton's Mill property. Canadian-born Jack Dueck, administrator of Penn Alps and a Mennonite storyteller and motivational management consultant, and his wife Eleanor bought the rundown house and property to save it from unwanted development. They commenced a no-expense-spared, two-year rehab that produced four elegant accommodations in the main house plus three in outbuildings.

The stained-glass front door of the beautifully restored house opens into a foyer and a living room and a library-parlor. One guest room on the main floor and three upstairs are done in Victorian florals and dark woodwork. Most of the original furnishings were purchased from the estate. The queen or twin beds are topped with Amish quilts. Pedestal sinks, Neutrogena toiletries, robes and hair dryers are in the updated bathrooms. A small coffee bar with a stocked refrigerator for guests is located outside the Stanton Room, which faces the old mill, and the Louisa May Alcott Room, named for Eleanor's favorite Victorian author.

Out back on the carefully landscaped property are larger guest accommodations. A walk made of old millstones leads to a restored tool house, now the Audubon House, with a beamed ceiling, queensize bed, a sofabed and a river-view deck. The Drover's House, once a wash house, features a living room with a sofabed and a kitchenette plus a queen bedroom upstairs with vaulted ceiling, loveseat and big windows onto the Casselman River across the meadow. The Amish built the benches and other elements of what Eleanor calls the Mission-style, "early settler" décor.

The Duecks' Canadian heritage shows up in the loony and two-ny coins embedded in a bullseye on the patio walk leading to the River View Room, part of a large new structure built as the innkeepers' cottage. An intricate and colorful quilt tops the room's queen bed. Furnishings include an antique secretary and a sofabed. The full-length rear deck juts out over the meadow toward the river.

Two porches and a rear patio with a hot tub are available for inn guests.

Rates include breakfast and lunch or dinner (Monday-Saturday 4 to 7 or 8) at the rustic Penn Alps restaurant across from the inn. The restaurant occupies the last remaining log tavern on the National Pike. The artisan village is close by, and across the meadow is the Casselman River, famed for its fly fishing.

(301) 895-4250 or (800) 272-4090. Four rooms and three cottages with private baths. May-October: doubles, $95 to $115, cottages, $115 to $130. November-April: doubles $85 to $105 weekends, $75 to $95 midweek; cottages, $105 to $115 weekends, $95 to $105 midweek. Two-night minimum weekends in season. Children over 12. No smoking.

The Deer Park Inn, 65 Hotel Road, Deer Park 21550.

Three large guest rooms are available above the top-rated restaurant (see Dining Spots) in the Pennington Cottage, a 110-year-old Victorian residence listed on the National Register of Historic Places.

Baltimore architect Josiah Pennington designed the shingled, seventeen-room house with wraparound porch as a summer home for his family on the grounds of the famed Deer Park Hotel, since demolished. The rooms are furnished with prized Victorian antiques, many of them original to the cottage or the old hotel.

Guests enter a foyer with fireplace, rich woodwork, stained glass, antique furnishings and a majestic staircase. Two candlelit dining rooms draw knowledgeable diners from near and far (see Dining Spots).

Sandy Fontaine, innkeeper with her husband Pascal, the chef from France, decorated the high-ceilinged guest rooms with Victorian flair. The bathrooms are private, although one is in the hall. Two rooms have decorative fireplaces. Sandy's artistic

Fine dining and lodging are offered in The Deer Park Inn.

sideline – she became a potter and a teacher of stained-glass production when they moved to this country from Paris in 1979 – is evident throughout.

Pascal prepares a full breakfast for overnight guests. A fruit plate and cereal precede the main dish, perhaps fruit pancakes, frittata or ham and cheese omelets.

(301) 334-2308. Three rooms with private baths. Doubles, $98 to $110.

The Oak & Apple, 208 North Second St., Oakland.

One of the handsomest houses in the Oakland historic district, this Colonial Revival Victorian built about 1915 commands a large lawn with mature fruit and shade trees in a prime residential area. Jana Brown and her ex-husband rescued it after it had been abandoned for two years, and burned out two power mowers just getting the lawn in shape.

A columned front porch and an enclosed sunporch surround the formal Victorian living room and a dining room with ten-foot ceilings.

The second floor holds a comfortable front sitting room with TV as well as two side queen bedrooms with private baths, one with a jetted tub. On the third floor are three bedrooms, one in front with a double and twin bed and a private bath. Two others with queen beds and in-room pedestal sinks share a hall bath.

Jana, who works during the day as an audiologist, offers a continental breakfast of fresh fruit, homemade granola, muffins, breads and scones.

(301) 334-9265. Three rooms with private baths and two with shared baths. Doubles, $65 to $85 with private bath, $60 with shared bath. Children over 12. No smoking.

Dining Spots

The Deer Park Inn, 65 Hotel Road, Deer Park.

Located off the beaten path in a summer colony that has seen better days between Deep Creek Lake and Oakland, this Victorian house is everyone's favorite locally for what one innkeeper calls "world-class dining."

Chef-owner Pascal Fontaine, who trained in Paris, struck out on his own after ten years as executive chef at the luxury ANA Hotel in Washington, D.C. His international travels influenced a cooking style that he describes as being "French with an American influence." Diners find the food and presentation exquisite, but the portions small.

Typical starters are cumin black bean soup with sour cream, sweet corn chowder with crabmeat, grilled portobello mushroom with goat cheese and pan-roasted scallops with asiago cheese and greens. Among the exotic salads is one with a terrine of layered yellow and red beets, greens and saffron oil.

The dozen main courses range from sautéed skate wing with lemon and capers to filet of beef with burgundy onion marmalade. Poached fillet of salmon scented with ginger, local rabbit with mushroom sauce and grilled veal chop with roquefort sauce are among the choices.

Desserts include a fragrant European-style plum tart, orange crème caramel with fruit garnish and, the chef's specialty, fresh crêpes with ice cream and chocolate sauce.

In the French tradition, Pascal leaves the kitchen after dinner to make the rounds through two small, intimate dining rooms as candles glow and classical music plays.

(301) 334-2308. Entrées, $14 to $19.95. Dinner nightly in season, 5:30 to 9:30. Closed Monday-Wednesday in winter.

McClive's, Deep Creek Drive, McHenry.
Seldom is a waterfront restaurant and lounge known for its food, but McClive's is a happy exception. For ten years, it has been packing in customers to the point it does not take reservations, and the seats begin filling up at 5.

Big windows look out onto the lake from the main dining areas, dressed with linens and candles. Downstairs is a courtyard lounge with a lakeside patio that inexplicably was not open the night we dined. We lucked out by asking to be seated on the upstairs lakefront balcony, starting something of a trend until an intermittent shower intervened (the braver souls among us simply put up the umbrellas and stuck it out).

McClive's is known for its specialty prime rib, mesquite-grilled steaks and fresh seafood. Two in our party tried the special "double dinner deal," $19.95 for two Sunday-Tuesday. It provided salads plus a good chicken dish and a highly recommended shrimp and garlic pasta that turned out to be mostly angel hair. Another diner made a meal of two appetizers, mushroom caps stuffed with crabmeat and baked scallops in garlic butter. A $14.95 bottle of Geyser Peak sauvignon blanc accompanied. Tuxedoed waiters provided smooth service that belied the bargain tab.

(301) 387-6172. Entrées, $10.95 to $16.95. Dinner nightly, 5 to 10 or 11.

Cornish Manor, Memorial Drive, Oakland.
Surrounded by tall trees on seven acres, this showy manor house at the edge of Oakland seats 100 in a couple of formal dining rooms and more on a delightful side patio. White lace runners accent tables dressed in pink or green, and French pans hang from a ladder suspended beneath the ceiling. A pianist entertains in the lounge on weekends.

French owner Christiane Bergheim and her husband Fred gave up their popular French Café Bakery and restaurant alongside Deer Creek Lake in 1997 to concentrate on this 50-year-old venture, of which they were only the third owners. Her son, Fabrice Du Four, manages the kitchen.

The extensive continental-American menu puts a highly rated appetizer of crab balls in spicy horseradish sauce amid such French standbys as country pâté, escargots and garlicky frog's legs. Main courses vary from salmon in parchment and broiled orange roughy with a pecan-frangelico sauce to chicken stuffed with crabmeat and French-cut lamb chops. Dessert could be crêpes suzette, bananas flambé or cherries jubilee.

(301) 334-6499. Entrées, $10.50 to $21.50. Lunch daily, 11 to 3. Dinner, Tuesday-Saturday from 5.

Pizzeria Uno Restaurant & Bar, Route 219, Deep Creek Lake.

If you're feeding a family or simply want to take out on a Sunday night when no liquor can be served in most of Garrett County, consider this stylish lakefront eatery and pizzeria with a deck overlooking the water. Awarded the Chicago-based franchise's pacesetter award, the local establishment offers an extensive menu from salads to pastas to baby back ribs. Deep-dish pizzas and California-style thin-crisp pizzas are featured.

We were quite happy with the house salads and a couple of pasta dishes – chicken pesto fettuccine and margarita chicken pasta. It being Sunday night, they were enjoyed with a bottle of wine on our own private patio back at our inn.

(301) 387-4866. Entrées, $10.95 to $17.50. Open daily, 11 a.m. to midnight.

Diversions

One-fifth of Garrett County's land area is devoted to state parks, forests and lakes. Visitors tend to be active, self-reliant souls who follow their own pursuits.

Deep Creek Lake, the center of recreational activity, was created in 1925 as a hydroelectric project by the Pennsylvania Electric Co. Twelve miles long, it meanders every which way, creating 65 miles of shoreline with no particularly long and broad stretch other than the busy section along Highway 219 between the Deep Creek and Glendale bridges. The water is deep and quite clear, providing good swimming and fishing. Power boats, especially pontoon boats for fishing, abound. Sailboats are few. Visitors get their best views of the lake along Highway 219 in the vicinity of McHenry and Glendale. Otherwise, trees and substantial homes (many available for rental through realtors) block views and access to the lake.

The mile-long shoreline at **Deep Creek Lake State Park** includes a 700-foot sandy beach, with grills and picnic tables and a nifty playground beneath nearby shade trees. Hiking trails and campsites are available. A new concert amphitheater was readied for **Garrett Lakes Arts Festival** events; the Tommy Dorsey Orchestra was a series highlight in 1997.

Swallow Falls State Park. About ten miles west of Deep Creek Lake near the West Virginia state line, the heart of this 300-acre mountain park contains tall hemlocks and white pines estimated to be 300 years old, the last stand of its kind in Maryland. From the parking lot, well-maintained gravel trails lead through the stand to four waterfalls, including **Muddy Creek Falls,** at 52 feet Maryland's tallest. A sign notes that Mud Creek originates in the brackish waters of Cranesville Swamp. The site where Henry Ford, Thomas Edison, Harvey Firestone and naturalist John Burroughs camped beside the falls is marked. The roughly mile-long trail on to Lower and Upper Shadow Falls and Tolivar Falls takes about twenty minutes. You may pass sunbathers on the rocks and kayakers in the water.

The cliffs covered with thick rhododendron and the sounds of various waterfalls and rapids are very cooling on a warm day.

Savage River State Forest. About a dozen miles east of Deep Creek Lake River site is Maryland's largest state forest, with 53,000 acres of forestland, wildlife habitat, a reservoir and two state parks. The aptly named Savage River is a narrow and harrowing stretch of whitewater for more than five miles. It was the site of the 1989 Whitewater World Championship races and the 1992 U.S. Canoe and Kayak Team Olympic Trials. A rugged hiking trail extends seventeen miles along the crest of Big Savage Mountain. A three-hour-long trail leads hikers through the gorge.

Whitewater Boating. Along with the Savage River, the upper Youghiogheny is one of the East's prime whitewater rivers. About twenty Class IV and V rapids challenge the experienced rafter and kayaker. Commercial outfitters run thousands of enthusiasts down the steep gorge each year. A scenic highway along the river leads to Ohiopyle Falls, just north of the Garrett County line in Pennsylvania. We've never seen so many rafters and whitewater-related activities in one place.

The Cranesville Sub-Arctic Swamp, near Cranesville. The most obscure of the area's natural phenomena is this 500-acre remnant of boreal forest producing growth normally associated with arctic regions. Even with a good map, we got hopelessly lost for more than an hour trying to find Cranesville, let alone the swamp. Then we traipsed for half an hour looking for the bog. We turned back when we found ourselves reaching a forest, having seen only two deer and hearing several bullfrogs. Other visitors told us the forest trail actually was the entrance to the bog and we had not gone far enough. We learned that a boardwalk takes hikers through the heart of the swamp. Is it worth it? "If you're into botany, it's really groovy," one teenager we met on the trail advised. Famed naturalist John Burroughs led the Henry Ford camping party from nearby Swallows Falls into the swamp in 1918 to examine the plant life. The Nature Conservancy owns the swamp, but apparently discourages visitors.

Penn Alps, Route 40 east, Grantsville.

This rustic restaurant and crafts store is housed in the last surviving log tavern on the first National Road. It's near the famed Casselman River Bridge, the largest single-span stone arch bridge of its kind when it was built in 1813. Now the tavern is a restaurant with five charming dining rooms and a crafts shop featuring the largest display of indigenous handicrafts in the Alleghenies, made in the homes and studios of tri-state residents. A stunning collection of Amish quilts, hickory rockers and hand-thrown pottery are featured. Nearby, other log cabins and rustic structures comprise the quaint **Spruce Forest Artisan Village,** where craftsmen work and show their wares. The annual **Music at Penn Alps** series offers classical and folk concerts Saturday evenings in summer in the Great Hall at Penn Alps.

(301) 895-5985. Restaurant open daily from 7 a.m.; Crafts Shop from 9 a.m. Artisan Village open Monday-Saturday 1 to 5, Memorial Day through October.

Shopping. Arrowhead Market, an upscale market and deli open 24 hours along Route 219 at Deep Creek Lake, carries everything a vacationing visitor needs, from full takeout meals to gasoline to camera supplies. Across the street is **The Tourist Trap,** a fairly stylish haven of local souvenirs. Its sweatshirts, coffee mugs, piggy banks and door mats all bear a Deep Creek Lake logo. Collectibles, crafts and country stuff are shown in three buildings at **Schoolhouse Earth,** where New Age music plays and a petting zoo in a rear barn keeps youngsters amused.

In Oakland, a hodgepodge of eight shops operates in one big red barn of building called **Grand Central Station**. The willow rockers and a line of yellow and black bumblebee kitchenware were nearly upstaged by all the beds in the sleep shop in the far corner at our visit. Oakland's old-fashioned main street is enhanced by the good little **Book Mark'et** and the **Book Mark'et Mezzanine** with antiques and collectibles.

Extra-Special

Fallingwater, Mill Run, Pa.
One of the surprises for many visitors to Deep Creek Lake is finding they are so close to architect Frank Lloyd Wright's most famous private home. Fallingwater, built atop a waterfall, is less than an hour's drive across the state line. The weekend home was designed in 1936 for the family of Pittsburgh department store owner Edgar J. Kaufmann. They had indicated the area around a waterfall as the location, but were unprepared for Wright's suggestion that it rise over the waterfall,

rather than face it. The house is open for hour-long guided tours, which reveal countless facets of the intriguing cantilevered structure (including, at our visit, the revelation that one of the unsupported concrete decks had just been given a support). The place is bigger than one expects and, from every angle inside and out, you can hear the waterfall, even if you can´t see it. Of all the rooms, we inngoers liked best the top-level guest house nestled in the rhododendron beside a stream-fed pool. At tour's end, visitors gasped when told the entire house with all the built-ins cost only $155,000. That was triple the Kaufmanns' budget, so Wright lowered his fee to $8,000. The place would cost millions today. During the close-up tour, you never really get to see the overall house the way it looks in pictures and postcards. That view is offered from the lookout at the end of the path below. A well thought-out visitor center contains a gift shop and restaurant.
(412) 329-8501. Tours by reservation, Tuesday-Sunday 10 to 4, $8 on weekdays, $12 weekends and holidays.

The drive to and from Fallingwater is particularly scenic, especially along the Youghiogheny River in the vicinity of Ohiopyle Falls in Pennsylvania. Also scenic is rural Route 1012 over Sugarloaf Mt. to the little town of Confluence, where the **River's Edge Café** at 203 Yough Street makes a good stop for lunch or dinner. The property slopes down to the Yough River, and butterflies flitted in the pretty gardens as we paused at midday on the porch for chicken salad and portobello mushroom sandwiches, accompanied by a couple of the chef's zesty soups. It's open seasonally, Tuesday-Sunday 11 to 9; closed in winter.

Stately architectural styles prevail in downtown Frederick historic district.

Frederick, Md.

'So Proudly We Hail'

"Our town has been here since 1745 and is still thriving on the same streets," said the woman at Frederick's visitor center. You can feel its longevity as you view the 18th- and 19th-century structures throughout the city's 33-block historic district. You can sense its prosperity in its downtown, enlivened by restaurants, boutiques and galleries.

And you can empathize with its new slogan, "So Proudly We Hail," borrowed quite appropriately from the anthem written by native son Francis Scott Key. Here's a town that possesses a strong sense of identity, as reflected in its slick monthly city magazine called, simply, Frederick.

This area is "heaven in Maryland for yuppies," extolled a state tourism promoter. They come here to go antiquing, tour the battlefields, enjoy the restaurants and walk the sidewalks tread earlier by George Washington, Abraham Lincoln, the Marquis de Lafayette, Stonewall Jackson and Barbara Fritchie.

Barbara Fritchie? She's the Civil War heroine who challenged rebel troops to target her rather than the Union flag she was waving as they marched the city's streets. "Shoot if you must this old gray head, but spare this country's flag," she pleaded, her defiance immortalized by poet John Greenleaf Whittier.

Whittier's tale of "the clustered spires of Frederick" comes alive as the visitor explores the sights, an experience made much more worthwhile by the guided walking tours offered weekends and holidays. Court House Square was the scene of the first official repudiation of the British Stamp Act in 1765, ten years before the Boston Tea Party. A century later, Frederick was a town divided by the War Between the States, its sympathies lying both north and south. Churches and public buildings became hospitals for the wounded from nearby Antietam, site of the bloodiest battle on American soil.

The local battle of Monocacy is credited with saving Washington, D.C., from destruction. Frederick itself was spared, after Confederate General Jubal Early occupied the town briefly and levied a $200,000 ransom for its salvation – an amount borrowed from local banks and finally repaid in 1951. Thus the city is a model of original architecture – "almost as fine as Williamsburg, and not reconstructed," in the words of our tour guide. Even the new downtown parking garages blend into the historic scene.

Steeped though it is in the past, Frederick wears well its latter-day theme as "Cinderella City." Its proximity to the Baltimore-Washington megalopolis has turned it into the fastest growing city in Maryland, an up-to-date community of 40,000 with a vision and a sense of place tied to its past.

Tourism is said to be the area's second largest industry. Many are attracted by Newmarket, a one-street town called the antiques capital of Maryland, just east of the city. Others head west to Antietam, the graveyard of the Civil War. At the center of it all is Frederick, a delightful blend of old and new.

Inn Spots

Tyler-Spite House, 112 West Church St., Frederick 21701.

History was made here in 1814 when Dr. John Tyler, who performed the nation's first cataract surgery, built this classic three-story Federal mansion to prevent the city from extending Record Street through to the National Pike. The foundation was constructed literally overnight out of spite: hence the name.

Owners Bill and Andrea Myer worked quickly, too, opening Frederick's first downtown B&B in 1990 and adding the adjacent Nelson House a year later. Bill, a retired Montgomery County school administrator, oversees the operation while his wife handles her medical transcription business based in Gaithersburg.

A beauty of a place is this, boasting thirteen-foot-high ceilings and full of price-

less antiques. It's blessed with a lush rear garden courtyard and the only swimming pool in downtown Frederick. The Philippine mahogany desk upon which guests register in the main hall was used by Gen. Douglas MacArthur to sign the peace treaty in Manila. The mirror in the hall is tall enough that Abe Lincoln is believed to have used it to adjust his hat during his Frederick visit. The chandeliers are reproductions from the Tryon Palace in New Bern, N.C. The stunning oriental screen in the library is a reproduction of the 14th-century "The Last Emperor." The Music Room harbors a Packard Victorian pump organ, a 1914 Ludwig grand piano and a victrola. Most of the eight working fireplaces sport imported carved marble mantels. Next door in the Lane House are crystal doorknobs, Chinese Chippendale beds and an 1820 chandelier of Waterford glass.

The inn has ten guest rooms, five with private baths and five that share – they generally are rented in pairs as suites so each has a private bath. "Once guests get here, a private bath is not an issue," Bill advises.

Guest rooms are commodious, most with queensize canopy beds and too many prized furnishings to enumerate. We were assigned originally to Bill's favorite Charles Parsons Room, third-floor front. It shares with the Barbara Fritchie Room a large carpeted hall bath, big enough to include a sitting area. The room comes with a queensize sleigh bed and a cane and rattan side chair made in the Philippines. The dresser was made of shipping cartons, the lamps are old sake bottles and a Japanese chest serves as a coffee table. We decided instead to settle in the Hood Room of what was then a two-bedroom suite, with an adjoining bath in between and a quieter, rear location overlooking the garden. (It since has been rechristened the Mosby Suite, the second bedroom having been turned into a living room with queensize sofa bed and the bath having been rehabbed with a whirlpool tub and a "rainforest" shower.)

Home of the honeymoon suite with private bath and three other fireplaced guest rooms, the 1820 Nelson House has a parlor and dining room with fourteen-foot ceilings, matching fireplaces and a bible door unique to the area in between. Guests here also enjoy an enclosed rear porch with a tin roof, sofas and a TV, a sleek black and white kitchen, and an outside deck on two levels surrounding a giant swamp magnolia tree.

Lately the Myers acquired the 1817 Ross Mansion across Court House Square at 105 Council St. and were hoping to open in 1998. Three guest rooms and a suite, all with private baths and working fireplaces, were approved to rent for up to $220 a night. Six more rooms may open there if approvals are granted.

Decanters of cream sherry are in every room, supplementing the exceptional teatime spread –at our visit, lemonade, tea, wine, watermelon slices, cookies, an extravagant strawberry cake, cheese and crackers. Sometimes there are tea sandwiches. Breakfast is a gustatory treat as well, served on the patio or, with some pomp and circumstance, in the large and formal dining room graced by fancy wallpaper and a Chippendale screen in the corner. Juice and fresh fruits precede such main dishes as Roosevelt eggs scrambled with cream cheese, baked apple dumplings, creamed chipped beef or, at our visit, airy belgian waffles topped with fresh peaches and whipped cream.

(301) 831-4455. Nine rooms with private baths and five rooms with shared baths. Doubles, $150 shared bath, $175 to $220 private bath, $200 honeymoon suite. Deduct $25 midweek. No smoking.

Turning Point Inn, 3406 Urbana Pike, Frederick 21701.
Set well back from the road on five nicely landscaped acres in the center of rapidly growing suburban Urbana, this Edwardian estate home with Georgian features is a full-service country inn known for its dining (see Dining Spots).

A gracious parlor is pretty in rose, pink and teal. It offers striped sofas, antique

Tyler-Spite House backs up to garden courtyard and swimming pool.

furniture, built-in bookshelves and a table with family pictures of innkeeper Charlie Seymour and his young son Tom as well as his mother and stepfather, Ellie and Bernie Droneburg, who founded the inn in 1985. The parlor separates the main dining rooms from the entry hall and a couple of small dining rooms on the other side.

Upstairs are five spacious guest rooms "out of the pages of House Beautiful," according to Charlie. All have private baths, TVs and telephones. The six-windowed Green Room contains two four-poster double beds and two upholstered chairs in a moss green decor. Steps are provided to climb into the queensize four-poster in the Blue Room. Fan windows overlook the countryside from two dormer rooms on the third floor, furnished in country style. The king-bedded Country Room here has a whirlpool tub.

Extremely popular are newer suites in outbuildings behind the inn. The three-level Carriage House cottage contains a living room with wet bar and small refrigerator, a bathtub with jets on the mid level, and a kingsize bed and formal country decor upstairs. Furnished in what the staff calls "country quaint" style is the spacious Dairy House room with kingsize bed and two reclining chairs.

A basket of fruit and a full country breakfast are included in the rates. The latter starts with assorted fresh fruit, juice and Swiss breakfast cereal. Then comes a choice of entrées, from eggs creole to corned beef hash with eggs. Last but not least are the breakfast meats, including spicy andouille and sometimes wild boar sausage.

(301) 874-8232. Five rooms and two suites with private baths. Doubles, $95 weekends, $75 midweek. Suites, $125 and $150 weekends, $100 and $125 midweek.

Stone Manor, 5820 Carroll Boyer Road, Middletown 21769.
Elegant suites of uncommon spaciousness, a fine dining experience and a rural location as part of a 114-acre working farm. These are among the attributes that distinguish this country inn in the rolling hills southwest of Frederick.

The majestic, eighteen-room farmhouse dates to the late 1700s, with additions built in 1830 and the 1970s. "It was always a private residence and we want to keep that feeling," said Judith Harne, general manager and one of the five local investors who bought it in 1991 to run as a B&B and restaurant (see Dining Spots).

They maintain the feeling of a country home – albeit one of considerable means – very nicely. The six suites are spaced well apart throughout the structure. Each is stylishly furnished with antiques and comes with extravagant bath facilities and tables for "in-suite dining" (used for breakfast and special-occasion dinners). Four have private porches and two have working fireplaces.

Largest and most formal is the second-floor Gardenia Suite with working fire-places in both the living room and bedroom, a queensize rice-carved four-poster bed, crown molding around the ceiling, and unusual window treatments in which swags and sheers are pulled to one side. The canopied queen bed in the main-floor Hibiscus Suite is draped entirely in white. Vintage clothing and toys, including a pair of old figure skates, are hung instead of artworks in the main-floor Trillium Suite, charming for its Shaker-style poster bed and colorful antique quilt and quilted pillows.

But it is the bath facilities that command most attention. The Gardenia comes with a whirlpool bath for two, a separate shower, a double vanity and the thickest carpet imaginable. The Thistle, the smallest, has a double whirlpool bath in a corner of the bedroom, opposite the poster bed and not far from the dining table. And the Laurel Suite in the oldest section of the original farmhouse masks well its antiquity with a jetted shower spraying from six directions, a room with pedestal sink, w.c. and bidet, and another vanity beside the oversize whirlpool, in which the waters are illuminated from below like a swimming pool.

Guests are welcomed with a plate of fruits and cheeses, delivered to the sitting areas of their rooms. In the morning, continental breakfast is served on the formal dining table in the room. The fare consists of juice, fruit, yogurt and breads.

There are lots of good magazines for perusing in the library at the top of the stairway. Outside are gardens, a pond, a stream, working farmlands and forests, from which deer might emerge to feed at the pear trees or drink from the fountain.

(301) 473-5454. Fax (301) 371-5622. www.ourhome.net/stonemanor. Six rooms and suites with private baths. Doubles, $125 to $250. No smoking.

Hill House, 12 West Third St., Box 4124, Frederick 21705.

A three-story Victorian townhouse embellished with Eastlake detailing on the façade at the edge of downtown was converted into an elegant B&B in 1996. Damian and Taylor Branson moved from southern Maryland to convert the structure's three apartments into a suite and three of the fanciest B&B rooms you ever saw.

The downstairs common rooms – a living room, sun room and dining room with their well-worn orientals on parquet floors – set the stage. Upstairs at the rear is the Mexican Room, a showplace from south of the border with twin beds, handpainted furniture and sponge-painted walls in yellows and burnt orange and reds. The enormous bathroom holds a stunning vanity washbowl that the Bransons "carted back" from one of their frequent trips to Mexico as well as a luxurious chaise lounge in a corner. It opens onto a second-floor gallery/porch overlooking the side garden, as does the Chesapeake Room, outfitted in floral chintz and tiger maple furniture, with an antique shaving mirror on the chest. Original oils and watercolors by Chesapeake artists are featured here. The front Victorian Room has a high step-up queen canopy bed and a deco-style bathroom in black and white.

The third floor holds the Steeple Suite, so called because "you can see a lot of the steeples of Frederick" from the rear windows, says Damian. Furnished in Colonial style, it has a living room with TV, a kitchen and a queen canopy in the bedroom.

Original drawings, paintings and crafts are evident throughout this much-decorated house.

Damian, whose hobby was cooking and catering, serves a full breakfast, from fried tomatoes to french toast. It's served at a table for eight in the formal dining room or outside in the garden.

(301) 682-4111. Three rooms and one suite with private bath. Doubles, $125 to $175. Suite, $235. Children over 12. No smoking. Open Wednesday-Sunday by reservation.

Middle Plantation Inn, 9549 Liberty Road, Frederick 21701.

The "rustic bed and breakfast" description on its brochure best describes this place ten minutes east of town in the village of Mount Pleasant. Or does it? Fronting on a suburban highway amid tract homes, it's really much more.

Shirley and Dwight Mullican tore down his grandfather's farmhouse on 26 acres and rebuilt in 1989 from the ground up, using logs, beams and floors from the original house. "So it looks old," says Shirley, "but has all the modern conveniences."

Guests enter through a rear keeping room, cozy with a tall corner stone fireplace, a skylight and built-in stained-glass windows separating it from the Mullicans' quarters on the main floor. Upstairs are three guest rooms with private baths, each bearing novel touches but contemporary amenities like plush carpeting and hidden TVs. Dwight's elaborate hand stenciling graces the Victorian Room, which contains a carved walnut bed, a Victorian loveseat and side chair. There's a modern shower stall beside the clawfoot tub. Old hunting prints and white pine country furniture are in the Hunt Room, where the TV is hidden in the corner washstand and an old icebox with a shelf is for storing clothes. The rear Plantation Room has more stenciling, a tester canopy bed and the original poplar floor.

The most private lodging is in the Log Room with its own entrance at one side of the house, finished inside and out with logs. A colorful quilt brightens the blue iron bed, the TV is found in a dry sink, a harness holds the mirror and a pottery bowl serves as the washstand. Mints and vases of dried flowers are in each room.

Breakfast in the keeping room is continental-plus, involving juice, fresh fruit, cheese, cereal, granola, and homemade breads and muffins.

(301) 898-7128. www.MPInn.com. Four rooms with private baths. Doubles, $110 weekends, $90 midweek. Children over 15. No smoking.

Strawberry Inn, 17 Main St., New Market 21774.

Innkeepers Jane and Ed Rossig used to go antiquing in New Market and then have dinner at the famed Mealey's restaurant, like thousands before and after them. They bought their 1837 farmhouse in the center of town in 1973 for retirement from New Jersey. "We started restoring it and the mayor said, 'why don't you open a place to stay in this little town?'" recalls Jane. They gutted the building and reopened as a guest house, which took off immediately. "We didn't feel right sending people off without even a cup of coffee," says Jane. But four years passed before they added the breakfast part of their B&B.

The oldest B&B in Frederick County weathered well as the Rossigs moved into semi-retirement. After Ed's death in 1996, Jane continued with the assistance of son Bud and his wife Sonya. They offer five guest rooms with private baths, all furnished in Victoriana. One on the first floor with twin beds has its own side porch. The large upstairs rooms contain queen or two double beds, and one has a sitting room with a Victorian loveseat overlooking the rear garden. Common areas include a living room, a small front porch with rockers up against the sidewalk, a formal dining room with individual tables and a lovely grapevine-covered back porch. A continental-plus breakfast of fruit, cereal and homemade muffins, banana bread or soda bread is served in the dining room or on the porch.

Wild strawberries still grow along Strawberry Alley beside the house, from which the inn derives its name. The long back yard includes a gazebo, a distant patio where tomatoes grow beside park benches and a log house containing Rossig's Art & Framing gallery and the owner's quarters.

(301) 865-3318. Five rooms with private baths. Doubles, $85 to $125. Two-night minimum on weekends in season. No credit cards.

National Pike Inn, 9-11 West Main St., Box 299, New Market 21774.

Almost next door to the Strawberry Inn and across the street from Mealey's restaurant, this B&B offers four rooms with private baths and two that share or can be rented jointly as a suite. The brown brick Federal house with a distinctive widow's watch atop is named for the nation's first federally funded highway. The house was built in three stages from 1796, accounting for the fact the upstairs bedrooms are on different levels. Owners Tom and Terry Rimel have furnished them in a mix of Federal and Victorian decors.

An oriental rug covers the original wide-plank floor in the attractive parlor, fashioned from two rooms and containing an organ. A full breakfast, perhaps pancakes or eggs, is served at a lace-covered table in the dining room or on a pleasant side courtyard, furnished with a table and lounge chairs and surrounded by azalea gardens, sculptured bird bath and fountain. Terry says guests rave over her banana-butterscotch bread and apple cider biscuits.

Two windsor chairs, a rocker and a queensize brass bed are in the red and white rear Colonial Room. Toward the front and up a bit from the smallish Antique Oak Room and adjoining Brass Americana Room (available separately with shared bath or together as the Country Suite) are the Victorian Room, where a floral comforter on the queensize spindle bed matches the draperies, and the Canopy Room with, of course, a canopy queen bed and a loveseat. Floral print fabrics cover the queensize bed and facing daybed and match the curtains in the newest room, lately vacated by one of the Rimel sons. Two mints are at each bedside.

(301) 865-5055. Four rooms with private baths and a two-room suite. Doubles, $85 to $125. No smoking. Children over 10.

Antietam Overlook Farm, Porterstown Road, Keedysville 21756.

From the large rear porch, guests can see the Antietam National Battlefield, the town of Sharpsburg and mountains in four states. The view isn't all they get at one of the more comfortably elegant new B&Bs we've seen in a long time. They get five queen-bedded suites, each with gas-burning fireplace, its own screened porch and a tub surrounded by plants; a plush common room that's made for conversation in front of a huge fireplace; a table of cordials from which to help themselves after dinner, and a "groaning plate" of a country breakfast.

"I didn't think I was the only person in the world who likes a porch and a bubble bath," Barbara Dreisch said after opening her B&B with husband John. They added

Private porches are among amenities at stylish Antietam Overlook Farm.

a contemporary wing to their existing 19th-century-style farmhouse on 95 acres and let the fun begin.

"Country but state of the art" is how Barbara describes it. The suites are carpeted, the fireplaces are operated by remote-control from the beds, the individual porches have two comfy chairs, the open steeping tubs fairly cry out for a bubble bath and there are sit-down showers in the bathrooms, where a basket of extras includes shaving cream, hair dryer and curling iron.

If you can tear yourself away from your own little heaven, you'll find a small kitchen area with welcoming wine or lemonade and an instant hot-water tap for tea or hot chocolate. Beyond is the Country Room, a vast sitting room with dining area paneled, like the rest of the house, in rough barnwood. Off this is the big rear porch with four-state view. The dining area is where John provides the "groaning plate" in the morning, perhaps pancakes with honey, muesli, hot homemade applesauce, bacon and homemade sausage balls, pitchers of orange juice and carafes of coffee. The day before our visit he served English broil with mushrooms and tomatoes and french toast made with thick raisin bread, coffee creamer and amaretto.

The house sits by itself atop a ridge in the middle of nowhere. The Dreisches give directions via a roundabout route so guests don't pass the shanties of hillbilly country that lie close to this fantasyland. The direct route from Sharpsburg is much shorter.

(301) 432-4200 or (800) 878-4241. Five suites with private baths. Doubles, $115 to $160. Two-night minimum weekends. Children over 12. No smoking.

Inn at Antietam, 220 East Main St., Box 119, Sharpsburg 21782.

A sign over the clawfoot tub in the rustic Smoke House suite here says "showers are for the strivers of the world." When guests see that, says innkeeper Betty Fairbourn, "they're content with the tub." And why not? The suite offers a fireplace, a loft bed, a wet bar, barnwood walls, oriental rugs on the floors and a sofabed in the sitting room.

Betty and Cal Fairbourn, GMAC transfers who moved here from Salt Lake City, took over a 1908 farmhouse that was "not as old as we'd like it to be." They've made do quite nicely, furnishing in country and Victorian styles with goods acquired from area estate sales. They offer four rooms they consider more like suites with sitting areas and private baths. Each is decorated gracefully and without clutter.

Guests enjoy a slate-floor solarium at the entry, a formal parlor and a front veranda that wraps around the house to an attractive rear patio. Breakfast is served at a long table in the formal dining room beside an ornate glass china cabinet. Juice, melon, waffles with local strawberries and bacon were the fare at our visit. Blueberry pancakes, egg dishes and blintzes might be available other days. Afternoon tea, snacks and homemade cookies are offered on the patio with a view of the Blue Ridge Mountains.

(301) 432-6601. Fax (301) 432-5981. Four rooms with private baths. Doubles, $105 weekends, $95 midweek. Two-night minimum on weekends. Children over 6. No smoking. Closed Dec. 21 to mid-February.

Piper House B&B, Route 65, Sharpsburg 21782.

Most people who stay here are serious Civil War buffs, say innkeepers Regina and Lou Clark. That's understandable, for this is the mid-19th-century log and frame farmhouse that Confederate General James Longstreet claimed as his headquarters during the bloodiest single day of the Civil War. The house evokes haunting memories, situated as it is, surrounded by the Antietam National Battlefield and just down the road from the park entrance.

The Clarks saved the B&B in 1994. Its former principals, Hagerstown residents whose occupation is restoring old buildings, had decided to give up their long-term lease from the National Park Service. When word got out among Civil War buffs regarding the planned closing of the house, protests came from all over the country. The Clarks learned about it, visited the property and quickly negotiated a new long-term lease. Of the potential lessees, "we were the only married couple who wanted to live on-site," Regina said. They moved in and found it "simply wonderful to live in an historic home on federal property."

They share their small treasure with overnight guests in three bedrooms with private baths. Each is simply but attractively furnished to the Civil War period. The Clarks have tried to make the rooms more comfortable, and their live-in presence adds a dimension heretofore lacking. There are a couple of small downstairs parlors and an upstairs sitting room and rear screened porch. Regina serves guests a continental-plus breakfast of juice, fruit compote, cereals, muffins, breads and pastries at a long table in the kitchen.

The old slave house, smoke house and stone root cellar out front add to the Civil War ambiance here.

Lately, the Clarks were proud that the Piper House was honored as one of the 50 best-kept travel secrets in the world in 1998 by Travel-Holiday magazine.

(301) 797-1862. Three rooms with private baths. Doubles, $95 weekends, $85 midweek. Children over 10. No smoking.

Dining Spots

Turning Point Inn, 3406 Urbana Pike, Frederick.

For a special-occasion meal out in the country, this glamorous and expanding spot is where many locals go. The view of the surrounding landscape from the large garden-style dining room through floor-to-ceiling windows is lovely. Rose tablecloths, rattan chairs and vases of alstroemeria add to the setting. Two small, formal dining rooms are located on the other side of the entry.

Executive chef Dean Winning, who helped Mark Miller open the trendy Red Sage in Washington, D.C., took over kitchen duties in 1996 to advance inn owner Charlie Seymour's plans to take the dining operation to a higher level. Under

Impressive fieldstone structure is home to Stone Manor, country inn and restaurant.

construction in 1997 was a basement tavern and wine cellar. The former was designed as a rustic English pub serving casual fare, while the latter was to be the venue for ultra-fine dining. A Japanese garden with a sitting area is just outside.

The new chef, known for unusual combinations and arresting presentations, tempts adventuresome palates with appetizers like carpaccio of tuna with a shiitake mushroom salad and wild morels with a garlic custard flan. Another dinner starter, a spinach-crabmeat tart with marinated tomatoes and cucumbers, turns up as a main course on the lunch and brunch menus as well. For main dinner dishes, he employs a spicy tropical fruit sauce and baby bok choy with his pan-seared rare tuna, and adds a bell pepper-crab relish and roasted onion sauce to his rainbow trout crusted with potato and garlic. A porcini mushroom crème fraîche dresses the pan-seared veal scaloppini.

Fresh strawberries and blueberries garnish the dark chocolate tower dessert, an ethereal stack of flourless chocolate cake rounds layered with pistachio cream.

(301) 831-8232. Entrées, $16.95 to $24.95. Lunch, Tuesday-Friday 11:30 to 2. Dinner, Tuesday-Thursday 5:30 to 9, Friday and Saturday 5 to 9:30. Sunday, brunch 11:30 to 2, dinner 4 to 8:30. No smoking.

Stone Manor, 5820 Carroll Boyer Road, Middletown.

For some of the most pure, exciting food in the area, drive fifteen minutes or so into the countryside southwest of town to this restored restaurant and country inn. It's in an impressive fieldstone manor house, and the experience is likened to that of dining in a private home – which it was, for its first 200 years.

Five local business investors have turned it into a refined restaurant of distinction. Dining is in the main beamed and stone dining room with an enormous fieldstone fireplace and damask-covered tables seating a total of 25 to 30, in a private room set for ten or twelve, or in the gracious living room, where lace mats top the fine polished tables.

Periodic cooking demonstrations, a remarkably extensive wine cellar and special wine dinners attest to the fact that this is a restaurant that takes food and drink seriously. Chefs Bryan Kimmett and Chris Grossnickle grow many of their own vegetables and herbs and acquire others from nearby purveyors.

The menu is prix-fixe, $45 for four courses with two or three choices in each course, or $55 for a pre-selected five-course dinner. Add $22.50 or $27 respectively for wines with each course.

A typical meal might start with an amuse-gueule, followed by a grilled vegetable terrine with pan-fried goat cheese and basil vinaigrette, pan-seared loin of rabbit with sautéed rhubarb and wild berries, or a lobster couscous salad. An intermezzo sorbet (and perhaps an adjournment for a short walk in the gardens) precedes the main course, which could be pan-seared emu with haricots verts, artichokes and roasted garlic and cambozola-stuffed new potatoes. For the grand finale, you might find lemon-ginger cheesecake with mango, papaya and nectarines.

Other main courses in this talented kitchen's repertoire could be pan-seared sesame tuna with a bok coy-jicama-cucumber slaw, spicy yam fries and coconut relish; grilled breast of duck with orange-cumin oil and yogurt and a salad of amaranth, walnuts and citrus, and pan-seared medallions of beef with coriander corn pudding and black bean salsa.

Lunch is offered in three courses for $25. Expect treats like a gratin of blue crab with creamed corn and crispy leeks, a frittata of curried sea scallops and sweet peppers, and black raspberry ice cream with a pineapple compote.

Because this is a favorite place for private functions and because of its out-of-the-way location, meals are served by reservation only and the schedule may vary.

(301) 473-5454. Prix-fixe, $45 to $55. Lunch, Tuesday-Saturday 11 to 2. Dinner, Tuesday-Saturday 6 to 9. Sunday, brunch 11 to 2, dinner 4 to 7.

Tauraso's, 6 East St. at Everedy Square, Frederick.

This is quite an establishment, from the old Jaguar sometimes parked in front of the entry to a sleek dining room to the enormous, high-ceilinged **Victor's Saloon & Raw Bar** in the original Victor's Home Remedies patent medicine business that paved the way for the old Everedy factory. The Jaguar is "our mascot – I drive it every day," said Dr. Nicola Tauraso, a physician who opened the restaurant in 1987 for his son Michael, a talented chef not long out of Rhode Island's Johnson & Wales culinary program. "This is the toughest business I've been in," says Nick, who's been involved in his share. The place seats 300 and is open every day except Christmas.

Although there's considerable show, the food is taken seriously here. We've seldom been served a better pasta dish than the luncheon special of linguini with seared grouper fillet, marinated green olives, roasted garlic and white wine, accompanied by a dish of grated parmesan cheese. We also liked the homemade seafood sausage with pepper and olive compote and the focaccia seasoned with sage, oregano and garlic. The cappuccino, dusted with fresh nutmeg and served like most drinks here in glass mugs, arrived with an amaretto cookie. All this was delivered by a tuxedoed staff at white wrought-iron tables on a large outdoor courtyard under a red, black and white canopy, beside a trickling fountain.

The soaring interior dining room is just as dramatic. Its high black ceiling contrasts with exposed ducts painted pinkish-mauve. The black marbled tables bear huge white service plates emblazoned with the Tauraso logo. An extensive list of daily specials supplements an ambitious menu categorized as pizzas, pastas and specialties ranging from chicken cutlets milanese to filet mignon with béarnaise sauce. Your only difficulty may be settling on a choice between gourmet pizzas fresh from the wood-fired oven and specials like peppered tuna with braised vegetable ragoût and sundried tomatoes or grilled rockfish with tomato-basil vinaigrette.

Bananas foster, chocolate mousse, warm peach cobbler, cannoli and Italian ice creams are possible dessert selections. A staggering wine list has great range in both price and origin and is computerized for changes every week.

(301) 663-6600. Entrées, $12.95 to $19.95. Open daily, 11 to 11.

The Province Restaurant, 131 North Market St., Frederick.

Billed as a bistro-style restaurant, this is not French as its name might suggest, but creative American and international, in the words of co-owner Nancy Floria. It takes its name from the 1767 deed to the property, when the area was known as the Province of Maryland. The brick walls of the first building on the site form the central part of the restaurant, which is cozy and historic in the front and middle, and opens onto an airy garden room addition in back.

The last is a stunning space for lunch, overlooking a flower and herb garden eked out between downtown buildings. New Age music plays against a backdrop of brick floors, comfortable snowshoe chairs and handmade quilts on the walls. Here we enjoyed chilled peach soup, a seafood pasta salad, a brie and almond pâté and a Greek salad. An orange mousse cake from a dessert tray bearing at least nine yummy desserts was a light and refreshing ending.

At night, the menu ranges widely from shrimp provençal and grilled salmon meunière to Parisian poulet, prime rib and veal piccata. Soft-shell crab with honey mustard-pinenut sauce and roast pork loin with fettuccine ragu were specials at a recent visit. The hummus and pita, antipasto plate, spanakopita and crab imperial in potato shells lend an international flavor to the appetizers.

Desserts range from hazelnut cream cake to derby pie to Washington apple cake. They are made daily at the Bake Shop at **Province II,** a caterer, baker and sandwich maker at 12 East Patrick St.

(301) 663-1441. Entrées, $12.95 to $18.95. Lunch, Monday-Friday 11:30 to 3. Dinner, Tuesday-Saturday 5:30 to 9 or 10. Saturday brunch, 11:30 to 3. Sunday, brunch 11 to 3:30, dinner 4 to 8.

The Brown Pelican, 5 East Church St., Frederick.

Pelicans are the theme of this elegant basement restaurant in a downtown building. They appear on drawings and paintings on the walls, in an etched-glass partition separating the bar from the dining room, and atop the oversize parchment menu that arrives rolled up like a scroll and refuses to lie flat. The atmosphere is serene: white-linened tables, captain's chairs, fieldstone walls and beamed ceilings.

Scallops scampi and crab norfolk might supplement the nearly two dozen entrées on the continental dinner menu, which seldom changes and appeals to traditionalists. It includes walnut bourbon chicken, shrimp czarina, lobster savannah, roast duckling with orange or green peppercorn sauce, mixed grill (filet, pork chop and German sausage) and New York strip steak. Appetizers cover all the bases from marinated herring and shrimp cocktail to baked brie and escargots. Six pasta dishes and caesar salad are listed under appetizers for two or more.

Some of the dinner entrées and pastas turn up on the lunch menu. Interesting salads and sandwiches also are available.

(301) 695-5833. Entrées, $12.95 to $18.95. Lunch, Monday-Friday 11:30 to 3. Dinner, Monday-Saturday 5 to 9:30 or 10.

Cafe Kyoko, 10 East Patrick St., Frederick.

Upstairs over Province II is this intriguing Japanese-Thai combination, a branch of Restaurant Kyoko in Washington, D.C. The high-ceilinged room could be any restaurant in Frederick, except for a couple of fancy chandeliers and some hanging lanterns on the landing and, of course, an authentic sushi bar. The third floor has a dining room with cushions on the floor.

The menu pairs Japanese tempura, teriyaki, sukiyaki and such side by side with Thai standards like goong-pad and seafood pattaya.

The sushi choices are extensive, and Japanese and Indian beers are on tap.

(301) 695-9656. Entrées, $8.95 to $13.95. Lunch, Monday-Friday 11:30 to 2. Dinner, Monday-Saturday 5:30 to 9 or 10.

Mealey's Restaurant, 8 Main St., New Market.

Dating to 1793, this old hotel turned into a dining institution is, as its name might imply, a place for a good meal. After a kitchen fire, owners Jose and Pat Salaverri rebuilt, to the approval of their large and loyal following. The main beamed dining room is dark, authentic and almost too atmospheric for words. Check out the vintage Wurlitzer jukebox near the entry in the bar.

The menu stresses seafood, from fried shrimp to crab imperial. Three cuts of prime rib, three steaks and three chicken dishes are alternatives. Crab bisque and smoked baby trout are among appetizers. Favored desserts are homemade cheesecake with raspberry sauce and bread pudding with bourbon sauce. Maryland selections are featured on the wine list.

(301) 865-5488. Entrées, $11.50 to $22.95. Lunch, Friday and Saturday 11:30 to 2:30. Dinner, Tuesday-Saturday 5 to 9, Sunday noon to 8. No smoking.

Diversions

Historic Frederick. The historic district embraces 33 blocks of central Frederick, but the important structures are concentrated along eight short blocks of downtown. The downtown Visitor Center offers a map for a short walking tour, but its 90-minute guided walking tour given weekends and holidays at 1:30 is well worth the $4.50 tab. Many of the fascinating sights (and insights) we were told about aren't detailed in the written tour. Among these are the unique top hats atop dormer windows, the cast-iron dog stolen by Confederate soldiers desperate for bullets and later returned and resting today in front of Dr. John Tyler's Home and the unbelievably realistic murals painted on downtown store walls under the city's Angels in the Architecture program. You see the law offices of Roger Brooke Taney and Francis Scott Key (famous brothers-in-law, one a Supreme Court justice known for the Dred Scott Decision and the other the author of the National Anthem) opposite City Hall and Court House Square. Other tour highlights: the oldest consecrated Catholic church in the country, the oldest ginkgo tree in the country across from the synagogue, the Barbara Fritchie House and Museum (open Thursday-Monday or by appointment, $2), the home of the first president of the

Antietam was scene of bloodiest one-day battle of Civil War.

Continental Congress, the Historical Society of Frederick County (same hours and price as Fritchie House, but free to walking-tour participants) and stately townhouses, mansions and public buildings shaded by trees and parks. Of particular interest are the stained-glass windows in All Saints Episcopal Church, one side of which is original Tiffany glass, beneath a ceiling that is a replica of Noah's Ark.

Carroll Creek Park. A new promenade and linear corridor – the result of a flood-control project – stretch nearly a mile and a half through the city's heart. Benches, fountains, plantings, wood sculptures and a bridge with trompe-l'oeil stone walls are among diversions for passersby. The annual **Frederick Festival of the Arts** is staged here, and more activities and commercial and office developments were planned along the creek banks. Already, an old mill has been turned into the **Delaplaine Visual Arts Center** at 40 South Carroll St. and the **Frederick Brewing Company** brews Blue Ridge beers and ales and gives weekend tastings and tours at its microbrewery at 103 South Carroll St.

War Memorabilia. Frederick, a city where families and friends were divided by the War Between the States, is a center for devotees of the Civil War. It's centrally located between Gettysburg, Antietam and Harpers Ferry, among the more significant sites. More than 500 Confederate soldiers are buried in the city's vast **Mount Olivet Cemetery.** The Revolutionary War **Hessian Barracks,** the only surviving structures of the Civil War hospital complex here, are nearby. The **National Museum of Civil War Medicine,** detailing the story of care and healing amidst all the death and destruction, opened in 1995 at 48 East Patrick St. A new visitor center serves visitors at **Monocacy National Battlefield,** where Confederate General Jubal Early's advance on Washington was delayed long enough to allow Union reinforcements to enter and save the city.

Antietam National Battlefield. One of America's best preserved (and least crowded) battlefields, this was the site of the bloodiest battle in U.S. history. More than 23,000 men on both sides were killed or wounded on Robert E. Lee's first invasion of the north on Sept. 17, 1862. Antietam Creek "actually ran red that day," we were told by our Frederick walking-tour guide. Pause at the visitor center to view the award-winning, 26-minute movie, "Antietam Visit." It's gripping, grisly and melancholy. An eight-mile-long tour road allows visitors to drive past important sites and more than 350 monuments, tablets, markers and cannons. Adults, $1.

Antiquing in New Market. Just off the interstate, this little one-street town crossed by alleys is heaven for antiquers. The village that originally served as a stopover for travelers on the National Pike between Baltimore and Frederick has staked its reputation on being a destination for those with a serious interest in antiques. More than 30 shops are tucked in and behind houses in a half-mile stretch. There's not a boutique in sight. Most shops are open only the latter half of the week or on weekends. You can stop for lunch or dessert at the cozy **Village Tea Room & Antique Shop,** 81 West Main St., where the owner-baker makes 22 kinds of pies and offers sandwiches and vegetarian fare in the $5 to $7 range.

Shopping. Frederick's downtown has never been lost, and even retained a local department store into the early 1990s. Although boutiques and crafts shops have sprouted up, it still has a barber shop located on the main street, where the window was filled with old glass milk bottles and seven men were waiting on a Tuesday morning for the three chairs. And people are apt to say hello; even the policeman bade us good morning and the meter maid awarded us a reprieve with a courtesy parking ticket. The owners of the **Museum Shop,** well-known for restoring museum paintings, moved from Washington to Frederick to open a gallery of exotic works, including a line of cards and plates with animal prints; Frederick proved so responsive that they moved to larger quarters at 20 North Market St. **The Country Way, Country Frills** and **Options of Frederick** are among the gift shops. **The Candy Kitchen** has dispensed candy made the old-fashioned way for more than 50 years.

There's another concentration of shops, some of them hard to find or get to, at the restored **Everedy Square & Shab Row** east of downtown. **Flights of Fancy** is a colorful place on several levels with a New Age atmosphere, handmade items, educational toys and our favorite Salt Marsh Pottery from Massachusetts. Wonderful specialty foods, chocolates, Maryland wines and gift baskets are among the offerings at **The Frederick Basket Company.** In between is the local branch of **Talbots.** Across the street from each other are the **Calico Fudge & Creamery** and the **Frederick Coffee Company Cafe.**

Extra-Special

Lilypons Water Gardens, 6800 Lilypons Road, Buckeystown.

Even if you've never been interested in water gardening, you should drive out to this fascinating aquatic farm and shop (incidentally named for Lily Pons, the opera star) eight miles south of Frederick. Here are 300 acres of tranquility, with pond after pond containing lilies and lotus with names like queen of whites, glorisa, rosy morn, floating heart and pink sensation. Holding tanks in back of the shop contain koi, the colorful Japanese carp (some as expensive as $250), comets, calico fantails and the like. The shop carries everything one needs to start a water garden, from books to filters, pumps and pool de-icers. Lectures and demonstrations are offered from spring to fall. The annual Lotus Blossom Festival occurs around the middle of July when the lotus begin to bloom, and the Koi Festival takes place in early September. Any time, you can take a picnic, stroll around the ponds, and dream of your own lagoon-shaped pool with the underground lights, the fan fountain and the black Japanese snails, tadpoles and clams to help keep it all clean.

(301) 874-5133 or (800) 723-7667. Open daily 10 to 5, March-October.

Solomons, Md.

The Ultimate Watering Place

Barely a mile long, this strip of watery real estate conjures up many an image in the minds of Marylanders. They think of the shore, boating, bugeyes, crabbing, watermen, the Patuxent River and the Chesapeake Bay.

They also think of a village bustling with belated tourism development – a far cry from its earlier description as a typical coastal fishing village.

Typical it is not, this narrow peninsula jutting from the foot of the graceful Governor Thomas Johnson bridge that arches over the Patuxent widewaters as they empty into the bay.

Airplanes soar overhead from the Patuxent Naval Air Station across the river. More boats seem to jockey for position in Solomons' deep-water harbor than in Annapolis. And more visitors from nearby cities descend during a summer weekend on what one booster calls "this sleepy little town" than it can possibly absorb.

Think of Ocean City – without the beaches and the high-rises – and you may

View from Calvert Marine Museum store.

get the picture. Life, though hectic on weekends, is quieter here along the bay and Maryland's western shore.

Solomons Island was named in 1870 for Isaac Solomon, who established the area's first oyster-packing facilities. The island part of the name was quickly dropped by the post office and Solomons really looks more like a peninsula than an island. It grew as a waterfront community, with a fishing fleet of more than 500 vessels, most built locally. More bugeyes – large, decked-over sailing canoes – were built here than in any bayside community.

Solomons gave birth to racing yachts of international fame. The maritime tradition continues today at the Calvert Marine Museum and the Chesapeake Biological Laboratory.

As with other resort communities of its ilk, this one is ever-changing. There were virtually no places to stay until a Holiday Inn opened in the mid-1980s. Today, Solomons has five bed-and-breakfast facilities offering a total of two dozen rooms. There are at least a hundred times that many restaurant seats. Singles jam the open-air Tiki Bar and whatever new restaurant and bar is au courant. "I've been here since 1977 and have seen a lot of coming and going," says shopkeeper Joann Kersey of all the changes.

What doesn't change is the inherent Solomons appeal – its watery aspects, the sailing, the charter fishing and the natural attractions of a special place.

Inn Spots

Back Creek Inn, Calvert and A Streets, Box 520, Solomons 20688.

Location, location, location. The Back Creek Inn has it, plus tranquility, beauty, artistry and sophistication. Artist Carol Pennock and gardener Lin Cochran offer seven elegant guest accommodations in a century-old waterman's house, a new addition and a great little cottage.

The pair were living in the area while their husbands were on military duty at Patuxent when the fledgling inn property became available. "It was love at first sight," Carol recalls.

The house is a couple of blocks off the island's main street in a residential section along the waterfront. Thick foliage blocks the front entrance; a gnarled paper mulberry tree along the side path makes you duck or go around. The verdant side lawn slopes gently to the deep waters of wide Back Creek. In the midst of lavish English-style gardens is a hot tub with a patio beside and a view of all the waterway goings-on.

Guests are welcomed with iced tea in big blue glasses bearing the inn's logo. It's served in a comfy, contemporary, brick-floored common room with floor-to-ceiling windows on two sides to bring the outdoor garden in. Beyond are an open kitchen and a stenciled dining room where four tables are set for breakfast. Lyn's beautiful herbal wreaths and Carol's paintings enhance both common and guest rooms. The art of the latter, who works in a variety of media, is so striking that we had to buy a couple of her small renderings of oysters and clams.

Off the dining room on the main floor is a room with a brass double bed and private bath. Upstairs are three rooms, two with queen beds and one with a double. All have private baths. They are nicely decorated with frilly curtains, an abundance of pillows and quilts made by Carol's sister-in-law.

Two suites are in the addition that also serves as a studio and living quarters for the innkeepers. Both suites have sitting areas, TV sets and oversize beds. One faces the vegetable-herb garden and the other the hot tub. But we'd splurge again to stay in the cozy, peaked-ceilinged cottage, with a queensize bed, a bathroom in shades of mauve, TV, fireplace and an idyllic screened porch from which to view the water and gardens.

Breakfast was a treat, even though an overnight rain had made things too wet for the usual service outside on the patio when we were there. Juice, coffee and fancy breads awaited on side tables in the dining room as Carol took orders for her

Innkeepers Lin Cochran and Carol Pennock are ready for breakfast at Back Creek Inn.

"Back Creek Bennies Our Way," superb eggs benedict with a sweet tang (ask her what the mystery ingredient is). These came garnished with fresh fruit, including kiwis and figs. Other choices might be a ham and cheese omelet, waffles topped with warm fruit compote or crab quiche – "when we have time to pick our own crabs off the pier," Carol advises. Sunday often brings a buffet with two different casseroles.

(410) 326-2022. Fax (410) 326-2946. Four rooms, two suites and one cottage with private baths. Doubles, $95. Suites, $125. Cottage, $145. Children over 12. No smoking. Closed mid-December to February.

Solomons Victorian Inn, 125 Charles St., Box 759, Solomons 20688.

New owners have upgraded this turn-of-the-century Victorian house on a rise overlooking water on three sides. Helen and Richard Bauer, sailing enthusiasts from Frederick, poured considerable resources and energy into the old Davis House, whose owners retired.

Originally the family home of Clarence Davis, renowned builder of early 20th century sailboats, the main floor holds a cozy sitting room outfitted in wicker and a more formal front living room.

Five second-floor guest rooms are named for Davis yachts, each bearing the appropriate picture. Furnishings vary from Victorian to casual white wicker. The front Orithia Room has a kingsize mahogany four-poster bed and a bay window yielding harbor views. The other rooms have queensize beds and three have water views.

The ultimate for views, however, is the huge third-floor Solomons Sunset suite, segmented into separate areas by sloping ceilings with skylights. Big windows front and side frame water scenes, enjoyed from two sitting areas. A double jacuzzi lies beneath another sloping window. The iron and wicker bed is kingsize. The suite comes with a fireplace, TV, a kitchenette and a dining area.

There's no need to cook, however, for the Bauers offer a hearty breakfast on a breakfast porch they refinished after "stripping about 25 coats of paint." The fare the day of our visit featured summer melon raised by the Amish near Annapolis and a shrimp puff incorporating eggs, mushrooms, cheeses and shrimp, followed by sour cream coffee cake and blueberry muffins. Stuffed french toast with peach preserves, blueberry bread and currant muffins were on the next morning's docket.

In 1997, the Bauers were adding two more suites in a carriage house behind the main house. They planned double jacuzzi tubs and gas fireplaces for both. They decorated the upstairs kingsize suite in gold and white for romance. The downstairs suite with queen brass bed was appointed in florals in shades of mauve and green.

(410) 326-4811. Five rooms and three suites with private baths. Doubles, $90 to $110. Suites, $165. Lower rates in winter. Two-night minimum on special weekends. Children over 13. No smoking.

By-the-Bay Bed & Breakfast, 14374 Calvert St., Box 504, Solomons 20688.
Owners Joan and Tom Hogenson spent six years renovating their Victorian house beside Back Creek before opening as a B&B in 1988. They stripped and refinished all the stained-pine woodwork. They painted the exterior a striking mulberry rose color with pink trim. She did the stenciling and he the stained glass in the front door and living room. Victoriana is the rule here – fairly dark in the living room and quite light and airy in the guest rooms.

The three bedrooms possess what Joan calls "an old-time flavor with modern comforts," such as private baths, queensize beds and TV sets. A main-floor bedroom off the dining room has a private entrance, a potbelly stove and a small refrigerator. It opens to an adjacent sitting room for optional use as a suite. Upstairs is a rear room with a step-up iron bed and plants in the windows. The front room has a recliner chair and a rocker. You'll find decorative touches like two old irons, but little of the clutter that fussies-up some Victorian inns.

A full breakfast is served at a lace-draped table beneath an elaborate old chandelier in the dining room. Fresh fruit or baked apples, Tom's muffins, hot or cold cereal and omelets, french toast or strata could be the fare. The Hogensons offer a deep-water dock, a swing on the wraparound veranda, a rear patio, lovely rear gardens with statue and fountain, and a screened-in sitting room and terrace down by the water.

(410) 326-3428. Two rooms and one suite with private baths. Doubles, $75 and $80. Suite, $95. Two-night minimum weekends in season. No credit cards. No smoking.

Solomons waterfront is on view from third-floor suite at Solomons Victorian Inn.

Webster House, 14364 Sedwick Ave., Box 1607, Solomons 20688.

Running a B&B was "an afterthought" for Peter and Barbara Prentice, who had envisioned opening a place for retreats for clergymen. "We were riding our bicycles and wondering where we'd live when we saw the old Webster house," reports Barbara. They demolished and rebuilt the house, designing it to look old in front. "We felt we were giving a new house a history."

Peter, a Navy physician, and Barbara opened their new/old house as a B&B in 1993. With their children gone, Barbara said, "I missed having people around." The prime accommodations are out back in The Haven, upstairs over a detached garage, where a private deck overlooks the long back yard and catches a glimpse of the broad waters in Back Creek. Here you'll find a queensize bed, private bath, a little kitchen with a dining table and cable TV.

Two large bedrooms on the front of the second floor in the main house share a hall bath (plus a half bath on the main floor). They also share a third-floor common room with TV, videos and exercise equipment. The bright and airy Lydia Beekman Room, named for Peter's grandmother, has a queensize English oak bedstead, lacy curtains on the windows and a loveseat with a Scrabble game at the ready. The Vanderpoel Room, stately in green, contains a cherry four-poster queen bed and two armchairs.

The Webster House brochure advertises "a homey Christian atmosphere," although we did not find it obvious. Artist Carol Pennock from the nearby Back Creek Inn stenciled the grape pattern around the entry. Barbara made the china dolls that line the window seat. She got Amish carpenters to build the built-in shelves in the dining room. A rear family room opens into the country kitchen. Here is where Barbara prepares a full breakfast – a fruit cup followed perhaps by puff pancakes with strawberries, waffles, or eggs benedict with asparagus or zucchini. The meal is often taken on the rear porch beside the patio and gardens.

Iced tea and shortbread are served in the afternoon. In the evening, Barbara puts out candles so guests can soak in the outdoor spa by candlelight.

Lately, the Webster House has curtailed its schedule, operating primarily on weekends.

(410) 326-0454. Fax (410) 326-5092. One room with private bath and two rooms with shared bath. Doubles, $85. The Haven, $140. Two-night minimum on weekends. No credit cards. Closed November-March.

Adina's Guest House, 14236 South Solomons Island Road, Solomons 20688.

A wide front porch with comfortable lounge chairs faces the Patuxent River and the soaring Governor Thomas Johnson Bridge across a cornfield at this B&B, which opened in 1993. Inside are a large living room with dining area, four bedrooms and the quarters of owners Adelaida and Glen Papure, who have done considerable renovations to the house. The expense was such that both had to resume fulltime jobs and, while officially open year-round, they concentrate on weekends.

The guest rooms come with queensize beds and cable TV. Two on the main floor have private baths, while two upstairs share a bath. The rooms have a variety of beds from sleigh to four-poster and are furnished with a few antique pieces in country style.

The Papures prepare a hearty breakfast of the guest's choice, including scrambled eggs with bacon, omelets or french toast, with fresh fruits and homemade muffins. Guests can make requests and "if I have it in my kitchen, I'll make it," says Adelaida.

The couple commute 90 minutes each way to their daytime jobs in Washington, D.C. They had the house up for sale in 1997. Who said running a B&B in your spare time is easy?

(410) 326-4895. Two rooms with private baths and two rooms with shared baths. Doubles, $65 to $80. No smoking.

Dining Spots

Dry Dock Restaurant, C Street at Back Creek, Solomons.

Part of the impressive Zahniser's Sailing Center, Dry Dock is upstairs over a small bathhouse with great views of the harbor. Innovative fresh seasonal cuisine is featured on the blackboard menu, which changes daily, and the food is considered the best in Solomons.

Decor is simple and nautical, with eight bare wood tables bearing paper napkins, pepper grinders and candles in globes. A lineup of signal flags frames large windows overlooking the busy waterfront. We watched with fascination the parade of boats finishing the weekly Wednesday night race. Racers accounted for much of the activity in the noisy bar, which is cheek to jowl with the tables in the small, L-shaped room.

Dinner began with a complimentary wooden board bearing Wispride cheese spread and assorted crackers. We liked the oyster stew better than the highly touted spinach salad with fruit and nuts.

Good main courses were lightly breaded pan-fried oysters with herbs de provence and grilled tuna with tomato-basil salsa. They came with rice, broccoli and an abundance of non-edible garnishes. Other possibilities included grilled mahi-mahi with sweet and sour sauce, grilled rockfish with Southwestern mushroom fricassee, and shrimp and scallops sauté with sundried tomatoes and pinenuts. Prime rib and sautéed chicken with curried carrots and tart cherries were the only non-seafood

Diners at window tables at Dry Dock Restaurant enjoy view of harbor scene.

items at our latest visit. Desserts included key lime pie, bourbon pecan pie and a number of chocolate extravagances.

Light dining is available in summer at the Dry Dock's jaunty outdoor **Pool Bar Cafe** beside the sailing center's pool. The menu includes salads, sandwiches and a few grilled items and specials.

(410) 326-4817. Entrées, $15.95 to $21.95. Dinner, Monday-Thursday 6 to 9, Friday and Saturday, 5:30 to 9:30. Sunday, brunch 10 to 1, dinner 5:30 to 8:30.

Lighthouse Inn, Patuxent Avenue, Solomons.

The bar here is in a skipjack, the Spirit of Solomons, custom-built in the restaurant. It's a conversation piece at a contemporary, high-ceilinged establishment with huge windows onto the harbor and an outdoor deck that takes full advantage of its waterside location.

The chef's cuisine has won awards for the restaurant, which was built in 1986. Seafood takes precedence on the menu, which ranges from a vegetarian platter to surf and turf. Scallops with mushrooms and cheddar cheese, crab in the usual guises, baked stuffed shrimp, seafood platters and filet mignon are favorites; flounder renaissance and snapper royale could be specials. Start with scallops wrapped in bacon, stuffed mushrooms or escargots.

Interior dining is on two levels on the main floor and on a spacious mezzanine. Oil lamps cast shadows on each shiny wood table. Sandwiches and light fare are served outside at the **Quarter Deck,** a separate entity run by the same enterprise.

(410) 326-2444. Entrées, $13.95 to $24.95. Dinner nightly, 5 to 9 or 10.

The C.D. Cafe, 14350 Solomons Island Road, Solomons.

Chef-owners Catherine File and Deborah Witmer used to cook at the Dry Dock Restaurant, so you'd expect the fare at their new cafe to be a cut above. And it is, according to all reports. Theirs is the full-service successor to a gourmet bakery and deli in the Avondale Center, a good-looking, contemporary retail complex built by Skip and Ellen Zahniser of the marina family. The Zahnisers thought the town needed another decent, casual restaurant serving dinner, and this is the happy result.

The sleek gray decor is minimal. Cane chairs are at butcherblock tables topped with gray inlays.

The dinner menu is eclectic, to say the least. Under appetizers and light fare are things like caesar salad with grilled salmon, a hummus and couscous sampler, creole andouille sausage and Catherine's savory cheesecake, a walnut-crusted blend of herbs, goat cheese and cream cheese. For entrées, Deb's favorite is pan-seared chicken with pecans, apples and onions, deglazed with apple schnapps and topped with crumbled feta. Other possibilities are smoked salmon cakes, scallops with sundried tomatoes and blue cheese over orzo, Mediterranean pasta and cajun shepherd's pie. No heavy dishes here – the meatiest is steak au poivre, unless you include a bistro burger.

Catherine's desserts are special: crème brûlée, bourbon-pecan pie, chocolate mousse cake, amaretto pound cake and decadent brownies. We got a taste of the last after a quick lunch of a curried chicken salad sandwich and potato salad that really hit the spot.

The espresso-cappuccino machine is the only one on Solomons, which makes this a good place for continental breakfast and coffee in the morning. There's a full bar for drinks later on.

(410) 326-3877. Entrées, $8.25 to $17.95. Continental breakfast from 9. Lunch, Monday-Saturday 11:30 to 2 or 3. Dinner, Thursday-Saturday 5:30 to 9. Sunday, brunch 11 to 3, dinner 5:30 to 8:30.

Captain's Table, 275 Lore Road, Solomons.

Good food at affordable prices is the hallmark of this hidden waterfront restaurant. You have to know about it and then find it, but the search pays off.

The setting is super: two nautical rooms, a bar and a waterside deck right beside Back Creek. The huge, eight-page menu is traditional plus: orange roughy parmesan, Chesapeake Bay rockfish, baked chicken cheddar. The specialty is baked stuffed shrimp with crab imperial, and the crab cakes were voted the best in Southern Maryland. The changing desserts are said to be some of the finest in town.

The deck is a great place for lunch, perhaps the specialty seafood quiche, a croissant stuffed with ham salad or a fried steak sandwich. An all-you-can eat breakfast bar is offered weekends for $5.99.

(410) 326-2772. Entrées, $12.95 to $19.95. Breakfast from 7. Lunch from 11. Dinner from 4.

The Naughty Gull, Lore Road, Spring Cove Marina, Solomons.

The view is everything from this nautical restaurant and pub, centered by a large bar in the middle, with tables on several levels. Alas, there's no deck for outdoor dining beside the water, but we lucked into the next best thing, one of the few window tables. The lunch menu yielded a soft-shell crab sandwich and an enormous, gloppy platter of aztec nachos, accompanied by plenty of guacamole, sour cream and hot salsa on the side.

Come nightfall, a varied menu is ranges from fish and chips to filet mignon. Crab imperial, a crab cake platter, three shrimp dishes and prime rib are among the possibilities. Dessert could be carrot cake, cheesecake or chocolate cake.

(410) 326-4855. Entrées, $11.95 to $19.95. Open daily from 11. Sunday brunch, 9 to 3.

Bowen's Inn, 14630 Solomons Island Road, Solomons.

Full of local color, Bowen's has been serving watermen since 1918 and looks it. Behind a three-story shingled building angled to the street lies an atmospheric bar and the newish Captain Mortimer Room, where a handful of small windows offer glimpses of the water. Problem is, the windows are too high for patrons seated at most tables to see out.

Locals laud Bowen's for what it is – a family-owned operation run by Captain Mortimer's granddaughter – and care not a whit that some tables sport lacy white cloths and others paper mats, all with fake flowers to brighten things up.

The menu is a typewritten sheet of mimeograph vintage. It ranges from spaghetti with meatballs through soft-shell crab and veal parmesan to New York strip steak and crab imperial. Salad and rolls come with. Those with hearty appetites can start with potato skins, Buffalo wings, nachos and such. Cheesecake and pies are favored desserts.

(410) 326-9814. Entrées, $6.95 to $14.95. Lunch and dinner, Tuesday-Sunday 11 to 9 or 10. Closed January to St. Patrick's Day.

Diversions

Solomons boasts an impressive new **Riverwalk,** a sixteen-foot-wide boardwalk stretching a third of a mile along the bulkhead of the Patuxent River. There are benches as well as a pavilion and an amphitheater. A 46-seat water taxi known as the Stars & Stripes shuttles passengers around the island on weekends in summer.

Sailing, boating and charter fishing are the big attractions. They are offered through various marinas, which seem to be the second most prevalent business activity here after restaurants. Hour-long cruises around Solomons Inner Harbor are offered by the 1899 log-built bugeye William B. Tennison, the oldest passenger-carrying vessel on the Chesapeake Bay. They're scheduled to leave at 2 p.m. Wednesday-Sunday, May-October, from the Calvert Marine Museum, but may depart early, as we found to our dismay upon arrival one afternoon at 1:56.

Calvert Marine Museum, Route 2, Solomons.

Started in the old school building, this growing museum specializes in local maritime history, the marine paleontology of the nearby Calvert Cliffs and the estuarine life of the tidal Patuxent River and adjacent waters. Its impressive exhibition building, dedicated in 1989, has extensive exhibits on the Patuxent, including 500 photographs, scale models and artifacts. Among them are a 28-foot-long, three-log canoe and an underwater mine and torpedo from World War II testing in the river. A permanent exhibit on the river and its life features seventeen aquariums, live otters and a discovery room with "please touch" area for children. A hall of fossils from the Calvert Cliffs traces ancient inhabitants of the region, including the enormous jaws and teeth of the extinct great white shark. Fascinating to visit is the Drum Point Lighthouse, which dominates the waterfront and is one of three remaining cottage-type lights from the bay. Fifteen visitors may go inside hourly on guided tours. Varied watercraft are on display in the small craft building or are afloat in the boat basin. Half a mile south of the main museum complex is the J.C. Lore Oyster House, which traces the region's commercial seafood industry and portrays the area's traditions of boatbuilding. Nautical and local items of interest are sold in the excellent Museum Store.

(410) 326-2042. Open daily, 10 to 5. Adults, $4.

Annmarie Garden, Dowell Road, Solomons.

Accented with contemporary sculptures, 30 acres of forests and gardens along St. John Creek are being developed into a world-class sculpture garden. Walkways in the woods take visitors past juried sculptures set in garden "rooms" cut out of the forest. A sculpture of an oyster tonger was a focal point at an early visit, followed by talking benches, a council ring and a surveyor's map. One local artist predicted the sculpture garden would ultimately rival the famous Brookgreen Gardens of South Carolina. The late Francis Koenig, who had donated the land and named it for his ailing wife, envisioned it as "a contemplative and creative place" for the public to commune amid floral and fauna. All kinds of visual and performing artists make the garden rooms come alive at the annual September Artsfest, which attracts 15,000 visitors and was named Calvert County's best event of the year in 1996. Gardenfest is a plant sale and exhibition staged annually in late April.

(410) 326-4640. Open daily, 10 to 4; closed weekends in winter. Free.

Calvert Cliffs State Park, Route 765, Lusby.

Nearly 30 miles of cliffs along the Chesapeake Bay's western shore north of Solomons hold one of the world's richest concentrations of fossil whales among more than 600 species of fossils up to seventeen million years old. A two-mile hike through the 1,460-acre wooded park takes visitors to the cliffs, which have been closed to fossiling lately.

(301) 872-5688. Open daily, sunrise to sunset. Donation, $2.

Jefferson Patterson Park and Museum, 10515 Mackall Road, St. Leonard.

Pre-historic and Colonial sites, nature and archaeology trails, farm exhibits and a visitor center with exhibits on history and nature are featured in this 544-acre preserve along the banks of the Patuxent River. Tractor-pulled wagon tours are offered weekends in summer.

(410) 586-0050. Open Wednesday-Sunday 10 to 5, mid-April to mid-October. Free.

Battle Creek Cypress Swamp, Grays Road off Route 506, Prince Frederick.

The northernmost natural stand of bald cypress trees in America distinguishes this 100-acre nature sanctuary. An elevated boardwalk covers a quarter mile of the swamp, now home to white-tailed deer, muskrats and other wildlife. The mysteries of the swamp are examined more closely in presentations at the nature center.

(410) 535-5327. Open Tuesday-Saturday 10 to 5, Sunday 1 to 5; to 4:30, October-March. Free.

Point Lookout State Park, Route 5, St. Mary's County.

The southernmost point in Maryland is at the tip of a 1,037-acre peninsula at the confluence of the Potomac River and the Chesapeake Bay. The park is so large and so far from the mainstream that it's almost always uncrowded. Attractions include miles of beaches on both river and bay, a fishing pier jutting 700 feet into the bay, a lighthouse, a swimming beach, a Civil War museum, an earthen fort built by Confederate prisoners and a Confederate cemetery. The Confederate Monument here is the only federal monument dedicated to those who died for the rebel cause. We liked the park's seclusion and the broad view across to the Northern Neck of Virginia.

(301) 872-5688. Open daily, 8 a.m. to sunset.

Shopping. Ensconced in a structure built right over the water along the boardwalk is **The Sandpiper,** a gift shop adjacent to the town dock, which also rents bicycles and sells ice cream. We picked up some clever Christmas cards from owner Joann Kersey's excellent selection at her other shop at the Holiday Inn Select. Handpainted clothing, T-shirts, jewelry, resort wear and gifts are featured at **Caren's Solomons Style.** Thousands of used and rare books are available **at Lazy Moon Book Shop,** where the owner is as interesting as his stock. The increasingly well-known **Carmen's Gallery** displays appealing artworks. Hoping to set a standard for future commercial development of Solomons, Ellen and Skip Zahniser of sailing-center fame erected Avondale Center, a retail and professional complex along the main street. Among its treasures are **Fine Things,** whimsically stocked with one-of-a-kind shell items, pottery, cut crystal, accessories and such, in exquisite taste. If we'd had a spare $155 we might have emerged with a gold-shell wreath. But it was on to **Solomons Mines,** where we ogled all the gems and jewelry.

Extra-Special

Historic St. Mary's City, Route 5, St. Mary's City.

Founded in 1634 by Catholic pilgrims, this National Historic Landmark was the fourth permanent settlement in British North America and served as the Colonial capital of Maryland until 1695. The abandonment of the town and the subsequent shift to agriculture was an archaeological blessing, for most of the 17th-century town was preserved under the plowed soils, awaiting excavation. A low-key, outdoor living-history museum opened on the 800-acre site in 1984, and work continues to uncover and restore the nation's only Colonial capital still undisturbed by development or erosion. Four main exhibit areas include the Visitor Center with an archaeology exhibit hall, a tobacco plantation, the Chancellor's Point Natural History Area (site of a Chesapeake Indian Lifeways Center) and the Governor's Field. We found the last to be of most interest. You can walk out on a dock in the St. Mary's River to board the square-rigged replica of a ship that brought the first settlers from England, hear your footsteps echo as you explore the reconstructed

State House of 1676 and stop for a lunch featuring traditional Colonial dishes and regional seafood specialties in the $5 to $10 range at Farthing's Ordinary. The remains of St. Mary's Chapel, whose excavation is in progress, marks the birthplace of the Roman Catholic church in America. The old town – what little there is of it – blends nicely into the waterfront campus of St. Mary's College, a liberal arts college of 1,500 students.

(301) 862-0990 or (800) 762-1634. Visitor center open year round. Exhibits open Wednesday-Sunday 10 to 5, April-November. Adults, $6.50.

State House at Historic St. Mary's City.

Tillie the Tug takes passengers for leisurely cruiise along Pocomoke River.

Snow Hill/Berlin, Md.

300 Years Along the River

Like a waterway in the bayous of Louisiana, the Pocomoke River lazes through the flatlands and forests of Maryland's Lower Eastern Shore. Stands of bald cypress trees define its path. Bald eagles, osprey, egrets and other wildlife populate its shores. The river – deep, languorous, mysterious and hauntingly beautiful – is Maryland's first to be designated "wild and scenic."

Such is the watery backdrop for little-known Snow Hill, founded by English colonists in 1642 and billed today as "the undiscovered treasure of the Eastern Shore." The county-seat town of 2,200 is not really on the way to anywhere. It claims more than 100 homes that are at least 100 years old, a way of life that's 40 years behind the times and almost no downtown at all. The big social events are church suppers and monthly dances in summer under the stars beside the river.

Snow Hill's counterpoint in the path of non-

discovery is Berlin, an old-fashioned town of 2,600 about fifteen miles to the northeast. The old houses here are not as compelling as the rejuvenated Victorian storefronts up against brick sidewalks on a maze of downtown streets. Berlin languished in the shadow of Ocean City until the late 1980s, when ten hometown boosters bought and renovated the Atlantic Hotel to wide acclaim. Now Berlin, pronounced BUR-lin by most natives, has a first-class restaurant, a restored theater, a working downtown, countless antiques shops and enough gawkers on weekends to qualify as the newly discovered "jewel of the Eastern Shore."

The attractions of Snow Hill, Berlin and environs are diverse: the Assateague Island National Seashore, canoeing on the Pocomoke, riverside parks, the site of a vanished 19th-century industrial village called Furnace Town. The coastal habitat and temperate climate produce the best bird-watching opportunities in Maryland.

Three centuries of history converge in Snow Hill. Its Presbyterian church is the first of the American denomination. All Hallows Episcopal Church, a brick antique surrounded by gravestones in the center of town, displays a bible and bell presented to the community by Queen Anne. Chain stores and fast-food outlets are noticeably missing here and in Berlin. The two small towns live up to their theme, "where the good life still lives on."

Inn Spots

The River House Inn, 201 East Market St., Snow Hill 21863.

A two-acre, 700-foot-deep lawn slopes down to the Pocomoke River behind this 1850 Victorian beauty, blessed with a wraparound veranda in front and screened porches upstairs and down in the rear. Larry and Susanne Knudsen from Ohio bought the residence and turned it into an elegant B&B with an expanding guest complex.

Besides the porches, they offer a bevy of attractive, comfortable public rooms on two sides of a green center hallway: a parlor with TV, a rosy red sitting and

River House Inn occupies ornate 1850 Victorian on two-acre lawn.

game room, a formal dining room and a breakfast room with draperies puddled on the floor. The breakfast room, which would be a fairly formal dining room in anyone else's lexicon, was the site for an impressive feast of orange juice, cantaloupe, blueberry muffins and a cheese omelet with bacon or sausage at our first stay. A recent visited yielded a choice of huevos rancheros and shirred River House eggs, both sensational.

Chocolates are at bedside at night. In the morning the Baltimore Sun was at our door outside the East Room, outfitted in Sheraton furniture with plush carpeting, fancy floral wallpaper coordinated with the curtains, and a high-ceilinged bathroom with windows. Three of the four guest rooms in the main house have fireplaces. All have queensize beds and private baths, one down the hall. The decor is French in the rear River Room and American Chippendale in the West Room. A third-floor suite with a wicker sitting area is done up in pastel pink and green in American country style.

Guests like to gather on the upstairs back porch full of wicker or its downstairs companion, smashingly appointed in tropical colors with bamboo-rattan furniture. The black decorative wrought iron on the front veranda could be straight out of New Orleans. Matching the wrought iron are the Knudsens' two friendly big black poodles, Bonnie and Winner, who love to go for romps down by the river.

Out back is the River Cottage, fashioned from an 1890s carriage barn. It's now a deluxe cottage with antique king bed, mini-refrigerator, entertainment center with radio and TV, and a neat wicker porch looking onto the lovely lawn with its Adirondack chairs and hammocks.

The newest accommodations are called the Riverview Hideaways, a new building with two substantial rooms offering queen beds, whirlpool tubs, gas fireplaces, thick carpeting and TV/VCRs, and each with a private 28-foot porch overlooking the Pocomoke River. The upstairs hideaway has a corner jacuzzi right in the room. The canopy bed in the downstairs unit is draped with ivy.

Dinner for house guests is available occasionally by reservation for $30, including wine. The meal might start with scallops seviche or crabmeat gratin and a salad. Barbecued steaks or salmon could be followed by frozen yogurt with fresh berries and homemade chocolate sauce.

The Knudsens have put in water gardens, lily ponds, fountains and walkways to supplement the lavish landscaping behind the main house. "Our objective is to make a home where guests feel comfortable," said Larry. It is a goal they quickly realized.

(410) 632-2722. Fax (410) 632-2866. Six rooms, one suite and one cottage with private baths. Doubles, $100 to $120. Cottage $160. Riverview, $175. Deduct $20 December-February. Two-night minimum summer weekends and holidays. Children accepted. No smoking.

Chaunceford Hall, 209 West Federal St., Snow Hill 21863.
Museum-quality furnishings – many of them made by the owner – are the hallmark of this refined B&B. Michael Driscoll lavishes as much attention on his custom furniture-making hobby that blossomed into a business as he and his wife Thelma devote to their guests.

The narrow, deep brick Greek Revival mansion dating to 1759 was built by Robert Morris, financier of the Revolution. Its three sections include the original house, a ballroom that's now the kitchen and a middle section joining the two. Beyond that kitchen, for which Michael made all the cabinets, is a stunning five-sided,

Elegant Greek Revival mansion dating to 1759 takes in guests as Chaunceford Hall.

high-ceilinged solarium shaded by the second biggest walnut tree in Maryland. Wine and hors d'oeuvre are offered here in the late afternoon, overlooking a brick patio with a 32-foot-long lap pool beneath a fiberglass roof.

Breakfast is served in an impressive dining room graced by Michael's sideboard and round tables in the Queen Anne style. Fresh fruit (strawberries, kiwi and bananas when we were there), apple-raisin muffins and eggs any style with sausage, bacon and potatoes O'Brien could be the fare.

The five guest rooms bear English names starting with the letter "C." Four have working fireplaces (the house has a total of ten), private baths, wing chairs, oriental rugs and canopied beds. All but one of the beds is queensize and all were made by Michael. Largest is the rear Carrington Suite with a loveseat and wing chair, a leather chair and rocker, and an extra twin bed. We're partial to the Chadwick, which has one of the two full baths as well as a crystal chandelier. The Chanceford Room on the main floor has the other full bath, a highboy, dark wainscoting and molding and a fancy medallion in the ceiling.

(410) 632-2231. Five rooms with private baths. Doubles, $115 to $135. Children over 12. No credit cards.

Merry Sherwood Plantation, 8909 Worcester Hwy., Berlin 21811.
Is this a museum or a B&B? The painstaking restoration and the priceless furnishings that owner Kirk Burbage lavished on his grandmother's grand antebellum beauty hint of the former, as does the sign "no guided tours today." But the run-of-the-house welcome for overnight guests and the energy of resident innkeeper Todd Durand attest to the latter.

Listed on the National Register, the Victorian showcase is a place where architectural historians, antiques enthusiasts and those into Victoriana are in their element. True, the place has its incongruities. Built in classic Italianate style, it also has Greek Revival and Gothic influences. The long main parlor (once a ballroom) holds both a grand piano and a square Victorian piano, while a pipe organ awaits in the front sitting room. The honeymoon suite comes with a marble bath and jacuzzi, yet the sunken bedroom with carved Victorian walnut double bed is the smallest in the house, and as for "suite," there's a little sitting room with uncomfortable chairs made for viewing rather than sitting. The other seven corner bedrooms on the second and third floors, all but two with private baths, seem quite spacious, particularly those with high ceilings on the second floor. The bathrooms are wallpapered and have marble floors and showers. The bedrooms are painted in lighter colors to set off the dark wood flooring. Most beds are dwarfed by heavy, ornate headboards and footers of solid walnut; "these beds need a lot of dusting," the chambermaid volunteered. On the nightstands are mints and Bibles. Fine oriental runners lead to the fourth-floor widow's walk, all windows with another Bible under the only seat.

Extravagant oriental rugs and carpets are particularly notable in the main ballroom/parlor, full of burgundy velvet sofas and settees. In the center of this expanse is a marble table topped by an enormous artificial floral arrangement in a three-foot-tall sterling silver vase imported from Germany, one of three in existence (and the owner claims two). The main-floor rooms are lit by no fewer than five huge brass chandeliers; a particularly striking one hangs over the table in the dining room. The house was in restoration for two years to the tune of $1½ million prior to its opening in 1992. The plaster walls, the loblolly pine flooring and a few of the furnishings are original. Kirk brought in the rest of the furniture, some of which had been in storage at his family's funeral home, oldest in Maryland, and had come from the area's finest estates.

"This is not a museum," innkeeper Todd stresses. "We want guests to play the pianos and read the books in the library." Tea and cookies are served in the afternoon. Next day in the great, dark dining room, guests sit down to a breakfast of apple pancakes, belgian waffles or egg casserole, served on fine china.

Although Kirk has no plans for expansion, he has enhanced the eighteen-acre property with seven formal Victorian gardens, a pagoda and a stocked pond, which make the place good for weddings and charity events. "We're doing our best to build the business to maintain this property the way my grandmother wished," says Kirk. "It's the most expensive hobby anyone could have, but she would be pleased."

(410) 641-2112 or (800) 660-0358. Five rooms and one suite with private baths; two rooms with shared bath. Mid-May to mid-October: doubles $150, suite $175. Rest of year: doubles $95, suite $125.

Waterloo Country Inn, 28822 Mount Vernon Road, Princess Anne 21853.

A bit west of the area but an early restaurant destination for visitors to Snow Hill, this is one of the more sophisticated small inns to open in the Mid-Atlantic region lately.

Therese and Erwin Kraemer from Switzerland came across the riverfront property while visiting friends in the area. They decided that very week to buy the three-story brick Georgian plantation house built in 1755 to run as a full-service inn and restaurant. She was a banker and he an electric company manager in Zurich. "We'd done a lot of entertaining and thought this would be easier," Therese said.

Many hours and more than $1 million in renovations later, they opened in 1996 with five elegant guest quarters and a 36-seat restaurant. A year later they closed the restaurant to the public, finding it "too much work" and the hours too long. "That was not what we came here for," Therese advised, although the Kraemers still serve dinners to house guests..

Major restoration preceded opening of Merry Sherwood Plantation as a B&B.

We were quite struck by two bedrooms in a main-floor wing. The Wicomico has a kingsize bed whose tapestry-look feather duvet matches the curtains, a fireplace that appears to be tiled in Delft, a handsome armoire, an antique sewing machine resting on a bureau, a sitting area and a full bath. The Manokin Room offers many of the same features.

It turns out the prime accommodations are upstairs, however. The Monte Room has a fishnet canopy king bed with fishnet quilt and pillows, two wing chairs, fireplace and a large bath. The Somerset is a two-room suite with queen bed, a fireplaced sitting room with a sofa and two chairs on beautiful hardwood floors, plus a bath with jacuzzi tub, separate shower and double vanity. The third-floor harbors the Chesapeake Suite with a kingsize bed and an enormous bathroom with a double jacuzzi, separate shower and double vanity. The sitting room with sofabed and a stunning antique Swiss buffet chest looks out onto a pond.

Each room is outfitted with TV, telephone, a closet with automatic lights and exotic fresh flowers. The decorative accessories, a mix of family Swiss pieces and American acquisitions, add personality and style. The stairway landing outside the Chesapeake Suite, for instance, harbors a huge fur-lined cowbell, a washtub with artwork that Therese hand painted and an old butter urn.

The main floor contains two parlors with fireplaces and a dining room, plus a large commercial kitchen. The owners hoped to reopen the restaurant as a leased operation. Meanwhile, Therese cooks dinner for guests by reservation, $30 for four courses. Zurich geschnetzeltes, a veal dish, is her specialty, but she's also known for salmon, lamb cutlets and an apple pie with almonds in puff pastry.

Erwin prepares a full breakfast of the guest's choice, which Therese serves elegantly on Rosenthal china in the fireplaced dining room. She also runs a little gift shop in the doctor's house outside, selling her artificial flower arrangements and handpainted accessories.

Waterloo Country Inn complex is reflected in placid waters of pond.

The Kraemers, who live in another house on the property, offer an angular swimming pool, a sizable pond, bicycles and canoes for paddling along Monie Creek across the road.

(410) 651-0883. Fax (410) 651-5592. Three rooms and two suites with private baths. April to mid-October: doubles $125 to $175, suites $205 to $225. Rest of year: doubles $105 to $155, suites $185 to $205. Two-night minimum on weekends. No smoking.

The Garden and the Sea Inn, Route 710, Box 275, New Church, Va. 23415.

For some time a restaurant of distinction (see Dining Spots), this out-of-the-way prize near the Maryland-Virginia line is now an overnight destination as well. Sara and Tom Baker from the Shenandoah Valley inherited a going concern when they bought the property in 1994. They offer three bedrooms in the showy Victorian restaurant building and three rooms in the oldest house in New Church, which was moved to the rear of the property in 1992. A handsome brick patio and rose garden with fountain and walkways connect the two.

Our quarters in the Vaucluse Room at the rear of the new Garden House could not have been nicer. The kingsize bed, loveseat, chair and desk were pretty in French wicker. The green wood floor was partly covered by a large oriental rug, while the pale green walls were accented by green floral print wallpaper trim along the ceiling. The floral print theme extended to the wallpaper and the cover of the Kleenex box in the bathroom, which was equipped with twin wash basins and a jacuzzi tub beneath a skylight. We shared a screened side porch outfitted in green wicker with occupants of the adjacent room, and never did see the honeymooners in the Champagne Room upstairs. The Garden House offered plenty of common space: a living room formal in swags and florals, a dining area and kitchenette with a refrigerator in which to stash your own goodies, and a front porch. Sherry, chocolate and fruit were at the ready.

Two more guest rooms of French country sophistication are upstairs above the restaurant. You might find a dressing table draped in paisley fabric, lace and ribbons, rugs patterned with flowers, painted furniture, porcelain doorknobs painted with flowers, and squares of colored glass around the windows. The Chantilly Room has a wicker queensize sleigh bed and the Giverny Room a headboard draped in lace. The modern bathrooms here include bidets. Lately, the Bakers converted a private dining room on the main floor into the deluxe Chardonnay Room with antique queen bed, loveseat sitting area, TV, a skylit double jacuzzi and a separate shower.

A continental-plus breakfast is served in the sun-porch section of the dining room. Ours included mixed berries and fruit, choice of cereals and granola, and melt-in-the-mouth croissants and blueberry muffins.

(804) 824-0672 or (800) 824-0672. Six rooms with private baths. Doubles, $145 to $165 mid-May through mid-October and all weekends; $65 to $95 midweek in off-season. Closed December-March. Two-night minimum weekends. Children accepted. No smoking.

Atlantic Hotel, 2 North Main St., Berlin 21811.

Built in 1894 and once the pride of what was the commercial capital of the Eastern Shore, this had seen better days before ten local partners got together to buy the building. Each put up $150,000 for its painstaking restoration in 1988. The hotel is now best known for its restaurant (see Dining Spots), but the upstairs lodging facility is no slouch.

The sixteen guest rooms on the second and third floors are the height of colorful Victoriana. Some are quite small, while others are large enough for two beds. All have private baths with clawfoot tubs and Gilbert & Soames toiletries. Beds come with dark and heavy wood headboards. The rooms we saw possessed wild floral carpets, Victorian lamps, mirrored armoires, fringed curtains and fishnet canopies. Decorated by one investor's wife who is an art teacher at Salisbury State College, each is distinctive for its antique furniture, window treatment and artworks. Telephones and clock radios are contemporary conveniences, and TV is available on request.

On the second floor is a small lounge for guests. A table contains a bowl of fruit, a scrapbook of area attractions and a photo album tracing the hotel's two years of restoration. A stark rear porch with a not particularly appealing view offers a couple of wicker chairs and rockers. More to guests' liking are the new sidewalk cafe and the lineup of rockers on the wide front veranda facing the goings-on in the heart of the rejuvenated downtown. Ditto for the Drummer's Café on the main floor, where the prevailing sedateness is enlivened by weekend singalongs.

Rates include a continental breakfast in the Drummer's Café.

(410) 641-3589 or (800) 814-7672. Fax (410) 641-4928. Sixteen rooms with private baths. July-August: doubles, $85 to $140 weekends, $75 to $95 midweek. November-March: $65 to $110 weekends, $55 to $75 midweek. Rest of year: $75 to $125 weekends, $65 to $85 midweek. Two-night minimum weekends in summer. No smoking.

Holland House, 5 Bay St., Berlin 21811.

A turn-of-the-century physician's residence at the edge of downtown was turned into the area's first B&B in 1986 by Jim and Jan Quick, he a chef at the Dunes Manor Hotel in Ocean City and she a dental hygienist. In 1997, they reconfigured some of the guest rooms and put on a rear addition. They now offer seven guest rooms, all with private baths and five with queensize beds. They are decorated simply with early American furnishings. Three are on the main floor, where a plaque designates the site of the former doctor's office and maternity ward.

One room favored by families has two double beds and an adjoining sitting/dressing room. In their renovations, the Quicks converted an old upstairs bedroom into an extra sitting and reading room and added a queen bedroom with private bath.

Breakfast is served on pink violet china in a pink dining room, decorated to match Jan's collection of pink depression glassware on the side shelves. The fare could be whatever Jim feels like preparing: perhaps blueberry pancakes, french toast or crêpes accompanied by fresh fruit and muffins.

Guests enjoy a comfortable living room, a paneled TV room, a wicker-filled front porch and a rear patio. They also have access to a picnic table.

(410) 641-1956. Seven rooms with private baths. May to mid-October: doubles, $80 to $90. Rest of year: $55 to $65. Children accepted. No smoking.

Inn on Market Square, 112 North Church St., Snow Hill 21863.

Built in 1904 by a prominent banker, this imposing neoclassic, white stucco structure is being converted into a B&B by Paul Stark, who was in hotel management for twenty years and finally decided that if he had to work 24 hours a day, "I'm going to do it for myself." He became the fourth owner of the house, opened in 1996 with three rooms and, at our visit offered six rooms going on eight. He was doing most of the painstaking renovations and meticulous decorating himself.

The main floor is a beauty. There's a huge foyer with a sitting area and one of two antique organs in the house. On one side is a square living room with windows on three sides, where classical music emanates from an elaborate stereo system.. On the other side is a dining room bearing a striking mural of a Colonial scene. This is where Paul serves a full breakfast, typically juice, fruit and an egg dish (from scrambled to florentine), or perhaps pancakes or waffles. Refreshments are offered in the afternoon.

The upstairs foyer includes a TV and sitting area. All the bedrooms have queen beds and private baths. Two come with fireplaces. After completing the second-floor rooms in 1997, Paul was moving up to the third floor, where he envisioned up to three more rooms and suites.

Architectural features include original brass and leaded glass light fixtures, beveled mirrors and maple floors.

(410) 632-3990. Five rooms with private baths. Doubles, $89 to $119. Two-night minimum weekends in peak season. Children accepted. No smoking.

Snow Hill Inn, 104 East Market St., Snow Hill 21863.

Acclaimed lately for its restaurant (see Dining Spots), this house dating to 1790 offers three guest rooms, one with in-room bath and two with private baths down the hall. A fourth room formerly used as a bedroom was turned into a much-needed upstairs common room by Jim and Kathy Washington, innkeepers since 1991. They also converted a downstairs bedroom into a cocktail lounge.

Though dining is their main thrust, they have upgraded the homey bedrooms, one of which has a working fireplaces. The Barrister Room features a double bed with a quilt, and a Victorian settee on the original 1790 floor. The Wicker Room has a queensize and a day bed. The Aydelotte has a kingsize bed and a fireplace.

Breakfast is continental-plus: juice and fruit, raisin bread or pumpkin muffins, quiche, cereal and cheese.

(410) 632-2102. Three rooms with private baths. April-September: doubles, $75 to $100. Rest of year: $75 weekends, $50 weekdays.

Dining Spots

The Atlantic Hotel, 2 North Main St., Berlin.

The local investors who renovated this "jewel of the Eastern Shore" knew what they wanted: a fine, special-occasion dining room. They searched the nation for

Victorian downtown Berlin is on view from veranda of Atlantic Hotel.

their first chef, who rewarded their trust with culinary honors (the Atlantic quickly became one of six four-star restaurants in Maryland as determined by the Baltimore Sun).

The 60-seat dining room is pretty in a hotel kind of way. Balloon curtains around tall etched-glass windows match the walls papered in deep rose, teal and dark blue. High-back upholstered chairs are at well-spaced tables topped with white linens.

The short, changing dinner menu ranges from scallion-crusted tuna with gingered bok choy, herbed mashed potatoes and bouillabaisse sauce to roasted rack of lamb with montrachet goat cheese, the last a house specialty. Salmon stuffed with spinach and oysters in puff pastry, grilled veal chop puttanesca and tournedos au poivre might be other choices. Crabmeat prevails among starters – crab stew with Smithfield ham, a crab cake on a blood orange coulis, crab phyllo plus curried quail at our latest visit. Finish with a selection from the dessert tray: perhaps Bailey's Irish Cream cheesecake, lemon-lime curd cheesecake, chocolate-raspberry ganache cake or homemade ice cream. The Wine Spectator award-winning wine list is on the expensive side.

At a Sunday jazz brunch in the dining room, we sampled shrimp Americaine and tomato concasse in an herbed crêpe as well as poached eggs Chesapeake, served on an artichoke bottom, surrounded by lump crab and topped with a delicate hollandaise sauce. A more traditional breakfast is now offered Sunday in the **Drummer's Café,** the Victorian lounge with a new sidewalk cafe that's stylish with wicker furniture and petunias in planters. Interesting, less pricey fare is offered here day and night.

(410) 641-3589 or (800) 814-7672. Entrées, $21 to $28. Dinner nightly, 6 to 9 or 10. Cafe, all-day menu from 11:30 to 9 or 10. Sunday breakfast, 8 to 2.

Snow Hill Inn, 104 East Market St., Snow Hill.

When Jim and Kathy Washington took over this restaurant in 1991, it had nowhere to go but up. And up it went, to the point where we heard nothing but raves. Jim mans the kitchen, while Kathy presides over the front of the house. This includes an airy dining room in the rear and a more intimate front room colorful with stained glass and a decor of hunter green with red accents. There are also a new lounge and a shady rear patio for dining al fresco.

Dinner selections include choice of tossed or spinach salad and homemade herbed bread or muffins, served with butter wrapped in aluminum foil – who said this was sophisticated dining? But it sure is affordable. At our first visit, we ordered a carafe of the house Sebastiani chardonnay. The waitress filled our glasses to the brim as we dug into tasty salads dressed with parmesan pepper and honey dijon. Main courses were the locally ubiquitous crab imperial and crab cakes, accompanied by red potatoes and mixed squash. We had no room for dessert, a choice of carrot cake, cheesecake or key lime pie. Entrée range from chicken marsala to a dish called Snow on the Hills, twin petite filets topped with imperial crab. Prime rib is far and away the most requested choice, according to Jim, and after sampling it at our latest visit, we understood why. The thick slab was succulent and sensational. Also good was the black and blue filet mignon

The restaurant is highly popular for lunch. Among the options are crab quiche, chicken caesar salad, sandwiches, pasta and shrimp scampi, with most items priced below $5. The lounge opens at 4 with a light menu.

(410) 632-2102. Entrées, $9.95 to $16.95. Lunch, Monday-Friday 11 to 2. Dinner nightly, 5:30 to 9, Sunday 4 to 8.

The Garden and the Sea Inn, Route 710, New Church, Va.

The polished restaurant here made quite a name for itself under the previous innkeepers, she in the kitchen and he out front. The roles were reversed when it was purchased in 1994 by Tom and Sara Baker. Tom, a Culinary Institute-trained chef, is in the kitchen and Sara oversees the front of the house.

The sophisticated dining room is pretty with pale peach walls, dusky pink pillars and trim, and remarkable window treatments. Delicate china, pink-stemmed glassware and shell-patterned silver are as refined as the service.

Diners order à la carte or from a couple of prix-fixe menus, four courses for $27.75 or four different courses and a tasting of three wines of the region, $39.25. One of us tried the lower-priced prix-fixe option, which produced a thick and tasty corn and crab chowder, a good salad of romaine lettuce with caesar dressing, and a superior breast of chicken dressed with pecans and dijon cream, served with slivered carrots and wild rice. The other ordered the sliced pork loin sautéed with backfin crabmeat and served with béarnaise sauce from a choice of seven à la carte options. Good rolls with two kinds of butter (one of them herbed) and a $20 bottle of our favorite Sanford sauvignon blanc from California (rarely seen on the East Coast) accompanied. Peach melba and crème brûlée were worthy endings to a memorable meal.

(804) 824-0672 or (800) 824-0672. Entrées, $16.75 to $24.50. Dinner, Thursday-Sunday 6 to 9, also Wednesday in summer. Closed December-March.

Globe Cafe & Deli, 12 Broad St., Berlin.

Just what the visiting lunch-goer ordered is served up at the deli counter adjacent to the Duck Soup Bookstore. Large, healthful sandwiches, bagels, soups, salads and quiche are ordered at the counter and delivered to tables scattered around the main-floor corridor outside the entry to the little Globe Theater. We liked the Globe sandwich (combining havarti, tomato, avocado, sprouts, cucumber and mayo on seven-grain bread for $3.25) and the chunky chicken salad sandwich called a chico ($3.50). Those and a couple of cafe lattes sent us happily on our way.

(410) 641-0784. Open Monday-Saturday 10 to 6, Sunday 11 to 5.

Diversions

The **Pocomoke River** is the area's principal attraction and defines its character. You can view it from two riverside parks, Byrd and Sturgis, in Snow Hill and from Milburn and Shad landings in Pocomoke River State Park. Otherwise, it's pretty much hidden from public view as it winds like a tropical jungle stream past thick forests and an occasional farm. The tidal river is the deepest (up to 45 feet) for its width in the United States.

The best way to experience the river is by canoe. The **Pocomoke River Canoe Co.** at the Route 12 drawbridge in Snow Hill rents canoes for $5 an hour and $30 a day. Groups can rent a pontoon boat for $65 for two hours. The less adventurous can settle for a tour on **Tillie the Tug,** an open tugboat that carries 22 passengers downriver from Snow Hill to Shad Landing and back. We saw lots of lily pads, duck blinds and stumps of bald cypress trees, but found the boat too low to see much – not that there was all that much to see. The odd bird and passing speedboat helped while the hour away. We got the distinct impression that life in the Snow Hill area moves just as slowly as Tillie the Tug and the Pocomoke River. Cruises available mid-June through Labor Day and fall weekends. Adults, $6.

Birdwatching. More than 350 species have been sighted in Worcester County from the Assateague coastline across the Pocomoke Forest and down the Pocomoke River. They are detailed in two brochures furnished by the country tourism office.

Historic Walking Tours. Maps for self-guided walking tours are available both for Berlin and Snow Hill. We like the shops and harmonious row of brick Victorian storefronts along Main Street in Berlin. The houses and the mix are more illustrious in Snow Hill, where most of the sights are concentrated along Market and Federal streets. Especially noteworthy are All Hallows Episcopal Church, established in 1692 and occupying its present structure since 1756, and nearby Makemie United Presbyterian Church, whose Gothic Revival facade hides the fact it was established in 1683 and is considered the birthplace of American Presbyterianism. The town's first three inns were among the houses opened for tours on Snow Hill's annual Heritage Weekend when we were there.

Viewtrail 100. About 100 miles of contiguous scenic bicycle trails along secondary roads are marked by Viewtrail logos and outlined on a map available through the County Extension Service.

Julia A. Purnell Museum, 208 West Market St., Snow Hill.

A former Catholic church houses local memorabilia involving Julia Purnell, a seamstress and storekeeper who lived here 100 years and took up folk art after breaking her hip at age 85. Because of her age and her penchant for relating stories of Snow Hill, her son opened a museum in her honor in 1942 and people flocked to see her and her creations before her death a year later. A few of her hundreds of needlework pictures are on display, but most of the space now operated by the town is devoted to a step-in boardwalk, a Colonial cupboard, the Purnell general store, a toy shop and Mrs. Purnell's sewing room.

(410) 632-0515. Open April-October, weekdays 10 to 4, weekends 1 to 4. Adults, $1.50.

Globe Theatre, 12 Broad St., Berlin, (410) 641-0784. The old theater in the center of Berlin has been restored and revived, encompassing a cafe, a book and gift shop and an art gallery. At the rear is a small theater of about four dozen seats, which started showing movies in 1989 "after a twenty-year intermission." It now schedules live musical entertainment of increasing distinction on many weekends. The Balcony Gallery shows interesting works of more than a dozen artists.

Shopping. Most of the area's shopping opportunities are in Berlin, and those primarily involve antiques. They have names like **Victorian Charm,** the **Brass Box,** which had quite a collection of brass candlesticks, and **The Last Straw,** with lots of wicker things. The pharmacy was converted into **Town Center Antiques,** a co-op of antique dealers. **Findings** is known for antiques, architectural details and glassware. We liked the handpainted designs on wine glasses, dishes, vases and such at **Ta-Da** among its eclectic gifts

Until lately, the best part of Snow Hill's downtown has been the little triangular park, lushly dotted with flowers, at Green and Washington streets. **The Green Street Shop** offers antiques and collectibles. The **W.W. Pusey & Sons Country Store** is a relic stocking gifts and practical stuff from boots to bird seed. A display counter featured 36 microbrews at our latest visit. The old Cannery beside the river houses antiques and craft shops and a restaurant was in the plans.

Extra-Special

Furnace Town, Old Furnace Road, Snow Hill.

Rarely can you see the remains of a 19th-century industrial village, least of all one that rose like a phoenix and thrived briefly on the gathering and smelting of bog iron ore. A short-lived boomtown of 300 people produced iron here in the 1830s, floating it on barges down Nassawango Creek to the Pocomoke River and the Chesapeake Bay. Almost as rapidly as it emerged it failed and became a ghost town. The Furnace Town museum shows the gathering of bog ore, archeological relics, a model of the mansion house and a loom, plus Snow Hill newspaper pages of the time citing the collective debt to "those enterprising strangers who have erected an iron furnace in our county" and the sudden notice of a sale involving 7,000 acres "embracing immense beds of iron ore." Visitors can tour an old print shop, peer into the Old Nazareth Church, inspect the crumbling Nassawango Iron Furnace, watch a craftsman making brooms in the broom house and a smithy at work in the blacksmith shop, and ascend the reproduction charging ramp for a four-story-high view of the countryside. Markers show foundations of long-lost buildings. We enjoyed the mile-long Nature Conservancy trail along a curved boardwalk through the adjacent, bayou-like swamp forest. We passed the stumps and "knees" of one of the northernmost bands of bald cypress trees, whose needles hang like grass clippings on trees below, and saw what remained of the twenty-foot-wide shipping canal. At appropriate times of the year you may see American holly and sweet gum trees, muscadet grape vines and fifteen varieties of orchids.

(410) 632-2032. Open April-October, daily 11 to 5. Adults, $3.

Lawn of The Inn at Perry Cabin faces Fogg Cove and St. Michaels waterfront.

St. Michaels, Md.

Waterfront Living in Style

Along the languorous shores of the Miles River, not far off the Chesapeake Bay, the historic town of St. Michaels has turned waterfront living into high style. The Eastern Shore's most upscale address is a mecca for visitors and second-home owners, some of whom eventually become year-round residents.

Tucked off the beaten path down a peninsula heading toward the bay, St. Michaels has long been known by yachtsmen and by affluent retirees who settled here for watery pleasures and a slower pace not far from the big cities. But it has been really discovered in the last decade. Large new inns have emerged (four B&Bs in 1997 alone), trendy restaurants and shops have opened, and waterfront properties sell at a premium.

Today's St. Michaels, still small and rather self-consciously quaint, is a far cry from that of a generation ago – before the Bay Bridge opened up the Eastern Shore to outlanders, before James Michener wrote *Chesapeake* in a rented house along the Miles River, and before the Chesapeake Bay Maritime Museum evolved into a major tourist attraction.

The first settlers in 1632 called its landlocked harbor "Shipping Creek," an apt reference for a place that would become a busy trading and shipbuilding center. Around the first Episcopal Church, named for St. Michael the Archangel, developed the town that took its name.

During the War of 1812, St. Michaels staged the first blackout in recorded history.

British warships gathered on the Miles River to shell this coveted target. Townspeople darkened their homes and hung lanterns in the treetops to trick the invaders into aiming high. When the shelling ceased, the ploy had worked; only the now-famous Cannonball House was hit. St. Michaels had earned a place in history as the town that fooled the British.

Now the year-round population of 1,500 is easily matched by visiting yachtsmen and landlubbers on summer weekends, and by even more decoy collectors and duck hunters in fall. A few skeptics pass off St. Michaels as something of a stage set – mainly fronts and no backs, at least along Talbot Street, the only thoroughfare. They obviously have missed the side streets, the boatyards, the undulating waterfront and the surrounding countryside that reflect the old St. Michaels, one of America's earliest port towns.

Inn Spots

The Inn at Perry Cabin, 308 Watkins Lane, St. Michaels 21663.

The first American innkeeping venture of Sir Bernard Ashley, widower of Laura Ashley, this is like no other inn on the Mid-Atlantic coast. With an idyllic waterfront location, beautiful grounds, sumptuous accommodations and a first-class restaurant (see Dining Spots), it's luxury to the max.

Many millions were spent redoing it for a 1990 reopening, even after multi-million-dollar refurbishings by previous owners of what started as a cabin for Commodore Oliver Perry ("we have met the enemy and they are ours") following the War of 1812. Still more millions went into a wing that more than doubled the inn's size in 1991.

Touring the inn on two occasions and staying on a third, we were stunned by the stripes, flowers, flounces, ruffles, fancy window treatments, beautiful colors, wallpaper, borders and painted furniture. Here is decoration to the nth degree.

From the dining room to the lounges to the bedrooms, all is plush, plush, plush. Stressing service, Sir Bernard is quoted as saying his philosophy is to welcome guests as he would to one of his homes. Each of the 41 rooms and suites is elegantly furnished in antiques, offset by what the promotion material calls "understated, classic Laura Ashley fabrics and wallpapers." Understated? Laura Ashley – in more

guises than we'd ever hoped to see – is splashed everywhere. On our tour of all the rooms, we got Laura Ashleyed out.

Admittedly, if you were staying in only one room, you would not find it overkill. You would likely find a four-poster bed topped by a draped corona, a wicker sitting area in a corner sun porch, a huge armoire imported from England, splashy colors, and a spacious bathroom with a striped ceiling and that most British of luxuries, a heated towel rack. Plus, of course, television, telephones, coffee-table books and magazines, terrycloth robes, fresh fruit and mineral water. In Room 5, you would sleep in Sir Bernard's unique kingsize four-poster from his home in Bermuda. In Room 16, you would raise the curtains by remote control onto soaring windows yielding the inn's best water view. A couple of prized two-story suites have living rooms on one floor, bedrooms on the next and jacuzzi bathtubs. They share a balcony overlooking the river and harbor. Evening turndown produces fresh towels, a refilled ice bucket and a couple of oatmeal-raisin cookies.

Rates include a full breakfast. Served in the dining room, ours was an unusual chargrilled "salmon ham" with scrambled eggs and scallions and a classic English mixed grill, from grilled tomato to kidneys to blood pudding, with a poached egg in the middle.

Three plush living rooms are filled with lovely antiques and spectacular flower arrangements. French doors lead to a brick terrace, where comfortable chairs invite sitting and looking at the water. House guests may take tea here or in the living rooms – a proper British one with little sweets and scones upon which to spread lemon curd and whipped cream. The newer wing adds an hibiscus-filled conservatory, where two model planes are suspended under the skylight, and a billiards room described as "a meeting room in disguise." An indoor swimming pool that we found rather tepid and an exercise facility with sauna and steam room are the latest attractions.

There's not even a check-in counter in the understated little reception area, where one of the friendly staff spots visitors through one-way glass doors and asks them to have a seat to check in.

The guest book at the concierge's desk is filled with superlatives, most relating to special occasions. "Perfection personified," one guest summed up.

(410) 745-2200 or (800) 722-2949. Fax (410) 745-3348. Forty-one rooms and suites with private baths. Doubles, $295 to $495 weekends, $195 to $395 midweek. Suites, $535 to $695 weekends, $435 to $595 midweek.

St. Michaels Harbour Inn & Marina, 101 North Harbor Road, St. Michaels 21663.

Opened in 1986 and redecorated and refurbished from top to bottom in 1997, this contemporary structure commands a prime location at the head of the busy St. Michaels harbor.

The L-shaped, three-story structure has 46 guest accommodations, 23 of them two-room suites facing the water. Each has a living room with a sofabed, desk, television and kitchenette with a sink and refrigerator, and a bedroom with one or two queensize beds, remote-control TV and a large bathroom with double vanities and thick towels. French doors lead from each room onto a private terrace or balcony with good-looking chairs and a table overlooking the harbor. One of us thought it quite a luxury to be able to watch her show of choice on the bedroom TV while her spouse was glued to a baseball game (this was playoff time) in the living room. Smaller quarters on the third floor have rooms with one queen bed, a refrigerator and a private balcony.

All rooms were redecorated and bathrooms updated throughout the hotel in 1997. Four suites on the third floor got expanded balconies and several bathrooms now have double jacuzzi tubs with separate showers.

Knight in armor keeps watch over occupants of Guinevere Room at The Old Brick Inn.

The pleasant **Windows** restaurant serves three meals a day (see Dining Spots). At breakfast, we enjoyed a stack of apple-pecan pancakes while watching the harbor activity.

A small outdoor pool beside the harbor is flanked by a jacuzzi and a bar for beverages and snacks. Overnight docking slips are available for 60 boats. There's a **Ship's Store,** and an aqua center offers canoes and aquabikes for adventuring around the harbor.

(410) 745-9001 or (800) 955-9001. Fax (410) 745-9150. Eight rooms and 38 suites with private baths. Memorial Day through October: doubles, $199 to $419 weekends, $159 to $339 midweek. Rest of year, $169 to $339 weekends, $139 to $269 midweek. Two-night minimum on weekends, May-October.

The Old Brick Inn, 401 South Talbot St., Box 987, St. Michaels 21663.

The largest B&B in St. Michaels was planned to be fully open in spring of 1998 in a couple of brick structures and a new addition.

Martha Strickland, who had been general manager of the old Pasadena and Kent Manor inns, and partner George Wilson purchased the property in November 1997 and readied the first four guest rooms within two weeks in what had been the Antiques & Such store in a carriage house along Mulberry Street. Five more bedrooms and suites were about to be fashioned in the handsome brick structure designated as the Old Inn on the St. Michaels walking tour. The building, listed on the National Register, once housed the St. Michaels Bank and lately Nina's Antiques. Five rooms were planned in a third-floor addition above and outward from the old inn.

The complex includes a small pool in a New Orleans-style, brick-walled garden courtyard, where tables were to be set for continental breakfast in season. The main inn contains a fireplaced dining room, in which Martha was thinking of running at tea room, and she was eyeing the cellar with its large cooking oven for a rathskeller.

The first four rooms with queensize beds in the old Antiques & Such store were eye-poppers – not the least of which were two high-ceilinged theme rooms on the ground floor with full-length windows up against the street that we think would need to be draped at all times for privacy. The Guinevere Room has a wrought-iron bed with a cathedral-style swagged tulle canopy against a brick wall, a brick floor and a life-size King Arthur suit of armor at the entrance to the full bath. Across the reception area is Annie Oakley's Room with a deer head overlooking the bed which is dressed in bright flannels, a holster and a cowboy hat on the wall and a sofa for seating. "I had a good time furnishing this room and found enough stuff to fill four more," said Martha, though she expected to vary the themes elsewhere. The second floor contains a small common sitting area in the hall, plus two carpeted bedrooms – one furnished in wicker and the other in "traditional" with a floral-quilted poster bed and two wing chairs. Each comes with a small balcony front and back.

Martha envisioned seven rooms with fireplaces in the main house and addition. One is a two-room corner suite with an existing marble jacuzzi tub and a handpainted sink, and another is a many-angled garret room on the third floor.

(410) 745-3323. Fax (410) 745-3320. Thirteen rooms and one suite with private baths. Doubles, $125 to $200 weekends, $100 to $175 midweek. Suite, $250 weekends, $175 midweek. Two-night minimum weekends in season. Children over 12. No smoking.

Black Walnut Point Inn, Box 308, Tilghman Island 21671.

This 57-acre portion of paradise at the end of Tilghman Island is surrounded by water on three sides. A gate blocks the entrance to the dirt road leading past a wildlife preserve and landscaped lawns to the secluded complex on a point between the widewaters of the Choptank River and the Chesapeake Bay. Once here, you're rather isolated, so it's understandable that this once was the summer retreat for the Soviet embassy. The state acquired the property in 1986 and ultimately leased it to Tom and Brenda Ward to run as a B&B.

In the charming main house, part of which predates the Civil War, they offer four guest rooms with private baths, each with a queen or a double bed as well as

Black Walnut Point Inn complex spreads over 57 acres on point at end of peninsula.

a twin bed. The Bay Room, with double poster bed, has a beamed ceiling and windows on three sides. Overlooking the pool is the refurbished Tilghman Room with a queensize bed. We stayed in the Choptank Cottage South, which has a spacious bedroom, small sitting room and a screened porch. With waves lapping at the rocky shore outside, it's just like the summer cottage of our dreams. Other cottage units raise the total number of bedrooms to seven.

The main house has a parlor with TV, VCR, games and grand piano, a chandeliered dining room and a summery sun porch with rattan furniture. Wine glasses and an ice machine are available in a room off the kitchen, where guests may help themselves to lemonade, iced tea, soft drinks or wine from the refrigerator. In the morning, Brenda serves a continental-plus breakfast with choice of juice, fresh fruit, cereal and homemade muffins.

Outside are a jacuzzi beside a delightful freeform swimming pool, with roses blooming all around, plus a lighted tennis court, a swing, rope hammocks and seemingly endless lawns. Once you stretch out in a hammock by the bay, perhaps watching one of the resident great blue herons, you won't want to get up. Tom may be persuaded to pilot guests around the island on a champagne tour in his speedy commercial fishing boat.

The Wards are outgoing hosts and energetic innkeepers. Their very special place has a casual, laid-back feeling in keeping with the St. Michaels of yesteryear.

(410) 886-2452. Fax (410) 886-2053. www.tilghmanisland.com/blackwalnut. Four rooms and three cottage suites with private baths. Doubles, $120. Cottage rooms and suites, $120 to $140. Two-night minimum weekends, three nights on holiday weekends. No children. Smoking restricted. Open weekends only in January and February.

The Hambleton Inn, 202 Cherry St., Box 1007, St. Michaels 21663.

New owners have upgraded and revitalized this established B&B in an 1860 house that occupies a prime harborfront site in the heart of St. Michaels.

Real-estate broker Steve Furman bought the B&B in 1995 and ran it himself for two weeks until a North Carolinian named Kimberly checked in with her younger sister. "I never checked out," Kimberly recalls. "Steve discovered I could cook." Soon married, they found the common space lacking and the guest quarters dark and dreary. So the Furmans closed for three months in 1997 to build a new wing for themselves. That freed up space for a handsome fireplaced dining room in which they now serve a full breakfast at a table for ten. The fare could be vegetable quiche, orange french toast or belgian waffles.

All five guest rooms, each with at least a partial water view, were refurbished and lightened up in decor. A bedroom in the original living room has a fireplace, kingsize poster bed, plump chair, sage green walls and fancy window treatments characteristic of the rest of the house. Another king-bedded room, this with a crown canopy, is pretty in mauve colors, with upholstered chairs and fine furniture on a refinished floor. Queen poster beds are in two other second-floor rooms, one with windows on three sides but the smallest bath in the house and the other with a large full bath and appointed in taupe and mint green. The old Crow's Nest on the third floor, where tall guests are warned not to bump their heads on the ceiling, is pretty in pale yellow. Chocolates are at bedside in each room.

The second-floor front porch serves as the common room here. Outfitted in wicker, Kimberly says it's "the best spot in the house." It certainly offers a great view of the harbor goings-on.

Newly renovated and expanded Hambleton Inn overlooks St. Michaels harbor.

The Furmans installed a new dock, landscaped the entrance and grounds, and provide bicycles for guests.

(410) 745-3350. Five rooms with private baths. April-December: doubles, $195 to $245 weekends, $115 to $145 midweek. Rest of year: $125 to $165 weekends, $85 to $145 midweek. Children over 13. No smoking.

Chesapeake Wood Duck Inn, Gibsontown Road, Box 202, Tilghman Island 21671.

Stephanie Feith was feeding ducks at the back door as we arrived. "We started with two and now have twelve," she said of the flock that has made the grounds of the inn their second home since she and husband David opened in 1993. "Now all we need is a pond for the ducks and a gazebo for watching them," she said.

The pond and the gazebo were in the planning stage for the long back yard leading to Dogwood Harbor, home of the last remaining working skipjack fleet in the country. You get the idea that they will soon be reality, given the speed with which the couple turned the 1890 boarding house and sometime bordello into an elegant seven-room B&B. Corporate dropouts from Atlanta, the Feiths scoured the country for the perfect B&B site and a simpler lifestyle. They found it on Tilghman Island.

Now David is a part-time working waterman, picking up substantial pin money to support the couple's penchant for dining out several nights a week. Cooking gourmet breakfasts, he goes all-out – arising at 5 a.m. to start prepping and baking fresh muffins from scratch, and you can taste the difference. Stephanie has turned her talents to interior decorating and dispensing Southern hospitality, which sounds trite but ends up true.

About those breakfasts. We started with a dish of cantaloupe, blueberries and kiwi and a glass of orange juice before digging in to some melt-in-your-mouth lemon-poppyseed muffins. The best was yet to come: an original that Dave calls a Tilghman omelet puff. Filled with cheddar and mozzarella cheeses, capers, tarragon and sundried tomatoes, it's wrapped in smoked ham and puff-pastry dough, then baked and topped with key lime-mustard sauce and raspberry puree, and served with fresh asparagus spears. Unforgettable! Sherried crab quiche, a crab pie that could well be a luncheon dish, and banana-stuffed french toast topped with cinnamon and roasted pecans are other specialties. Lately, Dave has added such side dishes as Spanish mackerel and crostini wrapped in bacon with caramelized brown sugar and mild chile pepper. Refreshments later in the day include 24-hour coffee and tea service, wine, soft drinks and sherry – the former available in the kitchen and guest refrigerator and the latter in a decanter in the hallway.

Stephanie has furnished the house in what she calls a "traditional/eclectic" style that's most comfortable except, perhaps, for the small antique double beds that she was gradually replacing with queensize beds. Each air-conditioned bedroom comes with private bath, assorted comforters, good artworks, savvy window treatments and fine antique furnishings. There are unexpected touches like a foxhunter's hat on the dresser in the Rutledge Room, which is handsome in deep blues and reds and paisleys, and a stunning Victorian stained-glass piece hanging in the window of the Magnolia Room, which is light and airy in shades of peach and green.

Lately, the Feiths have added a large suite with its own entrance and deck overlooking the harbor. French doors open into a living room with a sofabed and overstuffed chair, remote-control TV, CD player and stereo. Another set of french doors leads to a bedroom with queensize four-poster bed and a full bath with double vanity.

Interesting artworks – including a display of oyster plates – grace the walls of the kitchen, living room, dining room and sun room. Over the dining table is an antique chandelier that has followed the Feiths around from its original home in Charleston. There's plenty of space to spread out on the screened porch, the rear patio and soon, no doubt, in the gazebo beside the pond-to-be.

(410) 886-2070 or (800) 956-2070. Fax (410) 886-2070. www.wooduckinn.com. Six rooms and one suite with private baths. Doubles, $135 to $155. Suite, $165 to $195. No smoking.

Wades Point Inn on the Bay, Wades Point Road, Box 7, St. Michaels 21663.

Very Southern looking, this imposing white brick plantation-style home at the end of a long lane is surrounded by unusually attractive grounds and backs up to the Chesapeake Bay about five miles west of St. Michaels on the way to Tilghman Island. The original house was built in 1819 by Baltimore shipwright Thomas Kemp. A summer wing was added in 1890 and it has operated as a guest house in the old Bay tradition ever since.

"We've been updating but want it to stay comfy and homey," said innkeeper Betsy Feiler, who's owned the inn with husband John since 1984. Their prime accommodations are in the newer Mildred T. Kemp Building, which has twelve hotel-style rooms with modern baths, some with kitchenette facilities to encourage families and all but two with waterfront balconies that you may never want to leave. Each is furnished traditionally and individually with down comforters, plush carpeting and interesting window treatments, with Bibles on the night stands, and TVs noticeably missing.

The main house has fourteen guest rooms, two with private baths and several more with wash basin in the rooms. Most rooms here are interestingly if sparely furnished, and the annex that Betsy once candidly described as a "sophisticated Girl Scout house" is now called "a country farmhouse." The summer wing is what you'd expect to find around the Tidewater area: rooms with high ceilings (and

Porches of Kemp Building yield views of main house and bay at Wades Point Inn.

windows) open off the long corridor, the entrance to each containing a screen door inside the regular door, which guests tend to leave open for cross-ventilation on summer nights.

Guests enter a reception area in the original summer kitchen. The main parlor is furnished with two sofas, a piano, a tapestry over the fireplace and more books than a Southern gentleman could possibly have read. These rooms give little inkling of the astonishing Bay Room in back – a huge sun room that's a veritable sea of white wicker furniture with columns and arches, a fireplace, bleached floors topped with colorful patterned rugs and windows on all sides onto the water. Here is where guests linger over a continental breakfast of fruit salad, juice, cereal, muffins and french rolls or relax with a book and watch the boats go by. If you can stir yourself from the Bay Room or one of the hammocks and chairs spread out on the shady grounds beside the water, saunter along the special nature trail that curves along the shoreline and traverses the interior of the property. Be on the lookout for deer, rabbits, red foxes, terrapins, bald eagles, great blue herons, osprey and more. The prolific flower gardens in front of the Kemp House are worth a close look, too.

(410) 745-2500 or (888) 923-3466. Fourteen rooms with private baths and twelve rooms with shared baths. Doubles, $95 to $125 with private bath, $95 to $110 with shared bath, $150 to $230 in Kemp Building. Suite, $240. Two-night minimum weekends and holidays. Children welcome. No smoking. Closed January and February.

The Lazyjack Inn, 5907 Tilghman Island Road, Tilghman Island 21671.

Sailing enthusiasts Mike and Carol Richards from Reston, Va., have converted this 160-year-old house backing up to Dogwood Harbor into a charming B&B. The outbuildings serve as a base for their charter boat business.

All four accommodations come with modern baths, interesting decorative touches and heirloom quilts. A Victorian settee and a chair with ottoman face the water in the spacious, high-ceilinged Nellie Byrd Suite, which offers a kingsize brass bed, a built-in vanity in the bureau, a double jacuzzi tub and a shower with three sides of glass. Like the Nellie Byrd, the Garden Suite contains a jacuzzi tub and one of the inn's three in-room fireplaces. A good water view is afforded from the East Room, with exposed beam ceiling, heart of pine floors and Waterfall series furniture bearing shell hardware.

Mike, whose background is in residential construction, enclosed the big side porch to serve as a breakfast room. That and the rear deck with water view are the sites for the morning repast, which included a fresh fruit cup in a phyllo flower and baked stuffed french toast with cottage cheese and apricot glaze at our visit. Folded crab omelets, banana rum cake and sticky buns are other specialties. Sherry and chocolates are put out when the beds are turned down.

Mike can take up to sixteen passengers daily onto the Chesapeake Bay on the Lady Patty, his 45-foot classic ketch built in 1935. Two-hour, half-day and full-day sails can be arranged. www.bluecrab.org/members/mrichards

(410) 886-2215 or (800) 690-5080. Fax (410) 886-2635. www.bluecrab.org/members/ mrichards. Two rooms and two suites with private baths. Doubles, $140. Suites, $175 and $210. Two-night minimum at peak periods. Children over 12. No smoking.

The Inn at Christmas Farm, 8873 Tilghman Island Road (Route 33), Wittman 21676.

For a change of pace, stay overnight in a church. Not any church, mind you, but a little dollhouse of a chapel that David and Beatrice Lee moved to the side of their circa-1800 farmhouse about seven miles southwest of St. Michaels. The 1893 Methodist church belonged to their housekeeper's congregation down the road, but was available when it merged with another.

"We moved it, rebuilt it and renovated it to the Victorian period," said David. They converted the interior into two bright and airy, high-ceilinged suites. Each has a wet bar and refrigerator, a kingsize black iron canopy bed topped with frilly coverings, and double sinks in the bathrooms. The front Bell Tower Suite, entered through the double doors of the belfry, enjoys a brick patio running the width of the building. At the other end of the structure is the Gabriel Suite, where a hand-carved angel with trumpet presides over pieces from the owners' collection of farm furniture. Its french doors open onto a large, raised deck. Relax on the wrought-iron furniture on patio or deck, watch the goats, hear the farm sounds and look across the fields to the spring-fed farm pond with a dock for swimming and sunning and the distant waters of Cummings Creek. Here's contentment.

There's more. The Lees offer a suite with a kingsize bed, sitting room and a wood stove on the first floor of their main house. Another suite called Christmas Cottage was transformed from a little waterman's house they moved to the property and attached to the side of their house. It comes with a private entrance, a sitting room with a two-person jacuzzi at the far end and, upstairs, a kingsize bedroom and bathroom. The private courtyard here looks onto a cove where peacocks seem to spend a lot of time.

Now semi-retired in Beaufort, S.C., the Lees hire resident innkeepers. They serve a full breakfast, featuring perhaps poached pears, crab quiche or blueberry pancakes.

(410) 745-5312 or (800) 987-8436. Fax (410) 745-5618. Four suites with private baths. Weekends, $155 to $165. Midweek, $125. Two-night minimum weekends. Children over 13. No smoking.

Old Pasadena Inn has been grandly refurbished into The Oaks.

The Oaks, Route 329 at Acorn Lane, Box 187, Royal Oak 21662.

The former Pasadena Inn gave way in 1997 to this handsome yellow and green structure on seventeen waterfront acres along Oak Creek southeast of town. Paul Milne and Candace Chiaruttini, who own the acclaimed 208 Talbot restaurant in St. Michaels, gutted the manor house erected in 1748 as a private residence but retained the antebellum facade. They reconfigured the interior layout and reduced the number of rooms to produce fourteen guest rooms with king or queen beds opening off a maze of hallways. Eleven have jacuzzi tubs, eight have gas fireplaces and some contain TVs. Twelve yield water views and all are furnished, in Candace's words, with "antiques that came with the place."

The premier accommodation is a large waterfront room on the third floor with a king bed, a double jacuzzi at the edge of the room, a two-person shower in the bathroom and a private balcony overlooking the water. A floral comforter, floral carpeting and interesting window treatments add color here and throughout most guest rooms.

The pastry chef for 208 Talbot provides the baked goods for a continental-plus breakfast that includes cereals, breads, quiches and, when we were there, delectable blueberry muffins. It's served in a large dining room with the original center fireplace in the middle. The vast main floor holds banquet space, a common room with TV in the original section and a screened side porch furnished in wicker and overlooking a watery scene. More seating is on decks all around overlooking grounds where shuffleboard, horseshoes, badminton and such facilities are available. Canoes and bicycles are complimentary for guests. A pool was planned for 1998.

Eight basic rooms are available in an annex ($65 to $85), and more guest rooms were envisioned in other outbuildings.

(410) 745-5053. Fourteen rooms with private baths. Doubles, $150 to $225 weekends, $100 to $190 midweek. Two-night minimum weekends.

Victoriana Inn, 205 Cherry St., Box 449, St. Michaels 21663.

All is frilly and lacy at this inn that lives up to its name. A former private residence built in 1883 and facing the harbor, this elegant little gem opened as a B&B in

1988. The original owner sold it in late 1997 to Jim Gonden, who was "downsized in New Jersey and starting a new job and adventure here." He was familiar with the area from his service days in the Coast Guard and took over a turnkey operation.

Tiny sachets are on the beds, candies of the season are at bedside and fresh flowers are in the five air-conditioned guest rooms. Other thoughtful touches are embroidered pillows, toiletries and velvety towels folded up in baskets. The most coveted rooms are two on the main floor, each with canopied four-poster bed, fireplace and private bath. Three rooms on the second floor have in-room sinks but share two baths. Beds vary from antique double to queensize four-poster.

A collection of glass animals adorns the parlor mantel, and there's a sensational oriental piece in the upstairs hall. Victorian antiques and samplers are all around.

A small sun room facing the waterfront contains a TV and VCR. A front porch in gray and white wicker overlooks lovely flower gardens, one of the biggest magnolia trees we ever saw, a little fish pond and, of course, the boats in the harbor. Chairs are scattered about the lawns, and the setting is quite idyllic.

Breakfast is sumptuous: fresh fruit and juice, french toast, omelets or perhaps crêpes, and at least two homemade breads.

On adjacent lots, Jim planned to add two honeymoon cottages and a putting green.

(410) 745-3368. Fax (410) 745-6134. Two rooms with private baths and three rooms with shared baths. Doubles, $140 to $175 weekends, $125 to $150 midweek. Two-night minimum weekends. Children over 13. No smoking.

The Parsonage Inn, 210 North Talbot St., St. Michaels 21663.

Its entry tower topped by a steeple and flanked by two-story octagonal sections with paneled chimneys, this is one of the more architecturally striking structures along the main street. Check the unusual brick facade with its many inlay patterns and the Victorian gingerbread trim over the porches.

The house, built in 1883, was extensively renovated from a Methodist church parsonage in 1985. Five bedrooms were fashioned from the parsonage and three with separate entrances were added motel-style at the rear. All have private baths with Victorian pedestal wash basins and brass fixtures. Seven have king or queensize beds, plush carpeting and thick towels, Queen Anne-style furniture and Laura Ashley linens and accessories. Three possess working fireplaces. The two most appealing open onto an upstairs deck and two have television. A family suite contains a room with two double beds, a sitting room with TV and a bunk room with two twins.

Oriental rugs and fine Victorian furniture enhance the cozy fireplaced parlor and a large formal dining room, where a full breakfast is served by a resident manager for owner Willard Workman. The fare at our latest visit was waffles with sausage and peach crisp for dessert one day, and tomato strata and apple cake the next. Outdoors is a nicely landscaped patio with wicker furniture.

(410) 745-5519 or (800) 394-5519. Seven rooms and one suite with private baths. Doubles, $130 to $160 weekends, $110 to $140 midweek. Two-night minimum weekends, April-October. No smoking.

The Brick House, 202 North Talbot St., St. Michaels 21663.

This section of North Talbot Street got yet another B&B in 1997 when builder John Booth connected two brick shop buildings overseen by his wife Bonnie with a new section containing the latest B&B amenities.

The result is eight guest rooms with queensize beds, private baths and TV. Six offer jacuzzi tubs and four have balconies onto Talbot Street. The rooms we saw were summery and colorful, one in peach and blue and the other with a raspberry-colored wall.

John puts out a continental breakfast, including granola and yogurt, in the downstairs common room. Wine and cheese are offered here on weekend afternoons. Between contracting duties, John tends to the inn, while Bonnie runs B's Stitches, her needlecraft shop in the front of one brick house. Hollyhocks is an exceptional gift shop in the front of the other house.

(410) 745-2799. Fax (410) 745-2903. Eight rooms with private baths. Doubles, $145 to $175 weekends, $125 to $145 midweek. No smoking.

Kemp House Inn, 412 South Talbot St., Box 638, St. Michaels 21663.

This three-story clapboard house was the first B&B to open in St. Michaels (in 1982), and it's said that Gen. Robert E. Lee was a guest here long before that. Built in 1805, the eight-room B&B suffers from a lack of common facilities other than a rocker-lined front porch and a nice back yard.

Candles, low-light sconces and old-fashioned nightshirts create "an ambiance of romantic 19th-century life," according to owners Steve and Diane Cooper, who live in Philadelphia and hire a manager. They have improved the bathroom situation (now all but two are private, all with showers only) and the rates represent good value for St. Michaels.

Period furnishings, wingback chairs and Queen Anne tables are in each of the six original guest rooms, two on each floor. They have antique double four-poster rope beds with trundle beds beneath, patchwork quilts and down pillows. Beds in the two third-floor rooms are impossibly high, at least three feet off the ground and appearing rather ludicrous to contemporary eyes. The two third-floor rooms have washstands in the room and a shared bath. The four on the first and second floors have private baths and working fireplaces, which are lit on cool nights.

More modern comforts are offered in a new landing room with a balcony and a queensize brass bed, and in a rear cottage with cathedral ceiling, queen poster bed, sitting area and private patio.

Continental breakfast with pastries and cheese is taken on trays in the room or outside on the porch or lawn in summer.

(410) 745-2243. Five rooms and a cottage with private baths; two rooms with shared bath. Doubles, $70 to $110. Two-night minimum on weekends, March-December.

Dining Spots

208 Talbot, 208 North Talbot St., St. Michaels.

Since its opening in 1990 in a mid-19th-century house, this has become the area's best-regarded restaurant. A lounge with a marble bar leads into a serene main dining room and three smaller rooms, one a garden room with floral paintings on the white brick walls. Decor is crisp in teal green and white, and the staff is informed and suave.

Culinary Institute-trained chef Paul Milne was featured on the 1993 television series, Great Chefs of the East. He and partner Candace Chiaruttini present here what they call casual gourmet dining . Others call it quite sophisticated. Dinner is prix-fixe four courses on Saturdays and à la carte the rest of the week. Among dinner entrées might be seared sea scallops with creamy garlic polenta and tomato

Brick walls and sconces create sophisticated setting for dining at 208 Talbot.

coulis, yellowfin tuna with charred onions and burgundy butter sauce, New Zealand rack of lamb with roasted garlic and rosemary sauce, and grilled ribeye steak with homemade worcestershire sauce.

Start with a napoleon of smoked salmon with crispy wontons and wasabi sauce, fried Ipswich clams with oven-dried tomatoes and a brandy-tarragon mayonnaise or sliced oriental duck with a gingered pancake, mache and enoki mushrooms. Candace makes the delectable desserts, perhaps lemon tart, apple spice cake with warm caramel sauce, tirami su and assorted ice creams.

(410) 745-3838. Entrées, $21 to $24.50. Prix-fixe Saturday, $43. Lunch in season, Wednesday-Friday noon to 2. Dinner, Wednesday-Sunday 5 to 9 or 10; Sunday brunch, 11 to 2.

Bistro St. Michaels, 403 South Talbot St., St. Michaels.

This urbane new bistro was opened by chef David Stein and his parents from Washington, D.C. They converted a 125-year-old clapboard house into an intimate, 75-seat restaurant. The ambiance is authentic French bistro on the main floor with a zinc bar, banquettes and marble-top tables, with a semi-enclosed porch alongside. Upstairs is a more formal dining room with close-together white-clothed tables. Prized century-old French posters and artworks enhance the walls.

David and a couple of assistants do all the cooking, favoring local farmers and fishermen for indigenous products. The dinner menu is short but sweet. At our autumn visit it started with a white bean and ham soup, Wellfleet oysters with a shallot-sherry vinaigrette and an exotic salad of frisée, duck confit, goat cheese and beets with crispy onion rings and roasted garlic vinaigrette.

Main courses included pan-fried salmon with mustard-tarragon vinaigrette, sautéed jumbo shrimp with lobster butter sauce over spinach linguini, braised lamb shank with an apricot-mustard glaze, and grilled ribeye steak with crushed garlic potatoes, sautéed mushrooms and oven-dried tomatoes. Desserts were a classic crème brûlée, chocolate mousse with strawberries and streusel-topped apple pie with whipped cream and vanilla sauce.

We would gladly try every salad and sandwich on the with-it lunch menu.

(410) 745-9111. Entrées, $17 to $23. Lunch, 11:30 to 2 or 2:30. Dinner from 5:30. Closed Wednesday and month of February.

The Inn at Perry Cabin, Watkins Lane, St. Michaels.

The dining room setting is as perfect as the rest of the first Ashley House venture in the United States. And executive chef Mark Salter's food measures up, although at prices that mere mortals find staggering.

The peak-ceilinged dining room is a panoply of rose, green and white chintz. Tables, skirted to the floor and dressed to the hilt, are flanked by chairs upholstered in a burgundy fabric. Expansive windows and french doors look out onto a terrace and treed lawns leading to Fogg Cove.

The complicated, three-course dinner menu is strictly prix-fixe. Having over-indulged at afternoon tea, we asked if it were possible to eat lighter and were informed that we could order from the prix-fixe menu and be charged à la carte.

Three kinds of complimentary canapés – one with boursin cheese and another of salmon – whetted the tastebuds for treats to come. So did wonderful cheese-herb and sourdough rolls. Proper fish service was provided for our main courses, fillet of grouper with a pineapple and mint quinoa cake, mango chutney and pappadams for one, John Dory with wild rice, shiitake mushrooms and bok choy for the other. Presentation was in the architectural style, beautiful but small portions. An obscure (and perfect) Oregon pinot gris for $28 accompanied. A selection of four sorbets (mango, pineapple, apricot and espresso, topped with chocolate curls in a silver bowl) was a refreshing ending to a memorable meal.

High-rollers may enjoy à la carte luncheon fare at prices that would pay for dinner in most restaurants. The cheapest main course at our visit was a turkey club sandwich with vegetable chips and cornichons for $12.50.

(410) 745-2200. Prix-fixe, $68. Lunch daily, 12:30 to 2:30. Dinner nightly, 6 to 10, jackets preferred.

Windows, 101 North Harbor Road, St. Michaels.

The redecorated restaurant at the St. Michaels Harbour Inn and Marina was appropriately renamed and the food upgraded to rate with the tops in town. The contemporary, nicely angled dining room here is decked out in mauve tablecloths and blond wood chairs. Part is beneath billowing fabric and part beneath a pressed tin ceiling, but both areas command a great view across the harbor.

Executive chef Chris Moyer was earning accolades for such entrées as rockfish tandoori, cornmeal-coated salmon with a tangy artichoke vinaigrette, peanut-crusted sea bass with a creamed corn sauce, roasted cornish game hen scented with curry and grilled New York strip steak with bourbon molasses glaze. Oysters martinique and a garlicky cheese and crab dip with foccacia were favorite starters. Desserts included strawberry tartlets with crème anglaise and bourbon pecan pie.

A good but limited wine list offers many by the glass as well as pre-selected small samplings called flights, or you can create your own flights. A new manager also has added specialty martinis, microbrews and espresso.

(410) 745-5102. Entrées, $16.50 to $21.95. Lunch daily, 11 to 5. Dinner 5 to 9 or 10. Closed Monday and Tuesday in winter.

Town Dock Restaurant, 125 Mulberry St., St. Michaels.

The waterfront setting at this huge establishment is one of the town's best. The food was elevated by chef-owner Michael Rork, who had made a name for himself as executive chef at Baltimore's fancy Harbor Court Hotel. With his wife and three children, he sought a more rural location in which to run his own business. Although reviews were mixed, most locals felt he had succeeded in converting a touristy, 400-seat restaurant into his goal of "an upscale but casual dining destination."

The short daily specials menu is where the action is. Typical are grilled salmon topped with roasted leeks and peppers, soft-shell crabs with a tomato-herb cream sauce, grilled shrimp served over saffron orzo, and grilled duck breast with dried cherries and fresh currants. These are standouts on a seafood-oriented menu priced from fried oysters to Brazilian lobster tail stuffed with crab imperial.

We were impressed with the change at a summer lunch, served outside on the waterfront terrace. Cups of crab bisque and saffron bouillabaisse preceded the main events, crab monterey and a fried oyster sandwich with brabant potatoes and homemade coleslaw. All proved exceptional, brimming with assertive tastes. Two big chocolate-covered strawberries came with the bill, making dessert redundant.

Still in the planning stage was an elegant upstairs dining room with an open grill kitchen. That would be the showcase for the grilled specialties of Michael's contemporary regional cuisine. Meanwhile, the **Top of the Dock** upstairs lounge features light fare, live entertainment and dancing for the "over 30" crowd.

(410) 745-5577 or (800) 884-0103. Entrées, $15.75 to $21.95. Lunch daily, 11 to 4. Dinner, 4 to 10. Closed Monday and Tuesday in winter.

Diversions

Chesapeake Bay Maritime Museum, Mill Street, Navy Point.

Built on mounds of crushed oyster shells, this growing museum founded in 1965 is the town's major tourist attraction. Its focal point is the 1879 Hooper Strait Lighthouse, one of only three cottage-type lighthouses remaining on the bay. You learn what a lightkeeper's life was like and pass some interesting exhibits of fog signals, lamps and lenses as you climb to the top level for a bird's-eye view of the St. Michaels harbor. The Waterfowling Building contains an extensive collection of decoys and guns. The museum has the largest floating fleet of historic Chesapeake Bay boats in existence, including a skipjack, log canoe, oyster boat and crab dredger. They're maintained in a traditional working boat yard, where you get to see craftsmen at work and view a small display of primitive boat-building tools. Other attractions include the Small Boat Shed, a bell tower, a Victorian bandstand where concerts are staged in summer and a good museum shop.

(410) 745-2916. Open daily, 9 to 5; January-February, Friday-Sunday and holidays only. Adults, $7.50.

St. Michaels Walking Tour. A self-guided walking tour with a map is provided by the St. Mary's Square Museum. It covers the meandering waterfront, including the footbridge from Cherry Street to Navy Point (one wishes there were more footbridges to get from point to point), the Talbot Street business section and St. Mary's Square, an unusual town green laid out away from the main street and apt to be missed unless you seek it out. The map identifies 31 historic houses (none open to the public), churches and sites. We found equally interesting things along the way.

The St. Mary's Square Museum, On the Green, (410) 745-9561. One of the town's oldest Colonial houses was moved to this site, restored and furnished. It is joined to the 1860 Teetotum Building, so named because it resembles an old-fashioned top. The display areas of local memorabilia and history are open weekends and holidays from 10 to 4, May-October. Donation.

Shopping. Shopping is a big draw along narrow Talbot Street in St. Michaels. **Chesapeake Trading Company,** a bookstore and gift shop, is where you stop for espresso or great cold drinks as you browse among the wonderful collection of hats, apparel, jewelry, cards, music and paperbacks. Owner Linda Boatner stocks all the right things and displays them right. Those of us who like food spicy enough to bring tears to the eyes are in seventh heaven at **Flamingo Flats.** This shop must have every hot, spicy sauce or relish ever bottled, as well as numerous mustards and oils – more than 2,600, including many from the Caribbean. Now expanded into the former Celebrate Maryland space, it has a tasting bar, gifts and cards, cookbooks and entertainment. On Saturdays in season the staff barbecue out front on grills, and offer treats like smoked gouda with a cabernet, rosemary and thyme sauce. **Bags Aloft** stocks all kinds of bags from laundry to lunch. **Sailor of St. Michaels** offers sportswear and accessories of interest to the legions of sailing types that frequent this area. **Keepers-Orvis** appeals to the flyfisherman and carries clothing, equipment and decoys. Resort-type clothes are found at **Shaw Bay Classics, Chesapeake Bay Outfitters** and **Bleachers** (which also has some fun stuffed things like flamingos), while the **Broken Rudder** carries nice sportswear with a Chesapeake accent. A resident decoy carver works at **The Calico Gallery,** which has a large selection of local art posters. **The Mind's Eye Gallery** stocks unusual American crafts (check out the painted stools) and at the **Blue Swan,** we liked the nautical Christmas ornaments. **Canton Row Antiques** bills itself as an upscale antique mall, or at least a mews, with eighteen dealers. **The Cultural Art Gallery** has lovely things, including stained glass. We also liked the mobiles of stained glass at **Artiste Locale,** a showplace of local art

Extra-Special

Patriot Cruise, Navy Point, St. Michaels.

Since most of its meandering shoreline is very private and far from view, the best way to see and savor this part of the Eastern Shore is by boat. David Etzel provides a leisurely hour-long cruise up the Miles River on a two-deck boat carrying 180 passengers. He advised beforehand that he points out "birds, houses, duck blinds, whatever I see." We saw the Mystic Clipper in the distance, various kinds of bulkheading to prevent shore erosion, several osprey nests on channel markers, the ruins of St. John's Chapel, and some mighty impressive plantations and contemporary homes. We learned that James Michener wrote *Chesapeake* in a rented house along the river. Our only regret was that the boat didn't go closer to the sights the guide or the taped narration were pointing out on the eleven-mile round trip. (Smaller vessels like the workboat of **St. Michaels Lady Cruises,** 305 Mulberry St., can get closer and the waterman-captain tailors some excursions to special interests.)

(410) 745-3100. Cruises April-October, daily at 11, 12:30, 2:30 and 4 (weather permitting, minimum fifteen persons). Adults, $8.

Stately homes along Chestertown's Water Street back up to Chester River.

Chestertown, Md.

A Town that Has It All

The impression one gets upon entering Chestertown over the U.S. Route 213 bridge is unforgettable. Across the wide Chester River are grand brick mansions along the shore. In the center of town are great churches, squares and parks with monuments, the county courthouse, a couple of inns and suave stores. The streets in the nicely symmetrical downtown grid are lined with historic homes and townhouses, many dating to the 18th century.

Here's the perfect small town, you think – close to the water, with ties to the past, obviously prosperous, a manageable size, good quality of life. The first impression is not erroneous. Subsequent forays in and around the Eastern Shore town of 4,000 and conversations with its residents confirm that this is one great place to live, as well as to visit.

Local boosters are proud that Chestertown was rated in a national survey as the tenth favorite historic place in America. The lure is more than the fact that this small town claims the second largest district of restored 18th-century homes in Maryland, however.

Life is slower here, Chestertown lying well off the beaten path. As the county seat of Kent County, Maryland's smallest, it exudes an air of self-sufficiency and a sense of place that evades towns twice its size. The park fountain works, the clock tower is illuminated at night, tiny white lights twinkle in a downtown alleyway. Galleries, boutiques and shops, all owner-operated, purvey wares normally associated with metropolitan areas. Creative chefs have settled here to instill their culinary marks.

The good life is enhanced by the cultural offerings of Washington College, the nation's tenth oldest and the only one that George Washington allowed to use his name (he served as a trustee and received an honorary degree).

Not far away are attractions as diverse as the oldest Episcopal church in Maryland, the best bathing beach on the Chesapeake Bay at Betterton, a hokey but bustling auction house and Rock Hall, a once-sleepy fishing community that's become a happening place lately.

Who would challenge the claim that here is a small town that has it all?

Inn Spots

Brampton, 25227 Chestertown Road (Route 20), Chestertown 21620.

The thoughtful comments in the guest books in each room testify glowingly that innkeepers Michael and Danielle Hanscom do things right. Theirs is one of the more comfortable and elegant B&Bs in which we've stayed.

On 35 acres of plantation-like property about a mile out High Street (Route 20) south of town, the imposing three-story brick Italianate Greek Revival commands a hilltop set back from the road. Two gliders swing toward each other and an array of wicker chairs from either end of the pillared front veranda.

Inside the 1860 house, listed on the National Register, are a majestic living room with twelve-foot ceilings, high bookshelves and gray leather couches facing each other across an oriental rug next to the fireplace; a brick and paneled guest parlor and TV room (TVs also are available in guest rooms); a fireplaced dining room with peach draperies matching the wallpaper and four tables beneath a crystal chandelier, and solid walnut baseboards and doors that never suffered the humiliation of paint. What restoration needed to be done was ably handled during the six months prior to their 1987 opening by Mike, who had restored Victorian homes in San Francisco.

Danielle, a former flight attendant with Swissair, oversaw the decorating. The ten air-conditioned guest rooms and suites are classics. Each has a private bath and a queen or twin beds that can be put together as a king, and eight have fireplaces or Franklin stoves. They are tastefully decorated with period and reproduction antiques, many of them from Switzerland. Rooms are perfect down to the smallest details: plump pillows, duvet comforters, thick towels, night lights in the bathrooms, brass shoe horns on the closet doors. The bowl on our dresser in the Blue Room matched the blue and white wallpaper; a bird and butterfly from the stunning wallpaper pattern in the bathroom had been painstakingly cut out and pasted on the vanity. Most of the paintings in the house were done by Danielle's grandfather, an artist in Switzerland.

All rooms, with the exception of the Mezzanine Suite that is more cozy, are unusually airy and spacious. Even the two guest rooms on the third floor are surprisingly high-ceilinged and big for their location, each measuring twenty by

twenty feet. Choice new accommodations include the Fairy Hill Suite with a ground-floor sitting room and an upstairs bedroom notable for a Swiss cherry armoire and an antique chimney cupboard, and the renovated 19th-century Smoke House, now a high-ceilinged, beamed bedroom with couch, fireplace and an 1860 walnut armoire.

Italianate Greek Revival house is now Brampton, an elegant B&B.

The premier lodgings were fashioned in 1995 from an old horse barn out back. Now known as the Garden Cottage, it has two extra-large rooms, each with sitting area, fireplace, TV, private patio and double whirlpool tub with separate shower. Oriental rugs cover the shiny, random-width cherry floors. The East Room, furnished in Victorian style, has a king bed, while the West Room has a queen canopy bed and Colonial décor.

The Hanscoms, who live with their young daughters in an outbuilding on the property, offer afternoon refreshments and wine or sherry in the evening. Breakfast in their beautiful dining room starts with orange juice, fresh fruit and sticky buns. Our entrée was a delicate puffed pancake with a fresh plum sauce. Others could be french toast, blueberry pancakes, waffles or sausage, and cheese and green pepper quiche.

(410) 778-1860. Fax (410) 778-1805. Ten rooms with private baths. Doubles, $95 to $135. Suites, $115 to $155. No smoking.

The Imperial Hotel, 208 High St., Chestertown 21620.

Built as a hotel in 1903, the Imperial had been converted to apartments and shops before it was grandly restored into a small, urbane lodging establishment and restaurant by ex-Washingtonians Carla and Albert Massoni.

The hotel's eleven guest rooms on the second and third floors are decorated to the Victorian hilt with original art and period furnishings. All have private baths with heated towel racks and Gilchrist & Soames toiletries. Five have kingsize beds, five have twins and one has a queen. Armoires conceal TV sets and antique potty cupboards hide the telephones. Bold wallpapers, wild borders, ornate lamps, floral carpeting, coordinated fabrics, lace curtains and heavy draperies are the rule. Rooms vary widely in size. Some are rather small, but we found the third-floor suite big enough for a cocktail party, what with a living room that is total Victoriana, a bedroom with kingsize bed, a mini-kitchen and a porch the size of a volleyball court across the front of the hotel.

The Massonis think the best room in the house is No. 206 midweek, when rates are discounted. It's located in the front corner across from the guest parlor and beside the common second-floor porch, neither of which gets much use during the week. Two more accommodations are in the rear carriage house. A favorite is the spacious, country-style suite, a welcome break from the pervading high Victorian decor. It has a beamed cathedral ceiling, a skylit bathroom and a full kitchen.

The hotel has an award-winning restaurant (see Dining Spots) and a handsome little cocktail lounge with a fireplace. A rear parking lot has been transformed into a landscaped courtyard for lunch, lounging and Friday evening jazz concerts. Fine art is shown in the Courtyard Gallery behind the hotel, as well as at the Carla Massoni Gallery across the street. The cellar bakery is the temporary home of the Chester River Crafts & Arts Center's culinary school. There's a lot going on, as the Massonis continue to make their inn a stylish focal point for Chestertown.

A complimentary continental breakfast of juice and large, flaky croissants and other pastries is served in the Hubbard Room.

(410) 778-5000. Fax (410) 778-9662. www.chestertown.com/imperial/ Eleven rooms and two suites with private baths. Doubles, $100 to $125. Suites, $200 and $300.

Great Oak Manor, 10568 Cliff Road, Chestertown 21620.

Majestic. How better to describe this red-brick Georgian manor house grandly situated on twelve acres overlooking the Chesapeake Bay? Written descriptions, even photos, fail to convey fully the understated elegance and the alluring appeal of this winning B&B, as transformed by energetic owners Don and Dianne Cantor from California. They took over in 1993 from an absentee owner who owned eight area lodging facilities and quickly invested a quarter million dollars in refurbishing and upgrading what had been a tired, rather cold facility that catered to functions.

"What really attracted us was the large common rooms," said Don. "Our guests don't feel like they're intruding on the owners' quarters." The 25-room mansion, built in 1938 by an heir to the W.R. Grace shipping fortune, has regal public rooms, eleven guest rooms and plenty of space left over for the Cantor family at one end.

Guests enter a great hall worthy of the name, with a graceful spiral staircase on one side. Intricate carvings over the doorways announce each room's use (a rising sun over the entrance, a crab over the dining rooms). On the left are a formal living room, a rich-looking library with shelves of books, hunting prints and a huge oriental rug, and a side porch full of wicker and wisteria stenciling. On the right are the dining room and the Gun Room, dark and masculine with guns behind leaded glass doors, plush leather sofas and chairs, a TV/VCR and a small help-yourself bar hidden in a space beneath the spiral staircase. One of Dianne's stained-glass creations, a colorful parrot, stands sentry in a window.

The bedrooms vary in size and décor, but all are plush in an understated way. Each comes with full tiled bath, kingsize or king/twin beds, a sitting area with comfortable chairs, and bottles of Perrier water. Five have fireplaces and seven yield bay views. An artist hand-painted whimsical touches here and there: a squirrel on a desk in one room, an extra window on the wall of another. Even the third-floor rooms convey an unusual sense of space with their high vaulted ceilings. The Cantors provide TVs in one room that lacks a view as well as in the largest Russell Room, which has a sofa in the sitting area.

Handsome brick Georgian house known as Great Oak Manor looks onto Chesapeake Bay.

A continental-plus breakfast is served at individual tables amid lots of silver and china in the dining room. The fare includes fresh fruit, cereals, bagels and Dianne's special peach-pecan muffins. We took ours on trays to the back terrace to enjoy the broad expanse of tree-shaded lawn. A screened gazebo and a deck with rocking chairs await on a bluff above the bay.

The Cantors are hands-on innkeepers whose innkeeping savvy shows.

(410) 778-5943 or (800) 504-3098. www.chestertown.com/greatoak/ Eleven rooms with private baths. Doubles, weekends $95 to $145 April-November, $85 to $130 rest of year; weekdays, $76 to $116 year-round. No children. Smoking restricted.

Moonlight Bay Inn, 6002 Lawton Ave., Rock Hall 21661.

Guests at this B&B in a residential section along the Chesapeake Bay enjoy one of the more appealing water settings of any inn anywhere. A screened gazebo, garden chairs scattered about the large lawn and a wicker-filled porch take full advantage, as do the balconies of five deluxe rooms in a new structure opened in 1997 right along the shore. As the sun sets over little Swan Island, yellow lights outline docks in the foreground, white lights twinkle on the Bay Bridge in the distance and the glow of Baltimore to the west lights up the evening sky. The feeling is nothing short of magical.

So it may be difficult to comprehend why innkeeper Dorothy Santangelo "cried for two weeks" after her husband Bob bought the place in 1992. "I thought I'd be at Great Oak Manor or Tara," said she. "I wanted a B&B and he wanted a marina." What they got initially was a fantastic marina location and an abandoned house that had successively been a post office, a restaurant and a boarding house. They razed all but the front of the house and, after fifteen months of rebuilding and renovations, opened in 1993 with five handsome bedrooms, all with private baths and caring touches, from clock radios to diaries for guest comments.

The largest Magic Moon suite is on the main floor off a spacious guest living room. It comes with a sitting room, canopy queensize bed and windows onto the water. Even more windows onto the water were evident in our upstairs corner room, the Harvest Moon, comfortable with kingsize bed, a large and elegant bathroom, and an antique rocker beside a chair with a rush seat. If you're so inclined, says Dorothy, you can lie in bed here or in the adjacent room and "watch the boats pass outside." The adjacent room is large and lovely in white and blue, the patterned fabrics here matching some of the miniature vases displayed on a shelf on the wall. The cozy side Crescent Moon room that's summery in white lace and wicker, with accents of pink, "is every woman's dream." Each room contains a decanter of sherry, fancy window treatments and a framed wall hanging called "Inn Reminders," in which the usual guest instructions are rendered in poetry.

We'd happily stay in any of the five new rooms in a two-story structure at bay's edge. Each has a kingsize bed (one can be separated into twins), private bath with whirlpool tub and a private balcony with a wooden chair and lounge overlooking the water. Four balconies face the bay head-on. Moon Struck, upstairs in the rear, has a side balcony with views of both bay and an inlet known as the haven. It's dressed in striking black and white florals, and both the room and balcony are larger than the others. Beneath it on the main floor is a parlor for guests.

The entire inn has been lovingly furnished by Dorothy. The decorating is quite remarkable, given that she did it herself and is legally blind.

She's also quite the cook, as evidenced at breakfast in the dining room and enclosed atrium porch overlooking a showy English garden. Waffles in many forms are her specialty. We enjoyed belgian waffles after preliminaries of orange juice, a fruit cup with bananas and strawberries, and two kinds of muffins. English tea is served in the late afternoon.

(410) 639-2660. Fax (410) 639-7739. Ten rooms with private baths. Doubles, $98 to $134. Two-night minimum weekends. No smoking.

The Inn at Mitchell House, 8796 Maryland Pkwy., Chestertown 21620.
A long driveway leads, plantation-like, to this lovely old manor house seven miles west of Chestertown in the Tolchester section near Chesapeake Bay. The ten-acre property beside Stoneybrook Pond was part of a 1,000-acre working plantation. The manor, built in 1743 and expanded in 1825, is still fit for the landed gentry.

Jim Stone, a Washington native who summered here, his wife Tracy and their youngsters share the expansive house with guests in six rooms, all with private baths. They serve sumptuous breakfasts and offer weekend dinners to guests and the public.

Theirs is very much a family home, reflecting heirlooms and mementos from both sides of the family as well as the telltale signs of their youngsters. Jim acquired the eagle over the entrance from the cornerstone of a building in Baltimore. In one of the two parlors on the left is a portrait of Sir Peter Parker, a British commander who was wounded near here in the War of 1812 and was brought to the Mitchell House for aid; the portrait was found by coincidence many years later by Tracy's father. A signed Tiffany lamp graces the square baby piano converted into a desk. Family portraits cover a square grand piano, and a watercolor of Tracy and their youngsters hangs on one wall. Who can help but be fascinated by the lineup of framed White House Christmas cards dating from Tracy's years at the White House when she handled President Reagan's mail? The side-by-side parlors are attractive in pale yellow and deep green decor.

Art works from Jim's grandmother, who started painting oils at age 60, enhance the Joseph Mitchell Room, the largest bedroom with a queensize canopy bed, a fireplace and a sitting area with queen sofabed. The large Dr. William Ringgold Room has a queensize bed, a twin sofabed and a fireplace. On their way to other bedrooms, guests pass a refrigerator stocked with complimentary sodas and beer and a hallway decorated with flapper dresses and hats that belonged to Jim's great aunt. A king-bedded hideaway with private bath is up steep stairs in the beamed, low-ceilinged attic.

A country breakfast is served at five tables in the high-ceilinged dining room, where the floor is brick and plates and artifacts dot the walls. The main course might be french toast, omelets, featherbed eggs, peach-raspberry coffee cake – "everything you can think of that's bad for you I do," says Tracy.

The Stones also offer dinners on Friday and Saturday nights by reservation, a single seating for up to sixteen people at 7 o'clock. A classical guitarist plays as guests sip a complimentary rum cocktail. The $26 to $29 tab includes hors d'oeuvres and wine with the meal. You might start with steamed shrimp or cold soup and salad, move on to grilled tuna with mustard sauce or pork tenderloin with blackberry sauce, and finish with homemade apple pie (with apples from the couple's orchard), chocolate mousse or ice cream pecan ball with homemade hot fudge.

Outside, guests enjoy a screened porch containing a 1956 jukebox with old records that belonged to Tracy's father. The porch overlooks the pond, which you can traverse by means of two bridges. Jim put in the raised herb and flower garden, terraced gardens and a fish pond beside the old smokehouse.

(410) 778-6500. Six rooms with private baths. Doubles, $75 to $110.

The Inn at Osprey, Route 20, Rock Hall 21661.

Philadelphia Main Line investors who like to sail built this yacht club, marina, inn, restaurant and bar from scratch in 1993 along a section of Swan Creek known as "The Haven," an inlet from the nearby Chesapeake Bay. The place looks and feels new, although it was scrupulously designed with the Williamsburg look and patterned after the Coke-Garrett House, the mayor's house in Williamsburg, Va. It's all rather slick for Rock Hall.

On a still rather barren landscape that first strikes visitors as mainly sailing masts and parking areas, the endeavor suffers from a split personality. Overnight guests "register" at a second-story office that also serves the marina or, after hours, in the main-floor restaurant. The seven bedrooms are on the second and third floors of the main house. All equipped with modern baths and TVs, they are true to the Williamsburg look, from paint colors to wide-plank floors, and feature "showcase furnishings and gallery art throughout," according to the slick inn brochure. Amenities are "the finest that can be found, from our 250-count pima cotton sheets to our authentic oriental rugs," added one of the inn managers. We found the Windigo room fairly spacious but rather spartan, with queensize poster bed, a windsor chair at a writing desk, nautical and bird prints on the white walls, swagged curtains matching the pillows and the skirt on the night stand, and a couple of oriental scatter rugs on the floors. Coat hooks along one wall are pressed into service in lieu of a closet. Less chilly and more comfortable is the Carina room, equipped with two twin beds and a small TV between the sofabed and a wing chair. Prim but pleasant is the Cotton Blossom, with a queen poster bed, a wing chair and two window seats. The two-room Escapade suite with a jacuzzi in the

The Inn at Mitchell House is situated beside Stoneybrook Pond.

marble bathroom and the Bolero room with a gas fireplace and queen poster bed have the best water views, but the jacuzzi room "can be noisy due to the restaurant" below, the inn literature advises. A third-floor landing area, described as a common room, holds two wing chairs and some reading materials.

New innkeepers Herb and Christine Will offer a complimentary continental breakfast in the restaurant's Hunt Room. There's a nature trail along the woods in back of the inn, but the chief amenity here may be the large, club-like swimming pool and deck area with bathhouse.

(410) 639-2194. Fax (410) 639-7716. Six rooms and one suite with private baths. May-November: doubles $117 to $137, suite $157. December-April: doubles $105 to $120, suite $140. Midweek $10 less. Children welcome. No smoking.

The White Swan Tavern, 231 High St., Chestertown 21620.

Stay here if you're into history. The White Swan, dating to 1733, is full of it. Its restoration began in 1978 with an archeological dig and produced a "museum" room of the old bar, showing artifacts in a lighted display window.

Despite its lavish refurbishing, the place conveys a rather impersonal and commercial feeling. The hired innkeepers, who live off-premises, may or may not answer the locked front door. Afternoon tea is served by the fireplace in a chandeliered tea room for $2, with a plate of sweets available for $1.50. An article on the tavern's restoration is sold for $1. Occupants of the Sterling Suite find the bow window like that of a storefront, which it once was; though it's partially screened, one nevertheless feels on view to the street here.

Eighteenth-century period furnishings dignify the main-floor common rooms. An austere front parlor is set up as a game room. A more welcoming rear parlor, dressed in yellow floral chintz, contains a TV. All six guest rooms have private baths and at least an extra twin bed for additional guests. Various passages lead to the rooms, which range from the small Thomas Peacock with a lace canopy double bed and a twin under the eaves to the large T.W. Eliason Suite, with a twin bed in the entry, a kingsize bed with imposing wood headboard in the main room and a Victorian sitting room beyond. A favorite is the John Lovegrove Kitchen, a one-room dwelling that was the first building on the lot. It has a brick floor, dark beamed ceiling, twin beds and an old dining-room table in front of the enormous cooking fireplace. The room exudes atmosphere, but the fireplace (like those in other bedrooms) is not functional and the chairs aren't really comfortable for sitting.

Guests are served a continental breakfast at the time specified on a "breakfast preference card." The fare is "changing," but the innkeeper on duty at our visit would not be specific. It comes with a fruit basket and the morning paper.

(410) 778-2300. Four rooms and two suites with private baths. Doubles, $100 to $130. Suites, $140 to $150. No credit cards.

The Parker House, 108 Spring Ave., Chestertown 21620.

Personality pervades this B&B lovingly run by John and Marcy Parker, veterans of the New York publishing trade, who returned in 1994 to settle in the town he first knew as a student at Washington College. The personality comes from the outgoing innkeepers, he the author of three books and she a former director of administration for Time-Life, and from a 19th-century farmhouse that oozes history, including the first indoor bathroom in Chestertown, circa 1876. Not to mention their cocker spaniel Half Pint, who barks a greeting and kisses the feet of new arrivals.

The pale yellow house with black and white trim occupies a shady property at the edge of downtown Chestertown. From the wonderful rear screened porch overlooking a landscaped lawn with statuary, a barn and an old privy, you forget that you're in the heart of town. Guests also spread out near the fireplace in a large side parlor that had been two rooms and in a long dining room that had served as the original kitchen. From her new kitchen on the other side of this house that seems to stretch forever, Marcy prepares a continental breakfast that, their brochure advises, will have you "rise from the table with a spring in your step and a song in your heart."

All three guest rooms are spacious and equipped with private baths. One is ensconced in the original summer kitchen at the rear of the main floor. It's bright and cheery with a floral quilt on the kingsize bed.

Upstairs, beneath a 10½-foot ceiling, is the Queen's Room, with a loveseat at the foot of the queen bed. An adjoining single room can turn it into a suite. Occupants use the first indoor bathroom in Chestertown, obviously updated but still with the original marble sink and etched glass in the door.

The front Lincoln Room is so named for its carved antique double bed, similar to one belonging to Abe Lincoln. Bathrobes and bottled water are among the room amenities.

A stack of Time magazines from 1946 makes fascinating reading in the upstairs hall sitting area.

(410) 778-9041. Fax (410) 778-7318. Doubles, $105 to $110 weekends, $90 to $95 midweek. No smoking. No credit cards.

Swan Haven Bed & Breakfast, 10950 Rock Hall Ave., Rock Hall 21661.

This B&B in an 1898 Victorian cottage started operating weekends only with four bedrooms as owners Diane and Harry Oliver commuted from weekday jobs in Washington, D.C. An addition in 1997 produced three more guest rooms and meant Diane could be on hand fulltime.

The waterside location, with a pier on "The Haven" and a huge deck nearby, is a key asset. The new addition takes full advantage. The side Heron Room with

Porches mark facade of Imperial Hotel.

Clubby dining room at Imperial Hotel.

cathedral ceiling and kingsize iron bed has a private balcony overlooking Swan Creek and marinas, although the room itself has no chairs. The rear Cygnet Room has a kingsize bed, a jacuzzi tub for two and an antique wooden glider chair in the room, plus a balcony facing the Haven.

Other rooms in the original cottage have a distinctly older feel. All have private baths, central air conditioning and TVs. Two on the second floor, one with a queensize bed, open onto an old-fashioned screened front porch. Two more are up steep stairs in the attic. One here has a double and twin bed in the garrets; the other has a double bed beneath a skylight.

The main floor holds a living room with a fireplace plus a breakfast room notable for a wooden bar. A continental breakfast is put out on the bar.

(410) 639-2527. Seven rooms with private baths. Doubles, $85 to $115. Children over 10.

Dining Spots

The Imperial Hotel, 208 High St., Chestertown.

Two opulent, intimate dining rooms, one on either side of the main corridor are the setting for some of the area's finest meals.

The smaller room is dark and clubby in hunter green and Stuart tartan plaid, while the larger is light and feminine in shades of claret and celadon. Victorian round-back chairs are at tables draped in white damask with little fringed silver lamps on top.

Master of the kitchen is Chuck Reeser, former sous chef who returned after a stint as chef at the late Ironstone Café. The Zagat survey of Washington-Baltimore restaurants rates the Imperial among the tops in the region for food.

We certainly were impressed with our dinner. It began with a complimentary cheese straw. Starters were a rich cream of wild mushroom soup with port and chives and a wondrous plate of smoked shrimp, mussels and bay scallops with a cucumber and dill cream. Next time we'd like to try the pappadams layered with lump crab and wasabi mayonnaise or the grilled portobello mushroom topped with goat cheese, prosciutto and pesto.

Among entrées, our party sampled the sautéed lump crab cakes with a tomato-lemon-caper sauce, grilled fillet of snapper with sundried tomatoes, grilled scallops with fresh tarragon and fennel, and grilled New Zealand rack of lamb with artichokes, calamata olives and pinenuts, all superb. The pan-seared Atlantic salmon with a tropical fruit relish over wilted greens and the grilled filet mignon with a vidalia onion compound butter and cabernet-tarragon sauce were winners at another visit.

Desserts here earn much acclaim. The signature chocolate praline triangle with grand marnier sauce is heavenly. Ditto for the apple-ginger custard torte with caramel sauce, the chocolate cheesecake with a raspberry coulis and the chocolate-espresso torte with a vanilla bean anglaise.

At lunchtime, you might try pizza with grilled duck sausage, roasted vegetables and two cheeses; a grilled smoked chicken sandwich with chipotle mayonnaise on foccacia, or a grilled steak salad on seasonal greens with asparagus, wild mushrooms and a honey-cumin vinaigrette.

On Friday evenings in summer, light fare is served as top artists present live jazz in the hotel's garden courtyard.

Albert Massoni, hotel owner with his wife Carla, is an avid oenophile. His Imperial Wine Society sponsors periodic wine-tasting dinners and publishes an informative wine newsletter. The wine list earns an Award of Excellence from Wine Spectator.

(410) 778-5000. Entrées, $19.75 to $24. Lunch, Friday-Sunday 11:30 to 2:30, also Tuesday-Thursday seasonally. Dinner, Tuesday-Saturday 5:30 to 9:30.

Blue Heron Cafe, 236 Cannon St., Chestertown.

The old Ironstone Café gave way in late 1997 to this newcomer run by Paul Hanley, former general manager and partner in the highly rated Bayard House Restaurant in Chesapeake City. Previous owners Barbara Silcox and Kevin McKinney decided to concentrate fulltime on their newer restaurant, the Kennedyville Inn, eight miles north of Chestertown in Kennedyville.

The atmospheric, L-shaped dining room occupies an old carriage shop and glass company, which accounts for the garage door at the rear. The shelves that contained ironstone china now display Delmarva porcelain and stoneware commissioned by the Blue Heron for the restaurant. A local artisan obliged with a blue heron, skipjacks, chickens, Chesapeake workboats, redwing blackbirds and the like. An antique quilt from the 1920s hangs in the back dining room.

Paul says his team of chefs call their cuisine "traditional and innovative regional American." Typical main courses range from grilled swordfish with citrus-cilantro salsa to grilled veal chop with roasted garlic demi-glace. Pan-seared Atlantic salmon with oyster cream sauce, pasta Delmarva (with grilled chicken, fresh oysters, Smithfield ham, spinach and wild mushrooms in a romano cheese sauce over linguini) and honey-based roast duckling in a grilled pineapple and shallot sauce were early favorites.

Among appetizers were a barbecued shrimp cocktail on a bed of baby greens and red cabbage and an oyster fritter in lemon-butter sauce. The delectable homemade desserts include crème brûlée, hot milk cake with mandarin orange glaze, chocolate bourbon cake with white chocolate and raspberry sauces, pecan pie and assorted ice creams.

Some appetizers turn up on the lunch menu, which featured a delectable-sounding lump crab frittata at our visit.

(410) 778-0188. Entrées, $15 to $23. Lunch, Monday-Saturday 11:30 to 2:30. Dinner, Monday-Saturday 5 to 8:30 or 9:30.

The Inn at Osprey, 20786 Rock Hall Ave., Rock Hall.

The food at the handsome restaurant in this luxury inn receives high marks. White linens cover the well-spaced tables in the L-shaped dining room, which wraps around a small, historic-looking bar. A formal Colonial Williamsburg look is conveyed by french doors and tall, many-paned windows, a large fireplace, and white walls with Williamsburg blue trim.

The short dinner menu bears a contemporary Mediterranean touch. Among starters, we heard raves for the cream of crab soup, the lump crab cocktail on mesclun and baked oysters with sherry sauce and a touch of crabmeat.

Main courses include such winners as sautéed oysters with prosciutto and pistachio nuts in a cream sauce, served over linguini and "a masterpiece," according to our informant, and grilled swordfish over herbed polenta with chive pesto. Recent possibilities included crab cakes with caper aioli, grilled veal chop with onion chutney and rack of New Zealand lamb with mint vinaigrette.

The wine list spotlights boutique California wineries.

(410) 639-2194. Entrées, $15.95 to $22.95. Dinner, Thursday-Monday 6 to 9, March-December; Friday-Sunday, January and February.

Bay Wolf, Rock Hall Avenue (Route 20), Rock Hall.

A new sidewalk patio is a welcome summer addition to this well regarded restaurant, housed in a former funeral home and notable for church-like stained-glass windows. New owners Larry and Hildegard Sunkler (he of the Schaefer's Canal House family from Chesapeake City) mix a heavy dose of Austrian fare with an Eastern Shore accent in three pleasant dining rooms. They bill their bar as "the most convivial – and certainly the longest – in town."

A different theme is featured daily. Monday is German Wurst Night; Wednesday is Oyster Night. Otherwise, the dinner menu features such choices as Austrian pork roast with sauerkraut and dumpling, chicken hubertus with an Austrian mushroom sauce, duck a l'orange, wiener schnitzel and pepper steak nesselrotte with brandy sauce. Baked flounder stuffed with crab imperial, crab cakes and shrimp scampi appease seafood lovers.

Start with camembert fritters, fried mushrooms or a specialty chilled crab dip for two. Finish with apple strudel, black forest cake, key lime pie or "spumoni ice cream."

(410) 639-2000. Entrées, $14.95 to $23.95. Open daily, noon to 10.

Waterman's Crab House Restaurant, Sharp Street Wharf, Rock Hall.

The best waterfront location of any area restaurant is the draw of this oldtimer, which sprawls across a pier beside the landing for the Chesapeake Flyer, the catamaran passenger ferry that makes 75-minute trips to Annapolis and Baltimore.

You can see the ferry and lots of other marina activity from the heavy, six-sided picnic tables shaded by jaunty umbrellas on the pier, from another section with picnic tables under a vast canopy or from interior dining rooms that seat a total of 400.

On a sunny summer's day, we were quite happy with a cold beer and a frozen tequila sunrise. We were not so happy with the oyster sandwich, a travesty of four small oysters on a hamburger bun, and the "shrimpy caesar salad," a timid affair that lived up to its name in terms of size.

Perhaps things get better at night, when there aren't apt to be so many tour groups around. Crab and oysters are featured in various guises, along with ribs, chicken and prime rib. A widely advertised crab feast on Tuesdays and Thursdays was $10.99 for all you could eat, subject to a two-hour time limit.

(410) 639-2261. Entrées, $10.99 to $16.99. Open daily, 11 to 9 or 10:30.

The Feast of Reason, 203 High St., Chestertown.

This is a simple place across the street from the Imperial Hotel with eight round tables, bentwood chairs and a few posters on the wall. Geoffrey Riefe and his wife Kathleen, who were innkeepers at the Williamsville Inn in the Berkshires for two years, are in charge, he doing the cooking and she the baking.

To eat in or take out, they offer things like buttermilk-oatmeal muffins, spinach and corn quiche, flatbread pizza with shrimp or spinach and shrimp salad on a croissant. At our visit the soups were squash-honey and potato-scallion, and apple scrunch and butterscotch brownies were desserts of the day. We made a good picnic lunch of a roast beef sandwich with tomato-horseradish mayonnaise ($4) and a smoked salmon sandwich with dill and onion on pumpernickel ($4.75). Dinner entrées to go ($7 to $8) included chicken breast with pesto sauce and flounder with tomato-shrimp sauce. Beer and wine are available.

(410) 778-3828. Open Monday-Friday 10 to 6, Saturday, 10 to 4.

Andy's, 337½ High St., Chestertown.

For a change of pace, come here for a drink and a snack at the extra-long stand-up bar with high stools opposite or, better yet, in the rear "living room" with a fireplace, piano and numerous conversation corners with easy chairs, sofas and coffee tables.

Guest entertainers perform here on weekends and on some Thursday nights. The varied menu offers such things as a tomato-basil tart, ham and provolone sandwich, stuffed potatoes, burgers, quiche and gourmet pizzas in the $5 to $6 range.

(410) 778-6779. Light fare, Monday-Saturday 4 to 11, to midnight on weekends.

Diversions

Historic Chestertown. The orderly grid of streets leading from the riverfront is a living museum of homes that stood in Colonial times. The sights along Water, Queen, High and Cross streets are best appreciated on foot, guided by annotations on a walking tour brochure published by the Kent County Chamber of Commerce. More details are available in a booklet, "Chestertown: An Architectural Guide." A Kent County map outlines a 110-mile driving tour of this picturesque county, which includes the old-line waterman's community of Rock Hall and the beach at Betterton, considered the best swimming beach on the Chesapeake. Maps for nine bicycle tours are included in a Kent County Bicycle Tour brochure.

Chester River Craft and Art Schools, 105 South Cross St., Chestertown, (410) 778-5954. Local civic leaders and artists formed this venture in 1997 to foster the arts in the Chestertown area and give it a national identity. "We hope to become similar to Haystack," said catalyst Carla Massoni in a reference to Maine's famed Haystack Mountain School of Crafts. The project has an office, gallery and gift shop. As its first major venture in 1998, it was planning to build a replica of the 18th-century schooner Sultana, to be berthed on the Chester River as a floating exhibit and historical attraction. The ambitious, four-pronged approach will involve crafts, visual arts, performing arts and a culinary art school and café.

Dixon's Auction Barn, Routes 544 and 290 off 30l, Crumpton.

Every Wednesday is auction day at Dixon's, when you might find seven or eight pianos in a field, a tractor-trailer full of plants, a small Amish farm market and a warehouse stuffed with concession stands, furniture and antiques. Buyers and sellers of used and antique furniture come from across the country to deal here in something of a circus atmosphere. Auctioneer Norman Dixon takes no more than fifteen seconds to sell any item on his lot; if it's not sold, he gives it to anyone willing to take it. Table after table full of bric-a-brac leave some cold, and if you spot something you want, you have to wait until the auctioneer reaches that table and bid fast. When he and the crowd move in, things happen so fast the unwary bidder scarcely has time to think. As the typewritten handout says, "the auctioneer does not miss you, you miss him. So if you want something, holler out before he sells it, not afterwards."

(410) 928-3006. Open Wednesdays from 7 a.m.

Waterman's Museum, 20880 Rock Hall Ave., Rock Hall.

This little museum, nicely renovated from an abandoned house, was opened in 1993 by the owner of Haven Harbor Marina to preserve the history and lore of the watermen of Rock Hall. Three display rooms show exhibits on oystering and crabbing, plus fishing gear, local photographs, carvings and boats. "If it's been used on the water, we've probably got it," advised head curator Richard Burton, former marina manager who came out of retirement to oversee the well financed local venture. One of the more interesting exhibits involves a replica of a waterman's ark, a one-room shanty of a house on the scow of a boat. A pier was in the works to accommodate several workboats, including a skipjack, for visitors to board.

(410) 778-6697. Open daily, 10 to 5. Free.

St. Paul's Episcopal Church, 7579 Sandy Bottom Road, Chestertown. Actress Tallulah Bankhead, whose family lives nearby, is among the notables buried in the cemetery outside this historic church, built in 1713 and the oldest in Maryland. Giant oak trees, some more than 300 years old, rise among the boxwoods in the church yard. The interior is notable for embroidered kneelers and a beautiful stained-glass side window. A poster at our first visit piqued interest with word of an oyster roast celebrating the parish's 300th year.

Shopping. The shopping opportunities are wonderful in Chestertown. Start at the **Kerns Collection,** Susan Kerns's dramatic two-story showplace at 210 High St. next to the Imperial Hotel. The deep blue pottery by a local teacher intrigued us and now a lovely shallow bowl sits on our coffee table. Sensational stoles woven by the wife of the college president, art clothing, hand-blown glass, bonsai, jewelry made of Japanese rice paper, unique cards, colorful tiles and much more catch the eye. The **Carla Massoni Gallery** that originally occupied the Kerns space has moved to a loft across the street, where the hotelier displays the works of nationally known artists as well as the finest regional artists. She also offers fine art in the **Courtyard Gallery** behind her Imperial Hotel.

Rhodes at 241 High St. is a mecca of the impeccable taste of Holly and Frank Rhodes, he a cabinet maker who will custom-make any furniture, for instance an exquisite Queen Anne lowboy for $4,800. Wonderful china, linens, fire screens, decoys, oriental rugs and estate jewelry are some of the other traditional wares. **Dockside Emporium** has everything nautical, from cookbooks for the boat to sweaters with crabs thereon, and has expanded its clothing line. We admired an oyster plate in the window of **Bittersweet,** a consignment shop specializing in American country antique furniture. **The Finishing Touch,** which specializes in framing, offers nice prints. Unusual gifts are found at **Cornucopia of Treasures Ltd.** You'll find great sweaters at **Chester River Knitting Co.** Everything from gifts to cards to linens to books is available at **Twigs and Teacups.** We loved the birdhouses and things for the garden among the gifts and antiques at **The Village House.**

In the heart of Rock Hall, you can visit a restored corner drugstore, 1930s style, at **Durding's Store.** Ice-cream sodas made with real vanilla beans are served at the original marble soda fountain amidst a selection of cards, gifts and sundries. Fine furnishings for the home and yacht, Chesapeake memorabilia and clothing are carried at **The Cat's Paw,** a gift shop at The Sailing Emporium. Clothing of interest to boaters and nice gifts are carried at **The Ditty Bag,** the marine store at Haven Harbor Marina.

The Shops at Oyster Court, 5761 Main St., Rock Hall. This started in 1996 as a homey bookstore and gathering spot called the **America's Cup Café** at Rock Hall's main corner. Arlene Douglas manages the café, which specializes in coffee ("America's favorite beverage") and light meals day and night. Her husband Tom Sabol, a real estate lawyer, buys up old fishing shacks and outbuildings to move to the property and lease to merchants and craftspeople. The result is a charming alleyway lined with colorful enterprises, among them **Sweet Annie's** herbs and everlastings, **Smilin' Jakes** casual apparel, **Gepetto's Toy Store, One Nightstand** (for handpainted furniture and glassware) and **CoCoNuts** for the Banjo Man's folk art and pottery. Already, the second-hand bookstore spilled into an annex called **The Cup Runneth Over.** By 1998, Tom hoped to have twenty shops along the alley behind his café that began not with sailing races but coffee.

Extra-Special

Chesapeake Farms Wildlife Habitat, 7319 Remington Drive (off Route 20), Chestertown.

A driving tour leads through the 3,000-acre wildlife management demonstration area formerly known as Remington Farms, operated by the du Pont company in conjunction with Remington, the arms manufacturer. An informative brochure points out wildlife management practices being applied here. The self-guided tour takes one past ponds, swamps, woods and fields and involves fifteen marked – and some unmarked – stops for wildlife and plants. The leisurely drive is the closest thing we've found so far north to the famed J.N. "Ding" Darling National Wildlife Preserve on Florida's Sanibel Island, although the finds are neither so prolific nor so exotic. The quantity and variety of waterfowl you'll see depends on the season and the time of day. The habitat tour can take an hour or more, depending on stops. Other attractions of interest to nature lovers are the Eastern Neck National Wildlife Refuge in Rock Hall and the Millington Wildlife Management Area in Massey.

(410) 778-1565. Open free daily from February to Oct. 10, when it's closed to the public for hunting season.

Wide Lewes-Rehoboth Canal is on view from downtown Lewes.

Lewes, Del.

The First Town in the First State

Whoever thought up the "first town" slogan for Lewes was on the mark. The reference, of course, was to Lewes's founding by Dutch explorers in 1631, long before Delaware was to become the first state in the union. But age alone does not account for the popularity of this riverfront town that's pronounced "loo-iss" and takes its name from a town in Sussex County, England. As far as many are concerned, Lewes is first in charm and first in all-around appeal. For visitors, it's Delaware's most "visitable" – as opposed to its most visited – town.

Off the beaten path, Lewes is located on the lee side of Cape Henlopen, the strategic point where the Delaware Bay meets the Atlantic Ocean. It's long been home to skilled riverboat pilots who shepherd hundreds of cargo ships up the Delaware Bay to Wilmington and Philadelphia.

"This is a town with a beach – not a beach town," stresses the Lewes Chamber of Commerce. The distinction sets Lewes apart from its better-known neighbor to the south, Rehoboth Beach, with its glitzy sprawl of boardwalks and ballyhoo. This is a genuine town with a small but devoted year-round population (2,300), a working seaport town as opposed to a sailing or beachy town, a town that most folks would bypass on their way to or from the Cape May-Lewes Ferry.

No more. Now, restaurant waiters in Rehoboth are apt to steer their lunch patrons to Lewes for a rainy afternoon and innkeepers from across the bay in Cape May, N.J., come here for restorative day trips and overnights. In the last decade, Lewes has attracted fine inns and B&Bs, good restaurants and an uncommon array of small, sophisticated shops situated along Second Street beneath a canopy of unusual Bradford pear trees. It's now the side-by-side home of riverboat pilots, Delaware's first winery, the nation's first public park, an herb farm, some of Delaware's oldest homes, an inn offering lodging on a houseboat, World War II bunkers, "walking" sand dunes, a working blacksmith shop and a fascinating new residential development in which every structure is at least a hundred years old.

All are true, small-scale, understated places, as the town fathers have strived successfully to control development to avoid the all-too-evident fate of encroaching Rehoboth.

Once people discover the charms of Lewes, it seems, they become regular visitors or even residents. They like what one new innkeeper calls "a town of busy days and quiet nights."

Inn Spots

Blue Water House, 407 East Market St., Lewes 19958.

There are times when we veteran inn-goers don't even want to look at another Victorian sofa or chair, much less sit on one. That's why we heaved sighs of relief when we checked into our room at the comfortably but minimally furnished Blue Water House. The bed didn't have a headboard, much less a canopy (sacrilege!). The seats were deck chairs, the lamps weren't tasseled, the carpet was a dark industrial gray and the only amenity was a TV set. How refreshing! The air-conditioned room was large, the art was fascinating, the bathroom modern, and the french doors opened onto a wraparound deck from which we watched an incredible sunset.

The shingled inn was built from scratch in 1993 by Chuck and Karen Ulrich and their children, Charlie and Kayla. Chuck, an architect, designed it and it is wonderfully whimsical, with little touches of the tropics all around – it reminded us of places we've seen in South Miami Beach. The ground floor, nicely landscaped, is open because the inn sits on wetlands. It includes a patio, picnic table, grill, hammock, bicycles and refrigerator for guests, and we enjoyed taking out dinner from a local restaurant and enjoying it by candlelight here. The first floor is for check-in and the family. Guests congregate here around the long dining room table for a hefty continental breakfast complete with cereals, sticky buns and home-made breads. The table is covered with a wild floral cloth and the seats are folding bridge chairs. This is a children-friendly inn and the Ulrichs even provide fruit

loops for breakfast, to say nothing of all kinds of recreational equipment and the resident companions to go with.

Six ample bedrooms with private baths, four on the corners and all open to the wraparound porch, ring the third floor and are spaced for maximum privacy. Chuck has fashioned ingenious touches: the railing of the porch is a white picket fence. The decorative theme is

Makeshift sign and carved fish on mailbox greet guests at Blue Water House.

bright colors and fish, which turn up on the juice pitchers, the shower curtains and the covers of the room diaries. Some bedrooms can be combined to make family suites. On the fourth floor is a large quasi-widow's walk with good views of Lewes and the bay. Its big TV set and wicker furniture make this a gathering spot.

Chuck, who practiced in the Baltimore area, and Karen fell in love with Lewes when they visited and decided it would be a great place to raise the kids and to get out on the water. She has her own construction design business, but is on hand nights and weekends. He runs the inn the rest of the week and, having become a licensed Coast Guard captain, leads charter fishing and bird-watching trips on the Lewes-Rehoboth Canal and Broadkill River. In fact, if you catch some fish and want to eat them, the Ulrichs will provide a salad and a marinade for basting on the grill.

"It helped not going to B&B school," said Chuck, whose intuition makes him a good innkeeper. "We just opened our doors and did this by the seat of our pants." Again sacrilege, but it works. Staying here is "like joining old high school classmates and becoming part of the family," one guest wrote. Who knows? You could be treated to one of his great margaritas.

And if you miss your kitty, you might be comforted to find Bob, the inn's cat, purring on your bed. He spent most of the night with us. The Ulrichs say he is an outside cat, but Bob knows better.

(302) 645-7832 or (800) 493-2080. Six rooms with private baths. Mid-May to mid-September: doubles, $120. Mid-November through March: $80. Rest of year: $100. Two-night minimum in season and spring and fall weekends. Children welcome. No smoking.

The Inn at Canal Square, 122 Market St., Lewes 19958.
A coincidence led to the 1988 opening of the first and best-known new inn in Lewes. Bill Lucks, owner of a commercial real-estate firm, represented a client who was buying some rundown waterfront buildings. When the deal collapsed,

the sellers suggested that he buy the property. The result: ex-banker Bill and his wife Amanda, a shopkeeper extraordinaire, decided to open an upscale inn with rooms facing the wide Lewes-Rehoboth Canal.

The brown-shingled facade of the main, four-story complex looks like a contemporary Cape Cod condominium. Hidden from street view are nineteen guest rooms on the three upper floors, most with large balconies facing the water (though the views from some are screened by the adjacent lighthouse-turned-conference center). Rooms ascend in price and size by the floor. Ours on the top floor was quiet and comfortable and unusually spacious with 18th-century reproduction furniture including a kingsize bed, a sitting area with a loveseat and side chair, a dining table with two chairs and a TV hidden in the highboy. The two-part bathroom came with a separate vanity area and all kinds of toiletries. The balcony yielded a fine view over the lighthouse onto the busy canal.

The next morning, we were impressed with the continental breakfast spread set out in the ground-floor library/lobby. Four kinds of juices, three sliced fruits (kiwi, watermelon and pineapple), yogurt and a choice of a dozen assorted breakfast pastries put us in good shape for the ferry crossing to New Jersey.

Three guest rooms in the adjacent Courtyard Suites building compensate for their lack of balconies with more imaginative furnishings than rooms in the main inn. One draped romantically in mosquito netting has a brass bed. Another has an antique sleigh bed.

The most prized quarters are on the two-story houseboat moored on a barge alongside the dock. Here, guests find a full kitchen, a contemporary living and dining area with fireplace and floor-to-ceiling windows, two bedrooms with full baths on the second floor and a rooftop sundeck, reached by a ladder through a narrow hatch in the ceiling.

New management took over the inn in 1997.

(302) 645-8499 or (800) 222-7902. Fax (302) 645-7083. Nineteen rooms, three suites and a houseboat with private baths. Mid-June to late September: doubles $145 to $165, suites, $135. Rest of year: doubles $100 to $135; suites, $75 to $90. Houseboat, $225 daily, May-September, $175 October.

The New Devon Inn, 142 Second St., Box 516, Lewes 19958.

Built in 1926, the former Valley of the Swans Hotel had deteriorated into a seedy boarding house. The "Ugly Swan" is how one newspaper described it. And when Rehoboth Beach realtor Dale Jenkins showed it to her investor-partner, Washington attorney Bernard Nash, they were met at the front door by a boarder emerging on a motorcycle.

Dale envisioned the possibilities, however. Acting as her own contractor and decorator, she gutted the building except for the main staircase, the pine floors in the bedrooms and a rickety elevator, barely big enough for two people with any luggage. She removed the kitchenettes and added baths for each of 24 bedrooms and two suites. Part of the lobby became a fashionable sitting area, with plush sofas and a couple of elephant chairs carved from solid teakwood in Thailand. A grand piano, a glass chandelier and a ficus tree lit by tiny white lights add elegance. The pool hall in the basement was converted into a breakfast area and a TV room.

The result is a small downtown hotel of considerable sophistication, one that wears its National Historic Register listing with pride. The rooms, though small, are squeaky clean and modern but for their original floors and antique beds. Ours,

Wraparound porch at Wild Swan Inn features a corner gazebo.

the largest of the standard rooms, looked from its fourth-floor corner roost onto the cemetery beside St. Peter's Episcopal Church. The bed was small enough that one's extremities continually had to be draped over the edges. But there were thoughtful touches: in-room telephones, floral sheets, good prints on the walls, nightly turndown with a couple of small cordials, crystal glasses on a silver tray and windows that open. All the beds are doubles, except for two with twins and two suites with queensize beds and sitting rooms.

The TV in the basement is serviceable, so long as everyone wants to watch the same program. Coffee, orange juice and muffins are put out on the breakfast bar here in the morning. Those with heartier appetites can order a full breakfast in **The Buttery,** the swish restaurant on the hotel's main floor (see Dining Spots). Also available on the main floor and basement are a number of shops stocking everything from crafts to collectibles.

(302) 645-6466 or (800) 824-8754. Fax (302) 645-7196. Twenty-four rooms and two suites. Mid-June through August: doubles, $120 to $130 weekends, $85 to $95 midweek; suites, $170 weekends, $135 midweek. September to mid-October: doubles, weekends $110 to $120, midweek $65; suites, $155 weekends, $110 midweek. Rest of year: doubles $65 weekends, $50 midweek; suites $110 weekends, $90 midweek. Two-night minimum weekends in season. Children over 16.

Wild Swan Inn, 525 Kings Highway, Lewes 19958.

Pink with white gingerbread trim, this Queen Anne Victorian is long on personality and turn-of-the-century charm. Owners Mike and Hope Tyler moved here from suburban Wilmington to open a B&B with three bedrooms and private baths.

The breezy wraparound porch is notable for a corner gazebo, as well as a small refrigerator for guests' use hidden away at the far side. Also hidden from the street is a nice swimming pool flanked by a patio and another gazebo. Inside, a small front parlor is notable for a flock of five swans on a crystal chandelier. The parlor opens into a larger dining room, where one of the inn's antique brass chandeliers presides over the dining table and a number of the couple's collections, from a glass cabinet bearing old miniature liqueur bottles to a 1940 Zenith radio.

The stairway to the second floor is lined with colorful door stops, all fruits and flowers except for swans, exceptions that are repeated throughout. Hope named the front bedroom Nan's Room because it holds her grandmother's furniture. A queen bed is angled toward the center of the room from the far corner; its headboard matches the bureau. The bathroom is decked out in lace. The Delaware Room, overlooking the pool, features a wall quilt symbolic of Delaware as well as other local artworks. One prized work is an Andrew Wyeth print of a barn, framed in wood from the subject barn when it was razed. The side Rose Room takes its name from the wallpaper.

The dining room is the setting for some fairly fancy breakfasts cooked up by Mike, whose recipes have been included in three cookbooks. Besides a fruit dish like poached pears and fresh breads and muffins, expect such main courses as pumpkin waffles, asparagus pie or breakfast burritos, served with salsa made with ingredients from the Tylers' garden.

(302) 645-8550. Three rooms with private baths. July and August: doubles, $135. Spring and fall: $125. November to mid-May: $85. Two-night minimum weekends. No children. No smoking. Closed in January.

The Bay Moon, 128 Kings Highway, Lewes 19958.

Electic decor, modern conveniences and a casual ambiance are hallmarks of this B&B that opened in 1996 in a rustic-looking, brown clapboard Victorian house a long block south of downtown. Owner Laura Beth Kelly made good use of the original oak woodwork, from a massive mantelpiece and shelves surrounding the fireplace that separates the open living room and dining room to the wainscoting and even a bed headboard in the upstairs bedrooms.

"Amenities are our claim to fame," says Laura, who commutes periodically from her home in Harrisburg, Pa., but turns over day-to-day duties to resident innkeeper Tom Fisher.

Down comforters adorn the queen beds, each designed by Laura and built by her husband. All with private baths, the three second-floor rooms are bright and cheery, painted in pastel colors with bold accents. Each has a small TV/VCR atop a tall, slender mod chest of drawers. The top-of-the-line Silver Moon Suite comes with a draped kingsize bed, a sitting room with a day bed and a private rear balcony. A fourth queen-bedded room with private bath is on the third floor. Two additional rooms here share a bath and are rented as a suite.

Guests enjoy a complimentary happy hour with local wines and hors d'oeuvres, perhaps bean dips and quesadillas, in the side library and entertainment center. Equipped with books and videos, it adjoins a handsome bar room. Champagne may be poured at nightly turndown. The treats continue the next morning at breakfast, served at a table for ten in the dining room. The fare includes homemade breads and biscuits and perhaps a quiche, soufflé or artichoke strata.

(302) 644-1802 or (800) 917-2307. Three rooms and one suite with private bath. Doubles, $130 weekends, $110 midweek; suite, $150 weekends, $130 midweek. Off-season: doubles, $95, suite $110. Two-night weekend minimum in season. Open April-December and some winter weekends. Children accepted. No smoking.

1897 House, 801 Savannah Road, Lewes 19958.

After farming in upstate New York and Connecticut for 27 years, Jill Ruwet decided it was time to return to her home area to fulfill her dream of running a B&B. She acquired an ivy-covered, century-old Belgian block house in 1997 and opened it as a B&B.

Each of her three bedrooms, all with private bath, is painted in different colors. One room with kingsize bed is furnished in white wicker. A room with a queensize Stickley cherry four-poster bed has a matching highboy, while a third room has an oak and wrought-iron queen bed.

Guests enjoy a living room with a fireplace and a large dining room, but the main attraction in summer is the pool and deck at the side of the house. Here, Jill serves homemade ice cream in the afternoons and offers wine in the evenings.

Breakfast is a treat, perhaps belgian waffles, giant popovers stuffed with fruit or breakfast pizza, her own creation made with sausage, egg, cheese and mild salsa.

(302) 645-8363 or (888) 227-1897. Fax (302) 302-645-8323. Three rooms with private baths. Mid-May through Labor Day: doubles, $110 to $125. Rest of year: $80 to $95. Two-night minimum weekends in summer. No children. No smoking.

The Manor at Cool Spring/Lavender Farm Bed & Breakfast, County Road 290, RD 2, Box 238, Milton 19968.

Named for a hamlet about four miles west of Lewes, this farmhouse was converted into a three-bedroom B&B by new owners Joe and Pauline Palenik. "We wanted to run a B&B and this house was a perfect fit," Joe explained.

The heart of the house is a sunken sun porch at the side. It holds a large jacuzzi tub, a wood stove and a glass table flanked by rattan chairs, where breakfast may be served. Also available to guests are a formal dining room, a living room containing a lineup of Pauline's Toby jugs from England as well as a display cabinet showcasing her collections of owls and glassware, and a big, turreted corner library with a fireplace, gaming table and chess board ready for action.

Upstairs are three guest rooms with private baths, one with a whirlpool tub. They're furnished with what Joe calls 1920s and 1930s vintage furniture, enhanced by floral curtains that match the covers and pillows on the queensize beds. A third bedroom offers a small hot tub on a secluded second-floor deck.

Pauline's five-course breakfasts reflect her British background and her cooking studies at the Sorbonne. A typical meal includes fruit, eggs any style, and sausage and Canadian bacon. Special treats could be fruit crêpes or eggs benedict. Among the ingredients are herbs and vegetables the Paleniks grow on their rural four-acre property they now call Lavender Farm. Their lavender bath and massage oils and soaps proved so popular with guests that they have planted most of their acreage in lavender and now offer more than ten lavender products. Their seven cats also roam around the house and grounds.

(302) 684-8325. Fax (302) 684-8326. Three rooms with private baths. Doubles, $120.

Dining Spots

Kupchick's Restaurant, 3 East Bay Ave., Lewes.

Some of the area's finest and fanciest food is served in this unlikely looking building alongside the Delaware Bay beach. You'd expect burgers and frozen custard, perhaps. What you get is sophisticated continental and regional American fare, including some of the best crab dishes we've ever had.

Behind its undistinguished facade lie two dark, romantic dining rooms and a lively bar and grill. Traditionalists are partial to the formal restaurant, sedate with banquettes and windsor chairs at white-linened tables. Pink lalique-style shades over the candles and wall sconces and a few paintings provide accents of color.

The fare produced by chef-owner David Krasnoff is worthy of the setting. David is the grandson of Romanian immigrants who operated Kupchick's Restaurants in Toronto and Montreal in the first half of this century. His fairly lengthy menu features "Delmarva Rim Cuisine," which translates to such entrées as flounder imperial, grilled veal chop with a shiitake mushroom sauté, sirloin steak "au poivre congolese" and a handful of "vegetarian vagaries." with tri-colored peppercorn sauce. Blackened tuna, seared duck breast with port wine glaze and steak diane could be the night's specials.

Among starters are the family's special mushroom and barley soup, chiffonade salad, carpaccio, smoked bluefish and baked brie. Desserts could be Bailey's Irish cream cheesecake, grand marnier strawberry shortcake, chocolate-walnut pie and crème caramel.

An extensive grill menu featuring pastas and light entrées is offered in the bar, which was obviously popular the weeknight we were there. The staff could barely keep up with the demand, although the food proved to be well worth the wait. One of us enjoyed pastry chef Daria Horn's favorite salad with assorted lettuces, bacon, egg, onion and mushrooms and the crab platter, a succulent crab cake served with roasted potatoes. The other liked the zesty caesar salad and the lump crab linguini, tossed with sherry and mushrooms and simply sensational. The heavy, coarse bread was served with real butter (as opposed to the ubiquitous foil-wrapped slices) and a $14 bottle of Chilean sauvignon blanc accompanied.

(302) 645-0420. Entrées, $14.95 to $23.95. Lunch, Monday-Friday noon to 2, October to April. Dinner nightly, 5 to 9 or 10. Closed Jan. 1 to Valentine's Day.

The Buttery Restaurant, 142 Second St., Lewes.

This chic yet casual bistro in leased space at the side of the New Devon Inn proved to popular that it expanded into a back room. The original high-ceilinged space holds a small antique oak bar, a display case containing charcuterie meats and salads, and close-together tables for 36. The new skylight rear room has a fresh country air with high-back upholstered chairs. Bearing a coffee shop aspect at breakfast and lunch, the Buttery gets dressed for dinner. White tablecloths and candles lend a look of class, although we could have done without the rather raucous music in the background the night we dined.

Service was solicitous and highly professional as we enjoyed zesty house salads sprinkled with gouda cheese and dressed with fresh garlic and a basket full of crusty sliced French sourdough bread, more than we could eat.

Main courses range from grilled Norwegian salmon with cilantro-cashew pesto to filet mignon with chile-garlic marinade and hot pepper diablo. We settled for the Maryland crab cakes (very tasty with a rémoulade sauce), red bliss potatoes and an interesting dish of sautéed kale, and a rather strange bouillabaisse with a thick tomato sauce that masked the advertised "fennel-flavored tomato-saffron broth" and gave priority to the mundane fish fillet rather than the expected shellfish.

Appetizers were a specialty seafood chowder, a selection of house pâtés, ravioli filled with lobster and shrimp, and New Zealand mussels baked with pernod and

The Buttery Restaurant is chic but casual bistro in New Devon Inn.

roasted garlic butter. Chef Gary Papp's wife Lorraine, the pastry chef, is known for her desserts.

(302) 645-7755. Entrées, $16 to $24. Lunch, Tuesday-Saturday 11 to 2. Dinner, Tuesday-Sunday from 5. Sunday brunch, 10:30 to 2:30.

Second Street Grille, 115 Second St., Lewes.

This trendy newcomer was opened in 1997 by Ray Richardson, a chef from the Fenwick area, in quarters occupied by the old Jerry's American Café. One of his first special events was a week of French dinners in honor of the release of the year's beaujolais nouveau, an example of his priorities. He also upscaled the décor with white tablecloths, candles and framed French posters on the walls.

The contemporary fare ranges from oven-roasted pecan chicken to barbecued shrimp on a poblano quesadilla with tomato salsa or crab cakes with mustard slaw and hush puppies. Other main dishes could be sesame yellowfin tuna with cucumber salad and a spring roll, pork chops with bourbon sauce and apple fritters, and filet mignon with crispy onions and rosemary broth.

Starters could be Maryland crab soup, portobellos and brie in puff pastry, oysters rockefeller and coconut shrimp with pineapple chutney. Homemade desserts include raspberry cheesecake, chocolate mousse and lemon crème brûlée. There's an extensive wine list.

(302) 644-4121. Entrées, $12 to $23. Lunch, Monday and Wednesday-Saturday, 11:30 to 3. Dinner nightly except Tuesday, 5:30 to 9. Sunday brunch, 11 to 2.

Gilligan's Harborside Restaurant & Bar, Front and Market Streets, Lewes.

The kitchen is in a dry-docked boat, and the tropical bar, the side patio and the rooftop deck offer the best waterfront views of any local restaurant. New owner Patrick Shehan has upgraded the decor and carpeted the interior of this Canal Square standby.

The contemporary international fare is highly regarded, particularly the crab cakes served with varied sauces and baby greens, available as an appetizer or a main course. The with-it dinner menu starts with appetizers like a lobster tamale with a roasted tomato and chipotle pepper sauce. Main courses could be honey-pecan crusted red snapper with blackeyed pea relish, chile-rubbed chicken breast with tomatillo-mango salsa, and rack of lamb with warm citrus couscous. Hoisin-glazed swordfish on Asian ratatouille was to be a special the night we booked here, but a tropical storm cut the power and the restaurant closed unexpectedly for the evening.

Tarry with an after-dinner drink in the outdoor bar, with your back to a mural of a tropical island. Facing the boats passing by on the Lewes-Rehoboth Canal, you might think you were along the Intra-Coastal Waterway. Actually, you are.

(302) 645-7866. Entrées, $15 to $21. Lunch daily, 11 to 4. Dinner, from 5. Closed in winter, and Monday and Tuesday in off-season.

La Rosa Negra, 128 Second St., Lewes.

This long and narrow Italian downtown storefront restaurant is much loved by the locals, who rate the pastas the best around. The decor, a mix of black and white with red accents, is made more gala by tiny white lights at night. The food arrives on black octagonal plates.

Good starters are seafood focaccia, steamed New Zealand mussels and marinated blue crab claws. Pasta dishes are fairly standard, from spaghetti with meatballs marinara to fettuccine alfredo or puttanesca. More interesting were two specials of the day, red snapper with lump crabmeat topped with sundried tomato butter, and sautéed scallops with artichokes, prosciutto, parmesan and white wine over linguini. We also liked the chicken florentine gorgonzola, topped with sweet and sour bacon sauce and served with linguini. Other main courses run from chicken cacciatore to filet mignon and four veal dishes.

One couple we met, who were visiting Lewes for a week and had tried all the restaurants, liked this best and dined here twice.

(302) 645-1980. Entrées, $12.95 to $19.95. Lunch, Monday-Saturday 11:30 to 2:30. Dinner nightly, 5 to 9:30.

Diversions

The sense of history and the quiet waterside attractions are what lure most visitors to Lewes.

History. The historic section of Delaware's oldest town – usually missed by motorists rushing to or from the Cape May-Lewes Ferry – is compact and eminently walkable. Most of the historic sites are spread out along Front, Second and Third streets in a quarter-mile stretch between Savannah Road and Shipcarpenter Street. The Lewes walking tour brochure points out 40 sites of special interest in the area that was discovered by Henry Hudson and settled by the Dutch in 1631. They range from the 1730 **Fisher-Martin House**, a gambrel-roofed structure moved from nearby Coolspring in 1980 to become the information center for the Lewes Chamber of Commerce and Visitors Bureau, to the 1850's Greek Revival **Doctor's Office,** a medical and dental museum, one of six buildings in the Lewes Historical Society complex. Other attractions include the 1797 **Cannonball House,** the last remaining Lewes house bearing a cannonball scar from the War of 1812 and now occasionally open as a marine museum, and **St. Peter's Episcopal Church**

Cemetery, an unusual sight so close to downtown. Like many walking tour brochures, it neglects to point out some of the more interesting buildings. You'll enjoy chancing upon the 1790 **Rodney House,** home of one of Lewes's first families and now the site of the Surf and Sands Florist sandwiched between stores on Second Street. It looks much older than the better-known 1665 **Ryves Holt House** at Second and Mulberry streets, believed to be the oldest house still standing in Delaware. Two little finds are at the far end of West Third Street: one of the few remaining Dutch-style homes from the 18th century at 320, its fence brightened in summer by morning glories, and across the street at 321, an 18th-century Sussex County saltbox restored in 1981 as a private home. The **Lewes Historical Society Complex** at Shipcarpenter and Third streets, next to Shipcarpenter Square, harbors six buildings ranging from a 17th-century plank house, a log cabin that's one of the oldest extant buildings in the area, to the **Thompson Country Store,** where you obtain tickets for a guided tour of the complex. Open June-August, Tuesday-Friday 10 to 3, Saturday 10 to 12:30. Admission, $5.

Shipcarpenter Square. The developer of this novel residential complex eschewed the new construction prevalent elsewhere and moved 35 rundown or abandoned structures to the western edge of the Lewes historic district. Built between 1720 and 1880, they came from around the Delmarva Peninsula. Now these ramshackle buildings that most people wouldn't have paid a cent for are restored as private homes, upgraded with modern kitchens and bathrooms and surrounded by railed patios, fancy gardens and homey outbuildings. Some liken it to Colonial Williamsburg, but this close-together, close-in compound beats Williamsburg for livability, as attested by all the Mercedeses and Corvettes parked in the driveways. Particularly appealing are the looks of the 1795 timbered log house from Maryland and the dark red 19th-century school house from Milton, both now charming homes. You can walk or drive around the both the perimeter and the interior of the horseshoe-shaped community to see the unusual "telescope" house from Accomac, Va., or the colorful Victorian house from Wilmington College.

Zwaanendael Museum, Savannah Road and Kings Highway.
Built in 1931 for the town's Tricentennial, this exotic Dutch Renaissance building could be straight out of Holland. It is an adaptation of the town hall at Hoorn. Now a state museum, it devotes its main floor to the story of the H.M.S. DeBraak, a British warship with a Dutch name that sank in a storm off Cape Henlopen in 1798 after it had stopped in Lewes for supplies. Supposedly laden with gold, it had defied treasure-seekers for nearly 200 years until 1986. It was found beneath 30 feet of sand in water 80 feet deep. More than 25,000 objects – but no gold bounty – were recovered from the shipwreck. A few hundred are shown in a dozen vignettes, of which many find the one reflecting the life of a seaman aboard the ship most interesting. Artifacts from religious medallions to clay pipes to galley pots and plates are on display. Some credit the widely publicized recovery of the DeBraak with having first put on the tourists' map this quiet town steeped in maritime history and riverboat pilot lore. The museum's second floor contains changing local history exhibits (at our visit, one on African-American education in Sussex County, including an intricate little dollhouse-like, one-room school). History buffs also will find such relics as a stemmed drinking glass given to local governor-to-be David Hall and other Revolutionary War leaders by George Washington, an 1897 Lewes School class ring, a Delaware woman's collection of glass (inexplicably

from Sandwich, Mass.), and materials surrounding the 1926 collapse of the famed Cape Henlopen lighthouse, erected in 1763 as the second lighthouse in the new world but no match for the shifting sand dunes here.

(302) 645-9418. Open Tuesday-Saturday 10 to 4:30, Sunday 1:30 to 4:30. Free.

Cape Henlopen State Park, Lewes.

A mile east of Lewes, just past the Cape May-Lewes Ferry Terminal, lies this 4,103-acre park at the mouth of the Delaware Bay. It offers four miles of beach on ocean and bay, as well as nature trails, a bird sanctuary, the famed "walking dunes" shifting across the pine forest, and the Great Dune, at 80 feet the highest between Cape Hatteras and Cape Cod. The **Seaside Nature Center** has aquariums, a touch tank containing two horseshoe crabs and other exhibits of particular interest to youngsters. The bathhouse is large and modern, and the ocean beaches relatively uncrowded. When the surf's up here, families tend to prefer the town beaches along the calmer bay. Worth the effort is a short climb up a 115-step spiral staircase to the top of the restored observation tower, one of several relics from the abandoned Ford Miles military installation. Here, where patrollers watched for German submarines as arms were stashed in bunkers and gun emplacements below during World War II, you can scan the sea and landscape from the high-rises of Rehoboth Beach across the bay to New Jersey's Cape May. The views of the sunsets here are spectacular.

(302) 645-6852. Park open 8 a.m. to sunset, year-round. Cars, $5 in summer.

Nassau Valley Vineyards, 33 Nassau Commons.

The story of this fledgling winery, Delaware's first, is really that of 29-year-old Peggy Raley. A drama graduate of American University, the breathless and blithe blonde spent a couple of years "globetrotting" for Friends of Wine magazine before coming home to her father Bob's burgeoning office and retail complex in the Nassau section of Lewes. He launched her with 5 percent seed money. She borrowed the rest to open the winery after writing and personally shepherding the enabling legislation through the state legislature. Jill-of-all-trades Peggy, who's partial to red wines, touts her limited edition cabernet sauvignon, graced by an Old Testament painting by local artist Tom Wilson, first of an artist series. Her early wines also include chardonnay and rosé. Peggy pours samples in the tasting room after visitors take a self-guided tour alongside the production facility, an unusually showy and informative visual display that's almost like a museum on the history of winemaking. Peggy was talking of big things to exemplify the name of her winery, which she said is a play on the Napa Valley. Fifteen buildings that her father moved to the site "as a little restored Williamsburg" are to become shops.

(302) 645-9463. Open Tuesday-Saturday 11 to 5, Sunday noon to 5.

Shopping. For a small town, Lewes is blessed with unusually sophisticated shops and unusually friendly shopkeepers. Most are located along tree-shaded Second Street and a few along Front Street. Amanda Lucks, former owner of the Inn on Canal Square, started with a small gourmet and coffee shop, hence the name **Sugar & Spice.** It has grown like Topsy and now stretches back through a warren of rooms displaying local artworks, handpainted birdhouses and weathervanes into a huge Christmas shop. Some of the most interesting wares are stocked by Gavin and Lou Braithwaite, who own **Puzzles** (all kinds of puzzles), **The Stepping Stone,** where we coveted everything from carved egrets to great windsocks, and the adjacent **Union Jack** (all things British). We liked the umbrellas bearing cats and dogs, respectively, at **Nature's Touch of Lewes,** a boutique full of clothing, jewelry and gifts, many with an animal accent. A tall blue heron in the window lured us into **Thistles,** a wonderful trove of stained-glass lamps, hand-painted oyster Santas for Christmas tree decorations, silverware, children's clothing and a few items of women's apparel. Behind it is **Greenhorn,** featuring Southwestern jewelry, blankets and cookbooks along with enough vests, hats and mountain items to give it a distinctly Western flair. Underneath is **Auntie M's Emporium,** which the owners (one an antiquer and the other a writer) likened to "browsing in someone's basement." We were taken by all the old books and wrought-iron garden items here; the owners also have another store in the old firehouse and jail at 116 West Third.

Art, pottery and gifts with a statuary theme are featured at **The Saxon Swan,** where we liked a neat statue bearing bird feed in its outstretched hands. **The Gift Network** stocks handcrafts, quilts, wood crafts, dolls and miniatures, and the **Carolina Moon** unusual antiques and collectibles (check out the dollhouse furniture and the hand-dyed felt balls for kitties). The **Dockside Gift Shop,** here since 1977 ("long before Lewes was discovered by tourists," says owner Mary Perez), looks like your standard nautical gift shop but has unique touches, from shirts and bags silk-screened by a local artist to lighthouse replicas, birds and scrimshaw. Women's apparel is featured at **The Jetty, Figure Head** and **Twila Farrell.** Antiques are everywhere, but nowhere in such quantity as with assorted dealers at the **Lewes Mercantile Antique Mall.** Garden accessories, period furniture and a complete line of Cat's Meow villages, including 23 Lewes pieces, are among the offerings at **The Swan's Nest.**

Take a break from your shopping rounds with ice cream from **King's Homemade Ice Cream Shop,** a Delaware institution to which many folks repair after dinner as well as all day long. Or stop at the **Lewes Bakery and Roasterie** for a cinnamon roll to accompany your morning espresso. **Cinnamon Falls** offers pastries and a few lunch items to accompany its gourmet coffees at stand-up tables facing the canal or at sit-down, wrought-iron tables out front. Another place for a snack to eat in or take out is **A Taste of Heaven.**

Extra-Special

Punkin' Chunkin'. The world-championship (not to mention only) event of its kind lures television crews and upwards of 10,000 people – Lewes's largest crowd of the year – to a cornfield north of town the Saturday after Halloween. They turn out to see which team can hurl pumpkins the greatest distance. Over the years, contestants have employed homemade slings, crossbow catapults and centrifugal devices with names like The Mean Green Pumpkin Machine to chunk their leftover pumpkins weighing eight to ten pounds. Three teams participated in the first event in 1986, and the winning pumpkin soared 50 feet. The main event in a recent competition attracted twelve teams and the world-record throw was 2,508 feet. The defending champion team was led by John Ellsworth, who happened to be chairman and founder of the event. It seems folks were sitting around his local blacksmith shop – the Preservation Forge, a real, live, working blacksmith shop at 114 West Third St. and a special place in itself – and started talking about anvil throwing. One thing led to another and Punkin' Chunkin' was born. Chunk on!

Court House that served as first state capitol is centerpiece of historic New Castle.

New Castle, Del.

The Smallest of Wonders

In the state that proclaims itself "Small Wonder," surely New Castle is the smallest wonder of all. And perhaps its most choice wonder.

This is the town where Peter Stuyvesant laid out the green in 1651, the town where William Penn set foot in the New World in 1682, the town that became the first state's first capital. But its early importance was eventually overshadowed by Wilmington and Dover. A plan to restore the old town into a second Colonial Williamsburg was aborted in the late 1940s. And so New Castle remains – the living example of a rare Dutch-English-American river town from the Colonial era. The population of this historic district roughly three blocks wide and five blocks deep numbers 1,500, about the same as in its heyday.

The old town is often bypassed, hidden just off Interstate 95 south of the towering Delaware Memorial Bridge. The past is everywhere apparent along the cobblestoned, tree-lined streets clustered beside the Delaware River. Like the better-known historic district of Charleston, New Castle has a Battery park. It also has The Strand and The Green. There's a wonderful sense of access to a waterfront sheltered from the industrial disarray on all sides. Here you walk around the waterfront park, down Packet Alley, up the pedestrian path beside the Presbyterian Church to the green and the gravestones beside Immanuel Episcopal Church, and peer into the handful of stores along Delaware Street.

Two centuries of architectural styles are displayed in more than 50 landmark structures. Five are open to the public as museums showing the Dutch and English Colonial periods. Others, where life continues today amid a patina of yesteryear, are revealed to the several thousand visitors who come here the third Saturday of every May for "A Day in Old New Castle," a local tradition since 1924.

Still, only about 30,000 tourists visit New Castle annually, many of them on bus tours. It is not a visitor-friendly town. There is no information center for orientation purposes or brochures, and the fledgling New Castle Visitors Bureau operates impersonally through a post office box and a toll-free number, (800) 758-1550. Until the mid-1980s, there was only one guest house. Now there are five, but the lack of accommodations means that many visitors must head for motels along the Route 13 strip, the other New Castle more obvious to transients.

For New Castle really has two identities. One is the modern-day sprawl away from the river, not really New Castle but bearing its address since the New Castle post office serves a wider area, a situation that "gets everybody confused," according to one local historian. The other is the easily defined old town, separate and apart – a small National Landmark Historic Area of Colonial and Federal vintage, likened to that of Charleston and the French Quarter but considered unique in the country.

The old section of New Castle is one of those rare places where the hackneyed phrase "step back in time" truly means something.

Inn Spots

All but one of New Castle's guest houses have emerged in the last nine years. A town ordinance limits most new B&Bs in New Castle to three rooms.

Armitage Inn, 2 The Strand, New Castle 19720.

A walk-in cooking fireplace in a kitchen dating to 1670 testifies to the age of this handsome brick house facing the strand where William Penn set foot in the New World. Transformed into an elegant B&B in 1995, it was occupied by a Revolutionary War patriot who served as the early town's chief magistrate and began a tradition of hospitality when he provided sustenance for weary post riders passing through with news of the war's progress.

Steve Marks, a 25-year area resident who tired of the printing business, and his wife Rina did a masterful job of readying the 1732 residence for contemporary guests. On either side of a front foyer facing Battery Park and the river are a formal parlor notable for lovely oriental rugs and a wall of good-luck symbols, and a huge rose-colored dining room outfitted with a table set for ten. Both rooms are full of collections from the couple's travels. The rear of the house includes a library and a porch overlooking a walled garden and a cottage.

The original wide-planked wood stairs ascend to a suite and four guest rooms, all with private baths, featherbeds, TVs and telephones, hair dryers and other amenities. Newest is the Angelica Suite, second-floor rear, with a hand-crocheted cover on the queensize canopy bed and a sitting room that was once a

Armitage Inn faces the strand where William Penn set foot in America.

nursery. The White Rose Room has a king four-poster bed draped in white fabric, a bay window facing the river and a large bath with one of the inn's three whirlpool tubs. Queen beds are tucked beneath the sloping roof lines in the two third-floor rooms, one enhanced by floral stenciling.

Steve prepares and serves a gourmet breakfast to remember. Typical items are fresh fruit, homemade muffins and breads, apple-peach crisp and french toast. His maple-cream cheese pastries were featured in Bon Appétit magazine's Colonial Thanksgiving issue in 1996.

(302) 328-6618. Fax (302) 324-1163. Four rooms and one suite with private baths. Doubles, $105 to $145. Suite, $150. Two-night minimum at certain times. Children over 12. No smoking.

The Terry House, 130 Delaware St., New Castle 19720.

This Federal brick townhouse was built in the early 1860s by a banker for his family. It harbors comfortable lodgings and two lovely rear verandas, one above the other, with views across the Battery Park to the water.

Town residents Greg and Margaret Bell and her mother, Evelyn Watson, took over the B&B in 1997. In residence with their young sons, the Bells offer three guest rooms with queensize canopy or poster beds, private baths and cable TV, plus a small single room. Those in front look onto Market Square and the Old Court House; two in the rear yield views of the park and river when the foliage is off the trees. Fresh flowers, dried-flower wreaths, bedside chocolates, scatter rugs on bare redwood floors and period antiques are the norm. Decorative touches include a shelf displaying a collection of cups and saucers in one room.

Guests enjoy a handsome parlor, quite elegant with ornate carved friezes, swagged draperies and a brass chandelier. The side verandas on two stories and the deep, shady rear lawn are also furnished for relaxation.

A continental-plus breakfast is served at a table for eight in the formal dining room, full of mahogany pieces in the Queen Anne and Federal styles. The fare includes fresh fruit, cereal, muffins and breakfast casseroles, perhaps an egg dish or puff pancakes.

(302) 322-2505. Three rooms with private baths. Doubles, $80. Children over 10. No smoking.

Fox Lodge, 123 West 7th St., New Castle 19720.

The Gothic Revival mansion known locally as "The Castle" is on its way to becoming a European-style country B&B with a hunt theme. Elaine and William Class moved from Southern California in 1995 for a change in occupation and lifestyle. Elaine, an interior decorator, was undaunted by the challenge of restoring a 33-room mansion that had seen better days. "I'm taking it one room at a time," she said, opening the first three bedrooms in 1996. Building regulations stymied her plans for six more bedrooms, all with private baths, on the second and third floors.

Built by a physician named Lesley, the main floor with its thirteen-foot-high ceilings retains vestiges of its use as a doctor's office. Elaine pointed out the small waiting room, which was being converted by the Classes into their private family room, and the examining room, with its fireplace and pressed-tin walls. The physician obviously put more emphasis on his family living quarters than on his office. The original, eight-foot-high cast-bronze chandelier is a focal point of the manorial drawing room. Another is the two enormous neo-Gothic Revival wicker club chairs with tassels and ceramic legs. All but one of the nine fireplace mantels are made of marble, the exception being the one of carved walnut and Mercer tiles in the dining room. The wood shutters on the windows of the library are "so beautiful that we decided not to cover them up with velvet swags," Elaine said. In fact, this isn't what people expect of a Victorian B&B. She enhanced the Gothic colors and features with contemporary accents and California furnishings. "I'm not a slave to Bradbury and lace everywhere. The architecture here is so strong and masculine that I don't want the decor to detract."

Check out the trompe-l'oeil railing painted in the 1920s along the wall of the hand-carved, dark oak staircase. It's so real that many a guest reaches out to hold on.

On the second floor are three guest rooms with private baths, queensize beds, twelve-foot-high ceilings and décor that's unusual, to say the least. The master bedroom is named for Jane Lesley, the physician's wife, whose "ghost still visits us and goes to town on occasion," says Elaine (that's another story). She designed and built the bed's headboard of California yucca stems and a rope holding a mosquito net canopy. There are two wing chairs for seats, but only one bedside lamp other than lights on the ceiling fan for reading.

The Malvern Room, named for Elaine's mother, has a violet blue floor, tin ceiling and trim, a queensize wicker bed and a free-standing green washstand in the room. The Lisa Room, named for her daughter, is striking for the wrought-iron gates and antique porch posts that pass for the headboard of the queen bed. It opens into Zula, named for her daughter's Siberian husky, which may be rented as a rather spare living room with a sofabed, two twig chairs and no lamps to form a suite. Off it is an unfinished roof-top porch with a view of the Victorian and medieval gardens under restoration on the property.

A lodge-style, hunt breakfast adheres to the masculine theme of Gothic times. Juice and cereal precede such possibilities as fresh oatmeal soup (inspired by Jacques Pepin), kippers, cold sliced ham, a cottage cheese sundae, and grilled mushrooms and tomatoes. In the afternoon, guests are offered beer, wine, herbal teas and snacks in Piglets Tavern, a roving place that eventually will land in the former basement kitchen. Poetry readings, singing, music, seances and Gothic romance movies are scheduled periodically.

(302) 328-0768. Three rooms and suites with private baths. Doubles, $105 to $135, as suite $185. Two-night weekend minimum. Children over 12. No smoking.

William Penn Guest House, 206 Delaware St., New Castle 19720.

The restored 1682 house in which William Penn slept was the first of New Castle's modern-day lodgings. Irma and Dick Burwell bought the residence in 1956. "When I asked what I should do with it," Irma recalls, "someone suggested a B&B. I said I could do the bed, but not the breakfast." That's because she already was involved in the Coffee House, a restaurant next door.

Now retired, the Burwells do serve breakfast – continental style, with fresh fruit and homemade muffins or croissants – to overnight guests who stay in four air-conditioned bedrooms. It's taken amidst fancy lace and sterling in the dining room behind a pleasant parlor in this townhouse that's one room wide, a couple of rooms deep and three stories high.

William Penn slept in one room, second floor rear, now outfitted with quilt-covered twin beds, an oriental rug and a little black and white TV. It shares a clawfoot-tub bathroom with a front double-bedded room, also with TV. Two more bedrooms on the third floor share a tiled bath.

(302) 328-7736. Four bedrooms with shared baths. Doubles, $55 to $80. No credit cards. No smoking.

Rodeway Inn, 111 South du Pont Hwy., New Castle 19720.

Too bad this little local prize long known as the Dutch Village Motor Inn had to take on national airs with a Rodeway affiliation. But still special is this configuration of little duplexes that look not unlike haciendas, strung along a winding driveway back from the highway and amazingly quiet (testimony in part to the building techniques of the early post-war era). Lawn chairs are scattered about the grounds.

Two rooms go off an enclosed foyer in each duplex. The larger rooms in which we've stayed contain two double beds, large wraparound cantilevered windows that open and large closets with coat hangers and luggage racks. There's room to spare in each for a remote-control TV on a dresser, a table and two cushioned chairs.

Continental breakfast is included in the rates.

The Rodeway connection coincided with the arrival of new owners Pierre and Peggy Olivero, who formerly owned the Terry House B&B. They said that, despite high AAA and Mobil ratings and a toll-free number, a local motel with a local name was no longer viable. This remains a good spot to know about – when the old town's accommodations are fully booked or you simply want motel conveniences at a reasonable price.

(302) 328-6246 or (800) 321-6246. Forty rooms with private baths. Doubles, $54 to $69.

Blue and white dining room is dressed for dinner at The Arsenal on the Green.

Dining Spots

The Arsenal on the Green, 30 Market St., New Castle.

Built by the federal government as an arsenal in anticipation of the War of 1812, this handsome, cupola-topped building facing the green has served a variety of purposes, among them a school. In 1980 it was restored into a restaurant called the Newcastle Inn, nicely authentic and catering to bus tours and private parties.

The restaurant was abruptly closed in 1994 shortly after a fire at the David Phinney Inn and restaurant, leaving historic New Castle without its two key dining spots. Along came local caterer Mimi Pawlowicz, who was born and raised in New Castle and took her culinary studies at Johnson & Wales University. She reopened the restaurant in 1995 and revived its original name, saying the inn name was misleading.

Mimi inherited an elegant building with two large, high-ceilinged dining rooms on either side of the entry hall and more rooms for private parties upstairs. She converted the former rose dining room into the casual Cannon Tavern for lunch and dinner and added seating for dining in the bar. The more formal dining room in blue and white was reserved for elegant dining at night.

Traditional American fare is featured. The dinner menu includes seafood, steaks and chops, from chicken topped with lump crabmeat to classic surf and turf. Shrimp with sundried tomatoes in puff pastry, brandied chicken, veal oscar and New York strip steak au poivre or bordelaise are among the possibilities. Lighter, less expensive items are offered in the tavern.

(302) 328-1290. Entrées, $14,50 to $27. Lunch, Tuesday-Saturday 11 to 2. Dinner, Tuesday-Saturday 5 to 9, Sunday 1 to 8. Tavern menu, 11 to 10 or 11.

Jessop's Tavern, 114 Delaware St., New Castle.

The former Green Frog tavern, a dark pub with mediocre food, gave way in 1996 to this cheerful pub and Colonial-style dining room. It's named for Abraham Jessop, a cooper who built the original structure in 1724.

Top-to-bottom renovations added a fireplace, a modern kitchen, wood plank floor and nautical oil paintings. The locals were quickly impressed with the large portions of substantial American food at prices out of the past.

Proprietors Tika and Dick Day raise pub grub above the usual genre in classics like shepherd's pie and fish and chips, as well as hefty sandwiches and such appetizers as English flat bread and steamed crayfish. The chef shines at dinner, producing a variety from stuffed river trout and pepper-crusted fillet of salmon to chicken fricassee, turkey cutlets, porterhouse steak and prime rib with caramelized onions and brandy-glazed mushrooms.

Swedish apple pie with vanilla custard sauce, bread pudding, fruit cobbler and angel food cake topped with seasonal fruit and whipped cream are among the desserts.

(302) 322-6111. Entrées, $6.95 to $16.95. Lunch, Monday-Saturday 11 to 3. Dinner, Monday-Saturday 5 to 10.

Lynnhaven Inn, 154 North du Pont Hwy. (Route 13), New Castle.

Built years ago as a country inn/restaurant when this still was out in the country, the Lynnhaven remains a beacon of good food and serenity in the midst of the frantic commercial strip that developing New Castle has spawned. The colors of the handsome facade – beige with burgundy trim – are repeated inside the two main dining rooms, which contain well-spaced tables and booths for two and an early American decor. Horsey paintings grace the walls and plates, trays and decoys line shelves here and there. The pleasant brick and beamed lounge with its curving bar displays ship models and nautical antiques.

More decoys and wood-carved fish are shown in lighted display cases in the foyer. They're the work of Andrew Asimos, brother of owner-manager George Asimos, whose family has run the restaurant since 1957.

A team of four chefs, each with impressive credentials, prepares an extensive menu of basically American fare with an emphasis on local seafood. Shrimp aegean, Maryland crab cakes, seafood stir-fry over saffron rice, blackened chicken and shrimp, veal parmigiana, prime rib and steak diane are among the possibilities. House salads come with both the main courses and six pasta dishes. Start with escargots en croûte, clams casino or stuffed jalapeño peppers, or a cup of authentic snapper turtle soup. Finish with chocolate mousse, cheese cake or a changing selection of cakes and pies.

Some of the dinner dishes as well as selections listed under light fare turn up on the menu for lunch, which is popular with the business crowd.

(302) 328-2041. Entrées, $12.95 to $26.95. Lunch, Monday-Friday 11:30 to 3:30. Dinner, 3:30 to 10, Saturday 4 to 10, Sunday 1 to 9.

Air Transport Command, 143 North du Pont Hwy. (Route 13), New Castle.

Near the airport is this Disneyland of a theme-park restaurant, an incredible mélange that's most un-New Castle-like but immensely popular for the novelty of it all. Only someone who has been to any of this restaurant chain's other extravaganzas with military air motifs from Florida to Illinois knows what to expect.

Here a sign at the parking-lot entrance warns of bridge bomb damage. Tanks and military craft are scattered about the outside of a building that's a cross between a castle and a military camp. Wend your way across a bridge and through a maze to the dining room – make that three, seating 200 in a collection of World War II memorabilia. This is candlelit, white-tablecloth dining at tiered tables with views of the airport runways. Get yourselves ensconced in one of the intimate side-by-side booths for two and you can't get out – until the staff slides away the heavy table, which rolls on wheels.

At our visit, the "specialties maison" were as diverse as calves liver, chicken moutarde, shrimp stir-fry and lemon veal, but most people seemed to go for the seven kinds of steaks and prime rib. We went with the flow, choosing a large-cut prime rib and a petite filet mignon. Neither proved as memorable as the surroundings.

When we returned for a second gawk, we surmised the reason why. At one end of the sprawl was the largest lounge we've seen, comfy as could be with sofas and chairs and quite a crowd for 4 o'clock on a weekday afternoon. No mere restaurant this. It's an all-hours watering hole.

(302) 328-3527. Entrées, $13.95 to $23.95. Lunch, Monday-Saturday 11 to 3. Dinner, 3 to 10 or 11. Sunday, brunch 10 to 3, dinner 3 to 10.

Cellar Gourmet, 208 Delaware St., New Castle.
When a chiropractor purchased the 1802 Janvier House in the early 1980s, he was determined to turn the basement into a badly needed healthful and informal family restaurant. With a dirt floor and low ceiling, the project was quite a challenge and the front wall fell in. Now shored up with a new wall, the interesting room has local scenes etched into tables and benches built into the rocks.

We looked around and then settled down for breakfast at the counter between one of the old guard, who filled us in on the background of old New Castle, and a gadabout who kept interrupting to talk about places down the bay. One of us naturally had to try the "famous original tastiest-healthiest waffle in the world." It turned out to be overrated – a hazard of superlatives. Also merely adequate was the sunshine cereal, a hearty combination of oatmeal, almonds, sesame seeds and much more, served with whole milk rather than skim, for shame.

Under new ownership, the lunch menu offers salads, sandwiches, light bites and vegetarian items. Desserts range from a variety of ice creams to warm caramel-apple pie, and at one visit included a sticky bun à la mode.

(302) 323-0999. Open Tuesday-Sunday, 9 to 4.

Diversions

Not a reconstruction of replicas, New Castle is a living museum of superb restorations virtually unchanged since the mid-1800s. "The spirit of the town is not that of an antiquarian society at all," says the definitive book *New Castle on the Delaware,* a federal WPA writers' project compiled in the 1930s and revised in the 1970s. "The dwellers are as preoccupied with their own affairs as are Americans elsewhere. They take the town as a matter of course, a part of the background of their business, and like it as it is....The distinction of New Castle today is due to the busy daily life that has gone on in it without break through the centuries, achieving a fairly congenial blending of old and new in activity and interests. This is something rather rare in our country, rarer than in parts of Europe where a town normally has not only length, breadth and height, but also an imposing time dimension accepted as one of the realities of the place."

New Castle Heritage Trail. Most of the structures in the long two square blocks in the center of old New Castle are detailed in a brochure available at the municipal office. Walking is the best way to see the sites. Join New Castilians as they walk or jog around **The Battery** park beside the Delaware. Poke along the undulating brick sidewalks of **The Strand,** pausing to look at the vestiges of the old store with an early Ivory Soap billboard painted three stories high on the side of a brick dwelling along **Packet Alley.** Cut through a garden walkway beside the historic **Presbyterian Church** to the shady Green. Prominent Delawareans are buried in the graveyard at **Immanuel Episcopal Church,** which since 1924 has sponsored the famed A Day in Old New Castle the third Saturday in May on the Green. Other sights worth noting are the **Old Town Hall and Markethouses** with an unusual open archway connecting Delaware Street and the Market Place, the 1789 **Academy,** the 1809 **U.S. Arsenal,** the original **ticket office** for the old New Castle-Frenchtown Railroad, and the **Town Wharf,** where little remains to validate the claim that New Castle was once an important shipping and transportation center.

New Castle Court House, Delaware Street.

The largest structure in downtown New Castle, this is the oldest surviving courthouse in Delaware (1732) and also served as Delaware's first state capitol. The capital was moved to Dover and the county seat to Wilmington, and the scene of so much early history is now virtually still except for public tours offered by the Delaware State Museums. "We are interpreters, not docents," said the site supervisor. "We try to bring the building and the situations that occurred in it alive." The restored courtroom contains a judge's bench, witness stand and prisoner's dock.

(302) 323-4453 or (800) 441-8846. Open Tuesday-Saturday 10 to 3:30, Sunday 1:30 to 4:30. Free.

The Dutch House, 32 East Third St.

This improbably low-slung house with a door, two windows and overhang roof is New Castle's only complete surviving house built prior to 1700. It's also believed to be the oldest brick house in Delaware. Typical of Dutch Colonial architecture, it is furnished with early Dutch furniture and artifacts, including a Dutch Bible and a courting bench.

Another house museum run by the New Castle Historical Society is the **Amstel House,** Fourth and Delaware Streets. George Washington was a wedding guest in 1784 in this imposing Georgian house built a half century earlier. Later the home of Gov. Nicholas Van Dyke, it has antique furnishings and a complete Colonial kitchen on view.

(302) 322-2794. Open March-December, Tuesday-Saturday 11 to 4, Sunday 1 to 4; weekends in January and February. Adults, $2 each house; combination ticket, $3.50.

Old Library Museum, 40 East Third St.

Its fanciful hexagonal structure and three-level skylight make this an unusual site for a library. Philadelphia architect Frank Furness designed it in 1892 for the New Castle Library Company's collection of classics and law books. Today it is owned by the Trustees of the New Castle Common, which preserves 700 acres of early lands around the town in something of a civic coup for old New Castle. It's leased to the New Castle Historical Society for exhibits and a slide presentation on the town.

(302) 322-2794. Open Thursday-Saturday 11 to 4, Sunday 1 to 4. Free.

Shopping. Although this has always been a working town, most of the commerce has moved with suburbia up to Route 13. The Visitors Bureau guide to old New Castle cites sixteen places of interest, four lodgings and ten places to shop, one of them a realty office and others seeming to change every year or two. Biggest of the

George Read II House is one of the more exceptional Georgian house museums anywhere.

stores is **O'Donalds Variety & Souvenir Store,** one of the old school, with an ice cream parlor at the side. Antiques and collectibles are featured in the adjacent **Opera House Antiques Center.** High tea is served weekend afternoons in the Victorian tea room of the opera house in which Jenny Lind and Enrico Caruso once sang.

Specialty stores of interest are **Lauren Lynch Antiques & Co.,** four Colonial rooms with furniture, linens, art and such; the exceptional rare bookstore **Oak Knoll Books,** and **Gifts-n-Stuff Ltd.,** where the emphasis is on the latter.

Extra-Special

George Read II House and Garden, 42 The Strand, New Castle.

"The grandest mansion and oldest gardens in New Castle," says the sign outside. Actually one of the outstanding Georgian house museums anywhere, this was completed in 1804 by the prosperous lawyer-son of a signer of the Declaration of Independence. It's a huge house with an unimpeded view of the river, towering above its neighbors along The Strand. Now owned by the Historical Society of Delaware, it is a living museum of the decorative crafts from the Federal period. An iron balcony and palladian window surmount the handsome doorway, itself topped by a fanlight. Inside are incised marble window sills and lintels, a stunning Greek key trompe-l'oeil cornice decoration in the entry hall, and elaborately carved detailing in the woodwork, masonry and plastering. The house and its attached servants' wing are surrounded by formal gardens designed in the style of Andrew Jackson Downing, foremost landscape architect of the mid-19th century. The Colonial Revival taste of later owners is preserved in three rooms that contrast with the restored Read interiors. There is a small museum shop in the basement entry.

(302) 322-8411. Open March-December, Tuesday-Saturday 10 to 4, Sunday noon to 4; weekend hours in January and February. Adults, $4.

Old wagon is on view outside stone barn housing Chadds Ford Historical Society museum.

Chadds Ford, Pa.

Wyeth and du Pont Country

Although the Battle of the Brandywine stamped Chadds Ford's place in history, the Wyeth family has given it cachet.

This two-bit hamlet along the Brandywine is named for the farmer and tavern-keeper who ferried travelers across the river at "John Chad's fording place." Here is where George Washington made his stand in 1777 against British troops on the march from nearby Kennett Square to the new nation's capital at Philadelphia. Some of the British crossed here as expected; others outwitted Washington by outflanking him to the north. The biggest battle of the Revolution went to the Crown.

The bucolic landscape later inspired many an artist, among them Howard Pyle, father of modern American illustration. Most famous of his students in classes at Chadds Ford was N.C. Wyeth, who settled his family along the Brandywine early in the 20th century and launched three generations of artistic talent here. Andrew Wyeth was born in Chadds Ford and still is said to go out on foot daily to seek inspiration for his work. The works of America's foremost family of artists are the cornerstone of the famed Brandywine River Museum.

The Brandywine winds past forests, meadows and hillsides in a rural, almost Vermont-like strip through encroaching exurbia. Side by side with pastoral landscapes that are the backdrops of Wyeth paintings lie the du Pont estates, substantial tract houses, shopping areas and office parks of the Philadelphia-Wilmington corridor. Busy U.S. Route 1 traverses the area's midsection and crosses the Brandywine, as did the British, at Chadds Ford.

The hamlet's appeal derives partly from its scenic landscape, its trademark houses and barns of gray fieldstone and its abiding ruralness, utterly unexpected in the midst of so much development. Its winding, back roads are made for getting lost.

The appeal of the broader Brandywine Valley, which fans out on all sides from Chadds Ford, comes mainly from its uncommon concentration of sophisticated museums. Most owe their existence to one branch or another of the du Pont family, a name as strongly identified with the region as that of the Wyeths.

Together they lend sophistication to one of America's most celebrated landscapes.

Inn Spots

Accommodations range from country hotels and chain motels to small inns and home-stay B&Bs. We concentrate here on a variety situated near Chadds Ford or reflective of its particular ambiance. The geography involves a narrow section along the Route 1 corridor from Lima to Kennett Square and along the north-south Route 52-100 corridor from Chadds Ford to Fairville and across the state line into Delaware.

The Inn at Montchanin Village, Route 100 at Kirk Road, Montchanin, Del. 19710.

An historic 19th-century workers' village, built by industrialist E.I. du Pont to house laborers who worked at the nearby du Pont gunpowder mills and factories along the Brandywine River, now houses and feeds guests in high style. With an uncanny knack for anticipating the needs of sophisticated travelers, local preservationists Missy and Daniel Lickle set about creating 33 bedrooms and suites plus a 55-seat restaurant in eleven buildings.

The twenty-acre site, a terraced enclave sloping toward the Brandywine, represents the core of the old village named in honor of du Pont family matriarch Anne Alexandrine de Montchanin, and has been in the family for five generations.

Guest accommodations and amenities were dictated by the idiosyncrasies of a row of turn-of-the-century duplexes, dependencies, a schoolhouse, a blacksmith shop, a stone barn and the du Pont railroad station.

Most of the first 26 accommodations are one- or two-bedroom suites with sitting areas and wet bars. Our quarters in Belin, which turned out to be fairly typical, contained a cozy downstairs sitting room with plump sofa and chair covered in chintz, a TV atop a gas fireplace and a kitchenette area in the corner with wet bar, microwave and mini-refrigerator, complete with automatic icemaker and stocked with soft drinks and mineral water. Coffee and end tables were charmingly painted with flowers and rabbits. Everything was colorfully decorated in mix-and-match patterns that flow together. Up steep stairs was a skylit bedroom with a king bed dressed in Frette linens, about the most comfortable we've had the pleasure of luxuriating in, and a stunning, huge, all-marble bathroom. The latter came with chandelier, a deep tub embedded in marble, a separate

shower encased in thick clear glass and, if you turned on the right switch, heated towel racks. Wood-look venetian blinds covered the windows, padded hangers and ironing equipment were in the closet, and a country window had been painted whimsically on the wall beside a real window.

The inn's distinctive cowbird logo – a bird perched on the back of a leaping cow – was everywhere (monogrammed on the terry robes, embedded in the marble above the bath). The bed was turned down with chocolates and a copy of the weather forecast, and a thermos of ice water was placed beside.

Breakfast the next morning was served beside the front windows in Krazy Kat's, the inn's dramatic restaurant (see Dining Spots). Fresh orange juice and muffins were preliminaries to the main event, a choice including eggs benedict and an omelet with smoked bacon, brie and chives, tasty walnut-raisin toast, garlicky browned potatoes and garnishes of large blackberries.

Afterward, Missy Lickle led a tour of the six-acre site, a steeply sloping complex sandwiched between main road and train track. Golf carts are lined up to transport luggage from parking areas. All is artfully landscaped and full of surprises, from picket fences to gas lights to porches with wicker rockers.

Room sizes and configurations differ, but each appeals in its own right. The Jefferson offers wicker porches front and back and a bathroom walled in travertine marble up to the vaulted ceiling. Missy, who decorated with goods from her nearby gourmet emporium known as Everything But the Kitchen Sink, incorporated fine antiques and heirloom furniture, Staffordshire figurines, colorful animal print and floral fabrics, and a delightful sense of whimsy. Dan's penchant for architectural hardware shows up in antique Bennington doorknobs and iron door pulls and hinges commissioned from a local forger.

In 1997, four more rooms – smaller than most of the originals but still containing all the amenities – and a conference area were completed in the Carpenter House. Under construction in 1998 were four luxurious guest quarters and a common room in the 1799 Pink House and three rooms in the Gate House. The final project was to be conversion of the Barn into a new guest reception and gathering area with a walk-in fireplace in the great room, a gift shop and other facilities.

(302) 888-2133 or (800) 269-2473. Fax (302) 888-0389. www.montchanin.com. Eight rooms and eighteen suites with private baths. Doubles, $150 to $170. Suites, $180 to $325. Two-night minimum weekends. No smoking.

Fairville Inn, Route 52 (Kennett Pike), Box 219, Mendenhall 19357.
Fifteen of the Chadds Ford area's most comfortable and attractive accommodations are located in this welcoming, personal complex of a country house, a carriage house and a converted barn at the edge of Fairville, the heart of Château Country. The welcome and the personality come from Ole and Patti Retlev, he a fun-loving Swede and she a native Delawarean who moved here in the 1980s after selling their Deerhill Inn in West Dover, Vt.

The Retlevs relocated for the climate, the quality of life and a less-seasonal business. Success was assured by the combination of luxurious accommodations and the year-round demand for them by museum visitors and business travelers.

The inn in the main 1820s house, the rear carriage house and a small barn was designed by Patti's uncle, architect Rodney Williams, owner of Vermont's famed Inn at Sawmill Farm, who also had a hand in the Deerhill. Patti, who did the decorating, seems to have inherited her aunt Ione Williams's design flair.

Innkeepers Patti and Ole Retlev welcome guests to Fairville Inn.

The original 1826 house has a spacious living room with a stunning copper table bearing some of the magazines that are displayed throughout the inn, a tea and breakfast room dressed in pink and white with copper utensils hanging about and five upstairs guest rooms.

Most choice rooms are the ten out back in the carriage house, built by an Amish family, and in the nearby barn the couple named the Spring House. Accented with barnwood, beams and occasional cathedral ceilings, eight rooms have fireplaces, and all ten boast balconies or decks looking across three acres of fields toward a pond. All have spacious private baths (our suite had two vanities and a separate dressing area; the towels were thick and matched the decor), oversize closets, unobtrusive TVs, telephones, elegant country furnishings, crisp and colorful chintzes, and fresh flowers. Aforementioned suite had a balcony with wrought-iron furniture, a sitting room with a loveseat, and a bedroom with a kingsize bed and two wing chairs by the fire. Its pale yellow and moss green decor was altogether cheerful, enhanced by pink tulips in a green vase.

The Retlevs are forever embellishing their rooms, adding fireplaces and kingsize canopy beds, doing stenciling here and replacing fabrics there. They even repainted a room in the Spring House in one day for arriving guest Barbra Streisand. Hung in guest and public rooms are magnificent paintings copied from old masters by a New Jersey artist.

The owners and staff serve a continental-plus breakfast on fine linens and china in the main house. As classical music played, we enjoyed a generous cup of kiwi, melon, grapes and strawberries, as well as Patti's delicious homemade tomato juice, cinnamon-raisin buns, sticky buns and Swedish coffee bread. Not to be missed is afternoon tea, accompanied by at least ten kinds of yummy homemade Swedish butter cookies.

(610) 388-5900. Fax (610) 388-5902. Thirteen rooms and two suites with private baths. Doubles, $140 to $180. Suites, $185 to $195. Two-night minimum most weekends. Children over 10. No smoking.

Whitewing Farm, 370 Valley Road, West Chester, Pa. 19382.

One of the early occupants of the newest suite at this stylish B&B fashioned from the former estate of the treasurer of the du Pont Company was a Cabinet-level official from the Clinton administration. "We're calling it the Lincoln Room," quips Edward DeSeta, innkeeper with his wife Wanda. "Except you don't have to pay $50,000 or $100,000 a night."

In fact, the suite upstairs in the main house goes for $180 a night and represents good value, considering all the amenities at this lavish estate reflecting the good life in the heart of du Pont country. The DeSetas moved to their dream of a farm in 1992 with three children and no intention of running a B&B. An innkeeper/friend who had overbooked called breathlessly one day to ask the DeSetas to put up her guests in their pool house. "All you have to do is serve them breakfast," Wanda recalls being told. "And I've been serving breakfast ever since."

The 43-acre property is perhaps less a traditional B&B than a small resort, what with a swimming pool with a newly built-in jacuzzi, a twelve-foot-deep fishing pond, ducks quacking around lily ponds and a waterfall, a ten-hole chip and putt golf course, a tennis court, a greenhouse and perennial gardens for the growing of flowers. But for the new suite, the other accommodations are not in the sprawling fieldstone and clapboard mansion dating to 1796, but rather in four outbuildings where guests are left pretty much on their own. And, after showing guests to their rooms, the members of the busy DeSeta family go their various ways, although they're up early for the breakfast hour that starts at 7:30.

The family lives upstairs in the mansion, but share the lovely downstairs with guests. A knockout country kitchen with french doors onto a terrace was created from five small rooms. From it come the cookies that greet arriving guests, as well as gourmet breakfasts served in the formal dining room or on the terrace. Unfolding one after another are a paneled reading room with fireplace and TV, a living room full of substantial antiques and some of the couple's diverse collections, a huge beamed game room with fireplace, pool table, TV and even a small kitchen for refreshments, and a large sun porch overlooking the grounds.

Two comfortable guest rooms are in the converted stables, and three in the carriage house. Renovated for the purpose, each has a queensize bed (one is kingsize), modern bathroom (shower only) with marble floor, TV and a veritable library of books. They're decorated in a hunt theme with pale yellow walls, splashy fabrics and thick green carpeting.

Our quarters in the Gatehouse Suite included a skylit living room with a fireplace and sofabed, a book-lined den with one plush chair in front of the TV, a skylit bedroom with kingsize bed, a beauty of a bathroom done in marble with a bouquet of rosebuds (this in autumn) reflected in the mirror on the vanity, a modern kitchen and a terrace with a gas grill. We could understand why a Texas family considers it home during their annual six-week summer stay.

Two simpler rooms have been fashioned from the former men's and women's changing facilities in the pool house. The decor is garden style, the bed headboard is a picket fence and a patio with wrought-iron lounge chairs faces the idyllic fish pond, with its frogs croaking and its fountain lit at night.

A resident chef prepares and the DeSetas serve a breakfast worthy of the site. Orange juice, cream cheese and raspberry coffee cake and made-to-order omelets were the fare when we were there.

Guests like to ride around the property on a golf cart and pet the animals. "Ed

Main house and pool house look onto pond at Whitewing Farm.

wanted a cow for his birthday," Wanda said. "So I bought him one." Last we knew there were three cows, and horses were next on the agenda.

(610) 388-2664. Fax (610) 388-3650. Seven rooms and two suites with private baths. Doubles, $110 to $130. Suites, $180 to $225.

The Pennsbury Inn, 883 Baltimore Pike, Chadds Ford, Pa. 19317.

Listed on the National Register, this handsome B&B pairs contemporary amenities with slanted doorways, winding staircases, sloping floors and walk-in fireplaces in rooms spanning three centuries.. Frank (Chip) Allemann and designer James Pine, partners in local furniture and design company, restored and opened the house in 1996 as a showcase for their wares. The fieldstone and yellow brick house dating to 1714 is smack up against busy Route 1 but screened from passing traffic by a high, thick hedge. It offers decorator-quality common rooms and seven guest rooms furnished to one of the three periods in which the house was built and expanded.

The entire inn is furnished with antiques, Tibetan carpets, teak accent furniture and down-filled upholstered pieces that are for sale. Guest quarters range from a ground-floor single paneled in knotty pine and containing a twin bed to the rear Winterthur Room with vaulted ceiling and queensize cherry bed, loveseat, armchair and little deacon's bench. The cozy front John Marshall Room has a double bed and one of the three in-room fireplaces.

Feather beds with down comforters, TV sets and modernized baths with pewter or chrome fixtures are the rule. Décor is splashy – Pierre Deux or Osborne & Little wallpapers here, toile balloon shades and drapery panels there. But show sometimes upstages comfort. A solitary wing chair and three stiff wooden chairs placed strategically around the perimeter are the seats in the prized Lafayette Room, reached via an impossibly steep winder staircase in the original 1714 section of the house. The large palladian window and side windows in the Winterthur Room have no shades or curtains for privacy or to darken early morning's light.

The main floor offers three comfortable common rooms. One is a library with

Dating to 1714, the handsome Pennsbury Inn is listed on the National Register.

TV and stereo and another a magnificent garden room off the kitchen with a couple of dining areas and a sofa and chairs facing a huge fireplace. A manager prepares a full breakfast of juice, muffins or scones, granola and perhaps croissant french toast infused with fresh fruit or scrambled eggs with cream cheese and chives.

The inn offers lovely grounds, a swimming pool and eight wooded acres in back.

(610) 388-1435. Fax (610) 388-1436. Seven rooms with private baths. Doubles, $140 to $225 weekends; 15 percent off midweek. Two-night minimum weekends. Children over 13. Smoking restricted.

Hedgerow Bed & Breakfast Suites, 268 Kennett Pike (Route 52), Chadds Ford 19317.

Massed plantings of impatiens brighten the facade of the handsome Victorian home that had been in owner John Haedrich's family since the 1950s, and lately has been showy enough that passersby along Kennett Pike paused for a closer look. When John and his wife Barbara took possession in 1988, friends asked why they didn't open it as a B&B. With a "house full of kids," John said, it was more practical to use their rear carriage house instead.

The Haedrichs started modestly by offering two guest rooms sharing a bath in the air-conditioned carriage house, set well back from the road beyond a spreading sycamore that shades much of the back yard. We barely recognized the place at our next visit, such was the transformation. Beautifully landscaped, the entire carriage house is now used and looks like a small house. Upstairs are two rambling suites. Downstairs are a deluxe suite and common facilities, including an inviting parlor and a stylish dining room open to a designer kitchen.

We'd happily settle into the spiffy Longwood Suite, the latest ground-floor addition with its own entrance and screened patio, hand-inlaid cherry parquet floors and antique Victorian furniture made in Chester County. The entry hall with a floor of slate from Brazil opens into an elegant living room with a sofabed, a corner fireplace, a wet bar with mini-refrigerator and microwave, and french doors onto the patio. To the side is a large bedroom, lovely in white and pale green, with a kingsize iron and brass bed. At one end is an alcove with a writing desk and a marble-top bureau. At the other end is a smaller alcove with closet space and a vanity with wash basin. Beyond the living room is a two-part bathroom containing a jacuzzi in one section and vanity in the other.

Upstairs, the original two bedrooms are now the Winterthur Suite with a sitting room, a queen four-poster in one bedroom and two twin beds in a sun porch. The Brandywine Suite has a sitting room, a queen canopy in the bedroom and an alcove with a twin bed.

All accommodations come with TV, phone and central air conditioning.

From her dream of a kitchen, Barbara has supplemented her original hearty continental breakfast with main dishes like bacon and eggs or baked french toast. It's served in the dining room looking onto a brick terrace and, beyond, a gazebo and fish pond.

(610) 388-6080. Fax (610) 388-0194. Three suites with private baths. Suites, $125 to $160 for two; $20 each additional. Children over 15. No smoking.

Hamanassett, 725 Darlington Road, Box 129, Lima 19037.

What a manse is this! What gardens and grounds! What a nice place to stay, thanks to the heritage of an uncommon manor house and the straightforward, no-nonsense charm of its owner, a retired school teacher who has lived here since her marriage in 1949.

The mistress of the manor is Evelene Dohan – "every other letter is an E – when I was born, my mother must have screeched, 'eeee,'" quips this eminently quotable woman who must have been a memorable teacher. Here, single-handedly except for a commercial cleaning and grounds service, she offers six comfortable guest rooms and a suite, all with private baths and TV/VCRs and most with oversize beds. Her literature conveys the grace of an heiress as well as the strictures of a school marm.

"I want people to feel at home when they're not at home," says Evelene. We'd gladly stay in any of the guest rooms on the second and third floors of this manor house in which she raised five children. All are quite spacious, nicely furnished in traditional, unshowy decor and outfitted with "an abundance of antiquities, many of which have been in the family for centuries." Rooms have sitting areas, full baths, big windows, well-worn oriental rugs and an air of lived-in comfort. Three rooms contain small refrigerators stocked with wine, beer and snacks. A two-bedroom suite comes with a formal living room. A two-room affair with two double beds and a living room would be a suite anywhere else, but because the rooms are "connected through an open archway, it is not a suite," the lodging literature insists. It's quite a pad, nevertheless, for $95.

Guests spread out around the large Federal-era fireplace in the main living room/library, its shelves stocked with more than 2,000 volumes; in a cozier Green Room parlor with another fireplace outlined in Delft tiles (except for three substitutes made by her late father-in-law, and she defies you to determine which); in a huge, brick-floored and plant-filled solarium to end all solariums, and on the majestic front loggia overlooking the gardens. Guests enjoy strolling through the formal

English boxwood gardens with statues of Psyche and Aphrodite and inspecting the colorful flower gardens everywhere. "This is no Longwood," the owner apologized, but the plants are so prolific they keep the weeds at bay from July on.

Breakfast is taken at individual lace-covered tables in a chandeliered dining room open to the solarium. Evelene "studied at the Cordon Bleu, so cooking doesn't bother me." She prepares an extravagant buffet spread: juices, stewed fruit and melon, cereals, a couple of hot dishes such as tomato-mushroom omelets and pancakes with raspberries from the garden, Virginia ham, turkey sausage, Philadelphia scrapple, creamed mushrooms with basil sauce and assorted pastries from croissants to sticky buns.

You leave Hamanassett's 48 hilltop acres well-fed and restored, returning down the winding driveway past forests and gardens to Route 1, a half mile and another world away.

(610) 459-3000. Six rooms and one suite with private baths. Doubles, $90 to $125. Suite, $120 to $170. Two-night minimum required. Children over 14. No smoking. No credit cards.

Scarlett House Bed & Breakfast, 503 West State St., Kennett Square, Pa. 19348.

Victoriana reigns in this stone house with rust-colored shutters astride a hill at the edge of Kennett Square. Samuel and Jane Snyder, who ran a small B&B for eight years in Long Island, wanted a bigger place in which to entertain and display collections from their travels. "We saw the woodwork and fell in love with the inside of this house," said ebullient Jane. They are only the third family to occupy the house built in 1910 for the Scarlett family.

Guests enter a wide foyer notable for chestnut woodwork, doors and stairs. Each of two window nooks on either side of the door contains facing benches that are replicas of originals in the old Quaker Meeting House in Kennett Square. Off the foyer are two fireplaced parlors. One is a ladies' parlor sporting a collection of music boxes and the other a less formal setting where Jane chats with guests.

Upstairs is another sitting area, this one beside sunny windows full of plants on the landing, plus a suite and three guest rooms, two of which share a hall bath. Each comes with prized antiques, ceiling fans, bathrobes, toiletries and a long-stemmed rose. The rear suite offers an ornate Jenny Lind walnut queensize bed with matching dresser and a side sitting room. The front Victorian Rose room has an Empire chest and lacy pillows on the high-back walnut queensize bed. One of the shared-bath rooms has a sitting area in what used to be a sleeping porch.

"I love china, silver, lace and flowers," Jane says, "so this a great outlet for me." She leads the way to two chandeliered dining rooms in the rear, where lace-covered tables bear lavish displays of roses and floral draperies dress the windows. The tables are set with Limoges service plates, and Jane has a different china pattern for every day of the week.

Both she and Sam love to cook. Their three-course breakfast begins with a fruit and cereal course, perhaps fresh muesli with cantaloupe, honeydew and dried apricots. The main course could be "egg in the hole" garnished with crab, Kennett Square mushrooms, sour cream and caviar, accompanied by sweet-potato rounds spiced with cinnamon and nutmeg. Another day might yield a quiche of many vegetables and three cheeses, accompanied by cherry tomatoes stuffed with roasted garlic, basil and goat cheese. The dessert course could be a chocolate-macadamia coconut cake served with non-fat yogurt, bananas and star fruit.

Potted flowers on front loggia welcome guests to Hamanassett manor house.

In the afternoon, Jane offers complimentary refreshments in the second-floor sitting area. A hidden mini-refrigerator is stocked with cold beverages, and sherry, fruit and cookies are at the ready.

Outside are a broad, wraparound porch and English gardens. The Snyders have added a fish pond and a pergola in back.

(610) 444-9592 or (800) 820-9592. One room and one suite with private baths; two rooms with shared bath. Doubles, $85 to $105. Suite, $135. Two-night minimum weekends, April-December. No smoking.

Meadow Spring Farm, 201 East Street Road (Route 926), Kennett Square 19348.

Santas and dolls dressed in their Christmas best made this farmhouse-turned-B&B a highlight of the annual Candlelight Christmas tour in Chadds Ford. It's a bit of a Christmas fantasyland all year long. Innkeeper-collector Anne Hicks has turned her home into a gallery of whimsical animals in all guises, dolls and country antiques, from Noah's ark on the fireplace mantel to surplus dolls stored in the attic. We were charmed by the hundreds of cows of all varieties, many sent by guests.

The Hicks family has lived in the 1836 farmhouse for 50 years; daughter Sissy Hicks, chef-owner of the Dorset Inn in Vermont, grew up here. With her daughter Debbie and occasional help from one of eight grandchildren, Anne opens the farmhouse to guests in six air-conditioned rooms, each with TV and four with private baths. One queensize room has a fireplace and a sleigh bed and another, the Chippendale, has a crocheted canopy bed and a huge bathroom that was converted from a bedroom. Both beds are covered with Amish-made quilts. Antique wedding gowns hang on the wall in a twin bedroom featuring Laura Ashley linens and quilts. Two rooms over the garage are newer and furnished in more contemporary country style.

Guests enjoy the living room full of inanimate animals, a dining room with the long table centered by a carved cow and her calf, a lovely porch with garden furniture looking onto gardens and a swimming pool, and another enclosed porch with a hot tub. Fruit pancakes and mushroom omelets with scrapple or sausage are specialties at breakfast. It's served in the dining room or on the screened porch, where Anne offers tea or wine in the afternoons. She also puts up 200 jars of jam made with local fruit each year.

Guests are welcome to fish in the farm pond, feed the rabbits or play ping-pong or pool in the downstairs game room. Families particularly like the feel of a 200-acre working farm, although the rooster crowing at dawn jars some.

(610) 444-3903. Four rooms with private baths and two rooms with shared bath. Doubles, $75 to $85. Two-night minimum on weekends. Children welcome. No credit cards.

Brandywine River Hotel, Route 1 at Route 100, Box 1058, Chadds Ford 19317.

Claiming to be "the focal point of historic Chadds Ford village," this brick and shingle hostelry is set back on a hill away from busy Route 1. Opened in 1987, it's shielded from highway view by a cluster of rustic buildings called the Chadds Ford Barn Shops and the historic Chadds Ford Inn.

One of the restaurant's owners bought the hotel in 1996 and upgraded the room appointments, which were designed to resemble a wealthy Colonial home: Queen Anne reproduction furnishings in cherry and classic English chintz, wing chairs, oriental rugs, brass sconces and paintings in the Brandywine tradition. Bathrooms, telephones and remote-control TVs hidden in armoires are thoroughly up to date.

Among its 40 guest accommodations are ten suites with fireplaces and jacuzzi baths. Five new executive suites offer one double bed and a sitting area with a sofabed.

A complimentary continental buffet breakfast of granola and other cereals, corn or blueberry muffins, croissants, bagels and danish is served in the fireplaced hospitality room, decorated in the style of a Colonial meeting hall. It also is used for meetings and functions. Afternoon tea (iced tea on a warm day) or hot spiced cider and cookies are set out by the fireplace in the lobby.

(610) 388-1200. Twenty-five rooms and fifteen suites with private baths. Doubles, $125 to $135. Suites, $149 and $169.

Dining Spots

Chadds Ford Inn, Routes 1 and 100, Chadds Ford, Pa.

The house built by Francis Chadsey, the English Quaker who purchased 500 choice acres here from William Penn's commissioner of land grants in 1703, is now the Chadds Ford Inn. His eldest son, who lived nearby, ran the ferry that crossed the Brandywine. In 1736, John Chad turned the house into a tavern, a role it has upheld virtually ever since.

The place where Colonial officers were entertained during the Revolution now provides sustenance to Andrew and Betsy Wyeth, who live up the road, and to countless travelers who eat better here than they might expect.

The low beamed ceilings and wainscoting enhance the works of three generations of Wyeths hung on the walls of the restaurant. It has two main dining rooms on either side of the center entry hall downstairs and three more upstairs, plus an atmospheric tavern in back. Tables, each bearing a slender rose, are attractively

Works of three generations of Wyeths hang on walls of Chadds Ford Inn.

set in beige and brown. Candles are lit at lunchtime, even though sunlight streams through the windows recessed in the thick stone walls.

It was here we first learned that the area's ubiquitous snapper soup is made not with red snapper but with snapper turtle. It tastes like the turtle soup we've had in New Orleans and is thick and spicy. We also had chicken crêpes garnished with carrots and coleslaw. Roasted turkey salad served with marinated artichoke hearts and sesame seed dressing was another good choice from a changing menu that ranges widely from a grilled chicken and jack cheese sandwich to boboli with montrachet and crab cakes with lobster-chive sauce.

The much-acclaimed dessert tray held old favorites like pecan and pumpkin pies, chocolate éclairs, sour-cream peach pie, chocolate mousse cake and a strawberry-kiwi tart

At night, the historic atmosphere is grand, the presentation stylish and the service leisurely, at least the autumn midweek evening we dined. Everything on the contemporary dinner menu appealed, from baked salmon served over basil and spinach to grilled free-range chicken with sweet corn puree. The mustard-sauced Australian loin of lamb and the tender grilled venison steak topped with port wine and plum sauce were especially good. A hot popover came first; a key lime puff finished.

(610) 388-7361. Entrées, $15.25 to $24.95. Lunch, Monday-Saturday 11:30 to 2. Dinner, 5:30 to 10 or 10:30. Sunday, brunch 11 to 2, dinner 4 to 8.

The Gables at Chadds Ford, 162 Baltimore Pike, Chadds Ford.

The handsome, historic stone and frame barn that was once part of a dairy farm is now a stylish restaurant specializing in California cuisine with an Asian accent. Jack McFadden, area restaurateur for 30 years and known recently for successes at the nearby Marshalton Inn and at The Restaurant and The Bar in West Chester, invested more than $1 million in 1997 into what he considers his best effort so far. "This is my grown-up restaurant," he said, and early reviewers agreed.

The place is named for the 23 gables added to the barn in an 1897 Victorian facelift. An interior design aficionado who did the architectural renderings himself, he scouted up three art deco bronze chandeliers and matching sconces for the bar area, where the metal milking stools are cushioned in a deep red faux ostrich skin. Leaded glass windows separate the bar from the 120-seat dining room, where patrons view the cooks at work in an open kitchen. Jack calls the décor "barn chic." The linens are white, the floors heartpine, the walls are brick and crackle painted with gold tint, and dining is by candlelight. A canopied fieldstone outdoor dining patio with a waterfall and stone walls was planned for 1998.

Chef Mark Eastman and a crew experienced in leading area restaurants produce an extensive menu upon which every item appeals. We'd happily make a dinner of such appetizers as ahi tuna with Asian greens and crispy wontons, sautéed escargots over roasted orzo, crab cakes with seared scallops and coconut sauce, and seared duck confit served over lentils with a raspberry demi-glace.

Or we'd make a meal of a pasta like crab ravioli or fusilli with scallops, chèvre, leeks and roasted plum tomatoes. Main courses on the initial autumn menu ranged from Thai marinated grouper with wilted greens and citrus-glazed salmon with ancho chile rice to seared Long Island duck breast with pomegranate sauce, rosemary skewered pork tenderloin with roasted soy beans and grilled venison loin with roasted chestnuts.

Desserts include crème caramel, chocolate mousse and fresh fruit napoleon, presented like the rest of the courses on oversize white plates garnished and decorated to the hilt.

(610) 388-7700. Entrées, $15.95 to $23. Lunch, Tuesday-Saturday 11:30 to 2:30. Dinner, 5:30 to 10:30. Sunday, brunch 11 to 2:30, dinner 5 to 9.

Krazy Kat's, Route 100 and Kirk Road, Montchanin, Del.

This polished restaurant occupies the former blacksmith shop in the restored Montchanin village that once housed workers at the du Pont powder mills. Owner Missy Lickle chose the unlikely name for an eccentric spinster who once lived there "and was crazy as a cat," in the words of her grandmother. The feline theme extends from the cat sculptures clad in Japanese robes in each of the front windows to the tables set with zebra-print cloths and china in the colorful jaguar jungle pattern. The tables in two rooms are large and well spaced, the walls radiate a warm salmon color, and a fire burns in one of the original forges up near the ceiling.

Executive chef Scott Daniels modifies the contemporary American menu every few weeks.

One of us started with the zesty bluepoint oyster gratin teamed with prosciutto, tri-color bell peppers, shallots and parmesan cheese, while the other sampled the salad of field greens, a first-rate mélange dressed with toasted pinenuts, blue cheese and a zippy roasted garlic vinaigrette. Main courses ranged from sautéed shrimp and sea scallops Acadian to a mixed grill of muscovy duck breast, lamb chop and an ostrich medallion. The sautéed crab cakes were bound with a shrimp mousseline and served with honey-jalapeño tartar sauce and sweet potato fries. The melt-in-the-mouth Chesapeake rockfish was sauced with bluepoint oysters in a tomato-fennel cream and accompanied by crisp haricots verts and flavorful wild rice.

From a dessert repertoire that included a walnut-praline tart and crème de cassis crème brûlée, we settled for the intense raspberry and mango sorbets, architecturally presented with enormous blackberries and an edible orchid in an almond tuile.

Although this is a place for serious dining, the feline motif and lack of pretension impart a refreshing light-heartedness.

(302) 888-2133. Entrées, $22 to $25. Dinner nightly, 5:30 to 10. Jackets requested.

Dilworthtown Inn, Old Wilmington Pike at Brinton Bridge Road, Dilworthtown, Pa.

For historic atmosphere and fine food, locals head to the quaint hamlet of Dilworthtown and this rambling old wood, stone and brick structure dating to 1758. The French-inspired fare is classic and the wine list the area's best.

The original inn and its late 18th-century wing have been restored into an assortment of fifteen dining rooms, bar and lobby, complete with plate-glass windows and plantings in a mini-atrium. Eleven fireplaces, stenciling, oriental rugs, antique furnishings and candlelight combine for a romantic atmosphere.

The bound, eight-page dinner menu starts with fourteen appetizers, from shrimp cocktail to confit of duck spring rolls and ginger crisp lobster. Among entrées are three steaks, Australian lobster tail, lobster thermidor, breast of peking duck and chargrilled veal chop. The kitchen shines with the nightly specials: perhaps salmon poached with ginger, quail sautéed with fresh pears and New Zealand venison with a red wine sauce.

Desserts include chocolate mousse, crème caramel and homemade sorbets and gelatos of exotic flavors.

(610) 399-1390. Entrees, $17.25 to $25.95. Dinner nightly, 5:30 to 10:30, Saturday from 5, Sunday 3 to 9.

Half Moon Restaurant & Saloon, 108 West State St., Kennett Square, Pa.

Exciting new American cuisine at remarkably reasonable prices is featured in this new hot spot built – literally – by young restaurateur Scott Hammond from an old candy kitchen. With a few helpers, he constructed the 35-seat mahogany bar and back bar in the front of the long, high-ceilinged downtown storefront, a popular watering spot for a young crowd. He also built the booths and tables in the rear, where diners both casual and serious gather away from the hubbub to enjoy the inspired fare of Tennessee chef John Stewart, once the private chef for Gov. Lamar Alexander.

Scott named the place for a favorite after-ski haunt in Montana with the intention of opening a microbrewery called Total Eclipse. The restaurant proved so successful that the brewpub plans have been put on hold.

From an appealing menu made for grazing, we enjoyed the spiced bluefish wrapped in a potato crust with a shrimp and crawfish court bouillon, julienned mixed vegetables and melt-in-the-mouth mashed potatoes, and cashew-encrusted chicken sautéed with chevre, served with assertive curried vegetables and jasmine rice. With a bottle of Lost Horizon chardonnay, the dinner tab for two came to less than $40.

Sample a local mushroom napoleon with claret sauce, a crispy ginger-fried lobster salad with watercress and plum dressing, a crab melt sandwich, roasted duck and smoked portobello mushroom over chipotle pepper polenta, grilled rabbit loin in whole grain mustard sauce, grilled elk chop gremolata, chocolate chip cheesecake or apple-cranberry tarte. The tastes are great, and so are the values.

(610) 444-7232. Entrées, $8.50 to $17.95. Lunch, Monday-Friday from noon. Dinner, Monday-Friday 5:30 to 10, Saturday 6 to 10.

Chadds Ford Cafe, Route 1 at Heyburn Road, Chadds Ford, Pa.

Two sisters and their husbands opened this sprightly deli with a counter and quickly expanded to a full-fledged dining room. "We're family-owned and geared for family dining," said Joan Winchester, who's proud of her bright and cheery addition enhanced by Amish-made table tops, bench and corner cupboard.

The "family" description and the somewhat plain-Jane surroundings mask a rather ambitious menu offering three meals a day. Some of the area's most sophisticated fare emanates from the kitchen of chef-partner Frank Perko. His dinner menu starts with such appetizers as crab rangoon, wild mushroom polenta and walnut-coated fried brie with raspberry coulis and grilled focaccia. Treats like eggplant ravioli, mosticoli and spinach bake, and assorted mushrooms over mushroom ravioli tempt vegetarians. Lobster ravioli and shrimp shanghai (with bok choy and oriental garlic-ginger sauce) tempt the pasta-lovers. Up to a dozen entrées range from sea scallops Madrid to chicken wellington to veal citron.

We sampled a couple of appetizers for lunch: the signature split-bowl soups (half black bean and half cream of jalapeño with smoked pepper sauce, both wonderful) and the fresh spinach and mozzarella fritters, served on a pool of herb-tomato coulis.

(610) 558-3960. Entrées, $15.95 to $23.95. Open Monday, 8 to 2:30. Tuesday-Saturday, 8 to 9 or 10 p.m. Sunday 8 to 8. BYOB.

Buckley's Tavern, 5812 Kennett Pike (Route 52), Centreville, Del.

Built in the late 1700s, this consists of an intimate, noisy tavern in front, a pretty, white-linened interior dining room and an airy garden room at the back. There's also an open-air bar on two upper levels outside. Votive candles flicker on bare, rich wood tables flanked by comfortable, cushioned chairs in the garden room, our choice for dining on two occasions.

The former tavern and dinner menus have been combined into one short, interesting menu appealing to a variety of tastes and pocketbooks. That no doubt accounts for the fanciful juxtaposition of an expensive foreign car parked next to a pickup truck in the delightful drawing of the tavern exterior on the menu cover, as well as for the actual mix of singles, on-the-town foursomes, du Pont executives, foreign businessmen and couples that seem to pack the place every time we're there.

Burgers or hummus, barbecued pork sandwich or goat cheese bruschetta, chicken chili with black beans or Thai beef and noodle salad, farfalle with smoked salmon and roquefort or roasted Long Island duckling – here's the ultimate grazing menu. At one visit, we liked the crab cakes with a fresh coriander tartar sauce and the linguini with smoked chicken and red peppers. At another, the shrimp ravioli with tomatoes and rosemary and the shrimp and scallops with green peppercorns in puff pastry were winners.

The special cappuccino-pecan-praline ice cream was a hit among desserts, as was a fuzzy navel peach pie with a peach brandy custard sauce, which looked and tasted like a creamsicle.

The wine store located in the front of the building keeps the tavern's wine selection interesting and reasonably priced.

(302) 656-9776. Entrées, $13.95 to $18.95. Lunch, Monday-Saturday 11:30 to 2:30. Dinner nightly, 5:30 to 9; Sunday brunch.

Diversions

Museums are chief among the Chadds Ford area's myriad attractions. The big three:

Brandywine River Museum, Route 1, Chadds Ford. The Civil War-era grist mill converted into a modern museum is known for its incomparable collection of art by the Wyeth family as well as fine collections of American illustration, still life and landscape painting associated with the Brandywine heritage. Spectacular glass additions overlook the river as well as the adjoining wildflower gardens and nature trail developed by the Brandywine Conservancy, which marked its 30th anniversary in 1997 and preceded the museum by a few years. Andrew Wyeth's work, reflecting the valley and its people as well as the Maine coast, is shown in the special Andrew Wyeth Gallery, which constantly changes with additions loaned by the family. At our latest visit, a special exhibit told the story of the Wyeths' early relationship to Chadds Ford.

(610) 388-2700. Open daily, 9:30 to 4:30. Adults, $5.

Longwood Gardens, Route 1, Kennett Square. One of the world's great horticultural displays is showy year-round, thanks to the gardens and conservatories that once were the 350-acre private preserve of Pierre S. du Pont. Spring begins in January and the spectacle changes monthly through Christmas in the twenty Crystal Palace-type conservatories, which we find even more colorful and exotic than the outdoor gardens. Illuminated fountain displays are choreographed to music on summer evenings.

(610) 388-1000 or (800) 737-5500. Open daily, 9 to 5 or later. Adults, $10.

Winterthur Museum and Gardens, Route 52, Winterthur, Del. The world's premier collection of American decorative arts and antiques, assembled by Henry Francis du Pont, is displayed in 175 period room settings in the main house and in a new building with three exhibition galleries. Only some are on view at any one time, such is the scope of the collection and the size of the nine-story mansion. The interior can be seen on an assortment of guided tours, sometimes fully booked well ahead. The layman may be well enough served by Winterthur's new building dedicated to the art of looking at (and learning from) things. The Galleries at Winterthur shows 1,000 of the museum's pieces arranged in galleries on two floors. Trams take visitors on tours of the lavish gardens developed by "head gardener" du Pont on his 980-acre estate.

(302) 888-4600 or (800) 448-3883. Open Monday-Saturday 9 to 5, Sunday noon to 5. Adults, $8 to $21.

Brandywine Battlefield Park, Route 1, Chadds Ford.

In the biggest battle of the Revolution, 18,000 British and 11,000 Americans met at Chadds Ford. This one went to the Brits. They outflanked George Washington, who was defending Chadds Ford, and encircled his troops from the north. Now a 50-acre state park, it has a visitor center that presents a thirteen-minute slide show on the battle. Washington's headquarters in the Benjamin Ring House and Lafayette's quarters in the Gideon Gilpin House are open periodically for tours. The actual battlefield is on unmarked lands, "two miles north as the crow flies and five roundabout miles by car," according to a park guide.

(610) 459-3342. Open Tuesday-Saturday 9 to 5, Sunday noon to 5. Grounds open to 9 in summer. Building tours, $3.50; battlefield, free.

The **Chadds Ford Historical Society** has a museum and visitor center in a barn across from its **John Chads House,** Route 100, a quarter mile north of Route 1. The 1725 house is furnished as it was when the ferryman and farmer for whom the village was named lived here – that is to say, sparely. The society also operates the **Barns-Brinton House,** a restored 18th-century tavern nearby. Houses open May-October, weekends noon to 6, rest of year by appointment. Adults, $2.

Chaddsford Winery, Route 1, Chadds Ford.
This boutique-style winery with lots going on has been producing good wines since 1981. Operating from a converted barn, it imports grapes from around the area to make "new American classics from the Brandywine Valley." These include the Proprietors Reserve White (rated a model for regional whites), classic European varietals and a first-class chardonnay. Proprietor Eric Miller comes from a winemaking family (his father owns Benmarl Vineyards and Winery in New York's Hudson Valley); wife Lee has authored a book about wine.
(610) 388-6221. Open daily, noon to 6.

Shopping. The area's most sophisticated shopping extends along Kennett Pike (Route 52) from Fairville, Pa., site of a cluster of antiques shops, through Centreville to Greenville, Del. We're particularly partial to Centreville, where old buildings along the wide street have been converted to house such favorites as **Troll of Scandinavia** (for interesting takeout food), the **Jolly Needlewoman, The Sporting Gentleman** and **Wild Thyme,** all neatly detailed in a new brochure touting it as "still the perfect rest stop, from 1750 until today." We're drawn to **Communiques,** a great paper, book, card and gift shop, where coffee's always on tap and poetry readings are among the special events.

The largest selection of Wyeth reproductions anywhere is featured at **Chadds Ford Gallery,** in a brick house in front of the **Chadds Ford Village and Barn Shops.** Antiques stores and malls abound along Route 1 in Chadds Ford. Dealers are grouped at **the Brandywine River Antiques Market** and the **Pennsbury-Chadds Ford Antique Mall.**

Country wares are to be found in Dilworthtown, where the **Dilworthtown Country Store** is full of sophisticated American crafts and folk art.

Extra-Special

Hagley Museum, Route 141, Wilmington, Del.
The original du Pont mills and powder works, estate and gardens offer 230 acres of Brandywine history. More than the other museums, this lives up to its slogan, "something for everyone." A shuttle bus takes visitors around the tranquil grounds along the Brandywine. The Henry Clay Mill exhibits trace America's industrial expansion. Water flowing through the mill races power the massive stone mills in the powder yard. Pause for lunch in the simple Belin House Coffee Shop atop Blacksmith Hill and visit the workers' housing area. Then see how the boss lived in Eleutherian Mills, the first du Pont family home built by E.I. du Pont in 1803. The Georgian-style residence is furnished to reflect the tastes of five generations of du Ponts who lived there. Espaliered fruit trees set off the beautiful yet functional French garden outside. The Hagley, we think, is most evocative of the Brandywine heritage.
(302) 658-2400. Open daily 9:30 to 4:30, mid-March through December; weekends only 9:30 to 4:30 and one tour weekdays at 1:30 in winter. Adults, $9.75.

Curving driveway leads to The Cameron Estate Inn, one of county's finer properties.

Western Lancaster County, Pa.

Beyond the Tourists

Much of the Lancaster County of Pennsylvania Dutch fame is a land of strange names and quaint places – a sea of smorgasbords, outlets, motels and commercial enterprises taking advantage of the Amish-Mennonite connection and, alas, undercutting the very notion of "The Plain People."

That applies to eastern Lancaster County, where tourists arrive by the busload, three million a year strong. Western Lancaster County is, for the most part, a place apart.

Here, the picturesque rolling farmlands of the east flatten as they approach the broad ridge cresting along the Susquehanna River. The Amish and Mennonites are far less conspicuous. So are the trappings of tourism. The western section wears an historic face, but one unfettered by the commercialism of its eastern counterpart.

Mount Joy, Marietta and Columbia. These are the sleepy rural villages and river towns that dwell in the western county, surrounded by the ubiquitous farmlands that manage to survive in the face of creeping Lancaster suburbia.

Mount Joy, the biggest town, marks something of a dividing line between the frenzied quaintness of Pennsylvania Dutch country and the serenity beyond. Marietta is a long and narrow strip of a river town, as authentic as they come; nearly half the town is on the National Register. Columbia was a gateway to the west when it was Wright's Ferry, crossing point to the Susquehanna frontier. It was an important enough river site in the 1790s that it was one of the potential locations for the new nation's capital.

Congress ultimately chose a capital along the Potomac River, not the Susquehanna. The development of the area, which blossomed during the heady river and railroad days of the 19th century, was stunted in the 20th. Buildings now

Overseeing broad lawn is Mount Gretna Inn, the biggest house in town.

considered historic were bypassed by the building boom. They stand as mute testimony to an earlier era.

Betty Groff, the guru of Pennsylvania Dutch cookery, and her Groff's Farm restaurant put Mount Joy on the national culinary map. The sophisticates who came to this side of the county were charmed by its lack of clutter and tourism. The Groffs opened a country inn nearby, more inns and B&Bs followed and lately, western Lancaster County is becoming a destination in search of an identity.

No one – not tourism directors, innkeepers nor restaurateurs – has come up with a name for the area other than western Lancaster County. But they all see it as different from the rest of Lancaster County, a place apart.

Inn Spots

The Cameron Estate Inn, 1855 Mansion Lane, Mount Joy 17552.

New owners have enhanced the warmth and welcome at this landmark long associated with restaurateurs Betty and Abe Groff. The Groffs bought the historic Cameron estate in 1981 to open an inn in the grand manner, and sold in 1997 to Becky and David Vogt of Washington, D.C.

A grand manor it is, indeed, and the Vogts set about to capitalize on its potential. Out in the country on fifteen acres beside historic Donegal Church, the majestic 1805 Federal mansion was built by the great-grandfather of President McKinley and owned in the 1870s by Simon Cameron, Abraham Lincoln's first Secretary of War.

Hands-on innkeepers, the Vogts refurbished some of the common areas that they found dark and dreary, added personal accents and accessories to the guest rooms, and closed the restaurant operation. "We're focusing on elegant lodging," Becky stressed. They also were out to attract corporate business.

The inn is grandiose, from the sweeping entry foyer and central staircase to the third floor where an enormous skylight is filled with hanging plants. Rooms range from spacious baronial chambers on the first and second floors to third-floor hideaways tucked beneath dormers. All have private baths, king or queensize beds (except for one with two doubles) and eight have gas fireplaces. The Vogts have upgraded the linens and added telephones with data ports. They also discovered a couple of old fireplaces hidden behind upstairs walls. One, in the bathroom of the Simon Cameron Room, was cleverly enclosed in plexiglas at our visit with a sign saying that it would be restored to its 1805 appearance and face a soaking tub about to be installed – the only embellishment to bathrooms that appear dated.

Creature comforts there are, but most rooms are decorated in staid blue and brown colors and retain some of the starkness of earlier times. Becky has dressed them up with fresh flowers and artworks.

She redecorated the front library/sitting room with elegant Victorian furnishings from their Washington home. David's antique graphophone stands in one corner. Tea is offered here or in the formal dining room in the afternoon.

Instead of continental, breakfast is now a full, hot affair, served on the sun porch off the dining room. Belgian waffles, eggs benedict and quiche are among the main dishes.

The Vogts are restoring the grounds, a rural paradise of lawns, woods and artesian wells, one of them flowing into a century-old pool edged in limestone blocks. The herb garden was first, and an antique rose garden was next. "They're going to be wonderful," Becky said, "but it will take a few years."

Nearby, a trout stream meanders beneath an arched stone bridge. At the front of the property is Donegal Presbyterian Church, founded in 1721 and famous for its Witness Tree, a 350-year-old oak beside which the congregation gathered in 1777 to pledge support for the new nation.

The tranquil setting is appropriate for an inn that is quiet and refined.

(717) 653-1773 or (888) 722-6376. Fax (717) 653-8334. Seventeen rooms with private baths. Doubles, $125 to $175. Two-night minimum certain weekends. Children over 14. No smoking.

Mount Gretna Inn, 16 West Kaufman Ave., Mount Gretna 17064.

Opened in 1988, this is the only B&B in the Cinderella town of Mount Gretna, a hilltop aerie of pine groves, Lake Conewago, religious campgrounds, arts and music. And it's some B&B.

It was built in 1921 in the American Arts and Crafts style by local entrepreneur

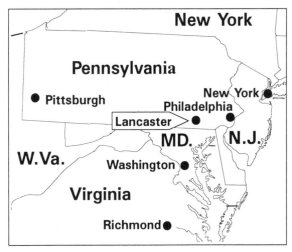

Abraham Lincoln Kaufmann, who developed the 50-acre subdivision known as The Heights. His was (and remains) the biggest house in Mount Gretna.

Robin and Keith Volker from nearby Elizabethtown purchased a turnkey operation in 1994. They had spent many a summer vacation in Mount Gretna, Keith said, and "for fifteen years my wife had been trying to talk me into becoming an innkeeper, when this perfect place became available." Keith continued as a field engineer for his own computer company while Robin is fulltime innkeeper.

The main floor is dramatic in lodge style with a fireplaced living room big enough for the occasional concert on the grand piano, two dining rooms set with china and crystal, and a great wide, deep front porch overlooking a manicured lawn.

Upstairs on the second and third floors are eight bedrooms of varying size. All have private baths and queensize beds. Stickley Arts and Crafts furniture and original paintings by local artists are featured. Most in demand is the Chestnut Suite with a Victorian bed from the Louisiana plantation owned by the former owner's family and two sitting areas amid oriental rugs, side table, dresser and armoire. Also popular are the Weeping Pines with burl maple furniture and private porch and the rear Black Walnut Room with antique poster bed made of a solid piece of black walnut and a plush chaise with matching ottoman. The Volkers call two third-floor rooms with gas fireplaces and soft canopies over the beds their romantic hideaways. Another third-floor room, decorated in an equestrian theme, includes a microwave and refrigerator.

Candlelight breakfasts are gala here. One autumn morning began with baked peaches and sour cream pound cake. The main course was angel puff incorporating four low-fat cheeses and fresh basil. Pumpkin-chocolate chip muffins were offered to finish. Other main dishes could be sausage casserole, Scottish griddle scones and stuffed french toast. Afternoon tea is served with crudités on the porch. Complimentary soft drinks, bottled water and packaged snacks are in the rooms.

For 1998, the Volkers were planning to redo two upstairs rooms, adding large baths with double jacuzzis and gas fireplaces.

(717) 964-3234 or (800) 277-6602. Fax (717) 964-3641. Seven rooms with private baths. Doubles, $85 to $115. Children over 12. No smoking.

Maison Rouge, 2236 Marietta Ave., Box 6243, Lancaster 17607.

Little wonder that the imposing – some say formidable – Second Empire Victorian structure near the main intersection in the hamlet of Rohrerstown has always been called the Red House. It's painted a shiny, wine red color with white trim and almost gleams in the sunlight. Rodney Petrocci chucked his budding career and a Victorian townhouse in Philadelphia for a different lifestyle in 1993. He bought the residence, long occupied by a physician,

from an interior design firm that had used it as a showroom. He added his furnishings and antiques to rooms that had been papered by Eisenhart as a backdrop for an advertising brochure. The decorative masterpiece is now a showplace B&B.

The foyer opens into a small but lavish parlor in which a crystal chandelier reflects in a gilded mirror above the fireplace. On the other side are a study fashioned from the former doctor's office and a cozy TV room, once the doctor's waiting room. Beyond is a formal dining room, where breakfast is served on antique china, silver and crystal beneath another glistening crystal chandelier. At our visit, the repast included fresh peaches and blueberries, banana muffins, and french toast stuffed with cream cheese and black walnuts and topped with orange sauce. Other main dishes include quiches, oatmeal pancakes with sausage and apples, and ricotta cheese wrapped in phyllo and baked with ham.

Upstairs are four spacious bedrooms, all with private baths and queensize beds. The master bedroom is dark and masculine in Ralph Lauren wallpaper and fabrics,

Imposing Second Empire Victorian structure lives up to its name, Maison Rouge.

all deep navy, hunter green and burgundy. It comes with a cannonball four-poster bed, two wing chairs in the bay window and an oriental carpet. The Garden Room, light and feminine in off-white tones, possesses a remarkable bed canopy "headboard" formed by the wallpaper pattern. Ralph Lauren floral chintz covers the bed and windows in the Elizabeth Room, which is outfitted with an oak antique bedroom set. Our favorite is the Empire Room in back, its chocolate brown walls contrasting with the cool blue sofa and comforter on the Chippendale canopy bed.

The prized antiques everywhere reflect Rod's passion for acquiring and living with fine pieces. Comments in the room diaries indicate that guests enjoy sharing them, too.

(717) 399-3033 or (800) 309-3033. Four rooms with private baths. Doubles, $95 to $125, May-November; $85 to $105, rest of year. Two-night minimum holiday weekends. No children. No smoking.

The Columbian, 360 Chestnut St., Columbia 17512.

A magnificent tiered staircase passes ornate stained-glass windows at the entry to this turn-of-the-century brick mansion with beige trim and a wraparound veranda. An outstanding example of Colonial Revival architecture, it was painstakingly restored in 1988 and converted into a B&B.

Young owners Chris and Becky Will offer four air-conditioned bedrooms, each with private bath, and a two-room suite with its own balcony. All have queensize beds, comfortable sitting areas, TVs, and fresh flowers and fruit. Three have gas fireplaces. They are decorated in Victorian or English country style, accented by paintings, crafts, needlework and quilts. Our room, though smaller than some of the others, came with a dainty window seat outfitted with lots of pillows. A rear suite offers a painted brass bed and large sitting area with sofa, plus a small adjoining room with a twin bed.

See-through fireplace and circular jacuzzi are features in cottage at The Olde Square Inn.

Centerpiece of the foyer is an antique victrola. At our visit, Chris "couldn't wait" for Christmas when it was to get quite a workout from his collection of old records. Principal listeners other than guests were toddlers Katy and Zach, whom their parents describe as "our entertainment committee."

Becky serves a hearty country breakfast. A typical repast could start with half a grapefruit, banana-nut or applesauce-raisin bread and a hot fruit dish, perhaps blueberry kuchen, for which Becky has printed copies of the recipe. The main dish could be baked egg casserole, strata, waffles or french toast. We were offered a choice of peach pancakes with peach sauce or a dish of hard-boiled eggs chopped in a cheese sauce on an English muffin with ham. Both were excellent.

In 1997, the Wills acquired a house up Chestnut Street and converted it into the **Clock Tower B&B.** It has three bedrooms, two with queensize and one with a double bed ($65 to $70). Guests have kitchen privileges and continental breakfast. It's designed especially for long-term visitors to the Watch & Clock Museum.

(717) 684-5869 or (800) 422-5869. Four rooms and one suite with private baths. Doubles, $80 to $95, May-November; $70 to $95, rest of year. Children welcome. No smoking.

The Olde Square Inn, 127 East Main St., Mount Joy 17552.

From the front porch, guests enter directly into the living room of this neoclassic residence built in 1917 by a local builder who apparently did not want a foyer. Later a boarding house, it was opened in 1991 as a B&B by Fran and David Hand, York County residents who drove by, saw the house for sale and knew it was for them. After two years of work, they were ready with four guest rooms, all with private baths, TVs and VCRs.

The largest is the Royal Room, which "we bill as fit for a king and his queen," says Fran, and is decorated with castles and such. The deep red wallpaper bears large blue flowers, and the twin beds can be joined as a king. The TV is hidden in an armoire. The Charleston Room, which Fran named for her favorite city, holds a queensize iron bed and is decorated in vivid florals with hats as accents. Its bathroom has a double shower with two seats. The Ivy Room comes with ivy and roses on the wallpaper and handpainted on the queen bed, the armoire and chest of drawers.

On the main floor are two living rooms, one with a fireplace. Beyond is a dining room elegant in beige and teal. Fran serves guests a full breakfast of fresh fruit, juice, homemade muffins and breads, and a main dish like baked sausage casserole, pancakes and sausage, or a baked egg casserole.

Out back is her pride and joy, the Enchanted Cottage, converted in 1997 from a brick carriage house. It's a large space with a circular jacuzzi tub in one corner. A three-sided glass fireplace faces the jacuzzi as well as the queensize iron bed and a sitting area with a sofabed. All the lights operate on dimmer switches. A kitchenette comes with a microwave and refrigerator. Hand-painted vines, flowers and brickwork decorate the sponge-painted walls. Thick carpeting, a ceiling fan and built-in stereo system are other attributes. The three-section bathroom has a double vanity and a shower area big enough to accommodate a wheelchair. Outside is a brick patio up against the sidewalk.

(717) 653-4525 or (800) 742-2533. Four rooms and one cottage with private baths. Doubles, $85 to $95. Cottage, $195. No smoking.

The River Inn, 258 West Front St., Marietta 17547.

They don't get much more historic than this 200-year-old house, lovingly tended by Joyce and Bob Heiserman and once featured in a Colonial Homes magazine cover story on Marietta.

The Heisermans live in half of the fourteen-room duplex house and turn over to guests the other half, including a parlor-library, tavern room and dining room. The entryway features magnificent crown molding and a painted checkered floor. All three guest rooms have queensize beds and private baths. They are decorated simply to the Colonial and Federal periods with oriental rugs, plaster walls and painted woodwork. The nicest, across the back of the house, has a fireplace, a canopy bed and two wing chairs. The largest is in front, facing the railroad track and the Susquehanna River. It contains both a queen and a twin bed.

Guests spread out in the cozy fireplaced parlor-library, well stocked with books and a TV set, and a tavern room with a reproduction bar modeled after one in Williamsburg. Here they can store food in the refrigerator, mix drinks and imagine themselves back in the 18th century.

The adjacent Colonial dining room is notable for a large pierced-tin chandelier, handmade wall sconces, braided rugs and a fireplace. Here or on the long rear screened porch outfitted in wicker, the Heisermans serve a full breakfast, perhaps herbed omelets, pancakes or french toast with bacon or sausage. The couple also have bicycles for guests to use, and Bob will take people fishing in his boat with advance notice.

The porch is a grand spot for taking in the 200-foot-deep back yard with its formal holly garden, Colonial herbs and flowers that turn up in colorful arrangements throughout the house.

(717) 426-2290 or (888) 824-6622. Three rooms with private baths. Doubles, $60 to $80. Children over 10. No smoking.

Country Gardens Farm Bed & Breakfast, 686 Rock Point Road, Mount Joy 17552.

The name here says it well, but let us embellish. The gardens are prolific, their bounty used to decorate the house and play a big role at breakfast. The 170-acre farm, primarily cattle and crops, includes a pen with four sheep, a goat and chickens. The bedrooms are homey and comfortable, and the breakfasts are something else.

Andrew and Dotty Hess, who have spent most of their lives working on the farm, raised seven youngsters in their house before turning it into a B&B in 1992. "We'd been doing B&B for 38 years," quips Dotty, "and figured it was time we were paid." They offer four bedrooms, two with private baths – one attached to the coveted Balcony Room, which comes with a queensize bed and an outside balcony for viewing the surrounding farmlands.

Quilted wall hangings are draped over the chairs and sofas in the extra-large living room. Made by an Amish woman, they're for sale, as are Dotty's floral wreaths and dried flower arrangements. The living room also holds quite a conversation piece – a photograph of the Hess family reunion, showing three generations and 213 people (of a possible 239) descended from Andrew's parents (he was one of nine children, each of whom had up to nine children, who in turn have had up to seven children). Most live in Lancaster County, and it turns out that Dotty is a cousin of noted restaurateur Betty Groff (see Dining Spots). Both grew up close to each other in eastern Lancaster County, were married about the same time and "moved up here about the same distance apart as before."

Most guests congregate in the family room off the dining area and country kitchen at the side of the house. Here is where the Hesses serve a bountiful country breakfast. The meal includes bowls of fresh fruit from the garden, baked oatmeal and a succession of main dishes served family style: perhaps scrambled eggs with cheese or cheese strata and ricotta cheese pancakes or french toast, accompanied by vegetables of the season, from asparagus and snap peas to corn and tomatoes. "Some folks go out of here thinking they've just had dinner," Dotty concedes.

After breakfast, Dotty takes any children to the "hen house pen" out back to gather eggs and feed the sheep.

(717) 426-3316. Two rooms with private baths and two with shared bath. Doubles, $65 to $75, plus $10 each child. No smoking.

Cedar Hill Farm B&B, 305 Longenecker Road, Mount Joy 17552.

Stay in this handsome 1817 fieldstone-stucco farmhouse and you're really on a working farm, out in the country on a wooded hillside beside Little Chiques Creek. Gladys and Russel Swarr (he was born here and his family has owned the property since the 1870s) raise thousands of chickens as well as corn and soybeans on 51 acres.

The five air-conditioned bedrooms with private baths are more elegant than city-slickers might expect at a farm. Each is nicely decorated with family heirlooms. One with a queensize, carved-oak bed (the bedroom suite was made by Russel's grandfather) overlooks the creek. Access to the front balcony belongs to the queensize honeymoon room, country pretty with a wicker sitting area. Its large bathroom contains a sit-down shower. A third room with a double bed is small and furnished in Victorian style. The largest room at the rear has two double beds, a full bath with a separate vanity under a skylight and a desk chair from the school Russel attended. The newest room has a kingsize brass bed and comes with a whirlpool tub.

Common facilities include a double parlor, a TV room with VCR and stereo, and a front porch furnished in wicker. Gladys serves breakfast in the original kitchen in front of a walk-in fireplace that's atmospheric as can be. She calls it continental-plus "because I don't serve eggs" – everything but, perhaps a fresh fruit and cheese

Original kitchen at Cedar HlI Farm B&B includes a walk-in fireplace.

platter, fruit cobbler, cereals, muffins and coffee cake. Baked oatmeal casserole is a recent guest favorite.

(717) 653-4655. Five bedrooms with private baths. Doubles, $75. No smoking.

The Belsnickel Inn at Morning Meadows Farm, 103 Fuhrman Road, Marietta 17547.

The driveway winds through cornfields as high as an elephant's eye. From the main road, owner Barbara Frey says, "you go three-quarters of a mile before you see a house." And it's quite a house, this stately brick edifice, with four soaring pillars and two stories worth of verandas. Not to mention room after room of "decorations" inside.

Barbara and husband Harold, who until lately worked this 240-acre farm of mostly cornfields along with nearly 1,000 acres nearby, opened their home to help put their children through college. They offer four air-conditioned bedrooms with private baths, each with queensize or two double beds, color TV, wing chairs and working fireplaces. The entire house is stylish in French country decor, except for the dining room, which is Victorian, and the country kitchen, where a collection of antique Santas adorns the fireplace year-round.

"Santas are my thing," says Barbara, especially German Santas that are called belsnickels. They became part of her B&B's name in 1997 as she moved from providing a farm-stay experience to catering to couples.

Decorations are her weakness, says this compulsive decorator whose Christmas extends from the day after Halloween into February. "I love the change of seasons because I get to change my decor." She does all the decorating herself, from a massive cornucopia of plants and vegetables on the kitchen table to the Raggedy Ann theme executed with red, white and blue abandon in Room 2.

The decoration is sophisticated and understated, except occasionally in terms of quantity. A simple canopy of white ribbon dresses the wall behind the step-up antique maple bed in the downstairs master bedroom.

The dining room table off the formal living room was set elegantly for breakfast at our visit, with all kinds of small Christmas trees atop hutches and sideboards. The fare that day consisted of fresh blueberries, granola and yogurt, bacon and french toast with blueberry sauce. It was almost like eating in the midst of a Christmas shop.

(717) 426-1425. Four rooms with private baths. Doubles, $75. No smoking.

West Ridge Guest House, 1285 West Ridge Road, Elizabethtown 17022.

Her children having left the nest, Alice Heisey decided to share with overnight guests the family home in an outlying residential section of West Donegal. That proved successful, so she and husband David turned the onetime chicken barn that had been headquarters for his contracting business into a guest house with five spacious bedrooms, a large living room with dining area and a carpeted room with a jacuzzi and exercise equipment.

This is not your typical B&B, even though it does everything a B&B should and more. The Heiseys cater more than others to corporate business and have outfitted their rooms accordingly. Each contains a queen or kingsize bed, modern bath, air-conditioning, TV and telephone. Some have private decks overlooking sections of the 23-acre farm, broad lawns, a gazebo, two fish ponds and a swimming pool.

The modern rooms in the guest house are individually decorated in different styles. The Williamsburg Room is the biggest, possessing a queen four-poster bed, cherry furniture, a blue and red color scheme, a sitting area with two stuffed chairs and a sofabed, and a whirlpool tub. The Wicker Room is in pale pinks, greens and whites – even the bed is wicker. Country curtains and spreads identify the Country Room, which has a queen and a double bed. Ornately carved chairs, fringed lamps and a crocheted bed cover mark the Victorian Room, a fantasy in teal and red. We liked our quarters in the Anniversary Suite, where the whitest, laciest kingsize bed imaginable is reflected in the mirrored headboard. Black floral wallpaper strips break up the white of the walls, mauve wing chairs and carpeting provide color, and a gas fireplace adds romance. Candles in many guises are the theme here.

Four more rooms are available upstairs in the Heisey home next door. They range from a small room with an oval bed built into the wall to a two-bedroom executive suite with two TVs, gas fireplace and a whirlpool tub in one bedroom. The main floor of the Loft Suite is all bath with forest green tiles, mirrors, double jacuzzi tub and separate shower. The upstairs loft is a knockout in mauves and greens with a large sitting area, sofabed and fireplace and a queensize bed on the other side of the room.

Bowls of assorted candies are placed in the rooms, which have such unexpected flouncy touches as little wool puffs on the coat hangers and artificial flowers around the candle bases. A refrigerator in the hallway is stocked with sodas and snacks for sale. Alice serves a full breakfast in the dining alcove off the large living room. Eggs any style, french toast and cereal were the offerings at our visit.

(717) 367-7783. Fax (717) 367-8468. Nine rooms with private baths. Doubles, $60 to $80. Suites, $80 to $120. No smoking.

The Country Stay, 2285 Bull Moose Road, Route 1, Box 312, Mount Joy 17552. Candles glow year-round in the windows of this beautiful 1880 brick Victorian

Main house and converted chicken barn face swimming pool at West Ridge Guest House.

farmhouse, and you may hear church bells chiming in the distance upon arrival. You also will no doubt be greeted by one of the barnyard cats, fifteen at last count.

Owners Darlene and Lester Landis, who have three children, raise beef and grain on their 98-acre farm. A Victorian suite in a separate section of the house has a private bath, while two other bedrooms share a bath. A hat is perched on one post of a carved Victorian headboard on the old rope bed in a room with thick brown carpeting, a bay window with frilly curtains and a window seat. Another bedroom contains braided rugs and a queen canopy bed covered with an Amish quilt. Homey touches, floral arrangements and country crafts abound in the bedrooms and in the small guest parlor adjacent to the breakfast room. "We try to make this feel like home for guests," says Darlene.

In the morning, she dons a period costume to serve a continental-plus breakfast of fresh fruit and homemade pastries, perhaps rhubarb bread, shoofly cake, blueberry buckle and coffee cake. She may add a more substantial dish like meat and potato quiche. She makes the crafts she sells in her Country Craft Cupboard on the premises, and her husband may entertain guests on the player piano in the family room.

(717) 367-5167. One suite with private bath and two rooms with shared bath. Doubles, $60. Suite $100. Two-night minimum holiday weekends. Children over 10. No smoking. Closed December-March.

Dining Spots

Accomac Inn, South River Drive, Wrightsville.

Dating to 1775, this fieldstone inn overlooking the Susquehanna across from Marietta at what used to be the landing for Anderson's Ferry is known far beyond the region for fine dining.

The historic dining room is all white with dark brown trim and a white fireplace at one end. White tapered candles stand tall on each well-spaced table, set with fanned napkins, pewter service plates and fresh flowers in pewter vases. Fine paintings adorn the walls, and window tables catch a glimpse of the river across a screened porch (everyone gets a water view when the porch is put into service in summer).

It's an altogether lovely, authentic 18th-century setting for classic French fare at prices considered high for the area. One of us started with an excellent warm salmon and shrimp terrine with a pernod-spinach-cream sauce. The other chose a salad of belgian endive, toasted pinenuts, grapefruit sections and watercress with a raspberry dressing. A small loaf of French bread, surrounded by an army of sweet-butter curls, accompanied.

Entrées range from tuna steak with tomato coulis to rack of New Zealand lamb. Good choices were grilled duck au poivre, served with wild rice and julienned peppers, carrots and leeks, and an outstanding dish of sautéed venison with duck liver mousse in a port cream sauce. Bananas foster made a worthy ending.

Prices on the extensive wine list were staggering. The teak wood bar in the small side lounge is the place for an after-dinner drink. We might have tarried had we not faced the roundabout way back to the highway – small signs mark the way in, but you're on your own going home.

(717) 252-1521. Entrées, $19.95 to $28.95. Dinner nightly, 5:30 to 9:30. Sunday, brunch 11 to 2:30, dinner 4 to 8:30.

Josephine's, 324 West Market St., Marietta.

The newest dining sensation in Lancaster County – some call it world-class – is this charming restaurant in an 18th-century building that originated as a log cabin. The log walls, beamed and paneled ceiling, gleaming hardwood floors and free-standing candles convey an elegant, historic ambiance in three dining rooms. Copper pans hung around the fireplace mantel in the oldest room add a French accent. Owner Jean Luc Sandillion chose the area because it reminded him of the rolling countryside of his native Poitiers. He named the restaurant after his wife's mother.

His chefs are known for superb, contemporary French food. People rave about the seafood gratinée, the baked salmon with strawberry coulis, the veal with morels in cream sauce, the filet of beef bordelaise and the rack of lamb, either roasted dijonnaise or sautéed forestière.

Good starters are the specialty crab cake with salmon mousse baked in a cassoulet, frog's legs provençal and an unusual salad of sautéed duck livers with a honey-sweetened balsamic vinaigrette served over mixed greens. Favorite desserts include crème caramel, raspberry napoleon and apple tart.

The lunch fare is like that which you'd expect to find in the French countryside. The choice, primarily French wine list is on the pricey side.

(717) 426-2003. Entrées, $15.95 to $22.95. Lunch, Tuesday-Friday 11:30 to 2. Dinner, Monday-Saturday 5 to 9.

Groff's Farm Restaurant, 650 Pinkerton Road, Mount Joy.

Betty Groff started serving weekend dinners in her home as a hobby more than 30 years ago for visitors who wanted to meet a farm family and taste the local cuisine. Betty, who grew up as a tenth-generation Mennonite on the other side of Lancaster County, had married Abe Groff and felt isolated without family and friends in Mount Joy, so this was her way of keeping in touch with people.

The rest, as they say, is history. They turned a 1756 fieldstone farmhouse into a thriving restaurant. They opened the high-style Cameron Estate Inn in 1981. A few years ago, they expanded their original restaurant with a glamorous sun porch and acquired a liquor license. Lately, they have converted their farmland into a championship golf course. Betty, the author of four cookbooks, is nationally known as the guru of Pennsylvania Dutch cookery.

Log cabin has been transformed into French restaurant called Josephine's.

Although housed on a farm, Groff's no longer is really a farm restaurant. Rather it is a fashionable, social place where the patrons ask after Betty and trade gossip with the waitresses. The food has taken on a sophisticated air, thanks to the lighter touch that Betty has given to the hearty dishes associated with the area as well as her son Charlie's additions of seafood and an à la carte menu to the traditional family-style menu. Charlie, a Culinary Institute of America grad, is the executive chef and manages the restaurant with his wife Cindy, although he's turned his attention to the golf venture lately.

Certain things never change, says Betty. All the coffee cups are turned up at each place setting, and the waitress asked "would you like coffee now?" as we were seated for lunch in the sun porch, pretty in peach and white. A platter of four relishes – corn, coleslaw, pickled celery and chow-chow – and apple butter for the bread arrived soon after. One of us had to try the house specialty, chicken stoltzfus, a luscious and filling dish of tender chicken smothered in cream sauce and served over flaky diamonds of buttered pastry – perfect for lunch. This came with thick stewed tomatoes and Southern-style green beans cooked in ham broth, served family style. Our other choice was a chicken and Canadian bacon melt, a bit dry and tough, garnished with chips and pickles. For dessert, we shared an excellent Amish vanilla pie embellished with butterscotch ice cream. The $13 tab wasn't bad for lunch in a country club setting.

The menu is considerably expanded at night. Most first-timers order off the family-style menu. Each person gets to choose an appetizer and dessert, but the whole table shares the main course – served family style, all you can eat. Main courses are chicken stoltzfus, hickory-smoked ham, prime rib and seafood, available singly or in various combinations. Prices ($16 to $26.50) include everything from soup to dessert. You may not want the latter, especially if you have sampled the moist chocolate cake and Betty's cracker pudding served as you are seated – "so you can enjoy these treats while you still have room for them," the menu advises.

If the entire table so decides, diners can order à la carte – much the same fare, plus broiled New York strip steak, baked stuffed flounder and broiled lobster tail.

After lunch, we perused copies of Betty's best-selling cookbooks, which are displayed in stacks here and there, and acquired some Groff's Farm relishes to take home.

(717) 653-2048. Entrées, $13.75 to $17. Lunch, Monday-Saturday 11:30 to 1:30. Dinner by reservation, Monday-Friday 5 to 7:30, Saturday seatings at 5 and 8. Sunday brunch, 10 to 2..

Alois's, 102 North Market St., Mount Joy.

The creative menu for six-course meals changes often in the old Central Hotel portion of Bube's Brewery. This is the nation's only microbrewery surviving intact from the 1800s and is now home to three separate restaurants under the ownership of young entrepreneur Sam Allen.

Named for Alois Bube, a German immigrant who built the brewery during Lancaster's heyday as the Munich of the New World, this section was the brewmaster's house. You think the hotel's brick exterior with its aqua and purple wood trim and shutters is colorful? Check out the flamboyant interior, four intimate dining rooms themed to their names (Canopy, Peacock, Dragonfly and Trophy), an upstairs banquet room with incredible handpainted walls and a Victorian bar to end all bars. Furnished like a Victorian parlor, it has an old gaming table with shelves underneath for drinks in one corner and, over the massive bar, a revolving silver ball like those from '40s and '50s dance floors, casting beams of light around the room.

Chef Ophelia Horn mixes cuisines and styles – Sam calls it all "interpretive international" for the leisurely dining experience that begins in the bar. Oil lamps flickered and New Age music played here as we had drinks and the hors d'oeuvre course, small portions of roast beef pâté with onion pastries, creole quiche and crabmeat nachos on white flour chips. We asked not to be seated in the Trophy Room, where patrons dine beneath the mounted heads of animals. Instead we were assigned to the Canopy Room, named for the ceiling shaped like a canopy. As in all the others, its walls were lavishly decorated with a mix of intricate handpainted and handstenciled art.

Our white-clothed table bore a candle, napkins and nothing else. Utensils came with each course, and salt only upon request.

The prix-fixe meal is presented course by course, with the only option being the main course (a choice of buttermilk chicken skewers or marinated shrimp skewers, one recent evening). Service was inordinately slow for a quiet night and a meal that was supposed to be paced. Gradually we got our soup course (cock-a-leekie), a mesclun salad with creamy pepper dressing and strawberry sorbet. Our main courses arrived on salad-size plates, the veal medallions with port and ginger accompanied by potatoes and the filet mignon by rice, carrots and zucchini. The blueberry cassis pie was chilled, intense and refreshing. Chocolate twigs came with the bill.

Although the meal is competently prepared and represents good value, be forewarned: the bar bill for a couple of house drinks and a bottle of wine likely will approach the tab for food.

(717) 653-2057. Prix-fixe, $26. Dinner by reservation, Tuesday-Sunday 5:30 to 9 or 10, Sunday to 8.

The Catacombs, 102 North Market St., Mount Joy.

If Alois's is the height of Victoriana, the Catacombs is positively medieval. A serf in medieval garb greets diners and leads them on a tour of the brewery as they descend 43 feet into the stone-lined vaults that were the aging cellars of Bube's Brewery. Here are round-ceilinged rooms totally lit by candles; in fact, the stone wall at the end of one room is covered with candle drippings, the better to hold steady more candles. Owner Sam Allen and his father made the heavy pine tables, dressed in white linens and set with pewter tankards and plates.

This is the setting for medieval feasts staged most Sundays at 5 year-round. The $30 tab includes wine and ale, live music and entertainment, tax and tip; everyone gasps as burly chefs carry in a whole roasted pig.

On other nights, a fairly versatile menu is offered. Entrées run the gamut from flounder stuffed with crabmeat to tournedos of beef with cracked peppercorns. Chicken satay, stuffed mushrooms and sausage en croûte are among the appetizers. Dessert could be chocolate-chip cheesecake or kahlua pie.

Upstairs in the brewery's original bottling plant is **The Bottling Works,** an atmospheric restaurant and tavern serving lunch and light fare. Interesting salads and sandwiches, gourmet burgers and bargain-priced entrées are featured. An adjacent outdoor **Biergarten** adds 80 seats to the 300 inside the brewery's three restaurants.

(717) 653-2056. Entrées, $16.95 to $23.95, Dinner nightly, 5:30 to 9 or 10. Lunch in Bottling Works daily from 11, Sunday from noon; dinner nightly from 5:30, weekends from 5.

Prudhomme's Lost Cajun Kitchen, 519 Cherry St., Columbia.

Yes, you read the name right. David Prudhomme, nephew of *the* Paul Prudhomme, and his wife Sharon opened this restaurant and entertainment center in 1997 at, of all places, the edge of Pennsylvania Dutch country. "We took a wrong turn, got lost and decided to stay," David quipped as he explained the name.

Actually, he grew up in Acadian Louisiana, worked in his uncle's sausage plant and met his Yankee wife while working in the area as a stone mason. The couple gutted the main floor of the old Rising Sun Hotel, put in a new kitchen and hung a Preservation Hall sign over the bar. The decor in two dining areas seating 90 is thoroughly cajun.

Besides renovating and hosting, the couple also do much of the cooking – "from scratch," David asserts. The recipes are their own, except for Enola's eggplant piroque, borrowed from Paul's older sister Enola, who attended their opening. Expect the usual suspects: gumbo, jambalaya, po'boys, crawfish étouffée, blackened catfish, fried or sautéed alligator platter. Plus some surprises: Sharon's chicken toes ("our version of chicken fingers"), shrimp fais do do (done three ways) and blackened pork chops, topped with homemade pepper jelly that the couple bottle and sell here. David makes a mean pecan-banana layer cake, while Sharon's specialty is sweet potato pie.

Cajun entertainment – "not the real stuff, but as close as we can get in Pennsylvania" – is offered three nights a week. You just know that everyone has fun here.

(717) 684-1706. Entrées, $6.95 to $17.95. Lunch, Tuesday-Saturday 11 to 2:30. Dinner, Monday-Saturday 4:30 to 10.

Railroad House, West Front and South Perry Streets, Marietta.

This architecturally significant, four-story Federal hotel was in its heyday when the trains stopped next door. It fell on hard times and was derelict when Donna and Richard Chambers restored it into a restaurant and tavern and fixed up the bedrooms.

Dining is in several venues. One is the Music Room, where handsome yellow and green swag curtains match the walls, oriental rugs cover the dark wood floors and a sheet of "America" is on the music stand next to a victrola. Another is the large Blue Room, stenciled and wainscoted. Beyond is the Country Room, where a collection of clocks is backlit on the mantel of the huge open fireplace that served the original kitchen. Light fare is available weekends in the downstairs **Arrivals Tavern,** where posters of the Orient Express and railroad memorabilia complement the beamed ceiling and the 30-foot-long copper bar. You also may dine on an appealing outdoor courtyard with black wrought-iron furniture overlooking flower and herb gardens. There are whimsical touches: a Victorian shoe on the wall here, two stuffed rabbits in an Adirondack twig loveseat there.

The same care extends to the kitchen, where Rick and his chef oversee a huge menu. A pasta dish called straw and hay – lobster, scallops and shrimp over spinach and egg fettuccine – is a favorite with customers. Rick also touts the broiled crab cakes, chicken moutarde, lamb chops and steak diane. Stuffed mushrooms, clams casino and caesar salad are among the starters. Desserts could be any number of flavored cheesecakes (oreo, mocha, amaretto and pumpkin-pecan), cappuccino torte and peanut-butter pie. Strolling minstrels play on Saturday nights.

The establishment also offers twelve guest rooms, eight with private baths (doubles, $59 to $99).

(717) 426-4141. Entrées, $16.95 to $24.95. Lunch and dinner daily, 11 to 9 or 10. Sunday brunch, 10 to 2.

Loreto's Ristorante, 173 South Fourth St., Columbia.

Mama makes the pastas and sauces here and her sons run this new Italian-American restaurant in a small corner restaurant with a brick facade. The owners advertise a beautiful hardwood Victorian bar, but it is the mother's pastas that draw most of the attention.

The menu is predictable. Favored appetizers are the antipasto salad and steamed clams. Pasta dishes are of the old school. Main courses run to broiled flounder, crab cakes, shrimp scampi, chicken marsala, veal parmesan, veal oscar and grilled sirloin Italiano. Tirami su, spumoni, amaretto cheesecake and cannoli are typical desserts. Espresso and cappuccino accompany.

(717) 684-4326. Entrées, $13.95 to $17.95. Lunch, Tuesday-Friday 11 to 2. Dinner, Tuesday-Saturday 4 to 9 or 10, Sunday to 8.

Diversions

All the attractions of Pennsylvania Dutch Country are at hand from a base in western Lancaster County. The tour buses head to Bird-in-Hand, Paradise, Intercourse and such; we prefer the more staid, picturesque towns of Ephrata and Lititz. Hershey and Gettysburg attractions are nearby.

A new heritage tour and map, called **River Towns and Roadside Stops,** suggests a sightseeing route to some of this area's historical sites. The map is available at most inns and attractions. The recommended route provides an overview of western Lancaster County as well as a close-up look at specific points of interest.

The Watch and Clock Museum, 514 Poplar St., Columbia.

Tick-tocking away the seconds in unison, the country's largest collection of precision watches and clocks draws visitors from across the country. Since opening in 1977, the museum has grown to more than 8,000 timepieces divided chronologically into galleries, from early pocket sundials to moonphase wristwatches. A turtle floating in oil in a silver bowl tells the time by swimming to the numbers on the side of the bowl of the tortoise clock. A mouse climbs along the numbers to show the time on the hickory dickory dock wall clock. A statue of a woman stands atop a pedestal and dangles the pendulum that drives a French clock. The masterpiece is the Engle Monumental Clock, whose creator called it the eighth wonder of the world, fourteen feet high with 48 moving figures illustrating Greek mythology and the twelve apostles.

(717) 684-8261. Open Tuesday-Saturday, 9 to 4; Sunday (May-September), noon to 4. Adults, $3.

Wright's Ferry Mansion, 38 South Second St., Columbia.

This stone house was built in 1738 for a remarkable English Quaker, Susanna Wright, whose pursuits spanned a spectrum from writing to the raising of silkworms. It contains an outstanding collection of Pennsylvania furniture and accessories in the William and Mary and Queen Anne styles from the early 1700s. Textiles, English ceramics and glass also are displayed to good advantage.

(717) 684-4325. Open May-October, Tuesday-Wednesday and Friday-Saturday 10 to 3. Adults, $5.

Veterans Memorial Bridge, Columbia. The multi-arched, reinforced concrete bridge stretches 6,657 feet across the broad, shallow Susquehanna to Wrightsville. When built about 1930, it was the longest of its type in the world. Ironically, the walls totally obscure any view of the river as you drive across. The bridge is closed one Saturday in October for the annual **Bridge Bust.** A double-decker bus shuttles back and forth the 20,000 area residents who turn out to enjoy arts and crafts, food and entertainment.

Chickies Rock County Park, Route 441, Chickies. Good hiking trails lead to the edge of the cliffs and what one enthusiast advises are a couple of the best overlooks in the East, high above the Susquehanna. Named for a native tribe that once lived here, the park won the award for "best view" in a Lancaster County magazine poll.

In 1997, the fledgling Starview Brewing Co., brewers of Chickies Rock Cream Ale, bought the old iron furnace along Furnace Road beneath Chickies Rock and planned to open a brew pub and restaurant.

Walking Tour of Marietta. Two and a half miles long and three blocks wide, this town of 2,700 grew up along the Susquehanna River. Basically unchanged from the 18th century, its eight-block center representing nearly half the town was placed on the National Register of Historic Places as a well-preserved example of a 19th-century industrial town. In 1997, the town received honorable mention for "exceptional aesthetic merit" in a Prettiest Painted Places in America contest. Two of the oldest-looking buildings we've seen, early log structures, stand out along East and West Market streets. A map with a detailed guide to 90 historic places is published by the Marietta Restoration Associates, which sponsors a popular candlelight house tour in December. There's also a walking path along the river.

Shopping. For real Pennsylvania Dutch flavor, you need head no farther than **The Country Store,** 906 Mount Joy-Manheim Road, Mount Joy. The Mennonites run – and also patronize – this place, where you'll find all kinds of bulk foods, cheeses, luncheon meats, pretzels, apple butter and Martin's handcooked potato chips, which we hear are the very best. Oh yes, you'll also find baseball cards and inspirational music tapes. Otherwise, western Lancaster County is not prime shopping territory, the eastern part of the county having cornered the market.

Mount Joy's strung-out downtown includes **Room with a View,** an interiors and gift shop, and **Elizabeth's,** an upscale women's apparel store. We liked all the handmade dolls and wreaths among the gifts and collectibles offered by Althea Johnson at her large **Country Haus Gift Shop,** located in her home at 558 East High St., Elizabethtown. In Columbia, **Hinkle's** combines a pharmacy, restaurant and gift shop of the old school. **C.A. Herr Family Hardware** is a three-story jumble where the basic hardware has been supplemented by household goods, work clothes and even a toy train display. It's been augmented by the **C.A. Herr Annex,** a co-op space that spreads antiques and collectibles through three buildings. The **Susquehanna Glass** outlet store also has a clearance center for extra savings; area innkeepers have had their B&B glasses engraved with their logo here. The **Poplar Street School for the Arts** includes an emerging crafts co-op and gallery.

Farmers' Markets. Shopping for local foods and crafts is usually best at farmers' markets, and Lancaster County markets are some of the best. Locals tout the **Columbia Market House** at Third and Locust Streets, built in 1869 and operating continuously since. Visitors can tour the dungeon underneath, originally storage space for farmers and the borough's lockup for drunks and felons during the Gay 90s. Also worth a look is the old opera house next door, newly restored as a municipal building. The market here operates Fridays from 7 to 4 and Saturdays from 7 to noon.

Extra-Special _____

Le Petit Museum of Musical Boxes, 255 West Market St., Marietta.

After David Thompson and George Haddad sold their gift shop and old country store in northern New Jersey and retired to Marietta, they found they missed their customers. Their trim green brick Federal townhouse also was overflowing with antique treasures they wanted to share. So in 1994 they opened a museum in their home. The name is a bit of a misnomer. The museum is not particularly petite and the 76 music boxes represent only the tip of the iceberg. Visitors will find such remarkable collections of New England art glass, clocks, Bennington pottery, baskets, toys, china and more tastefully displayed throughout the main floor that a special exhibit is mounted for each collection once a month. "Visitors are stunned – they're not ready for so much," says David. In the library he points out a rare American horse trough basket and a painting of Westminster Abbey that chimes. The largest Swiss 1896 disc musical box resides in the living room next to the museum's smallest music box, hidden in an album on a table. Lift the bread basket on the dining room table and it plays. Ditto for the seat on a child's chair and the statue of an inebriated man leaning against a lamp post, whistling "Show me the way to go home." The star of the collection is now a seven-foot-high Regina music box, the largest ever made in America. There's so much in this fascinating house museum that David guides up to eight people through on hourly tours, while George is at work downstairs producing their own antique music boxes for sale.

(717) 426-1154. Open March-December, Saturday and Monday 10 to 4, Sunday noon to 4. Adults, $3.

Monuments and cannons are everywhere in Gettysburg National Military Park.

Gettysburg, Pa.
Trappings and Treasures

There are two aspects to Gettysburg, the small town that embraces the decisive battlefield of the Civil War. One side is the tourist trappings that draw 2.5 million visitors annually and threaten to out-Niagara the Niagara Falls scene in the annals of tourism. The other is the rural tranquillity and sense of history that prompted Dwight and Mamie Eisenhower to make a Gettysburg farm their first and only permanent home. The two aspects manage to co-exist quite nicely, thanks in part to a semi-rural location and to the tenure of the National Park Service.

Sure, there are incursions that should not demean such hallowed ground: the domineering National Tower, the Civil War Wax Museum, the countless ancillary attractions ranging from war stores to a family fun center to a General Lee's Family Restaurant. Even the commercialism of the National Park Service's electric map and cyclorama programs is jarring. Not a particularly distinguished-looking town, Gettysburg gets downright tacky in places.

Yet there also are the treasures: the 1,432 monuments and markers that dot the rolling hills of the vast battlefield and cause Civil War buffs to choke up, the site of Lincoln's Gettysburg Address, the Eisenhower Farm full of poignant memories, the stately brick Gettysburg College campus, the rural byways that lead to all kinds of pleasures and discoveries.

The composite makes Gettysburg a classic middle American tourist destination, just as the Eisenhowers were the classic middle American couple of the post-World War II era.

The epic 1994 movie and mini-series on "Gettysburg," adapted from the Michael

Shaara novel *Killer Angels* and shown on Ted Turner's TV network, cast the town in the national spotlight and gave it a banner year for tourism.

Despite all its history, the inns and B&Bs of the modern idiom came late to a Gettysburg where high-rise motels were the rule. The first B&B emerged only in 1984. Many have followed, in town and in the surrounding countryside, especially to the south and east – the part of the area that we feature here. They make a choice base for experiencing the best that Gettysburg has to offer.

Inn Spots

Antrim 1844, 30 Trevanion Road, Taneytown, Md. 21787.

The most upscale inn in the area – indeed, one of the more upscale anywhere – is this expanding paragon of elegance twelve miles southeast of Gettysburg in the Maryland border town of Taneytown (pronounced Tawneytown).

The Antrim dates to 1844, when a Pennsylvania farmer began building the seventeen-room manor house and outbuildings for a working plantation. During the Civil War, Union Gen. George Meade made this his headquarters and watched Confederate troops move toward Gettysburg from its widow's walk. The house had been boarded up for 60 years when Dorothy and Richard Mollett, Baltimore restorationists, acquired it in 1988 to fulfill their dream of running an inn. They started in 1989 with four rooms and now have twenty, plus a restaurant of distinction (see Dining Spots), an enclosed wedding pavilion, a black-bottom marbleite swimming pool that looks like a reflecting pond, a gazebo, an Omni tournament tennis court, a croquet course and a putting green, all for people with means and leisure time.

Guests arrive to find their names calligraphed on cards with their room assignments at the entry. Fourteen-foot-high ceilings dignify the spacious common rooms on the main floor and four original bedrooms on the second. No expense has been spared to make everything perfect. Each guest room has a different personality but the same amenities – private marble baths, step-up canopy feather beds, oriental rugs, swagged valances. Crisp and pristine, they are cloaked in luxury. Men tend to favor the vast George Washington Clabaugh Room with a 19th-century half-tester bed from New Orleans. Women are partial to the Lamberton Room, pretty in white and floral prints. The footed, free-standing shower in the Meade Room is

like nothing we've seen. The posts on the 1820 Honduras mahogany canopy bed weigh 150 pounds each.

We enjoyed the Boucher Room, with a canopied kingsize feather bed, well-worn oriental rugs, a front morning porch and an evening garden porch from which we watched the sun set over the Catoctin Mountains.

What Dorothy calls four funkier rooms with

Handsome brick manor house is heart of plantation buildings at Antrim 1844.

canopies hanging from sloping ceilings and bathrooms with two-person jacuzzis now grace the third floor.

Most prized are newer fireplaced suites with jacuzzis or two-person steam showers in plantation outbuildings. The private decks beside the stream that come with the deluxe Sleigh and Carriage suites in the small yellow barn are perfectly idyllic. So is the Ice House Suite with queensize four-poster bed and chintz loveseat. Half-doors open onto the garden on one side and the pool on the other, and clouds are painted on the ceiling to complete the indoor-outdoor transition.

The Smith House, moved to the property from the center of Taneytown, contains three new deluxe suites. Top of the line is the Chamberlain, a main-floor beauty with a formal but cozy living room, a bathroom with corner jacuzzi and a glass-enclosed shower, and a step-up canopy featherbed facing the fireplace in the bedroom. Four more suites were in the works in a carriage house for 1998.

The main house is an architectural and decorative masterpiece. All shows to great advantage in the dining room with cobalt-blue lacquered walls and a crystal chandelier above a table for fourteen and in the two formal rear drawing rooms opening one onto the other, brimming with fine antiques, marble fireplace mantels and a profusion of fresh flowers. A corner of the library harbors a nifty English mahogany telephone booth that Richard found on an antiquing expedition and was just the ticket for sophisticated privacy. The library is "where everyone hangs out," in Dorothy's words, on facing plush leather sofas. That is, when they're not enjoying the formal gardens or the views of the Catoctin Mountains from the large, newly enclosed veranda dressed in plush tropical wicker.

The Molletts and their friendly staff pamper guests with a complimentary bar containing wine and champagne, turndown service with chocolates, port and a rose, and a wakeup tray placed on a butler stand outside the door of each room an hour before breakfast. Don't over-indulge on its muffins and fruit, however. Ahead lies a leisurely feast of belgian waffles, scrapple, ham and hash browns, or perhaps eggs benedict, beautifully served amidst fresh flowers, gold-edged china, silver and crystal goblets. Dorothy decorates the plates with all kinds of garnishes, just one more example of an innkeeper who cares.

(410) 756-6812 or (800) 858-1844. Fax (410) 756-2744. Eight rooms, eleven suites and one cottage with private baths. Doubles, $200 weekends, $150 midweek. Suites, $250 to $300 weekends, $200 to $250 midweek. Cottage, $225 weekends, $175 midweek. Two-night minimum on weekends. No smoking.

The Old Appleford Inn, 218 Carlisle St., Gettysburg 17325.

The town's oldest and largest B&B, this 1867 Italianate Victorian mansion is close to the Gettysburg College campus. Jane and John Wiley left careers in nearby Lancaster to move into the rear carriage house with their daughters and take over a successful B&B operation. They repainted the handsome house a stunning pale yellow and green, and added their own accessories and a musical accent.

A grand piano accents one end of the spacious, high-ceilinged living room. Jane, a classical pianist, can be coaxed into playing although she tries to defer to guests. John, a professional violinist, performs with local ensembles and offers instruction off site. Along the side of the living room are ten-foot pocket windows that slide up into the second-floor wall. Decanters of port and sherry await at the far end.

Across the gracious entry hall is a library/reception room with a fireplace. The Wileys' collections of assorted glass and decorative apples are on display here, and a portrait of Abraham Lincoln overlooks a breakfast table along one side. Jane's needlepoint samplers are hung in this room as well as throughout the inn. Her great-grandmother's collection of Haviland china is displayed in the adjacent dining room, where three more tables are set for breakfast by candlelight.

More common space is available in a small second-floor sun room, furnished in wicker and with a little TV "for those who cannot live without it," says Jane. Here, she sets out afternoon tea and snacks as well as early morning coffee.

Guests are well housed in ten guest rooms, one a two-room suite. All have private baths and six have queensize beds. Two chocolates are on the pillows, and homemade cookies are placed in each room.

The Abraham Lincoln Room, main floor rear, comes with a canopy queen bed, loveseat, antique gas fireplace and ornate armoire. Another favorite is the second-floor Judge McCurdy master bedroom with woodburning fireplace and queen poster bed. Among Jane's favorites is the stenciled General Lee Room, secluded and quiet at the rear of the third floor. It has a double bed, sofa and clawfoot tub. We liked the lavender clawfoot tub in front of the stained-glass window in the third-floor General Burnside Room. The General Pickett Suite has a double bed in each room on either side of a connecting bath. The country decor of the General Custer Room with its maple bed and a quilt wall hanging offers a break from the prevailing Victorian theme.

Given the inn's name, it comes as no surprise that apples turn up in some of the fare: Appleford french toast, apple-cinnamon poached pears and apple muffins, for instance. John, the cook, prepares everything from scratch. Guests are offered a choice between sweet and savory dishes. Eggs benedict, raspberry buttermilk pancakes and baked french toast are specialties.

(717) 337-1711 or (800) 275-3373. Fax (717) 334-6228. Nine rooms and one two-bedroom suite with private baths. April-October: doubles, $105 to $120 weekends, $95 to $110 midweek, Rest of year: $95 to $120 weekends, $85 to $95 midweek. Suite, $105 for two, $150 for four. Children over 12. No smoking.

The Gaslight Inn has been nicely transformed from ramshackle apartment house.

The Gaslight Inn, 33 East Middle St., Gettysburg 17325.

The most upscale inn in Gettysburg emerged Cinderella-like in 1995 from a ramshackle downtown apartment house. Dennis and Roberta Sullivan put the finishing touches on what they planned as "a deluxe in-town oasis" with eight custom-decorated guest rooms. All have queen or king beds and private baths, four with two-seat steam showers. Five have gas fireplaces. Telephones are in each room, and TV sets are available.

Each room is a beauty. A Louis XIV bedstead and a rococo table lend a French provincial look to the romantic, third-floor Lily Room in front. Its see-through gas fireplace is open to the double jacuzzi in the bathroom and the queensize bed in the room, where the walls are ragrolled in shades of taupe, shrimp and blue. The June Rose Room, incorporating roses on the comforter, is light and dainty. The Sweet William in the rear, rich in burgundy and cream, has a queensize brass bed with an antique Persian carpet for a bed cover, a sofabed, plus access to the third-floor balcony. That balcony is also available to occupants in the adjacent Aster Room, dressed in beige and blue with a kingsize featherbed, sofabed and chaise lounge. The handicapped-accessible Daisy Room at the rear of the ground floor opens onto a pleasant brick patio.

The rear of the second floor holds a small TV room with video library and a balcony for general guest use. Other common areas include a formal double parlor separated by pocket doors and decked out in oriental draperies that puddle on the floor, and an elegant dining room with a cherry gateleg table and four stained-glass wall hangings backlit for accents. Outside are a side porch and a gaslit brick patio beside lovely rear gardens and a fountain.

"Food is very much a feature here," according to Roberta, formerly a caterer in Montgomery County, Md. Breakfast can be a healthful, light continental affair or a full meal, always with an egg dish and perhaps crêpes with strawberries and champagne sauce. Coffee or cold beverages are served with a variety of baked goods in the afternoon.

Prix-fixe dinners for $24.50 are available to guests by reservation nightly except Sunday. The first guests to book select the menu, and drinks are BYOB. Dinner the autumn night we were there started with curried cream of pumpkin soup and a salad of mixed greens, accompanying bruschetta of montrachet cheese and sundried tomatoes. The main course was seared sea scallops and shrimp on a bed of baked leeks, with horseradish and scallion potato patties and fall vegetables. Bouillabaisse, stuffed roast pork and rack of lamb are other favorites. There's a choice of two desserts ("one light and fruity and the other drop-dead chocolate," says Roberta). She does catering out of her professional kitchen as well.

(717) 337-9100. Eight rooms with private baths. April to mid-November: doubles $110 to $140 weekends, $100 to $130 midweek. Rest of year: $100 to $130 weekends, $85 to $115 midweek. Two-night minimum certain weekends. Children over 12. No smoking.

The Brafferton Inn, 44 York St., Gettysburg 17325.

"Experience Gettysburg in the home where its history began," proclaims the advertising for this interesting inn. And history it has in spades. Built in 1786, the original fieldstone house was the first in Gettysburg's historic district. A ricocheting bullet fired during the Civil War battle left its mark on an upstairs fireplace mantel. Troops flanked the stairway as Catholics worshiped in a bedroom while their church became a hospital for the wounded. The dining room is encircled by a fascinating mural of eighteen local structures, painted by artist Virginia Jacobs McLaughlin, who lately was involved in the restoration of Mount Vernon.

All ten bedrooms have private baths and two are suites, their sitting areas equipped with pullout sofas and TVs. The sitting room of one suite on the main floor occupies what had been a small shop. A family suite on the third floor is a great space with beamed cathedral ceiling and a wall of stone and brick.

Six of the guest rooms are in a brick and clapboard house connected to the main structure by a glass-covered brick courtyard that the owners call an atrium. It opens onto the rear patio and a small garden, a pleasant refuge given that this is the heart of downtown Gettysburg. Some rooms in this house lack windows and are lit by skylights; they're small and somewhat stark in the Colonial style, with room for only one chair (for more comfortable seats, head to the atrium or the front parlor decorated in elegant early 19th-century style). The bedrooms have whitewashed walls with woodwork in Williamsburg colors, quilts, samplers and coverlets that match the remarkable stenciling. Benches and rockers, braided rugs, Civil War books, hats on racks and masks on the beds carry out the theme. A local potter made the salad bowls that form some of the sinks. We're partial to the quiet garden room in back with a carved four-poster queen bed. Upstairs in the main fieldstone house are the other four guest quarters with 200-year-old floors and walls. One of the three larger bedrooms here holds a queensize bed, as does the third-floor suite.

Tables in the appealing dining room are set with white ironstone plates and

Mural of local structures encircles dining room at The Brafferton Inn.

assorted bowls. Breakfast consists of juice, fresh fruit and a main course like strawberry or apple pancakes or peaches and cream french toast with bacon.

Innkeepers Sam and Jane Back, former education administrators in Connecticut, had the place up for sale in 1998.

(717) 337-3423. Eight rooms and two suites. Doubles, $90 to $105. Suites, $110 to $125. Two-night minimum weekends April-November. Children over 8. No smoking.

Battlefield Bed & Breakfast, 2264 Emmitsburg Road, Gettysburg 17325.

Costumed hosts, carriage rides, history programs and even artillery demonstrations come with your room at this B&B full of personality. It's located on 46 acres bordering the National Military Park and containing two small ponds, several streams and farmlands maintained as a wildlife preserve. The original 1809 section of the house "was in the midst of the Civil War battle," points out Florence Tarbox, owner with her husband Charles.

The rambling farmhouse, built of granite quarried on the property, has been expanded several times. Eight comfortable guest rooms in several sections are named for four Union and four Confederate units that fought on the South Cavalry Battlefield. They are tastefully decorated to the theme with Civil War historic art in décor ranging from Victorian lace to old country farmhouse.

Two guest quarters with fireplaces are in the original stone building with beamed ceilings and hooked rugs on the rustic chestnut floors. One on the ground floor comes with three old wooden chairs, one a potty seat. The upstairs suite has a step-up queen poster bed with comfortable chairs, a small sitting room and a large bathroom.

Upstairs in a 1971 addition is a large and airy room with vaulted ceiling and two

Monuments frame The Doubleday Inn, only B&B located on the Gettysburg Battlefield.

double beds. It's dedicated to the 1st Texas Infantry, although a cabinet display of miscellaneous collections render the Texas connection obscure until you note the artworks. A main-floor suite with a queensize bed in the main room and two twins adjacent is good for families.

You can sleep in a queen bed beneath portraits of Generals Jackson and Lee in the 7th Georgia Infantry Room upstairs in a 1993 addition. A wall mural sketches the pond outside the window. A sheer canopy queen bed and a stone wall enhance the Hart's Battery Room, while Rush's Lancers Room is light and airy with lace curtains and a matching decorative canopy.

The common areas are unusually spacious. There's a dark and historic living room with a walk-in fireplace and a TV in the original house. It opens off the main room, a huge one with a long table dressed for what looked to be a dinner party at our visit ("we set our breakfast table early," Florence advised). Around the perimeter are smaller tables, sitting areas and a quasi-office section with menus, brochures and the like.

The Tarboxes and their staff don Civil War-era costumes to serve breakfast. Fruit and pastries precede the main dish, which could be apricot cream french toast, heart-shaped pancakes or egg casserole with sautéed vegetables. Afternoon tea is available by appointment.

After breakfast, Charlie Tarbox, dressed as an artillery lieutenant, demonstrates the life of a soldier. He gives an artillery demonstration, may fire muskets or a cannon, and offers guests a ride in his horse-drawn courting buggy. Ghost story tellers and Civil War historians entertain periodically. Comments in the inn's guest book testify to the uniqueness of the experience.

(717) 334-8804. Fax (717) 334-7330. Eight rooms with private baths. Doubles, $122 to $142. Suites, $155 and $165. Children welcome. No smoking.

The Doubleday Inn, 104 Doubleday Ave., Gettysburg 17325.

The only B&B on the Gettysburg Battlefield, the Doubleday occupies a splendid location in a residential section atop Oak Ridge. On view are monuments and battle markers in front, the college campus and the town in back, and busloads of tourists going between.

Charles Wilcox, a Chicago area banker, and his wife Ruth Ann purchased the white clapboard house built in 1929 and have been redoing one room at a time. They offer nine guest rooms, five with private baths and two sharing at either end of the house. The Civil War is the theme and rooms are named after people involved, says Ruth Ann. "This was the site of the first day's battle and a lot of soldiers died on our grounds."

Rooms are rather small (one large enough only for a bed and a luggage rack) but sprightly, as the Wilcoxes have decorated for an English country look. Murals of two seasons are painted on the walls of the Loft Room, everybody's favorite, with a double and twin bed up a staircase from the bathroom. The two largest are on the main floor, the dainty Bell Jefferson Room in pink and green and the more masculine Marse Robert, with a paneled library air and an open bathroom screened by a lace partition.

The Doubleday makes up for any shortcomings in lodging space with marvelous public areas. Besides an elegant parlor and dining room, there are a rear patio, a side porch with a hanging swing and another patio, and a second-floor balcony. Civil War memorabilia is displayed throughout. Gary Gross, a licensed battlefield guide, holds forth in the parlor Wednesday and Saturday evenings with an entertaining two-hour dialogue on the war.

Accessories reflect some of the owners' several trips to England over the last few years. They also offer English tea in the afternoon or evening.

A country breakfast is served by candlelight on fine linens and china or, in summer, on the side porch. The meal includes juice, fresh fruit and a main dish like cheese strata, rum-apple french toast or blueberry pancakes.

(717) 334-9119. Five rooms with private baths and four rooms with shared baths. Doubles, $84 to $104. Children over 8. No smoking.

Baladerry Inn, 40 Hospital Road, Gettysburg 17325.

Once a field hospital for the adjacent battlefield, this restored 1810 farmhouse is nicely located out in the countryside and outfitted with the creature comforts that are important to the ratings guidebooks and their inspectors.

Ex-New Yorkers Tom and Caryl O'Gara try to provide the kind of accommodations they seek on their travels. They offer four bedrooms with private baths in the original main house and its addition, and four larger rooms (two with corner fireplaces) in a converted carriage house in back. All but one have queensize beds and come with tiled baths, light painted walls, plush carpeting and Pennsylvania House reproduction furniture.

The main inn's two-story, beamed great room is a manorial expanse with individual breakfast tables, sitting areas, wood stove and a decorative loft backed by a remarkable stained-glass window that is illuminated at night. Soft drinks are available in a help-yourself wet bar. Off the great room is a large, trellised brick patio, a good spot for relaxing and taking in the tranquil woodland scene. A common room and wicker-furnished sun porch in the new carriage house doubles as a conference center. The spacious grounds include gardens and a tennis court.

Breakfast in the great room or on the dining terrace consists of juice, a fruit plate, cereal and a main course such as french toast, griddle cakes or bacon and eggs.

(717) 337-1342. Eight rooms with private baths. Doubles, $94 to $125. Two-night minimum most weekends. Children over 14. No smoking.

The Old Barn, One Main Trail, Carroll Valley 17320.

John and Janet Lee Malpeli came well prepared for their new venture in an old barn. He was a landscaping contractor and she an interior designer in the Valley Forge area, so redoing the 1853 barn as a B&B and country inn "seemed a logical thing," in John's words.

Refurbishing the vast structure room by room, they have created quite an assortment of twelve lodge-style bedrooms, ten with private baths. Some are standard doubles; others have kitchenettes and some adjoin to become three-bedroom suites. One bedroom in the loft is light and airy with wicker furniture, floral bed covers and a green picket fence serving as a headboard. A downstairs suite offers a full kitchen, fireplace, a kingsize brass bed and a huge sitting area with sofabed and TV. The windows here are recessed into the original stone walls that are two feet thick.

The main-floor common rooms are uncommonly large: a formal sitting room with country and primitive furnishings and a large living room with fireplace and TV/VCR (in addition, an attic space is equipped with a billiards table and games). A meandering mural of area scenes by local artist Virginia McLaughlin graces a wall in the dining room, where three lace-covered tables are set for breakfast. The meal is billed as continental-plus but is really more, with quiche or omelets offered on weekdays. Sunday brings a gourmet feast – "always something exotic that nobody has ever had before," says John. "My wife likes to experiment. I'm just the waiter and I can't remember the names." Janet Lee also will prepare dinner by reservation for eight or more.

The four rural acres include a spacious rear deck, a 20-by-50-foot swimming pool and a new putting green. Youngsters like to explore the covered bridge nearby.

"The Old Barn may have been a barn formerly, but it is now a lovely country inn," said the blurb for the 1994 Pippinfest house tour, of which this was a part.

(717) 642-5711 or (800) 640-2276. Ten rooms with private baths and two rooms with shared baths. Doubles, $75 to $80. Suite, $100. Two-night minimum weekends, May-November. Children over 12. No smoking.

The Herr Tavern & Publick House, 900 Chambersburg Road, Gettysburg 17325.

Located atop Herr's Ridge, around which the Battle of Gettysburg began, the old Herr Tavern survived the battle but lost a war, so to speak, when a severe windstorm blew out its west wall in 1987. Owner Steve Wolf quickly rebuilt the restaurant and added five B&B guest rooms with shared baths in the Colonial style overhead.

Old-fashioned rooms sharing baths didn't work, he found, so a few years later the "new" rooms were upgraded to appeal to what a fellow innkeeper called "the new money crowd." All were given private baths, fireplaces and television, and two have jacuzzis.

That niche apparently worked. In 1997, seven deluxe rooms with queen beds, gas fireplaces, TVs and double jacuzzis were added above a new banquet hall. The

Tartan plaids and Civil War paintings dignify dining room at Antrim 1844.

fireplaces in the sitting areas are angled to be visible from the jacuzzi tubs in the bathrooms. Each room is furnished a bit differently with period furnishings. Some of the beds were built by a local craftsman.

In the main building, two large rooms facing the highway retain their Colonial feeling with creaky floors and period furnishings, stenciling and dried flowers. Three formerly small rooms that shared a bath have been converted into two rooms with private baths. One is small with a double bed; the other is big enough for a queensize canopy poster bed, VCR, a mirrored double jacuzzi with shower and twin vanities.

The crowning touch is the Garden Suite in the attic of the main house. Any semblance of Colonial style has been taken over by an oversize round bed, wicker furniture, gray carpeting, a mini-refrigerator, microwave and private deck, plus a day mattress covered with pillows on the floor beside the wood stove.

Guests have use of an upstairs sun porch with reading materials and card games. The downstairs sun room is the setting for a full breakfast, perhaps eggs or crêpes, fruit and danish pastries.

(717) 334-4332 or (800) 362-9849. Fax (717) 334-3332. Eleven rooms and one suite with private baths. Doubles, $90 to $150 weekends, $65 to $125 midweek. Suite, $170 weekends, $145 midweek.

Dining Spots

Antrim 1844, 30 Trevanion Road, Taneytown, Md.

Knowing diners are drawn from far and wide to this wonderfully restored plantation complex a dozen miles southeast of Gettysburg. Innkeepers Richard and Dorothy Mollett have fashioned three elegant dining rooms seating 65 in their old smoke house, summer kitchen and slave's kitchen – each a dramatic setting in brick, tartan plaid and hunter green – as well as an elegant dining room in which we first dined in the main inn. So successful have the Molletts been that they were building an addition to the smoke house with 60 more seats at our latest visit.

We enjoyed a fabulous, well paced dinner here prior to the arrival of talented young chef Sharon Ashburn, who's taken the restaurant to even greater heights. The experience begins at 6:30 with cocktails and complimentary hors d'oeuvres in the bar, where two loveseats face each other beside the huge brick hearth, and in various common areas where strolling waitresses pass the appetizers as classical music wafts through the inn. At 7:30, diners adjourn to the restaurant wing, where oil portraits of major Civil War generals watch over the proceedings and a pianist plays on weekends. Dinner is served in five courses, prix-fixe for $55. Our December meal started with an antelope picadillo burrito with papaya salsa and a green salad dressed with toasted nuts and fruited vinaigrette. Sorbet cleared the palate for the main course, a choice of wild rockfish baked with fennel and saffron, barbecued quail with hot German potatoes and braised cabbage, filet of angus beef tenderloin with wild mushroom-bourbon sauce and garlic mashed potatoes, and roasted rack of lamb with spaghetti squash and Smithfield ham.

Crème brûlée flavored with pumpkin and an apple strudel with crème fraîche completed what a Baltimore magazine reviewer called "a near-perfect dinner." A recent entry in the guest book touted "the best meal we've had west of Europe."

(410) 756-6812 or (800) 858-1844. Prix-fixe, $55. Dinner by reservation, nightly at 7:30.

Dobbin House Restaurant and Tavern, 89 Steinwehr Ave., Gettysburg.

Almost everybody's favorite restaurant locally is the 1776 Dobbin House, upstairs on two floors of Colonial dining rooms or in the basement in the stone-walled Springhouse Tavern that is most people's vision of what eating out in Gettysburg should be about.

The tavern is illuminated by candles even at noon. It was so dark we could barely read the menu, a lengthy affair with an historic theme. When finally we could see – and decide – one of us settled for an excellent baked French onion soup and a so-so spinach salad, accompanied by a glass of sparkling cider. The other was tempted by the tavern's special mile-high sandwich ($5.95), "meats and such piled almost as high as the stone walls of the Dobbin House but much straighter!" But with a choice of only two meats it seemed no bigger a deal than the No. 33 club sandwich, roast beef and swiss cheese, which also added bacon, for $5.25. There was no denying the atmosphere, although service was slow as molasses. And the roll that one of us requested to go with the salad turned out to be cold and stale and cost an extra 50 cents.

Afterward, we adjourned upstairs for a look at the main floor, a ramble of small rooms with bare tables and high-back or windsor chairs. Proceed to the second floor where you'll find more dining rooms, some with tables covered by glass. The largest called the Bedroom contains the startling sight of three tables for six under bed canopies, "wherein one can actually dine in bed," according to promotion materials.

For some, the gas-fired fireplaces diminish the otherwise authentic Colonial atmosphere. But most praise the food listed on a lengthy menu that rarely changes. Entrées run the gamut from "drunken scallops drowned in chablis" and crab cakes to veal madeira, roast duck and prime rib. Desserts run to cheesecake, pecan pie, black forest cake and warm gingerbread. The bound wine list contains affordable varieties, except for the special Chaddsford Gettysburg chardonnay at $42.

(717) 334-2100. Entrées, $16.75 to $21.95. Tavern open daily, 11:30 to 11. Dinner in Dobbin House, 5 to 9.

Upstairs dining room at Dobbin House.

Pedestal chairs in Herr Tavern dining room.

Blue Parrot Bistro, 35 Chambersburg St., Gettysburg.

The chef trained at the Culinary Institute of America and gives cooking lessons, so the food is a cut above. The menu is not all that innovative, however. And the surroundings are downright funky: a bar in front with three booths and some parrot paraphernalia to live up to the name (from a previous incarnation), a rear dining room with another bar and a pool table, and at the end of it all the kitchen, quite a hike from the front. Tables are covered with paper mats over striped cloths over white linens. Assorted lamps or candles and dried flowers in marmalade pottery jars complete the picture.

From a large lunch menu we sampled a hot chicken salad, a grilled brochette on a bed of tossed greens that left one of us still hungry. The other was more than satisfied with a delicious, hearty corn chowder and a vegetarian pita pizza, whose leftovers helped fill up the salad-eater. Each meal was served on a different platter, and ice water came in oversize glasses. Oyster crackers for munching at the bar were a pleasant extra.

The nightly specials are supposed to be the best part of the dinner menu, upon which eggs benedict, of all things, once headed the list of entrées. More recent possibilities were categorized under grills, seafood and pasta. Choices ranged from fried brown rice with beans and veggies or fettuccine tossed with pesto and vegetables to pan-fried catfish with bistro slaw, breaded chicken on creamed white beans with tomato and sweet pepper salsa, and two versions of steak.

Desserts could be crème caramel, mocha swirl cheesecake and fresh fruit with zabaglione.

(717) 337-3739. Entrées, $12 to $18. Open Tuesday-Saturday, 11:30 to 8:30 or 9:30.

The Herr Tavern & Publick House, 900 Chambersburg Road, Gettysburg.

Rebuilt in 1987, this establishment appears spanking new, in contrast with the creaky old of some of its compatriots. The biggest room is the contemporary-style tavern, light and airy with big windows and a long faux-marble bar.

The original tavern is known for a "salty past," according to old newspaper accounts. It's now the main dining room, pretty with green fanned napkins on white-over-salmon tablecloths, stenciled walls and a working fireplace. Most striking are the unusual wood and leather chairs on pedestals, which the hostess likened to those in church choir lofts. Altogether, 180 diners can be seated on the main floor and in the stone basement rooms.

The extensive menu covers all the bases and rarely changes except for specials. Recent food reviews were mixed. Dinner appetizers range from potato skins to escargots with prosciutto in puff pastry. Entrées include broiled rainbow trout, seafood creole, grilled swordfish, chicken kiev, veal parmesan or marsala, blackened prime rib and filet mignon béarnaise. Four pastas also are offered. Complimentary cheese and crackers precede the meal. The changing dessert tray might yield fuzzy navel peach pie, french silk pie and "berry sinful" pie.

Sandwiches, omelets and a few light entrées like scampi sauté and nutty chicken salad in a pineapple boat comprise the bulk of the lunchtime fare, served in the tavern. There's a pleasant outdoor patio for drinks.

(717) 334-4332. Entrées, $13.50 to $18. Lunch, Monday-Friday 11 to 4, Saturday 11:30 to 2. Dinner nightly, 5 to 9.

The Historic Farnsworth House Inn, 401 Baltimore St., Gettysburg.

This nice-looking theme restaurant, part of a complex of Shultz family enterprises, is devoted to the Civil War period. Oil paintings of opposing generals Meade and Lee hang over the fireplaces and the walls bear Civil War photos, letters and even a carpetbag in a frame. Pewter tankards and plates top the bare wood tables, dimly lit by lalique-style oil lamps. Taped Civil War music plays in the background, and sometimes it can be a bit much.

The chef adapts the menu to the period as well. Goober peanut soup, game pie, "real Virginia ham – salty and dry," Yankee pot roast, pumpkin fritters and sweet potato pudding are specialties. Baked flounder and prime rib are available for the less adventurous. The price includes a relish tray, homemade spoon and Jennie Wade breads with local apple butter and choice of vegetables. Among homemade desserts are rum cream pie, black walnut ice cream and walnut-apple cake.

Civil War period drinks are featured in the lounge.

(717) 334-8838. Entrées, $12.95 to $17.95. Dinner nightly, 5 to 9 or 9:30.

The Altland House, Route 30, Abbottstown.

Contemporary dining in an historic atmosphere is offered by the Haugh family in this landmark facing Abbottstown's Center Square. Michael Haugh has refurbished the restaurant started by his parents in 1954. The main dining room is a serene and sleek, hotel-style space with a few booths, round tables set with white linens, upholstered chairs and pinpoint overhead lighting rather too bright for our tastes.

The food and atmosphere are highly rated, drawing many from Gettysburg fifteen or so miles to the west. The extensive menu runs the gamut from meat loaf, shepherd's pie and creamed chicken with waffles to charbroiled tuna steak, shrimp scampi and filet mignon with béarnaise sauce. Oyster pie, jambalaya, chicken oscar and stuffed chicken Smithfield are among the specialties. A favorite starter is York County turtle soup served with sherry, and we liked the sound of the avocado egg rolls.

Downstairs is the **Underside Restaurant and Bar,** popular for sandwiches, burgers, light entrées and more casual dinners.

Upstairs are seven guest rooms with such modern comforts as kingsize beds, TVs and telephones, plus two new rooms with jacuzzis, one with a fireplace. They rent for $82 to $92 a night. A larger, third-floor executive suite and a rear cottage go for $125 a night.

(717) 259-9535. Entrées, $8.95 to $27.95. Lunch, 11 to 5. Dinner, 5 to 10, Underside to 11.

Diversions

The Civil War and the battlefields are the main attractions. All kinds of salient ventures, many of them commercial and/or hokey, capitalize on the theme.

Gettysburg National Military Park.
Gettysburg is virtually surrounded by 25 square miles of battlefields, where the Civil War's bloodiest battles were fought on the first three days of July 1863. President Lincoln delivered his Gettysburg Address later that year when he dedicated the Gettysburg National Cemetery. More than 1,400 monuments and markers, countless cannons and stone walls, three observation towers and 31 miles of marked avenues comprise the park. Start at the park visitor center to avoid being overwhelmed by it all. The best way to experience the site is to hire one of 90 licensed guides at the park visitor center for a two-hour tour ($25) in your own car. Most retired history teachers and Civil War buffs, they are passionate about their subject as they point out the obvious and not so obvious. You also can tour the battlefield on a double-decker bus ($12.95), one with a guide and the other with earphones for listening to a taped narration, or you can rent tour tapes for $12. A map points out highlights along a 23-mile self-guided tour that takes two to three hours, varying with stops and traffic. Bicycling may well be the most rewarding way to go. The Eternal Light Peace Memorial, the North Carolina and Pennsylvania memorials, Little Round Top and the optional Culp's Hill side tour are personal favorites. The visitor center contains a theater with an electric map program that shows with colored lights various troop movements during the battle (the 30-minute show costs $2.50). Nearby is the Cyclorama Center, where an 1884 painting of Pickett's Charge is displayed with a sound and light program inside a circular, 26-foot-high auditorium (adults, $2.50).

(717) 334-1124. Park open daily, 6 a.m. to 10 p.m. Free.

Scenic Drives. The Gettysburg Convention & Visitors Bureau details a **Scenic Valley Tour** covering 36 miles through the rolling orchard country of the west and north sides of Adams County. It also details an **Historic Conewago Tour** of 40 miles to the east and northeast of Gettysburg. Make your own tour to the southeast to include Taneytown, Littlestown, the horses at Hanover Shoe Farms, the lakes of Codorus State Park and the Stone Mill shop at Brodbecks.

Antiquing in New Oxford. East of Gettysburg is New Oxford, a Victorian town with a beautiful circle in the heart of downtown. It's a mecca for antiquers; 36 dealers within a few blocks of the circle are designated in a brochure.

Shopping. Gettysburg is full of stores specializing in Civil War memorabilia (the best is **Fields of Glory**) and tacky souvenirs. Some of the town's better shops are gathered under the **Old Gettysburg Village** umbrella at Baltimore Pike and Steinwehr Avenue. In the downtown center, good art and crafts by local artisans draw visitors to one side of **Gallery 30**; the other side offers a choice selection of books. Handcrafted jewelry and home and garden accessories are featured at

Presents. **Codori's Bavarian Gift Shop** is worth a look, as is the **English Rose Cottage** for dried flowers and pottery. South of town in Littlestown are three establishments linked in a country crafts shop tour, **The Quilt Patch, Koony's Barn** and **Smokehouse Crafts.**

For a break, stop for espresso at the **Gettysburg Coffee Company.** Healthful lunches and afternoon tea are offered at **Thistlefield's Tea Room.**

Our favorite shopping is a half-hour's drive away in Brodbecks at **Stone Mill Clay and Woodworks,** four levels with room after room of tasteful things. It's the gallery and shop of Inez and Jerry Fenster, she a potter and he a woodworker, who live upstairs in the old paper mill dating from the 1700s and whose studios and output flow through a most intriguing building. Her hand-thrown pottery and his inlaid tile tables and cupboards are showcased with the works of other artisans. Wooden spoons, Amish paintings, floral arrangements, quilts, linens, specialty foods, painted birdhouses, folk art, jewelry, decorative accessories – you name it, they've got it. The year's highlight is Stone Mill's annual Christmas show, when the shop is open Tuesday-Sunday. Otherwise, it's open Wednesday-Sunday, but closed in January.

Extra Special

Eisenhower National Historic Site, Gettysburg.

There's something altogether endearing about the Eisenhower Farm, a monument to the 1950s and the only home President Dwight D. Eisenhower and his wife Mamie ever owned. Fifty Norway spruce trees, birthday presents from each of the state Republican chairmen in 1955, line the long driveway into the 231-acre farm, which is reached by a five-minute ride on a shuttle bus leaving every fifteen minutes from the National Park Visitor Center. The rural site is very different from the Gettysburg that many tourists see; the bus driver pointed out two separate herds of deer as we arrived. The Eisenhowers bought a seven-room brick farmhouse in 1950 and added wings on either side for entertaining. The self-guided tour starts in the living room, where a guide notes that "the house was furnished in gifts" from friends and dignitaries. You learn that Ike considered this "the stuffiest room in the house," far preferring the long rear sun porch where the couple ate breakfast while watching the farm scene and had dinner in front of the TV. An easel bears a copy of the painting Ike was working on at his death. Among Mamie's collections are two gold plates from Tiffany & Co., juxtaposed with a plate she bought at Stuckey's and figurines of presidents and first ladies from cereal boxes. Ike's library contains favorite books plus U.S. Army Registers and volumes of Order of Battle Maps from operations in Italy. A glass door allows a peek into the linen closet, where most of the towels are pink, Mamie's favorite color, and monogrammed "MED" and "IKE." Past a funny little 1950s kitchen is Ike's paneled den, a favorite haunt. The self-guided tour ends outdoors with a look at Ike's brick barbecue, his putting green and a garage containing a Crosley runabout with a fringe on top, its front fender emblazoned with "Ike and Mamie" in stenciled script. Ike used the last to show guests like Winston Churchill and Charles DeGaulle around his farm. Visitors get to share part of the 1950s and the great middle American experience. Unfortunately, all the shades inside the house are drawn so you can't see the views the Eisenhowers could.

(717) 334-1124. Hour-long tours, daily 8:30 to 4. Hours and days may vary in off-season. Adults, $5.25.

Photo by Bob Lambert

On football weekends, Penn State's Beaver Stadium is focal point of the Happy Valley.

State College, Pa.

The Happy Valley

They call it Happy Valley, this long and lush valley nestled beneath Mount Nittany – a contented, rather inaccessible enclave that retains something of a Brigadoon-like innocence amidst the mountains in central Pennsylvania.

The Pennsylvania State University transformed its hometown into a burgeoning metropolis from its early years as center of the most important ironmaking region in the country. Penn State and the surrounding town are inevitably linked. Think of State College and most think of football weekends and the Nittany Lions. The university's 40,000 students equal the population of all State College.

Although Penn State is the dominant presence in the valley, the valley is more than Penn State. Its lure is so strong that it calls many alumni to make it their home. "This is a pulse point of the world, like a vortex," suggests Cheryl Bohn, who was drawn from Pittsburgh to take over one of the area's many new B&Bs.

There's much to appeal to visitors as well as residents, especially at times other than football weekends. That's when upwards of 100,000 fans turn the valley into a happy (if the Lions win) homecoming circus – the biggest by far in the East.

To the north of State College is Bellefonte, the prosperous Centre County seat, founded on ironmaking and home to seven governors. The Victorian treasures in its National Register historic district prompt some to call it "The Cape May of the Mountains."

To the east is Boalsburg, an historic village that defines the word quaint in Pennsylvania terms. It's the birthplace of Memorial Day and home to a house museum with the nation's closest ties to discoverer Christopher Columbus.

All around are mountains, streams and lakes that make this a happy place for recreation. Spring Creek is a fly fisherman's paradise. America's only all-water cavern can be toured by motorboat. Stone Valley Recreation Area is the center of hiking and boating activity.

"The Happy Valley is a 1970s thing," says local innkeeper Sara Songer. "It sounds like something we should have recovered from, but haven't."

In 1990, Garth Brooks earned $4,000 when he pinch-hit for an entertainer at the Centre County Grange Fair. In 1997, he made millions at five sold-out concerts in Penn State's sparkling new Bryce Jordan Center.

Mae McQuade, dean of the area's innkeepers, cites the change as "a metaphor for our happy valley. We are a treasure waiting to be discovered."

Inn Spots

As a university town, accommodations are booked far in advance for football and special-event weekends and may go begging at slow periods. Most rooms carry higher charges and minimum stays for special events, which include football weekends, graduation and the Central Pennsylvania Festival of the Arts.

Carnegie House, 100 Cricklewood Drive, State College 16803.

Patterned on the great country-house hotels of the British Isles, this luxurious establishment is one of the more welcoming we've encountered. Resident innkeepers Peter and Helga Schmid personally greet guests, show them their rooms and maintain hands-on oversight throughout their stay.

The German-born couple has an obvious love affair with their inn. They played key roles in its creation with principal Phil Sieg and partners, including William Schreyer, chairman of Penn State's board of trustees and chairman emeritus of Merrill Lynch, and Joe Paterno, Penn State's well-known football coach. Peter, whose career in hotel management included stints locally at the Toftrees Resort and the Nittany Lion Inn, dreamed of a place of his own as a retirement project.

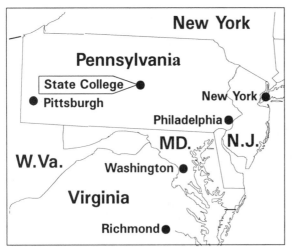

Phil Sieg owned the property, part of philanthropist Andrew Carnegie's farm, which inspired the name. He also had the vision for imparting the richness of Scottish country houses into a new architectural package that is indigenous to the Northeast, complete with dormers and cupolas.

The preliminary plans for an eight-room B&B blossomed into a full-scale inn that opened in

Carnegie House occupies tranquil location adjacent to Toftrees golf course.

1994 with 22 guest accommodations, a restaurant, elegant common rooms and a small gift shop.

The bedrooms are beauties, with an aura of spaciousness, comfort and luxury that belies their affordable pricetag. Each different, most have kingsize poster beds, sitting areas, TVs hidden in armoires, large closets with removable coat hangers and huge bathrooms with soaking tubs and walk-in showers. Woolen throws and colorful pillows are a decorating trademark. A tray of plump strawberries and a bag of homemade cookies wrapped in a pink ribbon were welcome goodies at our summer visit.

More culinary prowess was evident in the dining room. Dinner begins with cocktails and complimentary hors d'oeuvres in the richly paneled library, which is big enough for several conversational groupings at once. Peter Schmid enters the adjacent Thistle Bar, "the smallest bar in town," to mix "the biggest drinks in town," among them a mean martini. You order from the nicely varied, five-course menu ($35 prix-fixe) before entering the dining room, which overlooks the 17th green and fairways of the Toftrees golf course.

Appetizers at our visit were a stellar grilled shrimp with curry-yogurt dressing on a cucumber and melon salad and tasty slices of beef tenderloin on a potato and corn cake. Soups (the signature leek and a puree of broccoli) and a house salad followed. Among main courses, we enjoyed the medallions of lamb loin in a dijon and merlot demi-glace, paired with snow peas and a potato cake, and the grilled filet of beef with blue cheese and bourbon jus, served with roasted potatoes and grilled vegetables. Desserts were a lemon charlotte topped with wild blueberries and red currants and an assortment of Penn State Creamery ice creams and frozen yogurt.

New chef Kelly Shay added an à la carte menu for those who prefer lighter fare.

Continental breakfast includes assorted fruits, juices, homemade granola and light pastries. The Schmids go all-out on a Scottish breakfast on Sunday mornings.

(814) 234-2424 or (800) 229-5033. Fax (814) 231-1299. Dinner prix-fixe, $35. Entrées, $15 to $25. Lunch, Tuesday-Saturday 11:30 to 1:30; dinner, Monday-Saturday 6 to 8:30.

Twenty rooms and two suites with private baths. Doubles, $150 and $175. Suites, $275. $25 surcharge on special weekends. No smoking.

The Fairmount is a gray limestone house in residential section near downtown.

The Fairmount, 234 West Fairmount Ave., State College 16801.

A handsome, substantial gray limestone house in a residential section just south of downtown State College is the base for four comfortable guest rooms with queensize beds and private baths and common facilities of distinction. The residence is the home of Bonnie and Peter Marshall and their three offspring. The B&B is the pre-retirement project of Peter, State College's city manager, and Bonnie, director of development for Penn State's College of Liberal Arts. Amazingly, the couple, who travel widely in their professional lives, do all the work themselves, from preparing gourmet breakfasts to cleaning the ten bathrooms on the property.

The Marshalls opened their B&B in 1995 in preparation for the time seven years hence when their last child goes off to college. At this stage, they offer two rooms upstairs in the main house and two in a rear carriage house, with more in the plans as they become empty nesters.

The Centre County Room on the second floor bears memorabilia from the home area. The Pittsburgh Room, devoted to Peter's hometown, has a rare iron bed.

Out back are two larger, more private quarters. The Williamsburg-inspired Garden Room has a wicker-style bedroom set. The Chester County Room, depicting Bonnie's background, is outfitted in burgundy and plaids and hunting pictures. Both have TVs and telephones. Bonnie furnished all the rooms with family pieces in a mix of styles.

Beautiful oriental rugs dot the dark stained floors in the main house, where guests gather in a double parlor decorated with hunting colors and a TV/VCR in front and a more formal parlor in back. Alongside is a long enclosed stone porch with another TV and some interesting tiles above the fireplace. A rubbing of the tiles has become the Fairmount's unusual logo.

Breakfast is served in a sunny room overlooking the rear slate terrace or in a formal dining room. The Marshalls take turns in the kitchen, preparing perhaps grand marnier french toast, puff pastry with scrambled eggs and smoked salmon, sour-cream belgian waffles or baked eggs with tarragon and leeks. Abundant fresh fruit and juices come first. On weekdays, when the couple faces workday chores, one or the other is on hand to serve a continental breakfast.

(814) 237-1101. Four rooms with private baths. Doubles, $95 to $115 weekends, $75 to $85 midweek, $115 to $130 special events. No smoking. No credit cards.

Chatelaine at Split Pine Farmhouse, 347 West Pine Grove Road (Route 45), Box 326, Pine Grove Mills 16868.

Mae McQuade's beloved pre-Civil War home just southwest of town is filled with treasures, many collected during years of living around the U.S. and Europe with her late husband, an army officer. But cherished above all is the finely detailed corner cabinet in the dining room that he made for her. It holds her most precious pieces of china, from an astounding collection on display here and there around the house.

Years of entertaining military brass prompted this gracious hostess to open one of central Pennsylvania's first B&Bs in 1985 – the same year she graduated Phi Beta Kappa from Penn State after returning to college to finish her degree.

The Chatelaine has two bedrooms on the second floor with private baths, and two bedrooms on the third sharing, although they are usually rented as a suite or for one couple. "I started with a swan Christmas plate," says Mae of the Swan Room, which is the favorite. Now it is filled with swans, even to the fixtures in the bathroom and the shape of the soap. It has a kingsize bed.

In the Black Chintz room, the unusual walls are covered with shirred chintz fabric of flowers on a black background. The cannonball poster bed is queensize. A handsome chair that she got for ten cents, a stand that cost a quarter, and a Wells Fargo desk purchased in Kansas are accents. The room's hall bathroom has lavender art glass, lit from behind, in lieu of a window.

We slept in the third-floor Dawn Room, eclectic to say the least, with a king bed, TV and what Mae calls "happenstance decor." Some of the childhood clothes and toys of her four children are on display. Black and white bathrobes, to match the black and white wallpaper, are provided for the hall bath, a mini-museum under the eaves. Across the landing is the twin-bedded Twilight Room. A memorable piece here is the carved bear in two pieces. Mae's artistic daughter Amanda sketched the mural on the stairway leading to the third floor, a fantasy of childhood dreams. Her sister Delia painted the wonderful fantasy birds in the downstairs hall.

Guests relax in the comfortable living room, with its white sofas and many magazines, or at a table amid Mae's gardens on the wide front lawn. In the morning, juice and coffee or tea is delivered early outside the bedrooms. We savored our candlelit breakfast of cantaloupe with blackberries and incredibly rich meringue french toast (made with croissants) with orange sauce, served on a beautifully set table. Other dishes from Mae's extensive repertoire could be fresh fruit mélange with tamarind-ginger sauce, German plum cake, huevos verdes, Swiss omelet roll, Florentine crêpe cups and chocolate chip banana bread.

The trunk of the venerable white pine in front of the house is split, which accounts for part of the name. Mae considers herself the chatelaine, or "keeper of the keys." She turns the keys gladly, pampering guests in her charming house.

(814) 238-2028 or (800) 251-2028. www.virtualcities.com/pa/chatelaine.htm. Two rooms with private baths and two with shared baths. Doubles, $80 to $90; special events, $115 to $135. Two-night minimum for special events. Children over 12. No smoking.

The Reynolds Mansion, 101 West Linn St., Bellefonte 16823.

Charlotte and Joseph Heidt, both Penn State alumni (as are many innkeepers in this area) and now among the town's guiding spirits, bought the magnificent red sandstone Reynolds Mansion, built in 1885 by bachelor business tycoon William F. Reynolds, the town's first millionaire. They undertook several months of renovations and opened it as a B&B in 1994.

Guests have the run of the main floor with its marble vestibule, beautifully furnished parlor with a handcarved tiled fireplace, a large billiards room and a cozy snuggery filled with books and magazines that you can read in front of the fireplace. Stunning parquet floors, stained-glass windows, twelve-foot walnut ceilings and polished and intricate woodwork abound. But this is no fussy Victorian. Charlotte advises that they furnished with country Colonial pieces from their former home and Victorian pieces they have picked up in the area.

Three guest rooms are on the second floor. The choice Colonel's Green Room in which we stayed is almost a suite, with an entrance hall, a large bathroom with shower, and a huge jacuzzi tub in the corner of the bedroom. Its kingsize bed faces a working fireplace. Grace's Garden Room, light and airy with Laura Ashley fabrics, has a queen bed, loveseat, plants in the turret and a steam shower with a waterfall that pours cool water down one's back. Cherubs are painted on the ceiling of the mushroom white Louisa's Cherub Room, which has a delicate spread on the queen bed, fireplace, jacuzzi and separate shower.

Two more large rooms with jacuzzis and gas fireplaces were envisioned on the third floor for 1998. The spacious grounds include a rear carriage house that the Heidts were thinking of converting into an English country cottage.

Charlotte, one of the most calm and unflappable hostesses we have met, serves a pre-breakfast of mini-muffins and coffee on the upstairs landing. Joe makes the real breakfast for guests before he disappears into his office for his work day as a computer programmer. At the lace-covered table in the chandeliered dining room with walls of striped mahogany, a plate of eight kinds of fruit and a choice of four juices are standard. We feasted on french toast stuffed with apples and cream cheese, almost like a soufflé, with a side of sausage. Other main dishes could be zucchini frittata, quiche lorraine or a strata with asparagus and mushrooms. There is always dessert; heart-shaped sand tarts or perhaps cinnamon twists.

Decanters of bourbon and blackberry brandy await guests in the evening.

The Heidts do things up in style. For Christmas, they decorate their vestibule with an eighteen-foot-high tree so big it takes seven men to carry it in.

(814) 353-8407 or (800) 899-3929. www.nwiinc.com/rmbb. Three rooms with private baths. Doubles, $95 weekends, $85 midweek; $110 to $135, special events. Two-night minimum for special events. Smoking restricted.

Earlystown Manor, Route 45, RR1, Box 181A, Centre Hall 16828.

Built as a B&B, this substantial brick house set well back from the road eight miles east of town is the retirement project of Zane and Anne Smilowitz, both longtime Penn State employees. The vast grounds are being landscaped by Zane, whose avocation is gardening, and a farm pond was in the works at our visit.

The Smilowitzes offer four spacious bedrooms with private baths, queen beds and large closets. They are nicely appointed with traditional reproduction furnishings. A second-floor sitting area in the hall contains a guest refrigerator and snacks.

Showy red sandstone Reynolds Mansion offers deluxe overnight accommodations.

Besides family quarters, the main floor holds a living room and dining room. Zane cooks a full breakfast, his favorites being crêpes, a bread pudding casserole with apples that he likens to french toast, and an oven omelet with mushrooms, onions, green peppers and cheese. Fruit, cereal and pastries also are available.

(814) 466-6118 or (800) 644-4842. Four rooms with private baths. Doubles, $85 to $95; special events, $140 to $150. Two-night minimum for special events. Children over 12. No smoking.

Windswept Farm, 1000 Fillmore Road, State College 16803.

Sheep graze along the quarter-mile-long driveway leading up a hillside to this French country-style home in the midst of 65 acres of gently rolling hills. The expansive, whitewashed brick residence is the home of Tom and Sara Songer, who share it with guests in three bedrooms, living room, family room and dining areas.

The manicured lawn and gardens surrounding the house focus on a spacious rear patio beside a small pond. A gazebo overlooks bucolic hills and dales. Not a sign of civilization was in sight as we feasted on afternoon tea, lemonade and an amazing array of goodies: three kinds of fancy sandwiches, cheeses, cakes and cookies, all part of an area tour and tea program in which Sara participates. Enough food to feed an army (and far more stylish than army food), it was typical of the bedtime snacks that Sara plies on her guests. A guest refrigerator is stocked with complimentary beverages.

From the large, two-story-high entry hall a curved staircase leads to the sizable guest rooms sprawled across the second floor, each named for the couple's three children. At one end, Aaron's Room, once the master bedroom, has a kingsize iron canopy bed topped with an Amish quilt, a chaise for lounging in front of a panoramic view, and a couple of club chairs. At the other end, Tommie's Room is a two-room suite with a queen bed and a day bed. In the middle is Rachel's Room, cheery and cozy with a queen bed. Crabtree & Evelyn toiletries are in the bathrooms, two of which have double vanities. Carpeting is plush throughout.

Breakfast is a feast as well, and it's obvious that Sara makes good use of the 300 cookbooks in her family room. Fresh fruit, blueberry muffins, poached pears with raspberry sauce and almonds, and baked french toast were on the docket at our visit. Cheese blintzes with raspberry puree, pecan pancakes and western-style scrambled eggs with roasted pork chops are other favorites. The fare is served at a table for six in a formal dining room, which opens onto a more casual, sunny addition with a table for six more. That's because so many of their guests are parents of Penn Staters, and Sara likes to entertain entire families. "We know that may be the only chance they get to just sit and talk," she says.

The three-page information sheet that Sara puts in guest rooms is as full of wit and character as is the personable hostess.

(814) 355-1233 or (800) 450-1233. Fax (814) 355-4688. Three rooms with private baths. Doubles, $105 to $135 weekends, $75 to $105 midweek, May-November; $80 to $105 weekends, $65 to $75 midweek rest of year. Two-night minimum for special events. Children accepted. No smoking.

The Wagon Shed at Nittany Meadow Farm, Route 322, Box 311, Boalsburg 16827.

A large, lodge-like common room with kitchen, dining area and lots of comfy seating is the place to hang out or party at this nicely private B&B behind the farmhouse where Kate and Craig Kissell live with their five children.

Kate welcomes guests with cookies upon arrival and comes over in the morning to prepare breakfast for guests who stay in three spacious bedrooms opening off the common room. One day's fare might be baked grapefruit, pumpkin bread and ham and cheese au gratin. Another day could bring cantaloupe, orange crescent ring and breakfast casserole. Kate's sausage breakfast pizza, shredded wheat muffins and giant pecan sticky buns are favorites. Craig mixes in the blender a "power drink" incorporating orange juice, bananas, strawberries and vanilla.

The wagon shed, deceptively small from the front, is big enough for three bedrooms on the side and across the rear; each with queen bed and full bath and each smartly furnished. One has a private deck. Antique rug beaters decorate the wall of one, christening dresses the wall of another. Cookie molds and bobbins are on the wall of the dining area.

Although fine for couples traveling separately, the Wagon Shed with its party room is perfect for three couples wanting to get together – as is often the case on Penn State football weekends.

(814) 466-7550 or (888) 466-7550. Three rooms with private baths. Doubles, $75; special events, $125. Two-night minimum for special events. Children over 12. No smoking.

Springfield House Bed & Breakfast, 126 East Main St., Box 240, Boalsburg 16827.

Ensconced in the midst of quaint downtown Boalsburg is this 1847 structure, which derives its name from the era when the community was called Springfield because of numerous springs found in the area. A graceful porch wrapping around the Federal-Victorian house provides a vantage point for observing the passing scene.

Cheryl Bohn, a government worker from Pittsburgh, returned in 1996 to the

Lavish afternoon refreshment spread is served in gazebo at Windswept Farm.

Penn State area in which she had matriculated to fulfill her dream of operating a B&B. To a turnkey operation she added the frills, among them candies on the pillows, bathrobes and dainty décor. The five rooms are billed as suites because of their size. All have armoires, small TVs and private baths, three of which are side by side across the hall from the rooms. Three rooms occupy much of the second floor. The other two are in a rear carriage house; the one upstairs has one of the inn's two queen beds and a wet bar.

The main floor of the house holds a casual gentlemen's sitting room in what had been a doctor's office and a more formal ladies' parlor in what once was a one-room cabin.

Breakfast is served in the dining room, on the porch or in the garden. The meal begins with fruit, breads and muffins, and a tray of cheeses, cold cuts and vegetables in the European tradition. The main course could be apple dumplings, omelets or crêpes. "I like to cook on a whim," says Cheryl.

(814) 466-6290 or (888) 782-9672. Five rooms with private baths. Doubles, $85; special events, $115. Children over 12, small pets accepted. No smoking.

Starry Night B&B, 1170 West Branch Road, State College 16801.
Handsome oriental rugs everywhere are a feature of this new B&B in a 1920s farmhouse presented to Chet Esber and his bride by his grandfather, a longtime rug dealer. The house was renovated to provide four guest rooms with private baths and a living room with a fireplace. A long side porch yields a view of a stream cutting across the secluded, 40-acre property, known for its fireflies, sunsets and starry nights.

The beamed, main-floor Uncle George's Room comes with a double sleigh bed, gas fireplace and a private patio. Upstairs, Grandfather's Room has a queen sleigh bed and a full bath; Grandmother Ginny's Room a queen sleigh bed, Turkish rugs and many antiques, and Mother Betse's Room a queen bed, chaise lounge and purple tiles in the bath. The furnishings throughout might be called contemporary farmhouse, although Chet refers to them as an eclectic mix of antiques.

Breakfast is deluxe continental or, as Chet calls it, healthy. Expect fruits, cereal, yogurt, croissants, sweet breads and bagels.

(814) 234-8111. Four rooms with private baths. Doubles, $65; special events, $125. No children. No smoking.

Cooke Tavern Bed & Breakfast, Route 45, RD 2, Box 218-A, Spring Mills 16875.

"Welcome to Cooke Tavern, also known as the Money Pit," quip Greg and Mary Kay Williams of their handsome, red-brick Georgian property. The young couple have fulltime jobs as well as a hands-on renovation project that won the Centre County Historical Society's preservation award for 1995.

Theirs is a B&B with considerable charm, historic authenticity and a bathroom that must be seen to be believed.

Built in 1808 as a tavern, the house has a spectacular three-story open winding staircase, eleven-foot-high ceilings, seven fireplaces, original locks and hardware, and much hand-stenciling. The tavern room on the main floor retains its original yellow pine floor and now holds quite a collection of nutcrackers atop the piano. Mary Kay rag-rolled the walls of the elegant dining room in blue-green and gold and sponge-painted the walls of the parlor in the rear.

Two upstairs ballrooms have become bedrooms, one with a kingsize iron canopy bed and one with queensize bed, done in Williamsburg Colonial styles. They and the Peach Room with an antique brass and iron double bed share two baths.

But what baths! The principal one is a Roman bath, modeled on the ones they had experienced at the Baden-Baden spas in Germany. Complete with pillars and trailing vines, it has a corner jacuzzi with a fountain, a separate shower, a double vanity, and a small television set and refrigerator facing the toilet. Occupy this bath and it could well go unshared!

"The rest of the house was restored to the period, but there were no bathrooms here and no plumbing – only an outhouse – so we felt a Roman bath was fair game," explained Greg with a twinkle.

The dining room is the setting for a candlelight breakfast: fresh fruit, Sally Lunn bread and perhaps mushroom-cheese strata or baked french toast.

Mary Kay was thinking of converting a rear cabin into a shop.

(814) 422-8745. Three bedrooms share two baths. Doubles, $85 to $95; special events, $115 to $125. Two-night minimum for special events. Children over 12. No smoking.

The House on Top of the Hill, 1800 Earlystown Road, Boalsburg 16827.

This large contemporary ranch house, built of stone in 1989 on eleven hilltop acres, takes guests in two bedrooms furnished in country style. Each has a private bath, queensize bed and remote-control TV. One on the main floor has access to a screened porch. The other on the lower level has a private entrance and a terrace overlooking the Tussey Mountain ski area and the Elks Country Club.

Sharon Au, owner with her husband Jim, serves a full breakfast of seasonal fruits, homemade muffins or pastries, and a main dish. Her Christmas morning egg bake is a favorite.

(814) 466-2070. Two rooms with private baths. Doubles, $70; special events, $125. Children accepted. No smoking.

Rest & Repast, Box 126, Pine Grove Mills 16868.
Linda Feltman represents 60 mostly part-time B&Bs that take in guests by reservation, mainly on peak weekends. Energetic Linda knows each property well and prospective guests find her booking service a good matchmaker.
(814) 238-1484. Fax (814) 234-9890. Doubles, $50 to $100.

Dining Spots

The Hummingbird Room, Route 45, Spring Mills.
Arguably the area's finest dining is offered by Eric and Claudia Sarnow in a National Register landmark built in 1847. The couple left Philadelphia, where he was sous chef for six years at the renowned Le Bec Fin, to open a 22-seat Hummingbird Restaurant in the Woodward Inn in eastern Centre County in 1993. They purchased the Fisher House and moved the Hummingbird Room closer to State College two years later, retaining the name but expanding dinner service from three to five nights a week.
Dining is in a variety of small rooms on the first and second floors. Burgundy-linened tables are set with stunning Villeroy & Boch china. Dishes arrive under silver cloches and tablecloths are crumbed between courses.
The French menu is available à la carte or prix-fixe, $34 for three courses. The reputation of the lobster bisque, the house-smoked salmon with a lobster and artichoke salad, and the sautéed lobster with morels over homemade pasta preceded our visit. Good things also were said about the filet of beef rossini with black truffle sauce and the loin of veal with smoked veal sausage, cognac sauce and truffled mashed potato.
We were smitten by the wild mushroom ravioli and the cold seafood pâté with lobster and salmon for starters. The roast duckling with raspberry sauce and the filet of pork tenderloin with dijon mustard-tomato-cornichon sauce and a goat cheese soufflé were superior main dishes. Claudia prepares the desserts, which include an excellent chocolate-hazelnut dacquoise, orange cheesecake with grand marnier, rhubarb cobbler and kiwi sorbet. Eric uncorked the champagne with a saber in the napoleonic style.
(814) 422-9025. Entrées, $19 to $27.50. Dinner, Wednesday-Sunday from 5. BYOB.

The Gamble Mill Tavern, 160 Dunlap St., Bellefonte.
The first Bellefonte building to earn placement on the National Register, this three-story mill dates to 1785 as part of the earliest settlement in the Nittany Valley. Self-taught chef Courtney Confer and manager Jeanne Murphy started in 1986 with a soup and sandwich restaurant. Now the full-service facility heads most lists of favorite eating spots and includes a revolving art gallery.
Dining is on several levels in rooms of varying size. Tables are grouped in the cobblestone carriageway, where millstones are embedded on the floor. There are a tavern room of brick and wood, a loft-style dining area full of hanging plants, and a huge dining room for functions or overflow.
The mill is a sight to behold, both for its art and its history. The food measures up, as evidenced by our lunches of a chicken salad with honey-mustard dressing and a warm Polynesian chicken salad with avocado, melon and bell peppers in a fabulous orange-ginger dressing. Our tablemates liked their creole pasta, mesquite-grilled shrimp with black beans and roasted pepper salsa, turkey club croissant

and chargrilled vegetable pita. Cappuccino torte and an ice cream puff were tasty desserts.

At night, the setting is elegant for Courtney's specialty beef wellington, seafood strudel, grilled salmon caribe, crab cakes, chicken montrachet, mustard-crusted rack of lamb, and seared venison loin and sausage with raspberry sage sauce. The wine list is small but choice and affordable.

(814) 355-7764. Entrées, $14.95 to $24. Lunch, Monday-Saturday from 11:30. Dinner, Monday-Saturday, 5:30 to 8:30.

The Victorian Manor, 901 Pike St., Lemont.
The quaint hamlet of Lemont holds this handsome light green Victorian house with red and burnt yellow trim and a copper roof. Built in 1892, it has a variety of dining rooms, one with a different lamp on every white-clothed table, and a glassed-in, wraparound porch pretty in pink and cream. The service plates bear the restaurant's logo.

The extensive continental menu offers main courses like fillet of salmon with béarnaise sauce, dover sole meunière, chicken marsala, roast duckling with sweet and sour sauce and veal oscar. Châteaubriand and rack of lamb are prepared for two. About the only contemporary touches we noted were garden-herb ravioli with red pepper coulis and mesclun-stuffed swordfish marinated in ginger and lime juice.

The smoked seafood and hot appetizer samplers appeal for starters. The latter contains escargots, mushrooms stuffed with crabmeat, grape leaves stuffed with lamb and rice, and baked clams with crabmeat. The crab bisque is another favorite. Espresso trifle and ice cream pie are among the desserts.

Lily's cocktail lounge on the lower level is open on weekends.

(814) 238-5534. Entrées, $15.50 to $24.50. Dinner, Tuesday-Sunday from 5. No smoking.

Duffy's Boalsburg Tavern, 113 East Main St., Boalsburg.
Steaks and seafood are the specialties in this handsome stone building, a stage stop tavern dating to 1819. There's a good variety of menu choices, served in both formal and informal surroundings with appropriate Colonial atmosphere.

The extensive menu is heavy on snack food, from "porridge of the day" (homemade soup) to a "Colonial sampler" of Buffalo-style wings, potato skins, mozzarella sticks and fried zucchini. Eight kinds of burgers, twice as many sandwiches and croissants are on the all-day menu.

The tavern's specials include rainbow trout sautéed with a lemon-peppercorn sauce, grilled tuna steak with citrus butter, almond chicken and New York strip steak. The formal restaurant menu is more elaborate.

The 22-inch-thick stone walls are as solid as the day they were erected, keeping the interior temperatures a cool 68 degrees even in summer. The terrace is a favorite for outdoor dining in season.

(814) 466-6241. Entrées, $9.95 to $19.95. Lunch, Monday-Saturday 11:30 to 2. Dinner, 5 to 10, Sunday 4 to 9. No smoking.

The Tavern Restaurant, 220 East College St., State College.
This ramble of rooms along the historic walkway, beside the Centennial Pig sculpture and just below the Penn State campus, is dark and historic with wood paneling, green and white tablecloths and all kinds of university memorabilia. It's

Landmark mill is site of Gamble Mill Tavern restaurant.

of the genre that students and nostalgic alumni adore, and has been a State College fixture since its founding in 1948.

The menu, printed daily, features good old American fare with cajun and Italian accents. It lists spaghetti with marinara sauce for $7.45 and the optional Italian meatballs cost 75 cents each. Typical starters are shrimp cocktail, hot garlic and potato soup, marinated herring and escargots. Main courses range widely from sautéed sea scallops primavera, crab cakes and marlin steak with lemon-tarragon butter to blackened chicken, yankee pot roast with red wine, veal parmesan and New York strip steak. The price includes as many choices from the old-fashioned vegetable and salad menu as one wishes. The vegetable platter – also an all-you-can-eat, unlimited selection – goes for a bargain $5.95.

The Tavern's fans consistently vote it the area's best restaurant.

(814) 238-6116. Entrées, $8.95 to $15.95. Dinner nightly, 5 to 10:30, Sunday to 8:30.

The Allen Street Grill, 100 West College Ave., State College.
Located above the busy Corner Room Restaurant, another Penn State institution, is this large and more contemporary retreat with a second-floor porch overlooking "The Wall," a favorite campus gathering spot.

Where the Corner Room's ultra-extensive menu is rather basic, the upstairs gets upscale in the collegiate idiom with such main dishes as jambalaya, crab cakes rémoulade, chicken bordelaise and mixed grill. Pastas are interesting, as in tomato-vodka shrimp over orecchiette or fettuccine tossed with salmon gorgonzola.

Starters include tomato-pesto bruschetta, black bean and cheese quesadilla and a nacho platter billed as downtown's biggest and best, enough for two or more to share. Carrot cake and chocolate mousse pie are the desserts of choice.

The Corner Room serves three meals a day. It began as Jack's Road House in 1855, the year the agricultural predecessor to Penn State was founded. Both restaurants are in the landmark Hotel State College, most of whose original 70 rooms have been converted to apartments or shops.

(814) 231-4745. Entrées, $9.95 to $14.95. Lunch daily from 11. Dinner, 4:30 to 10 or 11.

Baby's Burgers & Shakes, 131 South Garner St., State College.

For a different slice of American life head to Baby's, a 1950s-style diner with friendly young waitresses who are actresses, the requisite jukebox and an antique Coke machine. No normal diner, this. It's a big place with a big menu billed as "one you can pronounce." The original one-third pound-burger goes for $3.29, most sandwiches are $3.99 and the most expensive item is a fried chicken dinner in a basket with fries and a roll, $4.99. Accompany with thick milk shakes, malts or a root beer float.

(814) 234-4776. Open Sunday-Thursday 11 to 10, weekends to midnight.

Diversions

Penn State is the focus for most visitors to the Happy Valley. The valley ranks high as one of the best places to live, with the state's highest education and lowest unemployment rates. Residents cite its metropolitan attractions amid small-town charm, with countryside and mountains nearby. Its middle-American status is highlighted by the fact that State College is home to the busiest Walmart store in the nation, so busy that it now has two.

Pennsylvania State University drives the Centre County economy and brings the world into the isolated valley. Its Bryce Jordan Center, the 16,000-seat basketball arena, draws major entertainers and quickly became the top-grossing venue its size upon opening in 1996. Beaver Stadium always sells out its 93,000 seats for football games.

Founded in 1855 by local iron tycoons as the Farmers' High School, it became a land-grant agricultural college in 1862 and much of its 5,000-acre campus consists of farm fields.

The focal point of the campus is a small area around the **Nittany Lion Shrine,** a replica sculpted in limestone of the North American mountain lion that once roamed the University Park campus. Nearby is the world-famous **Creamery,** the first to offer collegiate classes in making ice cream. Ice cream gurus Ben & Jerry got their start from a correspondence course here. People line up to buy one of the eighteen flavors, including peachy paterno, named for head football coach Joe Paterno, a Penn State icon, community benefactor and friend of everyone hereabouts.

Almost next door to the Creamery, bronze lion paws mark the entrance to the **Palmer Museum of Art,** the largest between Philadelphia and Pittsburgh. The post-modern Renaissance palace addition in 1993 by architect Charles W. Moore was his last work before his death. Many of the museum's collections, from Asian ceramics to rare coins, have been donated by alumni.

Check out the stunning **Land Grant Frescoes** around the stairwell and mezzanine of the administration building called **Old Main.** They were painted in the 1940s by Henry Varnum Poor to depict the founding, aspirations and early endeavors of Penn State. One mural shows Abraham Lincoln with a student. The shaded lawns of **Main Mall** with its double row of old elms leads to downtown State College. Across the mall is the **Earth and Mineral Sciences Museum,** with the country's largest collection of mineral art.

State College itself is known as Tree City USA. Trees line the downtown streets along the southern edge of the Penn State campus. The downtown has interesting stores and hosts the annual Central Pennsylvania Festival of the Arts in mid-July. South of downtown is Fraternity Row and large fraternity houses amid substantial residences. With 60 fraternities and 26 sororities, Penn State claims to be the largest Greek campus in the country.

American Philatelic Society, 100 Oakwood Ave., State College, (814) 237-3803. Stamp collectors from around the world visit the research library and view changing displays at the society's national headquarters. A glass case contains the membership application of the society's most famous member, Franklin D. Roosevelt. Its first executive director happened to live in State College, advised Bill Welch, State College mayor and editor of the American Philatelist journal, as he led a tour. "He was the grain of sand around which this pearl was built." The building has its own post office branch, with an antique postal window from Bellefonte. Tours are offered upon request.

Centre Furnace Mansion, 1001 East College Ave., State College.
The mansion where Penn State got its start is the only remaining building from the iron-producing industry that prospered around the wilderness site in the mid-1800s. Still visible is the stack built in 1847 of the Centre Furnace Ironworks. The community that existed around the ironworks was the first town in the region of significant size. Its co-owners and ironmasters donated 200 acres of land for a school to educate farmers, the forerunner of Penn State. Bequeathed to the Centre County Historical Society, the mansion houses original furnishings and exhibits artifacts and documents relating to the iron industry. The house and grounds are undergoing restoration.
(814) 234-4779. Open Sunday, Monday, Wednesday and Friday, 1 to 4.

Bellefonte. When French statesman Talleyrand, exiled from France during the revolution, came across the Big Spring here, he supposedly exclaimed "Quelle belle fonte." The hilly town of 6,300 has been called Bellefonte since. The underground spring, with a daily output of 11½ million gallons, is the source of Bellefonte's water supply. Now rather unspectacular, with no evidence of a fountain and surrounded by concrete walls next to the pumping station on Water Street, it looks like a large, clear pool. The adjacent Talleyrand Park at the foot of downtown is credited with the rebirth of Bellefonte. Townspeople turn out with box suppers for the Sunday evening band concerts here in summer.

Iron ore brought the town's founders here and contributed to its flourishing Victorian era. Penn State buildings bear names of Bellefonte benefactors who kept the fledgling college afloat. Its status as a county seat gave it political impact (seven governors, including one from Kansas and one from California, lived here). Several grand commercial buildings take up entire blocks of downtown, and impressive 19th-century mansions in a variety of styles line Linn and Curtin streets. The town once had five legitimate theaters, and the old Bellefonte Music Theater is being revived as a dinner theater and professional theater. The new **Bellefonte Museum for Children & Families** emphasizes local history and culture. Melady Kehm, local resident who gives guided tours, points out the barber shop run by the grandfather of the Mills Brothers. Adds energetic mayor Candace Dannaker: "We're excitement waiting to happen."

Fisherman's Paradise. One of the East's most famous catch-and-release fly-fishing areas is along a picturesque stretch of Spring Creek called Fisherman's Paradise southwest of Bellefonte. Licensed fishermen can try their luck near the Bellefonte Fish Culture Station. The area is the home of the Richardson Chest Fly Box Co., producer of top custom-crafted models.

Boalsburg. Four miles east of State College is this quaint hamlet settled in 1808 by Scotch and Irish. The cemetery here was birthplace in 1864 of Memorial Day, when three young girls started placing flowers on the graves of relatives who died in the Civil War and ended up decorating the graves of all war victims. Decoration Day grew from there. The original streets and structures around the village "diamond" remain much as they were a century ago, housing shops, B&Bs and restaurants.

Boal Mansion Museum and Columbus Chapel, Old Boalsburg Road, Boalsburg.

The 1789 mansion has been home to nine generations of the Boal family who were among the founders of Boalsburg and Penn State. Furnishings and paintings throughout the main floor testify to this well connected family's connections with the likes of Queen Isabella and Napoleon. A hallway portrait shows a grandson of Christopher Columbus posing with a globe, and an 1860 rosewood reed organ is said to be one of six in the world. The ninth-generation man of the house still lives upstairs, but had just left to go swimming, our guide advised. The tour's highlight is the Columbus Chapel at the side of the property. It ended up in Pennsylvania when a fifth-generation Boal married the niece of a direct descendant of Columbus. Mathilde de Lagarde Boal inherited the chapel attached to a castle in Spain. She transported its contents, including woodwork, artwork, confessional and choir loft, and rebuilt it here in 1909. The fascinating collection features religious artifacts, furnishings and the explorer's personal possessions dating to the 1400s. Mass is still said here every Columbus Day and Christmas for family and friends.

(814) 466-6210. Open Tuesday-Sunday 1:30 to 5, May-October; 10 to 5, mid-June to mid-September. Adults, $5.

Mount Nittany Vineyards & Winery, Houser Road, Linden Hall.

Retired Penn Staters Joe and Betty Carroll, who grew up on Hoosier farms, are literally Mom and Pop operators of this small winery downhill from their home. They planted their first grapes in 1984 on the southern slopes of Mount Nittany and opened their chalet winery in 1990. They now produce fourteen varieties and 10,000 gallons a year. The Tailgate Red and Nittany Mountain white and blush are most popular. Visitors can sample wines in the showroom above the wine cellar or on a small deck overlooking a pond.

(814) 466-6373. Open Friday 1:30 to 5, Saturday 10 to 5, Sunday 12:30 to 4.

Shopping. Downtown State College is where most of it's at, and there's more than the predictable chain stores and others appealing to university types. Everything Penn State for the Penn Stater, even a baby bottle emblazoned "I'm a Nittany Lion," is available at **Lion's Pride.** We never saw so many varieties of stuffed animals as at **The Animal Kingdom;** there's even a room with a collection representing endangered species. Handpainted furniture and adorable children's clothes are among the sidelines at **Lacey's Flower Box.** Look for gifts, accessories and handpainted birdhouses at **Beppa's** and handcrafts from many countries, some a little retro, at **Sunshine Imports.** Cute furniture for children, nice totes and aprons and engraved glassware impressed at **Initially Yours by BJ.** Check out the award-winning display windows at **Tinderbox Gifts. Tadpole Crossing** is one of the better nature stores we've seen. **Bostonian Ltd.** has offered preppy men's and women's clothing since 1957, when it opened as a men's shoe store. **Mr. Charles** goes back 56 years with ladies' apparel, though most of the stock now is quite mod. **The Artisan Connection** represents 140 artisans, most from Pennsylvania. **Appalachian Ski and Outdoors** is a great store for the sportsman. One of the most colorful shops is **Kitchen Kaboodle,** where we eyed Portuguese china, fused glass pieces (some with intricate lilacs), gadgets like a bacon press, cappuccino cups, pasta dishes and cookbooks.

In Bellefonte, **Adam & Art** is a spacious gallery, featuring distinctive art and sculptures from "Bellefonte's Creative Spirits," 23 talented local artists. **Temple Court Crafters** shows gifts from another group of local crafters. **Ruffles & Treasures** offers homemade crafts and gifts. An art teacher makes a lot of his jewelry at **Creekside Rocks & Gems.** Poetry readings and entertainment are among the draws at the **Cool Beans Coffee & Tea Shop.**

In Boalsburg, **The Federal House** offers wonderful gifts and garden accents, along with Christmas items, jewelry and boxes for the tooth fairy. **Caffe del Gatto** is an appealing little espresso bar. Collectibles and gifts are featured at **This 'n' That Emporium, The Colonels Ladies** and **Lindsay's on the Diamond. The Henley House** displays classic women's wear and accessories. Cookware and gourmet foods are among the wares at **The Country Sampler** and **A Basket Full Country Store & Gift Shop.**

Extra-Special

Penn's Cave, Route 192, Centre Hall.

A cave is a cave is a cave. Except when it's America's only all-water cavern, plus a wildlife sanctuary. Former Gov. Andrew Curtin from Bellefonte called the cave "Pennsylvania's greatest natural wonder" around the time of the Civil War. Visitors board flat-bottom motorboats for an hour-long guided tour through the half-mile-long cavern of limestone and shale carved by an underground stream. Boats go out through the underground cavern to Lake Nitanee for a glimpse of wildlife and then back through the cavern. Lit by the boat's spotlight or in color by hidden cavern lights, glittering stalactites and stalagmites appear in wild profusion. Some are clustered in formations given names like the Statue of Liberty, Garden of the Gods and the Strait of Gibraltar. Others are shaped like a buddha, an Arizona cactus, the Nittany Lion and a Chinese dragon chasing a tortoise. It sounds hokey, but isn't. It's quite a show. Bring a jacket, for the cavern temperature is a cool 52 degrees all year. Less compelling for adults but of interest to children is the 90-minute tour of the 800-acre Penn's Cave Farms and Wildlife Sanctuary. We saw Texas longhorn steers, baby bears, tiny white-tailed fawn, two timber wolves and four gray wolves. The resident elk and mountain lions didn't show up that day.

(814) 364-1664. Tours every half hour, daily 9 to 5, mid-February through December, 9 to 7 in summer. Cavern tour, $9; wildlife tour, $10.

Canadensis, Pa.

Heart of the Poconos

For all its glitz and glitter, its honeymooners and heart-shaped tubs and honky-tonk, the Pocono Mountain area suffers a bum rap. There's a section of the Poconos where the glitz image does not apply – a quieter, more old-fashioned and more rural refuge, less sullied by all that mars much of the region.

That refuge is the area around Canadensis, a dot on the map and a traffic light at a crossroads. Add its neighbors in the tight little stretch from Cresco and Mountainhome to Skytop and South Sterling. Country inns, restaurants, antiques stores, hiking trails, mountains and waterfalls are mixed in just the right blend for "unhurried leisure," as one innkeeper bills it.

Elsewhere in the four-season vacationland known as the Poconos, tourism has taken on immense proportions. Resorts, whirlpool tubs, golf courses, ski areas, souvenir shops, outlet stores, theme parks – you name it, they've got it, almost too much. Studies showed that by the millennium, the four-county region would host eighteen million visitors a year.

People come here from the cities for the outdoors – "the near country," the Pocono Mountains Vacation Bureau hypes it. But the onslaught threatens to blight the natural assets that are sought. Some of the Poconos are becoming rather like what visitors are escaping from.

Canadensis is a rural area many outsiders have heard of. Its name is taken from

the botanical name for the hemlock tree that furnished the bark for the leather tanning industry, which was the lifeblood of this region before tourism took hold. The area has managed to retain the natural attractions that originally beckoned Pocono-goers. It's a mountainous, forested retreat surrounded by three state parks, the home of the venerable Pocono Playhouse and the focus for a cluster of old country inns and new B&Bs.

Here, away from the fray, is the heart of the Poconos, the way they used to be.

Inn Spots

The French Manor, Huckleberry Road, Box 39, South Sterling 18460.

The crème de la crème of lodging spots in the Poconos is the fieldstone château built in 1932 atop Huckleberry Mountain for Joseph Hirschorn, the mining tycoon whose art collection is now housed in the Smithsonian. He modeled this house after his manor in the south of France. Later sold to Samuel Kress of department

Fieldstone château built in 1932 for Joseph Hirschorn is now The French Manor.

store fame, it was transformed in 1986 into a small country inn of distinction and was acquired a few years later by Ron and Mary Kay Logan, who had taken over the nearby Sterling Inn in 1982.

Despite its attributes, this is a low-profile establishment that's little known in the area and relatively unknown outside. Beneath its imported Spanish slate roof and beyond the Romanesque arched entry are a manorial restaurant (see Dining Spots) and six guest rooms and three suites, each with private bath, plus a downstairs lounge that looks like what it was: a huge, dark-paneled basement recreation room with a TV set in the corner.

Often kept open (perhaps to entice curious diners into a future stay?) is the Monte Carlo Room near the entry foyer. It is on the majestic side, its walls and ceiling paneled in cedar. A fancy headboard dresses the kingsize bed, two bright blue armchairs await nearby and there's a full bathroom. Go upstairs to the Florence Room with its canopied four-poster, massive dresser and elaborate bath-shower curtain and on to the spacious Venice Room. Here you'll find another ornate headboard and two armchairs, one on either side of the room.

The pièce de résistance is the Turret Suite, whose living room has a TV in the armoire and windows on three sides to take in the mountaintop view. Even that pales beside its bedroom, one floor above and again with windows on three sides. A colorful Southwest-looking quilt tops the kingsize bed, and baskets in recessed shelves provide decorative accents.

The woods throughout the house are cedar and pecky cypress. Leaded glass doors and windows, stone fireplaces, paintings, sculptures and antiques attest to the care lavished by Hirschorn and the 165 craftsmen and artisans he imported from Europe to build and furnish the structure, a task that took five years.

There's more. The main floor of the Carriage House is home to the lavish Genevieve Suite, with a canopied kingsize mahogany bed facing a gas fireplace and a sitting area with loveseat and TV. A corner of the room holds a double

Brookview Manor occupies hilltop property facing Brodhead Creek.

whirlpool tub on a platform and the bathroom contains a shower. Upstairs, the Brigitte Suite offers two more bedrooms, a living room, fireplace and jacuzzi.

The grounds contain trails for hiking and cross-country skiing. Guests also may use the recreational facilities of the Sterling Inn less than two miles away. A full breakfast is included in the rates.

(717) 676-3244 or (800) 523-8200. Six rooms and three suites with private baths. Doubles, $150 to $180 weekends, $120 to $145 midweek. Suites, $225 weekends, $175 midweek. No children.

Brookview Manor, Route 447, RR 1, Box 365, Canadensis 18325.

Built in 1911 as a summer vacation home for a prominent Scranton family on four hilly acres across from Brodhead Creek, this was renovated into a B&B in the mid-1980s and has had four owners since. The latest, MaryAnne Buckley, left the insurance business in New York to take over a going concern. She expanded and upgraded the place into one of Pennsylvania's nicer, more stylish B&Bs.

The entire first floor is given over to guests: a living room, a music corner with a grand piano in the turret next to three bowed windows with remarkable curved glass and window sills, a den and TV room, a game room, a wraparound porch containing rockers and what could be the biggest swing in the county, and a lineup of three adjoining rooms in which breakfast is served – a fireplace room, a sun porch and a picture-window room with striking stained glass.

That breakfast includes fresh fruit, muffins and perhaps french toast made with Italian bread or a soufflé of ham and eggs or sausage and tomato. Afternoon refreshments are served on the porch or in front of one of four fireplaces.

Upstairs in the main house are six accommodations, all with private baths and outfitted with country furnishings and antiques. A favorite is a side suite with a carved queensize bed, a sun porch outfitted in wicker and a spacious bath. On the third floor are two nicely renovated rooms, one with queen poster bed and corner fireplace and the other light and airy with floral fabrics and a step-up jacuzzi.

The rear carriage house had been a little used suite with three bedrooms sharing a large living room and a bath. MaryAnne reconfigured it into three guest rooms, all with private baths and two with jacuzzi tubs. They're now among the most in demand.

The main house, attractive in yellow with dark red and green shutters, is shaded by giant hemlocks. Behind the Brookview property are an additional hundred acres that guests can explore. Many taks the 30-minute hike to a hidden waterfall.

(717) 595-2451. Eight rooms and one suite with private baths. Doubles, $110 to $150 weekends, $100 to $130 weekdays. Children over 12. No smoking.

Crescent Lodge, Routes 940 and 191, Cresco 18326.

This refurbished, contemporary lodge in the Paradise Valley section offers a restaurant, fourteen upstairs guest rooms and twelve outlying cottages, some with kitchens, fireplaces, oversize jacuzzi tubs and private sundecks or patios. Run by the Dunlop family and upgraded lately, it has some of the facilities and feeling of a small resort.

The upstairs rooms, most with queen beds but a few with doubles, are lavishly furnished in the country inn style. The ones we viewed had vivid wallpapers, canopy four-poster beds with thick comforters, wicker chairs and antiques. All come with TVs, telephones and thick carpeting.

The colonial theme gives way to contemporary in seven individual and five duplex cottages, which come in nine configurations. These vary from deluxe rooms with two double beds to a deluxe jacuzzi cottage with queensize canopy bed, TV/VCR, fireplace, sunken jacuzzi and full country kitchen. One we saw was fancily decorated with matching wallpaper borders, swagged canopies and curtains around the in-room jacuzzi tub. A "jacuzzi villa" was done in Southwestern decor, with kingsize bed, ceiling fan, sunken jacuzzi tub and see-through corner fireplace.

The ultimate is the secluded mountain hideaway, a stone cottage up a pathway along a mountain. It has a queensize canopy bed, fireplace, sunken jacuzzi, country kitchen, balcony and sundeck.

Breakfast is available in the inn's elegant main-floor restaurant (see Dining Spots). The complex includes a gift shop, a cocktail lounge, large pool, "fitness trails," tennis court and shuffleboard court.

(717) 595-7486 or (800) 392-9400. Fax (717) 595-3452. Fourteen rooms and seventeen cottage units with private baths. Rates EP: Weekends in summer and winter: doubles $100 to $160, cottages $165 to $275. Weekends in spring and fall: doubles $90 to $140, cottages $150 to $275. Midweek in summer and winter: doubles $80 to $125, cottages $130 to $225. Midweek in spring and fall: doubles, $70 to $115; cottages, $120 to $225. Two-night minimum advance reservation required most of year.

Farmhouse Bed & Breakfast, Grange Road, HCR 1, Box 6B, Mount Pocono 18344.

An antiques collector and professional chef runs this restored 1850 homestead that's not like any farmhouse we've seen. Jack and Donna Asure turned the home of his parents, who formerly owned Memorytown across the street, into a B&B of character and comfort. Part of a complex of family residences on six treed, landscaped acres, this has five suites, all with private baths, remote-control television, telephones, small refrigerators and air-conditioning.

The enormous, wood-paneled living room-dining area is a showcase for the Asures' antiques and collections. "We collect everything," says Jack. That ranges from an authentic cigar-shop Indian in the entry to Stangl pottery to depression ware to shot glasses. A large TV is ensconced in the old bake oven. Guests take breakfast at a long table in a sunny corner of this wondrous room. "Donna bakes," perhaps carrot and pineapple muffins or blueberry croissants, says Jack. "I'm just the cook and bottle washer". He offers a choice of eggs, from benedict to broccoli and cheese omelet, or rum-raisin french toast, potato pancakes and belgian waffles.

The other side of the main floor contains the wood-paneled Parlour Suite with a queensize bedroom, a pretty quilt in peach and green, and a library-like living room with a stone fireplace. Upstairs is the Master Suite with a free-standing cast-iron fireplace in the living room and a queen bedroom. Outside, the farm's original ice house is now a cottage. You enter into a cozy living room, where a fireplace has been built into the now-whitewashed stone walls. Stairs lead to a balcony and a bedroom.

In 1994, the Asures divided a ranch house on the property into two suites. The Sundown offers a large living room with fireplace, a bedroom with queensize four-poster and a bath with a sunken garden tub. The Sunup lacks a fireplace but adds a full kitchen, a queensize bedroom and a combination tub-shower.

(717) 839-0796. Four suites and one cottage with private baths. Doubles, $85 to $105. Two-night minimum weekends. No children. No smoking.

The Sterling Inn, Route 191, South Sterling 18460.

This is the most with-it of the area's old country inns, and the recreational facilities on the 103-acre property give it a bit of a resort flavor. The place is as old as some of the buildings dating to the mid-19th century on its park-like campus and as new as the ten cottage suites with fireplaces and jacuzzi baths erected in late 1997.

Big draws are cross-country skiing, tobogganing, ice-skating, horse-drawn sleigh rides and an indoor pool and spa in winter and a small private lake for swimming and boating, the Wallenpaupack Creek, tennis, a nine-hole putting course and a 90-minute, self-guided nature trail in other seasons. Perhaps folks who hike the nature trails make use of all the walking sticks stowed in a milk pail beside the inn's front door.

Nearly half the 66 lodging units are in the sprawling main inn, where a large living room separates the reception area and restaurant (see Dining Spots) from the new indoor pool and bar area. Most rooms here are rather small and pleasantly old-fashioned, one with twin beds and two armchairs, others with king or queensize beds and perhaps a daybed.

Definitely worth the extra tab are the inn's four deluxe suites and the eight Victorian fireplace suites in converted buildings out back by the creek. Our corner suite on the inn's second floor was a nice surprise with two large rooms, two closets, television and lots of space to spread out. A mix of fancy French provincial off-white furniture blended with modern tweedy sofa and chairs, and two more chairs were available in a reading area with windows on three sides beside the kingsize bed in the bedroom.

The road noise that was the only disturbance here is not a problem in the eight fireplace suites in the Nearbrook and Wayside buildings out back. You'd never guess these deluxe, carpeted rooms with franklin stoves, queensize four-posters and decks or balconies onto the babbling brook started as garages.

The ultimate quarters are the ten new fireplaced suites in five duplex buildings, each with queen bed, sofabed, jacuzzi, kitchenette and outside deck. The rest of

Fresh snow provides mantel of white around main house at The Pine Knob Inn.

the accommodations include a new suite with fireplace and jacuzzi and standard rooms in an old lodge and guest house and four cottages of one or two bedrooms.

Three meals a day are served in the dining room. The day's breakfast choices are recited by the waitress and yield such dishes as eggs any style with local ham or sausage, pancakes and corned-beef hash.

(717) 676-3311 or (800) 523-8200. Fax (717) 676-9786. Fifty-six rooms, suites and cottages with private baths. Doubles, $120 weekends, $100 midweek. Cottages and suites, $150 to $200 weekends, $130 to $170 midweek. Add $40 for MAP.

The Pine Knob Inn, Route 447, Canadensis 18325.

New owners are at the helm of this 1847 inn that occasionally shows its age. Cheryl and John Garman from Harrisburg have redecorated a few rooms, added a wedding gazebo and installed in a corner of the dining room an unusual "dynamic wine rack" – so named because it's always changing.

The L-shaped common room in this homey inn is a real common room. It's full of Victorian and traditional sitting areas, with a Christmas village of ceramic houses on the fireplace mantel lighted year-round. People asked the owners not to take them down, so the holiday decorations remained up – slightly camouflaged by flowers interspersed in summer. Walls here and in other common areas are hung with artworks painted by participants in the annual art workshops the inn sponsors.

There are seventeen guest rooms (nine in the main inn and eight in the North and South guest houses out back), plus a two-room "honeymoon bungalow" for two. All have private baths, and most have brass, cherry high back or oak beds covered with cheery quilts. Most beds are twins or doubles, but the twins in two rooms can be joined as kings. Carpeting covers the floors, and rooms have accents of little wreaths, a stenciled stool here and poof curtains there. Furnishings include collectibles and pieces from of antique glass. Bathroom amenities amount to clean towels and a little bar of Ivory soap, plus the occasional quilted shower curtain. The clientele approves. "People they feel like they're in Grandma's house, it's so comfortable," reports John.

White Adirondack chairs are scattered about the lawn. The property includes a tennis court, volleyball court, a 60-by-40-foot swimming pool and a pagoda between the pool and Brodhead Creek, a mecca for fly-fishermen.

(717) 595-2532 or (800) 426-1460. Fax (717) 595-6429. Seventeen rooms and a cottage with private baths. Doubles, $120 to $140. Cottage, $150. Two-night minimum on weekends.

Skytop Lodge, Route 390, Skytop 18357.

Off by itself just north of Canadensis is this grand mountaintop resort built in 1928, commanding 5,500 acres of private woodlands, lakes and hills and a devoted repeat clientele. It's a favorite for conferences (one of us attended a newspaper seminar here a decade ago and found it perfect for the purpose, but not the kind of place to which we'd return for a tête-à-tête).

Skytop has all the sports facilities you could want, from a golf course by the lake to its own ski slope, a toboggan run, indoor and outdoor pools and a fitness center. Three meals a day, served in formal dining rooms, are included in the rates.

The tiered, angled fieldstone hotel contains 130 rooms and mini-suites. There also are 40 guest bedrooms in ten cottages – four bedrooms each with porches, refrigerators and laundry facilities. Half the cottage rooms have queen beds and the rest are twins. Thirty-one of the hotel rooms contain twin beds; 39 rooms have queen beds and 31, kingsize. Twenty mini-suites have king or queen beds and sitting areas, while four VIP suites come with a separate bedroom and parlor.

(717) 595-7401 or (800) 345-7759. Fax (717) 595-9618. One hundred five rooms, 24 suites and 40 cottage units with private baths. Rates AP: May-October: doubles and cottages $330 to $370 weekends, $315 to $335 midweek; suites, $460 to $540 weekends, $410 to $475 midweek. November-April: doubles and cottages $305 to $360 weekends, $215 to $270 midweek; suites, $420 to $495 weekends, $325 to $430 midweek. Two-night minimum on weekends.

Dining Spots

Homestead Inn, Sandspring Drive, Cresco.

Consistently good food in pleasant surroundings is the hallmark of the Homestead, established in 1980 and, at our visit, about to gain a view of a new manmade lake in back. Philadelphia caterers Drew and Susan Price converted a large barn-like skeleton into an attractive restaurant that's country casual. Three dining rooms in prevailing brown and white seat nearly 100 amid barnwood or redwood walls, an occasional aquarium, starched green floral linens, votive candles and Wyeth prints on the walls.

The Homestead gained a measure of fame when TV producer Woody Fraser, a Poconos vacationer and fan of the Homestead, featured the owners on ABC's Home show.

Susan oversees the kitchen, from which emanate such entrées as crabmeat-stuffed brook trout en croûte, scallops chardonnay, sautéed chicken wrapped with prosciutto, roasted pork tenderloin with peach sauce, filet mignon au poivre and rack of lamb in pesto sauce. Hot biscuits and breads, tossed salad and fresh vegetables accompany.

Among starters are snapper soup, escargots in puff pastry and smoked mozzarella with tomatoes and basil. Raspberry cheesecake, apple crisp, rum cake and

Artworks and hanging plants adorn rear dining room at Homestead Inn.

chocolate mousse are favorite desserts. The well-chosen wine list is priced from the teens to the $40s.

(717) 595-3171. Entrées, $18.25 to $29.95. Dinner, Monday-Saturday 5 to 9, Sunday 4 to 9. Closed Monday, September-May.

Pump House Inn, Sky Top Road, Canadensis.

The red pump in the original 1842 well outside the entrance provides the name for this elegant bastion of special-occasion dining. The imposing foyer inside is like a library, where proprietor John Keeney takes telephone reservations at an old desk and greets patrons upon arrival. He leads them to the Pub Bar, dark and intimate and atmospheric as can be, or to a couple of small, dark dining rooms brightened with pink linens, the front porch whose four tables are highly prized or the far grotto room with its waterfall wall and all kinds of nooks and alcoves. Trenton oyster crackers, flickering oil lamps and place settings of three forks and three spoons each are on the tables.

It's a sumptuous backdrop for French-American fare that has been pleasing a well-heeled clientele since the early 1960s. The short menu is supplemented by daily blackboard specials. For starters, you might try the sensational baked pecan brie over warm spinach, beer-batter shrimp with pungent fruit sauce or poached shrimp and scallops on a bed of grilled eggplant and tomatoes with a ginger-lime sauce.

Main courses range from chicken breast topped with grilled tomatoes, smoked mozzarella and tomato-basil sauce to rack of lamb. The poached salmon could be stuffed with grilled scallops and crabmeat, the basil shrimp served with garlic on a bed of pasta and the veal sautéed with shrimp and a mustard-marsala sauce. There's no wine list; instead the wines are displayed on racks between dining rooms. Patrons view the array, affordably priced from the mid-teens and up, and pick their choice.

To finish with a flourish, how about chocolate mousse, raspberry crème brûlée or white chocolate cheesecake?

The Pump House also offers three basic guest rooms above the restaurant, as well as four more modern rooms with queen beds and reproduction furniture in the rear Carriage House. A guest cottage with living room, sun porch and terrace serves two to four people. Continental breakfast is included in the rates.

(717) 595-7501. Entrées, $14.95 to $25.95. Dinner, Tuesday-Saturday 5 to 9, Sunday 2:30 to 8:30. Closed Monday-Wednesday, December-April. Doubles, $65 to $85.

The French Manor, Huckleberry Road, South Sterling.

The dining room in what was the great room in Joseph Hirschorn's manor home has 40-foot-high peaked and beamed ceilings and massive fireplaces at either end, each with a gigantic grape wreath above. The setting reminded us of a certain lovely pousada at which we once dined in Portugal.

A plush beige carpet with borders of burgundy and green covers the floor, the linens are pink and green, and a bouquet of carnations and baby's breath was on each table at our visit. From picture windows on one side of the room, you can see the slate terrace and mountains beyond. Oriental screens and lamps and a mix of chairs from ladderback to French provincial complete a look that's rather sophisticated for the area. Classical music adds to the splendid setting,

A pianist plays at night, when the haute French menu lists such appetizers as smoked trout, pâté of foie gras in brioche, escargots bourguignonne and a timbale of morel mushrooms and chicken. A green salad with balsamic vinaigrette and a sorbet intermezzo are included in the price of the entrées. Among the choices are red snapper on a bed of aromatic vegetables, roast pheasant on a puree of grapes with glazed apples and crème fraîche, grilled veal chop with a ragout of varietal mushrooms, and dijon-crusted rack of lamb on an escoffier mint sauce. The execution seems to live up to the pretensions of its prose, at least at our extravagant lunch (since discontinued). Desserts could be raspberry linzer torte, chocolate mousse, apple custard torte and cannoli. The wine list is short and expensive.

(717) 676-3244 or (800) 523-8200. Entrées, $19.95 to $32. Dinner nightly, 6 to 9; weekends only, November-April. Jackets required. No smoking.

Crescent Lodge, Routes 940 and 191, Cresco.

Here's a glamorous setting for dining in two large rooms with heavy leather and wood armchairs at well-spaced tables and artworks hung in gilt frames. A pianist plays on weekends, the service is polished and the ambiance is perfect for a special occasion, the kind where châteaubriand bouquetière is flourished tableside for two.

Chef Wayne Dunlop, representing the third generation of Dunlops at the family-owned lodge, oversees an ambitious continental menu. Here you'll find almost anything from broiled brook trout and Long Island duckling with orange sauce to bouillabaisse, veal oscar and beef wellington.

A complimentary bowl of marinated vegetables starts the meal. Appetizers include clams casino, lobster ravioli, veal cannelloni and batter-dipped alligator strips with a chilled curry dipping sauce. Strawberry ice cream pie, coupe romanoff and peach melba are signature desserts. The wine list is better than the area's norm.

(717) 595-7486 or (800) 392-9400. Entrées, $16.95 to $22.95. Dinner nightly, 5:30 to 9 or 10, Sunday 3 to 8. Closed Monday and Tuesday, November-April.

The Sterling Inn, Route 191, South Sterling.

A stone fireplace helps divide into two intimate sections the long dining room at this inn hidden behind towering rhododendron bushes. It's pretty in pink and white, but rather too brightly lit for intimate dining and with tables rather too close for comfort on busy nights.

The changing menu is printed daily. Among appetizers, we tried the chicken liver pâté with crackers and mussels on the half shell with tarragon and tomatoes. The tossed salad was mostly iceberg lettuce, but this lapse was redeemed by the savoyard potatoes and the excellent mix of sautéed snow peas and yellow squash that accompanied our prime rib with dijon cream sauce and broiled loin lamb chops with a homemade tomato chutney. A $19 Mirassou cabernet was one of the cheaper selections from the short wine list. Other entrée choices might include poached salmon on a five-onion sauce, roast pork loin in a bourbon pan sauce and osso buco that innkeeper Ron Logan calls "awesome buco." A perfect key lime pie was an excellent choice from desserts that covered the gamut from tapioca pudding and rainbow sherbet to walnut pie and honey cheesecake with raspberry topping.

Rockers line veranda of The Sterling Inn.

Although there's quite a range in prices on the menu given the public, all items on the same but unpriced menu are available to house guests on the MAP plan without surcharges – a rare policy that we find refreshing. Innkeepers Ron and Mary Kay Logan know how to keep their guests happy.

(717) 676-3311 or (800) 523-8200. Entrées, $15.75 to $22. Lunch daily, noon to 1:30. Dinner, 6 to 8:30. No smoking.

The Pine Knob Inn, Route 447, Canadensis.

The menu arrives in an old book in this inn's 65-seat dining room, sprightly in pink with white floral overcloths, rose napkins and lalique-style candle-holders. It makes for some interesting reading to embellish the short yet varied menu.

Main courses cover the bases from baked salmon with amaretto butter sauce and stuffed jumbo shrimp to pork tenderloin with a mushroom-brandy sauce to filet mignon with wild mushroom ragout. The cheapest item might be penne tossed with portobellos, grilled chicken and madeira wine sauce. The high end is grilled rack of lamb with shiitake mushrooms and sundried cherries.

Start with clams casino, teriyaki shrimp or wild mushroom tart. Finish with a seasonal pie or one of the specialty liqueured coffees.

Owner John Garman's "dynamic wine rack" has improved the wine situation here.

(717) 595-2532 or (800) 426-1460. Entrées, $14.95 to $24.95. Dinner nightly, 6 to 9; fewer days in off-season; Friday-Sunday in winter.

The Cook's Touch, Route 390, Mountainhome.

Dave and Cindy Cook lend youthful energy and considerable cooking talents to this newcomer, warmly received for American fare at affordable prices. They took over a large space that had been home to a succession of restaurants and "started from scratch," in Dave's words. He preps and does the cooking, while his wife oversees the 90-seat dining area with timbered walls and decor in beige and brown.

Dave hand-butchers his meats, obtains the freshest of seafood and singlehandedly cooks everything to order – no mean task, given the scope of the menu and the size of the dining room. Although featuring American cuisine, his chicken dishes vary from cajun to française to florentine. The veal comes marsala, parmesan, italiano or with pesto in lemon wine sauce, "our own creation." Baked stuffed flounder, hickory barbecue pork chops, lamb chops, teriyaki tenderloin and delmonico steak indicate the range. Soup or salad come with each dish.

Stuffed mushrooms, smoked trout and mussels marinara are among appetizers. Desserts include chocolate mousse, a cordial parfait and a birch beer float.

(717) 595-3599. Entrées, $9.95 to $15.95. Dinner, Tuesday-Saturday 5 to 10 or 11, Sunday noon to 8. Also open Monday in July and August.

Mountain Home Deli & Cafe, Route 390, Mountainhome.
This casual place is a good stop for a quick lunch. We ordered a ham and cheddar sandwich on a kaiser roll and a cashew chicken salad and took it to a side dining area.

Sandwiches and salads are in the $4 to $6 range. Baked goods accompany espresso and cappuccino in the morning.

(717) 595-3839. Open daily, 6 to 2:30.

Diversions

From golf courses to ski areas, fishing lakes to mountain trails, the Poconos are a four-season recreation destination. The specifics are outlined in countless brochures and periodicals, including "This Week in the Poconos" and "News of the Poconos."

Promised Land State Park, ten miles north of Canadensis, is the most popular of three state parks in the vicinity. The area along Route 390 into Promised Land is as notable for the profusion of rhododendron and mountain laurel, a majestic sight in the late spring, as it is for the funny little cabins that line the highway year-round. The 3,000-acre state park at an elevation of 1,700 feet is surrounded by 8,000 forested acres. Good fishing and swimming are available in a tranquil setting – power craft are banned from the lake, though you can rent rowboats, sailboats, pedal boats and canoes. For more exciting boating, head a few miles north to **Lake Wallenpaupack,** Pennsylvania's largest. **Gouldsboro** and **Tobyhanna** state parks also offer good swimming, boating and picnicking.

Waterfalls. Bushkill Falls is billed as the Niagara of Pennsylvania and is quite commercial. **Buck Hill Falls** is reached by a well groomed trail from a parking lot near the old Buck Hill Falls resort. The falls tumble 200 feet in three major drops along a mile of picturesque glen. It's not as spectacular as Bushkill, but most people like it better. Innkeepers at area lodging establishments can steer visitors to their own favorites.

Pocono Playhouse, Mountainhome, (717) 595-7456. One of the nation's longest-running summer playhouses has brought Broadway to the Poconos since 1946. The 1997 season opened in June with "La Cage aux Folles" and closed in mid-October with "Big River." Shows are staged Wednesday-Sunday nights, plus Wednesday, Thursday and Sunday matinees. Tickets, $17 to $20.

Shopping. Antiquing and the new Tannersville outlet stores have their devotees, but the main intersection of Canadensis tells something of its priorities. It has a service station, an Indian Trading Post, the Sunrise Foodmart, the Calico Kitchen, a Methodist church and that's about all, except for **The Kitchen Garden,** which features everything for the herb garden and herb enthusiast, plus herbal teas and tea gifts. The better shopping is along Route 390 in Mountainhome and Cresco.

Holley Ross Pottery at La Anna is widely advertised for "distinguished china and threefold entertainment" – demonstrations, woodland park and large factory showroom. Bus tours descend here, and you might find a nice bean pot, a mixing bowl or a coffee mug at a good price. As for the rest of it, take it, puh-leeze. Much more tasteful are the clothing, home accessories and artificial floral arrangements and outdoor furniture at **Viva** in Mountainhome. **Truly Tasteful** in Mountainhome bills itself as a unique country store, but stocks sophisticated cards, crafts, soaps, antiques, coffees and specialty foods among its wares. Also in Mountainhome, **Christmas Memories** claims to display the Poconos' largest line of collectibles. More collectibles, dolls, teddybears and gifts are on display at **Wonderful Things.** The relocated and expanded **Cooks Tour,** in something of a hardware store setting in Mountainhome, is a kitchen shop without peer, especially in terms of cookware, gadgets and utensils you can't find elsewhere.

Theo. B. Price Inc. at Cresco must be seen to be believed. It's part lumber company and part country store, with a mysterious jumble of things from oyster crackers to light bulbs, dried flower arrangements to carved decoys and Santas, all mixed in together. The **Ella C. Ehrhardt General Store** in Newfoundland is like a time capsule, purveying some of the same kinds of items it did when it opened in 1860. Also near Newfoundland is **Reece Pottery,** where Thomas Reece crafts interesting functional and sculptural stoneware.

Extra-Special

Callie's Candy Kitchen and Pretzel Factory, Route 390, Mountainhome and Cresco.

We never thought we'd see so much candy until we – and a few tour buses – met up with Callie's Candy Kitchen, founded in 1952 in Mountainhome and now a three-generation family enterprise that opened a pretzel factory in Cresco in 1985. The family patriarch still gives occasional candy-making demonstrations, which attract young and old, and there are plenty of free samples. We defy anyone to get through the huge store showroom without succumbing to one of the tempting fudge flavors from macadamia nut to piña colada. Or the chocolate-covered potato chips with the texture of chips and the taste of chocolate. Or the Pocono Mountain Crunch, a mix of butterscotch, crispied rice and ground cashews that is the best-seller. What next? Pretzels, that's what – plain or chocolate-covered, filled with peanut butter, available in bite-size chunks, sticks and rings, plus pretzel dogs and pretzel pizzas. The pretzel factory just down the road in Cresco also makes gourmet popcorn in 60 flavors, from hot jalapeño to apple pie. The pretzel factory is all glassed-in so viewers can watch the goings-on.

(717) 595-2280. Candy kitchen open daily 10 to 5, summer to 8; weekends only in January.

(717) 595-3257. Pretzel factory open daily 10 to 5, weekends only January-March.

The Inn at Phillips Mill, as depicted by artist Raymond E. Halacy.

Bucks County, Pa.

Romance Along River Road

What could be more special than the River Road section of Bucks County, sixteen miles of pristine paradise along the Delaware River? William Penn called it "the most beautiful of landscapes," even more beautiful than England's Buckingham, the shire in which he was born and after which this was named. We call it romantic, even magical, any time of year.

River Road, the winding state Route 32, hugs the river and its adjacent canal as it wends north from New Hope to Upper Black Eddy, linking hamlets that have changed little since the Revolution. The river remains largely untouched by development; its flow varies from rushing to gentle, depending on location and season. Beside it is the Delaware Canal, which flourished for a century as mules plied the towpath, drawing barges behind. The canal's quaint wooden bridges, moss-covered locks and stone aqueducts attest to times past.

There are treasures: Phillips Mill, the cradle of the Bucks County Art Colony. Centre Bridge, an area of substantial edifices in keeping with its English name. Lumberville, a string of houses, stores and inns up against the river. Point Pleasant, the area's

population center, if a few hundred souls can be called that. Erwinna, where large historic landmarks are spread across a river plain.

Hillsides awash with mountain laurel and rhododendron descend to the flatland strip along the river. Sturdy stone houses punctuate the countryside, looking for all the world like those of Britain's Cotswolds. Authentic country inns provide lodging and sustenance for travelers, as in the past.

This is Bucks County at its best, away from the hustle and bustle of touristy New Hope and the encroaching suburbia from Philadelphia and Doylestown. It's a place tailor-made for a rural retreat, for canoeing, walking the towpath, browsing the few shops, eating well and rejuvenating one's spirits at a country inn or B&B. Ramble along the river and succumb to its romance.

Inn Spots

The inns here, as well as the restaurants that follow, are covered in geographical order from south to north.

The Inn at Phillips Mill, North River Road, New Hope 18938.

Hanging pots overflowing with fuchsias, wooden casks filled with all colors of mums, wreaths of Christmas greenery or a profusion of spring bulbs – depending on the season, these mark the entrance to this small and adorable yet sophisticated inn. When you see its facade of local gray stone, smack up against an S-turn bend in the River Road, with its copper pig hanging over the entrance, you would almost swear you were in Great Britain.

That impression is heightened as you register at the reception desk and observe the low-ceilinged dining rooms (see Dining Spots). Upstairs are four charming guest rooms and a suite, cheerily decorated by innkeeper Joyce Kaufman, whose architect husband Brooks did the restoration of the 1750 barn. One has its own sitting room. Honeymooners request the third-floor hideaway suite, where fabric covers the ceiling. Most beds are four-posters or brass and iron and are topped with quilts. Antiques, handpainted trays, dried-flower arrangements and embroidered cloths on the nightstands abound. They don't advertise it, but sometimes the Kaufmans rent a cottage in back of the inn. A small swimming pool also may be used by guests.

A continental breakfast (juice, flaky croissants and coffee) is delivered to your room, wrapped in a blue and white checked tablecloth in a basket.

(215) 862-2984. Four rooms and one suite with private baths. Doubles, $80. Suite, $90. Cottage, $125. No credit cards.

Centre Bridge Inn, 2998 North River Road, New Hope 18938.

This striking white structure with red shutters built in Colonial Williamsburg style has a large restaurant-tavern, nine guest accommodations and an advantageous location beside the Delaware River across the bridge from Stockton, N.J. Fires destroyed inns that had occupied the site since 1705, so this reconstruction is of early 1960s vintage.

Overnight guests enter an enormous formal vestibule, with a fireplaced parlor on the river side. Ahead are a pair of two-room suites, one with a foyer leading into the main room with queensize canopy bed, two plush blue chairs on thick carpeting, TV set, cedar-lined bath and private river-view deck – "our nicest room," according to our guide. The other suite in front has a queen brass bed and sitting room with sofa, loveseat and TV.

Upstairs are seven more rooms, five with four-poster canopy beds (one with two canopied doubles) and all outfitted lately with TV. All are air-conditioned, have private baths and are notable for antiques and colorful Schumacher wall coverings, though some appear a bit tired.

A continental breakfast is served in the suites, the parlor or outside on a deck off the main floor, which has one of the nicest views of the river anywhere.

The downstairs tavern-dining room with beamed ceilings, stucco walls and huge open fireplaces could not be more attractive, nor the glass-enclosed porch overlooking the river more inviting. The food can be very good, but the dining room also has a reputation for inconsistency. The updated continental menu ranges from grilled yellowfin tuna with cilantro pesto to grilled lamb steak with rosemary-mint butter. We recall a happy evening sipping after-dinner drinks at the bar as a pianist entertained.

(215) 862-2048. Fax (215) 862-3244. Seven rooms and two suites with private baths. Doubles, $100 to $125 weekends, $80 to $105 midweek. Suites, $145 and $150 weekends, $125 and $130 midweek. Two-night minimum weekends.

Entrées, $18.95 to $26.95. Dinner nightly, 5:30 to 9:30 or 10, Sunday brunch.

1740 House, River Road, Lumberville 18933.

For serenity, motel-style privacy and a quiet location in a quaint hamlet beside the Delaware, this appeals to repeat visitors who book the same rooms year after year. The 1740 House was opened in 1967 by well-traveled New Yorker Harry Nessler and his wife. They built it to look old, each room in two wings opening from a front corridor and extending to patios or balconies perched out back at canal's edge.

Individually decorated, the 24 spacious rooms and a suite on two floors have king or twin beds, large bathrooms (some with showers only), comfortable chairs with reading lights, nightly turndown service, detachable wooden coat hangers, and pleasant outdoor seating areas overlooking the river. There are no televisions or phones to intrude.

Instead, enjoy the peace and quiet of the river from your balcony or porch, catch some sun around the small pool, read in a couple of small parlors, and meander up River Road to the center of

1740 House at Lumberville.

Lumberville to walk the canal towpath or cross the footbridge to an island park in New Jersey.

A buffet-style breakfast is served in the cheery garden dining room, where you're likely to end up sitting family-style with other guests. Help yourself to juice, cereal, croissants and a hot dish like scrambled eggs or creamed chipped beef, and toast your own homemade bread or English muffins.

Since the death of Harry Nessler at 92 in 1994 (he manned the front desk at the inn until the end), the 1740 House has been run by his grandson, Robert John Vris, who lives with his wife and children in nearby Ottsville. Robert continued the tradition, although he did stop serving dinners for house guests. He converted his grandfather's living quarters on the second floor into a two-room suite. At our latest visit, he was opening up the rear grounds to the river with a landscaped terrace.

(215) 297-5661. Twenty-four rooms and one suite with private baths. Doubles, $113 weekends, $75 midweek. Suite, $125 weekends, $113 midweek. Two-night minimum weekends. No credit cards.

Tattersall Inn, River and Cafferty Road, Box 569, Point Pleasant 18950.

This manor home of pale aubergine plastered fieldstone with wood trim of cream and dark green is set amid holly trees and rhododendrons. It was once the home of Ralph Stover, the best known member of the ubiquitous Bucks County clan of mill owners. The B&B originally was opened in 1983 by the owners of the Inn at Phillips Mill to accommodate their overflow. Herb and Gerry Moss have been running it for many years with aplomb, plus some fun music from Herb's assortment of ancient phonographs (he worked for RCA, which explains his interest).

They offer six bedrooms, all with private baths and queensize beds and two with gas fireplaces. The Highland Room is done in Black Watch tartan. The Royal Lavender Room has lavender moiré covering the walls and a lace canopy over the bed, and the Wintergreen Suite adds a sitting room. Gerry crocheted the canopy for the bed in the main-floor Squires Room, which also has a sofabed.

Cider and cheese are served in the afternoon in the beamed rear tavern room, now a common room with a wonderful big fireplace, old wood floors, hunting prints and comfy rust-colored velvet sofas.

Breakfast is taken amid Herb Moss's collection of early victrolas and talking machines. His 1903 Edison cylinder talking machine is the oldest, and the 1915 Edison retains its original diamond needle. A full breakfast featuring french toast, banana pancakes or cheese omelets is served in the dining room or on the veranda. Or you can have continental breakfast in your room.

(215) 297-8233 or (800) 297-4988. Fax (215) 297-5093. Six rooms with private baths. Doubles, $85 to $130 weekends, $70 to $115 midweek. Two-night minimum weekends. Smoking restricted.

EverMay on the Delaware, 889 River Road, Erwinna 18920.

Dating to the 1700s and enlarged in 1871, this three-story gold and tan Victorian mansion has the patina required for a listing on the National Register of Historic Places. It's set back from the road on a broad lawn facing the river, the perfect setting for the air of calm and quiet that the innkeepers try to project – though we were a bit startled to find chickens pecking away on the side lawn at one of our visits.

Evermay is the bed-and-breakfast and gourmet-dinner venture of William and Danielle Moffly, antiques dealers who acquired the inn in 1996 and live on the premises.

The sixteen guest rooms are located upstairs in the manor house as well as in a nearby carriage house and cottage. All with private baths and telephones, they are furnished with collectibles and antiques from the Victorian era. We found ours in the Carriage House a bit austere, despite the presence of fresh flowers and a large bowl of fruit. Some inn rooms retain the original fireplaces. Walnut beds, oriental rugs, marble-topped dressers, fancy quilts and lacy pillows are among the furnishings.

A fire often burns in the fireplace and decanters of sherry are at the ready downstairs in the double front parlor, where afternoon tea with cucumber or watercress sandwiches and cookies is served at 4. At bedtime in your room you may find fruit and candy and a liqueur in a little glass with a doily on top.

Although continental, breakfast in the rear conservatory room is quite special, with orange juice, incredibly flaky croissants and pastries, one with cream cheese in the center, and the pièce de résistance at our visit: a compote of fresh strawberries, red seedless grapes, bananas and honeydew melon, garnished with a sprig of mint and dusted with confectioners' sugar – colorful and pretty.

(610) 294-9100. Fax (610) 294-8249. www.everymay.com. Doubles, $95 to $175. Two-bedroom suite, $250. Two-night minimum weekends.

Bridgeton House, 1525 River Road, Box 167, Upper Black Eddy 18972.

With sweat and TLC, restorationists Charles and Bea Briggs have transformed this onetime wreck of an apartment house built in 1836 into a comfortable B&B with a great location beside the river. Although smack up against the road, the inn has been opened to the rear for a water orientation.

A rear parlor and upstairs balconies look onto a landscaped courtyard beside the canal. Lovely stenciling, fresh or dried flowers, a decanter of sherry and bowls of potpourri grace the dining room, where breakfast is served. Following a fruit course (perhaps baked pears in cream or a fresh fruit plate) comes a main dish: waffles with strawberry butter, eggs Roxanne, or mushroom and cheese omelets. Fresh lemon breads, muffins, and apple cake likely accompany.

Most of the eleven guest accommodations overlook the water. Each was exceptionally fashioned by Charles, a master carpenter and renovator, and interestingly decorated by Bea. Some contain four-posters and chaise lounges; all have private baths, country antiques, colorful sheets, fresh flowers and intriguing touches. Our main-floor room came with lovely stenciling and a private porch. Two small suites have gas fireplaces.

Bea calls the dramatic penthouse suite Bucks County's ultimate. It has a twelve-foot cathedral ceiling, a kingsize bed, black and white marble fireplace, marble bathtub, backgammon table, black leather chairs, a stereo-TV center and a full-length deck onto the river.

(610) 982-5856. Eight rooms and three suites with private baths. Doubles, $89 to $159 weekends, $69 to $119 midweek. Suites, $159 to $225 weekends, $149 to $179 midweek. Two-night minimum weekends. Children over 8. No smoking.

Dining Spots

Hotel du Village, River Road at Phillips Mill Road, New Hope.

The food is country French, but the chef-owner is Algerian and his hostelry is Tudor English in an early boarding-school setting. The main dining room in the former Lower Campus building of Solebury School looks like one in an English manor house, with a glowing fire at each end, a beamed ceiling, small-paned windows and a fine Persian carpet on the floor.

Delaware River is on view from second-floor balcony for guests at Bridgeton House.

Chef Omar Arbani arrived in Bucks County from Algeria by way of culinary endeavors in France, Denmark, London and Washington, D.C. His aim is "the kind of home-style country cuisine you'd find in the restaurants of Bordeaux or Burgundy on a Sunday afternoon," according to his wife Barbara, a former New Jersey teacher who manages the dining room, bar and a new banquet facility.

The menu and prices rarely change. We found the crusty, piping-hot French bread excellent, particularly when spread with the house pâté. Our tournedos with artichoke heart and béarnaise sauce were heavenly. So were the sweetbreads with green olives, mushrooms and madeira sauce. Potatoes sautéed with lots of rosemary, crisp beans and grilled tomato with a crumb topping accompanied. Moist black forest cake, crammed with cherries, and cafe royale were sweet endings to a rich, romantic meal.

Dining here takes precedence over the accommodations. Twenty rather spare rooms with private baths in a converted stable reflect their boarding-school heritage. Continental breakfast and access to a pool and two tennis courts on the ten-acre estate are included in the rates (doubles, $85 to $100).

(215) 862-9911. Entrées, $13.95 to $18.95. Dinner, Wednesday-Saturday from 5:30, Sunday 3 to 9. Closed mid-January to mid-February.

The Inn at Phillips Mill, 2998 North River Road, New Hope.

Looking as if it had been transported from the British Cotswolds, the quaint gray stone building right at the S-turn bend in the River Road has a copper pig above the entrance – a symbol of the stone barn's origin as a gristmill that stood next to the village piggery. Architect Brooks Kaufman and his innkeeper wife Joyce transformed it into a country French restaurant.

The dining setting is romantic as can be. Candles augment light from the fireplace in low-ceilinged rooms with dark beams and pewter service plates and water goblets. The menu, written in French with English translations, is executed by chefs whose names are listed at the bottom. The terrine of veal, pork and foie gras and the escargots with garlic-walnut demi-glace are favored appetizers. We enjoyed a springtime special, Maryland crabmeat in half an avocado, which was really special. We've never tasted such a tender filet mignon with such a delectable béarnaise sauce nor such perfect sweetbreads in a light brown sauce as on our first visit. We liked the sautéed calves liver in a cider vinegar and the veal medallions with roasted shallots in cognac sauce on another occasion.

Desserts are triumphs, among them a lemon ice-cream meringue pie, about six inches high and wonderfully refreshing, and a vanilla mousse with big chips of chocolate and chocolate fudge sauce.

(215) 862-9919. Entrées, $15.50 to $21. Dinner nightly, 5:30 to 9:30 or 10. BYOB. No credit cards.

Black Bass Hotel, Route 32, Lumberville.

For rustic charm, you can't beat this 1740 establishment straight out of England and so loyal to the Crown that, when George Washington crossed the Delaware just below here, the hotel supposedly wouldn't let him in. Wander around the dark, beamed dining rooms and look at all the British memorabilia collected by veteran innkeeper Herbert Ward, as well as the pewter bar that came from Maxim's in Paris.

Though we recall a memorable dinner from some years ago, we like the Black Bass best for lunch, when you can feast on the riverside scenery outside the long rear dining porch. Many favor the Charleston Meeting Street crab, a fixture on both the lunch and dinner menus. We enjoyed the New Orleans onion soup, thick with onions and cheese, which came in a proper crock. The crisp greens in the house salad were laden with homemade croutons and a nifty dressing of homemade mayonnaise, horseradish, dijon mustard and spices. Hungry after a lengthy hike along the towpath, one of us devoured seven of the nut and date mini-muffins that came in a basket.

The dinner menu ranges from seared salmon with leek compote and savoy cabbage to seared beef napoleon layered with potato crisp, walnuts and gorgonzola. Desserts here are exceptional: perhaps walnut cheesecake with sour cherry sauce and crème fraîche, or fresh fruit cobbler with wild turkey whiskey sauce. There's also a selection of homemade ice creams and sorbets.

Upstairs are seven bedrooms sharing two baths ($80) and two suites ($150 and $175).

(215) 297-5770. Entrées, $17.95 to $25.95. Lunch, Monday-Saturday noon to 3. Dinner, 5:30 to 9. Sunday, brunch 11 to 2:30, dinner 4:30 to 8:30.

Golden Pheasant Inn, 763 River Road, Erwinna.

The glamorous plant-filled solarium in this 1857 fieldstone inn was the setting for one of our more memorable meals, so we're glad that the rest of the restaurant has been fixed up as well.

French chef-owner Michel Faure, who was well regarded at the nearby Carversville Inn and Philadelphia's Le Bec Fin, and his wife Barbara have restored the two dark inner Victorian dining rooms to an elegant country French look of the 1850s, showcasing an extensive Quimper collection from Brittany.

Set back from the river on broad lawns is EverMay on the Delaware, known for fine dining.

We'd still choose the solarium, where you can see the canal and the trees illuminated at night, to enjoy some of Michel's dinner creations. Start perhaps with his renowned lobster bisque, pheasant pâté or smoked trout. Continue with such main dishes as crab croquette in the Brittany style, shrimp provençal, grilled duck, filet mignon béarnaise or rack of lamb with a rosemary-garlic-mint demi-glace. Worthy endings include cappuccino cheesecake, crème caramel, homemade sorbets and, a specialty, Belgian white chocolate mousse with a raspberry coulis.

The Faures, who live on the premises, offer up to six guest rooms with private baths, the total seeming to vary with the number of their offspring in residence (doubles, $85 to $145).

(610) 294-9595. Entrées, $19.95 to $26.95. Dinner nightly except Monday, 5:30 to 9 or 10. Sunday, brunch 11 to 3, dinner to 8.

EverMay on the Delaware, 889 River Road, Erwinna.
The weekend gourmet dinners offered by the former chef-innkeepers were acclaimed, drawing not only house guests but a local following. Their sous chef maintained the inn's reputation for contemporary American fare.

The six-course meal is prix-fixe, with little choice except between two entrées – grilled swordfish with papaya-mango salsa and rack of lamb with rosemary jus, at our latest visit. It's served at a single 7:30 seating, usually booked far in advance.

The meal is taken in a main dining room where the draperies match the upholstered chairs, in a rear garden room or at tables for two in an intimate porch-conservatory pretty in white and light brown, with windows onto the back lawn. Our meal here was one of the best we've had, nicely presented and paced. Hors d'oeuvres of smoked trout salad, sundried tomato crostini and country pâté with green peppercorns were served first. Next, in order, came a suave chicken and leek soup, sautéed chanterelles on a saffron crouton, and a salad of boston and mache lettuces, garnished with violets and toasted walnuts and dressed with a sherry vinaigrette.

These were mere preliminaries to the entrées: Norwegian salmon poached in white wine, served with hollandaise sauce and garnished with shrimp, and tender lamb noisettes wrapped in bacon and topped with a green peppercorn butter. These came with thin, crisp asparagus from Chile, rice pilaf and a sprig of watercress.

A cheese course of perhaps St. André, montrachet and gorgonzola precedes dessert. Ours was a perfect poached pear, set atop vanilla ice cream, butterscotch sauce, golden raisins and pecans.

(610) 294-9100. Prix-fixe, $52. Dinner by reservation, Friday-Sunday at 7:30. Jackets requested.

Bucks Bounty, 991 River Road, Erwinna.

The Adirondacks meet the Southwest in this restaurant and pub put together by Dutch chef Johan Van der Linden. It's notable for the unique vaulted ceiling, extravagantly colorful in yellow, red, turquoise and black – the design taken from

an Alaskan Indian blanket. Long, narrow mirrors atop the wood wainscoting that doubles as the back for banquettes are bordered by Adirondack scenes. Sturdy Adirondack chairs are at green-clothed tables covered, alas, by glass tops.

It's a trendy, unexpected setting for food that Johan calls American-continental with German influences and Italian specialties. He's at his best at dinner, when the affordable menu ranges from simple pastas to sautéed sweetbreads and filet mignon. Crispy roasted Long Island duck with his own Chinese barbecue sauce and chicken dijonnaise are signature dishes. Prime rib is a standby on weekends. Start with smoked trout, onion soup au gratin or

Adirondack motif prevails at Bucks Bounty.

wilted red leaf salad with feta cheese and sesame seeds. Favorite endings are peach cobbler, crème brûlée and shoofly pie.

The new weekend brunch menu is more enticing than was the fare offered at lunch the weekday we ate here. One of us had a good tuna salad sandwich, while the other got the soup and half-sandwich special. The caramelized onion soup was tasty and the half liverwurst sandwich with a big slice of raw onion more than substantial. But we would have preferred some of the interesting luncheon salads that had been added at a later visit.

(610) 294-8106. Entrées, $13.95 to $18.95. Lunch, Tuesday-Friday 11:30 to 4. Dinner, Tuesday-Sunday 5:30 to 10. Weekend brunch, 9 to 3.

Chef Tell's Manor House, 1800 River Road, Upper Black Eddy.

Chef Tell Erhardt of Philadelphia television fame has taken over the elegant Manor House along the Delaware River and is doing a land-office business. The 1830 manor is quite a sight, what with a long sun porch facing the river across the road and an elegant inner dining room with blue and white fabric upholstered chairs.

Chef Tell's German specialties – among them, sauerbraten and wiener schnitzel – are featured. The rest of the lengthy dinner menu takes on international overtones: baked shrimp in a ring of mousseline potatoes, sautéed Swedish-style pork loin, grilled chicken Bangkok, spicy oriental roast duck and filet mignon béarnaise. Ditto for the specials, perhaps seared Chilean sea bass with ginger-hoisin sauce or rum and molasses-glazed salmon with banana salsa.

Start with Thai dumplings, Swedish gravlax or conch fritters Cayman style from the chef's worldly offerings. Some of the same dishes are available at lunch.

(610) 982-0212 or (800) 424-3385. Entrées, $12.95 to $20.95. Lunch, Wednesday-Saturday 10:30 to 2:30. Dinner, Wednesday-Saturday 6 to 9. Sunday, brunch 10:30 to 3, dinner 4 to 8.

Diversions

The Delaware River and the adjacent Delaware Canal provide diversion enough for most. For action, New Hope and its galleries, shops and nightlife are just down River Road – but all that is a different world.

Walk the Towpath. The best way to experience both river and canal and their surroundings is to walk the towpath, which also is used by joggers and the occasional bicyclist. Start in Lumberville at the footbridge to Bull's Island, a New Jersey state park. The gardens, back yards and architecture of English-type manor houses intrigue. A footbridge leads to the Cuttalossa Inn, where the outdoor terrace begs one to pause for lunch or a drink. For the makings of a picnic, cross the highway bridge at Centre Bridge to Stockton, N.J., to pick up food to go at Errico's Market and a bottle of wine at the well-stocked Phillips wine store. Not far downriver is Phillips Mill, an ever-so-British looking cluster of stone houses hugging the River Road. The old miller's house and surroundings were taken over by artists around 1900, thus launching New Hope's reputation as an art colony. The 1756 grist mill has been preserved by the Phillips Mill Community Association as a landmark, cultural center and site for its highly regarded annual fall art exhibition. Not far beyond is Lenteboden, the business and residence of Charles Mueller, the bulb specialist whose gardens – lavish with daffodils, tulips and hyacinths – herald the arrival of spring. Like almost everything else along the towpath, they're free and open for the exploring.

River Pursuits. Canoeing, rafting and tubing are so popular here that the Bucks County River Country enterprise in Point Pleasant has become the East's largest water recreation facility. Tubing is its biggest operation, with up to 3,500 people a day renting inner tubes for floats of three to six miles. Canoeists are transported up to Tinicum, Upper Black Eddy or Riegelsville for trips downriver of six to twelve miles. The New Hope Mule Barge Co. hauls tourists on mule-drawn barges along the old Delaware Canal past Colonial homes, artists' workshops, gardens and countryside from downtown New Hope north to the Route 202 bridge and back.

Parks. The entire River Road area is so utterly unspoiled that it seems like one big park. And so some of it is. The aforementioned towpath is part of the **Delaware Canal State Park,** a 60-mile strip following the canal along Bucks County's riverfront. **Tinicum Park** offers picnicking, boating, hiking and more on its 126 acres beside the river in Tinicum, just north of Erwinna; here also are the historic **Erwin-Stover House** and the **Stover's Mill Gallery,** open to visitors on weekends.

Ralph Stover State Park, just north of Point Pleasant, has 37 hilly acres for fishing, hiking and swimming along Tohickon Creek. It adjoins **Tohickon Valley County Park,** one of the largest of Bucks County's parks.

Shopping. A complex of buildings centered by a picturesque red wood and fieldstone barn built in 1749 is part of **River Road Farms** in Erwinna. The barn houses **Chachka,** one of our favorite stores. An interesting gift shop, it also accents some unusual food items, including Thai and Indonesian. "People say they have to go to many different stores in New York to find what we have here," says proprietor Dick deGroot, who makes the wild and wonderful Gentleman Farmer preserves and relishes at his home next door. Chachka also hosts outdoor festivals with seasonal food and entertainment on certain weekends. The **Lumberville Store** is an institution in Lumberville, a country store with a post office, book section, sundries, antiques and a deli (great sandwiches). Point Pleasant is notable for **Kinsman Co.,** garden tools and gifts, and **Poor Richard's,** an in-your-face hodgepodge, indoors and out, of wicker, brass and copper antiques. Smaller antiques shops are scattered here and there along the River Road. If you want still more shopping, just cross the river to the New Jersey side (Milford, Frenchtown, Stockton and Lambertville) or head down river to New Hope.

Sand Castle Winery, 755 River Road, Erwinna, (800) 722-9463. Two brothers from Czechoslovakia moved to a 72-acre estate above the Golden Pheasant Inn to grow vinifera grapes – the "noble vines of Europe," they call them – in the old-world tradition. Paul and Joe Maxian offer wine tastings beneath a tent canopy and in a reception trailer on a hilltop overlooking the countryside. They lead tours through their underground wine cellar and show pictures of their planned winery building patterned after a 10th-century Czech castle. The winery started production of riesling and chardonnay before adding expensive barrel-aged cabernet sauvignon and pinot noir, priced at $18 and $19 respectively.

Extra-Special

Bucks County Covered Bridges.
Nostalgia and romance are triggered by covered bridges that preserve a vanishing piece of Americana. Bucks County still has eleven of its original 36 covered bridges, all excellent examples of the lattice-truss construction patented in 1820 by Ithiel Town, a Connecticut architect. The oldest bridge was built in 1832. Five of the bridges are in the River Road area between Point Pleasant and Frenchtown. One at Uhlerstown spans the Delaware Canal; the shortest, at Erwinna, crosses Lodi Creek. Another was relocated for preservation purposes but burned in 1991. A Bucks County Tourist Commission brochure touts the virtues of covered bridges and provides a detailed map for a day's tour. Make a wish as you enter a wishing bridge or steal a kiss on one of the kissing bridges.

Sign tells story of the swallows of Lambertville at Delaware River entrance to town.

Lambertville, N.J.

On the Verge of Chic

Some time ago, the New York Times referred to a village of our acquaintance as "on the verge of chic." The same could be said today for Lambertville.

This sleepy New Jersey river town, a product of the Industrial Revolution and the 19th century, languished until lately. It was at the edge of chic, overshadowed by New Hope, Pa., its better-known neighbor across the Delaware River. History, artists and an enduring quaintness gave New Hope the best of everything. But Lambertville? This was the town through which New Yorkers had to pass to get to New Hope. Even that need was obviated after the new Route 202 toll bridge bypassed Lambertville.

Time was on Lambertville's side, however. The three A's – arts, authors and antiques – strained New Hope's limits and spilled into Lambertville. They found a receptive host, one untouched by the 20th-century building boom and urban redevelopment.

The first restaurant of note opened in 1980; the first B&B in 1983. Next a group of investors turned the old train station into a restaurant and built an adjacent luxury inn-hotel. Suddenly, Lambertville was "in." Now its main streets are chock-a-block antiques stores and art galleries. It has a wider variety of quality restaurants than does New Hope. Visitors are discovering the advantages of staying in Lambertville – close to New Hope, but without the crowds and hassle.

Lambertville has its own identity, that of an emerging town of 3,900 on the way to becoming the little city it calls itself. Starting in 1994, its Chamber of Commerce has produced annually a helpful brochure to guide tourists. Just up river is Stockton, itself a class act, centered by the old inn with the wishing well immortalized in the song, "There's a Small Hotel." Beyond is Rosemont, a crossroads hamlet where

Landmark 1812 hotel has been restored as deluxe Lambertville House.

an old chicken farm is now a complex of business enterprises, one of them advertising the largest selection of handcrafted furniture in the country. Most of the area's riverfront with its parallel Delaware & Raritan Canal has been turned into the longest and narrowest strip of state parkland in the nation.

Although Lambertville is on the verge of chic, its surroundings are about as rural as they get in the nation's most densely populated state.

Inn Spots

Lambertville House, 32 Bridge St., Box 349, Lambertville 08530.

Lambertville's landmark hotel, which had been closed for eleven years, was grandly restored in 1997. New Hope developer George Michael bought the four-story structure dating to 1812 and added contemporary amenities as he returned it to its original luster. His son, Brad, became the innkeeper and set about attracting the high-end market.

The restored facade is a knockout with a two-story veranda along the stone front and walls above painted beige with green and burgundy trim.

An elevator serves the 24 guest rooms and suites on the top three floors, each with marble bath and jacuzzi tub (six are double jacuzzis). Twenty-three have gas fireplaces, eight offer balconies and six are suites. Touch pad telephones with data ports, remote-control TV hidden in armoires or in cupboards over the fireplaces, terrycloth robes, Gilbert & Soames toiletries, make-up mirrors, hair dryers and bottles of mineral water are among the amenities. Beds are queen or kingsize. Rooms come with a writing desk and one wing chair. The formal furnishings are period antiques and reproductions.

The six courtyard suites, two on each floor, are larger and have balconies overlooking the rear courtyard. The one we saw had a queen poster bed with an elegant quilt and a see-through fireplace serving bedroom and bathroom. The bathroom had a double jacuzzi, separate shower and a sitting area with a wicker chair to supplement the wing chair in the bedroom.

Two more courtyard suites, retails shops and conference facilities were under construction in a building across the courtyard.

A continental-plus breakfast, included in the rates, is offered in a quaint basement breakfast room designed to look like a French kitchen with tiled floor, tiled fireplace, original rafters and wall sconces.

The inn's main floor contains a reception foyer beside a stone wall and a couple of upscale retail shops, including the Greene & Greene Gallery.

(609) 397-0200 or (888) 867-8859. Fax (609) 397-0511. Eighteen rooms and eight suites with private baths. Weekends: doubles $189 to $249, suites $269 to $299. Midweek: doubles $159 to $229, suites $229 to $239. Two-night minimum on holiday weekends. Older children accepted. No smoking.

The Inn at Lambertville Station, 11 Bridge St., Lambertville 08530.

A group of investors spent more than $3 million in the 1980s to build this architecturally impressive, luxury hotel/inn on abandoned land that had been an eyesore along the Delaware River.

Check-in is at a counter resembling the ticket office of an old train station, but you'll probably be awed more by the soaring, three-story lobby, which is higher than it is wide. Prized antiques are in the 45 guest rooms and suites, each named for a major city and decorated accordingly by an antiques dealer who spared no expense.

Ours was the New York Suite, high in the trees above a rushing waterfall that lulled us to sleep. There were chocolates at bedside, the bathroom had a whirlpool tub and a basket of good toiletries, and around the L-shaped room were heavy mahogany furniture, leather chairs facing the fireplace and TV, handsome draperies, ornate mirrors and fine art. Afternoon tea or drinks from an honor bar are available in the lobby or on the adjacent creekside deck, a shady refuge in the trees. A small continental breakfast with carrot-nut muffins arrived at our door with the New York Times the next morning.

The large Riverside Room, facing the river with windows on three sides, is used for Sunday brunch ($18.95 for quite a spread).

(609) 397-4400 or (800) 524-1091. Fax (609) 397-9744. Forty-five rooms and suites with private baths. Doubles, $115 to $180 weekends, $85 to $135 midweek. Suites with fireplaces and whirlpool baths, $135 to $230.

Chimney Hill Farm, 207 Goat Hill Road, Lambertville 08530.

Three deer were grazing in the back yard the day we revisited this rural retreat. "There are lots more," said Terry Ann Anderson, owner and innkeeper with her husband Rich. "They ate every chrysanthemum and daisy off our porch this fall. We also have a brood of wild turkeys, rabbits and big fat groundhogs."

The animals are appropriate at this opulent manor house, sequestered atop a wooded hill beyond a high-rent residential area on the southeast edge of Lambertville. It was once a working farm, and the restored gardens put in by former owner Edgar W. Hunt, an internationally known attorney, are quite spectacular in season.

The inside of the house borders on the spectacular as well. Vacant when it was acquired by two aspiring innkeepers in 1988, they first put it on display as a designer show house to benefit the Delaware River Mill Society. The designers took everything with them but the living room wallpaper, however.

The former owners used their own restoration and design instincts to good advantage to create a B&B with great potential. They lost interest and ultimately the house to bankruptcy. It was left to the Andersons, who moved here in July 1994 from northern New Jersey to put the B&B back on track. All it took was live-in owners who decided this was to be their home, an infusion of money, a woman's touch and plenty of TLC.

The Andersons inherited most of the furnishings for the eight guest rooms, all but one with king or queensize beds and private baths and two in the north wing with fireplaces. Each is awash in splashy fabrics, all Schumacher or Colfax & Fowler, we were told. The smallest room has space enough only for a double bed and one chair. The rear Terrace Room is bigger with tapestry fabrics, kingsize bed, a large bath with clawfoot tub and its own balcony. We liked the looks of the Hunt Room master suite, where the covers and canopy on the step-up queen bed match the gently swagged curtains, and the sofa and the oriental carpet pick up the theme. As we peeked into the Library Room at the end of the North Wing, a large space with a queensize canopy bed, fireplace and two armchairs, a departing honeymooner returned to snap a photo. "We want to take every inch of this house with us," he said.

We also liked the looks of the sunken main-floor sun porch, with windows on three sides and floors, fireplace and walls of fieldstone. Warmth and color come from ficus trees and the floral chintz that covers four wicker loveseats angled around a huge glass cocktail table. The splashy sun porch makes the attractive living room pale in comparison.

Breakfast is served by candlelight at six tables for two in the 1820 dining room that was the original room in the house (the wings were added by attorney Hunt in 1927). Terry offers fresh fruit, cereals and plenty of homemade pastries, from muffins with farm-made raspberry jam to croissants filled with fruit or cream cheese. Baked french toast is one of the additional treats on Sunday mornings. In the afternoon, port and cream sherry await in the butler's pantry, where tea, cider and snacks also are available. The Andersons have added bathroom toiletries, and guests find in each room a "gift snack pack" with candy, goldfish and peanuts.

The new owners had their eyes on the rear carriage house, which they planned to renovate to provide four more guest rooms. They hoped to convert the barn into a conference and entertainment center, and to add a hot tub in the rear greenhouse.

(609) 397-1516. Fax (609) 397-9353. www/bbianj.com/chimneyhill. Eight rooms with private baths. Doubles, $130 to $175 weekends; $80 to $105 midweek. Children over 12.

The Stockton Inn, 1 Main St., Stockton 08559.

You want a sense of history plus contemporary comforts? At many inns, the two are mutually exclusive. The Stockton Inn offers both.

Manor house at Chimney Hill Farm is part of what once was a working farm.

History it has in spades, this stone edifice with the pillared veranda dating to 1710. Remember the Rodgers and Hart Broadway show song, "There's a Small Hotel?" This is that small hotel, the lyrics were written here and guests still make wishes at *the* wishing well.

Band leader Paul Whiteman used to sign off his national radio shows from Trenton with the announcement that he was going to the Stockton Inn for dinner (one of the fascinating murals in the dining room pictures Whiteman fallen from his horse on his way home to nearby Rosemont after imbibing too much). In 1935, the inn gained national fame as the press headquarters during the Lindbergh kidnapping trial.

Besides making history, the inn preserves it in its overnight accommodations and restaurant (see Dining Spots). The three guest rooms and eight suites all have private baths, lavish period furnishings and color TV. Most have queensize canopy beds and fireplaces. We were comfortably ensconced in the upstairs suite in the Federal House, one of three outbuildings holding the bulk of the accommodations. It was handsomely appointed in deep greens, with the fabric on the canopy and bedspread matching the curtains and the loveseat. A fireplace, a selection of timely magazines, a mini-refrigerator and a basket with packets of instant coffee, teabags and broth were among the amenities. More extras were found in the bathroom, where another basket offered everything from the usual shampoos and lotions to mouth wash, a mending kit and a toothbrush.

"New Yorkers love the creaky floors," our guide said when the floor underneath the thick carpeting squeaked with every footstep as we toured the Colligan Suite, upstairs in the inn. It and the adjacent Stockton Suite share access to the front balcony, from which guests get a straight shot down Bridge Street to the Delaware River and can see most of the goings-on in town.

The popular Loft Suite in the rear of the stone 1832 Wagon House is large and airy, thanks to high windows and a vaulted ceiling from which hangs a brass chandelier with a dimmer switch. Rich Williamsburg colors, striking trim (blue here, black in the Carriage House), good art works and mahogany furniture are the rule.

The range of accommodations includes a basement kitchenette suite running the length of the Federal House, entered through a rear garden.

A continental breakfast buffet is put out in the inn's dining room. We enjoyed quite a spread of fresh fruit (kiwi, strawberries, pineapple and cantaloupe), carafes of juices and an array of pastries from croissants to muffins to nut bread.

(609) 397-1250. Three rooms and eight suites with private baths. Doubles, $90 to $130 weekends, $65 to $95 midweek. Suites, $155 to $170 weekends, $105 to $130 midweek. Two-night minimum weekends.

The Woolverton Inn, 6 Woolverton Road, Stockton 08559.

Built in 1792 as a manor house by pioneer industrialist John Prall Jr., whose mill is nearby, this is a B&B on six bucolic acres – where curious black-faced sheep and goats may mosey up to your car from a field next to the parking area. Its location on a country road, atop a hill away from the river, guarantees a noiseless night.

Elizabeth and Michael Palmer, new owners in 1994, have been reconfiguring and upgrading eight bedrooms in the main house, all now with private baths – the lack thereof had been a major shortcoming since we stayed here a decade ago. The Palmers redecorated all the rooms, adding mostly king and queensize beds. Each room has been furnished to reflect the personality and era of its namesake, a past owner or local figure. Thick soft towels, monogrammed terrycloth robes and extra pillows are pluses.

The new Letitia's Repose suite, transformed from two rooms that shared a bath, has a kingsize canopy bed, fireplace and jacuzzi tub. Amelia's Parterre, the original master suite, has a king four-poster bed with sitting area, fireplace and dressing room. Another favorite is Stockton's Quay, containing a queen bed with a twig headboard, a slate tiled bath with jacuzzi tub and outdoorsy décor. Guests seeking seclusion might opt for the Bodine's Farm suite or the smaller Wilet's Garden room in the former barn that also contains the innkeepers' quarters.

Guests have the run of the grounds, plus an elegant large living room with a portrait of Michael's mother over the fireplace. Family heirlooms have been interspersed among the sofas, wing chairs and oriental rugs that testify to the Federal period and the traditional style of what Michael calls "a classic country home." The dining room is big enough for the banquets and wedding parties to which the inn caters. Elizabeth and her husband, who works in New York City, offer a full breakfast daily rather than just on weekends as in the past. Fresh orange juice, baked apple and a vegetable frittata with fried potatoes and bacon were served the day of our visit. Pocket french toast, stuffed with cream cheese and walnuts and sautéed on the grill, was on the next day's docket. In the afternoon, tea and cocoa or lemonade are served with homemade cookies.

(609) 397-0802 or (888) 264-6649. Fax (609) 397-4936. Ten rooms and suites with private baths. Doubles, $105 to $150 weekends, $80 to $120 midweek. Suites, $190 weekends, $140 midweek.

Coryell Bed & Breakfast, 44 Coryell St., Lambertville 08530.

Gingerbread trim and a small front porch holding an Adirondack twig couch grace this 1870 brick Victorian house, spiffed up by new owners Denise Kortunik and Garry Duda. The interior is eclectic and quite unusual, much of it with an arty, oriental theme. The decor is the work of live-wire innkeeper Denise, a counselor

Ornate railings mark facade of The Woolverton Inn.

by trade and an interior designer by heart. "Our guests get some of both," she advises.

The partners offer three "suites" with queensize beds and private baths. One bedroom on the first floor front comes with poster bed, armoire, chaise lounge and a long, narrow bathroom running along the side of the house. Overhead on the second floor is another bedroom notable for bright colors, floral prints and oriental rugs. A genuine suite has a small sitting room with a wicker loveseat and chair and a bedroom beyond, with an English pine bed, another wicker chair and a green Korean kimono displayed on the wall.

Interesting art prevails throughout the house. A door between living room and dining room is painted as a trompe-l'oeil bookcase, realistic as all get-out down to the copy of the New York Times on the bottom shelf.

Breakfast here is different from those B&Bs where guests eat what the inn-keeper chooses, Denise says. "We tell people what we can serve and then they make a choice." Fresh fruit, blended juices, blended Italian-American-African coffee, cereals and breakfast meats accompany such main dishes as blueberry pancakes and eggs benedict – "basically whatever anyone wants." Denise adds that Garry, who's involved in building construction by day, is a good cook who's known for "outrageous omelets."

(609) 397-8292. Two rooms and one suite with private baths. Doubles, $135. Suite, $160. Children welcome. No credit cards.

York Street House, 42 York St., Lambertville 08530.
This large Georgian brick home was opened as Lambertville's first B&B in 1983 after it had been glamorized as a designers' show house. It wasn't the first time it had received wide publicity – the Massey Mansion was featured in 1911 in House and Garden magazine shortly after a local coal merchant had built it as a 25th wedding anniversary gift for his wife.

Today's visitors are greeted by an imposing brick mansion set back from the street with pillared verandas on the front and side, nicely restored by new owners Beth Wetterskog, fulltime innkeeper, and Nancy Ferguson, an emergency room physician at a Trenton hospital. They bought the house unfurnished and have been gradually renovating the rooms and furnishing them as they go along, which explained their work-in-progress feeling at our 1997 visit. Amazingly, they did the plumbing and carpentry work themselves.

Mercer tiles compliment the working fireplaces in the main-floor common rooms and an original Waterford chandelier glitters over down-stuffed furniture in the living room, where there's an unusual chaise for two that's so comfy that "once you get on you don't get off," Nancy advised. Besides the living room, guests spread out on the side porch furnished in wicker overlooking the largest yard on the block.

Crystal knobs open the walnut doors to five large guest quarters. Three on the second floor have remodeled baths. Three on the third floor that shared two baths were being converted. One room was to have a private bath and the other was being joined through a sitting room to form a suite.

All with queen or kingsize beds, they were being outfitted with TVs and telephones. Still the favorite is the second-floor front room with a lace canopy step-up queen bed, two wing chairs in the corner, an extra sink in another corner and – a startling sight in the bathroom – a free-standing toilet in the front bay window of what once was a dressing room. The partners were redoing in Victorian gingerbread a side bedroom with a wicker bed, window seat and a clawfoot tub in the bathroom beneath original stained-glass windows.

Signs in each room warn of a $100 fine for violation of the B&B's no smoking policy.

A full breakfast is served in the fireplaced dining room. Fresh-ground coffee accompanied croissant french toast the morning of our visit.

(609) 397-3007. Fax (609) 397-9677. Five rooms and one suite with private baths. Doubles, $85 weekends, $75 midweek. Suite, $165. No young children. No smoking.

The Bridgestreet House, 75 Bridge St., Lambertville 08530.

A pair of pre-Victorian structures started in the 1980s as a restaurant with a B&B adjunct. The restaurant eventually failed, and owner Sharon Lykins from northern New Jersey offers seven cozy guest rooms on three floors of the B&B house.

Four bedrooms have private baths and three share. Each is air-conditioned and has thick carpeting and remote-control TV. Sharon and her husband Randy have redone one bedroom with a queensize bed; the rest have double. Victorian antiques embellish the rooms. A couple have beamed ceilings, and floral comforters and draperies brighten one room. The rear Garden Room has a private bath and a private entrance off a small stone courtyard. Elaborate stenciling decorates the doorways off the narrow corridors

Chocolate mints and a decanter of brandy await guests in each room. In the morning, Sharon sets out a continental breakfast buffet in the small parlor. It consists of juice, seasonal fruit and homemade muffins.

(609) 397-2503. Four rooms with private baths and three rooms with shared baths. Doubles, $75 to $95. Children over 12. No smoking.

Wall of mirrors and paneling are backdrop for dining at Anton's at the Swan.

Dining Spots

Anton's at the Swan, 43 South Main St., Lambertville.

Shortly after it opened in 1990 in the Swan Hotel, this was picked by the New York Times as one of the year's ten best restaurants in New Jersey. It's still going strong, thanks to the inspiration of talented chef Anton Dodel, who leases the space from Swan owner James Bulger.

Anton is, in his words, spontaneous and eclectic. He's also versatile; at one visit, he was sprawled on the floor preparing to rehang curtains an hour before a special wine-tasting dinner. His short menu changes monthly. We'd gladly have tried any of his six October entrées, but particularly the roast cod on ginger-pumpkin sauce, the sautéed lobster and apples over chive biscuits, and the grilled venison on persimmon and chile sauce. Starters included curried shrimp and pumpkin soup, garlic flan on warm black bean sauce, and grilled green tomatoes on herb bruschetta.

Desserts always include something chocolate and always a flan, but you might find a poached pear in caramel sauce or a cornbread pudding.

The backdrop for these culinary triumphs is a subdued room with paneled wainscoting, a wall of mirrors, step-down windsor chairs and white-linened tables topped with candles in hurricane chimneys. Anton rebuilt the hotel's kitchen in order to produce a sophisticated menu and style, "one like a well-established restaurant in France." He cooks more casual fare for the hotel's bar.

(609) 397-1960. Entrées, $22 to $28. Dinner, Tuesday-Saturday 6 to 10, Sunday 4:30 to 8. Bar, Tuesday-Sunday 5 to 11.

Hamilton's Grill Room, 8 Coryell St., Lambertville.

Former Broadway set designer Jim Hamilton opened this little gem, hidden at the end of an alley in the Porkyard complex beside the canal and towpath. Jim, an architect who designs restaurants, installed an open grill beside the entrance and built the wood-fired adobe pizza oven himself. Chef Marc BrownGold moved here from New York's Tavern on the Green to execute the Mediterranean grill concept.

Marc created the option of grazing portions to let weekday diners try "a little of everything." Most items are available in standard and smaller portions (at about half the price). You might start with fettuccine with duck confit and lentils or a salad of belgian endive, radicchio, gorgonzola and pears. Then it's on to an adobe oven pizza, or perhaps green risotto with mussels and ricotta salata. Or graze with half portions of entrées like grilled swordfish with anchovy and caper tapenade or grilled ribeye steak with crisped leeks and onion rings.

The menu is similar but pricier on weekends, when the open grill yields things like rack of lamb with white bean puree and mixed grill of quail, duck breast and rabbit sausage with macerated figs and apples in red wine.

Our convivial meal began with grilled shrimp with anchovy butter and a crab cake on wilted greens and sweet red pepper sauce. Main courses were an exceptional grilled duck on bitter greens with pancetta and honey glaze and sautéed calves liver with pancetta, scallions and wine. The oversize plates were filled with fanned razor-thin sliced potatoes and grilled zucchini and green and red peppers. The signature grappa torta and the grand marnier cheesecake were good desserts, and two biscotti came with the bill.

Patrons dine at tables rather close together in the grill room, the Bishop's Room beneath angels and clouds surrounding a huge gilt mirror on the ceiling, beside a sensuous mural of a nude in the dining gallery and, in season, outdoors around the fountain on the courtyard.

Hamilton's is BYOB with a twist. It serves its regular menu weekends at the **Wine Bar** annex, a small house across the courtyard for folks who want full liquor service from the adjacent Boat House wine bar. In the main grill, the white wine we toted was stashed in a pail full of ice, and red wines and even water are poured in large hand-blown globes made locally.

(609) 397-4343. Entrées, $16 to $30. Dinner nightly, 6 to 10 or 11, Sunday 5 to 10. BYOB.

Manon, 19 North Union St., Lambertville.

An air of whimsy reigns here, from the colorful exterior of burnt orange and blue-green with gingerbread trim to the ceiling painted like Van Gogh's starry night. With a relocated and expanded kitchen, there's more room for young chef-owner Jean-Michel Dumas, who grew up in Provence, to work his culinary wizardry. There's also an extra table for patrons in the intimate, 36-seat dining room in front, and the chef and his American wife Susan were thinking in 1998 of adding a garden terrace with a few tables in back.

Gutsy food is served in robust portions. The French menu often starts with his trademark anchovy relish and an assortment of raw vegetables, the house pâté, escargots in pernod and salads like warm goat cheese or watercress with pear, endive, walnuts and roquefort. Soup of the day could be garlicky mussel or pistou.

Among the eight entrées are a classic bouillabaisse, grilled salmon on a bed of cabbage with lobster mushroom sauce, breast of chicken with garlic sauce, calves liver with a shallot-wine sauce, and rack of lamb with herbs de provence. Desserts include crème caramel, tarte tatin, chocolate mousse, marjolaine and nougat ice cream with raspberry sauce.

Similar fare is offered in three courses at a prix-fixe Sunday brunch ($17.50). *(609) 397-2596. Entrées, $18.50 to $25 Dinner, Wednesday-Sunday 5:30 to 9 or 10. Sunday brunch, 11 to 2:30. No credit cards. BYOB.*

Heritage Cafe, 13-15 Kline's Court, Lambertville.

The hottest dining ticket in town in 1997 was this newcomer opened by widely traveled chef Mark Wexler. "I drove around here one Sunday afternoon with my girlfriend," he said, "and I literally moved here a week later." He took over a space along Restaurant Row that had housed a number of predecessors and created a handsome, refined space with gray chairs, white cloths, and a long horizontal mirror and track-lit artworks on the walls.

Mark cooked in leading hotels from Washington to San Francisco before a stop with Arnold Schwartzenagger at his private Schatzi on Main restaurant in Los Angeles. An Austrian restaurant in Manhattan prepared him for his own place, where he features modern American cuisine with an Austrian accent. Peppered swordfish with pinot noir sauce and barbecued duck with goat cheese are signature dishes. The chef is partial to his wiener schnitzel ("I eat schnitzels four times a week") with spaghetti squash sauerkraut, and offers a schnitzel sandwich for lunch and brunch.

He employs roast Long Island duck as an appetizer, perhaps with a caramelized onion-raisin bruschetta or with a couscous salad, enlivens his ginger-cured salmon with scotch bonnet chile crema and sides his cornmeal fried oysters with ancho-ginger sauce. Dessert could be mixed berry crumble, mocha chocolate cake or caramelized bananas with vanilla ice cream and pralines.

(609) 397-2656. Entrées, $15 to $20. Lunch, Tuesday-Saturday noon to 2. Dinner nightly except Monday, 6 to 9 or 10. Sunday brunch, noon to 2. BYOB.

Church Street Bistro, 11½ Church St., Lambertville, N.J.

This tiny space behind Mitchell's bar now is the stage for Europe-trained chef David Kiser, an instructor at the French Culinary Institute in Manhattan. He leased the quarters in 1996 to present what he called variously "new bistro cuisine" and "cuisine of the market.".

In two areas separated by a divider, he fashioned an appealing country bistro look with white-clothed tables, spaced nicely apart, and accents of copper pots. An outdoor courtyard featuring the chef's grill is pleasant in summer.

The short dinner menu offers some of the area's more interesting dishes, with an emphasis on low-fat preparation. Starters could be yukon gold potato and goat cheese pavé with black olive tapenade or warm smoked trout with celeriac rémoulade and horseradish crème fraîche. Expect main courses like pan-seared tilapia with wasabi crust, organic chicken stew, herb-grilled veal chop with forest mushrooms, and grilled sirloin of Australian lamb with a roasted garlic and tomato jam. Several come in small and regular sizes, and there's a special prix-fixe menu on Wednesday and Thursday nights.

Desserts might be warm apple tart with homemade vanilla ice cream, pumpkin cheesecake and ginger crème brûlée. The well-chosen wine list is affordably priced. *(609) 397-4383. Entrées, $16 to $23. Lunch, Friday and Saturday 11:30 to 2:30. Dinner, Wednesday-Saturday, 5 to 10. Sunday, brunch noon to 4, dinner 5 to 9.*

De Anna's, 18 South Main St., Lambertville.

Here's a small, convivial place in which De Anna Menzel continues the culinary magic launched by her predecessor, Paul Blasenheim. She took over the former Chef Paul's in 1990 upon his retirement. The only physical change involved partitioning off the open kitchen from which Paul liked to converse with customers. De Anna confesses to being too shy to be part of the dining scene. Her statement is her food, which is robust Italian.

The menu lists a dozen homemade pasta entrées, from basic with marinara sauce to extravagant with calamari fra diavolo. We were smitten by two flavorful pastas, one with prosciutto and peas and the other with sundried tomato and pinenut cream sauce, which came with zesty salads and a couple of robust breads. The portions were ample and the leftovers made a great lunch the next day.

Desserts, for those who leave room to indulge, include blackberry jam tart, belgian chocolate-espresso cake, ricotta cheesecake and Italian ice.

The place couldn't be smaller – six tables seating twenty. Illumination is entirely by candles that flicker in hurricane lamps, reflecting on the glass tabletops. Big pillows and cushions rest on the wall benches.

In 1997, DeAnna expanded, opening **Festival** next door at 20 South Main St. It's a small cappuccino bar, sandwich and gourmet takeout place, with five tiny tables, an outdoor picnic area and a changing array of treats to go.

(609) 397-8957. Entrées, $11.50 to $14.75. Dinner, Wednesday-Saturday 5:30 to 9:30 or 10, Sunday 5 to 9. Festival open Wednesday-Sunday 9:30 to 6, Friday and Saturday to 9. Both BYOB. No credit cards. No smoking.

Lambertville Station, 11 Bridge St., Lambertville.

Once abandoned, Lambertville's 2 1/2-story train station took on new life as a stylish Victorian restaurant and lounge. Diners on several levels of the glass-enclosed Platform Room watch geese glide by and lights reflect off the waters of the Delaware & Raritan Canal. And the food is so good and fairly priced that we've returned more than once – an unusual occurrence given our normal wanderlust.

The first time, our party of four sampled the unusual appetizer of alligator strips, which we dipped into a mustard and green peppercorn sauce. The carpaccio of buffalo also was very good.

Among entrées, the jambalaya was spicy, the boneless roast duck was properly crispy and came with a raspberry sauce and polenta, the medallions of buffalo sautéed with mushrooms and brandy cream sauce were more than ample and the veal medallions with jumbo shrimp in garlic butter were excellent. A superior honey-mustard dressing enchanced the house spinach salad; lime-almond cheesecake and key lime mousse pie were good desserts.

The Sunset on the Delaware special, served weekdays from 4 to 6:30, draws crowds for one of the best bargains around: soup or salad, entrée and dessert for $9.95. A Victorian lounge is on the mezzanine, and a dance club on the lower level is open every night.

(609) 397-8300. Entrées, $11.25 to $24.95. Lunch, Monday-Saturday 11:30 to 3. Dinner, Monday-Thursday and Sunday 4 to 9:30, Friday and Saturday 5 to 11. Sunday brunch, 11 to 3.

The Stockton Inn, 1 Main St., Stockton.

The food at this venerable inn rises and falls with the chefs in the kitchen, hitting a high point lately when the Stockton was invited to prepare a special dinner at the James Beard House Foundation in New York. That chef left following a management change, but the culinary tradition continues.

Murals enhance Stockton Inn dining room.

Our dinner began with a trio of salmon (vodka-cured gravlax, hot smoked salmon from the inn's smoker and salmon rillettes). It was a sensational presentation, thanks to an assortment of sauces, capers, red onions and delicious baguette toasts. We also liked the special salad, an arrangement of arugula, goat cheese, roasted red peppers and sundried tomatoes with a complex, smoky taste.

Among entrées, the boned and rolled chicken stuffed with mushroom duxelles and flanked by an array of green beans, carrots, braised red cabbage and layered potatoes was excellent. So was the veal sauté with sundried tomatoes and roasted garlic. Rain forest crunch ice cream with fresh raspberries was a refreshing ending.

The setting is comfortable and romantic in six historic dining rooms seating a total of 175. On chilly evenings, we particularly enjoy the intimate front rooms with fireplaces, crisp white tablecloths and candles, and subtly illuminated local murals on every wall. Painted by artists during the Depression in exchange for room and board, they are quite remarkable. In season, there's dining on five outside terraces amidst two waterfalls and a pond stocked with golden trout, near the wishing well made famous by the Rodgers and Hart song. The Old World Garden Bar on the upper terrace has a dance floor. The main inn has a glamorous bar and a cozy pub in front.

(609) 397-1250. Entrées, $17.95 to $26.95. Lunch, Monday-Saturday 11:30 to 2:30. Dinner, Monday-Thursday 4:30 to 9:30, weekends 5 to 10. Sunday, brunch 11 to 2:30, dinner 3:30 to 9.

Atrio Cafe, 515 Bridge St., Stockton, N.J.

Chef-owner Ricky Franco, a native of Brazil who cooked in New York at the Plaza and the Waldorf-Astoria hotels, is one of the trio that opened this appealing cafe named for their partnership, "a trio." The decor in hunter green and burgundy is simple. The eclectic cuisine with a Brazilian "flare," as they advertise, is quite sophisticated.

Appealing main courses range from pan-seared salmon with peppercorn sauce on a chickpea cake to roasted rack of lamb topped with a cannellini bean, mushroom wine demi-glace. The ravioli might be topped with a shrimp, tasso ham and chick pea sauce. The monkfish could be sprinkled with black pepper, splashed with mustard-curry sauce and served over watercress drizzled with a roasted shallot dressing.

Start with lump crab cakes with a sweet onion salsa or a salad of pepper-crusted scallops and grilled portobellos with watercress and shaved parmesan. Finish with key lime pie or a tart of poached pear with ginger-mascarpone cream.

(609) 397-0042. Entrées, $16.95 to $19.95. Lunch, Tuesday-Saturday 11:30 to 3. Dinner, Tuesday-Saturday from 5. Sunday, brunch 10:30 to 3, dinner 4 to 8. BYOB.

Meil's Restaurant, Bridge and Main Streets, Stockton.

Fresh American fare with an old-fashioned slant is the theme on the extensive menu at this Lambertville transplant, a cramped little bakery and restaurant fashioned from an old gasoline station. On a warm winter's day, we eyed the picnic tables on the blacktop parking lot in front before deciding to sit inside. The decor is simple but jaunty: colorful balloon curtains over the windows, quilts on the walls (one wall has a montage of black muffin pans) and tables covered with mint-colored oilcloths.

All kinds of interesting salads, sandwiches and egg dishes are featured at lunch. We sampled a classic salad niçoise and a not-so-classic huevos rancheros, with an unexpected and unwanted ton of chili between the eggs and the tortilla, and the accompanying salsa lacking fresh coriander.

Night brings some of the daytime fare as well as hefty pastas and main courses from meatloaf and mashed potatoes to peanut shrimp and grilled filet mignon with roasted garlic sauce.

The place packs in the hungry. You also can get almost anything from buttermilk biscuits and blueberry muffins to beef stew and chicken pot pie to go.

(609) 397-8033. Entrées, $12.95 to $19.95. Breakfast daily, 9 to 3. Lunch, 11 to 3. Dinner, 4:30 to 9 or 10. BYOB. No credit cards.

The Cafe, Route 510 at 604, Rosemont.

Lola Tindell and Peg Peterson moved their little cafe from Lambertville to Rosemont. In the 1885 old general store, they have a lot more room to offer "fresh food at its simple best," as their business card attests.

It's a casual, drop-in kind of place with bare floors, wooden tables and a mix of chair styles. Shelves are filled with the cookbooks they use, plus things for sale like gourmet foods, Botanicus soaps and striking ceramics, some done by one of the waitresses. A case along one side displays cheeses, desserts and baked goods. At night things get more formal with candles, cloth napkins and Lola's 1940s tablecloths on the tables.

Stop in for a breakfast burrito or the Adirondack breakfast, muesli and a bran muffin, which "gives you the strength to climb mountains," says the menu. Omelets include Russian peasant and rhubarb-ginger chutney with cream cheese. Potatoes from heaven are grilled with olive oil, rosemary, garlic, onion and cayenne. At lunch, we enjoyed an excellent turkey quesadilla and a hefty turkey sandwich on whole wheat.

At dinnertime, you can still order sandwiches and omelets. Or try broiled flounder with herbs, chicken brazilia or pasta wilhemina (named for the resident ghost) with chicken, broccoli, mushrooms and garlic. The Wednesday night ethnic dinners are a steal, $15 for three courses.

For dessert, consider mocha pot du crème or one of Peg's cheesecakes, perhaps rum raisin, apple cinnamon or lemon.

(609) 397-4097. Entrées, $13 to $16.50. Open weekdays at 8, weekends from 9. Dinner, Wednesday-Sunday to 9. Closed Monday. BYOB.

Diversions

A Lambertville phenomenon that's rather diverting is that of wine bars and pubs. Local entrepreneur James Bulger is the inspiration behind two, The Boat House and The Swan Hotel. **The Boat House** at 8 Coryell St. in the Porkyard is an elegant bar, where wines are featured by the glass and where the walls are paneled with old twelve-foot-high doors. Hamilton's Grill and the Boat House team up to provide food and drinks at the adjacent **Wine Bar.** Another good place for a drink and maybe a snack is **The Swan Hotel,** where the public rooms are filled with art and antiques. The main bar has comfortable leather chairs to sink into and a greenhouse wall looking out onto a small garden with a fountain, which is spotlit at night. A pianist plays show tunes on weekends. **The Inn of the Hawke,** 74 South Union St., is a neighborhood pub with a long horseshoe-shaped bar in the center room and a dining room looking onto a pleasant outdoor courtyard. Two young sisters have upgraded both the dining operation and the seven upstairs guest rooms, but this remains essentially a drinking establishment.

Walking Tour. The Lambertville Area Chamber of Commerce has published a walking tour for historic buildings and points of interest. The self-guided tour takes about 45 minutes. The map details 22 buildings, the oldest being the landmark Lambertville House, built in 1812, now nicely restored. Other buildings on the tour date to the late 19th century, and one is as recent as 1909. For more ancient history, visitors have only to walk across the bridge to New Hope, where 18th-century structures are much in evidence.

Delaware & Raritan Canal State Park. For nearly a century, the old D&R Canal was one of America's busiest. A 22-mile-long navigable feeder canal stretching from above Stockton at Raven Rock south through Lambertville to Trenton brought water from the Delaware River to the main canal, which ran from Bordentown to New Brunswick. The canal and its adjacent towpath by the Delaware River are now part of New Jersey's longest park. The towpath is a favorite of joggers and hikers.

The Prallsville Mills, Route 29, Stockton. Once a thriving little commercial center, the 18th-century mills were abandoned until 1973, when they were included on the National Register of Historic Places and became part of the D&R Canal State Park. Local citizens formed the Delaware River Mill Society to restore and interpret the mill site, which includes a four-story grist mill now used for periodic arts and crafts exhibits, lectures and concerts. Original mill machinery is on display.

Shopping. Antiques stores and art galleries are proliferating lately along Bridge and North Union streets, where the shopping seems to get better every year. Two of the nicest and newest are the avant-garde **A Mano Gallery** of contemporary crafts, an offshoot of one across the river in New Hope, and **Greene & Greene Gallery**, a specialist in contemporary crafts and the furniture designs of Jeffrey Greene, which moved here from New Hope. Lots of flowery and garden theme things are featured at **Joanna Hearts,** whose stock runs from cards and teacups to fabrics and aromatic home accessories. Not to be missed is the **Porkyard,** a former sausage factory complex now given over to a restaurant, wine bar, **Blue Raccoon** for great home and garden antiques and accessories, **Porkyard Antiques** and **Coryell Gallery.** A rear terrace overlooks the Delaware River behind **Rivergate**

Books; pick up a good book and start it outside. We like the cappuccino bar at **Lambertville Trading Co.** on Bridge Street, where you can quaff single or double espresso, cappuccino or mochaccino and the aromas are luscious. Pumpkin truffles, Bavarian espresso cake, black currant scones, oils and vinegars, cheeses and many varieties of coffee beans are available. Also on Bridge Street, **Pinch Penny & Dress Well** has some interesting casual clothes for men and women, including sportswear from Jackeroos. **The Sojourner** is a treasure trove of gift items from around the world; a huge selection of dangling and colorful fish earrings was $10 a pair. **The 5 & Dime** on North Union Street specializes in collectible toys, comic watches, plastic, paper, advertising and the like from 1900 to the '70s.

South of town is the **Laceworks,** a mill complex with a changing array of outlet stores, among them **The Gipsy Horse** for clothing and the **Cross-Country Ski Outfitter. Riverrun Gallery** here features contemporary art and was having a show of original artworks and crafts, all priced for under $300. **Prestige Antiques** operates out of a warehouse of a place. Antiquers in the know head for the **Lambertville Antique Market,** a mile and a half south of town along Route 29 and rated by the New York Times as one of the nation's ten best. This is where many local shopkeepers and innkeepers find their prizes, and dealers come from across the country to buy and sell authentic pieces. The market and its companion **Golden Nugget Antique Flea Market** operate weekends year-round.

In Stockton, **Charles Tiles** has a large and unique selection. Almost next door, **Rebecca's Gifts** stocks great cards, painted tin animals, Chinese mushroom birds and decorative items for the garden. If you need a bottle of wine for one of those BYOB restaurants, you'll find exceptional selections at **Phillips'** in Stockton and **Welsh's** in Lambertville.

Extra-Special

Cane Farm, Route 519, Rosemont.

Three generations of Canes have transformed a 94-acre farm once home to half a million chickens into a furniture-making center and a complex of crafts workshops and retail showrooms in old chicken coops. The idea was that of Charles Cane, who gave up one of New Jersey's largest poultry operations for more versatile pursuits upon his retirement in 1965. The implementation was left to son Phil Cane, a woodworker at heart. Lately joined by his two sons, Phil and staff make much of the handcrafted furniture on display in a 580-foot-long showroom called **Cane Farm Furniture.** You'd never know these were once chicken houses and hatcheries, so complete is the transformation with windows along one side, carpeted or brick floors, and classical music playing. One old coop after another stretches nearly the length of two football fields, showing what Phil calls the largest collection of country furniture in America. The stock ranges from reproductions of antique tables, Shaker cupboards and windsor chairs to decoys, pewter, brass light fixtures, hunting prints and, lately, aviation art. Talented Phil, who restores old cars and builds racing boats, says he's also "a collector and an accumulator." He needs little persuasion to show his antique guns, Indian relics, historic documents, old postmarks and what-not in an area marked "Ephemeral and Miscellaneous."

(609) 397-0606. Hours vary. Showrooms generally open daily 10 to 5, Sunday 1 to 5.

Typical Victorian structures lead to Gothic tower of The Abbey B&B in background.

Cape May, N.J.

Grande Dame of Victoriana

Bed and breakfast as an American phenomenon got its start in Cape May. It also has been elevated here to its highest form.

Tom and Sue Carroll are credited with launching the phenomenon in the early 1970s when they turned the Windward House on Jackson Street into a Victorian B&B in this most Victorian of towns. The registered National Historic Landmark community has since spawned about 100 more B&Bs. And entrepreneurs in what they call the B&B capital of the United States host seminars for prospective innkeepers from across the country. The phenomenon locally was raised to high art through formal teas, exotic breakfasts and even B&B house tours. Lately, some of the inns' brochures have become state-of-the-art and as showy as the rest of the B&B experience here.

In the 19th century, America's first seaside resort was the playground for no fewer than five presidents, and Benjamin Harrison made Cape May his summer White House. Less than a century later, it was down at the heels when citizens banded together to save the landmark Emlen Physick House from demolition. Thus was born the Mid-Atlantic Center for the Arts (MAC), a community dynamo that not only promotes the arts but restores structures, stages tours and sponsors events.

Thanks to MAC, Cape May seems to be a series of festivals all year long, from Crafts in the Winter to a Christmas Candlelight House Tour. Cape May's celebrated Victorian Week is now an annual ten-day extravaganza in October.

The year-round population of 4,800 swells many-fold in the summer in this town at the southern end of a peninsula, a point actually below the Mason-Dixon Line, where the Atlantic Ocean meets the Delaware Bay. Visitors come to ogle the largest collection of authentic Victorian structures in the country, to relax on the beaches and enjoy the wildlife, including some of the East's best bird-watching. At the heart of it all are the inns and B&Bs, an integral part of the Cape May experience.

Inn Spots

Almost every house in Cape May's historic district seems to be turning into a B&B. In a whimsical turn, a sign in front of the 1882 Christopher Gallagher House notes its distinction from all its Jackson Street neighbors: "a private residence." The Cape May custom is for the innkeepers to serve – and often sit with – guests at breakfast, and later to help with dinner plans as they review the menus during afternoon tea or beverages.

The Mainstay Inn, 635 Columbia Ave., Cape May 08204.
Preservationists Tom and Sue Carroll launched the B&B movement in Cape May at the Windward House, now under different ownership, and purchased the Mainstay in 1975. The 1872 Italianate villa was built by two gamblers as a gaming and entertainment club for gentlemen. It is one of the town's few Victorian structures that has gone through more than a century with no transitions. The fourteen-foot-high public rooms are lavishly furnished in Victoriana, right down to the sheet music on the piano. Especially notable is the ceiling of the entrance hall, where a stunning combination of seventeen wallpapers makes a beautiful pattern.

The twelve accommodations in the inn and in the pleasant 1870 Cottage next door are named for famous visitors to Cape May. Lace curtains, stenciling, brass and iron bedsteads, armoires and rockers comprise the museum-quality decor. The Henry Ford room has its own small porch and the Bret Harte room (with many of his books in a case) opens onto the entire second-floor veranda. Climb a steep ladder with a wavering rope for a railing to the tower on the third floor, where, with cushions on two sides and windows on all four, you get a good view of the town. The inn and the cottage, both with wide verandas and green rocking chairs, are separated by a brick walk and a handsome trickling fountain. The front gardens are brilliant with flowers.

Four modern, two-bedroom suites with queensize beds are located in the Mainstay's newer annex, the Officers' Quarters, a restored naval officers' building across the street. It's an appropriate addition, since Tom is a Naval Reserve

officer. Each suite contains a spacious living room with a dining area, a loveseat facing the gas fireplace and the TV in a corner cupboard, a kitchenette with a mini-refrigerator, and a marble bathroom with whirlpool tub and shower. They are decorated in country style, giving "a totally different experience than at the main inn – contemporary elegance rather than Victorian splendor," says Sue. The stairway railing came from the old Lafayette Hotel here,

Pacesetting Mainstay Inn is headquartered in landmark 1872 Italian villa.

thanks to a former mayor who had saved it in storage. The Mainstay's trademark green wooden chairs also appear on the front porches of each suite. Guests who stay here have tea at the main inn; continental breakfast is delivered to their quarters.

Sue's recipes for her breakfast and tea goodies are so sought after that she has published six editions of a small cookbook called "Breakfast at Nine, Tea at Four." In summer, breakfast at the main inn is continental-plus, served buffet-style on the veranda; other seasons it is formal and sit-down at two seatings at 8:30 and 9:30 at a table for twelve in the dining room. Chicken-pecan quiche, ham and apple pie, hash browns quiche, western oven omelet, California egg puff, cheese strata and stuffed french toast with strawberry sauce are among the specialties.

Tours of the Mainstay's ground floor ($7.50) are given Saturday, Sunday, Tuesday and Thursday at 4. Participants are invited to join inn guests afterward for a formal tea, the tea served from a copper container and accompanied by cucumber sandwiches, cheese straw daisies, chocolate streusel bars, spiced shortbread and the like.

"Young children generally find us tiresome," the inn's brochure advises sensibly. Except for the spiffy Officers' Quarters, the Mainstay is, as Tom Carroll says, "a total Victorian experience."

(609) 884-8690. www.mainstayinn.com. Twelve rooms and four suites with private baths. Doubles, $135 to $195 mid-May to mid-October and all weekends; $95 to $175 midweek rest of year. Officers' Quarters: $195 to $255, peak season and all weekends, $145 to $195 midweek mid-October to mid-May. Three-night minimum in season and most weekends. No smoking.

The Queen Victoria, 102 Ocean St., Cape May 08204.

Toned-down Victoriana and creature comforts are offered by Dane and Joan Wells in Cape May's largest B&B operation, the only one open every day of the year. The Wellses, who along with Tom and Sue Carroll are considered icons by their fellow innkeepers, started with twelve rooms and eight private baths in their original 1881 corner property. In 1989, they turned the Victorian house and carriage house next door into eleven luxury rooms and suites. Here they offer the niceties that many of today's travelers want: queensize brass or iron canopy beds, bedside clocks and reading lights, sitting areas or rooms, mini-refrigerators, whirlpool baths, television, fireplaces and air-conditioning.

In 1994, they took over the former Heirloom 1876 House across the street and renovated it for reopening in 1995 as **The Queen's Hotel,** a small European country hotel. It has beds without breakfast: ten rooms and a suite with private baths, TVs, affordable prices and more privacy. "Twenty percent of our guests have been looking for this kind of thing," said Dane, which he likened to a hotel's concierge floor. "It's for the person who wants historic surroundings without all the B&B trappings."

Back in the main facility, furnishings in both guest and public rooms are not so high Victorian as in other Cape May inns. They are authentic in the post-Victorian Arts and Crafts style. Each house has a parlor, one in the original building with a piano and a fireplace and the newer one with TV, games and jigsaw puzzles. Pantry areas are stocked with the makings for popcorn, tea, sherry and such. The library in the original inn contains volumes on architecture, art and history collected by Joan when she was executive director of the Victorian Society in America.

Breakfast at a recent visit included choice of juice, homemade granola, blueberry-cinnamon muffins and three kinds of homemade breads, a main course of hash-brown potato bake with ham slices, plus a basket of toasting breads. Baked eggs, cheese strata, spinach or corn casserole and stuffed baked french toast with warm strawberry sauce are other possibilities. The meal is served at a long table beneath a portrait of Queen Victoria in the dining room of the main house and in a dining room outfitted similarly in the addition. Joan presides at one breakfast table and Dane at the other.

(609) 884-8702. Fifteen rooms and six suites with private baths. April-October: doubles, $180 to $205; suites, $235 to $270; three- or four-night minimum stay. November-March: doubles, $80 to $180; suites, $125 to $235; two-night minimum weekends.

The Abbey, 34 Gurney St. at Columbia Avenue, Cape May 08204.

If all is prim and proper and rather like a museum at the Mainstay across the street, The Abbey is intimate, theatrical and laid-back. Jay and Marianne Schatz, corporate and academic dropouts, purchased the showy 1869 Gothic villa with its 60-foot tower and incredible gingerbread trim in 1979. It's their fourth restoration, and they've done a splendid job.

The parlor, library and dining room on the main floor have ornate twelve-foot ceilings and eleven-foot windows (decorated with lace curtains and striking lambrequins, designed by Marianne). Among their priceless possessions is the largest freestanding bookcase (which comes apart in 27 pieces) we've ever seen.

Fourteen people can sit around the banquet table in the dining room with its Teutonic sideboard. "We have the noisiest breakfasts in town," says Marianne. That's partly because Jay keeps guests regaled both with his stories and his selection

Co-owner Curtis Bashaw oversees Virginia Hotel (above) and restoration of Congress Hall hotel.

of hats from a closet that holds a choice of more than 350 – perhaps an Australian bush hat or a "Hagar the Horrible" beauty. His act and Marianne's repartee nearly upstage their breakfasts, which are continental-plus in summer and more elaborate at other times. You might have pink grapefruit juice, a dish of fresh peaches and whipped cream, an egg and ham casserole with garlic grits on the side, and buttered English muffins. Marianne's cream cheese strata with strawberry sauce and bacon or sausage also is popular.

Seven bedrooms on the second and third floors, all with private baths and interesting period light fixtures, are named for cities. We stayed in the Savannah, a sweet room with white enamel bedstead, oriental carpets, a white wicker sofa with purple cushions and a small refrigerator in the bathroom. The Schatzes also have restored the Second Empire-style summer cottage next door as a bright and airy adjunct, offering seven less formal guest rooms, all with private baths and refrigerators, and a couple of parlors and verandas.

Jay gives public tours of the first floor of the main house ($5) on Monday, Wednesday and Friday at 4, followed by tea and tidbits at 4:30. He and Marianne, who works during the day in real estate, join guests at 6 over beer, wine and popcorn on the porch or in the parlor, steering their dinner choices and the next day's itinerary.

(609) 884-4506. Fourteen rooms with private baths. Doubles, $100 to $280, mid-June to October; $80 to $175, rest of year. Two- to four-night minimum weekends. Children over 12. No smoking. Closed January-April.

The Virginia Hotel, 25 Jackson St., Cape May 08204.
Built in 1879 as Cape May's first hotel, the Virginia has been grandly restored as what general manager Curtis Bashaw, co-owner with his father, calls a deluxe "boutique" hotel. Tiny white lights frame the exterior year-round, newspapers

hang from a rack outside the dining room and appear at your door in the morning, and a pianist plays in the pleasant front library during the dinner hour in the acclaimed Ebbitt Room (see Dining Spots).

On your way upstairs check the stained-glass window in the landing; a local craftsman spent a year looking for old glass with which to restore it. The second and third floors contain 24 modern, comfortable guest rooms that vary widely in size and shape. Like the public rooms, they are furnished in a simple yet sophisticated manner. Bedrooms are equipped with private baths with new fixtures, telephones and remote-control TVs and VCRs hidden in built-in cabinets. Room service is available, terrycloth robes are provided and the hotel's guest services packet is one of the more informative we've seen.

The decor is mostly soft peaches and grays, for a restful look. There are eleven standard-size rooms, eleven premium and two extra-premium at the front of the second floor with private balconies. Five have a sofa and two upholstered chairs each, though we were surprised that one premium room with a kingsize bed had room enough for only one chair. The wraparound balcony on the second floor gave our already expansive room extra space and was particularly pleasant the next morning for a continental breakfast, delivered to the room at the time specified, of fresh orange juice, fruit, danish pastries and croissants.

At age 37, Curt is the oldest person on his talented staff. He sees this as the prototype for other small luxury hotels that he and his father want to develop along the East Coast. A fine prototype it is.

For another example, check out nearby Congress Hall, dating to 1816 and once of the nation's largest summer hotels. It's now undergoing a multi-million-dollar renovation under Curt's auspices, to produce 100 renovated hotel rooms. The main floor already offers some of Cape May's most sophisticated shops and the jaunty Congress Hall Cafe, an interim operation until the hotel dining room is up and running in 1999.

(609) 884-5700 or (800) 732-4236. Fax (609) 884-1236. www.virginiahotel.com. Twenty-four rooms with private baths. Doubles, $180 to $295 in July and August and weekends Memorial Day to mid-October. Rest of year, $130 to $250 weekends, $80 to $155 midweek. Three-night minimum weekends in season, two-night minimum weekends rest of year.

Manor House, 612 Hughes St., Cape May 08204.

Amid Cape May's haute Victoriana and large inns with owners usually around only at breakfast or teatime, the Manor House is a refreshing change. The impressive, gambrel-roofed house with warm oak and chestnut foyer and striking furnishings seems almost contemporary in contrast.

Innkeepers Nancy and Tom McDonald from Philadelphia, who had stayed as guests here many times, considered the B&B a model when they bought it in 1995. They've maintained the tradition of good food, and added a secluded lower-level room with kingsize bed, full bath and private entrance.

Upstairs are nine guest rooms and a suite with private baths. They are nicely furnished in antiques, with brass and wood king or queensize beds, handmade quilts and light Victorian print wallpapers. A third-floor suite stretches across the front of the house with a kingsize bed, a sitting area and a whirlpool tub by the window in the bathroom. There are handmade "napping" signs for each door knob. Nancy plays "cookie fairy" at night, stocking the cookie jar with treats, including her favorite chocolate chip pecan hearts.

The McDonalds serve sumptuous breakfasts, employing many of the former innkeepers' recipes. Among favorites are "asparageggs" (poached eggs and asparagus on homemade English muffins with mornay sauce), a corn and egg pie with jalapeño cheese and tomato relish, vanilla whole-wheat waffles, a french toast sandwich made with raisin bread stuffed with cream cheese, apple crêpes and corn quiche. Juice, fresh fruit and sticky buns, a house signature, round out the meal.

Afternoon tea time brings cheese spreads, bean dip, salsa, coconut-macadamia bars and chocolate streusel bars. Guests partake in a front room with a striking stained-glass-front player piano or a library with two plush loveseats in front of a fireplace.

(609) 884-4710. Fax (609) 898-0471. Nine rooms and one suite with private baths. Doubles, $135 to $187; suite, $217. Off-season: weekends $112 to $147, suite $177; midweek, $87 to $112, suite $147. Three-night minimum in July and August. Children over 12. No smoking. Closed in January.

The Inn on Ocean, 25 Ocean St., Cape May 08204.

A billiards table greets guests as they enter this B&B, which is furnished in light-hearted Victorian style. It's part of a billiards room just off the front entry,

Wide front porch at The Inn on Ocean.

where owner Jack Davis's model Pontiac racing cars line the fireplace mantel and two of his seven sets of golf clubs are stashed in the corner. The room has a distinctly masculine air, an aspect that sets it apart from most B&B rooms in Cape May. Also unusual is this inn's theme of accommodations: five suites with private baths, oversize beds, TVs, wet bars, microwave ovens and thick carpeting.

Jack, who retired from General Motors, and his wife Katha opened their B&B in 1993 after a total overhaul of a three-story apartment house that was "barely fit for human habitation," in Katha's words. The walls are colorfully painted in sage green, pale yellow or pink, with coordinated fabrics and comforters. The bath in the Veranda Room was designed around an elaborate pedestal sink. A working clawfoot tub occupies a rear corner of the Promenade Room, while the shower is located in the bathroom. Besides sitting areas and the aforementioned amenities, Katha's lilting decor includes straw hats and accents like a pin cushion here and an old shaving brush and bowl there. A third-floor suite with two bedrooms and a sitting room accommodates four.

Guests enjoy a wicker-filled front porch, an open porch on the second floor with a good view of the ocean at the end of the street, a parlor with a fireplace and a pleasant pink dining room, where the table can extend to seat twenty. This is the setting at 9 o'clock for some memorable breakfasts, employing different table settings every day. An apple baked in chardonnay, an omelet supreme with salsa and cornbread, and cinnamon coffee cake were the treats at our visit. French toast with fruit was the main event the next day. The professional nurse in her spurs Katha to "try to mitigate our sins with a lot of fresh fruit." She also offers heart-healthy breakfasts. Afternoon tea time brings sherry in front of the fireplace, lemonade and brownies on the front porch, and tea or wine and cheese.

Jack, who says his innkeeping wife is the toughest boss he ever had, gets in his licks as a golf instructor and as a basketball coach for local youth leagues. He also may tempt you into a game of billiards.

The Davises also rent a four-bedroom cottage a block from the ocean in Cape May Point for $2,000 a week in summer.

(609) 884-7070 or (800) 304-4477. Fax (609) 884-1384. www.bbianj.com/innocean. Five suites with private baths. Doubles, $155 to $165; two-bedroom suite, $195 for two, $295 for four, mid-June through September. Off-season: $135 to $175 weekends, $99 to $129 midweek. Three to four-night minimum summer weekends. Children over 14. No smoking. Closed January to mid-February.

Inn at 22 Jackson, 22 Jackson St., Cape May 08204.
Presiding over the front parlor at this B&B is Minerva, a lady (?) ensconced at the edge of the sofa with her shoulders wrapped in mink, a wine bottle in the pocket of her apron and a wine glass in hand. "Minerva was our resident house-keeper," says co-innkeeper Barbara Carmichael. "But guests kept sending her expensive gifts and she's too prissy now to clean house. So she minds Eliza, my mother's doll."

The presence of Minerva sets a whimsical tone for this B&B that was opened in 1992 by Barbara, an interior designer from Gettysburg, Pa., and her partner, contractor Chip Masemore. They won a 1992 county beautification award for their restoration of this former apartment house, whose facade is strikingly vivid in navy blue and bright purple with white trim. Five suites come with king or queen beds, TVs, wet bars, microwave ovens and such. "We wanted to serve a different niche in Cape May," Barbara explained. "We tried to determine what Chip didn't like about B&Bs. He missed having TV, a gin and tonic at 5 o'clock and not being able to reheat his doggy bag from dinner for lunch the next day. So we offer modern conveniences, yet retain the charm of Victoriana."

Victoriana there is aplenty, from the unusual curved armoire in the Holly Suite to the clawfoot tub in the bathroom of the Windward Suite. And there are collections everywhere: Barbara's are dolls and majolica; Chip's are toys, games and depictions of bawdy women from days of yore – "the higher up in the house you go," says Barbara, "the bawdier they get." A mounted boar's head and a life-size cardboard cutout labeled Betty Boop oversee the sitting room of the Jackson Suite, whose porch faces Jackson Street. The two-bedroom Turret Suite on the third floor comes with a deck and a bathroom yielding an ocean view and a secret balcony for two overlooking Jackson Street. In back of the house is a two-story apartment annex that the innkeepers advertise as a cottage. It has a living room with gas fireplace and a kitchen on the main floor and two bedrooms with bath on the second floor, where a balcony affords an ocean view.

A full breakfast is served in the stunning dining room with bleached solid oak furniture, deep red painted walls and a ceiling trimmed with several showy Victorian wallpapers. The fare could be blueberry buckle and baked omelet with Canadian

Victoriana and verandas reign in typical scene looking toward turreted Inn at 22 Jackson.

bacon, or baked apples with raisin-bread french toast and sausage. If you're so inclined, there's "fresh cereal right off the truck," a reference to the cereal boxes stashed in a truck on a shelf displaying toy vehicles and dolls. Afternoon tea also follows the alternating sweet and savory themes: chocolate-chip cake one day, baked crab spread the next.

(609) 884-2226 or (800) 452-8177. Fax (609) 884-0055. Five suites with private baths. Mid-June to mid-October and weekends except in winter: one-bedroom suites, $185; two-bedroom suites, $240 for two, $330 for four. Winter, one-bedroom suites, $145 weekends, $95 midweek; two-bedroom suites, $250 weekends, $160 to $180 midweek. Two-night minimum stay weekends and in summer. Children over 12, younger in cottage. No smoking.

Leith Hall, 22 Ocean St., Cape May 08204.

In their colorful Victorian B&B (moss green with accents of deep peach and mustard), preservationists Elan and Susan Zingman-Leith are working miracles with wallpaper and paint. "We're trying to create an 'aesthetic movement' house," says Susan. Since Japanese things were the rage at that time, the parlor, with its Bradbury & Bradbury wallpaper dotted with swallows, plum blossoms and the rising sun has an anglo-Japanese look.

Eight guest accommodations, all with private baths, reflect the fun the couple has had with the painting techniques popular at the time. The Iris Room off the parlor has rag-rolled walls and a dragonfly and butterfly pattern on the ceiling. The floors are stenciled with lily pads. New in 1998 was the two-bedroom Audubon Suite "with everything anyone has ever asked for," in Elan's words: a queen bed in one room and two twins in the other, a fireplace, whirlpool tub and color TV, not to mention a paneled Bradbury & Bradbury frieze of birds and flowers plus other bird-related accessories.

Bedrooms on the second and third floors have views of the ocean (especially good on the third floor) and beds have been positioned so you can lie in bed and see the water. There are exotic touches, such as the white net draped from a ring over the bed in the checkerboard-stenciled Empire Room and silver and gold stars painted all over the ceiling in the Turkish Suite. The latter has an Arabian Nights feel and a queensize bed. Bathrooms sport nifty reproductions of ads from magazines of the era.

Breakfast is served in the small parlor (and the even smaller library off it) at two seatings, 8:30 and 9:30. Elan, the cook, loves to serve big breakfasts of perhaps scrambled eggs with cream cheese and dill, mixed berry pancakes or apple and cheese crêpes. There are always granola and fresh fruit as well. At teatime you might find scones and crumpets, brownies or even chocolate mousse cake. In summer it's served outside on the big wraparound porch.

Let us not overlook the sub-theme of Scotland. There are engravings of the town of Leith. The Highland Room on the second floor has wonderful murals from the highlands, stenciled thistles and now handpainted Scottish angels looking down from the sky on the ceiling. And in December Susan wraps balls for the Christmas tree in tartan. After only a few years of decorating, she says, "already my tastes are getting more complicated." We can't wait to see what she and Elan come up with next.

Meanwhile, they've co-authored a beautiful, insightful coffee-table photographic book called *The Secret Life of Victorian Houses*. Their own house shares many of the secrets.

(609) 884-1934. Five rooms and three suites with private baths. July-August and weekends June-October: doubles $130 to $155, suites $185 to $250. Late fall to spring: doubles $85 to $125, suites $135 to $160. Three-night minimum weekends in season; two-night minimum weekends rest of year. Children over 12. No smoking.

The John F. Craig House, 609 Columbia Ave., Cape May 08204.

Some of the best breakfasts in town are served in this attractive carpenter gothic summer cottage dating to 1866. Frank Felicetti, formerly a lawyer in Wilmington, Del., and his wife Connie live in the house, so are more involved than was former owner David Clemans, who sold to open the Cucina Rosa restaurant here. The B&B came with most of its furnishings, so about the only changes for longtime guests are hands-on innkeeping and evening turndown service, accompanied by homemade fudge or cookies – "whatever we've baked that day," say the enthusiastic cooks.

The house, which comes in two sections, contains seven air-conditioned guest rooms and a two-room suite. They are done in typical Cape May style, with lots of wicker and oriental rugs, marble-top tables and elaborate period wallpapers. Victorian linens and laces grace every window and turn up on tables and dresser tops as well as in antique crocheted bedspreads. All beds but one are queen or kingsize. Eastlake and Renaissance Revival antiques and original gasoliers prevail. Guests have use of the parlor and the requisite Cape May porches.

Blended coffees and teas are put out for early risers at 7:30. Breakfast is served at 8:30 and 9:45 seatings in the pretty dining room with its lace tablecloth and scallop-shell wallpaper. There are always seasonal fruits on the table as well as homemade muffins and buttermilk coffee cake. The entrée, which comes out on a piping-hot plate garnished with fruit, could be anything from lemon french toast spiked with rum to a bacon and gruyère cheese casserole to eggs with cream cheese and scallions in a ramekin, accompanied by rosemary-flavored new potatoes. Blueberry-cornbread pancakes with grand marnier sauce are a house favorite.

Herbed popovers, homemade sourdough or dark molasses breads, biscuits and coffee cake might accompany. Frank does the cooking, while Connie serves.

She also bakes the pastries and the goodies that accompany afternoon tea, put out on the sideboard in the dining room. Ginger cake, lemon-poppyseed bread, French pineapple upside-down cake, mushroom pâté with swiss cheese, hot artichoke dip and guacamole are among her specialties.

(609) 884-0100. Fax (609) 898-1307. Seven rooms and one suite with private baths. Doubles, $85 to $155. Suite, $125 to $175. Two-night minimum stay. Children over 12. No smoking. Closed January and February.

Rhythm of the Sea, 1123 Beach Ave., Cape May 08204.

The name of this B&B derives, of course, from the ocean surf across the street. It also reflects the spring and fall concert series presented by visiting musicians in its huge living room centered by a concert grand piano. New owners Wolfgang and Robyn Wendt aren't musicians themselves –"somebody has to listen," quips Robyn – but they import professionals who stay at the B&B and entertain inn guests and invited friends at afternoon tea.

Besides music, the 1915 summer house is unusual here in that it is furnished simply in the Arts and Crafts style with Stickley furniture and Mission-style lanterns, wooden blinds and table linens. Almost everything is handmade in the Craftsman style. "Many guests say they're tired of Victorian clutter and frills," says Robyn. "They find this to be more masculine, more open and spacious."

Seven large bedrooms come with queensize beds and private baths, and the painted walls are done in the rose, pumpkin and olive palettes of the period. The look is spare and pure. The new Library guest room, hidden behind bookshelves off the second-floor hallway, comes with a wicker settee and an ocean view from the bed. The Wendts, who moved into the rear carriage house, converted the former owners' quarters in the main house into a two-bedroom suite with a sitting room.

The couple relocated here in 1997 from Rock Hall, Md., where they had run a restaurant and managed the Inn at Osprey. Avid sportsmen who love to sail, they had met at a ski lodge in Colorado. Robyn, a well-traveled New Zealander, is into hospitality. Her German-born husband, a European-trained pastry chef, shows off his baking talents during afternoon tea and cooks four-course dinners for inn guests by reservation. The price ranges from $30 to $50 per person, depending on the meal. He also teaches cooking classes. A full breakfast is offered from 8:30 to 9:30 at four tables in the huge dining room. Fresh juices and fruit precede the main course. One of Wolfgang's treats is baked brioche made with cinnamon swirl french toast topped with baked custard and seasonal berries, accompanied by peppered bacon.

(609) 884-7788 or (800) 498-6888. Fax (609) 884-4380. Seven rooms and a three-room suite with private baths. April-October: doubles $160 to $225, suite $250. Rest of year: doubles $89 to 175, suite $195. Two-night minimum most summer weekends.

The Southern Mansion, 720 Washington St., Cape May 08204.

For several years, all Cape May had been agog over the goings-on at the historic George Allen Estate, the town's largest and most elaborate mansion. In 1997, innkeepers and tradespeople got an inside look at a fancy ball celebrating the grand opening. Barbara Bray and Rick Wilde, newly wed and barely turned 30, had finished converting the 30,000 square-foot Italianate villa into an elegant boutique hotel, which she said would be "the biggest and best in town." The 100-room house, built in the mid-19th century for a Philadelphia department store owner, occupies much of a two-acre square block in the heart of Cape May.

With 30 bathrooms, ten fireplaces, shiny Honduran mahogany floors, twelve-foot-high molded ceilings, cast-bronze chandeliers, 23 gold mirrors and 5,000 square feet of verandas and solariums, this was hardly a typical South Jersey beach house. Amazingly, the original furnishings, chandeliers and artworks were intact, many stored in the basement and ready to outfit ten more guest rooms under construction in a new wing.

Financing the restoration with house tours and the backing of her father, a Philadelphia physician, Barbara opened in 1995 with the first of fifteen ample guest quarters on three floors of the main house. They vary widely but come with an assortment of ornate, step-up king and queen beds, televisions cosseted in armoires, gilt-edged mirrors and chairs, gold damask bedspreads and draperies, velvet recliners and settees, writing desks and telephones with modems. Some of the bathrooms are small with clawfoot tubs. Others have huge walk-in tiled showers with seats. The sink in one room is installed right in the room between two halves of an armoire.

Ten larger, more deluxe rooms in a new wing at the side have king beds. Some come with fireplaces, porches and double jacuzzis. Beside the wing is an Italianate pool with columns and a waterfall.

The main floor has a catering kitchen, a solarium restaurant seating 160 for sit-down dinners, and a ballroom with six gold mirrors that "looks like Versailles," as Barbara envisioned it. We got a hint of what was in store in the bright aqua and butter-yellow ballroom of the main house, now a breakfast room with three tables bearing vases of long-stemmed roses and end walls of 23-carat gold-leaf mirrors reflecting into infinity. This is the setting for a full breakfast for house guests. Afternoon tea and wine and cheese with crudités are served here later in the day.

Eventually, Barbara planned a full-service restaurant for house guests and the public in the solarium. "We'll offer the amenities of a hotel but retain the antiques and charm of a B&B," said she. Meanwhile, as part of a fanciful experience, guests could order a catered dinner for two, to be served in the solarium, the new ballroom or the rooftop cupola atop the fifth floor with a view across town.

(609) 884-7171 or (800) 381-3888. Fax (609) 898-0492. Twenty-one rooms and four suites with private baths. Summer and weekends off-season: doubles $225 to $250; suites $275 to $350. Off-season: $125 to $250 weekends, $99 midweek. Children over 8. No smoking.

Dining Spots

The Ebbitt Room, The Virginia Hotel, 25 Jackson St., Cape May.

Named for the original owners of Cape May's first hotel, the small, candlelit dining room in the restored Virginia Hotel is an exceptionally pleasant setting for some of the best food in Cape May. In a town where restaurants get noisy and hectic, this remains an oasis of calm and professionalism, one worthy of owner Curtis Bashaw's aspirations for a small boutique hotel. Elegant in peach and gray, the high-ceilinged room has swagged draperies, crisply linened tables, delicate wine glasses, art deco wall sconces and birds of paradise standing tall in vases on dividers.

Chef Christopher Hubert's progressive American cuisine is exciting and innovative. Main dishes range from grilled swordfish with caramelized lobster, shallots

Elegant Ebbitt Room provides fine dining at Virginia Hotel.

and arugula, served with a pomegranate vinaigrette to sautéed venison with spaetzle and caramelized pearl onions.

Excellent hot rolls with a crisp crust preceded our appetizers, one an eggplant and gorgonzola crostini served with red onion pesto and the other a very zesty caesar salad, served on black octagonal plates. The roast cornish game hen was heavily herbed and rested on a bed of caramelized vegetables on a parsley-flecked plate, and the filet mignon was served with a grilled three-onion salad and roasted potatoes. On another occasion we liked the shrimp margarita, flamed in tequila and served with avocado cream sauce and roasted tomato salsa, and the pan-roasted quail with grapes and green peppercorns. These came with a medley of zucchini and carrots, and potatoes shaped like mushrooms.

For dessert, we enjoyed an upside-down fig cake and pecan-praline cheesecake. The good wine list leans to the expensive side, but we've found a Danfield Creek chardonnay for $17 and a Rutherford Hill merlot for $22. Service by young waitresses is graceful and competent. And the live piano music emanating from the lobby lends a glamorous air to this fine addition to the Cape May dining scene.

(609) 884-5700 or (800) 732-4236. Entrées, $18 to $28. Dinner nightly from 5.

Water's Edge, Beach Drive and Pittsburgh Avenue, Cape May.
Chef-owner Neil Elsohn and his wife Karen, who is hostess, offer some of the most inspired dishes in town in this sleek, hotel-style dining room in front of La Mer Motor Inn. The well-tailored expanse of banquettes and booths is dressed in white cloths topped with rose-colored runners and flickering votive candles.

On one occasion, we enjoyed an appetizer of strudel with escargots, pinenuts and an ethereal garlic cream sauce before digging into poached fillet of Norwegian salmon with lime and salmon caviar, and sautéed sea scallops with tomatillos, cilantro and grilled jicama. On our second visit, we grazed happily through appetizers and salads. These included scallop chowder, spicy pork and scallion empanadas with pineapple-ginger chutney, fusilli with grilled tuna, oriental

One of few ocean views for dining in Cape May is offered by Spiaggi.

vegetables and szechuan vinaigrette, and grilled chicken salad with toasted pecans, grilled red onions, mixed greens and citrus vinaigrette.

Main courses include such standouts as blackened tuna steak with mango-lime hollandaise, seared shrimp with creole mustard sauce, and grilled pork tenderloin with spicy black bean sauce and crispy sweet plantains. Desserts could be raspberry cheesecake with citrus anglaise, banana-bread pudding with hot chocolate sauce and bittersweet chocolate-walnut pâté with espresso and vanilla sauces.

In summer, a lounge menu is served in the spacious bar. Salads and appetizers are available there anytime. The brunch menu contains some exotic items; the meal is quite salubrious when taken on the outdoor deck with ocean beyond.

(609) 884-1717. Entrées, $18 to $26. Dinner nightly, 5 to 9:30 or 10, May to mid-October; Friday-Sunday rest of year.

Spiaggi, 429 Beach Drive, Cape May.

Consistently good food and flawless service distinguish this place reborn by Maureen and Stephen Horn on the second floor of what once was a bath house and saloon. For fifteen years their Restaurant Maureen was the best fancy dining establishment in town. In 1997, Maureen said, "it was time for a change."

Their beachfront restaurant reopened after a winter of renovations as Spiaggi (Italian for beach), with "cucina nouveau, light and fresh, served in a light-hearted atmosphere." The evolution was a natural for Steve, the chef, who trained in Florence and is partial to Tuscan cooking. The Spiaggi menu was broadened to appeal to diners who wanted an affordable pasta and a glass of wine at the Mermaid Martini Bar as well as those who craved the signature rack of lamb and a great vintage in dressier surroundings.

Typical starters are a grilled portobello mushroom seasoned with pancetta and shallots, homemade ravioli stuffed with sonoma goat cheese, and caesar salad laced with lump crabmeat and gulf shrimp. Pastas and main dishes vary from shrimp and pancetta with penne and a classic Mediterranean bouillabaisse to hazelnut-crusted swordfish with a garlic mayonnaise, sautéed chicken with artichoke hearts and fontina cheese, and filet mignon with portobello mushrooms in barolo wine sauce.

Desserts include a signature walnut cheesecake with a warmed caramel topping and a wonderful strawberry tart.

(609) 884-3504. Entrées, $14.50 to $24.50. Dinner, Tuesday-Sunday from 5, fewer days in off-season. Closed November-March.

410 Bank Street, 410 Bank St., Cape May.

This restaurant's enclosed outdoor courtyard, enveloped in plants and tiny white lights, is a lovely setting for dinner. Owners Steve and Janet Miller, who also run an Italian restaurant called Frescos next door, are theater set designers and their background shows.

A Chinese chef presents a gumbo of New Orleans, French and Caribbean dishes, many grilled over mesquite wood and most with cajun-creole overtones. We loved the special seviche and butterflied quail on warmed greens for appetizers, which also included Bahamian yellowfin tuna beignets and fresh Jersey asparagus amandine in a puff-pastry cornet. Among entrées are shellfish filé gumbo, blackened prime rib and baby rack of lamb with foie gras. Our choices of blackened red snapper with pecan sauce and yellowfin tuna in Barbadian black bean sauce, served with crisp vegetables and rice pilaf, were too much to finish. After all, we had to save room for the highly rated key lime pie, which was the real thing. So is everything else, from crawfish bisque to possibly the best bread pudding with hot bourbon sauce you'll ever taste. There's even a French-style roast – a special meat, fowl or game dish offered nightly.

If you can't eat on the courtyard, settle for one of the screened porches or the small, intimate dining rooms adorned with New Orleans posters inside the restored 1840 house.

(609) 884-2127. Entrées, $20.95 to $27.95. Dinner nightly, 5:30 to 10. Closed November-April. BYOB.

The Washington Inn, 801 Washington St., Cape May.

Surrounded by shade trees and colorful banks of impatiens, this historic white building run by brothers David and Michael Craig is considered far and away the best of the larger restaurants in town. Originally a plantation house built in 1840, it contains four elegant dining rooms, including a Victorian garden room and a pretty wicker-filled front veranda done up in pink.

The fairly extensive menu starts with scallops on horseback, mushroom strudel and crab cakes with a roasted red pepper sauce. Entrées include flounder stuffed with crabmeat and monterey jack cheese and laced with brandy, pan-seared salmon with passionfruit sauce, grilled salmon with a six-onion compote, herb-crusted chicken topped with grilled eggplant and mozzarella, and grilled Kansas steak with horseradish butter. Desserts could be frozen key lime pie, pumpkin-pecan cheesecake and fresh strawberry napoleons.

The 8,000-bottle wine cellar earns the Wine Spectator Grand Award. The wine list is reasonably priced, and diners like to finish with international coffees.

(609) 884-5697. Entrées, $18.95 to $24.95. Dinner nightly, 5 to 10. Closed Monday and Tuesday, November-April.

Union Park Dining Room, 727 Beach Drive, Cape May.

The restaurant in the 85-year-old Hotel Macomber has been infused with new spirit and style by Crystal and Charles Czworkowski, she a hotel general manager and he an attorney in Boston. They moved to the town where she had summered with her parents to buy and operate the 34-room beachfront hotel in 1996.

Crystal oversees the interior dining room, a high-ceilinged, summery space appointed mostly in white and evocative of the Cape May of the 1930s. The chef's contemporary fare and presentation earn good reviews.

We liked the sound of everything on the menu, which ranges widely from pan-seared sea scallops with a saffron-infused lobster and wild mushroom risotto cake to roasted rack of Wyoming lamb with dijon herb crust, presented wigwam style with asparagus spears perched over garlic-mashed potatoes. Favorite starters are steamed lobster dumplings with ginger-plum and hoisin sauce, grilled

Setting is summery at Union Park.

portobello mushroom stuffed with lump crabmeat and cheese, and a layered parfait of Scottish smoked salmon and lump crabmeat with crème fraîche and bermuda onions, two chives rising like antenna with a dollop of black caviar between.

Amid the complexities are three signature dishes named for the owners' young children. One is daughter Cezanne's apple cloud, crisp phyllo triangles holding sautéed apples, flanked by a scoop of vanilla ice cream and a pool of hot caramel sauce.

(609) 884-8811. Entrées, $20 to $32. Dinner nightly, 5 to 10. Closed Tuesday and Wednesday in off-season and January-February. BYOB.

Peaches at Sunset, 1 Sunset Blvd., West Cape May.

Cape May's prettiest restaurant is this establishment with an offbeat name, derived from chef-owner George Pechin's nickname and its location at the head of Sunset Boulevard.

A nicely restored Victorian house, vivid in peach with aqua trim, holds two small dining rooms divided by a walnut-trimmed aquarium full of tropical fish. Overhead are a stained-glass panel and a wild tropical design on the ceiling. Dining is al fresco on a raised rear deck leading to a gazebo with a few pint-size tables.

The contemporary dinner menu might offer eight entrées, among them Caribbean-style shrimp with rum and mint sauce, Cuban chicken stuffed with prosciutto and plantains, grilled duck breast with peach sauce and tournedos of beef with twin tapenades of artichokes and olives.

Start with the creamy clam chowder that we once savored during lunch at the owner's former Peaches Cafe, the signature roasted garlic served with mascarpone cheese and grilled sourdough bread or Thai crab served in endive leaves. Finish with bourbon-pecan pie or crème caramel.

(609) 898-0100. Entrées, $17.95 to $24.95. Dinner nightly from 4:30, April-October; weekends rest of year. BYOB.

Cucina Rosa, 301 Washington St. Mall, Cape May.

David Clemans, who has a reputation as one of the best cooks in town, opened this authentic and popular Italian restaurant after selling the John F. Craig House, his B&B of many years. "We take relatively standard southern Italian dishes and make them very carefully," says David. Everything is done from scratch, from the marinara and meat sauces to semolina bread.

Main dishes run from basic pastas to lobster oreganata. Widely acclaimed is the chicken portofino, stuffed with mozzarella cheese and Italian sausage specially made for the restaurant, rolled and baked with tomato sauce and served with pasta. Other treats include grilled swordfish and lamb chops, each marinated in olive oil and Italian spices and served with fried potatoes sautéed with peppers and onions or pasta with a choice of sauce.

Desserts are David's forte. He makes fruit pies that change daily, lemon cheesecake and a rich chocolate cake. He also offers ice creams and sherbets.

The 64-seat restaurant in rose and green is at a corner location along the mall. It spills outside with sixteen tables on a sidewalk patio in season.

(609) 898-9800. Entrées, $7.95 to $21.95. Dinner nightly except Wednesday, 5 to 10, Sunday 4:30 to 9:30. Closed January to mid-February. BYOB. No smoking.

Diversions

Victorian Cape May. The nation's largest concentration of Victorian ginger-bread structures – some 670, ranging from tiny cottages to sprawling hotels – is on display in the historic district. The best way to see them is on foot or bicycle or, better, through a variety of tours offered by the Mid-Atlantic Center for the Arts, (800) 275-4278. MAC offers two distinct **guided trolley tours:** the East End (the best if you only have time for one) and the West End. Each takes about half an hour and costs $5. MAC guides also lead several **walking tours,** each 90 minutes and $5. MAC sponsors boat cruises, moonlight trolley rides, kitchen tours, an Inns and Outs of Cape May tour and Cape May INNteriors Tours and Teas. Individual inns are opened for tours under their own auspices as well as through Mansions by Gaslight, Victorian Sampler and Christmas Inns tours.

Emlen Physick House and Estate, 1048 Washington St., (609) 884-5404. The eighteen-room house designed by Victorian architect Frank Furness was the first to be saved by MAC and the property serves as its headquarters. Many of the original furnishings have been returned to the house for display purposes. Tour highlights include an upstairs library with Japanese wallpaper, even on the ceiling, the owner's bachelor bedroom and the fan collection in his mother's bedroom. Cape May's only Victorian house museum has restored the Carriage House Gallery for changing exhibitions. Hour-long house tours cost $6.

Cape May Point Lighthouse, Cape May Point State Park. MAC continues to restore this 1859 landmark, which has been reopened for tours. The hardy climb the 199 tower stairs to the Watch Room Gallery just below the lantern for a panoramic view (adults, $4). A visitor center in the restored Oil House on the lighthouse grounds contains a photo mural showing the lighthouse view, a twelve-minute video detailing the structure and a museum shop.

Performing Arts. MAC sponsors a spring series of chamber music concerts known as the **Cape May Music Festival.** The East Lynne Company, an equity group in residence here in summer, presents a **Victorian Theater Festival** July through September. **Cape May Stage** mounts a number of summer shows at the Welcome Center, while the **Chalfonte Cabaret** is staged weekends at the Chalfonte Hotel. A **Vintage Dance Weekend** including a ball and a tea dance in Victorian attire is scheduled in April. Live performances are part of three-day **Victorian Holmes Mystery Weekends** in March and November.

Birding and Wildlife. Cape May lies on the heavily populated Atlantic Flyway and more than 400 species of birds head north and south through Cape May Point. Good areas for nature-watching are South Cape May Meadow, Cape May Point State Park, Higbee's Beach Wildlife Management Area and the Cape May Bird Observatory.

Swimming is fine along Cape May's beach (the required beach passes may be purchased, and often are complimentary to inn guests), and at Higbee's and Sunset beaches and Cape May Point State Park.

Shopping. Despite its Victorian charm and influx of tourists, Cape May's forte is not shopping, although the situation has improved lately. The Washington Street Mall is where most of the action is. Our favorite here is **The Whale's Tale,** a ramble of rooms containing everything from shell magnets to an extraordinary collection of cards. Another good gift shop is **McDowell's Gallery of Gifts. For the Birds** carries excellent things for nature lovers and **Swede Things** speaks for itself. Check out the wallpaper borders and elegant fixtures at **Fralinger's** original saltwater taffy emporium, even if you're not into taffy. The **Cape May Linen Outlet** offers good bargains, especially in placemats. The Virginia Hotel's Curt Bashaw oversees the tenant mix in the new Shops at Congress Hall. We like the clothing at **The Best Vest Co.,** the home and garden accessories at **Environs,** and especially **Love the Cook,** a gourmet kitchen shop chock full of goodies, run by Rhona Craig of the Washington Inn.

Extra-Special

Cape May Diamonds, Cape May Point.

A lot of fuss is made over the quartz pebbles found only locally and known as Cape May Diamonds. The semi-precious stones of diverse colors vary from the size of little peas to marbles and walnuts. They're bright and clear when found in the wet sand, but, alas, they become dull as they dry. When cut and polished, they can be set in gold or silver to make attractive jewelry such as rings, bracelets and necklaces. One of the best places to find Cape May diamonds is at Sunset Beach in Cape May Point, where you'll also see the shell of the USS Atlantis, a World War I concrete ship that ran aground in a storm and has been trapped here ever since. We burrowed into the sand here looking for "diamonds" and finally latched onto someone who seemed to know what he was doing. He demonstrated how to separate the good stones from the bad, or we'd never have known.

Photo by Bud Benz

Landmark St. Catharine's Church faces parkland across Spring Lake.

Spring Lake, N.J.
Jewel of the Jersey Shore

Among the seaside towns strung out along the Jersey shore is one that stands apart. No boardwalk bric-a-brac. No honky-tonk. No video arcades. No hangouts for young singles.

Spring Lake planned it that way. A century of tight zoning regulations and community resolve has produced a genteel enclave of substantial homes, manicured lawns, a tree-lined shopping district, a pristine boardwalk and not one but three lakes a stone's throw from the sea. All this within a long hour's drive of New York City or Philadelphia.

Enterprising developers launched Spring Lake in the late 19th century. They planned four neighboring towns, each having its own railroad station and a lavish hotel catering to a wealthy clientele from Philadelphia, northern New Jersey and New York. Additional hotels, large guest houses and elegant estates followed. The four communities united to become Spring Lake in 1892 in 1992.

The town retains the elegance of its past. The Warren Hotel clings to its summer social season. The stately Spring Lake Community House accommodates a library and theater groups in manorial surroundings. The recreation commission sponsors summer concerts at the park gazebo and model-boat regattas on Spring Lake. The 1992 Centennial Clock, with benches and colorful flowers at its base, would be at home in a European town square.

This is an eminently livable community for those who can afford houses starting at $300,000 and oceanfront properties of $1 million or more. The two-mile shoreline is pristine, its boardwalk uncluttered by anything more than a few covered benches and pavilions containing swimming pools at either end. Weeping willows frame and wooden footbridges cross Spring Lake, the meandering, natural spring lake in the center of town. It and two other lakes at either end of town yield a landscape rare for a seaside community.

No chain motels are among the 26 lodging establishments, ranging from old hotels to B&Bs, and no more can be licensed. The number of rooms has declined recently from 1,000 to 500, so the population of 5,000 year-round increases only to about 6,000 in summer. "The town consciously chose to stay a community rather than become a resort," says Michael Robertson, former executive director of the Chamber of Commerce. "For a quiet, romantic getaway, this is the place – only an hour away from everything, but an island of tranquility."

Inn Spots

Hollycroft, 506 North Blvd., Box 448, Spring Lake 07762.

Hidden behind a curtain of holly in a wooded residential area, this 1908 mountain-style hunting lodge is unique in the area. You'd expect to find it in the Adirondacks, perhaps, but not at the Jersey Shore. When you're sitting in the living room, you can look out across Lake Como and see the Atlantic beyond. In summer it's like being in the country with an ocean view; in the winter, when the towering ironstone fireplace is ablaze, it's like a ski lodge with an ocean view. That's the way the original owners planned it – one partner wanted a shore house and the other a mountain house, so this oversize log cabin in the Arts and Crafts style was their compromise.

"We bought it in 1985 as a private home, tore it apart and have been putting it back together ever since," said Mark Fessler, an architect and innkeeper with his wife Linda. Their handiwork has produced one of the more inviting and charming B&Bs we've seen. The public areas on the sprawling first floor include a large and welcoming living room paneled in knotty pine, a log-beamed dining room and a brick-floored sun porch beside the flagstone terrace, all taking advantage of the lake/ocean view. Stylishly and with great taste, the house displays portions of Linda's multitude of collectibles, from miniature English cottages to a Sicilian donkey cart chair.

The Fesslers have decorated in eclectic country style eight comfortable guest

quarters with private baths. All but two have king or queen beds and four have fireplaces. Each room comes with bottles of Perrier and the Hollycroft's own soaps. Unusual touches abound: a custom-made iron bed with a twig bird cage atop the canopy and lace curtains around the headboard in the Grassmere room, a twig accessory hanging from the rafters and on the wall behind the queen bed in the Somerset. The Ambleside has an English

Huge square living room is heart of Hamilton House Inn.

scrub pine canopy bed shipped back from one of the couple's many trips to England, a clawfoot tub and a private porch with a hanging swing seat. A favorite room is the spacious Cotswold Cottage at the far end of the main floor. It has a king bed, ivy painted on one wall, a wicker sofa, a window seat, Cotswold cottages pictured on the wallpaper border and in prints on the walls, and floral fabrics on the bedspread, curtains and table skirts.

The newest is a cathedral-ceilinged suite, aptly named Lords of the Manor. It offers a queensize French iron canopy bed beneath hand-painted clouds and sky on the ceiling, a chaise and two leather chairs facing a massive stone fireplace, a small sitting room, TV and wet bar, and a wicker-furnished screened balcony facing the lake. The bathroom has a separate shower and a soaking tub for two beside an arched window looking onto the water.

Talented Linda decorates lavishly for the seasons and makes all the handicrafts, which are for sale in her little Hollycroft Country Store off the entry.

The Fesslers put out a substantial buffet breakfast on a sideboard and table in the dining room. It's likely to include juices, fresh fruit, black-raspberry crumbles, Irish soda bread, raspberry-chocolate chip muffins and creamy scrambled eggs or ham and cheese egg strata. Sherry awaits in a crystal decanter atop a silver tray in the living room in the afternoons.

(732) 681-2254 or (800) 679-2554. Fax (732) 280-8145. Seven rooms and one suite with private baths. Mid-May through September: doubles, $125 to $160; suite, $275. Rest of year: doubles, $95 to $140; suite, $275. Two-night minimum weekends in summer. Smoking restricted

Hamilton House Inn, 15 Mercer Ave., Spring Lake 07762.
Every room has a swan somewhere in this deluxe B&B fashioned by Anne Benz, who was born and bred in Spring Lake, which is known for its swans, and her husband Bud, who grew up in neighboring Belmar. The two longtime AT&T employees raised four sons and cooked many a meal for their sons' friends and later their wives before deciding to move across town to open a B&B. "Now we have paying guests and only have to cook breakfast," said Anne. "We're having the best time ever."

Theirs is Spring Lake's only B&B with a swimming pool, and it's also one of the closest to the ocean. The facade of the 1877 Victorian is rather plain, but the inside is a beauty. You'd never guess that before the Benzes opened in 1994 it was a wreck. Eighteen months of renovations created inviting public rooms and eight comfortable bedrooms, all with private baths.

Cross the threshold from a small porch and enter a huge, square living room, 27 feet by 27 feet, lovely with salmon-colored walls and groupings of Victorian-style sofas and chairs. An enclosed sun porch harbors a TV, a gas fireplace and a decanter of sherry waiting to be poured. The chandeliered dining room with five round tables is papered in a floral pattern that matches the Villeroy & Boch china put out each day for the candlelight breakfast. That breakfast is quite a spread. Our first began with orange juice and honeydew melon, plus honey french bread and apple strudel muffins. The main dish was belgian waffles with crisp bacon. The second visit produced a guest-named "peach squeeze coffee cake" and a mushroom and five-cheese omelet. Both times, the kitchen remained so tidy we marveled that any cooking actually had been done there.

Upstairs are five fresh and pretty guest quarters on the second floor and three on the third. Each is decorated according to its name. A wallpaper border of swans along the ceiling graces the Spring Lake Serenity suite at the front of the house. We found it a most stylish and comfortable spread with a kingsize bed and a side sitting room with fireplace, TV and fine prints of Spring Lake scenes on the walls. A border of seashells and sandcastles coordinates with the bedspread in the summery Seashells and Sandcastles room, which includes a private porch from which to view the sun rising over the ocean. We also enjoyed the extra-large Victorian Splendor with kingsize brass bed, elegant loveseat, and oversize bathtub and marble shower. The lack of Victorian clutter was manifest even in a room named for its splendor. Carrying out the swan theme here was an intricate twig swan resting on the bureau. Seawatch on the third floor harbors an old desk, a ship's model in a bottle, a ship's lantern and a gas fireplace. Poet's Retreat comes with a wallpaper border of Shakespeare books, a gas fireplace and a wall of Bucks County photos by Bud, a talented photographer. Each room has a sitting area and fine amenities. A downstairs refrigerator is stocked with ice and complimentary beverages.

At our latest visit, Anne was producing a cookbook of recipes from family, friends and guests, entitled "Only the Best."

(732) 449-8282. Fax (732) 449-0206. www.hamiltonhouseinn.com. Seven rooms and one suite with private baths. Mid-May to mid-September: doubles, $145 to $175; suite, $225. Rest of year: doubles, $115 to $135; suite, $175. No smoking. Two-night minimum weekends in season. Children over 14. No smoking.

Sea Crest by the Sea, 19 Tuttle Ave., Spring Lake 07762.
Energetic owners John and Carol Kirby from Short Hills have infused this oldtimer on a residential street half a block from the ocean with a sprightly new lease on life. In a town where Victoriana reigns only slightly less preciously than in Cape May, their B&B finds its own niche. "We're more eclectic," says John. "We're reliving memories from our past lives and catering to adult fantasy and romance."

That translates to a Christmas wonderland in the Sleigh Ride Room, the Velveteen Rabbit Room reflecting Carol's favorite childhood tale, a stars and stripes ribbon around the portrait in the G. Washington Room, a cocoon of butterflies in the Papillon and a beaded curtain through which you enter the Casablanca Room. A favorite is the third-floor Yankee Clipper, where windows yield a view of the

Guests are accommodated in high style in Normandy Inn and its rear carriage house.

ocean both to the east and south. The bureau contains John's original sextant and old sailing logs from his service in the Merchant Marine, and a Kings Point Academy pin and pennant rest on the Arts & Crafts bed. A card lists the furniture in each room and guest diaries reveal the thoughts of previous occupants.

The former library on the main floor has become the Queen Victoria Suite, with canopy feather bed, sitting room with fireplace and small refrigerator, and a bath with separate shower and jacuzzi for two. A soaking tub for two occupies space at the side of the sitting room in the similarly appointed Teddy Roosevelt Suite, which also has a private balcony.

All rooms possess queensize beds, private baths with Caswell-Massey toiletries and TV/VCRs. Eight rooms have fireplaces and several have feather beds. The beds are dressed in linens of Egyptian cotton, French damask and Belgian lace and have six pillows on top. Equally fetching are the common areas, from a graceful living room to a luxurious wraparound veranda to a dining room with a majestic French oak table and sideboard. The dining room has been expanded lately into what was once the original kitchen with a wood stove, so that when the inn is full, all 24 guests can be served at once.

The Kirbys serve a bountiful gourmet breakfast starting, as their brochure puts it, at the civilized hour of 9 o'clock. Fresh fruit, homemade granola, John's breads and muffins and Carol's scones are accompanied by a Scandinavian blend of coffee reduced in caffeine. The main event could be frittata, featherbed eggs or french toast. Afternoon tea is served beside the player piano.

(732) 449-9031 or (800) 803-9031. Fax (732) 974-0403. Ten rooms and two suites with private baths. Mid-May through September: doubles, $159 to $189; suites, $259. Rest of year: doubles, $145 to $159; suites, $235. Two-night minimum June-September (three nights on weekends). Two-night minimum weekends rest of year. No children. No smoking.

Normandy Inn, 21 Tuttle Ave., Spring Lake 07762.
Haute Victoriana reigns inside this five-tone olive green and gold Italianate villa with Queen Anne accents – the only Spring Lake B&B to be listed on the National

Register. Innkeepers Michael and Susan Ingino note that only two pieces of furniture remain from the inn they purchased in 1982. They have renovated and replaced with authenticity and prized antiques.

The mood is set in a pair of fancy pink and red common rooms containing a rococo damask parlor set, an antique English tall case clock and marble sculptures. A Chickering grand piano occupies center stage in the huge, pillared dining room, where there's an extensive breakfast menu as well as daily specials for house guests. Complimentary wine is available all day on the side sun porch, where there's a television set, baskets hang from the ceiling and wicker furniture makes a comfy retreat.

Upstairs on the second and third floors are fifteen air-conditioned guest rooms and a suite with crocheted bedspreads and lace curtains. Two large second-floor front corner rooms are most prized. One has a tester bed whose posts are at least ten feet high, two upholstered chairs beside a table and a private porch. The other has a queen bed with a nine-foot burled wood headboard. Among the treasures are an 1860 signed Herter bed, a woven Brussels carpet and a reproduction of the bedroom wallpaper from the home of Robert Todd Lincoln. Victorian lamps, old portraits and antique furnishings dignify the rooms. Some on the third floor are rather small, although two at the rear have been turned into a suite with TV in the sitting area, a gas fireplace, a kingsize bedroom and a soaking tub. Out back, two upstairs rooms in the carriage house have been converted into a deluxe suite with a more contemporary feeling: a queen-bedded room, a small kitchen, a marble bath with a family-size jacuzzi, a big cathedral-ceilinged sitting room with corner fireplace, a sofabed and loveseat, and two TVs with VCR and stereo.

Two new rooms on the rear of the main floor have been fashioned from the owners' quarters. The result is a mini-suite with fireplace and an impressive bathroom with peacock wallpaper, a marble jacuzzi, separate shower and a chocolate-brown w.c.

Telephones lately have been incorporated into all bedrooms, and the inn's Victorian Times newsletter polled guests as to whether they want in-room TVs. The verdict: half do and half don't, so the Inginos make them available for those who wish.

(732) 449-7172. Fax (732) 449-1070. www.bbianj.com/normandy. Seventeen guest rooms and two suites with private baths. June-September: doubles, $121 to $181, suites $250 to $286. Rest of year: doubles, $96 to $146; suites, $215. Two-night minimum in July and August (three nights on weekends); two-night minimum weekends rest of year except in winter. Well behaved children accepted.

Ashling Cottage, 106 Sussex Ave., Spring Lake 07762.

Every morning at breakfast in the gazebo-shaped solarium at the front of this engaging Victorian cottage, innkeeper Jack Stewart runs a contest. He asks folks to guess in 30 seconds how many window panes there are in the solarium. "No one ever comes within a hundred," says Jack. "They're always too low." We won't spill the beans, but the answer lies well into the hundreds.

Those windows, containing the original glass dating to 1877, yield views onto Spring Lake across the street and a glimpse of the ocean beyond. "You couldn't face a better way to start the day," says Jack, and few would disagree. Against that watery backdrop, he and wife Goodi serve a sumptuous breakfast, buffet style. The fare includes a fresh fruit compote, cereal, bread and muffins and perhaps a special egg dish like California cheese puffs with hot peppers or a corn quiche.

Gazebo-shaped solarium at Ashling Cottage contains hundreds of window panes.

The hospitable Stewarts are apt to pour wine for afternoon get-togethers in their living room, handsome with red ribbon walls, dark green velvet swagged draperies and a sectional in front of the TV/VCR.

Despite period touches, there's no fussy Victoriana here. All ten guest rooms hold queensize beds. Eight have private baths. Two on the third floor with in-room wash basins share a hall bath and often are rented as a suite. The front Peach Room, the largest accommodation, offers a lovely lake view as well as an armoire, dresser and headboard in old oak. Jack's favorite is No. 4 on the third floor, up in the treetops surrounded by century-old sentinel sycamores. Most in demand in summer is a rear first-floor room with a private porch.

(732) 449-3553 or (888) 274-5464. Fax (732) 974-0831. www.bbianj.com/ashling. Eight rooms with private baths and two rooms with shared bath. Doubles, $149 to $169 mid-June through mid-September; $119 to $129 in off-season. Two-night minimum weekends. Closed November-April. Children over 12. No smoking.

La Maison, 404 Jersey Ave., Spring Lake 07762.

"I wanted this to be everyone's house," says former IBM sales executive-turned-innkeeper Barbara Furdyna. And as a college French major and a francophile who studied for a summer at the Sorbonne, she wanted hers to be a house with a French accent.

She started in 1982 with four rooms and a cottage in what had been Spring Lake's oldest guest facility. Within ten years, she had left IBM and renovated the entire house to produce a spiffy, French-style B&B. She now offers five rooms and two suites, all with private baths, TVs, telephones, queensize French-style sleigh beds, country French reproduction furniture, all-white duvets and down comforters, balloon curtains on the windows, Monet prints or original artworks on the walls and cozy sitting areas. The honeymoon room on the third floor, enhanced by beautiful French wallpaper, is the only one with a tub. The Juan Carlos Room on the first floor has a new double jacuzzi, teak accessories and a TV/VCR.

Out back is a small efficiency cottage. It has a wicker and leather sitting room with a sofabed and TV, a queen sleigh bed in an alcove, a clawfoot tub in the skylit bathroom, a kitchen and a couple of porches. Barbara likens it to a French provincial cottage and says, "I could happily live here all summer" – except that guests are quick to snap it up.

The French theme continues during the champagne breakfast each morning. Mimosas and creative fruit dishes, perhaps poached pears in an orange-raspberry sauce, precede a main dish of belgian waffles, quiche lorraine or crème brûlée french toast. Tartes tatin, baguettes, breakfast pastries, granola and cappuccino or espresso accompany. The meal is taken in a chandeliered dining room, where a fanciful bird cage is situated in the corner, or on the wraparound front porch. In the afternoon, there's an open bar for happy hour, as Barbara hosts guests as she would for a private party.

Besides exuberant hospitality, La Maison is known for fine art. The walls of its entry and living room are hung with paintings, some by her British-born husband Peter Oliver, and others by watercolor artist Paula Jordan, who lives across the street and is the assistant innkeeper here. Another staff member's watercolors as well as paintings gathered on one of Barbara's frequent trips to France are also for sale. "We're selling 40 paintings a year in our gallery," she said.

As an extra fillip, La Maison offers guest privileges at a top-rated health and spa facility nearby.

(732) 449-0969 or (800) 276-2088. Fax (732) 449-4860. www.bbianj.com/lamaison. Seven rooms and one cottage with private bath. Mid-May to mid-September: doubles, $145 to $215; cottage, $285. Rest of year: doubles, $120 to $195; cottage, $200. Children and pets welcome in cottage. Three-night minimum in July, August and holiday weekends, two-night minimum rest of year. No smoking.

Victoria House, 214 Monmouth Ave., Spring Lake 07762.

Masses of impatiens and a giant hydrangea bush brighten the exterior of this gray-green, Queen Anne-style residence with white gingerbread trim and an extra-large wraparound veranda furnished in wicker. Built in 1882 and a guest house for some years, it was revived in 1993 by new owners Robert and Louise Goodall. "We've hung 250 double rolls of wallpaper and refinished all the floors," said Louise, who was busy performing both functions at our first midweek visit to get the house ready for Spring Lake's annual Christmas tour.

What do-it-yourself elbow grease, modest carpentry talents and a terrific eye for design can do is manifest throughout the Goodalls' house, but most particularly in their nine guest rooms. Two of the more popular make the most of their corner turrets. "There seems to be something about being in a turret that guests like," Louise surmises. Both turret rooms hold kingsize beds and sitting areas, and the newer Rose Rendezvous has a fireplace. An armoire made from a gun cabinet enhances the Garden Bouquet Room, while a colorful quilt tops the kingsize bed in Cottage. The antique armoire gives the rich blue and burgundy Eastlake Room its name. The Delft and Wicker Room lives up to its title with a blue and white decorative scheme and lots of wicker. Two rear rooms that had shared a bath recently were turned into the Victorian Hideaway suite with raised ceiling and a spiffy sitting area, as the Goodalls continue to upgrade.

The common areas are equally compelling. There's a TV in the turreted parlor, and four original stained-glass windows brighten the stairway landing. Hand-carved

Lavish landscaping and wraparound veranda greet guests at Victoria House.

Italian walnut chairs are at individual lace-covered tables in the dining room. A full breakfast is served here or on the side porch, overlooking the showplace small garden created by Robert, a landscape architect. Typical fare involves juice, fruit, granola and a main dish, perhaps cheese strata, quiche or french toast. One guest wrote in the hall diary that the waffles with peach sauce were out of this world.

Louise, who did the decorating, is a fulltime mother as well as a hands-on innkeeper. Her husband is on hand nights and weekends.

(732) 974-1882. Fax (732) 974-9702. Seven rooms with private baths and two rooms with shared bath. Mid-May through September: doubles, $90 to $173 weekends, $75 to $158 midweek. Rest of year: doubles, $85 to $135. Two-night minimum stay in July and August and weekends in season. Children over 12. No smoking.

The Chateau, Fifth and Warren Avenues, Spring Lake 07762.

Billing itself as the Tiffany of Spring Lake's small hotels, this is gradually becoming less hotel-like and more like a large B&B. The evolution involves a conscious decision of young owner Scott Smith to offer elegant accommodations, personal service and, given the size of rooms and their amenities, good value for Spring Lake. The main lobby has been expanded to include a showy breakfast area, full of chintz floral armchairs at pink-linened tables. Continental breakfast is offered here – free midweek in the winter and $4.99 the rest of the time.

The hotel, dating to 1888 and in Scott's family for 49 years, is located at the end of Spring Lake and overlooks two parks and the town gazebo. Thirty-nine guest rooms and suites are in three buildings characterized by lots of public spaces, from decks to porches to a second-floor gazebo. Ceiling fans, wicker furniture and Waverly fabrics are the common denominator in each room. All also have TV/VCRs, refrigerators, wet bars, marble bathrooms and two phones with data ports. The ultimate are ten luxury suites with wood-burning fireplaces and jacuzzis or soaking tubs for two. We were happy to be ensconced in a large "classic parlor" with a sitting area, wet bar and two double beds in the Villa. A former residence facing the town gazebo, it contains six rooms that had been the Chateau's best until they were surpassed by the addition built in 1989 to house luxury suites, some with private balconies or porches.

(732) 974-2000. Fax (732) 974-0007. Thirty-nine guest rooms and suites with private baths. Mid-June to early September: doubles, $135 to $190; suites, $200 to $240. Spring and fall: doubles, $79 to $139; suites, $115 to $160. Winter: doubles, $65 to $97; suites, $95 to $135. Three-night minimum weekends in summer; two nights in spring and fall.

The Hewitt-Wellington, 200 Monmouth Ave., Spring Lake 07762.

This turn-of-the-century lakefront condominium hotel was totally renovated in 1988 into the most inviting of Spring Lake's other small hotels. Twenty-nine rooms and suites are offered in two three-story wings connected by a breezeway beside a small heated pool. Suites consist of a bedroom and a living room with a queensize sofabed and can accommodate four persons.

Most of those in the east wing face a park and afford views of the lake and the ocean. Two in the front corner tucked into the turret are particularly intriguing. Rooms are light and airy, outfitted with Drexel-Heritage furniture and thick carpeting. Queensize beds, TVs, mini-refrigerators, telephones and marble baths with brass fixtures are the rule. All rooms are decorated in similar style. Rates vary with location and view.

A complimentary continental breakfast is served in season. Dinner is available in the hotel's leased restaurant, **Whispers** (see Dining Spots).

(732) 974-1212. Fax (732) 974-2338. Twelve rooms and seventeen suites with private baths. Memorial Day-Labor Day: doubles, $175 to $250 weekends, $140 to $210 midweek; suites, $250 to $270 weekends, $210 to $250 midweek. Rest of year: doubles, $115 to $155 weekends, $95 to $135 midweek; suites, $155 to $180 weekends, $135 to $150 midweek. Two-night minimum in season. Children over 12.

White Lilac Inn, 414 Central Ave., Spring Lake 07762.

Built around 1881 with a Southern look, this onetime seasonal guest house has triple-tiered porches accented with beautiful iron work in the New Orleans style. "The house looks like it belongs in the South," says Mari Slocum, innkeeper with her husband Charles. They undertook extensive renovations in 1995 to turn it into an eclectic Victorian B&B full of lace, lilacs, art and collections.

"I'm a pack rat at heart," says Mari, a former school art teacher. Her pale pink Victorian parlor offers evidence: a breakfront full of antique china and glassware, a two-tiered table holding carousel animals, a rare dual-view stereo opticon from 1857. The front library/TV room, notable for an elaborate ceiling she wallpapered herself, holds an album of progress pictures she calls her renovation book. Photos of family members are found in most of the common areas and ten guest rooms, along with lilac accents and lots of lace.

Stuffed animals holding welcome cards on the beds greet guests in the rooms, all but two with private baths and all but one with queensize beds. Five have TV sets. Gilbert & Soames toiletries and Poland Spring water are in every room.

Lilacs grace the comforter and pillows on the white iron bed in the second-floor White Lilac Suite, which offers a corner fireplace, wicker chairs, TV, a clawfoot tub in the room, a shower in the bathroom and french doors onto the wraparound

Seasonal hotel has been refurbished into the stylish Spring Lake Inn.

porch. The best view comes a floor above in the fireplaced hideaway called Room at the Top, where a private balcony yields a view of Wreck Pond and, when the leaves are off the trees, the ocean four blocks away. Most rooms follow a lacy Victorian cottage theme, but the Vermont Cabin is quite an exception. The last room to be refurbished, Mari wanted something different so it reflects her husband's family ties to Vermont. Two third-floor rooms, her family-oriented Three Sisters and the patriotic Hail to the Troops, share a hall bath.

A full breakfast is served at five tables for two in the lacy white Garden Room, which is warmed by a gas fireplace in cool weather. Fresh fruit and pastries precede the main dish, perhaps Mari's signature cinnamon-raisin french toast, a ham and cheese omelet or asparagus quiche.

(732) 449-0211. Eight rooms with private baths and two with shared bath. May-September: doubles, $99 to $159 weekends, $89 to $149 midweek. Rest of year: $89 to $129 weekends, $79 to $119 midweek. Children over 14. No smoking. Closed in January.

Spring Lake Inn, 104 Salem Ave., Spring Lake 07762.
"It didn't look like this when we bought it," Pat Gatens says in an understatement. She and husband Jim, New Yorkers both, took over the old seasonal Spring Lake Hotel in 1995 and refurbished it into a classy B&B.

The 80-foot-long Victorian porch lined with rockers and the large lobby full of rich wood harken back to the 1888 hotel's past. So does the vast square dining room alongside, a beauty with a twelve-foot-high ceiling and a handful of tables spaced well apart for breakfast. The handsome rear parlor with wainscoting is furnished with a mix of traditional and contemporary seating, oriental rugs and "a wee drop of Irish," says Pat.

Eight guest rooms off the wide second-floor hallway are quite different. All are stylish and comfortable with interesting wallpaper treatments, private baths and queensize beds. The Victoria Rose has a cannonball four-poster bed and, surprise, a floor lamp for reading in the w.c. alcove in the bathroom. The bathroom in Serenity is as large as the bedroom. The Canopy Room contains a step-up bed. The Corner Room has not one but two bathrooms for some reason. Pat points out the rooms in which priests and nuns have stayed (they seem to run in the family) as she gives a tour; "that's the nuns' room," she says of what otherwise is called Nostalgia.

A ninth guest room at one end of the third floor is so large it a double bed in each corner and, again, two bathrooms. Nine more rooms with shared baths are rented for the season, but the Gatens were planning to convert them into six additional B&B rooms.

Breakfast is continental in the summer, full in the off-season. Cinnamon french toast, blueberry pancakes and scrambled eggs inside a baked potato are favorite dishes.

Ebullient Pat, quite a character, sent us on our way with a loaf of her Irish sodabread and the distinct impression that the Spring Lake Inn would not long remain "the town's best kept secret."

(732) 449-2010. Nine rooms with private baths. May to mid-October: doubles, $110 to $135 weekends, $90 to $115 midweek. Rest of year: $75 to $110. Two-night minimum weekends in season. No smoking.

Dining Spots

Spring Lake's restaurant choices are limited by zoning regulations and a lack of liquor licenses. But there are plenty of options nearby.

Old Mill Inn, Old Mill Road, Spring Lake Heights.

Overlooking a tranquil mill pond with an eight-foot water wheel just west of town is this impressive establishment that's almost everybody's favorite for fine food and surroundings. If it no longer looks much like the grist mill it once was, that's because the restaurant established here in 1938 has burned five times, the latest in 1985. From the ashes emerged a behemoth with two main-floor dining rooms seating a total of 240, a lobby bigger than most restaurants and an upstairs function room that caters 100-plus weddings a year.

A remarkable stained-glass rendering of the New York skyline takes up most of one wall in **Joe's Place for Steak,** a serious steakhouse that's dark and plush in rich wood and hunter green. The larger main Green Room, frilly and feminine, offers water views and was obviously popular for Saturday lunch when we were there. Best of all at midday is a window table in the bar, away from the hubbub and seemingly perched over the water beside a flotilla of ducks. The taped piano music was so pure we thought it was live. We enjoyed a spicy Manhattan clam chowder, an abundant spinach and avocado salad, and two crab cakes on a pool of herbed cream sauce, nicely presented with a side of yellow and green squash, cauliflower and green peppers. A bread basket with good, crusty rolls and a blueberry and a bran muffin came with. The french fries were made by hand with the skins left on, and the excellent salad accompanying the crab cake was tossed with a zesty raspberry vinaigrette. It was obvious that the kitchen cares and maintains interest and quality along with quantity.

For dinner, owner Joe Amiel recommends any of the seafood dishes ("we have wonderful lobster, crab and fresh fish"), the extra-crispy roast duck with raspberry-port wine sauce and the prime rib with horseradish sauce. The steakhouse fare can be ordered in either venue. Start with lobster bisque, carpaccio or oysters rockefeller. Finish with cheesecake, Swiss chocolate pie or ice cream. Honored by Wine

Window tables in Green Room overlook pond outside Old Mill Inn.

Spectator, the wine list offers a good mix between high end and low end, with lots in between.

(732) 449-1800. Entrées, $18.95 to $27.90. Lunch daily, 11:30 to 3. Dinner nightly, 3 to 10 or 11. Sunday, brunch 11 to 3, dinner noon to 10. Closed Monday in off-season.

Sisters Café, 1321 Third Ave., Spring Lake.

Four sisters who grew up in Spring Lake are involved in this small new restaurant with innovative contemporary fare, incongruously served amid vestiges of its former status as a luncheonette. "We used to come in here when we were kids," said Culinary Institute of America-trained chef Marianne O'Hearne, spokeswoman for the four. She and Kris Dier, who had cooked in the area for years, staff the kitchen, while Suzanne O'Hearne handles the front of the house and an out-of-town sibling oversees the business end.

Opening in 1997 and gaining a receptive following, the O'Hearne sisters inexplicably retained the prominent lunch counter but upgraded the rest of the place with tables on two levels. White linens, oil lamps and fresh flowers are the norm at close-together tables, some in the rear along a side banquette. Family pictures and memorabilia are displayed in a handsome built-in bookcase running the length of the side wall in front.

The short dinner menu changes weekly. Typical starters are a crispy risotto cake with rock shrimp, herbs and roasted mushrooms and Maryland crab cakes with chipotle aioli. Entrées could be spiced mahi-mahi with tropical fruit sauce, roast chicken breast stuffed with spinach and provolone, and New York strip steak with green peppercorn sauce. Desserts include carrot cake with maple cream cheese icing, mocha fudge torte with white chocolate sauce, and apple-blueberry crisp with vanilla bean sauce.

Lunch selections intrigue as well, among them a grilled chicken, bacon and avocado salad with lemon-yogurt dressing, an open-face blue cheese sandwich with pears and walnuts, and a sweet potato, apple and cheddar turnover over greens.

(732) 449-1909. Entrées, $15 to $18. Lunch, Tuesday-Saturday 11 to 3. Dinner, Tuesday-Sunday 5:30 to 9 or 10. Saturday breakfast, 8 to 11. Sunday brunch, 8 to 2. BYOB.

Bella Luna, 703 Belmar Plaza, Ninth Avenue and Main Street, Belmar.

With a chef from the famed Bouley in New York City, this stylish restaurant and espresso bar was an instant hit upon opening in 1997. Owners Florence and Patrick Shalloo, both with hotel and hospitality backgrounds, fashioned a spare, high-ceilinged space with lemon yellow walls and white-clothed tables spaced well apart.

It proved a pleasant setting for an inspired meal on a slow autumn weeknight (usually, we understand, the place is jammed). A basket of peasant bread came with a zesty apple-rosemary olive oil and herbed shallot butter as we placed our order. The zuppa di vongole with clams, sausage and cannellini beans was almost a meal in itself, particularly when paired with the assertive salad of baby spinach with roasted red peppers, portobello mushrooms and goat cheese, and an appetizer of smooth lobster ravioli with marscarpone cream on a sweet red pepper coulis. Also a standout was the rigatoni with smoked salmon and pancetta, followed by a refreshing lemon torte with a raspberry coulis and fresh berries. With a bottle of BYOB wine, the tab came to about $40 for two for a memorable dinner of great tastes.

Those with hearty appetites choose among the likes of seared tuna with a mango-chile salsa, an acclaimed fisherman's stew, chile-rubbed pork chop with spiced apple chutney, and polenta-crusted rack of lamb with mustard and port wine.

(732) 280-7501. Entrées, $13.50 to $18.75. Dinner nightly except Tuesday from 5. BYOB.

The Avon Pavilion, Ocean Avenue, Avon-by-the-Sea.

They dole out hot dogs and hamburgers by day at this snow-white pavilion right over the beach. Come evening, they dress up the summery interior with tablecloths and candlelight and offer a menu featuring gourmet, low-sodium and low-fat entrée specials denoted by heart symbols.

The lapping waves are the backdrop for interesting pastas and main dishes like broiled salmon with citron verte sauce, grilled yellowfin tuna with spicy creole sauce, stir-fried shrimp and vegetables on steamed rice, chicken française and grilled strip steak smothered with mushrooms, sweet vidalia onions and garlic. Instead of salad, the place serves a tomato concoction with olives and onions in which to dip your bread; regulars say it's to die for.

The "New Joisey" clam chowder with a Jersey Shore zip is a favorite starter. Otherwise, begin with bay and booze shrimp (steamed in beer and Old Bay spice) or caesar salad with a unique chardonnay caesar dressing. Finish with key lime mousse or toll house pie à la mode.

(732) 775-1043. Entrées, $14.95 to $18.95. Dinner nightly from 6, summer only. BYOB.

Whispers, 200 Monmouth Ave., Spring Lake.

The owner of the up-and-down Sandpiper restaurant operates the highly regarded dining room in the Hewitt-Wellington hotel. The cream and pink room is a picture of elegance with a marble floor, upholstered chairs, and four crystal chandeliers that coordinate with the long-stemmed crystal vases and wine glasses on the tables.

Chefs come and go, but the contemporary fare remains consistently good. Main courses could be grilled mahi-mahi Caribbean style, horseradish-crusted roasted red snapper, grilled veal chop or filet mignon with port wine sauce. Butternut squash served in its natural shell and tuna carpaccio with wasabi sauce were among the starters at our latest visit.

(732) 449-3330. Entrées, $17 to $26. Dinner, Wednesday-Sunday 5 to 9. Closed in January and February. BYOB.

Armadillo Crossing, 1605 Main St., South Belmar.

The ice water comes with lemon wedges in mason jars, a muddy cowboy boot rests on a shelf and a stuffed beaver stands near the restrooms in this interesting little Southwest haunt just north of Spring Lake in South Belmar. The blackboard menu reads like Tex-Mex with a cajun accent, although young chef-owner Brian Mahoney demurs. "Up-and-coming Southwest food," the Spring Lake native calls it. "No tacos or burritos or anything like that."

The complimentary plate of white bean dip with tortilla chips, cucumber and zucchini slices and black olives nearly made redundant our dinner appetizers of roasted garlic with feta cheese and red peppers (sensational) and a salad of exotic mushrooms on assorted baby lettuces (sublime). The waitress who explained the ins and outs of the menu employed a lot of "very hot" qualifiers, which turned out to be particularly true in the jerked chicken with kiwi salsa, accompanied by interesting sweet potato fries and a zesty corn salad. Slightly milder, as it was supposed to be, was the grilled Arizona chicken with avocado and kiwi sauce and Mexican rice. Both main dishes were excellent and arrived in such abundance that part left in doggy bags for lunch the next day. Desserts included an acclaimed key lime pie, strawberry-amaretto cake and cappuccino-hazelnut cake, but alas no icy refreshments to cool such assertive fare. The peppermint candies that came with the bill had to suffice.

The place is tiny, the music soft and the barn-red walls glow at night when the lights are dimmed and the oil candles lit. You don't even notice that the tablecloths are mismatched and that the decor is of the tag-sale variety.

(732) 280-1880. Entrées, $13.95 to $16.95. Dinner, Tuesday-Sunday 5 to 10. BYOB.

Rod's Old Irish Tavern, 507 Washington Blvd., Sea Girt.

Favorite among a number of Irish pubs in an area only lately shedding its moniker as the Irish Riviera is this large green house with white trim and a canopied entrance at the edge of downtown Sea Girt, an attractive residential town on Spring Lake's southern border. Green and white is the color scheme inside as well, from the checkered tablecloths in the enormous pub to the curtains separating leather booths and tables in the dining room. There's a garden cafe beyond.

The same menu spanning the spectrum from a jumbo hot dog to blackened sirloin steak is served throughout the establishment. This means you can enjoy grilled swordfish or one of the famous chicken pot pies while watching one of the dozen or so big-screen TVs around the central bar, or a burger, sandwich or barbecued ribs in the dining room, and vice-versa. Mix and match shrimp scampi, fettuccine primavera, a nacho platter, chef's salad, oysters on the half shell and such. Portions are huge and prices affordable.

(732) 449-2020. Entrées, $11.95 to $17.95. Lunch daily, 11:30 to 2:30. Dinner nightly, 5 to 11.

Tara Lynn's Unique Cuisine, 217 Jersey Ave., Spring Lake.

The name is a bit of a mystery at this pint-size establishment opened in 1997 by chef Tara Bartz and partner Lynda Milligan in the former Victorian Bean Café. The tea room/coffee house/café offers a continental-style menu during the day and blackboard specials at night.

What's unique? "Look at the menu," we were advised. It offered a panoply of fancy sandwiches and salads in the $5.95 to $7.95. The former bear names like thon, poulet, jambon and oeuf (the last for roasted eggplant – the name at least is unique –with roasted red peppers and garlic, red onion and herbed goat cheese). Salades are of the de mozzarella, de épinard and de hummus variety. Tara Lynn's "unique shakes" are called butter rum, tirami su, chocolate espresso and the like.

The dinner menu is posted daily in the window and recited by a waitress who kindly gave us her notes. Cajun mako shark, baked chicken with dijon tarragon sauce and london broil with mushrooms and onions were among the main dishes that night. Three kinds of pies and a port wine pear tarte were the dessert choices.

The place seats up to 28 people at intimate tables or at a rear counter/bar.

(732) 449-3299. Entrées, $11.95 to $14.95. Open daily, 9 to 9, to 7 Tuesday-Thursday in off-season. BYOB.

Diversions

A New York Times article claimed that "it's not so much what there is to do, it is what there is not to do that makes Spring Lake special." The prime attractions, of course, are the quiet boardwalk and pristine beach, plus the parklands surrounding the town's namesake lake. One could spend hours walking the streets and admiring the gardens and manicured lawns of Spring Lake, where commercial lawn services must rank as the town's single most prosperous business niche. Check out the manicured masterpiece surrounding the residence at 301 West Lake Drive. The whole lawn is clipped to one-fourth inch high and maintained daily like a putting green.

Within easy striking distance are Atlantic City, New York, Philadelphia, gambling, racing, arcades and what have you. From these you can return quickly to the refuge of Spring Lake.

The Beach. Two miles of wide beach (continually restocked with fresh sand) and New Jersey's longest non-commercial boardwalk separate the Atlantic Ocean beach from sand dunes and Ocean Avenue. Unlike neighboring Belmar where a McDonald's occupies the prime boardwalk location, Spring Lake's boardwalk contains only a few pavilions with benches and two larger pavilions harboring saltwater pools, rest rooms and food stands at either end. Beach passes are sold here, although most inn guests are given passes by their hosts. Even on chilliest days, lots of people stroll or jog on the boardwalk.

Theater. The Spring Lake Theatre Company has expanded its repertoire and schedule to stage eight shows year-round in the Spring Lake Community House. The English Tudor building built in 1923 by a former mayor and state senator includes a library and a 360-seat theater. Tickets are in the $15 range and sell out early; they're available through the Chamber of Commerce, (732) 449-0577, or direct, 449-4530.

St. Catharine's Church, Third and Essex Avenue. Built beside the lake between 1901 and 1907 by a wealthy resident as a memorial to his daughter, this striking edifice resembles the Romanesque St. Peter's Basilica in miniature and is well worth a visit. Two 800-year-old bronze standards from Rome line the entrance to the church. The high altar is made of the same Carrara marble used by Michelangelo and the stained-glass windows were made in Bavaria. A professor from Rome painted the interior frescos. The church is one of two in the same parish in Spring Lake, a heavily Roman Catholic community once known as the Irish Riviera. The total enrollment of Spring Lake's single public elementary school is less than that of the parochial school.

Shopping. Four blocks of tree-lined Third Avenue are home to small stores run by committed owners and an unusually high number of real-estate offices. The only chain store is a branch of **Crabtree & Evelyn,** although the local **Karen's Boutique** has a branch at the Warren Hotel to display its women's wares. Perhaps the biggest drawing card is the **Irish Centre,** which features all kinds of Irish imports reflecting the resort's heritage. Another is the old-fashioned **Spring Lake Variety Store** filled to the brim with all kinds of things, including beach chairs hanging from the ceiling. Clothing and accessories are more sedate specialties of **The Camel's Eye, Village Tweeds** and **Courts & Greens,** whose names indicate their priorities. Adorable bears clad in little smock dresses are in the windows of **Teddy Bears by the Seashore,** where two former Macy's buyers offer discounted clothing for children and their parents. We admired the sweaters at **The Clover Leaf** and the cute clothes at **Samantha's.** Some of the most sophisticated cards, stationery, books and desk accessories we've seen anywhere are stocked at **Noteworthy By-the-Sea.**

New stores and galleries seem to pop up at every visit. We know innkeepers who covet every single item at **Kate & Company,** where country pine furniture and home accessories are imaginatively displayed. We admired an intricate cathedral bird-cage show table for $995. Fine American crafts are among the "irresistibles," some made by the owners, at **The Moon & Sixpence.** Colorful placemats and trays caught our eye at the retail shop of **Dan's Kitchen,** a catering service. Art enthusiasts admire the offerings of the **Spring Lake Gallery, Evergreen Gallery, ArtEffects** and **Thistledown Gallery.**

Sweets lovers get their fill at the **Third Avenue Chocolate Shoppe** and **Jean-Louise Homemade Candies,** where the day's special at one visit was chocolate-covered grapes. Snacks are available to eat in or take out next door at **Freedman's Bakery.** Afternoon tea and desserts are offered at four tiny tables in the front of the window of **Spring Lace,** a mercantile confection full of lace and Victoriana (much of the Victorian lace on windows and tables at local inns was obtained here). Gourmet pizzas and sophisticated entrée specials are offered at the **Spring Lake Gourmet Pizzeria,** a sleek and squeaky clean place that lives up to its claim of being "not just another pizzeria." The **Spring Lake Bottle Shop** is the place to pick up a bottle of wine for restaurants where you bring your own.

Extra-Special _____

Historic Allaire Village, Allaire State Park, off Route 524, Allaire.

This outdoor living-history museum re-creates the days of New Jersey's early iron industry. Interpreters dressed in the work clothes of the 1830s portray the daily life and times of early iron workers and their families at the historic Howell Works, an industrial community established between 1822 and 1850 when bog ore was smelted. They demonstrate early crafts and open-hearth cooking in some of the twelve houses and buildings in a restored village. Other buildings include a snack bar and a general store/museum shop. The Pine Creek Railroad displays six antique trains, two of which offer ten-minute rides. Listed on the National Register, this mini-Sturbridge is part of 3,000-acre Allaire State Park just west of Spring Lake.

(732) 938-2253. Grounds open year-round. Visitor center open Wednesday-Sunday 10 to 5, Memorial Day to Labor Day, Saturday-Sunday 10 to 4 in September and October. Buildings open Saturday-Sunday 10 to 4, May-October. Parking, $3 weekends.

East Hampton, N.Y.

Village Beautiful

East Hampton, let it be said up front, is too-too. Too posh, too trendy, too social, too expensive, too precious, too much.

At the same time, let it be said that it is also beautiful. Classy. And, at other than peak visiting periods, rather serene. Almost perfect. Not too-too perfect.

For New Yorkers, there is no better-known summer place than the Hamptons,

Old Hook Windmill frames Mill House Inn.

some 110 miles east near the tip of Long Island's South Fork. The Hamptons collectively embrace, from west to east: Westhampton and Hampton Bays, which for most are quite skippable. Southampton, perhaps the best known of the Hamptons, the Palm Beach of the North. Bridgehampton, which is consciously understated. And East Hampton, more subdued than flashy Southampton.

It's not hard to understand why this was called "America's Most Beautiful Village" in the early 1960s by a national magazine. Town officials differ over whether it was the Saturday Evening Post or National Geographic; their indecision suggests that to East Hampton it doesn't matter.

The wide main street of the historic village passes a long green with a pond and a graveyard, a windmill, English-style edifices and substantial old homes before it reaches shady, suave downtown East Hampton. Take Ocean Avenue down to the beach, arguably the nation's cleanest and one of its most beautiful. Meander along the side streets of the estate area, where thick privet hedges screen the manicured estates of the rich and famous. Some of the more illustrious – and less flamboyant – make up the Blue Book of the Hamptons, which is discreetly stacked for sale on the counter at the local bookstore. Pause for a look at Home Sweet Home, the Mulford House, Clinton Academy, Miss Amelia's Cottage, Guild Hall, the Tudoresque library and the Old Hook Mill, one among the nation's largest collections of windmills. This is the East Hampton that the transient visitor sees.

The East Hampton that the New Yorkers take over in the summer is the one where the scene is seeing and being seen: in chi-chi restaurants charging Manhattan prices, at inns demanding minimum stays of three to five nights, in boutiques catering to the celebrity and carriage trade, in the slick newspapers and magazines touting the Hamptons' social scene, in all the fitness centers and beauty salons and cosmetic makeover clinics that show where priorities lie.

Some New Yorkers would kill for a share in a house in the Hamptons each summer – or even for an invitation for a weekend. Others would be advised to visit at off-peak times to enjoy East Hampton's many charms, without its hassles.

Sculptures accent back lawn and gardens at The J. Harper Poor Cottage.

Inn Spots

Accommodations vary from old inns to small, home-stay B&Bs taking in guests on summer weekends. Weekends, when minimum stays of three nights are the rule, are booked far ahead. Many inns require four-night stays on holiday weekends and two-night stays on spring and fall weekends. Lately, many have added in-room telephones with voice mail and modems, presumably for high-powered business and social types who can't stand to be out of touch.

The J. Harper Poor Cottage, 181 Main St., East Hampton 11937.

If you want to stay in an East Hampton mansion, how about this, one of the more stately in town? Gary and Rita Reiswig, former owners of the nearby Maidstone Arms, acquired the stuccoed Elizabethan manor facing the village green in 1996. Six months of renovations produced five guest rooms with private baths and the most elegant common rooms in town.

The Reiswigs had had their eye on the house for years. It became available following the deaths of Sid and Mim Perle, who had run it as a low-key, three-room B&B in conjunction with the 1770 House inn and restaurant they owned down the street.

The core of the house, named for former owner

James Harper Poor, was built in 1650 as a tavern. It was expanded with servants' and master wings on each side in 1885. The sheer size, the mullioned windows, the skylit Colonial Revival staircase, the Arts and Crafts architectural embellishments and the carved lintel angels framing the front entrance lend irony to the name.

With great taste, the Reiswigs have done extensive refurbishing, favoring the simpler English Arts and Crafts style to the excesses of the earlier Victorian era. The sunken living room is a beauty with a grouping in the center of four arm chairs upholstered in fabrics matching the frieze of William Morris floral wallpaper atop the paneling, an oversize grand piano from the 1860s at one end and window seats overlooking the rear sculpture gardens at the other. The fireplace inglenook is decorated with a checkerboard of English Victorian art tile in blue and white. The beamed breakfast room with a huge fireplace also doubles as a tavern, its original purpose, where guests can enjoy their favorite beverage with afternoon snacks ranging from chips and salsa to handmade pizzas. In front is a fireplaced library/reception room with more decorative tiling and light wood paneling.

Upstairs are five regal guest rooms, all with private baths, queen or king beds, sitting areas, telephones and TV/VCRs. Four have working fireplaces. Understated décor follows a garden theme with William Morris wallpapers and plush fabrics. Room 3 in the 1650 section retains the original beams, a paneled door hung on hand-wrought hinges, huge fireplace, a clawfoot tub and separate shower, plus a front veranda that's a tight squeeze for two.

Out back are a spacious lawn and formal sculpture garden surrounded by twenty-foot-high arborvitae. Among the several lounging areas is an intimate breakfast nook hidden beneath a 200-year-old climbing wisteria.

That and the nearby patio are idyllic spots in which to linger over a hearty breakfast. Guests help themselves to fresh fruit, juice, cereal and baked goods before being served a main course, perhaps eggs, waffles or pancakes. The garden conveys such a European feeling that guests may forget they are in the heart of the Hamptons.

(516) 324-4081. Five rooms with private baths. July and August: doubles $325 to $425 weekends, $250 to $350 midweek. June and September: $275 to $350 weekends, $195 to $250 midweek. October-May: $195 to $280 weekends, $150 to $250 midweek. Three-night minimum on summer weekends.

The Pink House, 26 James Lane, East Hampton 11937.

Despite an abundance of established inns here, architect/builder Ron Steinhilber felt there was a market for an upscale B&B. "People will pay a little extra for something really luxurious, that goes the extra mile," he said. So he took over a National Register-listed house, built by a local whaling captain across from the village green and pond in the mid-1800s, and imbued it with taste and personality – except for the pretty pale pink exterior, which he inherited and cannot be changed. The interior is not the locally prevailing Victorian look but country light.

Ron and a friend renovated the house themselves in 1990 and his architectural genius shows. So do his collections, from a platform light from Brooklyn's Myrtle Avenue subway line in a corner of the living room to his grandfather's watercolors, and Salari bells from New Mexico. A row of lights illuminates the entry hall and focuses on collections in two shelves at the top of the stairs.

All five guest rooms come with private baths, telephones and TV. The Blue Room has a cushioned window seat, queensize pine pencil-post bed, and a huge marble shower and sink bearing the inn's own toiletries. Another favorite is the

Pine pencil-post bed is draped in lace in **Blue Room** at **The Pink House.**

Elk Room, with Southwest decor, a jacuzzi and TV. The Twin Room, where the beds with pretty pink and green sheets can be joined as a king, contains a wall of iron artifacts. The Green Room has an Adirondack chair and a wicker queensize bed. On the main floor is the Garden Room with a four-poster bed, a private entrance and its own flower-filled patio, where "guests feel like they're in a cottage at the Beverly Hills Hotel," says Ron. Calla lilies adorn the bathroom sink to carry out the garden feeling.

Recessed ceiling lights spotlight selected art in the living room with two facing loveseats and in the dining room, both of which have fireplaces. The front porch is furnished in wicker. Guests help themselves to soft drinks and ice from a refrigerator, and chocolates are on the beds at night.

Breakfast in the dining room or on the screened rear porch includes fresh fruit and juices, homemade granola and European roast coffee. The crowning glory might be banana-walnut pancakes, sourdough french toast with sautéed pears, heart-shaped waffles topped with raspberries or a cream cheese and chive omelet.

Outside is a lovely back yard, where guests enjoy a hedge-screened swimming pool. "Although our aim is to be elegant and deluxe," says Ron, "we're also rustic and homey. People feel at home here."

(516) 324-3400. Fax (516) 324-5254. Five rooms with private baths. Doubles, $265 to $325 in summer, $165 to $265 in spring and fall, $145 to $185 in winter. Three to four-night minimum on summer weekends, four to six nights on holiday weekends. Children over 5. No smoking.

Centennial House, 13 Woods Lane, East Hampton 11937.
This shingled Victorian hugging the main road at the edge of the estate district was built in 1876, the date having been inscribed in plaster in the Bay bedroom by one of the village's celebrated builders. It was owned by only two families before it was acquired in 1987 by David Oxford, a lawyer who had his office in the rear barn until he retired, and Harry Chancey, a PBS television executive in New York.

In the midst of restoration, they turned their home into a B&B when the owners of the 1770 House inn followed up a casual suggestion by calling one night with a problem, the need for overnight lodging for a desperate couple. Their friends obliged, and one thing led to another.

Now the partners offer five elegant bedrooms with private baths and a three-bedroom cottage. Each is decorated to the Victorian hilt with antiques garnered mainly from estate and yard sales. Fancy fabrics, down comforters, white embroidered waffle weave robes and Neutrogena toiletries are in each room. So are sherry and port, chocolate truffles, TVs and bedside telephones, and a small refrigerator at the top of the stairs is stocked with drinks and snacks.

The Bay Room with the builder's initials inscribed in the wall beside the bookcase is most in demand. Its queensize four-poster is topped by a comforter and chintz floral pillows that match the balloon curtains in the bay window, from which it derives its name. The bathroom has a clawfoot tub and a sink ensconced in a 19th-century pulpit hand-carved from pine. The Bay Room has one of two new gas fireplaces in the house. The other is in the Rose Room, where the spiral-turned four-poster bed is wrapped in Waverly chintz that matches the window treatments and the clawfoot tub is draped with heavy tapestry. The Lincoln Room is so named for its Lincoln bed, designed the year he became president. The third floor holds a loft bedroom, its ceiling sloping down to a kingsize bed. This is not for tall people, who have to bend over in the shower and are apt to hit their heads on the ceiling as they go down the steep, curving staircase. It's for those who value their own roof-top deck for private "dining, sunning, whatever," according to the owners.

The rear cottage, fully winterized, boasts a full kitchen, breakfast area, living room with a TV and stereo, gas fireplace, two baths and a front porch. It has a small twin bedroom and a queen bedroom downstairs, and a room upstairs with a king bed, TV and one antique rocker. The cottage, rented by the week in season, is available for two-night stays in the off-season.

The interior of the main house is done in the high Victorian style. Twin Czecho-slovakian crystal chandeliers illuminate the double parlor, where prized doggies Earl and Edwinna are apt to preside in front of the Italian marble fireplace. Outfitted in Williamsburg fabrics (the chair seats are coordinated with the wallpaper), the formal Georgian dining room is set as if for dinner with cut-linen napkins and Rosenthal china. Breakfast is served here at a lace-covered table for eight and a smaller round table in a corner beside the bookshelves. Guests rave about the buttermilk pancakes, french toast or omelets prepared by Harry, David or house manager Bernadette Mead. Fruits, muffins and breakfast meats accompany.

Out back are a small fitness room in a barn and a secluded pool behind Harry's rose and herb gardens, where you feel as if you're a guest at someone's summer home. The guestbook is effusive with praise: "Relaxing, quiet, romantic, lovely, friendly" are recurring adjectives. "Your hospitality is unbeatable," summed up one happy guest.

Happily, in terms of hospitality, Bernadette is the perfect stand-in for Harry and David, who now commute between the Centennial House and their deluxe new Kingsbrae Arms in St. Andrews, N.B., Canada's first five-star inn.

(516) 324-9414. Fax (516) 324-2681. Five rooms with private baths and a three-bedroom cottage. May-October: doubles, $200 to $375 weekends, $175 to $275 midweek. November-April: $150 to $250. Three-night minimum weekends in summer, two-night minimum weekends spring and fall. Children over 12. No smoking.

Wicker-furnished front porch at Bluff Cottage faces lawns and ocean.

Bluff Cottage, 266 Bluff Road, Box 428, Amagansett 11930.

"We felt this was a house to share," say owners Clement Thompson and John Pakulek. They'd bought the oceanfront place as a summer home in 1971 and had proceeded to rent it out from Memorial Day to Labor Day, so rarely got to use it. When they decided enough was enough and moved in, they converted the 100-year-old summer cottage into a year-round house. "For years people had wanted to see it," Clem says. "Our friends were after us to do a B&B, so we did."

And a very inviting one it is. The only thing cottagey about it is the name. It's situated amidst a stretch of substantial residences cosseted behind privet hedges with the open Atlantic across the street. The air-conditioned house, full of fine antiques, has four guest rooms with antique queensize rice poster beds and private baths, elegant common rooms and porches on two levels overlooking the ocean. A refined, house-party atmosphere derives from affable hosts, relaxed company and a posh setting beside the beach. "This was our retirement project," says John. "And we've never worked so hard."

Every guest gets a tour of the main floor. Enjoy the corner fireplace and learn the stories behind a couple of enormous portraits in the den. Admire the 18th-century confessional in the corner and an old French dome chair beside the fireplace in the living room. Note the parquet-inlaid refectory table and one of the last surviving French tapestry screens in front of the fireplace in the dining room. In the country kitchen are shelf after shelf of antique English ironstone dinnerware. "You can see we're partial to French provincial and English country," says Clem.

Upstairs, the bedrooms are color-coordinated around a specific color, some more coordinated than others. The rear Peach Room is peach from its carpet to its walls to its hand-ironed sheets, interrupted only by the antique English mahogany poster bed and the curved English armoire. The front Green Room is a Ralph Lauren hunt scene look-alike in burgundy and dark green, although this was done like the rest of the house with fabrics from Calico Corners. The front Blue Room takes its name from just one of the colors in the draperies and isn't particularly blue, "so we *could* call it the Cameo Room," advises Clem. The Beige Room is, well, mostly beige. Each four-poster bed is draped in down comforters and duvets. Sturdy antique furniture abounds, but the look is uncluttered.

You'll be well fed in the morning after John picks up the makings for continental breakfast from the nearby Amagansett Farmers Market: luscious croissants, blueberry or bran muffins, English scones, fresh grapefruit and juices. They're served buffet-style in the dining room, and often taken on trays to the front porch.

The special charm of Bluff Cottage is enhanced by the wide front porch awash in wicker and a smaller upstairs balcony big enough for four. Both are good for ocean-watching and soaking up the seaside air.

(516) 267-6172. Four rooms with private baths. Doubles, $210 to $230. Three-night minimum June-August, four-night minimum holidays. Children over 12. No smoking. Closed October-April.

The Maidstone Arms, 207 Main St., East Hampton 11937.

Nicely located across from the town pond and the gravestone-lined village green, this white clapboard structure looks the way a summery country hotel should look.

It was converted from a private home in the 1870s, and upgraded from a seasonal inn into a year-round hotel in 1992. A porch with white rockers faces the tranquil green. Inside two three-story buildings connected by a sun porch is a ramble of rooms, from restaurant and dining porches to sixteen bedrooms with private baths, TVs, phones and air-conditioning. Out back are three garden cottages that represent the crème de la crème.

New owner Coke Anne Saunders, a New York architect whose late father was Texan Clint Murchison, poured big bucks into a cosmetic renovation and refurbishing of the old inn. A major rehab was precluded by zoning restrictions, but visitors today find modernized bathrooms, new furniture and beds, new wallpapers and draperies, and what chef and general manager William Valentine calls "a brighter, more cheery feeling." Accommodations vary in decor and size. Two small rooms we saw in the main inn – one with a double bed and another with twins – retain a snug, understated look even with the upgrades. More impressive are the garden cottages, each large and airy. We liked the one with vaulted ceiling, queensize poster bed, angled fireplace, sitting area with sofabed and armchair, and Waverly wallpaper and fabrics. Another cheerful bedroom, its wallpaper patterned with seashells and paired with tartan lampshades, won an honorable mention in Waverly's Country Inn Room of the Year contest. Besides the usual toiletries, a little sampler bag of local fragrances from Antonia's Flowers is in each room.

Guests share the wicker-filled front sun porch that doubles as a sitting room and breakfast room. It opens into a plant-filled room leading to gardens out back. The new Water Room is a gathering place for games, drinks, light meals and smoking. A continental breakfast of scones, English muffins and such is included in the rates. Breakfast also may be ordered à la carte.

The kitchen has been renovated to enhance the restaurant operation (see Dining Spots).

(516) 324-5006. Fax (516) 324-5037. Sixteen rooms and three cottages with private baths. Summer: doubles, $195 to $295; cottages, $350; three-night minimum weekends. Off-season: doubles, $165 to $285; cottages, $325; reduced rates midweek; two-night minimum weekends. Children welcome. Smoking restricted.

Waverly wallpaper and fabrics enhance cottage at The Maidstone Arms.

Mill House Inn, 33 North Main St., East Hampton 11937.

Facing the parkland and gravestones surrounding the Old Hook Windmill, this is a country charmer of a B&B with eight guest rooms, all with private baths. The original 1790 colonial saltbox was turned into a Dutch Colonial during expansion a century later. Katherine and Dan Hartnett, former northern New Jersey social workers raising three children, have undertaken major renovations and upgrading.

The beamed living room and dining room are properly historic and nicely decorated, the latter with yellow and blue wallpaper bearing a stunning teapot pattern. When we first stayed here, the guest rooms on three floors could best be described as homey. Now six rooms have fireplaces, six have queen beds and four have whirlpool tubs. All come with telephones and TV.

Katherine redecorated with antiques and armoires in a Colonial style. She stresses the history and character of the area with an equestrian theme in the main-floor Hampton Classic Room (its queen bed and day bed make it good for families), a floral theme in the Hampton Gardens Room, an afternoon at sea in Sail-Away and mill memorabilia in the Dominy Mill Room. Top of the line are two third-floor hideaways, the Hampton Holiday with a cherry wood bed and a plush settee, and the Hampton Breezes with a pine bed, wicker loveseat and chair, and one of three antique armoires upon which a friend painted remarkable designs from a wallpaper sample.

There's room to spread out on a long enclosed front porch, which the Hartnetts opened up with french doors, and in a spacious back yard. They also added french doors in the dining room, which opens onto a rear patio. Afternoon tea is served by the living-room fireplace in the off-season.

The Hartnetts installed a commercial kitchen to prepare gourmet breakfasts. The fare the day of our latest visit was typical: juice, crenshaw melon, homemade peasant and lemon breads, and tomato and basil frittata. Katherine, a chef who trained at the New York Cooking School, is known for her blueberry blintzes and smoked salmon quesadillas. Breakfast is taken on colorful Mikasa china in the dining room, on the porch overlooking the windmill green or on trays delivered to the bedrooms.

The kitchen also provides a setting for local caterer Kristi Hood's series of cooking classes in summer and fall.

(516) 324-9766. Fax (516) 324-9793. Eight rooms with private baths. May-October: doubles, $200 to $325. November-April: $140 to $250. Three-night minimum weekends in season. Children welcome. No smoking.

1770 House, 143 Main St., East Hampton 11937.

Seven guest rooms with private baths and a culinary heritage are available in this white clapboard house beside the old Clinton Academy, New York State's first accredited high school.

The culinary tradition started with Mim Perle, a cooking instructor and caterer, who with her husband Sid bought the structure, which had seen many lives, in 1977. Planning this as a semi-retirement project, the Perles found it quickly became a hands-on, family operation. When they opened the nearby Philip Taylor House as a low-key B&B, they left the 1770 House in the capable hands of daughter Wendy Van Deusen, who shared cooking duties with Mim, and son Adam, who presided over the bar in the Colonial taproom with its old hickory beams and open dutch hearth.

Following Mim's death in 1996, the big house was sold to friends who reopened it as a B&B. And after a gala New Year's Eve dinner, Wendy announced that she was through in the kitchen. The dining room was closed throughout 1997, although Wendy's husband, Burt Van Deusen, said they hoped to lease the operation out to a chef. "The place is ready and waiting," he said.

Among the guest rooms, we liked Room 10, a junior suite that has a queen bed in a recessed alcove, a floral print on the walls and some of the period clocks and antique furnishings that abound throughout. It comes with a little sitting room with a desk and one of the inn's two working fireplaces, as well as a small dressing room and a private entrance. Three other rooms have queen canopy beds, two have double canopy beds, and one has twins that can be joined as a king. A suite in the carriage house with a queen canopy bed, a loft with twin beds, a cathedral-ceilinged living room and a 2,000-volume library is the only place in town, we're told, where Yoko Ono will stay.

Guests gather in the beamed taproom or in a paneled library with a fireplace. Breakfast consists of fresh fruit, cereal and perhaps french toast made out of challah bread, belgian waffles or fresh herb omelets with scones.

(516) 324-1770. Fax (516) 324-3504. Seven rooms and one suite with private baths. May-October: doubles, $150 to $280 weekends, $120 to $250 midweek. November-March: $120 to $250 weekends, $90 to $120 midweek. Three-night minimum weekends in summer, two-night minimum weekends rest of year. Closed in April.

The House on Newtown, 172 Newtown Lane, East Hampton 11937.

This modest 1912 house built by a sea captain doesn't look like much, at least by East Hampton standards. Owners Mike and Marianne Kaufman ran it as a low-key B&B for eight years, filling by word of mouth and then branching out to lease five other houses they own around town to summer renters. Their house-rental service, the first in town, made a difference.

In 1994, they received "a modicum of fame," as Mike tells it. First, the White House travel office called for accommodations for "some very important people" in connection with a fund-raising visit by Vice President Al Gore. Although their houses were already booked, the calls continued daily for possible cancellations. In the midst of all this, upon the recommendation of the Maidstone Arms, ABC News asked if it could use the Kaufmans' Victorian living room as a backdrop for an interview with White House counsel Lloyd Cutler on "This Week with David Brinkley." The next morning the TV crews arrived, as did Cutler from his nearby home on Georgica Pond. All the goings-on at The House on Newtown made the front page of The East Hampton Star in a story headlined simply "Certainly Never in Kansas" – a reference to Mike's quote that if they had a B&B in Kansas, they wouldn't have the same stories to tell. "East Hampton is so exciting. We're at the epicenter of everything here."

The Kaufmans are fonts of lore regarding the epicenter, Mike having been a seventh-grade teacher here for more than twenty years. Like its owners, the B&B is welcoming and down-to-earth. All four bedrooms have private baths. Three have queensize beds (one has twins that can be joined as a king). They're full of sturdy oak furnishings and a lived-in look. Over the bed in one is a nifty painting of sandpipers by an artist who had once lived in the house.

A continental breakfast buffet of bagels, croissants, muffins, cereals, yogurt and fresh fruit is taken at round tables for two on the front sun porch. Guests enjoy privacy in a small sitting room outfitted in wicker, with a shelf lined with antique telephones overhead. People are more apt to gather with the innkeepers in the larger Victorian living room. The latter has a shelf lined with tea kettles, Victorian side tables, three sofas and two chairs.

(516) 324-1858 or 329-0672. Four bedrooms with private baths. Doubles, $190 to $220; off-season, $150 to $160.

Lysander House, 132 Main St., East Hampton 11937.

Their travels to Mexico and Japan are much in evidence at this welcoming and colorful B&B in a cozy Victorian farmhouse not far from downtown. "He worked and I shopped," Leslie Tell Hillel says of all the exotic pieces she and her husband Larry acquired while he was posted with Citibank in foreign lands.

Dramatic masks are lined up along the top of the walls in the front parlor. A wall of Japanese prints is the focal point of the side living room and dining area. Therapeutic duxiana mattresses from Sweden top the beds in three upstairs guest rooms.

All the folk art and eclectic furnishings are notable, as are the colors painted on the walls. One side bedroom with a double bed is a summery blue. The front master bedroom with a king bed is a cheerful pale yellow. And the rear suite is lavender in the queen bedroom and lavender-pink in the adjacent sitting room with sofabed. The walls of the hall and stairway are painted two colors: yellow for the sun on one side and blue for the sea on the other.

The hostess is into cooking as much as she is into art and color. For breakfast, she might jazz up the pancakes with mangos and the french toast with oranges and pecans. Another favorite is cheese frittata.

Chatty Leslie offers afternoon beverages and sends guests home with a bag of biscotti.

(516) 329-9025. Two rooms and a suite with private baths. May-October: doubles, $170 to $250 weekends, $140 to $210 midweek. November-April: $140 to $180 weekends, $120 to $160 midweek. Children over 14. No smoking.

The Plover's Nest, 199 Main St., East Hampton 11937.

History permeates the hand-hewn beams, the beehive oven and all the other accoutrements of this B&B in a brown shingled house erected in 1774 on a foundation dating to the town's settlement in the 1650s. Owners Adele and Fred Filasky retained the original handcrafted woodwork and floors, but added private baths, cable TV and queensize beds to their four guest rooms with fireplaces.

All convey an historic feeling, from the four-poster bed and beamed ceiling in one rear bedroom to a rear suite with a small sitting room and an extra twin sleigh bed that doubles as a day couch. Adele considers the third-floor bedroom with antique white iron bed and wicker chairs her most romantic quarters.

Downstairs is a cozy parlor with beamed ceiling and barnwood paneling, where wine and hors d'oeuvre are set out in the afternoon. Four tables for two are set for breakfast in the dining room on either side of a long and narrow buffet table where an elaborate continental breakfast awaits. The fare ranges from yogurt, fresh fruit and cereals to hard-boiled eggs, croissants and scones.

Guests enjoy lounging on a brick patio beneath a 250-year-old beech tree in the shady side yard.

(516) 329-1120. Four rooms with private baths. Memorial Day through October: doubles, $250 weekends, $225 midweek. November to Memorial Day: $165 weekends, $145 midweek. Two-night minimum weekends. No smoking.

The Huntting Inn, 94 Main St., East Hampton 11937.

The closest inn to the center of town, this is within walking distance of stores and yet back from the street beside a shady English country garden, of which innkeeper Linda Calder is rightly proud. The only problem is that inn guests have to walk outside and halfway around the building to get to the garden retreat. The owners hope eventually to put in french doors allowing access from the sun porch to the garden, but in strictly regulated East Hampton such things take time.

Resembling a New England country inn, this white clapboard structure with green shutters is really ancient and protected (some would say prevented) from changes that would bring it into the 21st century. It was built as a home in 1699 by the Church of England for the Rev. Nathaniel Huntting. His widow turned it into a public house in 1751, a status it has maintained since. The front porch and main floor are given over to The Palm, one of two restaurants run here by co-owners Wally Ganzi and Bruce Bozzi. The other is at the associated Hedges Inn.

Upstairs, a narrow maze of corridors leads to eighteen air-conditioned guest rooms on two floors. Rooms vary widely in size and style. One of the largest harbors a beamed ceiling, kingsize four-poster bed and a velvet sofa. The bathroom has pine wainscoting stained to look like oak and a double jacuzzi and separate shower. Another is small with an old-fashioned tub. Most rooms are decorated with vivid floral prints and dark carpeting. One charming room, sprightly with yellow paint and yellow floral duvet that matches the draperies, was awarded an honorable mention in Waverly's Country Inn Room of the Year contest. Our room was part of a two-room suite with a small bath in the middle. It had the floral wallpaper typical of the inn, tied-back lace curtains, a kingsize bed, a TV hidden in a corner armoire, new carpeting and a dark sitting room in which only one of the three lights worked. Ice was delivered with a complimentary bottle of S. Pellegrino water and one of the bureaus displayed a basket of toiletries, a little bag of local Antonia's Flowers fragrances and lotions, and two Lindor truffles.

A good continental breakfast buffet is spread out atop the Palm bar or, at peak periods, in the restaurant. Those who get there first may eat on the front sun porch so coveted by diners at night.

(516) 324-0410. Fax (516) 324-8751. Eighteen rooms with private baths. April through mid-October: doubles, $195 to $275. Rest of year: $125 to $195.

The Hedges' Inn, 74 James Lane, East Hampton 11937.
Beautiful flowers line the brick walk leading to this yellow clapboard inn dating to 1774. It stands at the entry to the village at the west end of the town pond – where the road makes a turn from the city to country life, according to one writeup. The secluded setting is residential, although much of the main floor gets busy at night as the James Lane Cafe. Like the Huntting Inn, it's owned by Wally Ganzi and Bruce Bozzi of the Palm restaurants.
Some of the eleven guest rooms on the second and third floors here seem brighter and more up to date than those at the Huntting. Room 1, for instance, is light and airy with a queensize bed, a small fireplace, a dark red velvet loveseat, baskets of fruit and flowers, and a modern bathroom with a double black marble vanity. Room 6 offers a king bed against sky-blue wallpaper. A small upstairs corner room has a double bed with a wicker headboard, but has no chairs. Each room has a private bath and air-conditioning.
Fruit, cereal, bagels, muffins and croissants are put out in a cheery breakfast room. Wicker furniture on the front porch faces the pond.
The dinner menu has dropped the weighty steaks and lobsters of Palm days in favor of grilled pizzas, pastas and seafood with an Italian accent. The dining room has been lightened up in shades of pale yellow and white. The tented flagstone patio remains inviting as ever with rattan chairs, votive candles and fresh flowers on white-clothed tables, twinkling white lights and geraniums here and there.

(516) 324-7100. Fax (516) 324-5816. Eleven rooms with private baths. April through mid-October: doubles, $195 to $275. Rest of year: $125 to $195.
Entrées, $19 to $32. Dinner nightly from 5, May-October.

Dining Spots

East Hampton is a place for eating and eating well, often at prices approaching those in Manhattan. Many restaurants require gratuities in cash rather than on credit cards. Reservations often are hard to come by.

Nick and Toni's, 136 North Main St., East Hampton.
Nice and tony, this is one of East Hampton's "in" places, and not simply because of its wood-burning oven. We could tell the moment we arrived and were led through the entire place to a rear table, which was fine with us. We became aware of the Hampton glance – all eyes on new arrivals to see who they are and with whom. Even the deuces are angled with backs to the wall so each diner can watch the passing parade. And why not, when the restaurant's backer was Steve Ross, the late Time-Warner mogul who had a home in East Hampton, the place is run by his daughter and son-in-law, Toni Ross and Jeff Salaway, and the inspired cooks in the kitchen have a devoted following?
There's a variety of summery rooms with big windows and no curtains. Seating is on sleek, cushioned European chairs at tables set with crisp white cloths. The look is unadulterated: no candles, no flowers and fairly bright overhead lighting.

Sleek, summery look prevails in side dining room at Nick and Toni's.

Dinner begins with dense Tuscan bread served with olive oil for dipping. For starters, we tried the night's soup, grilled tomato with a very smoky flavor and a sensational wilted dandelion salad with a bacon and mustard vinaigrette. Among main courses, we fell for the loin of pork with nectarines and swiss chard and the fettuccine with rabbit, lemon and rosemary. The house wine we had with appetizers was poured from an Italian pitcher, and meals came on various pottery serving pieces. With our meal we chose a sauvignon blanc from the nearby Hargrave winery among a number of good, affordable choices. Dessert was the day's special blueberry-peach buckle from a selection that included tirami su, "serious" chocolate cake and homemade ice cream.

The changing menu involves about eight appetizers, four pastas, side vegetables and six main courses, ranging from pan-roasted striped bass with truffled potato puree to ribeye steak with chilled lobster ($65 for two).

Although the clientele is haute, this did not strike us as a haughty place, as many in the area are. But the reservation system is complex (those with unknown names may not get in), and the prices have risen lately. The owners opened a Manhattan outlet of the same name in 1997 at 100 W. 67th St.

(516) 324-3550. Entrées, $23 to $34. Dinner nightly, 6 to 10 or 11. Sunday, brunch 11:30 to 2:30, dinner 5 to 10. Closed Tuesday and Wednesday, September-May.

Della Femina, 99 North Main St., East Hampton.

In East Hampton, don't be surprised by the improbable. Here in 1992 was Jerry Della Femina, arguably the world's most famous ad man and full of Brooklyn bravado, opening a restaurant – named after himself – across the street from Nick & Toni's. Nine months later, he took over another restaurant on the waterfront, East Hampton Point. Soon followed an Italian food market and deli to go, also bearing his name. And a couple of years later he acquired a propitiously located lumber yard for, at the time, who-knew-what-purpose – not, wife-TV newscaster

Judy Licht hoped, another restaurant. As New York magazine put it in an article headlined "The Adman Who Ate East Hampton," Jerry Della Femina has a way of making his presence known.

His first restaurant is understated, except perhaps for the prices and the flurry of reservations that are taken ten days ahead and sell out in a few hours at peak periods (there's a "power list" for VIPs). The 80-seat dining room is stark white except for beige cane chairs at well-spaced tables, a wood-paneled ceiling, tall straw wall sconces that look like sheaves of wheat and, near the far corner, a decorative fireplace with colorful jugs on the mantel. Boxes of fruits and vegetables add color in an opening between the dining room and the skylit bar, its walls plastered ever-so-suavely with framed caricatures of restaurant patrons. Trying to make a spot on that wall quickly became part of the restaurant's cachet.

The menu changes monthly. Look for starters like green gazpacho, grilled Hudson Valley foie gras and tartare of ahi tuna with seaweed salad, wasabi tobikko and cucumber-kaffir lime sauce. Fettuccine with lobster, asparagus and sundried tomatoes is one of the stellar pastas. Main courses could be roasted Mediterranean daurade (a seldom seen fish) with tomato-thyme sauce, pan-roasted local chicken with grain mustard sauce, and wood-grilled loin of Colorado lamb with black olive-herb sauce. A six-course tasting menu, selected by the chef, is available for the entire table.

Summer desserts are refreshingly cooling, among them Italian plum and blackberry cobbler with blueberry ice cream, banana tarte tatin with ice cream, root beer float with chocolate ice cream and something called a fudge brownie and malted milkball ice cream sandwich.

(516) 329-6666. Entrées, $20 to $33. Dinner nightly, 6 to 10:30, fewer nights in off-season.

The Maidstone Arms, 207 Main St., East Hampton.

New ownership has enhanced the grande dame of East Hampton restaurants. A spectacular floral arrangement in the entry hall is the only showy accoutrement in the low-key refurbishment.

The front dining room with corner service bar is traditional and masculine with dark wood floors, a fireplace and ship's models and seascapes on the walls. The larger rear dining room is carpeted, light and airy. It's notable for Clarence House wallpaper imprinted with trompe-l'oeil shelves and panels of plates that match the real china displayed along the front wall.

Such is the setting for meals that measure up to the expectations of resident East Hamptonites, young and old, celebrating special occasions. Chef-manager William Valentine returned to his native Long Island and the Maidstone Arms after a stint in Los Angeles. California and Pacific Rim influences show up in his masterful roast lacquered duck, everybody's favorite hereabouts. Flavored with five spices and coffee-mandarin glaze, its crisp mahogany skin and tender meat are perched atop scallion pancakes or soba noodles tossed with julienned vegetables. Other choices vary from chilled lobster with Japanese vegetable salad and a chile-mango dressing to boneless quail stuffed with Chang Mai sausage on stir-fried soba noodles with curried coconut.

The rum-smoked salmon with toasted semolina baguette is a signature appetizer. Desserts could be blueberry cobbler, crème brûlée and a trio of homemade ice creams and sorbets. The wine cellar is one of the Hamptons' best.

The restaurant takes pride in being open for lunch and dinner daily year-round.
(516) 324-5006. Entrées, $19.50 to $29.50. Lunch, Monday-Friday noon to 2:30.
Saturday and Sunday brunch, noon to 3. Dinner nightly, 6 to 9:30, to 11 on weekends.

East Hampton Point, 295 Three Mile Harbor Road, East Hampton.

Formerly Wings Point, this used to be the place that everyone locally recommended for cocktails on an outdoor terrace beside the water. They didn't seem to eat here, which is why we were able to get an 8 o'clock reservation for a window table on a weekday evening when other restaurants were full.

Enter adman Jerry Della Femina, who whitewashed the dining room and removed walls so that every seat on two levels looks onto boats bobbing to and fro in the marina and the sunset across Three Mile Harbor – or into mirrors reflecting same. Now its tables are coveted as much for dining as for the view. The place looked appealing for a summer lunch, except that we (and other latecomers) were thoroughly ignored, we felt underdressed amid all the fashion and media peacocks, and we didn't care to spend $15 for a chicken BLT sandwich or a tuna niçoise salad. View carries only so far.

For dinner, the kitchen delivers such standouts as grilled yellowfin tuna with wasabi crème fraîche, penne with shrimp à la vodka and a perennial favorite, barbecued braised lamb shank over red onion and corn risotto. Start with a roasted vegetable and goat cheese terrine or king salmon and crab cakes with avocado tartar sauce. Some of the kicky desserts bring back childhood memories: root beer float with chocolate-chip cookies, and toasted marshmallow and chocolate s'mores with tahitian vanilla bean ice cream, at un-childhood prices in the $7 range.

(516) 329-2800. Entrées, $20 to $28. Lunch daily in season, noon to 3. Dinner nightly,
5:30 to 11. Sunday brunch, noon to 3.

Bostwick's Seafood Grill, 39 Gann Road, East Hampton.

This spacious seafood grill commands the same water view as its higher-profile neighbor, East Hampton Point, but without the prices and pretensions. It's named for young chef-partner Chris Eggert's favorite fishing area in Gardiner's Bay, which shows where his priorities lie.

The seasonal place seats 140, most on a covered outdoor deck that can be enclosed in plastic and heated for use on chilly evenings.

Tiny white ribbed lights on the canopy barely gave off enough light to read the menu as we staved off hunger with a basket of lavasch and hot rolls. The lobster ravioli was the meal's highlight, a superior appetizer with a divine basil and garlic cream sauce. The caesar salad also was good, and we liked the looks of the thin-crust, brick-oven pizza topped with spinach, bacon, garlic, tomato and more delivered to the next table. For main courses, one of us settled on a special of grilled yellowfin tuna, nicely charred and served on an oversize white plate bearing three swirls of mashed potatoes and a bed of sliced carrots and haricots verts. The other sampled the stuffed yellowtail flounder, a less successful dish with more of the same accompaniments. A $16 Buena Vista sauvignon blanc was a satisfying choice from the affordable wine list. Desserts included Mississippi mud pie, chocolate mousse cake, key lime pie and raspberry sorbet.

(516) 324-1111. Entrées, $14.95 to $17.95. Lunch, Saturday and Sunday noon to 3 in
summer. Dinner nightly, 5:30 to 10 or 11, Thursday-Sunday in off-season. Closed late
September to May.

Santa Fe Junction, 8 Fresno Place, East Hampton.
Tucked away on a back street (and rather hard to find) is this trendy year-round venture, opened in 1994 by Chris Eggert and Kevin Boles, who earned their spurs at Bostwick's. They undertook a substantial renovation, adding brick and rough-hewn cedar and french doors in place of windows.

The menu features Southwest fare – "not Tex-Mex," chef Chris pointed out. Dinner entrées include assorted fajitas, hickory smoked ribs, crab cakes, local seafood, blackened tuna tacos, barbecued chicken enchiladas and mesquite-grilled ribeye steaks. Start with quesadillas, tamales, black bean raviolis or cornmeal fried oysters. Finish with sopaipillas, flan, chocolate-pecan pie or pumpkin cheesecake.

Although Chris oversees the food in both restaurants, his summer priority remains Bostwick's, because he's a water person at heart.

(516) 324-8700. Entrées, $14.95 to $17.50. Dinner nightly, from 5:30. Closed Wednesday in winter.

Sapore di Mare, Montauk Highway, Wainscott.
This is one beautiful restaurant and the beautiful people usually keep it packed. Dining is on several levels inside and on a porch backing up to Georgica Pond. Up to 160 diners can be accommodated at well-spaced tables topped by white linens, mod dispensers of extra-virgin olive oil and balsamic vinegars, and sleek glass oil lamps in a variety of styles.

The contemporary Italian menu changes seasonally. Most opt for the antipasti selection from the display table, although you also can start with carpaccio, grilled calamari or fresh mozzarella with roasted peppers. There are seven complex pasta dishes. Main courses vary from spicy seafood stew and grilled, sautéed or whole roasted fish of the day to grilled ribeye steak and veal scaloppini, the preparation changing daily.

Among desserts are tirami su, chocolate mousse, country-style apple tart, soft polenta cream with strawberry sauce and espresso granita with whipped cream.

Owner Pino Luongo also owns restaurants in New York, Dallas and St. Barts. He has published a cookbook, *A Tuscan in the Kitchen,* and has run a summer cooking school here.

(516) 537-2764. Entrées, $23.50 to $34. Lunch, Saturday and Sunday noon to 3. Dinner nightly, 6 to 10:30 or midnight. Closed Tuesday and Wednesday in off-season.

The Farmhouse, 341 Pantigo Road, East Hampton.
Situated on four beautiful acres and framed by masses of zinnias, the historic Spring Close House has new owners, new decor and a creative kitchen featuring American bistro cooking with a French influence. In the late 1600s, this dining room was the center of a 55-acre working farm. Today it specializes in farm-fresh food, and grows its own herbs and vegetables. From a wood-burning oven come chicken, local fish and gourmet pizzas.

The short menu starts with items like local mussels with smoked tomato sauce, roasted eggplant caviar and olive tapenade with wood-fired focaccia crisps, and crab cake with saffron-garlic mayonnaise. Main courses could be grilled Atlantic salmon with sweet corn and tomato ragoût, oven-roasted organic chicken with white cheddar polenta and grilled Australian rack of lamb.

Save room for dessert, perhaps pear cobbler, banana tart with vanilla ice cream and caramel sauce, the brûlée du jour or assorted homemade sorbets.

Canning jars and cans hold fresh flowers on each table in various dining rooms, outfitted in beige with dark green accents. Owners Fred and Susan Lieberman designed the country casual decor, augmented with antique toys from his collection and a delightful mix of whimsy, barnyard nostalgia and sophistication.

A large screened porch with flagstone floor has a billowing white canopy and Japanese lamps for outdoor dining in season.

(516) 324-8585. Entrées, $19 to $32. Dinner nightly, 6 to 10 or 11.

The Laundry, 31 Race Lane, East Hampton.

Only in place like the self-assured Hamptons could a restaurant converted from a commercial laundry call itself that. This really was a laundry, and you still can see the big extractor outside. Inside all is dark and glamorous, with seating on two levels, a long bar against the outside wall, and seating in green leather-like booths or on red chairs and banquettes. A spectacular flower arrangement at the entrance is a trademark.

The menu changes daily and is very with-it. You might start with carpaccio of local tuna with mustard sauce, grilled shrimp "in a country dress" or a choice of two tapas for $11. The soup could be Tuscan tomato or chilled cantaloupe.

Entrées range widely from sautéed calves liver grilled New York sirloin strip steak "dry aged 14 days." Pan-seared Nova Scotia halibut with spicy Asian stir fry, Japanese-style crab cakes with wasabi mayonnaise and grilled mahi-mahi with avocado salsa were among seafood possibilities when we were there.

Desserts run to strawberry sour cream brûlée, vol-au-vent of lemon curd with raspberry coulis, fresh fruit crisp and banana bread with chocolate crème anglaise and pistachio ice cream.

Locals consider this a good late-hour dining spot. It's also popular with singles.

(516) 324-3199. Entrées. $18 to $27. Dinner nightly, 5:30 to 11 or midnight.

Palm Restaurant, 94 Main St., East Hampton.

Everybody raves about the Palm Restaurant at the Huntting Inn, one of a chain extending from Manhattan to ritzy points south and west. They love the huge steaks and chops and lobsters. They warn about being talked into ordering more potatoes and vegetables than you need (the menu says they're served family style for two or more but they can feed an entire family). And they love the scene, dark and clubby and masculine, with lots of booths and caricatures framed on the walls. And, of course, they love it for the celebrities. "Billy Joel would go there, not here," we were advised by an insider at the Hedges' Inn, whose former Palm Restaurant recently was converted into the James Lane Cafe.

This is a typical Manhattan steakhouse, transported to the summery Hamptons by the Huntting owner, whose grandfather was the founder of the Palm. We can't imagine why New Yorkers would come out here to pay $29 to $31 for a steak or prime rib ($60 for a 36-ounce New York strip for two), add $6.50 for hash browns or fried onions or string beans ($7.50 for creamed spinach that we hear is great), and $30 or more for a cabernet sauvignon. But thousands do, even lobster-lovers who always come at least once a summer to order lobsters weighing four or more pounds. Who's to question why?

(516) 324-0411. Entrées, $16 to $31. Dinner nightly, 5 to 11. Closed Monday and Tuesday in off-season.

Diversions

Many people come to "America's most beautiful village" for the beaches, which have been ranked among the nation's cleanest. But there is much more to see and do.

Beaches. Parking at any village or town beach along Long Island's south shore is limited to fifteen minutes or requires a parking sticker indicating residency. All parking is banned from 10 a.m. to 4 p.m. on the residential streets lined with great estates near the beaches. For those without stickers, parking is available at Main Beach and Atlantic Avenue Beach for $15 on weekdays. Many inns have beach passes for guests.

Walking Tour. Walk Main Street in the heart of East Hampton's historic district from Montauk Highway to Newtown Lane. The **Town Pond** is a tranquil spot at the end of the village green, between Main Street and James Lane. Tombstones date back to the 17th century in the adjacent **South End Cemetery,** where many gravestones are so worn they are no longer legible. **Home Sweet Home,** the 1680 saltbox that was the boyhood home of poet John Howard Payne, who wrote the song of the same name, is open for guided tours and features fine furniture collected over three centuries. Nearby is an early windmill. The **Mulford Farmstead,** long the center of a working farm, also is open for tours in summer. **Guild Hall,** given to the town in 1931, is an art museum with three galleries and the John Drew Theater, the oldest playhouse on Long Island, the site for plays, musicals and concerts. Across the street is the charming brick and stucco, English-looking **East Hampton Library.** There's not a computer terminal in sight, but stacks of newspapers and two old typewriters can be seen through the front office windows of the **East Hampton Star,** the thick and newsy local weekly. Beside it is **the Wild Flower Garden of Long Island,** a shady oasis of native plants, the gift of the Garden Club of East Hampton. **Clinton Academy,** built in 1784, is marked as the oldest "academical" institution in New York State. It's used for Historical Society exhibits of period furniture, artifacts, decoys and dolls. School desks, hand-writing lessons and quill pens are on view next door in the shingled **Town House,** a former school and town hall built in 1731. The 1735 **Osborne-Jackson House** is the headquarters of the East Hampton Historical Society. In the triangle between North Main and Pantigo Lane is the **Hook Mill,** a still-operable windmill open to the public for tours in summer.

Driving Tours. Residential streets in the estate area between Main Beach and Georgica Pond are worth a look-see. Tall trees, privet hedges and deep lawns screen some estates from view, but others are visible from the road and most show signs of big money and good taste. Another pleasant drive is along the dunes on Further Lane to Bluff Road in Amagansett.

Shopping. East Hampton's tree-shaded shopping district along Main Street and Newtown Lane is quite villagey and low-key, as opposed, say, to Southampton. Garden benches provide welcome seating every thirty feet or so. Two stores that everybody seems to like are the ultra decorated **Polo Country Store,** the second of summer resident Ralph Lauren's country stores, and the **Coach Factory Store,** where the handsome and expensive bags are sold at a slight discount (we got a discontinued model for half price, however). There are so many designer clothing shops that you wonder if visiting New Yorkers are simply too busy to shop in

Manhattan; ditto for antiques and interiors stores. The options vary from **Cashmere Hampton, Bonne Nuit** (lacy lingerie and children's outfits), **Whitewash** (almost all white clothing) to **Victory Garden** ("antiques, etc." for garden and home) and **Long Island Sound** (music store). We coveted the incredible carved wood sculptures and acrylics (one of Noah's Ark and all the passengers for $2,400) at **Anne Kolb Gallery.** More to our price range were the handful of upscale outlet stores, spread out around sculptures and benches flanking the large lawn at **Amagansett Square.** The trendoids pick up their gourmet foods at **Jerry and David's Red Horse Market,** owned by Jerry Della Femina and a partner from Dean & DeLuca, at 74 Montauk Hwy. One of the more exotic salad bars is located across the plaza at Red Horse to Go. Other good lunchy spots with salads, focaccia sandwiches, gourmet foods and such are **JL Bean** and **Barefoot Contessa,** both along Newtown Lane.

Farm Stands. Long known for potatoes and ducks, eastern Long Island has become a center for fresh produce. **Round Swamp Farm** at 184 Three Mile Harbor Road was featured in the New York Times as one of summer resident Craig Claiborne's favorite markets. It sells everything from fruits and exotic vegetables to preserves, fish, cheese, baked goods and more, and we picked up a couple of jars of their good salsas. We thought Round Swamp couldn't be topped, but it was – at least in terms of size and crowds – by the **Amagansett Farmers Market** on the Montauk Highway in Amagansett, a privately owned "stand" bigger than any we've seen. Here, at what is obviously a local gathering spot, everyone was buying cut flowers for the weekend, picking up oyster mushrooms and baby pattypan squash, and sifting through every salsa, mustard, oil and vinegar ever made. An incredible bakery produces the best sticky buns, and folks sit out front with croissants and cappuccino from the espresso bar. There also are a section of prepared foods and a great meat market.

Extra-Special _____

Sag Pond Vineyards, Sagg Road, Sagaponack. (516) 537-5106.

Long Island has become known for fine wines, since the Hargrave Vineyard pioneered on the North Fork in the 1970s. Lately, the South Fork is diverting attention from North Fork vintners. Here, a stunning new state-of-the-art winery opened atop hill above the Atlantic Ocean in 1997. It looks like something straight out of Tuscany with its blue shutters on a sand-colored façade, imposing gates, colorful gardens and a fountain at the entry. Windows in the cathedral-ceilinged tasting room look onto the tanks in the fermentation room. Christian Wolffer, German-born international venture capitalist, bought the property on the north side of the Montauk Highway to raise horses, and his Sag Pond Farm is considered the top stable on the South Fork. He then planted 50 acres of grapes in 1987. Winemaker Roman Roth from Germany produces award-winning chardonnays and pinot noirs in the European style. Bone dry rosé, champagne and dessert wines are newer releases among Sag Pond's production of 7,000 cases a year. Prices range from $11.99 to $20.99. It claims to be the only New York State winery whose offerings are carried in all five of Manhattan's highest ranked restaurants.

(516) 537-5106. Showroom daily, 11 to 6; tours, Friday-Sunday 11 to 6.

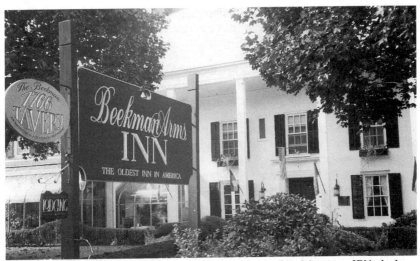

America's oldest continuously operating inn, Beekman Arms, is landmark in center of Rhinebeck.

Rhinebeck, N.Y.

History Along the Hudson

Among New York State towns, few are so old – and noticeably so – as Rhinebeck.

Located in the northern Hudson Valley a couple of miles inland from the river, the village was settled in 1686 by the Dutch as Kipsbergen. German immigrants who moved there around 1713 named it for their native Rhine river and "beck" meaning cliffs. The Livingstons, the Astors, the Vanderbilts, the Roosevelts and others of America's landed gentry followed.

Rhinebeck claims eight miles of the Hudson Valley's Sixteen Mile Historic District, whose great riverfront estates from the Gilded Age are well known. Less known is the fact that Rhinebeck – with 437 sites listed on the National Register, most out of the public eye on side streets – embraces one of the nation's largest historic districts.

The Beekman Arms, America's oldest continuously operated inn, occupies a prime corner at the village's main intersection. Across the street is an old-fashioned cigar store and newsstand, which still advertises cigars on its façade and displays pipes and tobacco inside and, sign of the times, a walk-in cigar humidor. On another corner, the old-line Rhinebeck Department Store with updated apparel claims to "continue tradition." Fanning out from the main intersection are a variety of stores, some with a New Age bent, and restaurants old and new. Most reflect a simpler past or pace rather than a gentrified, hectic present.

Farther from the center are other attractions. The Dutchess County Fairgrounds is home of New York State's second largest agricultural fair, plus periodic crafts and antiques shows of considerable renown. Antique airplanes perform stunts at the Old Rhinebeck Aerodrome. The heritage of the grand estates lives on at the Wilderstein Restoration, the Mills Mansion, Montgomery Place and Clermont. The Omega Institute links people with self fulfillment and the New Age.

Tiny Rhinecliff, where the train still stops, slumbers alongside the Hudson. Away from the villages, the rural landscape that attracted the Hudson River School painters remains pastoral – remarkably so, given its proximity to the nation's largest metropolitan area.

What the New York Daily News headlined "the renaissance of Rhinebeck" has vaulted the village lately into a destination for tourists.

"When people think of Rhinebeck, they think of the Beekman Arms," notes Nikola Rebraca, a New York restaurateur who recently restored the Belvedere Mansion into an inn and restaurant. "It's like the anchor store. They have history behind them. Everybody else plays second fiddle."

That may be changing. At least four restaurants give the Beekman dining operation a run for its money among knowing diners. Other inns and B&Bs have emerged, most in the last few years. Some on the fringe tend to come and go.

"Rhinebeck is rapidly becoming the focal point of everything in the Hudson Valley," notes architectural historian Ward Stanley, who moved with his wife from Philadelphia to open the Veranda House B&B in a mansion listed on the National Register.

Yet this is no slick, cutesy, movie-set town. Rhinebeck goes its own way. Visitors so inclined may come along.

Inn Spots

Beekman Arms, 4 Mill St. (Route 9), Rhinebeck 12572.

America's oldest continuously operating inn ages gracefully. It dates to 1766, and nowhere more noticeably than in the dark and beamed, low-ceilinged Tap Room, where candles are lit even at noon. In the newer rooms in the separate Delamater Courtyard area, the accommodations are up-to-date, some even verging on the luxurious. The food in the Beekman 1776 Tavern is often at the cutting edge.

The Beekman (or the Beek, as it's called locally) claims history, obviously, among its many facets. The feeling of antiquity is tangible in sections of the main building, which doesn't look all that old, what with its restored Georgian pillared facade and a contemporary solarium dining room facing the front lawn where George Washington and his troops drilled during the Revolutionary War. But the

requisite wide-plank floors, overhead beams and stone hearth greet guests in the lobby, often the busiest place in town. A guest log from 1887 is embedded in a coffee table in the far parlor, where we marveled over the glass-enclosed, table-top replica of an old tavern. Everything is in miniature, down to the most intricate tiny liquor bottles and bar stools.

Gingerbread-trimmed house built in 1844 is focal point of Beekman's Delamater Courtyard complex.

Upstairs in the main building, the thirteen guest rooms on the second and third floors were remodeled and redecorated with fresh Colonial décor and folk art accents in 1995. We were shown a couple of rooms that were described as typical. Each has twin beds, plump matching chairs, a TV hidden in a chest, a wash bowl inlaid in a wooden cabinet in the bathroom and a wooden butler with a tray holding a few amenities. All contain English pants presses, telephones and a decanter of sherry. Most remain dark and historic, as you'd expect from their 18th-century heritage.

Behind the main inn are six motel-style rooms with in-room refrigerators. Restaurant owner Larry Forgione's American Spoon Foods are featured in the Beekman Country Store at the side of the inn. An Antique Market and Art Gallery occupies a barn in back.

The most comfortable accommodations are the 40 of later vintage in the Delamater complex a block up the street from the main inn. The gingerbread-trimmed Delamater House was built in 1844 in the rare American Gothic style for the founder of the local bank. The original marble fireplace warms its guest parlor. The spacious front-corner bedroom opposite offers one of the inn's few kingsize beds and a plush wicker sitting area. Television sets are hidden in the armoires of it and the five upstairs guest rooms. Sherry awaits in decanters, a rear kitchen is available for guests, and front and rear porches are great for relaxing.

Behind the house are top-of-the-line rooms in the cathedral-ceilinged Carriage House and five other guest houses scattered around the perimeter of the Delamater Courtyard. All have beige facades with brown trim and colorful red roofs. Each holds four to eight rooms. The Germond House, which was moved to the site, contains a conference center as well. Rooms we toured in the carriage house have two Shaker-style double beds or a king bed on a level slightly raised above the sitting area, with sofabed, TV, antique chests and writing desks. Crossbeams accent the ceilings. The bathrooms are modern and outfitted with the amenities one expects. Twenty-three rooms contain working fireplaces.

Guests here take continental breakfast in a side building with a gift shop and tables overlooking the interior courtyard lawn.

Charles LaForge Jr., owner since 1958, turns out to be the longest-lasting of the Beekman's fourteen landlords listed on a plaque at the entry. He oversees the main inn. Innkeeper Doris Masteen handles the Delameter complex, which seems to go its own way with a separate telephone number and reception area.

(914) 876-7077. Delameter House (914) 876-7080. Fifty-seven rooms and two suites with private baths. Inn and motel: doubles, $80 to $120. Delamater complex: $85 to $150. Children accepted.

The Mansakenning Carriage House, 29 Ackert Hook Road, Rhinebeck 12572.

The Manhattan celebrities and CEOs drawn to this luxury hideaway in the country view it as a place for escape and romance. They don't want to chat idly with other guests or eat breakfast at a big communal table, says owner Michelle Dremann. "They cherish their privacy and independence, so they have everything they need in their rooms."

Michelle started in 1990 with two rooms and a suite in the main 1895 Colonial house that actually was the carriage house for a larger estate listed on the National Register and hidden in the woods some distance away. She now has four more suites, a husband and a child, and two fulltime innkeepers to assist.

The seven romantic hideaways here range from a small bedroom with a hall bath in the twelve-room main house to a sumptuous suite fashioned from four horse stalls in the former Stable. Five suites have fireplaces, three have jacuzzi tubs and four have private balconies or decks.

A Philadelphia artist painted the remarkable stencil designs in each room, and Michelle decorated each to the hilt. The queen or kingsize beds are dressed with Ralph Lauren linens and down comforters. TV/VCRs, telephones, Caswell-Massey toiletries, terry robes and a basket of extra towels are the norm. A coffeemaker, a decanter of sherry and a refrigerator stocked with complimentary beverages are in each room.

Michelle says Joan Rivers prefers the original Manaskenning Suite, light and airy with a kingsize bed beneath a beamed cathedral ceiling and eleven windows on three sides. An oriental rug accents the polished wide-board floor and two casual chairs face the fireplace. French doors open onto a narrow wraparound balcony.

Others like the largest Country Covert Suite on the main floor of the Stable. The corner fireplace is positioned to face the kingsize bed, and the jacuzzi is enclosed in wainscoting that matches the bedroom ceiling. A bird's nest is handpainted under a sheer half canopy above the Victorian trundle bed in a sitting room in one of the former horse stalls. The bedroom desk is next to a built-in ladder and a grain feeder from the original hayloft.

A wall in the Stable's upstairs hallway is a garden delight of handpainted flowers, birds, butterflies, a squirrel on a wheelbarrow and even a ladybug tucked in a blossom. Guests in the Huntsman's Hideaway find trompe l'oeil books painted on the fireplace mantle and incredible handpainted walls that look like wallpaper in the bathroom. At the other end of the hayloft is the sunny Fox Den with kingsize canopy bed, fireplace, jacuzzi and private deck.

Breakfast is delivered in a hefty basket with the local newspaper to the guest rooms at the decadent hour of 9:30. Guests, most still in their robes, take it at a table in their room or on a balcony. The fresh orange juice is in a chilled glass flask

Mansakenning Carriage House is ready for overnight guests.

and the homemade croissants, scones, mini-bagels and rugelach are in a heated cookie tin. The exotic fruit is a work of art surrounding the main dish, in our case diminutive slices of french toast stuffed with pecans and cream cheese, garnished with edible flowers and so good alone we passed on the side of peach-apricot sauce. The menu, printed daily, might yield cheese blintzes or buckwheat crêpes filled with smoked salmon. Their recipes have been included in a couple of inn cookbooks.

Guests rarely venture forth from their quarters into the huge living room with game tables that go begging most of the time in the main house, where the family occupies the first and third floors. They may walk around the five acres of wooded grounds, relax on Adirondack chairs or play croquet or badminton.

(914) 876-3500. Fax (914) 876-6179. Two rooms and five suites with private baths. Doubles, $125 and $250 weekends. Suites, $295 to $350 weekends, $195 to $250 midweek. Carriage House reserved for family Sunday-Thursday. By reservation only. Two-night minimum on weekends. Children over 17. No smoking.

Belvedere Mansion, Box 785, Rhinebeck 12572.

There are nine mansions in the mid-Hudson Valley that you can visit but only one in which you can stay, say Nikola and Patricia Rebraca, who claim the distinction. Longtime New York City restaurateurs, they took over the hilltop mansion overlooking the Hudson in 1993 and launched an ongoing restoration to turn it into a restaurant and country inn.

Erected in 1900 after fire destroyed the original home built in 1760, the pillared, Greek Revival mansion is named for its beautiful view. The interior is a fantasy reflecting the Gilded Age, lavishly decorated with 18th-century French antiques, trompe l'oeil and a cloud-painted ceiling. Sumptuous silk and damask fabrics adorn the walls and vintage fixtures light the rooms.

Upstairs are five guest rooms of mansion proportions. The rear Roosevelt Room with an English Tudor canopy bed is masculine in chocolate brown with gold trim. "There are a lot of pictures to get crooked around here," Patricia noted as she

Veranda House occupies 1845 Federal residence that was once a church parsonage.

straightened a couple while showing us around. All rooms have private baths with abundant marble, ceiling fans and matching French Empire beds (most queensize) and mirrored armoires. The Astor and Lafayette in front offer fireplaces and river views. Art deco lighting fixtures and a gilded clawfoot slipper tub grace the Vanderbilt Room. Two twin beds are joined as a king in the Livingston Room, where a writing desk occupies a private nook beside an oval window and the walls of the fanciful bathroom are painted blue to look like the sea.

Behind and to the side of the mansion is a motel-like lineup of accommodations with separate entrances in the former carriage house. Euphemistically called cottages, they're decorated differently with as much pizzazz as their simplicity and space would allow (a handpainted bureau here, a wicker chair there). The most popular is the River Queen, devoted to the riverboat era and boasting a handmade canopy kingsize bridal bed. Six have king beds. Four "cozies" each have a double bed tucked away in an alcove, a bathroom and not much more. They're perfectly serviceable, but not exactly the kind of place where you'd want to hang out and, at any rate, most have no places to sit.

Breakfast in the dining room generally includes a choice of omelets with Coach Farm goat cheese and oven-dried tomatoes, walnut-crusted french toast or Hudson Valley pear pancakes.

The ten-acre property includes a rear pool with new cabanas, a tennis court and a pond. "We have a long way to go," Patricia acknowledged after four years of restoration. But they're off to a promising start.

(914) 889-8000. Fax (914) 889-8811. Five rooms and ten cottages with private baths. Doubles, $175 to $195. Cottages, $85 and $125 to $145 weekends, $65 and $95 to $125 midweek. Two-night minimum on weekends. Children welcome.

Veranda House, 82 Montgomery St., Rhinebeck 12572.
Once an Episcopal church parsonage, this attractive 1845 Federal house listed in the National Register took on a new role in 1993. Ward and Linda Stanley of Philadelphia bought the residence at the north end of the village's historic district to run as a B&B.

They offer four air-conditioned guest rooms with telephones and private baths. One contains an original marble sink like one at the nearby Clermont mansion, a guest told Ward. Three have a variety of queensize beds, from four-poster Shaker with lacy canopy to antique brass. A side room that gets both morning and afternoon sun has old-fashioned wood twin beds convertible to king. Two bedrooms, one downstairs in what had been a dining room and the other above, are architecturally notable for their bay windows attached to a five-sided bay.

The Stanleys have outfitted the common areas with rather modern furniture from their Philadelphia home. The fireplaced living room opens onto a breakfast room as well as a TV room/library with books specializing in art and architecture. The original parquet floors and pretty glassware are on display throughout. Ward, who recently retired from a university job teaching architectural history, hosts lively wine and cheese hours for weekend guests on the wicker-filled front veranda or on a new terrace off the dining room.

Linda serves a full breakfast, starting with juice, a fruit plate and a homemade pastry, perhaps fresh scallion and gruyère muffins or sour-cream coffee cake. Orange-yogurt pancakes, zucchini and feta cheese crêpes or eggs Veranda (her own version of eggs benedict with portobello mushrooms) could be the main course. Apple or pecan strudel might follow. Ward's special coffee from New Harmony Coffee Co. of Philadelphia is freshly ground each morning.

Breakfasting on the terrace, a couple from South Africa said they felt right at home. The response was prompted by the mythical rhinoceros sculpted by the Stanleys' daughter and lurking under the trees in the side yard.

(914) 876-4133. Four rooms with private baths. Doubles, $95 to $120 weekends, $75 to $100 midweek. No smoking. No credit cards.

Whistle Wood Farm, 11 Pells Road, Rhinebeck 12572.

Tucked away in the wooded section of a rural horse farm is a rambling ranch house full of character, not the least of which reflects the owner. Maggie Myer opened her house as a B&B in 1983, offering rooms with shared baths and cupcakes for breakfast. She's come a long way. Her four rooms and two cottages now have private baths, queensize four-poster beds and ceiling fans. And her hearty buffet breakfasts, pictured in magazines, even entail desserts.

"How about a piece of apple pie or lemon-poppyseed cake?" Maggie asked as we arrived at mid-morning, pointing to treats left on the buffet table from the breakfast spread just finished. Her guests had demolished her mixed fruit platter and french toast with bacon before leaving for the day's sessions at the Omega Institute nearby.

The homey, much-lived-in farmhouse holds a front sun room, a barnwood living room with a big stone fireplace and a dining area with a striking horse mural. The country pine table here seems to play second fiddle as a breakfast venue to the front sun room and the front or rear decks. Baskets, pans and lanterns hang from beams in the country kitchen that's the heart of the house.

Three guest rooms in one wing range from the small Tumbleweed Room with a pastel quilt, ruffled curtains and a hall bath to the rear Juniper Room with quilts on the walls, an extra day bed and its own deck onto a berry patch. The other end of the house harbors the spacious Wyoming Room named for Maggie's western accessories, including an antique quilt, Indian blankets and a stained-glass rocking horse. A canoe rests on the rafters above the sturdy pine bed, and a twin bed is around the corner in an alcove. Sliding glass double doors open to the front and side gardens complete with fountain.

With the passing of her mother, Maggie has moved into the main house. She turned over her Corral Cottage, sandwiched between two stables, to guests. They have a front bedroom with a Shaker-style poster bed, a living room/dining/kitchen area with a queen sofabed and a wood stove, and a rear terrace with a hot tub looking onto the horse pastures. She also puts up guests a few miles away in a two-bedroom Lake Cliff Cottage at Beaver Point on a small lake, where turtles, beavers and a mute swan named Harold hang out.

Here, guests share the property with up to twenty horses, three dogs and a donkey. "One guest called me Martha Stewart with spurs," volunteered Maggie. She likens herself to Johnny Appleseed: "I'm always planting flowers everywhere."

(914) 876-6838. Fax (914) 876-5513. Four rooms and two cottages with private baths. Doubles, $135 to $180 weekends, $95 to $135 midweek. Corral Cottage, $200 weekends, $135 midweek. Lake Cliff Cottage, $575 for minimum two-night stay. Two-night minimum on weekends. No smoking.

The School House Bed & Breakfast, 112 River Road, Rhinebeck 12572.

Built in 1887, this functioned as a two-room school until 1951. Later restored and expanded into two apartments, the structure caught the eye of grande dame Elizabeth Blow, who used the original school room with high ceiling and big windows for her art studio. Maintaining the place proved costly. So in 1996, shortly before her 80th birthday, she started taking in overnight guests.

"This is a lot of work," said Elizabeth, a Boston Yankee who does it all herself and requires a two-night minimum stay to make things worthwhile. "It's also fun. I've found that people who frequent B&Bs couldn't be nicer."

Talkative Elizabeth loves to point out features of her quirky property, from the original tin ceiling over the entry to the old school outhouse in the barn, where she now raises chickens. "There's nothing like fresh eggs for breakfast," she volunteers.

An addition in the front houses a common room soaring 25 feet high. Alongside is a guest bedroom with a beamed ceiling and a duvet-covered canopy double bed in the corner almost up against the road. A full bathroom is adjacent.

The owner now climbs the spiral staircase to occupy one of the two small upstairs front bedrooms that had shared a downstairs bath in the laundry room. That bath is now private for guests in a large air-conditioned bedroom above the art studio. Here, beneath a skylit vaulted ceiling, are a queen bed, futon, TV and a writing desk.

Elizabeth, who trained at the Boston Art School and lived in Paris, paints watercolors and designs interiors in her professional life. Her new sideline includes cleaning rooms and preparing breakfast for guests in a small kitchen that formerly served as the school library.

"I experiment because I have guinea pigs," says she. For two well-traveled couples who departed just before our visit she had served banana-pecan pancakes one day and a complicated polenta dish topped with poached eggs, smoked salmon and chives the next. "They raved about the pancakes," she recalled, "but didn't say much about the polenta dish. I wonder whether they liked it." We like to think they did.

(914) 876-3194. Two rooms with private baths. Doubles, $100. Two-night minimum stay. Children welcome. No credit cards.

The Mulberry Street Guest House, 25 Mulberry St., Rhinebeck.
Local antiques dealer Kristine Stein and her husband Ray share their lovely, antiques-filled home with overnight guests.

The 1880 Victorian house, located in the historic district, is furnished to the period. Upstairs are two air-conditioned guest rooms with private baths. The Bay Room features a rice-carved queen canopy poster bed and a loveseat in the handsome side bay window. A carved mirrored armoire is a prized possession here. Two twin beds can be joined as a kingsize in the Charleston Room, which has two chairs upholstered in floral and Victorian floral decor throughout.

A full breakfast is served in the large, formal dining room with a side bay window and French toile wallpaper. Fruit and muffins precede a hot main course.

Guests relax in the elegant, formal parlor or a small, more casual library with a TV and an upright piano.

(914) 876-5478. Two rooms with private baths. Doubles, $115 weekends, $95 midweek. Two-night minimum in season No smoking. No credit cards.

Dining Spots

Le Petit Bistro, 8 East Market St., Rhinebeck.
Chef-owner Jean-Paul Croizer has retired, but this long-running establishment didn't miss a beat. Two of his waiters bought the place in 1997. Head waiter Brendan Callan moved into the kitchen and partner Dan Bleen manages the front. Brendan has quietly updated the fare, although he insists the menu remains the same. And Yvonne Crozier stayed on, so regulars still get a hug and a kiss upon arrival.

Pine walls and floors give the 40-seat dining room and half-circle bar at the side a country-French look. Except for globe lamps inside wooden frames, the decor is simple and the atmosphere convivial and intimate.

The French menu starts with classics like onion soup, pâté maison, smoked trout and escargots. Dover sole meunière is a house specialty. Sea scallops with crushed black peppercorns and cream sauce, duck with orange sauce, veal piccata, frog's legs, rack of lamb provençal and steak au poivre are among the choices. Grilled tuna niçoise, poulet marengo and rainbow trout with crabmeat and grenobloise sauce were specials at our latest visit.

Desserts include crème caramel, mocha mousse, raspberry frappe and peach melba.

(914) 876-7400. Entrées, $16.75 to $21.95. Dinner, Thursday-Monday 5 to 10, Sunday 4 to 9.

Belvedere Mansion, 10 Old Route 9, Rhinebeck.
New York restaurateurs Nikola and Patricia Rebraca, who have run Panarella's restaurant on Manhattan's West Side since 1979, now operate this fancy new restaurant. Patricia oversees the cooking here as executive chef, while her husband commutes to Manhattan.

The hilltop mansion seats 60 diners in three high Victorian dining rooms of the chandelier, fireplace and gilt-framed painting variety. Forty-five more can be accommodated at tables beneath green umbrellas on a spacious side deck in season. There's also a romantic table for two or four in a little tea room at the head of the stairway landing.

It's an elegant, formal setting for contemporary regional food. The dinner menu is straightforward and quite affordable. Look for starters like minted sugar snap

Hilltop Belvedere Mansion is named for its beautiful view of Hudson River.

pea soup with avocado salsa, a timbale of diver scallops and peeky toe crab, and marinated local quail with tagliatelle and lobster nage. Goat cheese from nearby Coach Farm enhances the organic arugula salad with toasted walnuts.

Main courses could be sake-marinated sea bass with a tat soi spinach and shiitake sauté, breast of muscovy duck with a fig and mango salad, and rack of lamb with lavender perfumed jus. Homemade desserts include a rhubarb and strawberry tart with chantilly cream, crème caramel with almond lace and a trio of sorbets.

(914) 889-8000. Entrées, $18 to $24. Dinner, Thursday-Sunday 5:30 to 9:30.

The Beekman 1776 Tavern, Route 9, Rhinebeck.

The restaurant at the Beekman Arms reopened to unprecedented fanfare after it was leased in 1991 to celebrity chef Larry Forgione, owner of An American Place in Manhattan. Forgione, who since has opened a third restaurant in Miami Beach and seldom is in the kitchen here, regularly updates a menu that incorporates American classics and regional ingredients. A chef from Argentina, Tony Nogales, executes his commands.

The classic Tap Room and Colonial dining rooms glow with the patina of age. Quite in contrast is the large, plant-filled solarium dining room overlooking the main street.

The dinner menu ranges widely, from a burger on a sesame bun to Colorado leg of lamb with an oven-dried tomato compote. Cedar-planked Atlantic salmon, seared mahi-mahi with couscous, applewood-grilled pizza and roasted free-range duck vie with such basics as country-style meatloaf (updated with roasted ketchup gravy) and free-range turkey pot pie.

Starters could be jumbo gulf shrimp louie, a deviled crab cake spring roll or fried Carolina rock shrimp with spicy rémoulade. Desserts include old-fashioned double-chocolate pudding, fruit crisp, homemade ice cream and sorbet of the day.

Obviously, the menu implies excitement, many of the accompaniments are interesting and unusual, and the prices are far lower than they would be in Manhattan. But the food critics' raves seem to fall on deaf ears locally.

(914) 871-1766. Entrées, $15.95 to $23.95. Lunch daily, 11:30 to 3. Dinner, 5:30 to 9 or 9:30. Sunday, brunch 10 to 2, dinner 3:30 to 9.

Calico Restaurant & Patisserie, 9 Mill St. (Route 9), Rhinebeck.

A perfect five-star rating from the Poughkeepsie restaurant reviewer followed the opening of this intimate little charmer in a twenty-seat storefront across from the Beekman Arms. The stars were for the food offered by Culinary Institute of America grad Tony Balassone and the baked goods of his wife Leslie.

The patisserie in front opens at 7 a.m. for croissants and brioche from a display case stocked with delectable treats. Come lunch time, the kitchen offers a handful of interesting choices, perhaps seafood chili with cornbread, house-smoked salmon fillet served on a mixture of greens and roasted porcini mushrooms, pizza of the day and sliced flank steak on a toasted baguette. The gratinéed vidalia onion soup laced with Anchor Steam ale makes a good starter. So does the roasted garlic soup with crème fraîche and herbed brioche croutons.

At night, Tony prepares such entrées as bouillabaisse, sesame-crusted salmon fillet with baby bok choy, breast of duck with cranberry-champagne cream sauce and rack of lamb with ratatouille.

Artifacts and calico items adorn a shelf above the pale blue wainscoting of this pure and simple place beloved by the locals. It has a full liquor license.

(914) 876-2749. Entrées, $15.95 to $19.95. Lunch, Wednesday-Sunday 11 to 3:30. Dinner, Wednesday-Sunday 5:30 to 9:30 or 10:30.

Cripple Creek Café, 30 Garden St., Rhinebeck.

Three partners with ties to a farm of the same name in Colorado opened this trendy little café to good reviews in 1996. The L-shaped room is sophisticated with pale gray walls and carpeting, white china, black tablecloths and accents of black faux marble. A pleasant, umbrellaed outdoor patio is pressed into service in summer.

A Culinary Institute-trained chef oversees the contemporary fare. The ten main dishes on a recent dinner menu included fettuccine with smoked salmon, English peas and dill cream sauce; roasted free-range chicken with wild mushrooms and orzo, and pan-seared lamb chops with red wine reduction. Three vegetarian choices were offered.

Expect appetizers like lobster and herbed mascarpone ravioli, truffle-scented escargots in puff pastry and oriental roasted pork wontons with a spicy peanut dipping sauce. Dessert could be a creamy chocolate-hazelnut torte, fruit cobbler or a cookie sampler.

Much the same menu is available for lunch, when the day's specials could be shrimp miso soup, fried soft-shell crab sandwich and lobster ravioli.

(914) 876-4355. Entrées, $15.95 to $21.95. Lunch, 11:30 to 3; tapas 3 to 5. Dinner 5 to 9 or 10. Closed Monday and Tuesday.

Osaka, 18 Garden St., Rhinebeck.

This hole-in-the-wall establishment down a side street is mostly sushi bar, and an ever-so-authentic one at that. It's the first Japanese restaurant we've encountered to have more seats at the sushi bar than at the tables. A warm washcloth was presented as we sat down. Mellow Japanese music played as we sampled some great sashimi ($8.95 for lunch), a yellowtail and scallion roll, exceptionally mellow ginger, and the bento lunch box with beef maki, dumplings and rice.

The usual suspects, from shrimp tempura to beef teriyaki, are offered on the dinner menu. But the sushi and sashimi assortments reign supreme.

(914) 876-7338. Entrées, $10.95 to $17.95. Lunch, Monday-Friday 11:30 to 2:30. Dinner nightly.

Diversions

The area's history and rural environment are the main drawing cards for visitors.

Rhinebeck Walking Tour. Copies of a walking tour developed in 1980, just after Rhinebeck was listed on the National Register as "among the most cohesive and best preserved historic environments," is still distributed by the Rhinebeck Historical Society at the Chamber of Commerce visitor center. The tour points out prime examples among the more than 400 Colonial and Victorian structures listed on the National Register, especially along residential Montgomery, Livingston, Chestnut and Mulberry streets. "In walking through Rhinebeck," it advises, "one must be aware of the varying architectural details. These are found not only at eye level, on first floors, but on upper stories as well. Be sure to notice peripheral pleasures, such as slate sidewalks, hitching posts, carriage stepping stones, wellhouses, fences, outbuildings and large shade trees."

Rhinebeck claims half of an area known as the Sixteen Mile Historic District, composed of 30 contiguous riverfront estates associated with the landed gentry of the 18th, 19th and early 20th centuries.

Wilderstein Preservation, Morton Road, Rhinebeck.

This towering, 35-room Queen Anne Victorian on a 40-acre riverfront site was owned and occupied until 1991 by the Suckley family, descendants of the early Livingston and Beekman families. Its opulent interiors were decorated by J.B. Tiffany and its grounds landscaped by Calvert Vaux, Frederick Law Olmsted's partner in the design of New York's Central Park. The estate's intricate network of paths, rustic gazebos and sheltered garden seats offer walkers scenic adventures and contemplation. Interior visitors are intrigued by the legacies of its last occupant, Margaret Lynch Suckley, a distant cousin of Franklin Delano Roosevelt. She worked with the president as archivist at the Presidential Library in nearby Hyde Park and often kept him company in Washington and on train trips. FDR called her Daisy and she gave him his famous little dog, Fala. After her death in her 100th year in 1991 at Wilderstein, friends cleaning her cluttered bedroom found a battered suitcase beneath the bed. Inside were Daisy's diaries and the letters the pair exchanged. The resulting book, *Closest Companion,* details their intimate friendship.

(914) 876-4818. Open Thursday-Sunday noon to 4, May-October. Adults, $5.

Mills Mansion, Old Post Road, Staatsburg.

A few miles downriver from Wilderstein, this Beaux Arts mansion of 65 rooms was the country estate of Ruth Livingston Mills and her husband, financier Ogden Mills. Built in 1832 and expanded in 1895 by architect Stanford White, it contains gilded ceilings, marble fireplaces, ornate furniture and art objects from around the world. The grounds sweep down to the river, offering some of the best views along the Hudson. A paved path leads to an old boathouse.

(914) 889-8851. Open Wednesday-Saturday 10 to 5, Sunday noon to 5, May to Labor Day, Wednesday-Sunday noon to 5 through October. Adults, $5.

Montgomery Place, Annandale-on-Hudson.

This 23-room Federal mansion dating to 1805 is furnished with 200 years of Livingston family possessions. The 434-acre riverfront property contains working pear and peach orchards, towering black locust trees, ornamental rose and herb gardens. Woodland carriage and walking trails wind through the property and down to the river.

(914) 758-5461. Open daily except Tuesday, 10 to 5, April-October, also Saturday-Sunday 10 to 5 in November and December. Guided house tour, $6; self-guided tour of grounds, $3.

Other Mansions. The foregoing landmarks are the closest to Rhinebeck, but more are nearby. Just to the north lie **Clermont,** oldest of all the Hudson River estates and occupied by seven generations of Livingstons from 1730 to 1962, and **Olana,** the Persian-style hilltop home designed by and for Frederic Edwin Church, one of the foremost Hudson River School artists. To the south are the opulent **Vanderbilt Mansion, the Home of Franklin D. Roosevelt National Historic Site** and the companion **Val-Kill,** Eleanor Roosevelt's retreat.

Rural Pleasures. Motorists beholden to busy north-south Route 9 miss the discoveries that await on either side. To the west, awesome views accompany the road toward sleepy Rhinecliff, a two-bit riverfront hamlet from days gone by with an Amtrak station, quaint houses and not much else. A viaduct leads across the tracks down to a boat ramp and dock at the Rhinebeck Town Landing. To the east, civilization rapidly disappears into the relative wilds, woods and vineyards of the eastern Hudson Valley. Bicycle touring is one of the best ways to see and savor the landscape.

Ferncliff Forest Preserve, River Road and Mount Rutsen Road, Rhinebeck, (914) 8765-3196. This 192-acre sanctuary was part of a vast estate owned by John Jacob Astor. Extensive trails lead to a pond, a lookout tower and foundation stones from the original 59 farms that made up Astor's 2,800 acres. Picnic tables make it a good stop for hikers and bicyclists.

The Old Rhinebeck Aerodrome & Museum, 44 Stone Church Road, Rhinebeck.

Endearingly indigenous to old-fashioned Rhinebeck is this collection of hangars, bleachers, booths, signs and antique "aeroplanes" that looks on busy days like an old county fair, when pilots in biplanes barnstormed the countryside. When our children were young, we joined the multitudes for one of the weekend air shows and found it a lot of laughs. The oldtime melodrama revs up the skies, as World War 1-vintage planes perform daredevil stunts in a flying circus that culminates in a climactic dogfight. Fifteen-minute barnstorming flights in a 1929 open-cockpit biplane are available before and after the shows for $30 a person. The Aerodrome's new museum building and hangars are full of old airplanes, engines, vintage cars, motorcycles and memorabilia.

(914) 758-8610. Open daily 10 to 5, mid-May through October; adults, $5. Air shows weekends at 2:30, mid-June to mid-October; adults, $10.

Entertainment. In its 200-seat tent out Route 308 east of town, **The Center for Performing Arts at Rhinebeck** stages upwards of 50 performances, from musicals to magic shows, in July and August. A permanent year-round structure was in the works. From fall through spring, the **Rhinebeck Chamber Music Society** presents Saturday night concerts monthly at the Church of the Messiah. **Upstate Films,** hailed the ultimate in way-off-Broadway for moviegoers, shows alternative and international films not often seen in this country in one-going-on-two screening rooms at 26 Montgomery St. It's in the rear of the Starr Building, from which **Starr Cantina** dispenses Mexican fare and entertainment out front. Across the street, **La Parmigiana** offers pizzas and Italian food inside a renovated church.

The ever-busy **Dutchess County Fairgrounds** entertains half a million visitors at its annual agricultural fair in late August. It also hosts weekend crafts, antiques and folk art shows and special events.

Shopping. The **Antiques Market & Art Gallery** behind the Beekman Arms displays the wares of 30 dealers on two floors. An old wooden sign inside the front door at our visit advertised the Beekman Arms: "modest rates, dinner $1." Forty more dealers show at the **Rhinebeck Antique Center,** 7 West Market St., and serious antiquers will find plenty of other haunts.

Shopping is best along East Market Street. The **Rhinebeck Department Store** "continues the tradition" of the former Hudson Valley Department Store. You'll find a Rhinebeck T-shirt among its wares, which seem to be mostly clothing. **Identities** offers women's apparel and sportswear. Offbeat designer apparel is shown at **Haldora** and **The Elegant Villager.** Side-by-side stores are **Summer Moon** ("a natural place for home and body") and **Winter Sun** with handworks and clothing from around the world. The **Omega Bookstore** sells texts of particular interest to those who attend the workshops in personal growth and development at the lakeside campus of the Omega Institute for Holistic Studies, 260 Lake Drive. **Earth's Rewards** offers New Age gifts, crystals, incense and a group meditation room.

Around the corner on Mill Street, beyond the corner **United Smoke Shop,** are the **Heritage Art Gallery** and **Habitu** for home/life/gifts. "There's a lot to see," the shopkeeper advised, as we eyed everything from cards to picture frames to handpainted bird cages. Hidden down Garden Street are **The Hamlet of Fine Craft and Art,** featuring Hudson Valley works; **Galeriá Borikén,** showing Puerto Rican and Latin arts and crafts; **Kiddlydivy,** a children's boutique specializing in natural fibers, and **Rhinebeck Health Foods.**

Extra-Special

The Rhinebeck Post Office, 14 Mill St., Rhinebeck.

Who'd expect a post office to be a special place? Adjacent to the oldest inn in America, this was erected in 1939 as a replica of the first home in Rhinebeck, built in the late 17th century by Dutchman Henrick Kip. Open the old wood door of the stone building and you're in a most un-post-office-like fantasy land of paneled walls and brass chandeliers. Antique airplanes are suspended from the beamed ceiling, lintel stone is displayed in a glass cabinet, and historic photos and documents are framed on the walls. All around the perimeter of the upper walls are what everyone locally calls "the murals." They were painted by artist Olin Dows and depict – somewhat obscurely for the uninitiated – the story of the people, landmarks and development of Rhinebeck. The thirteen panels show such sights as the Kip brothers buying Rhinebeck from the Indians and John Jacob Astor's first car being towed uphill by a team of farm animals. The panel of "contemporary Rhinebeck" (1939) includes a group listening to radio news. The post office was dedicated by none other than Rhinebeck neighbor Franklin D. Roosevelt in the company of the Crown Prince of Denmark, Cabinet Secretary Henry Morgenthau Jr. and Postmaster General James A. Farley. The foreword to the Rhinebeck Historical Society's little picture book about the murals called it "without doubt the most thoroughly dedicated small-town post office in the western hemisphere."

(914) 876-4073. Open Monday-Friday 8 to 5, Saturday 8 to 3.

Georgian Revival brick buildings present attractive vista in Saratoga Spa State Park.

Saratoga Springs, N.Y.

The City in the Country

Ever since George Washington came here following the decisive battle of the Revolutionary War nearby and tried – unsuccessfully – to buy one of the Saratoga springs, the high and the mighty have been drawn to Saratoga.

They come for the restorative powers of its mineral-water springs, the only carbonated waters east of the Rockies. They come to watch the horses at America's oldest and most scenic thoroughbred race track. They come for the amenities of the meticulous Saratoga Spa State Park, a complex of columned brick Greek Revival buildings and archways harboring a resort hotel, a theater, swimming-pool pavilions and baths, all set among lawns and towering pines sheltering a golf course, a skating pond and more. They come for the concerts at the Saratoga Performing Arts Center, summer home of the New York City Ballet, the Philadelphia Orchestra and many a visiting pop-rock performer. They come to eat and drink, to bet and be merry, to see and be seen.

Saratoga, recently promoted as "the city in the country," is many things to many people. It's too many to be totally encompassed unless you come – as the Vanderbilts and Whitneys, the Paynes and the Phippses do – for the season. The season here is August, the traditional thoroughbred racing period (lately extended to five weeks and five days and opening in late July). With Saratoga's increasing emphasis on the arts, however, a secondary season is all summer long.

Many a superlative applies to Saratoga. A Fortune magazine cover article in 1935 said the convergence of society and big money in Saratoga each August creates "America's dizziest season in America's daftest town." From the Gay Nineties on, more than 20,000 visitors could be housed in one of the world's great concentrations of grand hotels (all but two long since torn down). The rich and famous built "cottages" of 30 to 40 rooms along North Broadway and Union Avenue.

Some of those Victorian mansions are still occupied by the moneyed regulars who come each summer. Others are rented out by Saratogans who flee the August frenzy. Still others have been turned into lodging establishments.

Lately, Saratoga "has become a haven for B&Bs," according to Kate Benton, a native who returned with her husband to open her own. Indeed, B&Bs are opening "faster than we can keep track of them," adds Linda Toohey, executive vice president of the Saratoga County Chamber of Commerce. The Chamber has adopted guidelines that new B&Bs must have innkeepers living on the premises, must serve breakfast and must operate at least six months a year.

Saratoga bills itself as "the August place to be." But that's Saratoga at its most frenetic and most expensive. Go to Saratoga in August if you're into the racing scene. If not, go at less crowded, less pricey times to better savor the splendors of this urbane small city in the country.

Inn Spots

Accommodations are at a premium during the racing season, now the last week of July and all of August, and for major Skidmore College weekends, when prices may double or triple. Almost as quickly as the crowds descend, however, they leave. Accommodations tend to go begging from after foliage season until June.

The Mansion, 801 Route 29, Box 77, Rock City Falls 12863.

When Gary Collins televised ABC's Home show live from The Mansion a few years back, innkeepers Tom Clark and Alan Churchill put on an outdoor buffet breakfast for the TV entourage of 40 under the lights at 4 o'clock in the morning. "We had a full house, too," Alan said. The overnight guests got the usual breakfast spread a little later that day, after the excitement was over.

The incident tells two things about this remarkable establishment seven miles west of town. One is that of all the possible Saratoga settings, this was the one chosen for a national telecast from Saratoga. The other is that breakfast here is quite an event, TV crews or not.

The setting is the 23-room Venetian villa built in 1866 as a summer home by

self-made industrialist George West, known as "The Paper Bag King" for his invention of the folded paper bag. It was acquired in 1986 by Tom, a former college president, who had restored four other houses in Saratoga. He and Alan converted it into a fine Victorian B&B with four guest rooms and a suite, all with private baths.

The mansion is full of striking details, like six marble fireplaces

Double parlor at The Mansion.   **Statue of St. Francis in Mansion library.**

with massive carved mantelpieces soaring to the fourteen-foot-high ceilings, brass and copper chandeliers with etched Waterford globes, etched-glass doors, parquet floors of three woods, and Currier and Ives prints. The monogram of George West is inscribed near the top of the front parlor's fireplace mantel, a hefty combination of black marble, walnut, ebony, rosewood and beech, all inlaid with gold. Two matching etched-glass doors stand side by side at the end of the entry foyer. Covered with dirt and grime in the basement, "they were one of those magical finds you come across when you're doing restoration," Tom says. Another was the array of original chestnut shutters stashed in the attic. Now in place inside all windows, they obviate the need for draperies, keep interior temperatures stable and keep out unwanted early morning light.

A double parlor goes off a central hall striking for an unsigned Tiffany chandelier. One parlor is furnished in Empire furniture and the other in Eastlake. Tom built the handsome floor-to-ceiling shelves in the front parlor and in the suite to hide utility pipes. Three chairs in the front parlor came from Saratoga's old Grand Union Hotel and have been refurbished with the original tapestry fabrics. Ditto for the hotel's couch. It's now ensconced in the sitting room of the main-floor suite, which has parquet floors, marble fireplaces and a pink marble sink in the full bath. The bed here is a double four-poster; the partners deemed a queensize bed too overwhelming for a room we thought large enough for a kingsize.

Queensize beds are attributes of the four upstairs guest rooms, where small private bathrooms (showers only) were fashioned from dressing areas. Mahogany four-poster beds, mirrored armoires, wing chairs and puffy comforters are among the furnishings. Each room contains a dish of hard candies plus fresh flowers and plants that attest both to Alan's green thumb and his knack for arranging the results in his collection of 200 vases. The second floor also harbors a small, plant-filled area, where guests may sit on bentwood rockers and admire the river across the road.

Classical music from Alan's extensive collection of tapes plays in the front library, a fascinating room with a beautiful life-size carved wood statue of St. Francis in a window area and so full of coffee-table books and magazines that one of us could hardly be pried away for breakfast.

A bowl of exotic fruits centered by an alstroemeria blossom was followed by fresh orange or grapefruit juice. Next came a platter of half a dozen breads – lemon, zucchini, banana-bran, applesauce, pumpkin and six-grain toast. Cooked to order was an entrée of the guest's choice. We enjoyed a masterful eggs benedict and a vegetable omelet with a slice of ham. Chocolate-almond coffee was poured throughout at five rose-linened tables graced with fresh roses and tulips (this in January). A flame flickered from an Aladdin's lamp in front of the mirror on the fireplace mantel.

All is not inside. The cupola is open for a rooftop drink, if you'd like. There's a restored side porch, and the four acres of landscaped grounds include a swimming pool. The roaring waterfall that gives Rock City Falls its name is within earshot across the street.

(518) 885-1607. Four rooms and one suite with private baths. Doubles, $95, $185 in racing season. Suite, $120, $210 in racing season. No children. No smoking. No credit cards.

Batcheller Mansion Inn, 20 Circular St., Saratoga Springs 12866.

The outside of this drop-dead B&B is a sight to behold, as befits what historians variously call Saratoga's most spectacular, conspicuous and architecturally fanciful residential landmark. Park on the side lawn where your special grass-covered parking space is posted with a sign bearing your name. Open the arched mahogany doors and prepare to be overwhelmed. The living room with its gilt-edged mirrors and enormous crystal chandelier is extravagant. The mahogany-paneled library with its plump red velvet sofas beside the fireplace and towering ficus trees by the tall windows in the bay is dramatic. The impressive dining room holds a long table set for twelve and four side tables for two. Just when you think you've seen everything, you enter a kitchen to end all kitchens. It's a breathtaking space, long and narrow and 26 feet high – contemporary and stark white except for three soaring, twenty-foot-tall arched windows that bring the outside in. Oh to have a kitchen like that, except surely the cook must feel on stage as passersby along Whitney Place stop to gawk. After all this, the nine guest bedrooms may be a bit of a letdown, even though they are decorated to the utmost and one is so large it holds a billiards table in the middle.

The house was built in 1873 in what has variously been called flamboyant French Renaissance and High Victorian Gothic styles with Moorish minarets and turrets. Original owner George S. Batcheller was a lawyer, judge and ambassador, who eventually spent most of his life abroad but retained the 28-room castle as his pied-à-terre. It had been condemned and abandoned as a rooming house when a bachelor attorney bought it for $25,000 in 1972. He started a restoration that culminated in 1994 in two whirlwind months of conversion from a sometime residence into one of the grandest B&Bs of all.

The current owner, local developer Bruce J. Levinsky, had failed in efforts to sell the mansion as a residence and ultimately decided a B&B would be more feasible.

The nine bedrooms on the second and third floors come with private baths, queen or kingsize beds, fancy wallpapers and coordinated fabrics, oriental rugs atop thick carpeting, writing desks, television sets, telephones, mini-refrigerators, monogrammed bathrobes, thick towels and Haversham & Holt toiletries.

Saratoga's most conspicuous residential landmark is now The Batcheller Mansion Inn.

They vary widely in size from two small front rooms with hall baths to the third-floor Diamond Jim Brady Room, outfitted with a billiards table, kingsize iron canopy bed, a sitting area and a huge bathroom with an oversize jacuzzi, large stall shower and mirrored wall (two other rooms have smaller jacuzzis). Some rooms, with their TV sets and phones prominent atop their large working desks, would be at home in a business hotel. The Lillian Russell Room has two queensize beds and only a single settee for seating, while the Katrina Trask Room comes with a circular porch – reached by ducking through a window. The Rip Van Dam Room with its horsey theme and maple furniture is the only non-Victorian room.

An elaborate continental breakfast is served during the week, with a full breakfast on weekends. Resident innkeeper Sue McCabe offers a choice of french toast or eggs any style to accompany the continental offerings of fresh fruit and pastries on the side table.

(518) 584-7012 or (800) 616-7012. Fax (518) 581-7746. Nine rooms with private baths. May-October: doubles, $150 to $250 weekends, $125 to $210 midweek. Racing: $240 to $380 weekends, $210 to $380 midweek. November-April: $120 to $200 weekends, $100 to $180 midweek. Two-night minimum weekends; four-night minimum racing weekends. Children over 14. No smoking.

The Westchester House, 102 Lincoln Ave., Box 944, Saratoga Springs 12866.
One of Saratoga's oldest guest houses, this Queen Anne Victorian structure has been accommodating guests for more than 100 years. But it has been greatly enhanced since its purchase by Bob and Stephanie Melvin of Washington, D.C. They had traveled extensively and stayed at B&Bs before they opened their own,

and Stephanie said they approached the endeavor differently than others in town. "Comfort was paramount to us," she advised. "So while we have very fine things, we encourage people to feel at home. We want the rooms to be restful and our guests to feel special." The hallmarks here are hospitality, plus attention to detail, amidst a residential garden setting.

Hospitality comes easily to Stephanie, an opera singer who performs occasionally in Saratoga. She has arranged antiques, "old" art and contemporary artworks to co-exist in a welcoming environment. Brass and copper chandeliers, oriental paper-cuttings on the walls, high ceilings and gleaming wood floors topped with oriental rugs dignify the common rooms. Rich woodwork, oak newel posts on the staircase banister, blue tiles, two elaborate fireplaces and distinctive wainscoting are all original.

All seven upstairs guest rooms have handsome private tiled baths and all but one have king or queensize beds, except for one with two three-quarter beds. We were comfortable in the Jefferson Room, where the new kingsize iron bed is dressed in fine linens. Air-conditioning, ceiling fans, fresh flowers and chocolates embossed with the Westchester House logo are among amenities in all the rooms.

Guests relax in six distinct sitting areas amid terraces and Victorian gardens on the extra-large side lawn bordered by a thick hedge of spirea – a real in-town oasis in summer. Or they gather on the wraparound porch overlooking the Melvins' colorful, old-fashioned perennial borders for tea and cookies or wine and cheese. They relax at other times in either of the two main-floor parlors, where decanters of sherry are at the ready.

A continental breakfast is served stylishly and with lively conversation amid pink linens, china, crystal mugs and stemmed glasses in the dining room or on the porch. Juice, fresh fruits, fresh breads and muffins and sometimes cheese are the fare. After breakfast, Bob snaps photos of guests, which he and Stephanie forward with a thank-you note to remind them of their stay. Happy customers, they know, are repeat customers.

(518) 587-7613 or (800) 581-7613. www.westchester-bb.saratoga.ny.us. Seven rooms with private baths. Doubles, $95 to $150. Racing season: $195 to $250. Off-season: $85 to $115. Closed December and January. Two-night minimum weekends. Children over 10. No smoking.

Saratoga Bed and Breakfast, 434 Church St., Saratoga Springs 12866.

Some of Saratoga's most luxurious B&B accommodations are offered by Noel and Kathleen Smith in their recently opened 1850 Brick House. The four sumptuous suites there are a far cry from the simpler 1860 farmhouse in which they got their start as Saratoga's first B&B, or their basic motel that gives them an unusually broad range of accommodations and prices. Not to mention The Saratoga Arms, the small downtown concierge hotel they were about to open in 1998. As Noel proudly describes it, "we've now got all the bases covered."

When the Smiths started, four of the Saratoga B&B's five rooms shared baths. The original farmhouse now has four lodgings, all with private baths. They vary from a couple of small rooms with double beds and maple and oak furniture to two larger rooms with fireplaces, wicker furniture and queensize beds topped by colorful quilts made by a local church guild.

Kathleen prefers to dwell on – and in – the 1850 Brick House with its four suites, three with kingsize beds. All have splashy coordinated fabrics, antique walnut and mahogany furniture, glistening hardwood floors, TVs, telephones and bottles of Saratoga water. The most lavish is the rear Irish Cottage Suite, quiet and private with two queensize beds and two curved loveseats facing the TV and fireplace. The Waverly violet fabrics match the curtains and wallpaper; even the clawfoot tub is painted violet. One man who stayed here claimed it was like "waking up in a Bonwit Teller shopping bag," Kathleen reports.

The sun porch here is the summertime setting for a full breakfast for guests in both houses. Noel might prepare french toast with sausage one day and cream-cheese omelet with bacon the next. Juice, fresh fruit and corn muffins or toast round out the fare.

The Smiths recently added a water garden and lots of Adirondack chairs to their grounds. Ever innovative, Kathleen prints the front page of their hometown newspapers off the Internet for guests each morning.

(518) 584-0920 or (800) 584-0920. Fax (518) 584-4500. www.saratogabandb.com. Four rooms and four suites with private baths. Doubles, $65 to $95, racing $85 to $145; suites, $110 to $145, racing $160 to $225. Two-night or three night minimum stays on summer weekends. Children over 10. No smoking.

The Saratoga Arms, 495-497 Broadway, Saratoga Springs 12866.

The owners of the Saratoga Bed and Breakfast were restoring a hotel built in 1873 by Gideon Putnam's grandson for opening in June 1998. Noel and Kathleen Smith acquired the four-story building that had been used lately for transient housing. "It was horribly neglected but never abused," said Kathleen. "We found the original chandeliers, fireplaces and woodwork beneath layers of subsequent renovations."

Kathleen spent months at auctions to furnish sixteen guest rooms in high Victorian style. All rooms have kingsize beds, TVs, telephones and tiled baths, some with two-person jacuzzi tubs, and six rooms have fireplaces. Her aim was for a "clean-cut Victorian look," on the order of her 1850 Brick House at the Saratoga B&B.

The main floor was to have a black and white marble entry, black floral carpeting and public rooms with fireplaces. At least a continental breakfast was to be included in the rates, which had not been precisely determined as this book went to press.

(518) 584-1775. Sixteen rooms with private baths. Doubles, $95 to $350.

Adelphi Hotel, 365 Broadway, Saratoga Springs 12866.

One of only two of the great old Saratoga hotels still standing, this is the place to stay if you want to relive Saratoga's glory days. The four-story beauty with the columned veranda in the heart of downtown was built in 1877. The Adelphi had been closed for four years when Gregg Siefker and Sheila Parkert of Nebraska bought it in 1978 and started its ongoing restoration into a fantasy of Victoriana.

"It was a complete wreck, but we were lucky because it was never modernized," said Sheila, who made the curtains, sought out the antiques and now arranges the spectacular towering floral arrangements that grace the lobby.

We've seldom seen so much lace or so many crazy quilts in the 34 air-conditioned guest rooms and suites, each with private bath, telephone and television. All are spacious and feature lofty ceilings, ornate woodwork, antiques and lavish doses of Victoriana. For a change of pace, check out Gregg's favorite Adirondack Mission Room with its twig furniture, a sitting room in Stickley Arts and Crafts style, and a bathroom paneled in dark wood slats. Across the hall is a suite furnished in French country style.

Flanked by pergola and flagstone terrace, Adelphi Hotel's pool is sylvan oasis.

A complimentary continental breakfast of fresh fruit and coffee cake is served in bed, on the second floor in the High Victorian Parlor or outside on the Grand Piazza, the geranium-bedecked porch overlooking Broadway.

The owners recently overhauled the elaborate Victorian lobby, bar and upstairs parlor. The sight-to-behold lobby is an extravaganza of palms, crystal chandeliers and plush sofas and chairs. The walls and ceiling have been newly hand-stenciled in an exotic, over-the-top Neoclassic style by a stencil master from California.

Cocktails, tea, supper, dessert and coffee are served seasonally in the **Cafe Adelphi,** a Victorian bar incorporated into the rear of the lobby and extending beyond to a back porch and a charming courtyard garden. The latest addition here is a swimming pool surrounded by an elaborate pergola and flagstone terrace, a sylvan oasis in the heart of Saratoga.

(518) 587-4688. Fax (518) 587-0851. Thirty-four rooms and suites with private baths. Doubles, $90 to $145; racing, $145 to $225. Suites, $115 to $190; racing, $225 to $310. Three-night minimum on race weekends. Closed late October to mid-May.

Union Gables, 55 Union Ave., Saratoga Springs 12866.

Locally known as the Furness House, this three-story mansion with a corner turret was converted in 1992 into a ten-room B&B, Saratoga's largest and one of its more laid-back and comfortable. Local realtor Tom Roohan, his wife Jody and four children make the restored house their home.

The Roohans offer ten bedrooms with private baths in the circa 1901 Queen Anne Victorian with a corner turret and wraparound veranda, and out back in a renovated carriage house. The rooms – spacious, airy and uncluttered – have been professionally decorated with partial-canopy beds and colorful fabrics. Each is named for one of the couple's brothers or sisters. Annie, a front-corner turret room, has a painted sideboard, interesting periwinkle glaze painted walls and a white floor painted with ribbons, a kingsize bed and a single wicker chair. Edward also has a king canopy bed, two armchairs and a bay window awash in pillows. Kate's room is dark and horsy; a horse's collar is wrapped around the mirror in the bath, and a great wreath hangs above the queensize bed.

All rooms come with king or queen beds, TV and telephones, air-conditioning, mini-refrigerators stocked with a sampling of Saratoga's sparkling waters and a Victorian country – as opposed to haute – decor. "We want to provide the best of both worlds," Tom said, referring to the contemporary amenities in a Victorian masterpiece. There's an exercise room, and outside are a tennis court and a hot tub.

Rich paneling abounds throughout the house, especially in the large foyer and the huge living room/dining area, where you may be left to rattle around on your own. The Roohans put out a continental breakfast of fresh fruits, yogurt, cereals and pastries from the Bread Basket in the morning. It can be taken at a table for eight or outside on the great veranda with 80 feet of frontage on storied Union Avenue.

The house, designed by noted Saratoga architect R. Newton Brezee for a local manufacturer, blends Richardson and shingle styles. The variety of exterior surfaces (limestone, sandstone, pressed brick, wood shingles and slate) and their diverse planes produce an ever-changing play of lighting effects enhanced by the deep red, beige and dark green color scheme.

(518) 584-1558 or (800) 398-1558. Fax (518) 583-0649. www.uniongables.com. Ten rooms with private baths. May-October: doubles, $95 to $120. Racing, $225 to $260. Rest of year: $95 to $105. Children and pets accepted. No smoking.

The Wayside Inn, 104 Wilton Road, Greenfield 12833.

Built as a stagecoach inn and farm in 1789, this B&B reflects the much-traveled background and enthusiasm of owners Karen and Dale Shook. In the main house, they offer four bedrooms, all furnished with exotica. Their big blue barn (the largest in Saratoga County) was home to assorted sheep, goats, chickens, cats, dogs and an evolving "arts in the country" center until it was destroyed by fire in 1994.

The Shooks lived in many parts of the world while he taught on military bases before he came here in 1987 as a professor of international business at Skidmore College. The oriental screen and a shelf display of collections in the large fireplaced living room hint at things to come.

Upstairs, puppets are pinned to the curtains in the Toy Room. Canadiana prevails in the Captain St. John Room. Furniture from China and Korea marks the Madame Butterfly Room, which has an incredible screen framing an equally incredible chair in the corner, a queensize brass bed, TV set, oriental throw rugs atop the carpeting and an enormous bathroom-dressing area with double vanity, shower and small jacuzzi.

On the main floor in what had been the summer kitchen is the Maria Theresa Room, with a queen brass bed, private entrance and windows on three sides. It provides reminders of the Shooks' days in Holland, Belgium, Germany and Italy. All rooms share a vivid decor of quilts, curtains, pillows and such in lush deep colors, many reds and greens. Each contains a mini-refrigerator, which you could easily miss because there's so much to look at.

Karen has compiled a good little cookbook of her breakfast menus and recipes. A typical day's fare could be layered granola and strawberries, Mexican eggs, potatoes with onions and cheese and pineapple upside-down cake, along with juices (guava and passion fruit), yogurt, cereal, fruit, bagels and pastries. Sunday might bring fig-peach tarts, bacon popovers, and layered mushrooms and eggs. The feast is taken at a table in the formal dining room, at rattan tables on a sun porch or at a couple more tables in the entryway off the kitchen, which used to be a woodshed.

The ten-acre property includes an herb garden and a wildflower layout with paths and benches beside a creek, plus a fountain and gazebo beside a pond.

Until the fire, the front of the former dairy barn had been home to an artists' cooperative. The Shooks continue to show works of regional artisans, but the rebuilt barn has been serving primarily as an education and meeting center and the home for the State University at Albany Saratoga Weekend MBA Program.

(518) 893-7249 or 800-893-2884. Fax (518) 893-2884. Four rooms with private baths. Doubles, $85 to $100. Racing: $125 to $160. Off-season: $75 to $85. Children over 12. No smoking.

The Six Sisters Bed & Breakfast, 149 Union Ave., Saratoga Springs 12866.

Saratoga native Kate Benton, daughter of a former mayor, didn't want to leave Saratoga during the August racing season, as so many locals do. Upon returning to her hometown after fourteen years in Hawaii, she and her husband, Steve Ramirez, sought to be where the action is. So they opened a B&B in an 1890 Victorian facing Union Avenue, the main route to the racetrack. Verandas on the first and second floor give front-row seats onto all the comings and goings.

They named the architecturally unique building with a scalloped-edge roof for Kate's sisters; "my six brothers are still waiting," she quips. The four air-conditioned guest rooms, all with private baths and TV, are quite large (two have kingsize beds, one a queen and one has two queens) and are furnished in different styles. The master bedroom comes with a small sun room with etched-glass windows and a private front balcony. Wicker and floral prints mark a room furnished in the style the couple enjoyed when they met in Hawaii. The Elizabeth Marie has a tropical look with pastel colors, wicker chairs and pictures of flowers. The rear Agatha room offers a kingsize bed, a wet bar, a huge back porch and one of the B&B's two new whirlpool tubs.

Steve, an accomplished cook, prepares a family-style breakfast in the large dining room. Fresh fruit and baked apples might be followed by vegetable quiche or frittata, a side plate of bacon or sausage, and zucchini or nut breads. Kona macadamia nut coffee accompanies.

The pleasant front parlor with new flooring, oriental carpets and Italian marble around the fireplace harbors considerable local information, plus Steve's chatty little offbeat guide to Saratoga dining.

(518) 583-1173. Fax (518) 587-2470. Four rooms with private baths. Doubles, $125 to $150. Racing: $225 to $265. Winter: $85 to $115. Children over 10. No smoking.

The Lombardi Farm Bed & Breakfast, 34 Locust Grove Road, Saratoga Springs 12866.

A solarium with a hot tub/jacuzzi, gourmet breakfasts and Nubian and French Alpine goats in the barn are diverse attractions at the B&B that Kathleen and Vincent Lombardi run on the outskirts of town. The focal point is the large solarium that joins two houses, one old and one new. Here is where Kathleen serves her leisurely breakfasts at four lace-covered tables overlooking a jungle of plants and a jacuzzi.

Off one side of the solarium, in the new house to the rear, is a guest living room with a TV and a piano. Off another side in the new wing is a large main-floor bedroom with a canopy queensize bed, a wicker sitting area and a private bath outfitted with all kinds of lotions and colognes. This room has doors to an outside deck "so private that guests can sit out in their pajamas and enjoy their first cup of coffee," says Kathleen. Upstairs in the rear wing are two guest rooms with private baths. One decorated in a native American motif has a kingsize bed. The other has a double and a twin bed with hand-carved headboards..

Off the front of the solarium is the new country kitchen, the heart of the old house (circa 1840). Guests gather here around the wood-burning stove for hot mulled cider and home-baked goodies.

Upstairs is a master bedroom with kingsize canopy bed and private bath. Vince built an ingenious partial canopy decorated with silk roses above a queen bed tucked between the chimney and an outside wall in another bedroom. The bed in a nearby room has a lace canopy hand-crocheted by Kathleen's great-grandmother. An attic suite comes with a kingsize bed, a sitting room and a Niagara massage chair. Although they have a choice of seven accommodations, zoning regulations allow them to offer only four at a time.

Kathleen's "heart-smart" breakfasts start with an individual fruit platter, presented like a picture. Then might come coeur à la crème featuring the goat cheese made on the farm or toffee toast that is like candied bread – made with thick slices of french bread dipped in an egg batter and baked with a toffee syrup. Corned-beef hash with poached eggs, chocolate crêpes, ham soufflé with raspberry meringues and peach strudel, crème caramel and orange-oat waffles are among her imaginative dishes. There are always four or five courses.

(518) 587-2074. Four rooms with private baths. Doubles, $100. Racing, $130. Children welcome except in racing season.

The Eddy House, Nelson and Crescent Avenues, Saratoga Springs 12866.

"Welcome home...to your private Saratoga estate," begins the brochure for Saratoga's first B&B, a winner of a place operated by Barbara and Tom Bertino. "Staying home should be this good!" it concludes.

We agree, but don't let their "home away from home" theme mislead. This is a sophisticated house where a continuing house-party atmosphere draws a sophisticated repeat clientele partial to horses and the nearby tracks. The only drawback is a lack of private baths, the five guest rooms sharing two in a rather home-like situation.

The Bertinos – he a retired athletic director and she a former interior designer on Long Island – used to summer in Saratoga so their children could be exposed to the ballet, arts and horses. When the children left the nest, Barbara recalls, they urged their parents to move to Saratoga "and do what you like best – to cook and entertain." That was in 1984, and they've been cooking and entertaining since in a house and property that are suited to the role.

Guests may use every downstairs room in the 1847 Federal house. They include a summery parlor, pretty in pale yellow and blue with a collection of rare flow blue china on the wall, another living room in pink and teal, a cozy wormwood-paneled library with TV and a winterized rear porch. The formal dining room is a sight to behold, what with a large oak parquet table, the original white brick fireplace, an unused corner staircase upon which figurines and pictures are displayed and a table with every imaginable cordial to which guests may help themselves. Between the pre-dinner setups and vegetable dips and the after-dinner nightcaps, the house-party atmosphere is understandable.

Two acres of grounds make for plenty of party and activity space for guests at The Eddy House.

Upstairs in the rear are three rooms sharing a bath. They're named Lavender, Yellow and Teddybear for their decor. The Lavender is particularly striking for its floral-print wallpaper on walls and ceilings, nicely color-coordinated with a rainbow of towels. In the front of the house sharing a bath are two larger corner bedrooms. One has a queensize bed and an antique fainting couch that opens to a double bed. It's a fantasy in black and burgundy against pink walls. The other is in navy and white with a kingsize bed and white wicker.

Barbara's buffet breakfasts are such a hit that friends of guests often show up for the meal. Fresh berries and fruits from the Bertinos' organic gardens in back get things off to a good start and turn up in her homemade preserves that get lathered on the bran muffins and breads. The main course might be Swedish pancakes with lingonberry sauce, frittatas, oat waffles or orange french toast. Smoked pork chops or ham steaks cooked on the outdoor grill might accompany.

The party continues outside with volleyball, badminton, bocce and even a golf ball net, plus a game room in the garage. A twelve-foot-high hedge surrounds the nicely landscaped, two-acre property.

(518) 587-2340. Five rooms with shared baths. Doubles, $90 to $100. Racing, $140 to $160. Two-night minimum stay. Smoking restricted. No credit cards.

Brunswick Bed & Breakfast, 143 Union Ave., Saratoga Springs 12866
Their simple brochure notes "B&Bs are not for everyone. We have no television, private phones, room service or a swimming pool. We do have much warmth and concern."

Alinda and Kirk Nichols, who managed this former guest house for eleven years, bought the deteriorating 1886 Victorian Gothic structure in 1995 and began a gradual upgrading. They carefully renovated and redecorated all rooms to the period, updated the bathrooms and eliminated the shared-bath situation.

By 1998 they were offering ten rooms, all with private baths and queen beds. A couple of rooms open onto porches, and one has a gas fireplace. Three bedrooms on the first floor have mini-refrigerators. Guests also can use a guest kitchen with full refrigerator, stove and microwave.

The décor is simply but sprightly. Talented Linda handpainted the walls in two rooms with stripes that look like wallpaper. She sponge-painted walls in another room in multiple colors coordinated with the wainscoting.

There's a small rear sitting room for guests. The Nicholses offer a continental breakfast of sliced fruit, cereals and homemade muffins, drop biscuits and coffee cake.

(518) 584-6751 or (800) 585-6751. Ten rooms with private baths. Doubles, $95 weekends, $75 midweek. Racing: $175. Winter: $65 to $75.

Gideon Putnam Hotel and Conference Center, Saratoga Springs 12866.

Head deep into Saratoga Spa State Park past verdant golf-course fairways barely visible through the trees along the glorious Avenue of the Pines. Around the corner is this impressive, five-story Georgian brick structure that looks as if it's been there forever. A long green awning extends out from the entry between Corinthian columns to a circular drive upon which carriages and limousines once arrived. The latter still do, of course. The marbled, chandeliered lobby contains lighted cabinets displaying porcelain and china collections. Beyond are five dining rooms and countless lounges.

This is a state-owned resort of the old school, built as part of Franklin Roosevelt's WPA project in the 1930s and named for the man who sensed the springs' potential and opened Saratoga's first guest house. Lately, the resort has been upgraded and turned into a year-round facility by a concessionaire that also runs the national park lodges at Yellowstone, Bryce and Zion. The $5 million investment includes new and renovated bathrooms, better air-conditioning and heating, and new carpeting and lighting. The concessionaire also renovated and manages the nearby Lincoln and Roosevelt Mineral Baths.

Each of the 132 guest accommodations has at least a glimpse of the park. Rooms are furnished in Colonial reproductions and wicker in rose or blue color schemes. Because two double beds didn't fit well, most rooms combine a queensize and an extra-long twin bed, although some have a king or queen bed or two twins. All have enormous closets, television sets and telephones. Guests who spend the season usually snap up the eighteen parlor and porch suites. The latter have large screened porches furnished in bamboo overlooking a forest.

For meals, the fare is traditional in the former Georgian Room and lighter in the casual Saratoga Grille.

(518) 584-3000 or (800) 732-1560. Fax (518) 584-1354. One hundred fourteen rooms and eighteen suites with private baths. Rates EP: Mid-April to mid-November: doubles $130 to $150, suites $170 to $190. Racing: doubles, $250 to $285, suites $430 to $465. Mid-November to mid-April: doubles $89 to $110; suites, $125 to $160.

Dining Spots

43 Phila Bistro, 43 Phila St., Saratoga Springs.

Culinary excitement issues from this suave American cafe-bistro that's considered the best in town. Michael Lenza, an ex-South Jersey chef, cooked locally at Sperry's before launching his own venture. His wife Patricia oversees the 50-seat dining room, which is lovely in peach and terra cotta. The bar and banquettes are custom-made of bird's-eye and tiger's-eye maple. Caricatures of local folks brighten one wall.

Arriving almost as we were seated for dinner was a dish of assorted spicy olives marinated in olive oil, the oil useful for soaking the accompanying bread from Rock Hill Bakery, an area institution. Among starters were a smooth chicken-liver pâté served with crostini and cornichons, a terrific trio of smoked seafood (with capers in a little carrot floret and roasted red-pepper crème fraîche) and an enormous pizzetta, a meal in itself.

Had we eaten more than a sliver of the pizzetta we never would have made it through the main courses, a choice of four pastas and risottos and eight entrées. The Tuscan chicken pasta with roasted peppers, olives and white beans was a lusty autumn dish. The fillet of sole in parchment on a bed of julienned vegetables and rice, a signature item, turned out a bit bland. Other possibilities might be sesame-crusted yellowfin tuna with a wasabi-miso vinaigrette, veal rib chop milanese with crabmeat and saffron risotto, and grilled filet mignon served on focaccia toasts with gorgonzola butter. A $15 bottle of our favorite Hogue Cellars fumé blanc accompanied from a varied, well-chosen list that earned the Wine Spectator award.

The pastry chef is known for distinctive desserts, including a white chocolate raspberry tart, bananas foster and a peanut butter mousse in a chocolate ganache shell with mocha crème anglaise. We settled for a dish of plum-port sorbet, a refreshing ending to an uncommonly good meal.

In season, the chef offers some mighty good crab dishes, from soft-shell crabs with Thai curry sauce to Maryland crab cakes with rémoulade, corn piccalilli and hush puppies. He also bottles for sale the 43 ketchup that accompanies his black angus steaks.

(518) 584-2720. Entrées, $22 to $28. Dinner nightly, from 5. Sunday brunch in off-season, 11 to 3.

Eartha's Court Street Grill, 60 Court St., Saratoga Springs. (518) 583-0602.
This small grill and wine bar has been on everyone's list of favorites since it was opened in 1985 as Eartha's Kitchen, serving assertive fare in congenial surroundings. Carolyn Male, a chef who prefers to be in the front of the house, took over the restaurant in 1996. The dining experience slipped, according to the local consensus, although only those who had been there before recognized the difference.

The name derives from the half-ton, cast-iron wood stove and grill the founder called Eartha. From it come eight or nine entrées, mostly grilled but with an occasional sauté or pasta dish combining grilled vegetables and chicken or shrimp. Seafood is stressed, and the menu changes frequently.

When we were there, the huge wood stove was ready for mesquite, charcoal and applewood. It produced a super grilled mahi-mahi with avocado mousseline and a remarkable grilled catfish with pickled ginger and a mango glaze. They were accompanied by good rice and the best zucchini we've tasted in a long time. Preceding these were appetizers of salmon roulade with horseradish cream sauce and grilled belgian endive with basil aioli, served on nasturtium leaves.

The new owner has added such starters as smoked salmon fallen soufflé and grilled portobello mushroom with vegetable salsa and goat cheese. Recent main dishes included grilled pork medallions with roasted jalapeño-mustard cream and grilled black angus strip steak with a red onion jam and mushroom ragoût.

Desserts include chocolate timbale with a hint of Bailey's on a hazelnut tuile, blueberry-oatmeal crumb pie, fresh fruit terrines and a homemade ice-cream sandwich. We enjoyed a creamy cheesecake with strawberry puree on top.

Carolyn has brightened up the decor a bit, painting the walls, adding salmon-colored tablecloths and comfortable chairs with cushioned seats.

(518) 583-0602. Entrées, $16 to $23. Dinner nightly, 5:30 to 10. Closed Monday and Tuesday in off-season.

Sperry's, 30½ Caroline St., Saratoga Springs.

Once owned by Charles "Chubby" Sperry, a thoroughbred owner and trainer, this unlikely-looking establishment attracts a racetrack crowd in summer and locals the rest of the year. It looks like a gin mill, and only those in the know would venture inside. The decor is quite forgettable: a long bar, a black and white tile floor and, at either end of the room, dark old booths and tables covered with blue and white checked cloths. Beyond is a large covered patio for additional seating in season.

Chef-owner Ridge Qua is known for consistently good food at reasonable prices. The menu rarely changes, but the preparations and specials do.

For lunch, one of us enjoyed a great grilled duck breast salad with citrus vinaigrette and the other a cup of potato-leek soup with an enormous open-face dill-havarti-tomato sandwich, served with a side salad. Unfortunately, service was so laid-back as to be slow and disinterested. We had to go to the bar to ask for – and then to pay – the bill.

The dinner menu ranges from jambalaya to steak au poivre. Grilled Atlantic salmon with Thai sauce and wasabi, cajun-spiced catfish with southwestern salsa and guacamole, and grilled chicken with roasted peppers, ham and aged provolone were specials at a recent visit. Desserts include seasonal fruit tarts, cheesecakes, crème caramel and chocolate-cointreau mousse.

(518) 584-9618. Entrées, $13.95 to $18.95. Lunch, Monday-Saturday 11:30 to 3. Dinner, 5 to 10, Sunday to 9.

The Springwater Inn, 139 Union Ave., Saratoga Springs.

The food at this restored Victorian coach house has been upgraded lately by owners Leslie and Peter DeCarlo and their chef, Darren Veiche.

Their kitchen delivers some inspired contemporary continental fare, including such appetizers as shiitake mushroom ravioli with roasted red pepper coulis, Adirondack smoked trout, Greek scampi and escargots forestière. Main courses could be grilled salmon with sundried tomato beurre blanc, chicken and shrimp marsala over egg fettuccine, roast Long Island duckling with raspberry demi-glace, grilled venison flank steak with merlot wine sauce and veal saltimbocca.

Dining is in a book-lined main dining room, all very plush with skylights, arched windows and bentwood chairs, reflecting the building's heritage as a onetime carriage shop along fashionable Union Avenue. Light fare is available in the Adirondack Tavern, which has a fireplace.

(518) 584-6440. Entrées, $15.95 to $23.95. Lunch seasonally. Dinner, Tuesday-Sunday from 4.

Hattie's, 45 Phila St., Saratoga Springs.

After 55 years as Hattie's Chicken Shack, this well-known institution changed hands, shortened its name and raised its culinary aspirations. Hattie Austin, still doing the baking here at age 93, sold in 1993 to Christel Baker, then a 33-year-old Wall Street investment banker. "We're old friends," explained Christel. "Our families go way back."

Personable Christel, who was making apple butter in the kitchen at our first visit, has gradually broadened the emphasis from soul food to southern home cooking to "bayou" cuisine with a distinct New Orleans bite. She kept the homey, cozy, checkered-tablecloth decor, but added a brick patio surrounded by a Southern-style garden out back. She expanded the hours, added po'boys for lunch and live blues in season, offered the traditional side dishes à la carte and won a liquor license, featuring southern drinks like mint juleps. She also offers specialties through her new **Hattie's General Store,** based on the premises and featuring mail-order chutneys, pies and free-range pork and pasture-raised aged beef from her 110-acre farm near the Vermont border.

The whole enterprise is decidedly with-it and upbeat, the ambiance appealing and the food highly rated and affordable. At night, you can order Hattie's famous southern fried chicken with two sides (perhaps collard greens and candied yams), a green salad and homemade biscuits for $11.25. The new bayou specialties include creole jambalaya, low-country crab cakes, bourbon shrimp mandeville, shrimp étouffée and blackened farm-raised strip steak. Four of the southern side dishes with a salad and biscuits make a vegetarian sampler. Christel urges patrons to mix and match appetizers, soups and salads for a light meal. Finish with the peach cobbler or sweet-potato pie.

(518) 584-4790. Entrées, $11.95 to $14.95. Open daily in summer, 11 to 10:30 or 11. Breakfast, 8 to 11:30 in racing season. Closed Monday and Tuesday in off-season.

The Olde Bryan Inn, 123 Maple Ave., Saratoga Springs.
All gray stone and flanked by tubs full of geraniums and white petunias, this is the oldest building in Saratoga, a tavern and inn dating to 1773 and located near the High Rock Spring that George Washington tried unsuccessfully to buy. The place is jammed day and night, no doubt because of its moderate prices (the same menu is served all day) and a pleasant atmosphere of brick, brass and booths, plus a covered outdoor patio that we found torridly hot on a summer day.

For lunch, try a grilled chicken BLT, a cajun burger, a french dip sandwich or one of six salads served with homemade nut muffins or garlic bread. Dinner entrées range from an old-fashioned turkey dinner to blackened steak and New York sirloin, with plenty of options in between. The signature dessert is chocolate oblivion, a dense, fudge-like creation topped with whipped cream and resting on a pool of raspberry sauce.

The atmosphere is as casual as the menu, but locals consider the food outstanding.

(518) 587-2990. Entrées, $10.95 to $16.95. Open daily, 11:30 to 11 or midnight.

Longfellows at Saratoga Farms, 500 Union Ave., Saratoga Springs.
The owners of the Olde Bryan Inn took over the famed Caunterbury restaurant complex in 1996. They gave the old horse and dairy barns a facelift and toned down the former Disneyesque theme to create a pleasing Federal-style steakhouse and grill.

A new mesquite grill produces a variety of steaks and other items, such as swordfish steak with melon-lime salsa, bourbon-glazed salmon fillet, barbecued ribs, chicken with ancho-chile barbecue sauce and pork chops with homemade apple chutney. Slow-roasted prime rib is a specialty.

The menu also offers a trio of pastas, salads and appetizers from fried blossom onions to mesquite-grilled quesadillas.

(518) 587-0108. Entrées, $8.95 to $16.95. Dinner, 4 to 11, Sunday 2 to 10.

Maestro's, 371 Broadway, Saratoga Springs.

This storefront space on the ground floor of the landmark Adelphia Hotel building has been home to several restaurants. The latest was opened in 1997 by Joseph DeVivo Jr., a Saratoga native who offers new American cuisine with Italian and French accents. He seats 36 diners at white-clothed tables inside, with fourteen more seats on the sidewalk out front.

Defining maestro as "master of an art," he prepares three meals a day in season. The short dinner menu might offer homemade crabmeat ravioli with red pepper cream, chicken stuffed with prosciutto and sundried tomatoes and grilled filets of beef tenderloin with roasted garlic, plum tomatoes and goat cheese. A lobster cake with tomato-basil cream is the signature starter.

Banana-cinnamon pancakes and Texas-style french toast with maple-sweetened strawberries are specialties for summer breakfast.

(518) 580-0312. Entrées, $15.50 to $17.50. Breakfast in summer, 8 to 11. Lunch daily, 11:30 to 4. Dinner, 5 to 10.

Diversions

There are so many things to do and see here that we cannot possibly do them all justice. And visitors who tried to do them all in one trip would wear themselves out. Here is a brief selection:

The Horses. Drive around the east and south sides of Saratoga and you'll be amazed at the number of stables, racetracks, horses, horse people and hangers-on, especially in August. Louisville has its Kentucky Derby and Baltimore the Preakness, but the real high-rollers come to Saratoga for six weeks of racing and allied activities. Socialite Marylou Whitney's annual gala at the Canfield Casino to benefit the National Museum of Dance launches a whirlwind of balls and fundraisers all through August. The **Saratoga Race Course** off Union Avenue, oldest thoroughbred flat track in the country (1863), attracts the highest average daily attendance of any track (about 28,000) for its recently extended season from late July through August. As many as 50,000 show up for its major Travers Stakes race. Because so many winners of Triple Crown events have lost at Saratoga, the track has become known as "the graveyard of favorites." The place is massive: 17,000 seats, hundreds of stables, five restaurants and an infield with a pond upon which floats an Indian canoe, painted the colors of the owner of the last Travers winner. Breakfast at the track – watching the morning workouts and mixing with the trainers – is a tradition. Folks eventually move into the sprawling grandstand, rife with red and white striped awnings, gilded cupolas and thousands of geraniums and petunias, to bet an average of $3.5 million a day. Races, daily except Tuesday at 1. Admission, $2 to grandstand, $5 to clubhouse.

Open from mid-January to late November is the **Saratoga Equine Sports Center,** near Crescent and Nelson avenues. Considered by some the world's most beautiful half-mile track, the standardbred harness track opened on a former Whitney estate in 1941. Races are staged Tuesday-Sunday in July and August. Tours are available, and the **Saratoga Harness Hall of Fame** has exhibits in an old horseman's building. World-class polo is offered at the **Whitney Polo Field**.

National Museum of Racing and Hall of Fame, Union Avenue and Ludlow Street.

Enter not through a turnstile but a set of starting gates next to a life-size fiberglass horse and jockey frozen at the moment of a race's start. The sounds of horses loading, jockeys yelling and stalls flying open propel you into an arena that does for horse racing what Cooperstown's Hall of Fame does for baseball. It relates the past, present and future of thoroughbred racing through the latest in you-are-there museum gadgetry. An impressive, fifteen-minute film called "Race America," a montage of racing from coast to coast, is shown in the Hall of Fame auditorium. Famous jockeys and trainers explain their techniques through videos in a simulated racetrack area.

(518) 584-0400. Open daily in racing season, 9 to 5; rest of year, 10 to 4:30, Sunday noon to 4:30. Adults, $3.

Saratoga Spa State Park, off Route 9 South.

Perhaps the grandest park of its kind, this is a 2,000-acre island of serenity at the edge of the Saratoga hubbub. Enter through the soaring Avenue of the Pines past one of two golf courses. All the Georgian Revival brick pavilions, arched promenades, domed ceilings and marble arcades are flanked by pools, fountains and deep, pine-shaded lawns. Of special interest are the Hall of Springs, the Spa Little Theater, the classical Victoria Pool and the larger, Olympic-size Peerless Pool. Besides swimming, there are places for walking, running, cross-country skiing and ice-skating. The park was created to protect the springs, which at the turn of the century were in danger of being commercialized into oblivion. Most of the construction took place in the mid-1930s as a WPA project. "The park is unique in the state and maybe the world," said the manager. "You couldn't build this today."

(518) 584-2535. Open daily, 8 a.m. to dusk. Parking $4, Memorial Day to Labor Day.

Saratoga Performing Arts Center, Saratoga Spa State Park, (518) 587-3330. An amphitheater at the edge of the state park has seats for 5,100, and up to 25,000 more crowd the lawns for performances here. The New York City Opera is in residence in June, July brings the New York City Ballet and August the Philadelphia Orchestra. The Saratoga Jazz Festival and the Saratoga Chamber Music Festival also take place here. Special-event superstars range from Bonnie Raitt to James Taylor, Linda Ronstadt to Steve Winwood.

The Springs. Long before racing took hold here, Saratoga was renowned for its carbonated mineral springs. What made Saratoga different from other watering spas was the racing and the high-rollers it attracted. The fizzy waters, often smelling like eggs gone bad, can be sampled at more than 50 springs around town. A pavilion recently was built around the original Congress Spring in Congress Park, the downtown layout designed by Frederick Law Olmsted. Nearby are the domed Columbian Spring pavilion and the Hathorn Spring on Spring Street. North of downtown near Excelsior and High Rock avenues are the High Rock Spring and Red Spring, named for the color of its water. The heaviest concentration is in Saratoga Spa State Park. You can drink the waters, if you like, or soak in them (see below).

Mineral Baths. Opened in 1935, the **Roosevelt Baths** in Saratoga Spa State Park offer mineral water baths and massages year-round. (They were being renovated and upgraded by the concessionaire that runs the Gideon Putnam Hotel, but the baths and the facility still looked fairly primitive – the purists say authentic – at our visit.) You pay $15 for a mineral bath, taken in small private rooms in the men's or women's wings. Each is equipped with a tall bathtub and a cot with a sheet on top. Bubbly, brown water from the springs is heated and pumped into the tubs; you soak for twenty minutes, then wrap yourself in the sheet on the bed and nap for half an hour. For $26 more, you can add a half-hour massage by appointment (584-2011). Open May through August are the **Lincoln Baths,** recently redone by the state and offering semi-private baths. For more upscale surroundings (Italian marble and crystal chandeliers), head for the privately owned **Crystal Spa** at 92 South Broadway, fed by the Rosemary Spring outside the Grand Union Motel.

Yaddo Gardens, Union Avenue.

A private estate turned into a working arts community, the 55-room mansion just east of the flat track has played host since 1926 to 200 artists, writers and composers each year in an environment free of distractions. Some get their inspiration from the atmospheric rose and sculpture gardens, which are open to the public and well worth seeing. Modeled after formal turn-of-the-century Italian gardens, they have a colonnaded, rose-covered pergola as the dominant feature. On the terrace below are four oblong beds of red and white roses joined by a central Florentine fountain. Tucked among pine trees above the pergola is a rock garden of Japanese design.

(518) 584-0746. Grounds open daily, 8 a.m. to dusk. Free.

Shopping. Most of the good stores in this real, working downtown are stretched along wide, tree-lined Broadway with its massed plantings of colorful impatiens and a couple of side streets, Phila and Caroline.

Except for a new **Starbuck's,** about the only "chain" store is a branch of the **House of Walsh,** the classic clothing store based in Williamstown, Mass. Nearby on lower Broadway is **Symmetry,** where we ogled some of the most beautiful works in glass we have seen. It's really more like a glass art gallery. **Nostalgia** is a good place to pick up a gift, perhaps a scented candle, a wreath, a picture frame or a mohair throw. **G. Willikers** is quite a toy store, and **Celtic Treasures** speaks for itself. **Designers Studio** shows fine contemporary American crafts. The best hats for the track, many made on premises, are available amidst the "vintage ladies' finery" at **Saratoga Trunk.** Gifts for the horse lover are featured at **Impressions of Saratoga;** many convey an animal or a local theme. A scaled-down version of **Mabou,** a mini-Bloomingdales here back in the 1970s and '80s, has returned to Saratoga with trendy gifts, antiques, fashions and home accessories. **Lyrical Ballad Bookstore** qualifies as one of the better antiquarian booksellers. Stop for a coffee, latte or pastry at **Madelines Espresso Bar** or **Uncommon Grounds,** both classics of their genre.

Extra Special

Caffé Lena, 47 Phila St., Saratoga Springs.

The oldest continuously operated coffeehouse in the country, this was run from 1960 until her death in 1989 by Lena Spencer, called "the Mother Teresa of folk music." Her friends and patrons have banded together to continue the tradition since. "It's been a struggle, but we've endured," said one. Her legacy remains in the small upstairs room full of atmosphere as patrons enjoy the music along with good coffees, teas and homemade pastries (no smoking and no alcohol). Many is the name folksinger and cabaret singer who has entertained at Lena's. Bob Dylan and Don McLean first found an audience here; Arlo Guthrie sang here long before the rest of the world heard his music. The tradition, as they say, continues.

(518) 583-0022. Open Thursday-Sunday from 6 or 7.

Westport/Essex, N.Y.
Where the Adirondacks Meet Lake Champlain

Is there a less likely place than a corner of the nation's second most populous state to find quaint 19th-century villages relatively unscathed by time? This is the region where the Lake Georges, the Lake Placids and the Old Forges have been marked by wanton commercialism on the edges of the East's largest forever-wild area. So it is an agreeable surprise to leave the Adirondack Northway and head east through unspoiled countryside to the area where the Adirondack Mountains meet Lake Champlain.

Here is Westport, a hillside village where a library, rather than a town hall or a church, dominates the village center and the green is called the Library Lawn. A tradition of local beneficence began with the gift of both library and lawn in the early 1800s. It continued in 1991, when the land across the street was given for a village park leading down to the Northwest Bay of Lake Champlain and a sandy swimming beach open to one and all.

Here is Essex, an old-fashioned place containing one of the most intact ensembles of pre-Civil War village architecture in America. The entire village is on the National Register of Historic Places and persists as a living history museum. One cannot help but be impressed by the beauty of its lakeside setting as well as by its architecture.

Both Westport and Essex occupy particularly scenic sites beside Lake Champlain. Looming behind are the Adirondack High Peaks. Across the lake are the Green Mountains of Vermont.

History gave this section of Lake Champlain pivotal roles in the American Revolution and the War of 1812. The lake became the primary route for travel and commerce between Canada and the growing American republic. By 1850, Westport

and Essex were among the largest and busiest communities on the lake, each with populations of 2,300. The coming of the railroad brought summer visitors, who filled the area's hotels and inns to overflowing. "Social Notes from The Westport Inn" was a feature in the New York Times and the Boston newspapers. Prestigious Camp Dudley prospered here as America's oldest summer camp for boys.

The reduction of train service and the rise of the interstate highways freeze-dried the area's development in the 1950s. One finds here not mere vestiges but rather the essence of the look and the lifestyle of half a century or a century ago.

Picket fences and flowers surround All Tucked Inn.

Contrary to trends elsewhere, most of Westport's old inns have been converted into private residences of distinction. The railroad depot is now an equity summer theater. The yacht club is a public restaurant. The country club is open to the public. Boats are launched from public launching sites and busy marinas. The Lake Champlain ferry arrives in Essex every half hour in summer from Charlotte, Vt. Tourists find excellent brochures for walking tours of Westport and Essex and their historic sites.

What these villages don't have is traffic lights, chain stores or fast-food outlets. Such things weren't needed in days of yore, nor are they needed here today. Westport and Essex offer other virtues. They are two of the more appealing lakefront towns we know of, far from the hordes yet with touches of sophistication interspersed amid the charms of yesteryear.

Inn Spots

All Tucked Inn, 53 South Main St., Box 324, Westport 12993.

The new name was "the first thing that dawned on me," Tom Haley said of his 1993 purchase of the former Gables adjunct to the Inn on the Library Lawn a few doors away. He entered it in a national contest and, lo and behold, the name won fourth place.

The cutesy name perhaps does not do justice to this rather stylish, full-service inn with a guest dining room and nine bedrooms, all with private baths. Or perhaps it does. Energetic Tom, a former lobbyist for the state Civil Service Employees Association in Albany, shelters guests in rooms with sitting areas, caters to their every whim and plies them with caloric afternoon refreshments, home-cooked dinners and ample breakfasts. "Eating here is not a low-cholesterol event," he says.

He'll prepare anything from a back-yard cookout – perhaps chicken and ribs, or filet mignon –to a candlelight dinner with soup, salad, entrée and dessert, $20 for four courses. The day we were there he was serving black bean soup, tossed salad,

Three architectural styles are combined in The Victorian Lady.

chicken with stilton and sundried tomatoes in a port wine sauce, and three-berry cobbler. He might make peasant soup (sausage with white beans and leftover veggies) or clam chowder ("which people tell me is the best they've ever had"). Dessert is likely to be an ice-cream sundae. "Sweets are my weakness," he explains, "and I make what I like." Dinner is optional and BYOB, served by reservation around 7.

Breakfast is not optional. Tom prepares fruit, homemade raspberry or apple muffins, sausage and bacon, and offers a choice of three main courses: eggs (from omelets to eggs benedict), pancakes or french toast.

Bedrooms are scattered about the summery, country-style house and reached by different stairways. Most have queen or king beds and sitting areas with wing chairs, and three have fireplaces. A main-floor suite comes with a private porch. They're cheerfully decorated down to their coordinated sheets, quilts and bed covers. Horse prints and memorabilia reflect the owners' love for the Saratoga racing season.

Tom runs the inn on weekdays while his wife, Claudia Ryan, a lawyer, is in Albany. Claudia sheds her lawyer's mantle on weekends and becomes a waitress, serving Tom's meals to receptive guests.

(518) 962-4400 or (888) 255-8825. Nine bedrooms with private baths. May-October: doubles, $65 to $110. Rest of year: $55 to $100.

The Inn on the Library Lawn, 1 Washington St., Box 390, Westport 12993.

This is the largest inn in a village that once had many, including the storied Westport Inn across the street. The Westport was torn down in 1966, and its abandoned site was given to the village as a public park with a swimming beach beside the lake in 1991. The site of the old inn's foundation has been a public ice-skating rink for years.

Actually, this inn occupies what used to be annexes of the Westport Inn. The inn, whose entry is on the side across from the Library Lawn, wears its age well. Susann and Don Thompson took over in 1995 and have reinvigorated the place, gradually upgrading the rooms and reinstating lunch service on weekends.

All ten air-conditioned bedrooms have private baths and seven have television sets. Decor is simple but fresh. Susan has stenciled some of the floors and added accent pieces like wallpaper borders and straw hats. Rooms have high ceilings (some twelve feet), period furnishings and braided rugs, and five yield views of the lake. The largest is now a suite with a wicker loveseat and chair, a queen brass and iron bed, and a sitting room with a sofabed. Rates vary according to size, type of bed (twins, double and queen) and view.

Guests share an old-fashioned common sitting area full of books and magazines in the upstairs hall. The spacious main room on the front of the ground floor, long the site of the inn's restaurant, is now a fireplaced lounge area where complimentary beverages are served, as well as a dining room open to the public for lunch on weekends. The fare is salads and sandwiches in the $5 to $7 range, plus blackboard specials. The meal also may be taken outdoors on a pleasant side deck overlooking the lake.

In the morning, the dining room and deck are the setting for a full breakfast. Typically, juice, fruit and breads precede choices like eggs with salsa, ham quiche, apple french toast and blueberry pancakes. Don cooks the main courses and Susan handles the fruit course and the baking.

(518) 962-8666 or (888) 577-7748. Mid-April to mid-October: doubles, $69 to $95; suite $115. Rest of year: doubles, $59 to $85; suite, $105. No smoking. Lunch, Friday-Sunday 11:30 to 12:30.

The Victorian Lady, 57 South Main St., Box 88, Westport 12993.

Colorful in shades of pale yellow with light blue and brick red trim, this charmer dating to 1856 combines three architectural styles. The original 1856 home is Greek Revival, the front facade with mansard roof and three-story tower is Second Empire, and the full veranda added in the 1880s is of the Eastlake style. Wayne and Doris Deswert, who winter in Florida, took over the former Doll House B&B and spent a year refurbishing before reopening in 1994.

The main floor contains a formal, high Victorian parlor furnished with antiques, plus an informal living room outfitted with TV and modern wicker. The parlor is notable for its English embossed wall coverings. Rich paneling and woodwork are evident throughout.

Upstairs are three bedrooms with private baths, plus a two-bedroom suite good for families. A front room offers a queensize brass bed and a day bed, while a second room opens onto a wicker-furnished porch. Making up part of a suite, Grammy's Room in the back comes with a canopied double bed, a few dolls and stuffed animals. It has an old dresser converted into a lavatory sink and a long closet for a bathroom, which may be shared with occupants of the adjacent Garden Room.

The premier accommodation is a suite on the top floor of a newly constructed rear carriage house. It holds a kingsize bed and a sitting area with TV.

Continental breakfast is served upon request in an upstairs sitting room. Most guests wait for the four-course breakfast served by candlelight in the formal dining room, however. Fresh fruit, orange juice and homemade muffins precede the main event, perhaps quiche or blueberry waffles.

Tea is served in the afternoon. It's often taken on the 1,200-square-foot front veranda that catches a glimpse through the trees of Lake Champlain. The veranda contains a swing and a hammock, just like at Grandma's house – to which many guests liken The Victorian Lady.

(518) 962-2345. Three bedrooms and two suites with private baths. Doubles, $95 to $115. Suites, $130 and $140. Closed mid-October to Memorial Day. No credit cards. No smoking.

The Gray Goose, 42 North Main St., Box N, Westport 12993.

Shades of gray and geese are the decorative themes for this homey Victorian B&B and gift shop lovingly run by Elizabeth Kroeplin, a New Jersey transplant who had spent summers here. She offers three guest rooms with private baths, one with a double bed and the others with twins. Two on the first floor on either side of the shop open onto a front porch, with a view of Lake Champlain beyond buildings across the road. Each has its own private entrance and is decorated with period furniture, white frilly curtains and gray, geese-covered bedspreads that match the shower curtains. A third bedroom on the second floor has antique maple beds, a wicker loveseat and a clothing hook in the form of a wooden goose.

Guests may use Elizabeth's skylit sun room, cozy with a wood-burning stove, as well as the front porch. She offers an optional continental breakfast for $3, including juice and homemade muffins, served at a table set with cloth placemats in her shop or on the front porch.

The shop is a family affair. She and her sister and an aunt make most of the handicrafts for sale. Grapevine wreaths are Elizabeth's specialty.

(518) 962-4562. Three rooms with private baths. Doubles, $65 to $75. Closed mid-November to mid-May.

Champlain Vistas, 183 Lake Shore Road (Route 22), Willsboro 12996.

You want vistas? From this hilltop B&B two miles north of Essex, Lake Champlain and Vermont's Green Mountains are the front yard, so to speak, and the High Peaks of the Adirondacks are the back yard. The views were what prompted Barbara Moses to move here upon her retirement as business manager of the computer center at Rensselaer Polytechnic Institute in Troy.

She had sailed on Lake Champlain for years, so was quite keen to buy part of the historic Owens Farm on the western shore, renovate its mid-18th-century farmhouse (listed on the National Register of Historic Places) and make it her year-round home and B&B. She offers four guest rooms, two with private baths and the others sharing, plus a small single room. The rooms are named for their views. The main-floor Champlain room has a queen bed and a private bath, as does the Green Mountain Room with its original wallpaper of yellow jonquils on the second floor. Closets hold bathrobes for the occupants of the Mount Mansfield and Adirondack rooms, with a double or twin beds.

A striking mahogany table made by Barbara's father-in-law graces the formal dining room. A delightful sun porch adjoins. Guests also enjoy the square, beamed living room that is both stylish and homey. Quite spacious, it has a spinning wheel in one corner and a fireplace made from fieldstones gathered on the 300-acre property.

The property also houses a large barn with an attached shed and a peaked-roof grainery, which Barbara recently converted into a small art gallery with a smattering of antiques. Behind her house is a prolific grape arbor furnishing the makings for

Side lawn is the place for relaxing and taking in views at Champlain Vistas.

preserves and wines, and behind that a storage shed that has been transformed into a small exercise and fitness center. "It faces the most wonderful pastoral setting," she says, "so you can work away and not feel miserable."

Barbara serves a full country breakfast of fruit, juice, cereals, homemade muffins and a main course of perhaps bacon and eggs, french toast or waffles. In the evening, guests sit on the side lawn and watch the moon shimmering across the waters of Lake Champlain.

(518) 963-8029. Two rooms with private baths and two rooms with shared bath. Doubles, $75 to $95. No smoking. No credit cards. Closed in January.

The Stonehouse, Church and Elm Streets, Essex 12936.

This restored 1926 Georgian stone house looks as if it's been transplanted from the British countryside. Which is why it attracted Sylvia Hobbs, who lives in England and spends the summer and holidays here.

She shares her gracious home full of antique furnishings with overnight guests in five bedrooms, with a variety of bed sizes. Two rooms on the second floor, one with double bed and one with twins, share a bath. We liked the looks of the master bedroom with its coffered ceiling, crown canopy bed, full bath and more chairs and sofas than two could possibly occupy. Some might prefer to escape to the attic hideaway with a queen bed and sofa and a bath with clawfoot tub, shared with a double-bedded room adjacent. For 1998, Sylvia was planning to raise the attic roof and install four rear windows and a rooftop terrace.

On the main floor are a large and elegant living room, a formal dining room and a small room for TV, "which we don't encourage," advises Sylvia. Wine is offered at the end of the day on the candlelit porch, and sherry is poured on chilly evenings in front of the fireplace.

Breakfast is a treat at individual tables on the sunny garden terrace. Sylvia calls it "superior continental," which translates to a fresh fruit platter, juices, cereals, homemade breads and muffins, and bagels obtained from Montreal.

(518) 963-7713. One room with private bath and four rooms with shared baths. Doubles, $65 to $125. Open Memorial Day to Columbus Day and some holidays. No credit cards.

The Essex Inn, Main Street, Box 324, Essex 12936.

Its pillars and verandas on the first and second floors running the length of the house, this 1810 Federal structure with a Greek Revival colonnade lends quite a presence to Essex's little main street.

For some years, the inside was a presence as well under the ownership of a Burlington artist and restaurateur. A more mainstream presence was instilled by new owners John and Trish Walker from downstate New York. They toned down the eccentricity, upgraded the guest rooms, revived the restaurant operation (see Dining Spots) and instilled a much-needed personal touch.

"We're trying to turn it back into an old inn again," says Trish. Gone are the kitchenettes and the huge stuffed alligator that formerly surprised guests on a built-in bed. Antique beds, quilts, period pieces and traditional artworks are the décor now. The Benjamin Franklin Room contains matching antique twin beds. The Fitzgerald has an antique double bed. The e.e. cummings suite offers a kingsize

Pillars dignify facade of The Essex Inn.

bed as well as an alcove with a twin trundle bed leading onto the veranda.

For 1998, the Walkers were adding a handicapped-accessible guest room with its own entrance on the first floor. It also will accommodate pets. The common room was being converted into another dining room for the expanding restaurant operation. The new common room was to be in quarters vacated by the small **Essex Inn Book Shop** that was relocated to another section of the inn.

A full breakfast, served on the veranda in season, is complimentary for overnight guests. Specialties include blueberry or raspberry pancakes and french toast with brandied fruit sauce.

(518) 963-8821. Five rooms with private baths and two rooms with shared baths. May-October: doubles, $80 to $115. Rest of year: $70 to $95. Children and pets welcome. No smoking.

Dining Spots

Le Bistro at the Westport Yacht Club, Old Arsenal Road, Westport.

Long a focus of Westport social life with its dances and regattas, the old yacht club was sold in the 1940s as Westport experienced a decline in tourism and was converted into a private home. After a disastrous fire in 1982, the place was rebuilt as a public restaurant.

Perched like a yacht club along the shores of Northwest Bay, it enjoys a panoramic water view up and down the lake. A front cocktail platform, a side deck, a lovely canopied porch and a serene inner dining room take full advantage. That the decor is so sophisticated and the food so good is a bonus.

Chef-owner Bernard Perillat, co-owner of the popular Chez Henri at Sugarbush in Warren, Vt., moved here in 1996 when his lease for Le Bistro du Lac in Essex expired. Here he offers a similar bistro-ish menu, which is quite like the Sugarbush model and changes periodically.

We lunched on his house pâté with a side salad and a salade niçoise, tasty but different with cauliflower substituting for the usual potatoes and bits of bacon, anchovy and warm tuna. A signature dessert – frozen sorbet cake ($5), layers of passion fruit, raspberry and black currant topped with frozen kiwi and served on a raspberry coulis with lady fingers – was a sensational ending.

Dinner entrées range from changing preparations of chicken and pasta to rack of lamb with rosemary herb sauce. Duck with fruit or pepper sauce, salmon with beurre blanc and filet of beef au poivre are standards. They're supplemented by such nightly specials as blackened tuna with mustard sauce, grilled mahi-mahi with salsa, pork tenderloin charcuterie and ragoût of sweetbreads and shiitake mushrooms. The classic onion soup gratinée, country pâté, escargots in puff pastry and endive salad are popular starters. Desserts run to mousses, crème caramel, ice cream and sorbet.

(518) 962-8777. Entrées, $13.95 to $23. Lunch daily in summer, 11:30 to 3. Dinner, 5 to 9 or 9:30. Open mid-June to mid-September.

The Westport Hotel, Pleasant Street, Westport.

If its unprepossessing exterior in a commercial area prompts you to pass on, don't. Hidden behind the evergreens is an elongated restaurant of great appeal, particularly the rear porch screened by trellises and evergreens and looking like something you might find in California – or in an old Adirondack lodge.

Hanging bushel baskets contain the lamps. Brightly painted wooden tulips are on the tables and shelves, and there's quite an assortment of mismatched chairs. All the wooden posts and beams and greenery provide lots of atmosphere. There's additional outdoor dining on the front and side porches.

The interior dining rooms are more traditional, with white-clothed tables, beamed ceilings and walls enhanced with paintings by local artists. A pot of impatiens decorates each table, inside and out. A huge picture of a dog team and sled dominates the bar.

Chef-owner Ralph Warren used to own the College Inn Restaurant and Lounge in South Hadley, Mass. Here he's gone more upscale with a fairly extensive, changing dinner menu featuring healthful, low-fat choices. Entrees run from vegetarian dishes and raspberry chicken to Montreal peppered sirloin steak and New Zealand rack of lamb with honey, garlic and thyme. Clams casino, marinated herring and chilled shrimp and salsa are among the appetizers. The house wines are some of our favorites from Corbett Canyon.

Upstairs off a long central corridor are ten guest rooms, clean but spartan ($45 to $85). Six have private baths.

(518) 962-4501. Entrées, $12.95 to $18.95. Breakfast daily, 8 to 2. Lunch, 11:30 to 2. Dinner, 5 to 9.

The Essex Inn, Main Street, Essex. (518) 963-8821.

The expanding restaurant taking up the front veranda, three main-floor rooms and a little bar has been upgraded by new chef-owner John Walker, a Culinary Institute graduate. The food has improved, too, and three meals a day are served on a more consistent basis than under previous ownership.

Antiques and period art enhance the candlelit dining rooms, which Trish Walker, the chef's wife and hostess, has tried to make "relaxed and early American."

The short dinner menu features main dishes like sautéed shrimp with sundried tomatoes and mushrooms over angel-hair pasta, boneless pork loin with cider sauce and filet mignon with béarnaise sauce. House salads come with. Starters vary from shrimp cocktail to escargots, grilled portobello mushrooms over greens and bruschetta with mozzarella. Trish prepares the desserts, her signature being warm apple crisp with vanilla ice cream. Chocolate tarts, cheesecakes and fruit pies are others.

Light fare is also available at lunch and dinner.

(518) 963-8821. Entrées, $12.75 to $16.95. Open daily except Tuesday in summer: Breakfast 7:30 to 10. Lunch, 11:30 to 2. Dinner, 5:30 to 9. Off-season: Breakfast Saturday and Sunday, lunch Friday and Saturday, dinner Thursday-Sunday.

Upper Deck at Willsboro Bay Marina, 68 Klein Drive, Willsboro.

This stunning, summery waterside restaurant is the inspiration of sailors James Arvay, a Plattsburgh architect, and Denise Mavor, who has a restaurant background. They combined talents in 1997 to produce a contemporary main dining room on two levels. Six garage doors open to the outside, complimenting a canopied deck on one end and an open deck on the other. The boats in the marina and the Adirondacks across the bay provide all the décor one needs, and the sunsets across the water are spectacular.

Even dreary weather that forced us inside failed to mar a summer lunch. One of us enjoyed a mandarin chicken salad, while the other was happy with a mozzarella flatbread pizza that came with a tasty rice salad.

The highly acclaimed fare is called "casual contemporary," as in dinner dishes of cioppino, tandoori salmon, rotisserie chicken and mixed grill kabobs with Thai peanut marinade over couscous. Starters vary from shrimp rémoulade to escargots bourguignonne. Desserts at our early visit were limited to Minnesota cheesecake, tirami su and vanilla ice cream.

(518) 963-8271. Entrées, $12.95 to $18.95. Lunch and dinner daily in summer, Friday-Sunday through mid-October.

The Galley, Westport Marina, Foot of Washington Street, Westport.

What owners Dee and Bob Carroll call Lake Champlain's most active marina includes a busy restaurant operation in the old sea plane hangar, whose arched roof gives it something of a boathouse feeling. It's a cavernous place, made more cozy with such personal touches as a gallery of Westport waterfront scenes along one wall, newspapers and games in the restored desk from the old freight office on the dock, and a free paperback book exchange in the pigeon-hole pass-throughs once used for selling tickets to steamboat passengers.

The Carrolls keep the place jumping with activities like weekly lakeside barbecues with visiting entertainers on summer Saturday nights.

The extensive, all-day menu is affordably priced. Among specialties are tortilla salad, chicken-chutney-curry salad and teriyaki sirloin sticks from an old family recipe. Complete dinner platters include poached salmon, shrimp and scallop kabobs, and ribeye steak with Montreal pepper sauce.

All this is taken on redwood picnic tables inside or outside under umbrellas beside the boats.

(518) 962-4899. Entrées, $8.50 to $13.25. Breakfast daily, 8 to 11, Sunday to noon. Lunch and dinner, 11 to 8 or 9. Open mid-June through Labor Day.

Diversions

Westport's prime location on one of Lake Champlain's largest bays has always offered a protected port for boats of all kinds. The old steamboat Ticonderoga – now on display across the lake at the Shelburne Museum – berthed here nightly early in the century. Visitors today have considerable access to the lake from the new Ballard Park, the public boat-launching site, the Westport Marina and the Westport Yacht Club.

Westport Walking Tour. An exceptional guide to the town was prepared in 1989 by the Westport Historical Society and the Westport Chamber of Commerce. A 36-page booklet with photos, descriptions and maps outlines the tour, which totals five miles and can be covered in two to three hours. The starting point is the landmark **Westport Library,** a restored beauty whose all-wood interior with cathedral ceiling resembles an Adirondack lodge. The library is as much the dominant force as it is the dominant structure in town. The Library Lawn is the setting for concerts each summer. You'll likely be struck by the number of buildings that at one time served as inns; today, most are private homes.

The Depot Theatre, Pleasant Street, Westport, (518) 962-4449. Westport's refurbished Delaware & Hudson railroad station now serves as a town museum and as the summer home of the professional Depot Theatre (the Amtrak train also stops here daily in each direction on its run between New York and Montreal). Founded in 1979, the equity theater presents four shows a season, one of them sometimes a new American musical, in the old freight room. There are also special mid-week shows and art shows in the depot. Shows generally run for two weeks over long weekends. Adults, $15 to $18.

Meadowmount School of Music, Lewis-Wadhams Road, Westport, (518) 873-2063. Students ranging in age from 8 to 30 converge each summer on this summer school for accomplished young violinists, violists and cellists training for professional careers. You might hear a budding Itzhak Perlman or Yo-Yo Ma, both alumni, at free concerts given in the Memorial Concert Hall Wednesday and Sunday evenings at 7:30.

Essex Tour. This is one interesting village, from the sunburst of mustard and maroon splashed across the facade of the 1800 firehouse greeting visitors at the main intersection in town to the 1790 Wright's Inn now serving as a town office across the street. Twenty-eight village landmarks are detailed in "Essex: An Architectural Guide;" 24 more also are shown in the outlying town. The descriptions plus the accompanying maps make your travels more informed. The entire village is on the National Register and claims one of the more prized collections of Federal, Georgian Revival and Greek Revival architecture in the country.

Sunburst Tea Garden, South Main Street, Essex, (518) 963-7482. The Sorley family serve English cream teas at tables beside a garden with a fountain on their back lawn overlooking the lake in summer, Wednesday-Sunday 2 to 5, weather permitting. Homemade scones with jam and fresh whipped cream, cakes and a variety of teas are featured. They also offer a modest room for overnight guests in their 1813 Cape Cod house.

Shopping. There's not a lot, but the situation is improving – particularly in Essex – and you will find a few places in which to spend your shekels. In Westport, we liked **The Westport Trading Co.** at 2 Pleasant St., where Kip Trienens makes gorgeous stained-glass hangings and lamps. Pottery, baskets, twig furniture, windchimes and birdhouses abound here. **The Bessboro Shop** at 26 Main is a small department store with classic clothing and gifts. Everything for boats and cottages and those who reside in them is available at the **Ship's Store** at the Westport Marina.

If you need a pick-me-up after shopping or walking tours, stop at **McQueen's Food & Fountain** in Westport, a restaurant and ice-cream parlor from yesteryear. Order a fried egg sandwich for $2 or an old-fashioned banana split for $3.50.

Essex, which as recently as the early 1990s had only a couple of stores of note, is experiencing a mini-burst in retailing. **The Store in Essex** on Main Street has changed from an old-fashioned emporium into an upscale center of eclectic folk art, featuring works of New York and Vermont artisans. Sophisticated country woodsy merchandise, collectibles and crafts are offered at **Adirondack Spirit.** Potter Judy Koenig claims her **Sugar Hill Pottery** is the oldest business in town; we particularly liked her teapot with iris, garlic bakers and bowls, all hand-thrown and appealing in earth colors. Hand-dipped candles and accessories are featured at **Adirondack Chandler.** Look for antiques, paintings, garden items and more at **Neighborhood Nest.** At **Natural Goods & Finery,** Sharon Boisen stocks wonderful candles, Vermont honey lights, herbal items, vintage jewelry and clothing with flair. Furniture, clocks, linens, china and collectibles are among the offerings at **Margaret Sayward Antiques.** The works of area artisans, from loon items to sweaters to jewelry, are nicely displayed at **Hand Made.** The little wood cats with the sign "Better to feed one cat than many mice" intrigued at **Wade's Woods and Crafts.** Jim and Mary Wade also design wooden replicas of Essex's Main Street.

Extra-Special _____

Camp Dudley, Camp Dudley Road, Westport. (518) 962-4720.

The historic marker near the entrance designates this as the oldest boys' camp in continuous service in the United States (1885). It's extra-special to one of us, who was a happy camper back in the late 1940s when half the fun was getting there on the special Camp Dudley train from Albany, New York, Syracuse and points beyond. Today's campers fly in from Sri Lanka and St. Louis or drive in with their parents, who boost occupancy rates at local inns and B&Bs. To a venerable alum, the sprawling complex looks the same except for a new-fangled curving slide at Swim Point and an indoor gymnasium with two basketball courts and, sign of the times, a weight-lifting room. Still the same are all the eight-bunk fireplaced cabins spread along the lakeshore and the perimeter of the 250-acre campus, the cavernous Dining Hall, the nightly shows at Witherbee Hall, the activity at Avery Boathouse and enough sports facilities to accommodate 480 campers whose parents spend a small fortune for the month or two-month stay. Casual visitors can introduce themselves at the main office and ask for a look around.

Cooperstown shows its patriotism and serenity in Lakefront Park.

Cooperstown, N.Y.
The All-American Village

Few places its size (population, 2,200) are so embedded in the American consciousness as the upstate New York village of Cooperstown.

Native son novelist James Fenimore Cooper gave it and Otsego Lake, his "Glimmerglass," a romantic place in the history of literature through his *Leatherstocking Tales*. Abner Doubleday supposedly invented the game of baseball here, and the Baseball Hall of Fame stands as the shrine to America's national pastime. The Farmers' Museum captures the spirit of New York State's rural life of the 19th century.

Although Cooper and Doubleday get most of the credit, the impetus for the Cooperstown we know today stemmed from latter-day native sons, the Clark family of Singer sewing machine fame. The house that Edward S. Clark built in 1932 on the Cooper property beside Otsego Lake is now the Fenimore House Museum, a showcase for the New York State Historical Association's masterful collections of folk and decorative art. Stephen C. Clark Sr. paid $5 for an early baseball that led to the formation in 1939 of the National Baseball Hall of Fame. He founded the Farmers' Museum in 1943, the third prong in his visionary effort to develop for Cooperstown a clean industry, tourism. Another prong has emerged with the evolution of the Glimmerglass Opera, thanks to more local benefactors, the Busches of beer fame. A fifth prong arrived in 1993 with the opening of the Corvette Americana Hall of Fame, one newcomer's astonishing tribute to cars and pop culture.

The four museums – celebrating baseball, art, rural life and pop Americana – reflect the essence of small-town America and inspire for Cooperstown the logical moniker, "The Village of Museums." But Cooperstown is no mere display-case relic. It's the living Norman Rockwell town where flower baskets hang from the downtown lamp posts, flags fly in front of homes large and small along its tree-shaded streets, there's only one traffic light and no outside chain store or motel has been allowed to sully its all-American purity.

"Time has stood still here and people fight tooth and nail to keep it that way," says Laura Zucotti, the ex-New York restaurateur who now operates the J.P. Sill House here as a B&B. And well they should. Cooperstown is a neat and tidy-looking community with an air of obvious prosperity. The Bassett Hospital, affiliated with Columbia University, is the village's biggest employer and a training site for doctors. The impressive Clark Sports Center is a multi-purpose counterpoint to baseball's historic Doubleday Field. Main Street is dominated by the institutional presence of the Hall of Fame and the lakeshore by the stately Otesaga resort.

The Otesaga, a few old inns and small up-the-lake motels monopolized visitor accommodations until 1984, when the first B&Bs emerged. That year, four pages in the 36-page Cooperstown Area Guide were devoted to accommodations; a decade later, the guide had swelled to 72 pages, 32 of them for lodgings. Many were opened by former metropolitan New Yorkers who found nirvana here away from the mainstream.

Cooperstown, enveloped in hills, is not really on the way to anywhere else and therefore access is difficult. That helps explain its singularity, but scarcely prepares unsuspecting visitors for what they find – a picturesque lakeside village that's far more than a baseball shrine. Here is a Brigadoon dreamland suspended in time.

Inn Spots

Thistlebrook, County Road 28, RD 1, Box 26, Cooperstown 13326.

Except for a few Gothic-patterned windows, nothing about the facade of this big red barn prepares one for the treasures found inside. Paula and Jim Bugonian, corporate types from the Kingston area, crossed the mountains to visit her parents in Cooperstown, found the 1866 barn, bought it the same day and started creating one of the more dramatic, stylish and all-around comfortable B&Bs anywhere.

"We don't have children," says Paula, "so everything we've done – all the gifts we've given – have been for our home. And we love to share it."

The shared home is also a work in progress. The Bugonians opened with two guest rooms, had five at our last visit, and were finally readying their own quarters in the rear of the barn. In the process, they've thought about, and provided, just about everything a guest could want.

The interior spaces, formerly occupied by working artists who used them as galleries,

Pillared living room of Thistlebrook is an unexpected sight inside an old barn.

soar to ceilings sixteen feet high in the living room. French doors and tall windows open onto an expansive deck, overlooking gardens, trickling water fountains and, beyond, a meadow, stream and hillside alluring to deer, ducks and red-wing blackbirds.

The large living room is elegantly outfitted like the rest of the place in a mix of European and American furnishings and antiques. The dining room holds an antique table big enough to seat twenty, an intricate Queen Anne bar cabinet from which sherry or port are dispensed in the evening, and a 200-year-old Chinese china cabinet that is Paula's pride and joy. The library alcove on the stairway landing harbors an array of books and upscale magazines to occupy guests "since we don't have TV," Paula notes. Sit there beside the window, take a batch to your room, the common areas or the sunken sun room with exercise equipment and a jacuzzi – you'll find the perfect nook or cranny since, as the hostess says, "I love little groupings of seats where people can sit and read or chat."

Such groupings are evident in the spacious guest rooms, all sited on different levels for utmost privacy. Two at the side are light and airy, with windows onto the meadow, white walls and floral prints. One, Paula's favorite, comes with a queen bed set between French kidney-shaped night tables, a comfy chaise and wing chair, a little French armoire and a unique writing desk hidden inside a chest of drawers. Upstairs in the darker front of the house is the master suite, where a kingsize bed resides on a raised platform beneath a nicely angled, vaulted ceiling. It's flanked by plush chairs and faces a wall of books and a sitting area with sofa and an overstuffed chair and ottoman big enough for two. Gothic-style doors lead into a sight-to-behold bathroom with tub, separate shower, bidet and a long double vanity in front of mirrors implanted in a Gothic window frame. Downstairs in front is another bedroom with a kingsize bed and a sitting area. The newest is the former owners' quarters in the upstairs Loft Suite at the far end of the barn. A far cry from its onetime status as a hayloft, this is a substantial, cathedral-ceilinged space with a kingsize mahogany bed (raised to take advantage of the view through wide rear

Opera performers Gwen and Fred Ermlich entertain at Creekside Bed & Breakfast.

windows). Paula has decorated it in rust and soft green for a country gentleman look. The sitting area contains two sofas, an arm chair and a wicker settee.

The Bugonians' brand of hospitality matches their luxurious accommodations. They put out coffee and fruit at 7:30 in the morning, prior to serving a full breakfast with fresh fruit cup, banana or corn bread and a main dish like french toast with ham and browned cinnamon apples, blueberry-orange pancakes, vegetable omelets or lemon-dill scrambled eggs with mini bagels or croissants. Afternoon libations are offered, followed by sherry, chocolates and cookies in the evening.

(607) 547-6093 or (800) 596-9305. Two rooms and three suites with private baths. Doubles, $110 to $135. Closed November-April. No smoking.

Creekside Bed & Breakfast, Fork Shop Road, RD 1, Box 206, Cooperstown 13326.

The hosts at this elegant B&B on the delightfully named Fork Shop Road beside the delightfully named Fly Creek are among the most interesting people around. Fred and Gwen Ermlich – he a former priest and she a onetime Playboy centerfold – helped found and still perform with Glimmerglass Opera. And their B&B digs are a bit theatrical in two rooms, two suites and a cottage, all with private baths, queen or kingsize beds and TV/HBO.

"This is my Saints and Sinners gallery," Gwen said as she led us up the stairs lined with photos from her shows and modeling career, including one as a centerfold (clothed) in the Japanese edition of Playboy magazine in 1970. We were to be ensconced in the Penthouse Suite, an open, third-floor hideaway complete with sitting room and dining area. That was more spacious for a rainy evening than the one we'd booked, the Bridal Chamber, a mostly white cocoon of lace and frills, plus a canopied queen brass bed, a skylight and a beautiful curved armoire. This room has since been enlarged into a suite with an 18-by-22-foot living room harboring a year-round Christmas bridal tree decorated in wedding memorabilia, a parquet floor, tapestries, bisque lamps and a grouping of leather chairs and sofa beneath a crystal chandelier – not to mention a Romeo and Juliet balcony. Less extravagant but functional is the three-room cottage out back, where there's lots of room to spread out on peach-colored sofas in the living room with wet bar beneath a dramatic twenty-arm brass chandelier. The bedroom has a canopied bed, and the dining room and a spacious side deck overlook lawn and creek. The new Garden Room comes with an antique kingsize bed and picture windows overlooking the garden.

The Ermlichs share with guests the rest of their home, including an atrium entry and a wraparound deck off the beamed and paneled rear family room – an expansive space that's perfect for the opera parties the Ermlichs frequently host. "This house is so happy when it's filled with people," Gwen says.

The actress in her demands that she serve her husband's lavish breakfast on a dining-room table set with lace cloth, dainty china, elaborate silver, lit tapers in the candelabra and a showy centerpiece of dried flowers. Tiny white lights twinkle here and there to add to the charm, and she changes the place settings daily so that "the meal becomes as dramatic as an opera." At our visit, orange juice, fresh fruit cocktail and coffee cake preceded Fred's dilled scrambled eggs, bacon, baked apple slices and English muffins, on which we tried Gwen's three sensational liqueur-flavored butters (peach, raspberry and strawberry).

(607) 547-8203. Three rooms, two suites and a cottage with private baths. Doubles, $85 to $100. Suites, $105 and $145. Cottage, $145. Two-night minimum on peak weekends. No smoking.

Angelholm, 14 Elm St., Box 705, Cooperstown 13326.

Painted mint green with dark green trim, this 1805 house on a residential street backs up to Doubleday Field, and guests can frequently hear – if not see – baseball games being played. Fred and Jan Reynolds retired here from Ridgefield, Conn., in 1992 after having stayed frequently with the original owners over five years. "This was almost like moving into our own house," says Jan. They changed the decor from Victorian to Federal, built a small addition to expand the rear side veranda and two rear bedrooms, and added two private baths.

They now offer five air-conditioned bedrooms with private baths, good swivel reading lights over the beds, countless oriental rugs and runners, and collections of dolls here and there. Most in demand are three large corner rooms, two with queensize beds and one with antique twins joined as a king. The Reynoldses have added queen beds and reconfigured the two smaller center bedrooms so that their former hall baths now open en suite. The rear Doubleday Room with antique iron bed and a day bed comes with plush carpeting made out of recycled pop bottles. "We use only recycled stuff in this house," Jan points out.

The hosts share the main floor with guests. The fireplaced living room with fine oriental rugs opens into a snug library with TV and another fireplace. The library opens onto the side veranda, where formal tea or iced tea and lemonade are served in the afternoons and the guests help themselves to Jan's "never-empty cookie jar."

Breakfasts are an occasion. A former caterer who loves good food, Jan offers assorted juices, a fruit course like blueberries with lemon-yogurt sauce or peaches with honey-cinnamon glaze, braided coffee bread with pecans and cinnamon or croissants, sausage or bacon and a main dish like blintzes filled with sour cream and topped with toasted coconut or country egg scramble incorporating red potatoes, leeks, and red and green peppers. Fred, the raconteur, holds forth in the dining room.

(607) 547-2483. Fax (607) 547-2309. Five rooms with private baths. Doubles, $95 to $110. No smoking.

Duke's Oak Bed & Breakfast, Route 80, Box 406, Springfield Center 13468.
On a hillside eight miles north of Cooperstown, this large tan house with beige trim is almost within hearing distance of Glimmerglass Opera House. Which is why Don and Mary Ellen Fenner bought it in 1986 and gradually rescued it, she said, "from wrack and ruin." Glimmerglass boosters (he's treasurer of the Opera Guild), they put up opera crews in their house for years until their daughter and son-in-law, Cynthia and David Staley, returned in 1997 to operate it as a B&B.

Running the turn-of-the-century house was a godsend for Cynthia, who studied hotel and restaurant management at the University of Denver. All the renovations and decorating were completed, and there was room on the third floor for both families. The Staleys operate the B&B, although Mary Ellen says she irons the sheets and plays the breakfast music. The last means she plays the grand piano or the harpsichord in the music room while guests eat breakfast across the hall in the dining room.

The music room is the heart of the house, and it's the room that guests enter through a new rear entrance. Shelves near ceiling level both here and in the front foyer are home to eye-catching collections of bottles, plates and what-not. "Dad's a collector," explains Cynthia. "We have at least three of everything, and that's in the house. There's more of everything stored in the barn." Cynthia was eyeing the barn for another role: a couple of future guest rooms or suites.

On the second floor of the house are three bedrooms with private baths, one with an adjoining queen-bedded room that's rented as a suite. There's a TV and telephone in each room, and each is tastefully outfitted with antique furniture and a secretary desk. The smallest has a double bed. The largest is the master bedroom with queen bed and spacious bath with double vanity.

Out back is the barn-red Acorn Cottage, hidden in the woods up the hill and overlooking a stream in a ravine. Fresh and light, it has a living room and kitchen, bedroom and sleeping loft with double-bedded accommodations for six.

Cynthia cooks pumpkin waffles, blueberry pancakes, omelets or quiches for breakfast. Fresh fruit, homemade granola and muffins accompany.

. The two-bedroom suite is named for its last owner, Thomas Goodyear, "patron saint of Duke's Oak" and donor of the turkey farm property that is now the Glimmerglass site. The Duke's Oak property was home to the late Duke's Oak Theater, which took its name from an obscure quote in Shakespeare's "A Midsummer Night's Dream."

(607) 547-2179. Three rooms and a cottage with private bath. Doubles, $85 to $105. Cottage, $155; two-night minimum. Children over 10. No smoking.

The Bassett House Inn, 32 Fair St., Cooperstown 13326.
Built in 1816 as an inn, this was long occupied by the Bassett family for whom the local hospital is named and is directly across the street from the Hall of Fame. "With a history and location like this," says former Wall Street lawyer Steve Collins, "we couldn't miss." He and wife Peggy were living in Greenwich, Conn., when he decided to quit his job. "We could have just moved to our lake house and died," quipped Peggy. "But my parents and grandparents still go to the Otesaga and I had been coming here since I was a kid, so I said, why not go up to Cooperstown and buy one of those big beauties for a B&B? This was waiting for us and it was a perfect fit."

The Collinses fitted out the handsome Federal-brick house with their Greenwich houseful of antique furnishings, collections (from American clocks and game tables

Ex-banker's Italianate Victorian home is now The J.P. Sill House.

to miniature cannons and guns) and a dash of ingenuity. Everyone seems to want canopy beds, Peggy learned, so she found some netting in the Spiegel catalog and fashioned fancy mesh canopies for beds that lacked them. The second floor has five spacious bedrooms with private baths, all but one with queensize beds (it has two twins joined as a king). All have sitting areas, TVs and antiques, and a couple are appointed in high Victorian style. We think the nicest is the rear room with windows on three sides, light and airy in white, where versatile Peggy has painted trees on the walls and draped ivy over the lace curtains.

Continental breakfast is served stylishly in the Victorian dining room. Cut-up fruit comes in a crystal punch bowl and coffee and tea in silver pots. Cereals, danish pastries and donuts complete the repast, which may be taken on trays to the large dining table or out to the enclosed side brick piazza and flagstone terrace, facing a hedge-rimmed lawn, geraniums, a fountain and sturdy cedar lawn chairs that Peggy picked from a catalog. Several dozen clocks tick and board games and a pool table occupy prominent positions in a games room that once was a living room. The seating area is now in the enclosed piazza solarium, exceptionally stylish with plants, artworks and Peggy's stenciled willow branches on the walls.

(607) 547-7001. Fax (607) 547-6009. Five rooms with private baths. Doubles, $115 to $135. No children. No smoking.

The J.P. Sill House, 63 Chestnut St., Cooperstown 13326.

The architectural magnificence of this yellow brick Italianate Victorian built in 1864 by Cooperstown bank president Jedediah P. Sill has landed it on both the state and national historic registers. Add its remarkably lavish handprinted Victorian wallcoverings, prized antiques and an aura of status cultivated by the innkeepers, former owners of New York's famed El Morocco restaurant. The accommodations are fit for royalty, though it's hard to imagine royalty sharing bathrooms, as do people in four of the seven guest quarters here.

Angelo and Laura Zucotti literally stumbled upon Cooperstown shortly after they closed El Morocco in 1988 because of a decline in their carriage trade. "I'd always wanted a B&B," she said. "We found this house and thought, wouldn't it be nice to fix it up?" The sale was closed in three weeks and they started restorations designed to make the carriage trade take note.

The most striking aspects of the decor are the reproductions of Victorian wallpaper designs created by William Morris and others. The front parlor sports seven different papers on the walls and even the ceiling; the dining room has eight. The parlor is awash in oriental rugs, Victorian furnishings, bookcases reproduced by a preservationist and a replica of the house holding a TV inside. Decanters of port and sherry await guests here, and the Zucottis offer complimentary drinks from a full bar.

Japanese-Italianate paper adorns the dining room, where El Morocco's first menu from 56 years ago hangs framed near the kitchen door. Here is offered a bountiful buffet breakfast: perhaps strawberries and cream, fresh juice, homemade granola and a savory entrée, maybe a puff pastry, salmon en croûte or ham and cheese. Laura, who studied at the Cordon Bleu, is known for her lemon and coconut breads. On Sundays she likes to serve a smoked salmon platter and cream cheese along with the New York Times. The repast is taken around the formal table, set with tapestry mats atop a lace cloth, or on the wicker-filled side porch off the dining room.

A front corner of the main floor is given over to a suite that's arguably the most extravagant in town. It's the only guest accommodation with a private bath in the main house. And what a bathroom – a huge space with a whirlpool tub and a vibrator for one's back, a wicker rocker and chair, floral wallpaper and windows onto the side lawn. The suite, decorated by Laura Ashley's son, is papered with eight different patterns to represent the Iris and the Dragonfly. A Laura Ashley duvet covers the ornate queensize brass bed angled in a corner and an armoire hides the TV/VCR and stereo system facing an armchair and two wicker chairs.

Upstairs are four more guest rooms, all with queensize beds and more showy wallpapers. One has a wicker sitting area. Another has a fireplace, a signed Eastlake armoire and a new powder room with Laura Ashley appointments. The four rooms share two bathrooms, one containing the original pewter tub and a new shower and the other with shower only.

Constantly upgrading, Laura has acquired Frette bedspreads from Italy for summer, to stand in for the Laura Ashley quilts and goose down comforters she favors in winter. She also furnishes linen bathrobes for summer, Ashley robes for winter. All bathrooms are outfitted with hair dryers, shaving mirrors and a complete line of Perlière toiletries.

The Zucottis aren't through yet, however. On the third floor are three servant's rooms that they hope to convert into one long gaming room with a billiards table. At the side of the house is a carriage house they recently converted from apartments into a pair of two-bedroom suites designed for families. Each has sitting room, dining area, kitchen and bedrooms with queen and double beds. They're furnished with antiques and wicker in what Laura calls "Laura Ashley Welch cottage style in the palest primrose colors." Telephones and TV/VCRs are among the extras.

(607) 547-2633. Four rooms with shared baths and three suites with private baths. Doubles, $100. Suite, $150. Two-bedroom suites $175, $225 for four. No smoking.

The Inn at Cooperstown, 16 Chestnut St., Cooperstown 13326.
Built in 1874 in Second Empire French style as the annex to the old Fenimore Hotel across the street, this is the baby of Michael Jerome, a Cornell Hotel School

Strawberry Hill Farm faces field of wildflowers and backs up to English gardens.

grad and preservationist from Elmira, who occupies an apartment on the property with his wife. He acquired the hotel in 1985 and quickly received a state historical preservation award for a painstaking restoration that is ongoing.

The exterior is strikingly handsome. Inside, the eighteen rooms with private baths on two upper floors vary. One rear room with a queensize bed was barely big enough for a chair and a dresser. Rooms are advertised as having twins or queensize beds, although a couple we saw were set up differently: one with two twins and a matching day bed, and another with a kingsize bed that we were told was available only for walk-ins.

Frilly sheer curtains, country decor and basic furniture are the rule, although Michael points out that he is continually adding furnishings. Half have renovated bathrooms with hair dryers and toiletries, and more baths are being redone each year. Some have unusual tiled corner showers with new terrazzo bases that, except for the wraparound curtain, are open to the rest of the bathroom.

The main floor offers two pleasant sitting rooms in a double parlor, where a television set and telephone are available. Complimentary coffee, juice and home-made breads and muffins are served in a couple of small breakfast rooms. Rocking chairs on the wide front veranda offer relaxation and a view of the passing scene.

(607) 547-5756. Fax (607) 547-5756. Eighteen rooms with private baths. Doubles, $98 to $110 in summer, $95 to $102 in spring and fall, $85 in winter.

Strawberry Hill Farm, Greenough Road, RD 3, Box 245, Cooperstown 13326.
"Peace and quiet" are what Jocelyn Rauscher and her husband Andrew, a physician at Bassett Hospital, like most about their 120-acre farm. They offer two grand rooms with private baths and television, as well as abundant common space and gardens. With their children off to college, the Rauschers have plenty more room options, although Jocelyn says she quite likes her sitting room and her husband likes his, so further guest rooms in the rambling three-story Federal farmhouse with seven working fireplaces are in limbo.

Meantime, guests enjoy their own handsome rear living room with fireplace and a formal dining room and frequently spill into the enormous country kitchen, which opens onto the hosts' family room. A front main-floor bedroom has a lace canopy queensize bed and a small bathroom with a stunning European sink handpainted with flowers. Upstairs is a secluded bedroom with queen wicker bed, ivy stenciling and dark green carpeting, and Gilbert & Soames toiletries in the full bath. A connecting bedroom with twin beds is available for families.

The British-born Rauschers' floral interests are manifest in the delightful English gardens they have created in back. Water trickles in fountains, morning glories climb a trellis and a rope hammock beckons. If you don't become immobilized here, you can amble along the walking path they have blazed through the eight-acre field of wildflowers across the road.

Jocelyn prepares a continental breakfast with fresh fruit salad, croissants, and homemade zucchini bread or muffins.

(607) 547-8619. Two rooms with private baths. Doubles, $75 ($85 in August). No smoking. Closed November to April.

Overlook Bed & Breakfast, 8 Pine Blvd., Cooperstown 13326.

Another family home, this one along a stately boulevard near the heart of town, the Overlook has been taking guests since 1989 when six of Jack and Gayle Smith's seven children had left the nest. The main section of a manse that required five servants in its heyday dates to 1888.

A harmonium in the foyer and an extensive collection of music boxes hints at this family's musical interests. A spacious, fireplaced living room has lots of seating and oriental rugs. A corner TV room contains a leather sofa and a wall of family pictures. Guests help themselves to an extended continental breakfast on the sideboard in the fireplaced dining room; they can eat there at a table for six or head outside to one of the commodious porches.

Upstairs are three light and spacious guest rooms and a suite, created when the Smiths vacated the master suite and "moved up to the servants' quarters – which was quite fitting," Gayle quips. That opened up a huge room with queensize poster bed, a sitting area with a beige leather sofa that converts to a bed in front of a console TV, a large bath and walk-in closet. A room in the front corner has a double four-poster bed; it shares a hall bath with a larger turret room, pretty in blue and pink with twin poster beds, a floral sofa and a wall of decorative plates from the musical "Annie." A rear room with a double poster bed enjoys a private bath and small sitting area.

(607) 547-5178. Fax (607) 547-7052. One room and one suite with private baths; two rooms with shared bath. Summer: doubles, $80 to $95; suite, $125. Rest of year: doubles, $75 to $85; suite, $99. Two-night minimum weekends most of year. Children accepted.

Toad Hall, Route 28, RD 1, Box 120, Fly Creek 13337.

A dead tree carved into a totem pole with all kinds of critters marks the entrance to one of the more unusual B&Bs we've encountered. The tree was planted around 1820, when the house was built near the hamlet of Oaksville. Allen Ransome and Randy VanSyoc, owners of the fabulous Toad Hall store in Cooperstown, bought the house in 1988 and have turned it into a mini-folk-art museum that was the subject of a photo spread in Country Living magazine.

The living room walls are covered with murals in the style of Rufus Porter. In the book and art-filled library is a Thai temple guardian. A collection of Pennsylvania redware decorates the dining room, and even the kitchen is filled with folk art. On the 80 acres of property are walking trails and a trout pond. The men raise and show Newfoundland dogs.

Staying in one of the four upstairs guest rooms would be like staying in a museum, a rather eclectic one. Paintings from Allen's travels in India adorn the India Room, outfitted with a tiger maple queensize bed, a chaise lounge and a TV. Its hall bath is shared by a small single room. The walls and floors of the other two baths, both private, are made of slate. The Bovine Room with another queen bed has, you guessed it, cows painted on the dresser and on a twig chair, plus a collection of frogs. The Trinidad Room is named for a friend, Trinidad Gilmore, who painted its incredible wall mural of animals toting furniture to Toad Hall. The room has a queen poster bed, a French Victorian loveseat and an armchair.

At breakfast, taken on the long wooden table in the fireplaced dining room, a big espresso machine provides frothy cappuccino or caffe latte. Seasonal fresh fruit, juices, waffles, pancakes, french toast with homemade bread and New York maple syrup make up the fare. The hosts like to use local eggs, butter, milk, cheddar, ham and sausage.

On the pillared veranda out front, even the Adirondack chairs are the background for some wonderful art.

(607) 547-5774. Two rooms with private baths and two rooms with shared bath. Doubles, $85. No smoking.

The White House Inn, 46 Chestnut St., Cooperstown 13326.

A large back-yard swimming pool, screened from neighbors by tall hedges, is a draw at this new B&B in an 1835 Greek Revival house listed in the national historic registry. So are the fancy breakfasts offered by Marjorie and Edward Landers, who took over the former dentist's office and residence in 1996.

Gregarious Ed refers to four "areas" rather than guest rooms as he leads a tour of the rambling, 21-room structure, which is deceptively small on the outside and strikes some as a hodgepodge inside. One area is a family apartment above the former dental office with a living room, kitchen and two bedrooms, one with twin day beds and the other with a queen bed and a crib. Another area is on the main floor of a wing off the Greek Revival structure. Here are a more traditional configuration: a front bedroom with queen bed, chocolate brown walls, antique furnishings and private bath, and a mini-suite with a small library/TV room, bath and a bedroom with a queensize bed that Marjorie draped with a curtain-like canopy to cover up an unused door. Upstairs in this wing are the third and fourth areas, actually a family suite with a room with twin beds, a hall bath and a sitting room with futon and TV. Beyond, available separately or jointly, is another bedroom with queen bed and private bath.

Marge, an artist, has decorated with her paintings and creations made with artificial flowers. Her artistry takes another dimension at breakfast, served formally on Rosenthal china in the smallest dining room you ever saw, a windowless affair sandwiched in the middle of the house between a front parlor, the mini-suite and a large, fireplaced gathering room at the rear. Typical fare includes juice, homemade muffins, a pineapple boat filled with fruit and a main dish, such as scrambled eggs with cream cheese and chives or baked french toast with a caramel bottom.

Marge was about to turn her artistry to a stairwell when Hall of Fame inductee

Rockers on circular porch are great for taking in view of lake at The Otesaga Hotel.

Phil Niekro stayed here in 1997. He and other athletes left their signatures for posterity on the bare wall, prompting Ed to start a Wall of Fame. He was converting a rear house carriage into a small conference area.

(607) 547-5054 or (607) 547-1100. Three rooms and two family suites with private baths. Doubles, $95 and $100. Family suite and apartment, $165 for four. No smoking.

Cooper Inn, Main and Chestnut Streets, Box 311, Cooperstown 13326.

On broad lawns in the center of town, this distinguished brick mansion dating to 1812 is owned by the famed Otesaga resort hotel. It's quite inn-like, with a graceful double parlor and TV/game room off the entry foyer, and a cozy breakfast room in which donuts and danish are served at five tables.

The facility's ten rooms and five suites are all quite different, furnished in period hotel style with double or twin beds, desks, TV sets, telephones, walk-in closets and non-working fireplaces. The wing hidden behind dense trees contains five two-bedroom suites. Guests here have access to all the facilities of the Otesaga, a short drive away.

For 1998, all public and guest rooms were being totally redecorated, with spiffy new fabrics and window treatments. As a result, the entire inn is now non-smoking.

(607) 547-2567 or (800) 348-6222. Ten rooms and five suites with private baths. Doubles, $150. Two-bedroom suites, $225 for four. Lower rates in off-season. No smoking.

The Otesaga Hotel, 60 Lake St., Cooperstown 13326.

No mention of Cooperstown lodging facilities would be complete without a reference to one of New York's grand resort hotels, opened in 1909 and still owned by the Clark family. A doorman beneath a columned portico and a palatial lobby in green and red chintz greet arriving visitors; a pianist plays in the lobby during afternoon tea. A sweeping rear veranda looks across the pool, a luncheon terrace and the broad lawns to Otsego Lake, with an eighteen-hole golf course beside.

The four-story brick hotel offers 124 rooms, six parlor suites and eight two-bedroom suites. The standard rooms are nicer than we had been led to expect, fresh in pale blue with twin beds, two armchairs, yellow floral spreads and curtains, lamp stands painted with flowers, television sets and large, modern baths. The six deluxe parlor rooms are quite spiffy in wicker with matching fabrics.

A sumptuous breakfast buffet and prix-fixe dinners are served in two beautiful, connecting dining rooms, while a lunch buffet is available on the Lakeside Patio. Lunch and dinner also are served in the casual new Hawkeye Bar & Grill (see Dining Spots), a favorite of locals. There's live music with dancing nightly in the Templeton Lounge. Jackets are required for the evening meal in the dining room and are strongly recommended after 6 p.m. in all public rooms except the Hawkeye Bar & Grill, which is now open year-round..

(607) 547-9931 or (800) 348-6222. Fax (607) 547-1271. One hundred twenty-four rooms and fourteen suites with private baths. Rates MAP: doubles, $270 to $295 in summer, $260 to $285 in off-season. Suites, $345 to $390 in summer, $325 to $370 in off-season. Open mid-April through October.

Dining Spots

Gabriella's On the Square, 161 Main St., Cooperstown.

Albany waitress Donna Marquardt found she liked the restaurant business so much that she and husband Bob opened their own in 1997. They gutted a former restaurant facing a main downtown intersection, redesigned it with what Donna called a country French provincial look and prevailed upon Albany chef David Neil, a Culinary Institute of America graduate, to join them. They offer haute contemporary cuisine with an Italian accent for lunch and dinner.

Heavy white linens and cut-glass shaded oil lamps on the tables, swagged lace curtains on the windows, pale yellow walls and gas fireplaces convey a warm, elegant look in two dining rooms seating about 80. The seasonal menu offers pasta dishes like shrimp and scallops with crimini mushrooms and peas in lobster cream sauce with linguini. Main courses could be grilled ginger swordfish with fruit salsa, tuna steak au poivre, roast duck glazed with honey and Old Slugger pale ale, and herb-crusted rack of lamb with roasted garlic jus, each with its own distinctive accompaniments.

Starters include a pan-fried lump crab and crawfish cake that one partaker said was to die for, and a grilled portobello mushroom topped with provolone cheese and roasted peppers. Laura Neil, the chef's wife, makes a signature tirami su along with a chocolate terrine, granitas and lemon soufflé.

(607) 547-8000. Entrées. $17.95 to $19.95. Lunch daily in summer, 11:30 to 2. Dinner, 5 to 9 or 10, to 11 in summer, Sunday 1 to 7:30.

The Blue Mingo Grill, West Lake Road (Route 80), Cooperstown.

The area's hottest seasonal dining ticket lately has been this lakeside establishment with the odd name (taken, co-owner Michael Moffat says, from the local Indian tribe of Blue Mingo who appeared in the works of James Fenimore Cooper).

Now featuring the creative grill cuisine of a chef from New York's famed Arcadia Restaurant, this started simply in 1987 as a hot-dog stand called Dot's Landing behind Sam Smith's Boatyard, about two miles north of Cooperstown. The original cook's brother is now the chef, Larry Kohn, who spices the cuisine with the fruits of his off-season travels through the Far East. The hot-dog stand's founders, Sam Smith's daughter Cory and husband Michael, now run the restaurant and boatyard (plus several Cooperstown retail ventures) in partnership with another daughter, Robin, and her husband Jaime Butchard.

Here, two Adirondack-style dining porches open off the marina store. The Moffats polyurethaned the tables with local memorabilia, hung watery artifacts on the walls and dress the place with linens and flowers at night. Diners look across the lake to Kingfisher Tower as they sample such starters as Indian griddled corn cakes with smoked salmon and sour cream, oven-roasted quail with grilled sweet potato and port, and wild mushroom and goat cheese napoleon.

The contemporary/fusion menu changes nightly, but expect main courses like grilled salmon with red pepper marmalade, grilled lobster with roast corn butter, roast duck with chipotle sauce, and coriander-crusted New York strip steak with oven-roasted tomatoes. House salads, grilled mixed vegetable skewers and roast garlic mashed potatoes or house rice accompany.

The lunch menu ranges equally widely, from Asian grilled chicken on vermicelli to the boatyard dog, the hot dog that made Dot's Landing famous.

(607) 547-7496. Entrées, $15.95 to $22.95. Lunch daily in summer, 11:30 to 2:30. Dinner, 5 to 10. Closed Monday-Tuesday in off-season and Columbus Day to Memorial Day.

The 1819 House, County Route 11 at Greenough Road, Cooperstown.
Local consensus anointed the old Terrace Café as best in town during its heyday. Now relocated to a larger, more historic structure several miles south, it seems to be a case of out of sight, out of mind. People mention it when prompted, but seldom volunteer it in their list of dining favorites.

Owner Robert Paul and Baltimore-trained chef Lynn Hathaway have maintained the Terrace's culinary tradition in a trio of nicely restored upstairs dining rooms and a downstairs tavern with a stone fireplace. "We try to do things nobody else around here does," says Lynn, citing particularly his seafood and veal dishes, including veal london broil with mustard sauce, a specialty.

If not exactly cutting-edge, Manhattan style, the fare has its moments, as in the tangy goat-cheese lasagna, layered with prosciutto and marinara sauce, a dish we found surprisingly refined, and the veal scaloppine sautéed with zucchini, tomatoes and pernod. The crab cakes and grilled andouille sausage with creole mustard are favorite starters. The specialty dessert, bread pudding with a delicious whiskey sauce, is so rich that a little goes a long way.

A tavern menu offers lighter fare.

(607) 547-1819. Entrées, $12.95 to $17.95. Dinner, Tuesday-Sunday 5 to 9 or 10.

The Hawkeye Bar & Grill, Lake Street, Cooperstown. The casual American grill on the lower level of the Otesaga resort has leapt into the forefront of local dining favorites lately, so much so that it's now open year-round.

As compared with the fancy upstairs Dining Room and Lakeside Patio, which are considered special-occasion places and rather stodgy, the grill fare is more contemporary and the decor casual in pink and dark green with white exposed pipes overhead. It's immensely popular with people who like the Otesaga cachet, the lakeside setting and the reasonable prices. They speak highly of such dinner entrées as Eastern salmon steak with orange vinaigrette, grilled shrimp wrapped in prosciutto, spice-rubbed chicken with peach relish and marinated lamb london broil. You can settle for a burger, a sandwich, a caesar salad or a risotto, or graze on appetizers like an onion blossom, crab cakes, green chile wontons or an antipasto. Sandwiches, salads and some of the dinner appetizers are available for lunch.

Like most resorts of its ilk, the Otesaga's upstairs is a local favorite for a summer lunch or Sunday brunch on the outdoor terrace or in the beautiful, chandeliered dining room all in pristine white with red accents. We headed here for lunch, until we found they weren't serving outside on a mild September day and the lunch buffet in the dining room cost $13 for an array that looked like a glorified salad bar with seafood newburg, rice and green beans at the end.

The fancy setting lends itself less to a quick weekday lunch than to a leisurely Sunday brunch. The extra tab for brunch ($17.50) yields scrambled eggs, roast turkey and steamship round as well as the salad-y fare and the venue is usually on the outside terrace overlooking the lake.

The printed dinner menu (prix-fixe, $29) changes daily. Au courant choices are mixed in with traditional fare, offering a range from fresh fruit cup with sherbet to belgian endive with ham mousse, prime rib with yorkshire pudding to broiled lamb chops with baked tomato and mint jelly, bread pudding with English sauce to chocolate ice cream pie with marshmallow topping.

(607) 547-9931. Hawkeye Bar & Grill, entrées, $13 to $18.50, lunch daily, 11:30 to 3; dinner nightly, 6 to 9:30. Dining Room, lunch or brunch on Lakeside Patio, depending on weather, noon to 2; dinner nightly, 6 to 8:30; jackets required.

Black Bart's B-B-Q, 64 Main St., Cooperstown.

"It ain't for sissies," says the trademark for this long, narrow downtown storefront that serves specialties of the South and Southwest. Local foodies gave it high marks for solicitous service and quality fare.

Pass the open kitchen and settle at one of the booths and tables in the back, where colorful papier-mâché Mexican figures soar overhead. The chef does a lot of Texas and Louisiana specials, from jambalaya to baby back ribs, smoked in the restaurant's own smoker. Everything is made from scratch except for the potato chips, the manager advised. Highly rated are the barbecued beef and pork and the smoked beef, pork and turkey, served on French bread, with a choice of baked beans, potato salad, coleslaw or "papafritas." Expect to find also the usual Tex-Mex items, as well as salads and sandwiches.

There's a beer and wine license. Ice-cream sundaes head the dessert list.

(607) 547-5656. Entrées. $7.95 to $16.95. Open Monday-Wednesday 11 to 8, Thursday-Saturday 11 to 10.

Diversions

In baseball land, you'd expect to find a baseball theme, from the Short Stop restaurant and the Walker Gallery ("the fine art of baseball") to the Cooperstown Bat Co. But there's much more to this appealing village, some of which we concentrate upon here.

National Baseball Hall of Fame and Museum, Main Street, Cooperstown.

Enshrined here in 1939 on the apparently erroneous theory that Abner Doubleday invented the game in Cooperstown a century earlier, the four floors dedicated to America's national pastime are what draw most visitors to Cooperstown. This is a museum in which hordes of men and boys stand mesmerized for hours – in front of an old uniform, a signed baseball, a recital of statistics. Since a major addition in 1979, it has been transformed from a primitive museum with tabletop glass cases and encyclopedic sweep into a scattershot, state-of-the-art story of the game. The zoom-in, flashback approach is tailor-made for today's attention spans and the increasing enormity of the subject matter. Ever expanding, the museum opened a new National Baseball Library & Archive complex with exhibits on "Scribes and Mikemen," and in 1997 launched a major exhibition featuring Jackie Robinson and the African-American baseball experience. Everyone has his favorites (ours include the section on baseball parks and the lifelike statues of Babe Ruth and Ted Williams carved from single pieces of laminated basswood); others prefer the awesome cathedral dedicated to the more than 200 Hall of Famers or the statistics spewed out by IBM computers. Who can fail to appreciate the magic of the animated, thirteen-minute multi-media presentation in the Grandstand Theater? The audience sits in grandstand seats, shouts of "play ball" and "get your popcorn here" punctuate the ever-so-realistic crowd noise, the organ pumps up the fans and, well, it's almost like being in the old ballpark. Little wonder that everyone joins in the rousing "Take Me Out to the Ballgame" finale. Visitors exit through the ultimate baseball gift shop.

(607) 547-9988. Open daily, May-October 9 to 9, rest of year 9 to 5, to 8 on weekends except January-March. Adults, $9.50.

The Farmers' Museum, Lake Road, Cooperstown.

This, not the Hall of Fame, was the primary destination for our seventh-grade class trip back in upstate New York in the late 1940s. The museum, only five years old at the time, was already known among educators and made a worthwhile outing for a day's immersion in early New York State history. The main barn displays agricultural artifacts and early crafts. Nearby is the relocated resting spot of the memorable Cardiff Giant, originally foisted on an unsuspecting public as a petrified prehistoric man and looking mighty big to seventh-graders. Beyond is the Village Crossroads, a dozen historic buildings assembled from within 100 miles of Cooperstown, nestled against the hillside with cows grazing and chickens wandering about nearby. Buildings are furnished and staffed for the period. The Toddsville Store has a cast-iron stove, a printing office issues leaflets and the old Bump Tavern ought to dispense food and grog instead of relegating visitors to the mundane but reasonably priced fare of the nearby snack bar called the Herder's Cottage Restaurant, which has picnic tables out front. But on a gorgeous autumn day, strolling the grounds, admiring the old buildings and looking across the stone walls to the golf course, Otsego Lake and the flaming hillsides, we grownups felt this was close to paradise.

(607) 547-1450. Open daily 9 to 5, June-August; daily 10 to 5, September-October; Tuesday-Sunday 10 to 4, April and November; Friday-Sunday 10 to 4 in December. Adults $9.

Fenimore House Museum, Lake Road, Cooperstown.

Magnificent, yet somehow personal and homey, is the lakeside edifice built in 1932 on the site of novelist James Fenimore Cooper's farm. It's been the home of the New York State Historical Association since 1945. The stately portico leads to room after room of fine and decorative arts. A twelve-minute slide show provides a good orientation, and the descriptions throughout the galleries are unusually informative. The paintings in the ballroom include many from the Hudson River School. Thomas Cole's landscape scene from Cooper's *Last of the Mohicans* is especially appropriate in a gallery holding works associated with the novelist. Changing portions of the association's unsurpassed collection of folk art are displayed. The American Indian Wing exhibits the acclaimed Eugene and Clare

Thaw Collection of more than 500 works of American Indian art. The new Fenimore Café offers a light, Italian-based menu.

(607) 547-1400. Open daily, June-August 9 to 5; daily 10 to 4, September-October; Tuesday-Sunday 10 to 4, April and November; Friday-Sunday 10 to 4 in December. Adults $9.

Corvette Americana Hall of Fame, Route 28 South, Cooperstown.

What could be more related than "baseball, hot dogs, apple pie and Chevrolet," as the old ad campaign suggested? The first three were already associated with Cooperstown, so this was a logical site for Allen Schery's one-man tribute to Corvette and American pop culture. The son of a New York City fireman, the graying, pony-tailed Corvette collector, cultural anthropologist and former rock band manager spent more than $7 million to realize his life-long dream in a warehouse-style arena that's bigger than the Baseball Hall of Fame it emulates. He personally oversaw every detail, from photographing the mural backdrops on two whirlwind 1991 cross-country jaunts to editing the lively audio-visual presentations that accompany. His 35 heavy-hitter collector Corvettes are displayed each in their own color-coordinated Hollywood sets that Allen calls "time tunnels," complete with TV, movie, news and sports snippets and commercials from the year involved. The extravaganza starts with the first 1953 model (the year he was born). It shows Allen's first white convertible bearing a sticker price of $3,860 (it's now worth $125,000) and a life-size cutout of Marilyn Monroe, plus posters and artifacts of her films from that year. The museum integrates each Corvette into the cultural milieu from which it emerged. The backdrops (from Ebbets Field to the Golden Gate), the featured pop heroes (from James Dean to Madonna) and the memorabilia (from hula hoops to pet rocks) are the images and symbols of Americana as portrayed by Schery. His collections are awesome; the 1978 display of Chevrolet billboards touting the 25th anniversary of Corvette stresses that "these are the original billboards – they are not reproductions." The museum also contains an interior display room featuring every Corvette sales brochure, plastic model, magazine, wheel cover and owner's manual ever made. The whole astonishing affair is dedicated to Woody Guthrie of "This Land Is Your Land" fame: "What Woody did with a guitar and a song has been done here with a camera and a car." Baseball star Reggie Jackson was so impressed that he put his 1963 Corvette on indefinite loan here.

(607) 547-4135. Open daily, 9:30 to 8 in summer, to 6 rest of year. Adults, $9.50.

Sightseeing. Catch the **Cooperstown Trolley** for a scenic ride between three free outlying parking lots and the village's major attractions. The trolley runs daily from 8:30 a.m. to 9 p.m. in summer and 8:30 to 6 on weekends in late spring and early fall. An all-day pass costs $1.50. This may be the best way to get around on busy days, when visitors outnumber the resident population. The Lake and Valley Garden Club publishes a brochure outlining a walking tour of 44 local sights. **Classic Boat Tours** offers daily hour-long excursions on Otsego Lake aboard an all-wooden boat that cruised the lake at the turn of the century for the Clark and Busch families; adults, $8.50.

Shopping. Baseball cards and paraphernalia are on sale everywhere, of course, from the **Seventh Inning Stretch** to **Mickey's Place** (for Mickey Mantle memorabilia) to **Cap City,** which sprung up to capitalize on the baseball cap craze. Even the venerable **Church & Scott Pharmacy** sells baseball bats. Check out the suave, decorated Christmas tree with a baseball orientation in the window at **A**

Cooperstown Christmas. A long garden path leads to the hidden courtyard outside **Moon Dreams,** an inspirational music, book, crafts and jewelry store; it offers a pleasant tea room and café with pastries, international lunches and light suppers. The prime place for deli items, cheeses, Artisan breads and baked goods from an open-hearth bakery, gourmet coffees and specialty foods is the upscale **Danny's Main Street Market. Tin Bin Alley** offers gourmet jelly beans and bins of candies along with gifts. Other good shops include **Global Traders, Muskrat Hill** for gifts and specialty foods, **Willis Monie** for used and rare books, **Homescapes** for decorating, and **Metro Fashion** and **The Purple Star** for women's clothing

Three of the best shops are on Pioneer Street. The works of 50 artisans are shown at **Leather Originals,** which displays Native American crafts, wood carvings, leather gameboards and purses. **Lake Classic Designs** stocks select gifts and, upstairs, fine women's apparel. **Toad Hall** is a showcase for the most incredible pottery, crafts, gourmet foods and more. Here are imports from across the world, as well as many items by local artists. We coveted a table with frogs for legs, not to mention a bed with bears at the head and foot. From fancy soaps to Hudson Bay blankets, everything here is fascinating and fits in with that certain look sought by owners Allen Ransome and Randy VanSyoc, who also operate the stylish Toad Hall B&B here and a Toad Hall branch at ABC Home Furnishings in New York.

Just north of town in Fly Creek are two worthy side-by-side destinations. **Fly Creek Cider Mill** is a complex of weathered buildings dispensing a variety of ciders, plus apple bread, apple butter, apple pies, candied apples, specialty food items and much more. You can watch cider being made from a vantage point upstairs off the gift shop, where the owner sells pretty dried arrangements from flowers and weeds she collects and air dries. Exotic ducks frequent the pond out back. At the nearby **Christmas Barn** you'll also find really special Christmas things. Dozens of trees, all with different themes, display hundreds of ornaments. Just about everything else for Christmas decorating is here as well.

Extra-Special

Glimmerglass Opera Festival, Route 80, Cooperstown.

The high retractable walls roll down as the lights dim in the 900-seat Alice Busch Opera Theater on Thomas Goodyear's former turkey farm above the lake that James Fenimore Cooper called Glimmerglass. The sense of drama heightens as another performance by one of the nation's best regional companies begins. Founded in 1975, this has become a major attraction. The $5 million, semi-open-air theater funded in 1987 by the Busch family represents the first major opera house built from scratch in America in several decades. And a sophisticated place it is for so rural a setting. The gilded ceiling is staggered in a quilt pattern for acoustical purposes, lamps adorn the balconies and the European-opera-house look is elegant and intimate, remarkable for a building designed to resemble a hops barn. Catered picnics may be ordered ahead and consumed beside a reflecting pond or on the hillside across the road, overlooking Otsego Lake. "Opera previews," free 35-minute programs, are scheduled one hour before performances. Thirty-eight performances of four operas run in repertory from early July to late August.

(607) 547-2255. Box 191, Cooperstown. Matinees, Sunday, Monday and occasionally Tuesday and Saturday at 2; evenings, Thursday-Saturday at 8. Tickets, $19 to $70.

Cazenovia Lake is on view from balcony outside Harden Room at Brewster Inn.

Cazenovia, N.Y.

Picture-Perfect Place

There's little commercial hoopla surrounding Cazenovia and its lake. No visitor information center (not even a tourist booth or a Chamber of Commerce office). No brochures touting its attractions. No marinas or amusement parks. No chain stores or fast-food restaurants, a solitary McDonalds at the far edge of town excepted. The weekly newspaper claims on its masthead to be Cazenovia's oldest industry.

And yet the knowledgeable traveler has likely heard of this picture-perfect village, much of it still wrapped in the 19th century, at the end of Cazenovia Lake. It offers three full-service inns of considerable renown, and bed and breakfasts are popping up. It possesses enough historic structures to prompt the Cazenovia Preservation Foundation to produce a brochure outlining five walks in the village of Cazenovia and another detailing five drives in the surrounding township. It harbors a small college that adds activity to an already sophisticated community. It has a much-photographed main street whose storefronts are occupied by local entrepreneurs, most of them thriving. An outlying suburb of Syracuse but with an identity of its own, it exudes an unmistakable air of prosperity.

Despite its lakeside setting beside sylvan hills 1,250 feet above sea level, this is no summer resort. It did have something of that reputation in the late 1800s when lakeside farms gave way to estates with their summer "cottages" and some of the nation's first tennis courts and golf courses were laid out here. Today, summer greenery blocks water views for motorists who circle the four-mile-long Cazenovia Lake along East and West Lake Roads to look at the substantial year-round homes. Lake access is limited to town residents and their guests.

The opening of the New York Thruway some twenty miles to the north in the 1950s stifled the development of Cazenovia and nearby towns along U.S. Route 20, the old Lincoln Highway that spanned the continent on the path the stagecoaches took.

This area turned its isolation to advantage, however. Cazenovia retained much of its early character, which had been inspired by young Dutch naval officer John Lincklaen. He established a Holland Land Company office beside the lake in 1793 and named his new community in honor of Theophilus de Cazenove, the Philadelphia-based banker for the Dutch investors. Most of the village is listed on the National Register of Historic Places.

To the east, sleepy Bouckville and Madison have become a mecca for antiquers, lining Route 20 with 39 antiques shops in the space of a few miles and staging the East's second largest outdoor antiques show every August.

Visitors are drawn by Cazenovia's character, its lakeside setting, its varied architecture and historic charm. They sense what the Syracuse Standard was alluding to in a newspaper article a century ago: "Amid the vast aggregation of summer resorts, of spas, beaches, points and harbors, Cazenovia stands by itself...for certain distinguishing characteristics,...for its individuality." It is, indeed, a place apart.

Inn Spots

The Brewster Inn, 6 Ledyard Ave. (Route 20), Box 507, Cazenovia 13035.

Gloriously situated at the southern end of Cazenovia Lake, the old Lake Meadows inn and restaurant gave way to the Brewster in 1984. Syracusan Dick Hubbard, who had managed the Sherwood Inn in Skaneateles for five years, and his wife Cathy have upgraded into a class act the 1887 summer home built by financier Benjamin Brewster, who with John D. Rockefeller established the Standard Oil Co.

Not that everything is perfect. The inside of the house is finished entirely in hardwood, and the lobby with its deep-coffered ceiling is particularly dark. Trooping up two long flights of stairs to our third-floor room was gloomy. And the room with two double beds and a tiny bathroom (shower only) – despite a lake view through a couple of tiny windows – turned out to be small and undistinguished.

Fortunately, no one seemed to know about the third-floor common room to which our room was attached, so we took it over and quietly made it our suite.

A tour the next morning proved our room to be an aberration. For half again more money, we could have stayed in the Harden Room, newly fashioned from former servants' quarters. It has a crocheted canopy queensize four-poster bed, elegant Harden furniture set against cherry walls, a two-section bathroom with brass fixtures, two reclining armchairs in front of a huge TV set and a balcony overlooking the lake. Also on the second floor is a cheery room in mint green and pink with a kingsize brass bed and, the first thing you notice, a double jacuzzi beside the bay window. Dark and more formal with oriental rugs and an ornate carved wood double bed is another second-floor suite with a sun porch. The three-room Stickley suite on the third floor has a jacuzzi and a magnificent lake view.

All nine inn guest rooms and suites contain private baths, TVs and phones, but vary markedly in size and spirit. Six offer lake views. Ours, in the mid-price range, actually was not the smallest.

Eight more air-conditioned rooms are on two floors of the renovated Carriage House Annex at the side of the main inn. Here, all have queensize beds (except for one with two doubles) and full baths. Two on the main floor boast jacuzzis; two on the second floor, cathedral ceilings.

Everyone gets to enjoy the lawn leading down to the lake where sailboats bob up and down, although it was taken over for a private party by a business group when we were there. A buffet spread of juice, cereal, mini-bagels (which you can toast in the toaster provided) and pastries is set out for continental breakfast in the lovely dining room (see Dining Spots). There's an appealing cocktail lounge, where we picked up after-dinner drinks to sip on the lawn, and a small gift shop.

(315) 655-9232. Fax (315) 655-2130. Sixteen rooms and one suite with private baths. May-October: doubles, $90 to $160 weekends, $75 to $140 midweek; suite, $195 to $225. Rest of year: $75 to $140 weekends, $60 to $130 midweek; suite, $175. Two-night minimum weekends.

Notleymere Cottage, 4641 East Lake Road, Cazenovia 13035.

When her parents decided to sell their lakeside Victorian Shingle-style mansion, they didn't have to look far for a buyer. Susan Cannon McCarvill and her husband, John, were living in Virginia Beach and waiting for the opportunity to run a B&B. They acquired the property, updated the bathrooms, hunted up furnishings at estate sales, and opened for guests in 1996. John oversees the B&B full time, while Susan, a special education teacher, is on hand weekends and in summer.

Listed on the National Register, this is one beauty of a year-round "cottage" situated on two acres of landscaped grounds sloping to the lake. A porte-cochere at the entry leads into an oak foyer with one of nine working fireplaces in the house. Off it is a guest living room with a turn-of-the-century victrola. A baronial stairway with elaborate balustrade rises past stained-glass windows to the second floor. In one rear corner is a two-room suite with two fireplaces, large sitting room, a kingsize iron bed, a new bathroom with a double jacuzzi and separate shower, and a wonderful deck overlooking gardens and lake. At the other rear corner is a spacious room with two wing chairs and a loveseat, a queen bed and a bathroom with its original marble sink and clawfoot tub. Another prized accommodation is a third-floor room with a queen bed dressed in a floral comforter, a wide window seat with the best view in the house, a clawfoot tub and marble sink, and a tiny balcony for watching the sunset. The McCarvills offer two smaller guest rooms, both with private baths and one with a fireplace, and have plans for two or three more rooms. Each has TV and telephone and is furnished to the period.

Breakfast is served at a table for eight in the majestic dining room, its walls and ceiling paneled in rich mahogany and cherry. Frittatas are the specialty among egg

Rear of Notleymere Cottage overlooks grounds sloping to Cazenovia Lake.

dishes, accompanied by fresh fruit and homemade coffee cakes and pastries. In season, the meal may be taken on the rear veranda overlooking the gardens and lake. Down at the shore are a dock with a canoe and a fireplace for barbecues.

(315) 655-9419 or (800) 704-4753. Fax (315) 655-8110. Four bedrooms and one suite with private baths. Doubles, $85 to $125; suite $150. No smoking.

The Brae Loch Inn, 5 Albany St., Cazenovia 13035.

"As close to a Scottish inn as it can be this far west of Edinburgh," says the brochure for this dark brown gabled landmark across from the park near the head of Cazenovia Lake. Occasionally attired in kilts, longtime innkeeper Grey Barr and his son Jim oversee a bustling establishment with a good downstairs restaurant and lounge (see Dining Spots), banquet facilities, a large Scottish gift shop and fifteen guest rooms.

Grapevine wreaths wrapped in tartan ribbons adorn the doors to the rooms, which vary from small (with two three-quarter beds) to deluxe with kingsize canopy beds. All but two have private baths, and all have telephones and remote-control TVs. Nicest are the luxury rooms on the second floor in front and in a new section in back. The Adam and Eve suite harbors a hand-carved king canopy bed and a double jacuzzi, while the Queen Elizabeth room has a lace-topped king canopy bed, fireplace and window seat.

Grey Barr was ebullient as he pointed out special touches: Stickley furniture, prized antiques, in-room coffee-makers, reclining chairs, a mix of carpeting and oriental rugs, extra insulation and firm mattresses ("because I have a bad back and want the best beds one can get").

A continental breakfast is served buffet style in the entry lobby, much of it displayed in an antique serving cupboard Grey had just acquired after seeking one for years. Guests have swimming privileges at the town park across the street.

Recently, the Barrs added a selection of antiques to supplement the Scottish gift items in their "Wee Hoose" and called it the Wee Gift and Antique House. With Grey in semi-retirement, Jim and his wife Val have taken up innkeeping duties.

(315) 655-3431. Fax (315) 655-9232. Thirteen rooms and one suite with private baths; two rooms with shared bath. Doubles, $80 to $130. Suite, $140.

Lincklaen House, 79 Albany St., Cazenovia 13035.

The handsome brick landmark that bears Cazenovia founder John Lincklaen's name was built in 1835 by a group of investors who felt the village needed an elegant hotel to care for its prominent visitors, who were to include Grover Cleveland and John D. Rockefeller. Dating to horse and buggy days, rooms vary from small, for those arriving by horse in back, to spacious, for those arriving by carriage in front. Some of the smallest rooms have been joined to make fewer but larger rooms.

Each of the eighteen air-conditioned rooms and three suites comes with private bath, phone and TV. Rooms are generally light and airy, with stenciled borders, floral curtains, antique highboys or armoires, and Lord & Mayfair toiletries. They look surprisingly comfortable, despite their age, although those in front suffer from street noise. One suite we saw had a queensize Hitchcock stenciled bed, an armoire with a TV, and a sitting room with a couch, an armchair and a table for three.

Afternoon tea and a continental breakfast, including cereals and pastries, are put out in the East Room off the main lobby. An aura of history and elegance pervades the entire main floor with its high ceilings, large fireplaces, classical carved moldings and chandeliers. Before or after dinner (see Dining Spots), some guests like to pause downstairs in the intimate, often smoke-filled little tavern, **Seven Stone Steps.**

The establishment was in transition after its purchase in 1997 by Dan Kuper, a chef from the Brewster Inn, with backing from Cazenovia College.

(315) 655-3461. Fax (315) 655-5443. Eighteen rooms and three suites with private baths. Doubles, $99. Suites, $125.

Cleaveland Manor, 3504 South St., Madison 13402.

An elegant brick Federal mansion dating to around 1800 has been restored with great taste into a seasonal B&B by owners Cheryl and Jim Breeding from Florida.

The Breedings happened on the house during a long weekend at the annual Madison-Bouckville Antiques Show. "We'd always dreamed of having a small summer house in the country," said Cheryl, originally from Buffalo. "But we didn't mean this big." She's one of those people who craves company (they put up foreigners in their home in Fort Lauderdale), so it was not long before they started a B&B in Madison in 1997.

They share their summer home with guests in three bedrooms. One is a two-bedroom family suite with sitting area and bath, and the other a master bedroom with kingsize bed and private bath. The suite, which is booked most often, has a queen bed in the larger bedroom and antique cannonball double and twin beds in the room beyond.

The house, with ten-foot-high ceilings, is handsomely furnished in the antique Empire style. The downstairs common rooms include a formal twenty-by-twenty-foot living room/salon with a fireplace and an Empire settee, and a matching dining room of the same size with fireplace and a huge chandelier. Cheryl expected guests to hang out with TV and stereo in the comfortable library, but finds they prefer "to absorb the experience of the living room" with all its antiques. In back is a porch and a new terrace overlooking four acres of countryside.

Cheryl prepares a breakfast of the guest's choice, from granola to bacon and eggs poached in spicy tomato sauce. Based on her experience of catering formal teas in Florida, she was planning in 1998 to offer a four-course tea at Cleaveland Manor for $14.95, regularly the second Sunday of each month and other times by reservation.

The Breedings spend their winters in Florida, but returned for the 1997 holiday season to cater a private New Year's sherry party in a house that was meant for entertaining.

(315) 893-7510. One room and a two-room suite with private baths. Doubles, $100 with private bath. Suite, $175. Children over 12. No smoking. Closed mid-October to mid-May.

Ye Olde Landmark Tavern, Route 20, Box 5, Bouckville 13310.

At the antiquey end of Madison County near Colgate University is this landmark. It's an imposing, curving polygonal building with four cobblestoned facades and a peaked roof topped by a gingerbread-trimmed cupola with six sides. Legend has it that the builder's wife wanted an octagonal structure and only half of it would fit on the pie-shaped lot, so what she got was one-half an octagon.

Visitors today get a good restaurant (see Dining Spots) plus four second-floor guest rooms, all with private baths. The rooms ooze history, but are thoroughly up-to-date with canopy four-poster beds, carpeting, cable TV and air-conditioning. Each is stenciled and furnished in antiques. A suite offers a canopied queen bed and a sitting room with blue accents and a writing desk.

Juice, fruit, yogurt, cereal and danish are put out amid the magazines in a small dining-common room in the morning.

(315) 893-1810. Four rooms and one suite with private baths. Doubles, $80 weekends, $65 midweek. Suite, $90 weekends, $75 midweek. Closed January to mid-March.

The Horned Dorset Inn, Route 8, Leonardsville 13364.

Next door and across a garden from their famous restaurant (see Dining Spots), the owners of the Horned Dorset have restored a once-decrepit late 19th-century house into a handsome B&B. They offer two bedrooms, two suites and a distinct sense of isolation and privacy. An off-site innkeeper comes in to serve a continental breakfast with linens, china and a silver coffee pot on a silver tray to the bedrooms in the morning. The fare includes juice, coffee and croissants with homemade preserves.

Otherwise, guests are on their own. There's a dark and elegant, richly paneled living room with a grand piano occupying a corner alcove and an abundance of antiques, as is the case throughout the house. The main floor also holds two main-floor bedrooms, one with a double four-poster bed and a full bath with a black tub and black sink, and the other with twin beds and a shower. Up a curving staircase are the suites, one over the living room with a table in the alcove, a kingsize bed and a pullout sofa. The other has twins joined together as a king bed and a bathroom with a bidet and lots of amenities.

Two of the original partners left in 1988 for Puerto Rico to open the Horned Dorset Primavera, a secluded 24-room inn that has won rave reviews. The hearts of the two owners who stayed seem to be in their restaurant.

(315) 855-7898. Two rooms and two suites with private baths. Doubles, $105. Suites, $125.

Oneida Community Mansion House is blend of inn, restaurant and museum.

Oneida Community Mansion House, 170 Kenwood Ave., Oneida 13421.

Here's a switch: A National Historic Landmark that's a blend of a living museum, a comfortable inn and a cafeteria-restaurant.

It began as the home of an early religious/utopian society called the Perfectionists who settled here as the Oneida Community. The hilltop mansion was built in stages from 1862 to 1914 as the community grew to more than 250 people. Its large scale – more than 300 rooms – reflected the needs of a group that lived as one family. Guides conduct tours through seven historic rooms, ranging from the Big Hall and Upper Sitting Room to the Nursery Kitchen and Old Library. Family portraits, Empire and Victorian furniture, costumes, artifacts and photographs are shown. The community abandoned its communal way of life in 1881, but its silver company, Oneida Ltd., now publicly owned, still manufactures fifteen percent of the world's flatware. The mansion has been maintained by a non-profit educational organization since 1987.

Some community descendants still rent apartments in the mansion, which varies from three to four stories and reflects a variety of architectural styles, including Italianate, French Second Empire, high Victorian and Colonial Revival.

Overnight guests are housed in eight extra-spacious, high-ceilinged guest rooms in a separate wing. Each has a queen or two twin beds, a modern bath, TV, telephone and solid traditional furnishings. Executive director Bruce Moseley describes them as "elegant, though not posh, and very comfortable." He says they often are booked by Oneida Limited for executives and visitors, and the new thrust is to make the mansion a destination for "travelers looking for a somewhat different place to stay."

Three meals a day are offered residents and the public in two dining rooms that also serve as an unofficial executive dining room for Oneida Ltd. The food, served cafeteria style, is prepared by a Culinary Institute-trained chef. Several choices change daily, and locals report the food is remarkably good. Full meals cost $3.50 for breakfast, $6 for lunch and $7.50 for dinner. There's a liquor license, and the inn's version of a hotel minibar is a basket full of miniatures in each guest room.

Overnight guests enjoy a large lounge and a library, and have the run of the public areas that museum visitors pay to see.

(315) 361-3671. Fax (315) 361-4580. Lodging and meals by reservation. Eight rooms with private baths. Doubles, $70. Breakfast, 7 to 8:30, weekends to 9. Lunch, 11:45 to 12:45 (Sunday dinner, 12:30 to 1:15). Dinner, 5:45 to 6:45.

Tours, Wednesday-Saturday at 10 and 2, Sunday at 2.

Dining Spots

The Horned Dorset Inn, Route 8, Leonardsville.

Wow! That's the first-timer's initial – and lasting – impression of this dramatic space carved out of a two-story commercial establishment that started as a 19th-century stagecoach stop and became a general store and an antiques store. It had been unoccupied for ten years and its roof was falling in when four partners acquired it and converted it into a restaurant in 1977.

Out in the middle of nowhere, this had to be good – and good it is, earning acclaim (and fame) far beyond the territory. It takes its name from the horned Dorset sheep that original partners Harold Davies and Kingsley Wratten raised here after they graduated from Colgate University in nearby Hamilton.

Replicas of horned Dorsets are scattered throughout the bigger-than-expected establishment (the only real ones are pictured in the men's room). The side dining room with three palladian windows is a stunner, its well-spaced, white-clothed tables flanked by windsor chairs and topped with fresh flowers, candles in hurricane lamps and gleaming crystal and sterling. Black walnut woodwork accents the soaring room that's otherwise all pristine white.

Chef-owner Don Lentz calls the decor Victorian; we call it medieval or baroque, more at home in Europe than Leonardsville. Church-like elements are seen in the paneled banquet room and the main dining room on two levels, one beside a library of bookshelves. It's paneled, has stained glass and a great hanging tapestry. Upstairs is a cocktail lounge with more bookshelves and high-backed Victorian furniture.

Such is the spectacular backdrop for the food, which is classic, high-cholesterol French and has won even more accolades than has the architectural restoration. The changing menu is recited nightly and includes five or six appetizers and an equal number of entrées. One evening's dinner started with broiled scallops in a superb sauce and tossed salad with a dressing whose recipe the chef guards jealously. Main courses were sweetbreads and twin tournedos, extra-tender and served in ample portions. Chocolate bombe and a chocolate roll wrapped around chocolate mousse were desserts of choice. Neither the menu nor the prices were shown, and this is not the place to ask. The wine list was pricey and the service leisurely.

At a recent visit, Don was preparing appetizers like cold marinated mussels with lime vinaigrette, sautéed scallops and lobster in phyllo with green onion beurre blanc, and slices of smoked duck breast with apples, cabbage and peppers. Main courses that night included swordfish with basil beurre blanc, chicken with cream sauce and sundried tomatoes, filet of lamb with brown sauce, ginger and raisins, and loin of veal stuffed with peppers, onions, prosciutto, brie and served with curried brown sauce. Raspberry mousse cake in genoise, frozen lemon soufflé, strawberry-blueberry tart, homemade apricot ice cream in a cookie cup and five sorbets were on tap for dessert.

Head chef Don and partner Bruce Wratten, who runs the front of the house, met at Ithaca College and have been here from the beginning. Bruce's brother Kingsley

Room with a medieval look is setting for fine dining at The Horned Dorset Inn.

and Harold Davies have left to operate the Horned Dorset Primavera in Puerto Rico. But the original still draws a knowing clientele from Cazenovia, Cooperstown, Syracuse and beyond.

(315) 855-7898. Entrées, $20.95 to $28. Dinner, Tuesday-Saturday 6 to 9; Sunday 3 to 7:30 in summer, 5 to 7:30 in winter.

The Brewster Inn, 6 Ledyard Ave., Cazenovia.

Sliding glass windows open onto the lake in the wraparound dining room elegant in white and mint green. Swagged curtains top the windows, candles flicker in oil lamps and our only quibbles are that the atmosphere is fairly close and track lights make the window tables overly bright. An interior dining room is serene in white and beige, with windsor chairs at well-spaced tables, and a fireplace.

Innkeeper Dick Hubbard, who has a restaurant background, acts as host and puts together the excellent wine list honored by Wine Spectator. A choice of good salads comes with the meal: in our case, romaine with mandarin oranges, almonds and a creamy dijon dressing and a classic caesar salad with homemade croutons. Entrées on the sophisticated menu range from sautéed chicken roulade with fontina cheese and prosciutto to broiled veal chop stuffed with mushroom duxelles and finished with bourbon sauce. House specialties are veal atlantis (sautéed veal cutlets with lobster and béarnaise sauce), blackened swordfish and tiger shrimp tossed with portobello mushrooms and asiago cheese over linguini. We found the pork tenderloin au poivre a bit heavy handed, but the accompanying three-potato terrine layered with imported cheese was super. So was the pan-seared salmon sprinkled with sesame seeds and served on a tahini and peanut sauce with rice and nicely julienned vegetables. Raspberry crème brûlée was the most interesting of many desserts.

(315) 655-9232. Entrées, $17.50 to $19.95. Dinner nightly, 5 to 8:30, Saturday 6 to 8:30. Sunday brunch, 11 to 1:30.

Kilt-clad proprietors Jim and Grey Barr welcome guests to The Brae Loch Inn.

Brae Loch Inn, 5 Albany St., Cazenovia.

Back in the days when we lived in the area, this was our place for special-occasion dining. A summer ritual was a trip to Cazenovia, roast-beef dinners in what we remember as the Wee Little Pub, and then nightcaps at the Seven Stone Steps at the Lincklaen House across the way.

The Wee Little Pub has given way to a series of three dark, cozy dining rooms paneled in butternut or pine, the one in the middle called the Grill Room because of the open brick grill at the side. In front is a large Victorian cocktail lounge. The motif remains Scottish, from the tartan carpeting on the floors, the white tablecloths with red napkins and the pewter service plates to the staff wearing kilts and Glengarry hats.

Beef remains a fixture on the menu, as it has since the Barr family opened the restaurant in 1946. Prime rib and filet mignon are the priciest items on the menu. Other choices include shrimp scampi, baked Boston scrod, chicken stuffed with crabmeat en croûte, roast Long Island duckling and veal piccata. Specials could be mustard-fried catfish with cajun mayonnaise, chicken Tuscany or tournedos of lamb in phyllo with spinach, garlic and feta cheese.

Start with coconut shrimp with drambuie marmalade, escargots en croûte, baked brie or, the first time we've seen this as an appetizer, lobster newburg. Finish with a choice of sundaes and parfaits, cheesecake, pastries or ice cream pie.

The Friday night surf and turf buffet packs in the crowds.

(315) 655-3431. Entrées, $12.95 to $17.95. Dinner nightly, 5 to 9:30 or 10. Sunday, brunch 11 to 2 (no brunch in summer), dinner 1 to 9.

Lincklaen House, 79 Albany St., Cazenovia.

In our college days and for a while afterward, one of us considered the Lincklaen dining room a bit stuffy. But the **Seven Stone Steps** tavern in the basement was such a quiet, impressive place for a few drinks that we sometimes made a night out of it. Seven stone steps lead from the sidewalk to an intimate tavern with wood tables in which many a name has been inscribed.

Nowadays the columned, high-ceilinged dining room seems quite romantic, dimly lit with an oriental screen gleaming in the fireplace at the far end and windsor chairs at nicely spaced tables set with white linens and floral china. Under new ownership in 1997, the short dinner menu was scaled down from its recent nouvelle heights. Among entrées were grilled swordfish with roasted pepper coulis, pesto scallops served over fettuccine, chicken marsala, duck à l'orange and charbroiled strip steak. Starters included crab cakes with rémoulade sauce and deep fried brie.

A screened, shaded outdoor courtyard is a pleasant setting for lunch in season.

(315) 655-3461. Entrées, $12.95 to $15. Lunch daily, 11 to 2. Dinner nightly, 5:30 to 9. Tavern, 4 to 11.

Wheatberry, 63 Albany St., Cazenovia.

One oldtimer calls Wheatberry "bohemian, serving things like quiche and salads." We and the standing-room-only crowd that jammed it one weekday lunchtime call it neat.

The decor orchestrated by owner Susan Carpenter is something else, all right. Fake leopard skins frame the door and the pastry freezer and cover the chair seats and bar stools. The long, narrow room on several levels is dark in hunter green and brick, its high ceiling bearing gold designs. Lighting is from upside-down, parasol-like hanging glass lamps. There are assorted marble-top tables and banquettes in the rear.

It's a witty backdrop for a with-it international menu. At lunch, we enjoyed a combination salad platter (curried chicken, crunchy tuna and tabbouleh served on romaine) and the chilled gazpacho with a spinach, bacon and mushroom salad. Everything was served in glass cups, bowls or plates. The spiced iced tea packed a punch. The day's Wheatberry News on each table offered quotable quotes, a secret-word contest and a handful of ads. In short, this is fun, noisy and convivial.

At night, you can still get sandwiches and salads. You'll also find a dozen more substantial entrées, from eggplant parmesan and spanakopita to shrimp à la griglia, oriental salmon, Greek chicken, veal marsala and strip steak stuffed with blue cheese and scallions.

The homemade desserts are delectable, and a good little wine list is easy on the wallet.

(315) 655-2102. Entrées, $13.95 to $15.75. Lunch daily, 11 to 3 or 3:30. Dinner, 5 to 9 or 10. Sunday brunch, 11 to 3.

Ye Olde Landmark Tavern, Route 20, Bouckville.

This odd-looking landmark (half an octagon, with four cobblestoned facades) has been a restaurant since 1970, when it was acquired by Andrew Hengst, head of the food service department at Colgate University. His son Steve runs the establishment today.

It's an attractive operation, seating 120 in four beamed and stenciled dining rooms, the wainscoting and trim in each painted a different color.

The menu is basic upstate New York traditional, starting with baked stuffed chicken or broiled steer liver with a rasher of bacon and topping off with New York strip steak or filet mignon. In between are roast duckling à l'orange, chicken cordon bleu, broiled pork loin, broiled or deep-fried sea scallops, brook trout amandine and three versions of turf and surf.

Curving polygonal buiding houses Ye Olde Landmark Tavern, an inn and restaurant.

The dessert list includes five kinds of parfait, cheesecake, apple crisp à la mode, pies and bread pudding with bourbon sauce.

(315) 893-1810. Entrées, $9.95 to $17.95. Dinner nightly, 5 to 9 or 10, Sunday 1 to 8. Closed January to mid-March.

Diversions

Cazenovia and environs are a do-it-yourself kind of place. Guests at some inns have lake privileges; otherwise Cazenovia Lake is generally viewed from afar. Swimming in Lakeland Park is reserved for village residents.

Sightseeing. The Cazenovia Preservation Foundation, whose land-use guide is a model for groups across the country, publishes two self-guiding maps. One details five walks in a village known for its architecture. Founded in 1793, the planned community was laid out by Holland Land Company agent John Lincklaen, whose taste in building kept the Federal style in Cazenovia long after it was out of favor elsewhere. Although Greek Revival and Gothic styles also are prominent, the village reflects the gamut of 19th-century architectural styles. One tour takes in the out-of-the-way village green and the campus of Cazenovia College, a former seminary and junior college for women, now a co-ed four-year institution with more than 1,000 students. The other map outlines five driving tours, one around the lake and the others taking off in all four directions. Not to be missed is **Chittenango Falls,** a 167-foot cascading waterfall taller than Niagara. In the mid-19th century, the upper portion of the falls helped power factories. Today, more than 100,000 visitors annually enjoy the state park's recreational and geological facilities. There are trails to the brink of the falls and to the bottom.

Shopping. Another Cazenovia self-guiding map called Shopper's Walk details most of the downtown stores along tree-lined Albany Street. Seemingly every other store has the name Cazenovia in it, from **Cazenovia Jewelry** to **Cazenovia Fabrics** to **Marjorie of Cazenovia,** a women's specialty shop housed in an old post office. One of our favorites, **Cazenovia Abroad,** displays European and Asian giftware, including a double-decker checker bus for kids, nutcrackers resembling

Scotsmen and Mounties, stained-glass vases and paper weights, sterling silver tree ornaments and Cazenovia tote bags. The store opens into **P.E. Mulligan's,** an updated dry goods store with handknit sweaters and cute children's clothes. **Complements** offers contemporary women's clothing and accessories, while **Waldman's Basics** gets back to basics in casual clothing. **Details,** an interior design studio, stocks the fabulous hand-painted china from MacKenzie-Childs in nearby Aurora; we coveted a small pitcher but balked at the price. The emphasis at **Serendipity** gift shop seems to be on dried flower creations. The most versatile gift shop is **The Cheshire Cat,** with a mix of toiletries, kitchenware, cards, Cazenovia T-shirts, Lorenzo towels and a small Christmas shop.

Special Events. A brochure titled "Spend a Day in Cazenovia" details quite a list of special events, from the Cazenovia Foot Races around Cazenovia Lake to a Christmas Walk called Joy to the World. Many, such as the annual horse and carriage driving competition and the Lorenzo Family Garden Fest, take place at Lorenzo State Historic Site (see Extra-Special). The annual **Franklin Car Trek,** an exhibit of antique Franklin cars manufactured in Syracuse in the early 1900s, attracts trekkers from far and wide to the Cazenovia College campus for a week in mid-August. Six **Thursday Evening Concerts in the Park** are scheduled beside the lake from early July to mid-August in Lakeland Park.

Antiquing. The Cazenovia area has ten antiques shops, but the biggest concentration is along Route 20 to the east in Bouckville and Madison. A guide details 48, some of them harboring a number of dealers. More than 1,000 dealers from 26 states and Canada come to the annual mid-August **Madison-Bouckville Antiques Show,** the biggest in New York State.

Extra-Special

Lorenzo State Historic Site, Route 13, Cazenovia.

Every area should be so lucky as to have a treasure like this in its front yard. The showy brick mansion was built in 1807 by John Lincklaen, the Holland Land Company agent who founded Cazenovia. He is thought to have named it for Lorenzo di Medici, the Renaissance patron of Florence, whose work he admired. The visitor center in the restored carriage house is an excellent introduction to the man, the house and the times. Here you see a huge curtain quarter coach and other carriages and sleighs. Guided tours leave here every half hour for the mansion, which was occupied by Lincklaen descendants, including Ledyards, Fairchilds and Remingtons (of Remington Arms), until it was given to the state in 1968. The mansion is a restoration in progress. Many furnishings are original, reflecting the different periods and styles of the occupants over 160 years. Visitors can't help but be impressed by the majestic entry hall with its vivid pink patterned wallpaper, the Federal-style drawing room, the bedrooms and a library of 4,000 volumes. A brochure details a self-guided tour of the formal gardens and grounds, site for numerous community events. From the rear garden walk, it's possible to see Cazenovia Lake through the mansion's central hall and out the front door. Although Route 20 passes in front, nothing was allowed then or since to block Lorenzo's view.

(315) 655-3200. Open mid-May through October, Wednesday-Saturday 10 to 5, Sunday 1 to 5. Grounds open all year, 8 a.m. to dusk. Free.

Ithaca, N.Y.
The Little Apple

"Ithaca Is Gorges," say the ubiquitous bumper stickers hereabouts. The play on words is apt. Gorges slice through and around the biggest city in the Finger Lakes region, creating waterfalls that cascade almost into downtown. And the scenery is gorgeous, thanks to all the gorges, the surrounding hills and Cayuga Lake. The Cornell University campus, which straddles some of the most gorgeous of the gorges, is to our minds the most scenic in America.

Cornell landmarks overlook Cayuga Lake.

Hills rise sharply all around this city cradled at the southern end of Cayuga Lake. Only the downtown and west side are flat. Everything else in Ithaca is on hillsides, some as steep as any in San Francisco. The views from parts of the Cornell campus and the posh Cayuga Heights residential section are as dramatic as those in Berkeley.

Ithaca is also called "The Little Apple," a reference to its big-city status as a cultural and arts center. Ithaca is home to both Cornell (an Ivy Leaguer with 12,500 undergrads and 5,600 graduate students) and Ithaca College (the largest private residential college in New York State with 6,400 students). The ivied Cornell and the modern Ithaca campuses sprawl across hilltops on opposite sides of town, though Cornell is much the larger presence. Together their student bodies nearly equal the year-round population of the city (29,500). The students and their top-notch faculties make for a lively academic and arts community.

Ithaca remains a small town at heart, however. One of our visits coincided with a flying trip by then Vice President Dan Quayle to visit his son at a summer soccer camp and to take in the panoramic view of Ithaca, as everyone does, from the fifth-floor gallery of the Herbert F. Johnson Museum of Art. The Ithaca Journal ho-hummed the story the next day under a one-column inside headline, "Quayle Drops In."

Where there is such scenery and sophistication, good restaurants, shops and inns are sure to follow. Ithaca harbors more than its share. One block of North Aurora Street in downtown has five restaurants in a row for starters. Downtown, with its main street turned into a pleasant pedestrian mall, bustles at all hours, thanks to good shops, galleries and eateries. The area has the only four-diamond,

Sherry and Charles Rosemann have built Rose Inn into highly rated inn and restaurant.

four-star country inn in New York State as well as more than 30 B&Bs at last count. Ithaca has the largest farmers' market on the East Coast for a city its size. It also has a winery inside the city limits, and is the starting point of the Cayuga Wine Trail. Three large state parks have Ithaca addresses, as do the spectacular Cornell Plantations gardens and the Sapsucker Woods wildlife sanctuary.

All these assets add up to a quality of life that ranked Ithaca first in the East in a book, "Rating Guide to Life in America's Small Cities." Little wonder that the Ithaca area is one of the fastest-growing in New York State.

Inn Spots

The Rose Inn, 813 Auburn Road (Route 34), Box 6576, Ithaca 14851.

In less than a decade, the old "House with a Circular Staircase" was transformed into New York State's first four-star, four-diamond country inn, as rated by Mobil

and AAA. That comes as no surprise to those who know Charles Rosemann, who moved to Ithaca to manage the Cornell University hotel school's Statler Inn, and his dynamic wife Sherry. The classic Italianate mansion they bought in 1983 had such potential that Charles left his Statler job to devote full time to the inn that Sherry seemingly had started somewhat as a lark.

Located in the hilly countryside twelve miles

north of Ithaca, this has become a destination for travelers. Starting with five guest rooms and mostly shared baths, the Rosemanns have worked constantly to improve the guest quarters. They now have twelve rooms with private baths, plus five glamorous suites with fireplaces and jacuzzis for two. A parlor with a game table, a living room with Victorian furniture, TV, books and games, outdoor terraces and a rear rose garden are also available for guests' enjoyment. As is a prix-fixe dinner to remember.

The Rosemanns' latest addition is **The Carriage House,** a casual yet stylish restaurant and jazz lounge in their new conference center, discreetly located out of the way on the main floor of a carriage house at the side of the property. The conference center, which accommodates up to 44 people for meetings and meals amidst original barnwood walls and oriental carpets, is used during the day. On weekend evenings, it becomes a hunt-themed restaurant – open to the public and offering a short à la carte menu, with entrées ranging from grilled tuna to roast duck to osso buco milanese. Live music is offered from 7:30 to 11:30.

With the expansion, the Rosemanns have added a fulltime manager, a chef and two cooks. Yet the man who answers the inn's phone and welcomes guests may well be Charles, a hands-on innkeeper if ever there was one, and Sherry still oversees the kitchen.

The inn's guest rooms are individually decorated by Sherry. Those in a newer two-story addition capture the classic flavor of the rest of the house. They are luxurious, from their lace curtains, ceiling fans and fresh flowers to their luggage racks, terry robes, Vitabath and other amenities. In two, the bathroom fixtures (including a stretch-out tub) are from the Eastman House in Rochester. Folk art and antiques abound. Our rear suite contained a sunken jacuzzi in a garden-like space filled with plants, a majestic kingsize bed and antique furnishings in the bedroom, a large closet and a modern bathroom. At nightly turndown, a candle is apt to be lit beside the bed, the towels replenished, your toiletries neatly lined up on the bath vanity and your clothing hung in the closet. A thank-you note bids "Sweet Dreams."

Breakfast is an event worthy of the rest of the Rose Inn experience. It's served in the parlor, the dining room, the carriage house or in the foyer with its beautiful parquet floor. Rose mats are on the polished wood tables, as are white baskets full of seasonal flowers. The juice glasses sport the Rosemann crest. Because fifteen varieties of apples are picked from their orchard, homemade cider is often poured. Also on the table are Sherry's jams and preserves – maybe spiced blueberry or strawberry-rhubarb. Local fruit is served in summer (we loved the raspberries), often with the Rosemanns' own crème fraîche. The main dish could be an omelet with smoked salmon and croissants, or perhaps cream cheese, bagels and lox. Charles's specialty is his puffy Black Forest apple pancake with raspberry syrup, which we found absolutely yummy. The coffee is his own blend of beans, including Kona from Hawaii.

The Rosemanns set an elegant dinner table in the main house as well, with candles, flowers, sterling silver and sparkling wine glasses. The many-course dinner at $55 per person is optional for inn guests and must be booked in advance. A few non-guests may reserve if space is available.

Our dinner started with smoked oysters in a puff pastry and a hot artichoke strudel on a bed of pureed tomatoes. The colorful salad was a work of art: Boston lettuce with snow peas, radicchio, watercress and sprouts, dotted with red and

Hanshaw House B&B occupies restored 1830 farmhouse with a second-story addition.

yellow peppers and red and yellow tomatoes, and dressed with a raspberry-dijon vinaigrette. The rack of lamb, done on an outdoor grill and served on a glaze of madeira with red currant jelly and cumin, and a veal chop with chanterelles were garnished with baby ears of corn. Scampi Mediterranean style is served on a bed of acini, the sauce including a touch of curry with pinenuts on top. Our favorite vegetable was the potato basket, which comes with every dinner. Individual grand marnier soufflés with chocolate or a foamy brandy sauce are a perfect end to the meal. The wine list is well chosen and affordably priced.

Whether it be for lodging or food or both, the Rose Inn is a class act.

(607) 533-7905. Fax (607) 533-7908. Twelve rooms and five suites with private baths. Doubles, $125 to $175. Suites, $200 to $275. Two-night minimum weekends. No smoking. Prix-fixe, $55. Dinner by reservation, Tuesday-Saturday at 7. Carriage House, entrées, $13.95 to $18.95, dinner Friday and Saturday 6 to 10.

Hanshaw House B&B, 15 Sapsucker Woods Road, Ithaca 14850.

She loves country inns, decorating and entertaining, so the wife of an Ithaca College dean put it all together in this sumptuous country B&B. Helen Scoones, who used to work for a decorator, did the decorating herself in this restored 1830 farmhouse with a second-story addition and a new rear wing for the couple's living quarters.

Hanshaw House has four air-conditioned guest rooms, all with private baths and two with sitting areas. Each is furnished with great panache and an eye to the comforts of home. We lucked into the second-floor suite, with a queensize feather bed, down comforter and pillows, English country antique furnishings, a modern bath and plenty of space to spread out. We didn't need so much space, for we had the run of the house – a stylish living room outfitted in chintz and wicker with dhurrie rugs all over, a side TV room with gardens on view on both sides, and Adirondack chairs in a pleasant yard backing up to a small pond and woods full of deer, woodchucks and other wildlife.

In the new wing is Helen's "pièce de résistance," a formal dining room with a crystal chandelier, oriental rugs on pegged floors and french doors opening onto the rear patio and gardens. It's the setting for a gourmet breakfast served on blue and white china. Ours included fresh orange juice, an orange-banana yogurt frappe and Swedish pancakes puffed in the oven with peaches and crème fraîche. Other main courses could be quiche, frittata with homemade popovers, baked french toast with caramel sauce, baked eggs and heart-shaped waffles.

Early-risers are pampered with a choice of exotic coffees. In the afternoon, Helen greets guests with iced lemon tea or mulled cider and cookies in the living room.

Always upgrading her rooms, at a recent visit she showed the newly tiled bathroom, the floral sheets and the new curtains in a main-floor bedroom that she decorated in "MacKenzie-esque style," a reference to her favorite pottery from the nearby MacKenzie-Childs studio.

(607) 257-1437 or (800) 257-1437. Fax (607) 266-8866. www.wordpro.com/ hanshawhouse/ Four rooms with private baths. April-December: doubles, $90 to $125 weekends, $77 to $105 midweek. Rest of year, $72 to $84 weekends, $68 to $78 midweek. Two-night minimum weekends in season. Children over 8. No smoking.

Buttermilk Falls B&B, 110 East Buttermilk Falls Road, Ithaca 14850.

Guests leave this very personal B&B with full stomachs and hugs from innkeeper Margie Rumsey. You'd expect no less, for breakfast is quite a riot with guests in the dining room bartering and exchanging jams, seconds and whatnot with those on the porch, and Margie encouraging it all as she cooks up a storm on her AGA cast-iron cooker in the kitchen in the midst of all the fun.

First you help yourself to juices, including local grape and apple cider. Then you build your own "cereal sundae" with a hot whole grain (rye, at our visit), several kinds of fruits, local honey, yogurt sauce and four kinds of milk from skim to heavy cream. A big loaf of French or Italian bread is placed on each table, where people break off chunks and lather them with butter and one of Margie's homemade jams, perhaps gooseberry or apricot with ginger (here starts the bartering). There follow sticky rolls (as if anyone needs them), bacon and scrambled eggs jazzed up with herbs Margie manages to pick from the garden between courses. All the while she keeps up a steady chatter with guests on all sides.

Such is the start of a typical day – if there's any such thing as typical here – at this attractive white brick 1825 house, the closest private building to the foot of Buttermilk Falls. Energetic Margie, a one-woman dynamo, came to the home of her late husband's grandfather as a bride in 1948. When her youngest son graduated from Cornell in 1983, she opened it as Ithaca's first B&B and has been improving it ever since.

Now all four guest rooms have private baths, and some retain a homey look (including built-in cupboards like those one of us grew up with). Good art of Finger Lakes scenes, oriental rugs and early American antiques grace each room. We enjoyed the large and luxurious downstairs bedroom with a woodburning fireplace and a double jacuzzi surrounded by plants in the corner, from which Buttermilk Falls can be glimpsed through a hedge. Recently, Margie painted pink the mahogany walls of an upstairs room with a little kitchen and out came the fancy Rose Room. She also redid the living room in a Colonial English tavern look, with Queen Anne loveseats facing each other in front of the fireplace. A rear carriage house contains a two-room cottage good for families.

Classical music plays throughout the public rooms. They include the plant-filled dining room notable for a long cherry table flanked by twelve different styles of

Side porch at The Federal House overlooks park-like setting.

windsor chairs made by her son Ed, the aforementioned eat-in kitchen and an attractive screened porch where we had breakfast, facing a garden in one corner.

(607) 272-6767. Five rooms with private baths. June-October: doubles, $150 to $185 weekends, $85 to $150 midweek; jacuzzi room, $250 weekends, $195 midweek. November-May: doubles, $95 to $150 weekends, $85 to $135 midweek; jacuzzi room, $250 weekends, $150 midweek. Children accepted. No smoking.

The Federal House, 175 Ludlowville Road, Lansing 14882.

Antiques collector Diane Carroll closed her former Decker Pond Inn south of Ithaca and reopened north of town in the historic mill hamlet of Ludlowville. Here, instead of a pond, Diane has Salmon Creek Falls within earshot, plus a park-like setting. She has fashioned a great side yard, complete with prolific flower gardens, a gazebo, a trellis and an old bench. There's an expansive wicker-filled side porch for taking it all in.

Diane stripped the interior of the gracious 1815 house to its original woodwork and floors before decorating it elegantly in the Federal style. The fireplace mantels are believed to have been hand-carved by Brigham Young, who worked as an apprentice carpenter in the area in the early 1800s. Candles flicker by day in the handsome living room and at breakfast in the formal dining room.

From her enormous country kitchen that stretches across the back of the house, Diane prepares lavish breakfasts for guests. One day it might involve fresh orange juice, an apple-banana crisp with sour cream sauce, banana bran muffins and orange french toast with cinnamon-peach sauce. Another day could bring cantaloupe with lime-yogurt sauce and fresh mint, a zucchini frittata, bacon and blueberry muffins. Individual vegetable soufflés are served with steamed asparagus and broiled tomatoes on the side.

Upstairs in the rear of the house is the new Seward Suite, named for William

Seward of nearby Auburn, secretary of state under Abraham Lincoln. He courted his future wife in this, her uncle's summer house. It has a large and high-ceilinged bedroom with a queensize wicker bed and spiffy green and white decor, plus a sitting room with gas fireplace, day bed and TV. Also with air-conditioning and private baths are two more bedrooms, one with queen bed and one with king/twins, reached by a steep rear staircase. Each is decorated with flair and appointed with antiques. The front Lincoln Suite has a queensize canopy bed, gas fireplace and TV.

A collector with great taste, Diane sells antiques and gifts in her little Blueberry Muffin Gift Corner at the side entrance.

(607) 533-7362 or (800) 533-7362. Fax (607) 533-7899. Two rooms and two suites with private baths. Doubles: May-November, $85 to $125 weekends, $65 to $75 midweek; rest of year, $70 to $85 weekends, $60 to $75 midweek. Suites: $125 to $175 weekends, $80 to $100 midweek. Two-night minimum weekends in season. No smoking.

The Hound & Hare, 1031 Hanshaw Road, Ithaca 14850.

Lace, antiques and family heirlooms abound in this stately white brick house in a residential area, surrounded by tall trees and manicured lawns and gardens. Innkeeper Zetta Sprole's ancestors built the house in 1829 on property given them by George Washington for service in the Revolutionary War.

The configuration of guest rooms and rates get confusing because each of the three main rooms joins an adjacent room for possible use as a suite.

The new Valerie room in the east wing of the house has a queen bed and a private bath with jacuzzi tub. A spiral staircase leads to a planned new bedroom with a jacuzzi tub and private entrance below. The queen-bedded Victoria room uses the original hall bath, and can link up as a suite with the Carolina room with a double bed and its own bath. Facing the rear gardens is the Vanessa with a high brass queen bed. It adjoins the porch-like Christina room with antique step-up twin beds, so its occupants have a choice of sleeping accommodations or they can use it as a sitting room.

Zetta bills as "a Victorian fantasy" her well-dressed living room and a cozy library with TV and stereo. She offers afternoon tea and crumpets, and directs guests out to the back yard to enjoy herb gardens, rose beds a lily pond and fountain.

Morning brings a candlelight breakfast served with fine china, silver and crystal in the dining room or on the porch. Apple pancakes or quiche could be the main course, supplemented by turkey sausages and fruit compote.

(607) 257-2821 or (800) 652-2821. Fax (607) 257-3121. Three rooms with private baths. Doubles, $85 to $125 in summer, $150 in spring and fall, $110 in winter. Two-night minimum fall weekends. No children. No smoking.

La Tourelle, 1150 Danby Road (Route 96B), Ithaca 14850.

A French-style country inn or a glorified motel? We've heard plenty of references to both, though this white stucco building trimmed with brown certainly looks more like the former than the latter. The points of interest on a walking map of the grounds given to guests are listed in French, and what could be more French country inn-like than that?

La Tourelle was built in 1986 by Walter Wiggins, a partner in the well-known L'Auberge du Cochon Rouge restaurant next door (which was damaged by fire in 1994 and reopened as the John Thomas Steakhouse). The building is set back from the road on a 75-acre property descending to Buttermilk Falls State Park.

The plant-filled lobby is notable for colorful tiled floors. Three comfy sofas are in front of a stone fireplace, blazing in winter. Thirty-three spacious rooms and two suites are handsomely appointed in elegant country French style. Each has king or queen beds, good art, color TVs, VCRs (movies are available at the front desk), and tiled and marble bathrooms. A decanter of Spanish sherry awaits in each room.

The most memorable are the two round "romantic tower suites," which must be seen to be believed. Each has a sunken circular waterbed, a double jacuzzi just behind it, a TV mounted over the door and a mirrored ceiling. One has a fireplace.

An optional continental breakfast will be delivered to the room for $5.95 per person. Meals from the restaurant are available through room service.

(607) 273-2734 or (800) 765-1492. Thirty-three rooms and two suites with private baths. Doubles, $85 to $110 weekends, $75 to $95 midweek. Suites, $125 weekends, $110 midweek.

Peregrine House, 140 College Ave., Ithaca 14850.

This 1874 brick Victorian located three blocks from the Cornell campus has been a B&B since 1986. At our latest visit, the cozy parlor with its two wing chairs beside the fireplace was decorated with vases of black-eyed susans and Queen Anne's lace, and fresh fruit and candy were set around for guests.

Each of the eight bedrooms on the second and third floors (four with private baths, four with w.c. and sink and sharing showers) are different. Most have a fresh Laura Ashley look. All are air-conditioned, and all have TVs and clock radios. Pretty linens, thick towels, soaps and shampoos (and even Woolite) are nice touches. Room 203, the largest, has tulips on the comforter and cabbage roses on the shower curtain.

Innkeeper Susan Vance took over the business lately from her mother, the founder. She offers "a plethora of choices" for breakfast, including juices, fresh fruit and eggs, french toast and blueberry pancakes. Specialty items on weekends could be belgian waffles or a tomato, cheese and bacon omelet. In the afternoon, tea or lemonade and gingersnaps are served on the front or side porches or in the parlor.

(607) 272-0919. Four rooms with private baths and four rooms with shared baths. Doubles, $99 to $109, mid January to mid-November; $59 to $79, rest of year.

Thomas Farm, 136 Thomas Road, Ithaca 14850.

Electric candles glow in the windows year-round at this trim white farmhouse along a rural road southeast of Ithaca. Glenn Schneider and his wife Edie, whose family has owned the house since it was built about 1850, offer four bedrooms, two with private baths, and a coveted main-floor suite with a kitchenette and hand stenciling on the ceiling. All are handsomely appointed with antique wallpaper, quilts and brass beds, all but one of them queensize.

Edie Schneider greets guests with lemonade or tea and cookies on the side porch or on a patio on the other side of the house. In the morning, she prepares a hearty breakfast. Typical fare includes juice, fresh fruit, homemade muffins and a main course, perhaps an omelet, french toast or scrambled eggs with hash browns.

Guests enjoy sitting on the porches or relaxing beside the pond. The wooded, 120-acre farm property is laced with walking trails.

(607) 539-7477. Two rooms and one suite with private baths; two rooms with shared bath. Doubles, $85 to $105.

The Statler Hotel, Cornell University, Ithaca 14853.

It's obviously not an inn, but no lodging guide for Ithaca would be complete without mention of the old Statler Inn. Like a phoenix reborn after an infusion of untold millions from the hotel industry, the three-story inn was transformed in 1989 into a nine-story monument to the Statler dream, quite appropriate for the operation that is part of Cornell's renowned School of Hotel Administration.

All is state of the art, from the richly paneled lobby with bowls of dried flowers grown at Cornell Plantations to the 150 guest rooms and suites. Computerized TV sets hidden in armoires allow you to order room service and settle your bill before check-out. Lord & Mayfair toiletries, Saratoga water, minibars stocked with New York wines and local art enhance the rooms, the rear half of which afford incredible views over Cornell landmarks toward Cayuga Lake.

The hotel's **Banfi's East Avenue Grill** offers a Sunday brunch that is a Cornell tradition, and dinners ($13.50 to $16.95) with Cornell specialties and northern Italian overtones. The room is serene and pleasant with damask linens on well-spaced tables, black lacquered chairs and banquettes, and full-length windows with a view of the campus. Half the staff are students.

(607) 257-2500 or (800) 541-2501. Fax (607) 257-6432. One hundred thirty-two rooms and eighteen suites with private baths. Doubles, $150 to $170. Suites, $225 to $350.

Benn Conger Inn, 206 West Cortland St., Groton 13073.

A restaurant of distinction for some time (see Dining Spots), this 1921 classic revival mansion is becoming a destination for inn-goers as well. Innkeepers Peter and Alison van der Meulen have been improving the accommodations and plan eventually to quadruple the number of rooms.

For the moment, the upstairs of their handsome pillared mansion offers three suites and one small bedroom. Together, they encompass about 3,500 square feet, and guests have been known to comment that the suites are larger than many a small apartment.

Consider the Dutch Schultz suite, named for the infamous bootlegger and racketeer who found it a safe haven following the departure of original owner Benn Conger, a state senator, banker and founder of the Corona Corporation (later Smith-Corona). The brass bed is outfitted with 310-count percale sheets and down or feather pillows, and the TV is hidden in an armoire. You may get lost in the bathroom, surely one of the world's largest – it seemingly goes on forever in assorted rooms and alcoves. Another suite with fireplaced sitting room and queensize brass bed is furnished in Cape May wicker and comes with a clawfoot tub. A smaller suite with a sleeping porch has a bath with a European shower. The Caswell-Massey and Gilchrist & Soames toiletries are stashed in little ceramic bathtubs. Each room contains period furnishings appropriate to the 1920s.

Guests share a small, wicker-furnished common area in the hallway at the head of the stairs. They also can join outside diners in the cozy library/bar with fireplace and piano.

The complimentary breakfast in the pretty conservatory dining room is a five-course feast. Look forward to a choice of juices, fruit (crenshaw melon with mixed berries at our visit) and a pastry course, perhaps Danish aebleskiver, crêpes or blueberry-buttermilk pancakes. Then – can you stand it? – comes the main course. It could be eggs benedict or a frittata with three kinds of wild mushrooms, cheddar and chèvre. The last course is breakfast meats (surely you weren't expecting dessert).

Paintings by chef-owner's wife enhance walls at Dano's On Cayuga.

With their renowned dining operation well under control, the van der Meulens were looking to add guest bungalows around their eighteen-acre hilltop property. "We want to get up to fifteen rooms," Alison advised.

(607) 898-5817. One room and three suites with private baths. Double, $90 to $120. Suites, $145 to $220 peak, $110 to $150 off-season. Two-night minimum on weekends. Smoking restricted.

Dining Spots

Dano's On Cayuga, 113 South Cayuga St., Ithaca.

Nearly everyone in Ithaca agrees that Dano's is tops on the city's dining list – for food, value and atmosphere. It's a remarkable accomplishment for a former European ballet dancer who took over a downtown storefront dive in 1990.

Dano (pronounced Dan-yo) Hutnik was born in the Ukraine, grew up in Czechoslovakia and was a ballet dancer for fifteen years in Vienna before entering the restaurant business in New York and San Francisco. A classified ad in the New York Times led him to Ithaca and this old space that he and his wife, artist Karen Gilman, transformed into a French-style bistro in peach and blue-gray. There's seating for 44 at white-linened tables topped with white paper against a backdrop of her striking artworks on the walls. Desserts are displayed in a nook at the side, and Edith Piaf music plays in the background. Dano table-hops at meal's end and proves to be quite the talker and philosopher.

The short menu of Central European, French and northern Italian fare is handwritten daily. Those in the know go for such specialties as oxtail stew with black and green olives and grilled brine-cured pork chop with spaetzle and braised red cabbage. We shared an appetizer of melted raclette with boiled potatoes, cornichons and pearl onions, the classic version and plenty for two.

Main courses range from veal sausage to filet mignon in a five-spice sauce with eggplant potato strudel and savoy cabbage slaw. We found superlative both the sautéed chicken breast with artichokes and sundried tomatoes and served with mouth-watering polenta sticks, and the linguini with shrimp, peas and scallions. We also liked the Hermann J. Weimer dry riesling, the only Finger Lakes choice on a fine wine list specializing in imported wines and rarely seen Californias. Crème brûlée and a bittersweet chocolate gâteau with raspberry sauce were fantastic endings to one of our more enjoyable meals in a long time.

(607) 277-8942. Entrées, $12.95 to $21.95. Dinner, Tuesday-Saturday 5:30 to 9:30 or 10.

Renée's, 202 East Falls St., Ithaca.

Within earshot of Ithaca Falls, the highest of the city's many waterfalls, lies this pristine bistro. It's run by Renée Senne, who cooked in a couple of local restaurants upon her return from studying at La Varenne in France and teaching at the New York Cooking School.

Candles flicker and classical music plays in her airy dining room, where hanging plants and ficus trees thrive, and in a small bar area beyond. We sampled Renée's work at a fine spring lunch (since discontinued). The cream of onion soup, a slice of French bread topped with fresh mozzarella, sundried tomatoes and basil, and a special of fettuccine with grilled shrimp and garlic cream sauce hinted at the treats in store at night.

The possibilities for dinner range from herb-roasted game hen to beef tenderloin with sautéed mushrooms, bacon and gorgonzola. Innovative seafood preparations are highlighted: broiled salmon with yellow pepper coulis, grilled swordfish served with shrimp-filled ravioli, and grilled halibut with beurre blanc on steamed spinach.

Starters could be smoked salmon quesadilla, shrimp cakes with roasted pepper sauce, and a salad of warm new potatoes with chèvre on baby greens.

Renée's background as a pastry chef is reflected in such treats as mille-feuille, peach shortcake, apricot genoise with puree, and profiteroles with vanilla ice cream and dark chocolate sauce.

(607) 272-0656. Entrées, $16.50 to $21.50. Dinner, Monday-Saturday 5:30 to 10.

John Thomas Steakhouse, 1152 Danby Road (Route 96B), Ithaca.

A kitchen fire closed L'Auberge du Cochon Rouge, a French restaurant of renown, in 1994. When owner Walter Wiggins rebuilt, he surprised almost everyone by turning the hilltop farmhouse overlooking the Cayuga Lake valley into a New York-style steakhouse. He also surprised local skeptics, some of whom were persuaded that this was even better than its predecessor.

The restaurant's traditionally masculine decor lent itself to the steakhouse concept. L'Auberge sous chef William Peterson stayed on as chef, presenting a predictable menu ranging from roasted half chicken with mashed potatoes to T-bone steak. Prime beef is featured and the house specialty is porterhouse steak, $45 for two. There are grilled or blackened tuna, broiled swordfish, broiled salmon, shrimp scampi, a vegetarian platter and a couple of chicken dishes for non-beef eaters. Although all entrées come with a fresh vegetable, the usual salads and side orders cost extra.

Appetizers include smoked trout, baked deviled crab, shrimp cocktail and clams casino. Desserts range from old-fashioned bread pudding and assorted ice creams to triple berry strudel.

The fire destroyed L'Auberge's acclaimed wine cellar, but the inventory was being restocked slowly.

(607) 273-3464. Entrées, $12.95 to $26.95. Dinner nightly, 5:30 to 10 or 11.

Trattoria Tre Stelle, 120 Third St., Ithaca.

This striking Italian trattoria is the home of wood-fired pizzas and a winning Mediterranean decor. The owners are designer-architects who did the sculptures in the corners of the dining room, rag-rolled the walls, designed the metal chairs and orchestrated the marble look on the bar. One also is a mushroom expert who picks the chanterelles that turn up in various dishes.

Vicki Romanoff's printed menu is short but sweet and most affordable: a couple of antipasti, five changing pizzas, a couple of side dishes and four desserts. At our visit, the chalkboard entrées included herb and cheese lasagna, lamb shanks with tomatoes and orzo, braciola (flank steak rolled around sausage and egg) and an acclaimed rabbit dish simmered in white wine and bearing a smoky taste from the wood oven. The favorite of the pizzas is the della casa (wild mushrooms with sundried tomatoes, caramelized onions and parmesan). Among desserts are ricotta cheesecake with blueberries, polenta cake served with whipped cream and cherry sauce, and almond biscotti.

The excellent all-Italian wine list is priced mostly in the teens.

(607) 273-8515. Pizzas, $7.50; entrées, $9.75 to $11.50. Dinner, Thursday-Monday 5 to 9:30 or 10:30.

The Heights Cafe & Grill, 903 Hanshaw Road, Ithaca.

Plainer than plain is this new popular new storefront operation in the Community Corners shopping plaza in tony Cayuga Heights. Black upholstered chairs are at mottled gray tables, each topped with a votive candle in a little flower pot. A few paintings and wall sconces complete the decor.

Diners pack the place for the affordable American-Mediterranean fare of chef-owners James and Heidi Larounis. Prices have risen lately, but you can still get things like fish plaki (Greek-style Boston bluefish with tomatoes, feta and olives), pesto grilled chicken and grilled pork chops with a dijon wine sauce in the low teens. The pasta dishes and brick-oven pizzas are downright bargains. At the high end of the menu are grilled leg of lamb and blue cheese-crusted beef tenderloin. Everything comes with choice of Greek or caesar salad.

Starters could be tomato-basil bruschetta or grilled octopus. Desserts range from baklava to crème brûlée. The wine list, mainly from the Finger Lakes and California, is pleasantly priced as well.

(607) 257-4144. Entrées, $11.95 to $19.95. Lunch, Monday-Saturday 11:30 to 2:30. Dinner, Monday-Saturday 5 to 9 or 10.

Oldport Harbour, 702 West Buffalo St., Ithaca.

The waterside setting is great, but consistency in food and service tends to be a problem at this neat place billed as "a little bit of Europe on the Cayuga inlet." Although there are several interior dining rooms with bentwood chairs at light wood tables with blue mats, we'd dine outside any time we could, on the far garden terrace beside an outdoor bar or on the near deck with the MV Manhattan tour boat moored beside.

The latter was the setting for a Sunday jazz brunch that brought back memories of New Orleans. One of us tried the clams monte carlo and the pâté maison, while the other splurged on poached eggs Oldport with smoked salmon, brie and hollandaise sauce, accompanied by roast potatoes, onions and fresh fruit garnish. Everything was adequate, but secondary to the canalside setting and the music.

Dinner entrées run from grilled swordfish brochette to steak au poivre. Shrimp scampi, chicken with jerk seasoning, roast duckling and veal homard are among the offerings. Linzer torte, fresh fruit tarts, cheesecake with strawberries and German chocolate cake are possible desserts.

(607) 272-4868. Entrées, $9.95 to $18.95. Lunch, Monday-Saturday 11:30 to 2. Dinner nightly, 5:30 to 9 or 10. Sunday brunch, 11 to 2:30.

Thai Cuisine, 501 South Meadow St., Ithaca.

Knowledgeable Thai-food lovers consider this the best Thai food in upstate New York. It's served in a serene, white and pink linened dining room in a commercial plaza by a Thai family in the kitchen and a mainly American staff out front.

There's a staggering choice of soups, salads and appetizers at dinner – anything from shrimp chips with special house dip to yum-ta-lay, a salad of shrimp, clams, scallops, squid, mint leaves and fresh chile peppers.

It's difficult to choose among such entrées as panang-neur, sliced tender beef simmered in panang sauce with sweet basil and pineapple, served with a side of pickled cauliflower, and gaeng-goong, shrimp simmered in Thai green curry with coconut milk, baby corn, straw mushrooms, chile peppers and kaffir lime. Only a few of the chef's specials cost more than $13.95.

(607) 273-2031. Entrées, $9.95 to $13.95. Dinner nightly, 5 to 9:30 or 10. Saturday lunch, 11:30 to 2:30. Sunday brunch, 11:30 to 2.

Moosewood Restaurant, 215 North Cayuga St., Ithaca.

This 1960s-ish establishment on the lower level of the downtown Dewitt Mall is known to vegetarians around the country through the *Moosewood Cookbook,* written by one of the former owners of the co-op operation. Visitors come from all over, some deciding that the cookbook is better than the restaurant. Which is a hazard of a laid-back operation in which chefs rotate in the kitchen and the menu changes twice daily.

Along with regulars like pita sandwiches, lasagna and tofuburgers, the black-board menu lists an imaginative selection of casseroles, curries, ragouts, salads and luscious homemade desserts like walnut baklava, chocolate glazed hazelnut cake and a plum tart with whipped cream. At one visit, we liked the sound of tagine, a North African vegetable stew simmered with lemon and saffron on couscous. Moosewood is not strictly vegetarian – varied seafood dishes are offered Thursday through Sunday. Fresh pasta is featured Wednesday nights, and Sunday nights are devoted to different ethnic cuisines. Beer and wines are available.

Folks sit in a row of chairs outside to wait for tables inside the recently refurbished dining room. A canopied patio is used for outdoor dining in season.

(607) 273-9610. Entrées, $9.50 to $11.50. Lunch, Monday-Saturday 11:30 to 2. Dinner nightly, 6 to 9 or 9:30. No credit cards. No smoking.

Benn Conger Inn, 206 West Cortland St., Groton.

The dining operation put this renowned inn on the map, and Ithacans often make the short trip to enjoy special-occasion splurges. Chef-owner Peter van der Meulen mans the kitchen, while wife Alison does the baking and oversees the front of the house.

The main floor of the Colonial Revival mansion holds a cozy library/lounge and three elegant dining rooms enhanced by fine artworks done by a family friend. Along the side is a smashing porch/conservatory in white and green, where tables are set with white linens and fresh flowers. The colorful candlesticks and flower pots that grace each table, handpainted by a local artisan, are for sale.

Peter's Mediterranean-inspired cuisine includes appetizers like fish-shaped ravioli filled with smoked salmon and served in a light tomato cream sauce, coquilles St. Jacques and marinated artichoke hearts served hot with gruyère and chèvre. Main courses are as varied as shrimp, scallops and mussels in cognac cream, served over black lobster-filled ravioli; rainbow trout stuffed with lump crabmeat, grilled pork tenderloin with raspberry salsa and rack of lamb with raspberry-mint sauce.

Alison's desserts prove worthy endings, among them an acclaimed crème brûlée with blackberries, a classic French cheesecake with mascarpone and cream cheese, and profiteroles with varied ice creams. The wine list earns the Wine Spectator award of excellence.

(607) 898-5817. Entrées, $17 to $24. Dinner, Wednesday-Sunday 5:30 to 9.

Diversions

The beautiful Cornell University campus and its gorges and Beebe Lake are not to be missed. Pick up a city or a campus map to avoid getting hopelessly lost.

The Gorges. Cascadilla, Fall and Six Mile creeks slice through the city, and Ithaca Falls plummets 150 feet near the Ithaca High School campus. At the edge of town is **Buttermilk Falls State Park.** Buttermilk Creek drops more than 500 feet through dramatic rock formations in a series of cascades and rapids into a swimming hole at the foot of the falls. Nearby, trails in **Robert H. Treman State Park** wind through Enfield Glen for three miles, passing twelve cascades, sink holes and 115-foot-high Lucifer Falls. Just up Cayuga Lake is **Taughannock Falls State Park,** where the 215-foot-high falls are higher than Niagara. All have swimming, picnic areas and hiking trails.

Sapsucker Woods Sanctuary, 159 Sapsucker Woods Road, Ithaca.

Home of the famed Cornell Laboratory of Ornithology, the sanctuary has 200 acres and more than four miles of trails through woodlands and over swamps and ponds. Huge picture windows in the Lyman K. Stuart Observatory look onto a garden filled with bird feeders and a ten-acre pond abounding with wildlife. Chairs and telescopes are provided. Original works by renowned artist Louis Agassiz Fuertes are hung in the hallways, and the Crow's Nest Birding Shop has a large selection of bird-related items.

(607) 254-2473. Observatory open Monday-Thursday 8 to 5, Friday to 4, weekends 1 to 4.

Ithaca Farmers' Market, Steamboat Landing, Ithaca. Ithacans are justly proud of one of the more flourishing farmers' markets in the East. All items for sale are grown, baked or produced by vendors within a 30-mile radius. We've been particularly impressed with the juried crafts and the ethnic foods. Entertainers perform and a festival atmosphere prevails. The market off Route 13 north of downtown is open seasonally, Saturdays 9 to 2 and Sundays 10 to 2. A smaller version operates Tuesdays from 9 to 2 in Dewitt Park at Buffalo and Cayuga streets.

Cayuga Wine Trail. The only Northeastern city we know of with a vineyard inside its limits is Ithaca. **Six Mile Creek Vineyard,** one of the region's newest, is nestled on the slope of a valley at 1551 Slaterville Road (Route 79). Picnic tables look across the vineyards and hills, a European-style setting for the sampling of chardonnays, rieslings, seyvals and such, priced in the $6.50 to $10 range. Seven other wineries on the west side of Cayuga Lake, including **Knapp, Hosmer, Swedish Hill and Cayuga Ridge** form the Cayuga Wine Trail. A special attraction for lunch and dinner is the fine **Three Seasons Restaurant at Knapp Vineyards.**

Museums and Galleries. Housed in a stunning eleven-story building designed by I.M. Pei, the **Herbert F. Johnson Museum of Art** at Cornell University is one of the country's leading university art museums. The late Johnson Wax Co. chairman gave the building, best known for its Rockwell Galleries of Asian Art, nicely displayed on the fifth floor where wraparound windows offer awesome views in all directions and visitors can lose sight of the art for the scenery. Other notable collections are those of American art and decorative arts, including 200 pieces of Tiffany glass. Special exhibitions show its diversity and quality; we found one on "American Clothing: Identity in Mass Culture" to be of great interest. Other galleries are scattered about town and downtown. We were particularly impressed by the **Gallery at 15 Steps** and the **State of the Art Gallery.**

Shopping. The Downtown Ithaca Commons, formed by closing a section of State Street to vehicular traffic, is a downtown pedestrian marketplace that works. Trees, landscaping, benches and sidewalk cafes provide a pleasant people place, and plenty of people seem to be around at all hours. The Thursday night Concerts on the Commons are popular in summer. Most of Ithaca's better stores are not in the suburban malls but here. Among our favorites is **People's Pottery,** particularly strong on jewelry. We loved the special cat show at **Handwork,** Ithaca's co-op crafts store – crafted cats in all forms from tea cozies to enamel pins to stained glass to a scare cat for the garden. The expanded **Now You're Cooking** offers hard-to-find gadgets, classic cookware and unusual accessories. All kinds of outdoor equipment and clothing are available at **Wildware.** Check out the unusual women's fashions at **Angelheart Designs** and the men's apparel at **Benjamin Peters. The Plantation** offers tropical plants, home accessories and collectibles along with fine dinnerware and crystal. **Alphabet Soup** is a good children's store.

Extra-Special

Cornell Plantations, One Plantations Road, Ithaca.

The arboretum, botanical garden and natural areas of Cornell University are collectively known as the Plantations. They total nearly 3,000 acres of woodlands, gorges, gardens and lakeside trails bordering the campus. We were quite unprepared for their size or their scope. The Robison York State herb garden, for instance, has sixteen theme beds and 400 species surrounded by antique and shrub roses. Nature lovers could spend hours here. A driving tour past sculptures, ponds, test gardens and tree collections (many of them marked as Cornell class gifts) gives a quick overview, but all the cyclists and walkers have the right idea. If time is short, at least take the self-guided walking tour around Beebe Lake. The Garden Gift Shop in the headquarters building offers all kinds of things from pressed-flower notepaper and magnets to floral glass window hangings.

(607) 255-3020. Gardens open daily, dawn to dusk. Free.

Sonnenberg Gardens and Mansion are a major drawing card for visitors to Canandaigua.

Canandaigua/Bristol Hills, N.Y.
The Chosen Place

The Seneca Indians were on the mark when they named this area Kanandagua, "The Chosen Place."

The settlement at the northern end of Canandaigua Lake became the capital of the western frontier. It was the seat of the vast Phelps-Gorham land purchase, the shire town of Ontario, mother of all counties west of Seneca Lake. In 1789 the first office was established here for the sale of land directly to settlers. Leaders of the young nation, four cabinet members among them, lived in stately mansions that still line the broad main street 200 years later.

The westernmost of New York's major Finger Lakes lies cradled between hills. They are particularly majestic at its southern end, an area that has been called "The Switzerland of America." The village there was renamed Naples after a French dignitary said during a visit two centuries ago that the only area of comparable beauty was Naples, Italy. New York's wine industry was born in Naples, and the town paints its fire hydrants purple for the annual Grape Festival in September.

Canandaigua, the western gateway to the Finger Lakes, is a busy summer resort town. Its location beside a lake at the edge of the Rochester metropolitan area makes it the fastest-growing city in upstate New York State (approaching 15,000). The workaday world and the world of summer cottages co-exist side by side. The redevelopment of Lakeshore Drive and Kershaw Park in 1997 improved a once tacky lakefront. The renewal of waterfront activity contrasts with the sound of outdoor music at the Finger Lakes Performing Arts Center and the unexpected show of opulence at Sonnenberg Gardens and Mansion.

Just minutes away is the rural tranquility of the Bristol Hills, rising sharply to the south and west of Canandaigua Lake. Here are hidden towns, country shops, the highest ski area between the Adirondacks and the Rockies, and a couple of the wineries that help make the Finger Lakes famous. The area holds a fond place in our hearts from our frequent visits when we lived nearby in Geneva and Rochester.

Poke along Canandaigua Lake's west shore and the hills and byways above. You'll know, as we do, why the Senecas called this their chosen place.

Inn Spots

Morgan-Samuels Inn, 2920 Smith Road, Canandaigua 14424.

Actor/farmer Judson Morgan, not J.P. Morgan as was originally thought, built this lovely English-style stone house in 1810. A brick wing was added in the early 1900s, and eventually it became the home of Howard Samuels, the plastic-bag inventor and manufacturer who ran unsuccessfully for governor of New York State. Julie and John Sullivan left jobs in Geneseo to buy the house in 1989 and convert it into a masterpiece of a B&B. "We had just visited another B&B," said bubbly Julie, "and knew we were meant to run one." They named it the J.P. Morgan House, only to discover they were in error and, honest to a fault, they renamed it the Morgan-Samuels in 1993.

At the end of a quarter-mile drive lined by maple trees, the house sits like a plantation on a rise with 46 acres of hay fields all around. The scene is truly bucolic. Ducks, turkeys and chickens roam around, and a heifer calf named Kimberly punctuated the tranquility with her mooing as we sat in the garden room.

The serenely lovely garden room, a well-furnished living room, a cozy library with TV, a stone-walled and glass-enclosed tea room with potbelly stove, a tennis court and no fewer than four landscaped patios (one with a trickling fountain and another with a lily pond and waterfall) are available for guests.

The house contains five guest rooms and the Morgan Suite, a beauty with early 18th-century French furniture, kingsize bed, an extra-long loveseat in front of the TV and a double jacuzzi in a corner of the bathroom. The Antique Rose Room has a fireplace, a flowered carpet and one of the first kingsize beds ever made. The sunken Garden Room, where the eight Samuels children used to play, has been transformed into a house favorite with a queensize four-poster, a handmade patterned rug from Romania, a cut-lace bedspread from China and a parlor stove in the angled fireplace. The Victorian Room on the third floor, all in burgundies and greens with a tapestry look, has another fireplace, a wonderful bathroom with old stone walls, a kingsize canopy bed, a jacuzzi and lots of Italian marble, not to mention french doors onto a pleasant balcony.

A fountain sounds like a babbling brook beneath Evy's Chamber, which

Porch-like garden room at Morgan-Samuels Inn looks onto lawns and rural vistas.

Julie recently transformed into a Victorian fantasy and named for her mother. It has a rosewood queensize bed, a corner closet ingeniously fashioned from the sideboard of a bed, and a bathroom with raised shower and ceiling in a former closet.

Our room on the third floor, small but exquisitely done, featured a pretty Gothic window beneath a cathedral ceiling. The king bed, awash with fourteen pillows, nearly filled the room. It was neatly tucked into a niche between built-in shelves. The black floral rug matched the wallpaper border.

All rooms are air-conditioned, have private baths and are equipped with reproduction radios and tape cassettes.

Breakfast is served in the beamed dining room, in a small breakfast room, in the garden room or on the patio. If the inn is full, all these spaces may be called into use. John is in charge of cooking – he and son Jonathan make an early-morning run to the supermarket to pick out the perfect fruit for the fruit platter, which usually contains two dozen varieties, depending on the season. We counted 26 (and Julie promptly added, "he forgot the blueberries") on the exquisitely put-together silver platter, including local Irondequoit melon, mango, two kinds of grapes, papaya, persimmon, figs, kiwis and prunes sautéed in lemon sauce. With that come fresh orange juice served in delicate etched glasses, a baked apple, muffins (the carrot muffins were huge and delicious) and sticky buns.

The main event involves a choice of fluffy buckwheat pancakes with blackberries, blueberries or pecans (or all three), scrambled eggs with herbs, french toast or a six-cheese omelet. We've tried them all but are partial to the omelet, one of the best breakfast treats we've ever had – it looked like a pizza with slices of tomato, scallions, red peppers, onions, jalapeño peppers, mushrooms and lots of herbs and parsley. Monterey jack, mozzarella, parmesan and blue cheeses were on top, and spicy sausage patties and sunflower seed toast (from bread made by Trappist monks) accompanied, as did hazelnut coffee.

Tea (iced or hot) is served in the afternoon. John will do dinners Thursday-Sunday by reservation for six or more guests ($30 to $50 each, depending on number and selection of courses). The birds were chirping, the fountains trickling and classical music playing as we enjoyed dinner by candlelight with fine silver and china in the garden room. Our meal, which John said was typical, produced a procession of whitefish with horseradish sauce, pasta shells in a hot Bahamian sauce, garlic bread, a fabulous chilled peach soup and a mixed salad bearing everything from strawberries and apples to beets, snow peas and artichoke hearts, dressed with raspberry vinaigrette studded with bacon and capers. The main course was filet mignon with a sherry-herb sauce, sided with green beans, mushrooms, cauliflower, potatoes, and broccoli and cheese. Dutch apple pie with ice cream ended a spectacular meal. "I cook the way I like to cook," says John, who has no formal training. He certainly cooks the way we like to eat, although we would have had to be super-human to finish it all.

Music, mostly classical but perhaps New Age in the morning and haunting Gregorian chants at breakfast, is piped throughout the house and across the grounds. The Sullivans display quite a collection of oil paintings, and the bathrooms at their extra-special inn win a prize for the most amenities ever, including toothbrushes. Enchantment, it seems, is in the details.

(716) 394-9232. Fax (716) 394-8044. Five rooms and one suite with private baths. May to mid-November: doubles $129 to $189, suite $225. Rest of year: doubles, $119 to $179, suite $195. Smoking restricted.

The Oliver Phelps Country Inn, 252 North Main St., Canandaigua 14424.

This 19th-century Federal beauty was "the worst-looking house on Main Street" when Joanne and John Sciarratta bought it in 1987. You'd never know it today, such is the transformation the energetic couple have given it. John painted and stenciled every room, his wife decorated with taste, and now it stands out as one of the best-looking houses among many lining the broad main street. The gazebo John built on the wooded side lawn is strategically placed for an advantageous view. The latest addition for guests is a hot tub on the back porch, overlooking the back yard.

The house was once owned by Judge Oliver Phelps, grandson of Oliver Phelps, a Revolutionary War leader who was responsible for the Phelps-Gorham land purchase of 1788. A Tiffany-style lamp with 1,200 pieces of colored glass hangs over the dining-room table. Here Joanne serves a full breakfast of fresh fruit and perhaps a soufflé, omelet, frittata or french toast. Blueberry pancakes and sausages were the fare the morning we visited.

Beyond is an enormous parlor, having been enlarged when a wall was removed during the era when this was a Christian Science church. A group of dolls and teddy bears is ensconced beside one of the sitting areas. Unusual clocks from the couple's collection are located throughout the house.

Upstairs are four air-conditioned guest rooms with private baths. Each bears John's intricate stenciling. Oliver's Suite has a sitting area with a working fireplace, a kingsize four-poster bed, a three-quarter brass bed and, for good measure, a cradle. There's a stenciled bench in a bathroom that is as big as many a bedroom, plus stenciling on doors of closets. Geese are the stenciling motif in the Country Duck Room, which has a queensize poster bed and a single bed. Floral stenciling and an Amish painting enhance the Tulip Room. A fourth room with a sloping ceiling has a white brass queen bed, stenciling in pinks and blues, and the only in-room TV.

(716) 396-1650 or (800) 724-7397. Four rooms with private baths. Doubles, $80 to $105. Suite, $145. Children over 6. No smoking.

Sutherland House occupies renovated Victorian-Gothic structure west of town.

Sutherland House, 3179 Route 21 South (Bristol Street Extension), Canandaigua 14424.
Diane and Cor Van Der Woude realized a lifelong dream when they opened this B&B in 1994. Diane, who had been an executive in gourmet food sales with the Wegman's supermarket chain, and her Dutch husband, a carpenter, purchased the deteriorated 1885 Victorian-Gothic summer house, one of five built by Sutherland brothers along rural outer Bristol Street on outskirts of Canandaigua. They undertook a painstaking renovation, knowing exactly what they wanted every step of the way (extra insulation between walls, for instance) and rebuilding accordingly.

The result is five guest accommodations, all with new bathrooms and TV/VCRs. The largest is a suite with a white wicker kingsize bed, a Vermont Castings stove, a sitting room with baskets hung on the wall, a trundle couch, dressing table and a double whirlpool tub, and a bathroom with shower. The rear Lillian's Lodge, a cathedral-ceilinged loft recently vacated by the couple's son, also has a king bed, fireplace, tulip stenciling and an unusual chair bed with an ottoman that opens into a twin bed. Another double whirlpool tub is a feature of the Dutch Treat room with queen bed. Two smaller rooms with queen beds and telephones also feature Diane's stenciling and the country and romantic touches evident throughout the house. One has a two-person shower.

Afternoon refreshments are served in the front parlor, notable for four Victorian sofas. Guests also help themselves to the contents of two stocked refrigerators, and enjoy the porches and grounds in summer.

As you might expect, Diane prepares an elaborate breakfast, of which she and her husband may partake with guests, at a large table in the dining room. Expect a choice of juices, fresh fruit (baked apple in winter, "which we're tiring of but guests enjoy because they're having it for the first time") and a fancy casserole, french toast or Canadian bacon and eggs. A fresh fruit medley with orange yogurt and blueberry-banana muffins were prefaces to a sausage hash-brown frittata at our summer visit.

Diane, whose recent business experience had been in human resources, took readily to innkeeping. "I feel like I open a new novel each night as I meet and greet," she reports. "People want to talk and I like to listen."

(716) 396-0375 or (800) 396-0375. Fax (716) 396-9281. www.dreamscape.com/canbba/ sbbhome.htm. Four rooms and one suite with private baths. Doubles, $90 to $150. Suite, $170. No smoking.

The Acorn Inn, 4508 Route 64 South, Box 334, Canandaigua 14424.

Pink impatiens, geraniums and petunias accent the greenery around this handsome, dark brown shingled Federal stagecoach inn built in 1795 in the hamlet of Bristol Center. It's the home and antiques shop of Louis and Joan Clark, he a Canandaigua investment broker and she a specialist in antiques and decorative arts. The grounds include a rear terrace, perennial and rock gardens on two levels, brick walks, mulched nature trails and a creek that meanders into a town park with a jogging track. A jacuzzi spa is a focal spot in the gardens.

The centrally air-conditioned interior is striking as well, appointed in 18th- and early 19th-century English and American formal and country pieces, each priced and for sale. Guests wander through five rooms of antiques shops downstairs before retiring to their rooms, which also are period pieces.

The Clarks offer four elegant guest rooms, each with private bath and canopy queen or kingsize bed. All have reading lamps for the side chairs, large closets and thick insulation to muffle noise. The largest is the Bristol (the former ballroom) with king bed, sitting area with TV and a spacious, well-appointed bath with a soaking tub and separate shower. The new Hotchkiss Room comes with floor-to-ceiling windows overlooking the gardens, a sitting area with TV/VCR and a whirlpool tub.

Part of a research library of 5,000 books on art, antiques and architecture enhances the living room. Another common room contains a large 18th-century fireplace ready for hearthside cooking.

The attractive dining room and the garden terrace are where the Clarks serve a full breakfast. It might be fresh orange juice, melon garnished with raspberries, french toast and sausages. Pancakes and herb omelets are other entrée choices.

Tea and sherry are offered in the afternoon. Chocolates and a carafe of ice water accompany nightly turndown service.

(716) 229-2834. Fax (716) 229-5046. www.dreamscape.com/canbba/acorn.htm Four rooms with private baths. Doubles, $105 to $165. No young children.

Enchanted Rose Inn, 7479 Routes 5 & 20, East Bloomfield, Box 128, Canandaigua 14424.

Her background in the flower business helps explain all the fresh and dried flowers at this B&B run with TLC by Jan and Howard Buhlmann. "I love flowers," notes Jan, stating the obvious. "So I have them everywhere."

You'll find fresh flowers in the bedrooms and the bathrooms, floral patterns on some of the draperies and bedspreads, garnishes of flowers on the breakfast dishes and a heart-shaped rose garden among the gardens in back.

The Buhlmanns share their 1820s Federal-style home in East Bloomfield with overnight guests in three air-conditioned bedrooms, all with queensize beds and private baths. They're filled with antiques and decorated in an English country style. Each features paintings of local artists. The First Lady's Room offers an

Flowers and plants are decorative theme at The Enchanted Rose Inn.

antique bed and dresser and two comfy chairs. The Royal Rose Room has a cherry four-poster bed and two antique wicker chairs (one a rocker). The Victoria suite comes with a cherry hand-carved canopy bed draped in lace and awash with pillows, a sofa, a TV with VCR and a small dressing room with another sitting area.

Guests have access to the formal living room but most gravitate to a common room that's open to the kitchen. It has a fireplace, TV and a bay window yielding views of the gardens. A handsome display cabinet, obtained from a jewelry store in Rochester, holds quite a collection of bone china and pressed glass in the formal dining room. Breakfast is by candlelight at a table for six. The meal begins with fresh fruit, perhaps fruit salad sprinkled with mint or cantaloupe with raspberries, juice and homemade muffins. The main event could be heart-shaped pecan waffles with brandied peach sauce or an egg soufflé with ham, cheese and mushrooms. Jan garnishes her plates with edible pansies, rose petals and johnny jumpups, and finds that some guests say hers are the first flowers they've ever eaten.

Outside and screened from the highway is a nicely landscaped side and rear yard, full of arbors and gardens. An English garden flanks the rear post-and-beam barn.

(716) 657-6003 or (888) 657-6003. Fax (716) 657-4405. www.servtech.com/public/ enchrose/ Two rooms and one suite with private baths. May-December: doubles $95 to $105, suite $135. January-April: doubles $85 to $95, suite $125. No smoking.

The Maxfield Inn, 105 North Main St., Box 39, Naples 14512.

Only six families have owned this pillared 1841 mansion in the center of Naples. The latest are Russell and Alice Cochran, retirees from the Rochester area who "wanted a big dining room for all our kids and grandchildren." They bought it as their home, and inherited a recently renovated B&B vacated by local school teachers who had their hands full with three young children. The former innkeepers "said we'd love running a B&B, and we do," Alice advised. "The guests are the best part of it."

The Cochrans have seven air-conditioned guest rooms, three with private baths and four sharing two, one of the latter sporting a jacuzzi. Rooms are outfitted with period pieces in pine, cherry or mahogany and have new wallpaper and carpeting or oriental rugs. A two-bedroom suite with a bathroom between is good for families.

Alice is so fascinated by the heritage of the inn she was writing a book about its original owner, Hiram Maxfield. He owned the area's first winery and had a 2,000-bottle cellar in the basement. He also ran the first bank in town, and its original door leads into the kitchen. The barn was part of the underground railroad.

The high-ceilinged front parlor and library, both light and airy, are full of the Cochrans' diverse collections of glass. Guests relax on the columned front porch or at an umbrella-covered table on the side lawn.

The Cochrans have removed the carpet and restored the original oak and chestnut floors in the dining room, an unusual pattern of squares that look like tiles. Here they serve a breakfast that starts with fresh fruit – a bowl of blueberries and straw-berries with whipped cream (red, white and blue) for the July Fourth holiday when we were there. Next came french toast with sausage. Scrambled eggs, hot breads and popovers are other favorites.

(716) 374-2510. Three rooms with private baths and four rooms sharing two baths. Doubles, $65. Children welcome. No smoking.

The Vagabond Inn, 3300 Sliter Road, Naples 14512.

So you "vant to be alone," as Greta Garbo used to say. Here's the place, high on a remote mountaintop in the hills northeast of Naples. Just you and your significant other and up to four more similarly inclined couples cosseted in a luxurious, contemporary house designed for romance. With your own jacuzzi and a TV/VCR with a 400-movie library, and perhaps a fireplace to warm the night air. And a swimming pool, secluded patios and exotic landscaping just outside.

Celeste Stanhope-Wiley started in 1987 with a three-bedroom ranch house in an unconventional location, "alone on a mountain" with a sharp 1,000-foot drop to the Italy Valley below. Now she shares 7,000 square feet with guests on two floors. You enter a 60-foot-long "great room" rich in natural woods with a seating area facing a stone fireplace at one end. At the other end is a dining-room table set for ten beside full-length windows onto a deck with a glorious view beyond. Although it's daytime, the room is dimly lit and little lights simulating candles flicker here and there.

The hostess shows you the well-equipped guest kitchen, employed by many guests for dinner since the nearest civilization is ten miles away by roundabout rural roads. Then she directs you to your room, perhaps the pine-paneled Lodge on the lower level, where the tulips handpainted on the headboard of the kingsize bed match the patterns on the pillows and bedspread. Two plush wing chairs flank the fireplace and a terrace awaits outside. Also in the room is a dining table for four – she had a lot of space to fill, Celeste explains. In the corner alcove beyond the bed is a whirlpool spa, right in the room, beside a bar, mini-fridge and microwave. Once ensconced in the Lodge, you may not be seen again until it's time to leave.

"Everybody needs to run away overnight," says Celeste. She knows. She relates that she was "thrown out of a convent in Greenwich," Conn., as a teenager and ran away from home in nearby Darien. She "went back to my roots" in the Caribbean, settling in Haiti and eventually turning up on her mountaintop. Vagabond, she calls it.

For those of a mind, the finest magazines vie with VCR movies for attention. A collection of recent Bon Appetit issues is in the queen-bedded Shannon (one of two bedrooms named for her grown daughters), blessed with a 27-inch TV set, garden patio, fireplace and a bathroom of cedar and mirrors with dimmer lights,

Terrace with view at The Vagabond Inn.

hot tub and separate shower. National Geographic Travelers are in the Mahogany Room, where a stuffed gorilla peeks over the double four-poster bed. Architectural Digests grace the Bristol Suite, a grand main-floor space with a kingsize canopy bed, ironwood twig-style furniture on the screened porch, a private deck and an enormous bathroom containing a palm-bedecked jacuzzi for two, a fourteen-foot mirrored dressing area with twin vanities, and a separate shower.

Coffee and tea are available around the clock, as much to satisfy Celeste's needs as those of her guests. She serves "a very full breakfast" between 8 and 11 a.m.; "your arteries start hardening as you sit down." Fresh orange juice and fruits precede such baked goods as homemade muffins and "piña colada sweets," served with winery jams. Next comes the main course, perhaps crab and vegetable omelet or a 24-egg pie. By then it may be time for a nap.

Next time, Celeste may rent you her new garage suite called Heaven's Gate, into which she had moved, with privacy screens onto the pool area, walk-in closets and a mirrored bathroom to end all bathrooms, complete with a customized jacuzzi good for all the aches that ail you.

Lately, Celeste has turned portions of her great room and two adjacent rooms into a showcase for the sale of fine international crafts and jewelry.

(716) 554-6271. Two rooms and three suites with private baths. Doubles, $105. Suites, $160 to $192. No children. No smoking.

Dining Spots

Lincoln Hill Inn, 3365 East Lake Road, Canandaigua.

Everybody's favorite restaurant hereabouts is Lincoln Hill, and with good reason. It has a grand setting on a hillside overlooking Canandaigua Lake within earshot of the outdoor Finger Lakes Performing Arts Center shell. It has tables inside and out. It has an extensive menu. And the food is consistently good.

Cheryl and Bill Ward, who were teaching at Monroe Community College in Rochester, bought the 1804 brick homestead and converted it into a large restaurant, opening fortuitously in 1983 on the same day as the arts center shell. Inside are several small, cozy dining rooms with pastel linens, antique lace curtains and soft lighting. One room is strung with little white lights. A lounge contains remarkable modern American primitive paintings of the lake and the area as it was in the latter part of the 19th century by Adelaide Cook Kent, who was influenced by Rufus Porter.

But it was the open front porch with its white over floral clothed tables, citronella candles and fresh field flowers to which we were attracted on a summer's evening. It, plus an enclosed side porch and a back patio called the Garden Room, seat 120 outdoors, half again more than the number inside. For dinner, you can order light: an appetizer and a salad, an open-face prime rib sandwich or perhaps the ultimate appetizer platter, a sampling of eight. Or you can order scampi tuscany over angel-hair pasta, baked whitefish provençal, chicken and cheddar crêpes, sautéed pork tenderloin or four versions of prime steak.

Dinners come with salad, including an excellent one with greens, mandarin oranges, walnuts and a honey-poppyseed dressing, and a garden salad with dijon vinaigrette. We liked the tender calves liver, grilled with onions and bacon, and the prime rib, a thick slab with horseradish sauce. The ample plates, garnished with edible nasturtiums from the gardens out back, yielded potatoes or rice, garlic cloves and zucchini stuffed with vegetables and cheese. French chocolate decadence is one of the good desserts.

(716) 394-8254. Entrées, $14.95 to $24.95. Dinner, Tuesday-Sunday 5 to 9 or 10. Closed Sundays in winter.

Koozinas, 699 South Main St., Canandaigua.

A fish is sculpted out of the wall at the entry and waves ripple across the walls of this ultra-colorful restaurant with a mod nautical look. It takes its name from the Greek word for kitchen, according to chef George Stamatis. He and his wife Christine opened their contemporary Italian-Mediterranean restaurant in the former Wegman's store in mid-1997, just in time for a roaring summer season.

There's a lot to look at in the large, high-ceilinged space: faux columns, colorful angles, a tiled kitchen and hanging fisherman lamps from Greece.

"We tried to give it flair," says George, whose food follows suit. He, a chef and six cooks man the open grill, producing a wide variety of wood-fired pizzas, pastas, panini, salatas and the like. The choices are staggering. You might start with bruschetta, polenta portobello, spanakopita or calamari salad. A cup of soup and half a panini sandwich makes a light supper. So does one of the thin-crust pizzas, or any of the dozen pastas, from pignoli with banana peppers and ziti to scallops sautéed with spinach, diced tomatoes, black olives, feta cheese and fusilli.

Main courses are fewer in number, but cover the bases: grilled shrimp with vegetables, wood-fired chicken topped with mozzarella, twin veal chops and Grecian T-bone steak topped with kalamata olives, plum tomatoes and scallions.

George makes most of the desserts, among them baklava, kahlua torte, berry tart and tirami su.

(716) 396-0360. Entrées, $11.50 to $13.75. Open Monday-Saturday, 11:30 to 11 or midnight. Sunday, noon to 10.

Nicole's Dining Room, Canandaigua Inn on the Lake, 770 South Main St., Canandaigua.

Taken over by the owners of Canandaigua Wine Co., the old Sheraton Inn was renamed the Canandaigua Inn on the Lake. They redid some guest rooms, but concentrated their efforts on the dining operation. An innovative chef elevated the fare, and the elegant dining room with upholstered armchairs, shaded candles and fanned napkins atop service plates is quite stylish. Big windows look onto the lake.

Porch with view of Canandaigua Lake is favored by diners at Lincoln Hill Inn.

For dinner, expect such entrées as grilled salmon with ginger-black bean vinaigrette, roulade of chicken with tasso ham and roasted garlic sauce, and grilled center-cut pork chops with braised red cabbage and sweet potato casserole. Starters could be roasted red peppers with grilled bread, kalamata olives and New York State goat cheese and grilled vegetable napoleon with roasted red pepper sauce.

Locals love the restaurant's lakeside terrace and Sandbar for a summer lunch. The lounge is Baco's wine bar.

(716) 394-7800 or (800) 228-2801. Entrées, $12 to $22.50. Lunch, 11 to 4. Dinner, 5 to 10, to 9 in winter.

Casa de Pasta, 125 Bemis St., Canandaigua.

People come from miles around for the pasta in this red brick townhouse at the edge of downtown, we were advised. And the restaurant received the highest rating from a newspaper reviewer.

Owner Bruce Warren's menu is surprisingly bland, however. The pastas include five kinds of spaghettini or ziti with meatballs or mushrooms and such, linguini with garlic and parmesan cheese, lasagna, tortellini alfredo and ricotta stuffed shells. The specials are really special, said the reviewer: pasta puttanesca, gnocchi gorgonzola and veal madeira with pasta the night we were there.

Entrées run from whitefish marinara to shrimp scampi and filet mignon. Veal parmesan, braciole and chicken parmesan are menu fixtures. An Italian platter for two brings antipasto, garlic bread and a platter of lasagna, stuffed shells, meatballs and homemade Italian sausage. Pizzas are available except on weekends.

Diners enter through a bar presided over by the convivial owner-host. Beyond are two intimate, noisy dining rooms with pine wainscoting and red and white oilcloths and curtains – a spirited place for regulars who relish homemade Italian cuisine.

(716) 394-3909. Entrées, $11.95 to $17.95. Dinner nightly, 5 to 9:30 or 10.

The Holloway House, Routes 5 & 20, East Bloomfield.

As it has for years, the green neon sign still glows outside this historic tavern and restaurant dating to 1808 and facing the green in a charming hilltop town. Owners Fred and Doreen Wayne haven't changed the menu much since we found it somewhat dated in the 1960s. But folks love it, particularly the oldtimers who dress up for lunch and make it their dinner.

There's a ramble of Colonial rooms with ladderback chairs at bare wood tables and frilly sheer curtains on the windows in this landmark on the National Register of Historic Places. The dinner menu starts with roast turkey (our informant said she'd had the best turkey dinner ever here the week before) and fried half chicken with biscuit to surf and turf and twin lobster tails. Specialties include broiled sea scallops with tartar sauce, baked stuffed flounder, seafood newburg en casserole and, on Saturdays, prime rib – ladies' cut or regular cut. Complete dinners (add $2.50) start with tomato juice, soup du jour or fruit shrub. They come with au gratin or mashed potatoes, two vegetables that are passed, tossed or fruit salad with French, Russian, Italian or blue cheese dressings, Sally Lunn bread and homemade orange rolls, and desserts like pies, angel food cake, strawberry shortcake and hot fudge sundae.

A Friday night summer buffet packs the crowds in at $15.50 for adults, $8.50 for children, with more than 25 items to choose from. The lunch menu features chicken fricassee, turkey à la king, and chicken livers and bacon. Who says the '60s are out of style?

(716) 657-7120. Entrées, $11.45 to $16.45. Lunch, Tuesday-Saturday 11:30 to 2. Dinner, Tuesday-Saturday 5:30 to 8:30, Sunday noon to 7:30. Closed December-March.

Bob's and Ruth's, Route 21 at Route 245, Naples.

A legend in the area, this started in 1950 as a diner and takeout stand, made its name with grape pie, and grew like topsy. The diner and takeout counter remain in front, where you can get a basic American sandwich (starting at $1.95 for egg salad) or a meal of roast chicken or prime rib, $5.95 to $14.95. Eat at the counter or one of the booths or outside at a picnic table in the adjacent Old Town Square Park.

In the rear and reached by a separate entrance is the Vineyard Lounge on one side and on the other, the **Vineyard Room** with two walls of windows looking onto a sea of grapevines and a great new outdoor dining deck. Decor is solid, green and brown, to match a solid menu. Most diners opt for the complete dinner, which includes a locally famous salad bar (homemade preserves, pickled fruits and vegetables, garden vegetables and more). The offerings run from turkey dinner to prime rib, which the menu used to tout as "the traditional celebrant dinner of this area." Now it's simply "a local favorite." Other possibilities include broiled rainbow trout, baby back ribs ("a Canadian treat"), broiled ham steak with pineapple and fruited sherry sauce, roast duckling flambéed tableside, veal parmigiana and filet mignon. Grape pie, famous all over the state, is the obligatory dessert in season.

(716) 374-5122. Entrées, $9.95 to $19.95. Bob's & Ruth's: open daily from 6 a.m. The Vineyard: lunch 11:30 to 3:30; dinner from 5, Sunday from noon.

Diversions

Finger Lakes Performing Arts Center, Lincoln Hill Road, Canandaigua, (716) 325-7760. Since 1983, the outdoor shell on the Finger Lakes Community College campus has drawn thousands for summertime concerts by the Rochester

Philharmonic Orchestra and visiting entertainers. The RPO presents Saturday evening concerts, seating 2,600 in the shell and another 10,000 on the lawn, although financial shortfalls curtailed the orchestra season lately. Guest entertainers over the years have ranged from Huey Lewis, Sting and John Denver to Steve Lawrence and Eydie Gorme, and Peter, Paul and Mary.

Sonnenberg Gardens and Mansion, 151 Charlotte St., Canandaigua.

What a treasure is this – and so unexpected in little old Canandaigua. Restored in 1973 after 40 years of neglect, the Victorian gardens are recognized by the Smithsonian as some of the most magnificent ever created in America. The 50-acre garden estate around their 40-room summer home was planned at the turn of the century by Mary Clark Thompson, a Canandaigua native who married Frederick F. Thompson, a New Yorker whose family started Chase Manhattan and Citibank. Widowed at 67, she traveled the world to create nine formal gardens, an arboretum, a greenhouse complex and more as a memorial to her husband (who, we were told, rather preferred his fishing cottage down Canandaigua Lake to Sonnenberg, German for "Sunny Hill"). Some 75,000 visitors a year admire the Japanese hill garden and tea house, the vast Italian garden with four sunken fleur de lis parterres and the Rose Garden launched with 4,000 bushes from the former Jackson and Perkins Rose Gardens in nearby Newark. Other attractions are Mrs. Thompson's favorite Blue & White Garden, a Pansy Garden in which even the bird bath is shaped like a pansy, and a rock garden entered through a canyon of puddingstone and including 5,500 feet of streams, waterfalls and pools fed by geysers and springs. In the middle of one particularly dry summer, we found the flowers a bit lackluster (not surprising, since a staff of only seven plus volunteers maintain what 75 fulltime gardeners did for their founder). Still we marveled at the accompaniments: belvederes, statues, gazebos, arbors, a temple of Diana, a sitting Buddha, a fountain with a statue of Hercules and even a Roman bath. The vast South Lawn with its rare specimen trees is remarkable: Mrs. Thompson liked to give house parties and asked guests to bring trees to plant, each guest trying to outdo the other. A walking map guides visitors, but more informative are the guided tours of up to two hours in length, offered daily at 10 and 2. The mansion, a testament to the extravagances of the Gilded Age, has its own delights, among them the Lavender and Old Lace gift shop. Sonnenberg also has launched a summer lawn concert series, five Sunday concerts at 6 p.m., and a chamber music series. **The Festival of Lights,** in which the mansion is decorated and the gardens are gloriously illuminated with lights and themed figures, extends the season from Thanksgiving to New Year's.

(716) 394-4922. Gardens open daily, 9:30 to 5:30, mid-May to mid-October; also nightly in holiday season, 4:30 to 9:30. Adults, $6.50.

Canandaigua Wine Company Tasting Room, Sonnenberg Gardens. Striking stained glass embellishes the winery tasting room and sales area at the entrance to Sonnenberg Gardens. The largest of the Finger Lakes wineries is located in a plant and showcase headquarters on the western edge of town. This is simply a tasting and sales room, which gets mighty crowded when a bus tour stops by. Open daily, noon to 4, mid-May to mid-October. Free.

The Granger Homestead and Carriage Museum, 295 North Main St., Canandaigua.

Gideon Granger, who was postmaster general for Thomas Jefferson, moved here in 1813 and resolved to build a homestead that would be "unrivaled in all the nation." This pale yellow Federal mansion is the result and its period rooms with original furnishings are on display. More than 50 horse-drawn vehicles, from coaches and sleighs to an undertaker's hearse, are shown in the Carriage Museum.

(716) 394-1472. Open Tuesday-Friday 1 to 5, May-October; also Saturday and Sunday 1 to 5, June-August. Adults, $4.

Boat Tours. Canandaigua is known as a summer resort and the best way to experience it is by boat. Town native Gray Hoffman gives enlightening narrated tours five times daily in summer under the auspices of **Captain Gray's Boat Tours,** from the dock at Inn on the Lake; adults, $7. He gives the history of the lake and tells who lives in which cottage on an hour-long tour that even natives find informative. The **Canandaigua Lady,** 169 Lake Shore Drive, the only authentic replica of a paddlewheeler in the Finger Lakes, offers lunch, dinner and sightseeing tours daily in summer, $12 to $38.

Shopping. A big stuffed pig wearing sunglasses sits outside on a wicker chair at **Renaissance – the Goodie II Shoppe** at 56 South Main St. Here are all the socially correct gifts, from jewelry to porcelain dolls, bath things, Port Merion china and lovely Christmas ornaments. Teddy bears, cookbooks (we picked up Linda McCarthy's for a vegetarian son) and nifty paper plates and napkins abound. **The Country Ewe, Ltd.** specializes in handknit sweaters from around the world among its outstanding array of sportswear, outerware, accessories and gifts. From handloomed blankets to golf wear, this expanding store has something for anyone of style. North of town at 1901 Route 332 is **The Five Seasons,** two floors of a log building housing a gift shop to end all gift shops. Owner Sue Ellsworth is known for her handpainted crockery.

A fun shop to explore on the west side of Canandaigua is **Cat's in the Kitchen** at 367 West Ave. Here Laurel Wemett has collected, from tag sales and auctions, all the things our mothers and grandmothers used in the kitchen. She specializes in the Depression era to the 1960s, and it's fun to check the old canisters, cookie jars, china, pots and pans and the corner full of old cookbooks.

Farther afield is **Cheshire,** billed as "a little bit of New England awaiting discovery." **The Cheshire Union,** Route 21, is a renovated schoolhouse containing a gift shop, antiques center, the Schoolhouse Deli and the Company Store. Thousands turn out for its annual folk fair and antique show. "Everything Grape and More" is the theme of **Arbor Hill Grapery,** a delightful place at 6461 Route 64 in Bristol Springs. John and Katie Brahm, he a former Widmer's Wine Cellars executive, are proof that wines aren't the only good use for grapes. They sell grape-filled cookies, hot grape sundaes, fillings for grape pies, wine-motif wallpaper, vinegars, gewürztraminer wine jelly and their Arbor Hill Winery wines.

Tiny Naples is the home of some interesting shops around **Old Town Square.** The new Village Corner complex is the home of **Classics,** an exceptional gift store. Owner Anne Schneider stocks its several rooms with an assortment of sophisticated wares, from linens, pottery and jewelry to cookbooks, candles and Christmas ornaments. Naples offers a Saturday afternoon summer concert series at the Old Town Square park. The year's highlight is the annual **Naples Grape Festival** in late September with arts, crafts, entertainment, food and, of course, those sugary-sweet grape pies.

Widmer's Wine Cellars, 1 Lake Niagara Lane, Naples.
Swiss immigrant John Jacob Widmer, whose home is still on view, launched

this hillside winery in 1888. We remember it fondly from its days under the aegis of the R.T. French Co. Lately sold to Canandaigua Wine Co., Widmer's is now part of the nation's third largest wine-producing firm. Its winery tour, one of the best in the East, starts with a twelve-minute video shown through the end of a wine barrel. The half-hour guided tour takes you through ancient subterranean passageways where wine is aged in oak barrels, past the famous rooftop sherry barrels and into the fascinating bottling and labeling room. The publicity notes "there are a number of stairs to traverse." The visitor may choose instead to relax in the air-conditioned Widmer's Wine/Food Center for an extensive wine-tasting and sales of wines, juices, jellies and Finger Lakes items. In the adjacent **Manischewitz** cellars, which moved in 1986 from Brooklyn, two rabbis are employed fulltime to oversee the making of kosher wines. Tours are offered Monday-Thursday except Jewish holidays.

(716) 374-6311. open Monday-Saturday 10 to 4, Sunday 11:30 to 4:30; November-May, daily 1 to 4.

Living Wall Gardens, Tobey St., Naples. (716) 374-2870. Quite a sight are all the colorful flower growing up walls and around gates at this new enterprise, a division of Curious Research Corp. We were there after hours, but poked briefly around the property to ogle all the modular growing systems – marigolds, begonias, petunias, impatiens and more – blooming and showing up in profusion like never before. The company offers eight models for exterior or interior use. If you're not in the market, you can simply look.

Extra-Special

The Wizard of Clay Pottery, 7851 Route 20A, Bristol.

Out in the middle of nowhere in the Bristol Hills are seven geodesic domes that are home to ex-Rochester teacher Jim Kozlowski's pottery empire. Visitors come

from across the world – they mark their hometowns with pins on a map in his workshop – to see "the workshop where the wizard works wonders." The Wednesday we visited was his afternoon for golf, according to an assistant who called herself a wizette. So we had to be satisfied reading lists of the 29 steps to making a Bristoleaf pot and the twenty most often asked questions and their answers, both garnished with a sense of humor. Jim makes each piece individually, but a staff helps with the decoration. His trademark Bristoleaf pottery is decorated with delicate imprints from all kinds of leaves picked in the surrounding hills. He's most proud of his signed and numbered limited editions, particularly those decorated with leaves handpainted in gold and selling for up to $225 a bowl. Two domes house more than 1,000 pottery lamps with shades; another, bakeware and planters; still another, a zoo craft gallery of arts and crafts reflecting the animal kingdom. There are even a gazebo and a nature trail. It sounds hokey, but isn't really.

(716) 229-2980. Open daily, 9 to 5.

Index

H

I

R

Rabbit Run B&B, Gordonsville, VA 56
Railroad House, Marietta, PA 291
Ranson-Armory House, Harpers Ferry, WV 143
Rebecca's, Cape Charles, VA 103
The Red Fox Inn, Middleburg, VA 133
Reedville Fishermen's Museum, Reedville, VA 92
Renée's, Ithaca, NY 506
Rest & Repast, Pine Grove Mills, PA 321
The Reynolds Mansion, Bellefonte, PA 316
The Rhinebeck Post Office, Rhinebeck, NY 434
Rhythm of the Sea, Cape May, NJ 377
The River House Inn, Snow Hill, MD 193
The River Inn, Marietta, PA 283
Rodeway Inn, New Castle, DE 254
Rod's Old Irish Tavern, Sea Girt, NJ 399
La Rosa Negra, Lewes, DE 246
The Rose Inn, Ithaca, NY 497

S

Sag Pond Vineyards, Sagaponack, NY 420
Sam Snead's Tavern, Hot Springs, VA 14
Sampson-Eagon Inn, Staunton, VA 18
Sand Castle Winery, Erwinna, PA 350
Santa Fe Junction, East Hampton, NY 417
Sapore di Mare, Wainscott, NY 417
Sapsucker Woods Sanctuary, Ithaca, NY 509
The Saratoga Arms, Saratoga Springs, NY 441
Saratoga Bed and Breakfast, Saratoga Springs, NY 440
Saratoga Spa State Park, Saratoga Springs, NY 452
Savage River Inn, McHenry, MD 157
Scarlett House Bed & Breakfast, Kennett Square, PA 268
The School House Bed & Breakfast, Rhinebeck, NY 428
Sea Crest by the Sea, Spring Lake, NJ 388
Sea Gate B&B, Cape Charles, VA 97
Second Street Grille, Lewes, DE 245
1740 House, Lumberville, PA 342
1770 House, East Hampton, NY 410
Seward House Inn, Surry, VA 69
The Shadows, Orange, VA 54
Shirley Plantation, Charles City, VA 76
Silver Thatch Inn, Charlottesville, VA 37 and 43
Sisters Café, Spring Lake, NJ 397
The Six Sisters Bed & Breakfast, Saratoga Springs. NY 444
Skytop Lodge, Skytop, PA 334
Sleepy Hollow Farm, Gordonsville, VA 54

The Smithfield Inn, Smithfield, VA 74
Smithfield Station, Smithfield, VA 70 and 74
Smithfield Gourmet Bakery & Café, Smithfield, VA 76
Snow Hill Inn, Snow Hill, MD 200 and 202
Solomons Victorian Inn, Solomons, MD 183
Sonnenberg Gardens and Mansion, Canandaigua, NY 523
The Southern Mansion, Cape May, NJ 377
Sperry's, Saratoga Springs, NY 449
Spiaggi, Cape May, NJ 380
Spring Lake Inn, Spring Lake, NJ 395
Springfield House Bed & Breakfast, Boalsburg, PA 318
The Springwater Inn, Saratoga Springs, NY 449
St. Catharine's Church, Spring Lake, NJ 400
St. Luke's Church, Smithfield, VA 78
The St. Mary's Square Museum, St. Michaels, MD 221
St. Michaels Harbour Inn & Marina, St. Michaels, MD 207
St. Paul's Episcopal Church, Chestertown, MD 235
Starry Night B&B, State College, PA 319
Statler Brothers Complex, Staunton, VA 28
The Statler Hotel, Ithaca, NY 504
The Sterling Inn, South Sterling, PA 332 and 336
Sting-Ray's Restaurant, Cape Charles, VA 102
The Stockton Inn, Stockton, NJ 354 and 362
Stone Manor, Middletown, MD 169, 175
Stonegate Bed & Breakfast, Hamilton, VA 132
The Stonehouse, Essex, NY 459
Stratford Hall Plantation, Stratford, VA 91
Strawberry Hill Farm, Cooperstown, NY 473
Strawberry Inn, New Market, MD 171
Sunburst Tea Garden, Westport, NY 463
Sunset Hills Farm, Washington, VA 113
Surrey House Restaurant, Surry, VA 75
Sutherland House, Canandaigua, NY 515
Swan Haven Bed & Breakfast, Rock Hall, MD 230
Sycamore Hill House & Gardens, Washington, VA 111

T

Tara Lynn's Unique Cuisine, Spring Lake, NJ 399
Tarara Vineyard & Winery, Leesburg, VA 139
Tastefully Yours, Too, Cape Charles, VA 102
Tastings, Charlottesville, VA 44
Tattersall Inn, Point Pleasant, PA 343

Also by the Authors

Inn Spots & Special Places in New England. The first in the series, this book by Nancy and Richard Woodworth tells you where to go, stay, eat and enjoy in New England's choicest areas. Focusing on 35 special places, it details the best inns and B&Bs, restaurants, sights to see and things to do. First published in 1986; fully revised and expanded fifth edition in 1998. 524 pages of timely ideas. $16.95.

Getaways for Gourmets in the Northeast. The first book by Nancy and Richard Woodworth appeals to the gourmet in all of us. It guides you to the best dining, lodging, specialty food shops and culinary attractions in 22 areas from the Brandywine Valley to Montreal, Cape May to Bar Harbor, the Finger Lakes to Nantucket. First published in 1984; fully updated fifth edition in 1997. 570 pages to read and savor. $18.95.

Waterside Escapes in the Northeast. This new edition by Betsy Wittemann and Nancy Woodworth relates the best lodging, dining, attractions and activities in 36 great waterside vacation spots from Chesapeake Bay to Cape Breton Island, from the Thousand Islands to Martha's Vineyard. Everything you need to know for a day trip, a weekend or a week near the water is told the way you want to know it. First published in 1987; revised and expanded third edition in 1996. 474 pages to discover and enjoy. $15.95.

Weekending in New England. The best-selling travel guide by Betsy Wittemann and Nancy Woodworth details everything you need to know about 24 of New England's most interesting vacation spots: more than 1,000 things to do, sights to see and places to stay, eat and shop year-round. First published in 1980; fully revised and expanded fifth edition in 1997. 448 pages of facts and fun. $16.95.

The Restaurants of New England. This book by Nancy and Richard Woodworth is the most comprehensive guide to restaurants throughout New England. The authors detail menu offerings, atmosphere, hours and prices for more than 1,200 restaurants in the same informative style that makes their other books so credible. First published in 1990; revised second edition in 1994. 490 pages of comprehensive information. $14.95.

The Originals in Their Fields

These books may be obtained from your local bookstore or direct from the publisher, pre-paid, plus $2 shipping for each book. Connecticut residents add sales tax.

Wood Pond Press
365 Ridgewood Road
West Hartford, Conn. 06107

Tel: (860) 521-0389
Fax: (860) 313-0185
E-Mail: woodpond@ntplx.net
Web Site: www.getawayguides.com

ON LINE: Excerpts from these books are found at **www.getawayguides.com.** Check out this Web site for continuing updates on selected inns, B&Bs and restaurants in destination areas throughout the Mid-Atlantic states and New England.